D0615438

# COMPUTER MODELS IN MANAGEMENT

# COMPUTER MODELS IN MANAGEMENT

BARBARA BUND JACKSON

Graduate School of Business Administration
Harvard University



1979 RICHARD D. IRWIN, INC. Homewood, Illinois 60430
Irwin-Dorsey Limited Georgetown, Ontario L7G 4B3

Case material of the Harvard Graduate School of Business Administration is made possible by the cooperation of business firms who may wish to remain anonymous by having names, quantities, and other identifying details disguised while basic relationships are maintained. Cases are prepared as the basis for class discussion rather than to illustrate either effective or ineffective handling of administrative situations.

ISBN 0-256-02225-9
Library of Congress Catalog Card No. 78–61189

*Printed in the United States of America*

1 2 3 4 5 6 7 8 9 0 MP 6 5 4 3 2 1 0 9

*To Chuck*

# PREFACE

Over the past 10 or 20 years, computer hardware has become more powerful and less expensive, programming languages have become increasingly powerful and widely available, and the supply of computer professionals has increased. Time-sharing services have made computer power available even in small quantities. As a result of all these changes, the potential for constructive computer use in management has increased rapidly and the start-up (or entry) costs for computer users have decreased very substantially. Actual computer use has also increased.

Training is needed to help ensure successful use of computer analysis. In the past, as was appropriate, most of the training effort focused on those who would provide computer services—on the programmers, designers, and maintainers of computers. Even when courses were offered for a more general audience, they tended to be the beginning portions of the materials used in the more advanced courses for specialists. In other words, generalist courses would teach a little computer programming and a little bit about hardware design.

The basic premise of this book is twofold. First, I believe that we have reached the point in the development and use of computer technology where it is important to provide tools designed specifically for educating the consumer of computer analysis, who may have neither the time nor the desire to learn the material more specifically intended for the computer-services provider. Second, I believe that the design or planning of computer analysis is different from the coding or implementation of plans or designs and that the two parts of a successful computer application (design and implementation) can be separated for teaching purposes.

Let me expand a bit on these two points. First, most people with any experience in the general computer area have heard numerous tales of unhappy computer applications or attempted applications. Projects take longer than they were supposed to. Or, finished projects do not do what the managers who sponsored them expected them to do. Or, programs are designed and written by the computer specialist and only later does someone realize, with horror, that a major piece of the problem was omitted from the analysis. Much of the attention in books and in journals in the computer field focuses on the question of how computer professionals can achieve successful implementations. They consider efficient management of large-scale programming efforts, and they worry about the need to provide sufficient documentation of finished programs. The computer professionals' attack on the problem from their end is necessary and certainly admirable. I believe that the problem must be attacked, simultaneously, from the other side as well. Part of the problem described by computer horror stories may have come from the side of the technical specialist, but certainly another good part of these problems arises because most non computer-specialists do not understand computer potential well enough to be intelligent consumers of the powerful new tools. Yet these managers must be able to specify, intelligently and clearly, what the computer should do for them. One can almost guarantee that whatever program is written by a computer specialist who has not been given adequate direction will not solve the right problem. Thus, the first part of this book's premise, as outlined above, is that we need books and courses designed for the generalist user of computer analysis. Those educational tools should bring the nonspecialists to the point where they can define their problems in such a way that well-trained computer professionals should be able to understand and act.

The second part of the premise arises from my analysis of just what it is that such generalist consumers of computer power must in fact be taught. Although, as I noted above, most education in the computer software field has centered almost exclusively on programming, I believe that coding is neither a necessary nor a sufficient part of the education of computer consumers. In particular, the generalist unfortunately usually has a limited amount of time to devote to education about the computer. If we use all or most of that time teaching generalists to code, we will at best make them capable of coding, correctly, rather small problems of the sort that are routinely used in beginning computer courses. There is, certainly, some value to their going through such an exercise. For one thing, anyone who has taken such a beginning computer coding course learns very quickly about how much pain can be involved in getting all of the commas and parentheses correct in a computer program. It is quite desirable for managers to understand how much pain their professional helpers may have to go through in implementation. On the other hand, the limitation of coding to relatively small problems is, to my mind, a major flaw. The generalist will eventually find a problem that needs computer analysis in the course of some real-world decision problem. That computer analysis will almost invariably be extremely more complex or, at the very least, larger than any of the problems that could have been analyzed through programming in a beginning course. Yet, if generalists are to obtain computer programs that satisfactorily analyze their problems, they will have to know how to give their technical support staffs clear directives as to what must be done. They must have a good grasp of what constitutes a well-defined algorithm or model, even for a relatively complex problem. They must know how much detail is involved in making a model specification clear.

Thus, the premise of this book is that today's generalist students should be trained to create general designs of models or programs and to communicate those designs to programmers who can implement them. Perhaps more importantly, they should be trained to be able to move from an understanding of a management situation to a consideration of how much, if any, computer analysis is appropriate for the problem; they then must be able to abstract the design of a model from their general understanding of the problem.

In some cases, this training in design will be coupled with some training in simple computer coding. Certainly, if the student has the time to learn both design and some coding, so much the better. On the other hand, the material in this book has been used successfully in an elective second-year course at Harvard Business School, where the students do not learn how to program. Both students with and students without previous computer programming experience have taken the course. In fact, the student group has ranged from some students who have never coded at all to others who have had work experience in the computer software industry and who have returned to that field after graduation. The students without experience learn what models and algorithms are. Those with experience learn additional modeling techniques and also have a chance to create designs for considerably more complicated situations than they studied in their prior courses in programming.

Because of the emphasis on model design rather than on the use of existing models (such as linear programming or other optimization models) the book emphasizes simulation models (in a very general sense of that term). It begins with a discussion of deterministic models in Chapter 1. Chapters 2 and 3 proceed to discuss probablistic models. These chapters consider a number of technical topics, such as correlation, Markov models, and queueing theory. The technical topics are not treated exhaustively. Rather, they are discussed in the context in which they fit into the design of computer programs. For example, there is a brief general description of Markov processes followed by a discussion of how Markov models can help in building serial correlation into probabilistic simulation models. After the basics of deterministic and probabilistic models are covered in the first three chapters, Chapter 4 can turn to a consideration of large-scale models, mainly through case material. Finally, Chapter 5 briefly considers some basic ideas from data analysis. These topics are included because the ideas and even the specific techniques of cross tabulation and regression are so often useful in modeling. The fifth chapter does not provide a complete discussion of these topics but rather serves as a review for readers who have had at least some exposure to some statistics (such as a section on regression in a quantitative methods course).

The book contains text material, exercises, and cases. The exercises are generally stated as exercises in design although, because they cover smaller more easily defined problems than do the cases, many of the exercises are appropriate for computer coding for those teachers or readers who want to consider coding as well as design. The cases are an important part of the book because they provide the examples on which students can test their developing design skills. In essence, the text can be viewed as an outline. Considerable substance is added to that outline through the cases. The great majority of these cases are descriptions of actual modeling situations; a few of the cases have been disguised. In some of the cases, a decision problem is described and the design of a model for analyzing that problem is left to the student. In other cases, the description covers both the decision problem and also an existing model intended for the analysis of that problem. In such cases, the student's job is to figure out what the model does, to decide whether it is useful for the problem at hand, and, often, to decide whether there are interesting opportunities to extend or modify the existing model.

The book was written for use at the graduate and advanced undergraduate levels. Its focus on management problems makes it particularly suited for use in business curricula. While its prime purpose is to help in the education of competent consumers of computer analysis, the focus on design and the consideration of complex problems suggest that it can also be useful as a nontraditional piece in the educational program of a computer professional.

## Acknowledgments

This material was developed while I was teaching at Harvard Business School. The school administration, including the Division of Research, has provided support and encouragement. In addition, my students in the course Designing Models for Use in Management have been very important in helping me test and develop the material.

I would also like to thank especially a number of colleagues who have given generously of their time in reading and commenting on the course plan and on specific material as it was developed: Charles Jackson and Professors Howard Raiffa, Roy Shapiro, and Paul Vatter deserve special thanks.

I give special thanks to the various companies that served as sites for my cases, and the managers who worked with me.

Some of the cases included here were written by others. Gordon Donaldson wrote the Upstate Canning case and Thomas Piper designed the program for its analysis. Stanley Buchin wrote the original cases on which the Green Cap cases were based. D. S. R. Leighton and J. D. Pearson of the University of Western Ontario wrote the Hudson Chemical (A) case. Paul Vatter and Howard Pifer wrote the Marsh and McLennan cases. Both Crimmins Distribution and Great Western Steel were adapted from problems written by Robert Schlaifer. The Clarke's Markets case and supplement were written by Steven Wheelwright. The Crosstabs Exercise on Bonds contains some material by Arthur Schleifer. I am very grateful to all of these individuals and to the University of Western Ontario and Harvard Business School for use of the materials. I would also like to thank Nancy Hayes, Frances Charon, and Carol Covington for their consistently excellent help with the typing and preparation of the book and of the preceding material on which it is based.

*January 1979* BARBARA BUND JACKSON

# CONTENTS

chapter 1

# DETERMINISTIC MODELS

## O. INTRODUCTION

A major advance of 20th-century technology has been the development of the electronic computer. The development of computers and then their rapid improvement and growth during the 1960s and 1970s have made fundamental changes in the type and extent of calculations that can be performed and can be used by persons working in fields as diverse as business, engineering, and the humanities. This book is intended to help teach a set of skills necessary for using computers effectively. In particular, it is intended to help bridge the gap between the way computers operate and calculate and the way humans think. Computers can be thought of as extremely rapid instruments for performing numerical and logical operations, which are also extremely rigid, totally unimaginative, and without intuition. Taking the thought processes of humans, which are often creative but also usually not thoroughly precise, and translating those processes into instructions for computers is not easy. Individuals must learn to judge just what a computer could possibly do in a particular situation to help human decision makers by providing useful results of calculation. In addition, individuals must learn to express their requests for calculations in forms which computers can understand. This book helps with the first of these tasks and with a portion of the second. It discusses the art of analyzing a real-world problem, deciding what computer analysis is appropriate, and then specifying the instructions for that analysis in a form which can relatively easily be translated (perhaps by someone else, acting as the computer programmer) into the language of the computer.

This first chapter discusses the simplest type of computer models, called deterministic models because they do not involve the explicit consideration of probabilities or uncertainties. It begins by considering definitions for the terms *model* and *algorithm* and it then proceeds to a brief discussion of computers and computer languages. At that point, the necessary basics are in place and we can proceed to consider the process of specifying computer models, some of the issues that arise in that process, and some of the technical suggestions available to facilitate model design and use.

## I. MODELS AND ALGORITHMS

The word *model* has a number of different common uses. It may mean a pattern or design; it may be used for a three-dimensional representation, usually in miniature, of some physical thing. Alternatively, model may refer to a person or thing considered worth imitation, to a person or thing that acts as a pattern, or to a person who displays clothes. Model also has scientific or technical meanings. For example, the Bohr model of the atom is a description of the structure of atoms (involving a nucleus of protons and neutrons surrounded by orbiting electrons) which was meant to help facilitate scientific understanding. Thus, some scientific models are meant to describe (often in an abstract and simplified manner) something in nature. Often, the thing that is being modeled cannot be observed directly. (Such was certainly the case for the atom when Bohr proposed his model of atomic structure.)

A second type of scientific or technical model is the kind with which we will be concerned in this book. Webster's Third International Dictionary defines this variant as "a theoretical projection in detail of a possible system of human relationships (as in economics, politics or psychology)." There is no particular reason to restrict the definition to human relationships; in addition, we will tend to focus on the specification of the system of relationships rather than on their projection (which, once we make the relationships sufficiently precise, is a relatively straightforward matter for a computer). As a very simple example, consider an extremely simple view of the operation over time of a bank account at .5 percent interest per month. A model of the bank account will include the three main components present in any model: what we will call *inputs, relationships,* and *outputs*. The inputs for the bank account might be given as the starting balance, the date of that balance, and an ending date. We call these inputs *variables* to reflect the fact that we will be able to specify (and investigate the results of) different sets of values for them as we use and re-use the model. The relationships might specify that each month the balance should be multiplied by 1.005 to reflect the earning of interest. The output would probably be the ending balance. Note that the system of relationships in this example is really just a statement of the intuitively simple idea of compound interest. If we specify values for the variables (such as a starting balance of $100 on May 1, 1978, and an ending date of September 1, 1978, then we can apply the relationships to the inputs (or, in common jargon, run those inputs through the model) to obtain the output (an ending balance of $102.02).

There is considerable latitude in specifying models and often different individuals would construct a model for the same situation or problem in very different ways. Also, there is latitude in the decision as to what becomes an input and what is a relationship. The very simple model described above assumed (in the relationships, or "inside" the model) an interest rate of .5 percent per month. We might, alternatively, have let the monthly interest rate be an input variable to the model (which would then have started with a beginning balance, a starting date, an ending date, and an interest rate). In general, however, a model will consist of a set of inputs (often called *parameters* of the model), an explicit system or set of relationships for combining and manipulating those inputs, and the definition of the outputs which will be used to summarize what happens when a specific set of values for the inputs is subjected to the relationships of the model.

When a computer is used to investigate a model, the computer is instructed to take the inputs, to apply the relationships sequentially (in a specified order), and then to print out the results or outputs. Hence, the computer programmer will tend to think of a model in terms of a series of instructions or steps for calculating the implications of a model. S/he is more likely to think in terms of procedures or methods or techniques than in terms of sets of relationships. Programmers speak of *algorithms,*[1] which might best be thought of as specific sets of instructions for calculating the projections or results of models. For the simple bank account example, an algorithm might be: Take the starting balance. Start a counter for time at the starting date. Advance that counter by one month and multiply the balance by 1.005 (assuming this fixed interest rate). Check to see if the ending date has been reached. If so, print out the balance. If not, advance the counter by another month, multiply the balance by 1.005, and go back to check again for the ending date . . . continue in this way until the ending date is reached.

When they are intended for implementation on computers, algorithms must be extremely precise (for computers are precise and have essentially no ability to interpret ambiguity). The algorithm to investigate or implement a model must specify the variables which will be inputs to the model, the relationships which should be applied to the inputs (and the exact order in which those steps should be taken), and the output which should be provided. Once such an algorithm has been put into computer language (or programmed), you would run the program: being very careful to specify values for the variables in exactly the form expected (decimals if the program wanted decimals, percent if it wanted percent), you would give values for all

---

[1] The term comes from the name al Khuwarizmi or al Khowarizmi, a famous 9th-century mathematician who wrote a book on algebra with Arabic numbers.

of the input variables and the machine would then carry out the algorithm and print the output values for you.

For most of this book we will be concerned with specifying models of various business situations. As do many users, we will generally talk in terms of *models* rather than of algorithms. We will assume, however, that our aim is to learn to specify the model in enough detail that it would be reasonable to expect a programmer to be able to convert it into a computer program; the programmer will most likely think of *algorithms* or procedures. As preparation for the main task of the book, which is to teach the art of model design, we turn first to a brief consideration of computers and computer programming.

## II. COMPUTERS AND COMPUTER PROGRAMMING

In discussing the general structure and operation of electronic computers, it is useful to put aside for the time being the rich assortment of computer designs that are available today and to begin by considering a simple computer structure that was typical of early machines (in the 1950s, for example). In describing computers it is customary to distinguish between what are called hardware and software. *Hardware* is the term used for the physical computer, with its electronic circuits, storage devices, and related parts. *Software,* by contrast, refers to the programs or sets of instructions which are given to the computer and which it carries out or *executes.*[2] We begin by considering simple computer hardware and then, later in this section, proceed to show how the computer software provides instructions for the hardware to follow. The remainder of the book can be considered further discussion of the design and use of computer software.

The simplified diagram in Figure 1–1 shows the main parts of the hard-

**FIGURE 1–1**

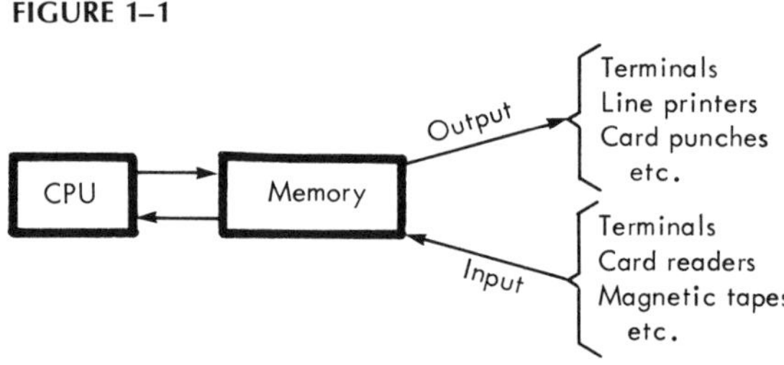


[2] In fact, in the 1970s the distinction between hardware and software became somewhat blurred as what is called "firmware" became common. To begin this discussion, however, it is useful to make a clean distinction between hardware and software.

[3] In fact, the basic set of operations is even simpler than this description suggests, since some arithmetic operations are performed as combinations of simpler ones. For example, multiplications are accomplished through series of additions and shifts. For our purpose, however, it is sufficient to think of the CPU as performing all the basic arithmetic operations.

ware of a typical early computer. The term *CPU* in Figure 1–1 stands for *central processing unit.* This portion of the computer carries out the basic calculations which form the core of the machine's work. In particular, the CPU performs its work through combinations of a very small number of basic numerical and logical operations. It can add two numbers or can subtract, multiply, or divide.[3] It can also compare two numbers and determine which is the larger (or whether the two quantities are exactly equal).

Clearly, for it to be worthwhile to have a CPU with capability to perform these basic operations, it must also be possible to provide the computer with interesting numbers on which the CPU can operate. The function of the second basic computer building block, called *memory,* is to hold information (or data) on which the CPU can then call. In Figure 1–1 the arrows in both directions between CPU and memory indicate that the CPU must be able to obtain data from memory on which it can then perform its basic operations, and that the CPU must also be able to store or save the results of its operations in the memory, either for future use by the CPU or for presentation to a human computer-user in the form of what is called *output*. Conceptually, it is useful to think of the computer memory as a collection of well-identified slots or bins (or *words,* in computer language). Each word can hold a single number, with some set number of digits specific to the particular computer model. Even when computers are used to handle letters rather than numbers, as is the case when they process mailing labels, for example, the alphabetic information is actually coded within the computer in terms of numbers. Words are identified by numeric names or labels, generally called "addresses." When we now consider combining a CPU with a memory unit in building a computer, we find that we must add a few more capabilities to the CPU to allow it to use the memory effectively. In particular, the CPU must be able to request specific information from memory; for example, it must be able to issue requests such as "fetch the information in memory location 101." The CPU must also be able to store or save the results of its computations in specified memory locations; it must be able to issue commands such as "save the result in memory location 102."

Computer memory can take many different physical forms. In earlier machines computers often had some memory built from magnetic cores, or small, toroid-shaped pieces of material that could be magnetized in either of two directions. One direction was interpreted by the computer logic to represent a 0 and the other direction was interpreted as a 1. All of the computer's most basic calculations are performed in terms of zeros and ones, in what is called *binary* or base-two arithmetic. Because magnetic core memory was expensive, early computers also typically had one or more forms of what was called *secondary memory* or storage. An example was magnetic tape. Secondary storage was slower than core memory in that it took the CPU many times as long to receive requested information from such storage devices as was needed to obtain information from the primary memory, but the enormously reduced cost of the secondary media made them appropriate for storage of large quantities of data. The secondary devices also use a binary representation for data, recording information in terms of zeros and ones.

As computer architecture has developed over time, there have evolved many new forms of memory. The basic high-speed computer memory today is no longer built from magnetic cores. Often, integrated circuit memories, using the technology that has allowed extensive development of calculators and other electronic equipment, are used for memory. Other technologies are available or being developed. There are also many new forms today for secondary storage, including disks, floppy disks, and bubble memories. Today's wide range of computer capabilities and prices means, in addition, that what is considered satisfactory as the main memory technology for a less expensive computer might be considered suitable only for secondary storage, if that, on a faster, more expensive machine. The specific details of computer memory technology are not at all necessary for our basic concern with computer model design. It is sufficient to know that computers can hold and operate on large amounts of data and that the cost of memory is falling rapidly, as are the costs of other parts of the computer hardware.

The CPU, with its basic operations and the ability to fetch from and store in memory, together with the memory and its ability to save useful data, provides the central portion of the computer. To make the design complete, we must add two further capabilities. First, there must be some mechanism for a human computer-user to convey to the machine the information to be stored in its memory and operated upon by its CPU. In addition, there must be a mechanism for the computer to present to the human user the results of its calculations. The portions of the computer hardware that handle these two tasks are generally called the *input/output* part of the computer or, often, simply the *I/O*. Many mechanisms are available for accomplishing I/O. First, consider the input task. A very common input medium on early computers consisted of punched computer cards. Such cards are still in use today (they are used by telephone companies in customer billing and record-keeping, for example, with a punched card enclosed with each customer's monthly bill), but the importance of cards is declining. Information on cards is recorded when small rectangular holes are punched in the card. Sensors on card-reading computer hardware translate the pattern of holes into numbers. A more modern form of computer input uses computer terminals. These devices have keyboards on which the user types information. In addition, they are linked in some way to a computer, so that the information typed by the user can be converted into a pattern of zeros and ones and then conveyed directly to the machine. Some terminals having printing mechanisms for providing typed (or hard-copy) records; other terminals use cathode ray tubes, like TV screens, to show the user what has been typed. The CRT's are faster than hard-copy terminals but do not in general provide a written record for the user of what has been typed. In some situations magnetic tapes serve as input for one computer, providing information to the machine that has come from some other computer. Other input devices are also used. Output devices on computers are similarly diverse. Output can be provided in the form of punched cards by card punches. Printed output can be provided on terminals or on high-speed printing devices called line printers. Output can also involve magnetic tapes and other devices.

For today's user, the main points to understand about I/O media concern the impacts that different media have on the way users interact with computers. In particular, some devices are more appropriate for what is called *batch processing,* others for what is called *time sharing.* We will return to a description of these two fundamental modes of computer operation after a bit more discussion of how the basic computer building blocks fit together.

In order for a computer to perform useful computations and provide valuable output information, the human user must be able to give the machine one more type of information. S/he must tell the machine what sequence of basic operations to perform on the input data s/he has provided. A set of instructions for a computer is called a *computer program;* in writing or creating such a set of instructions, a human user is said to be *programming.* As we noted above, the computer itself stores data in the form of zeros and ones in its memory. Computers also store programs as series of zeros and ones in memory, with particular patterns of these two digits representing specific machine instructions. For example, on one machine the sequence 101110000 10011 might tell the CPU to request that the contents of location 10011 be fetched from memory. The very first computer programs ever written were written as such sequences of zeros and ones. Further, they were written in terms of the basic operations such as fetch, store, add, subtract, compare. To tell the machine to multiply sales and price together to find revenue, the user would first have to decide which memory locations were to correspond to sales, to price, and to revenue. Assume that 10010 is sales, 10011 is price, and 10100 is revenue. Assume further that the sales and price numbers have already been input to the appropriate memory locations. A very small set of instructions for finding revenue might be

101110000 10010

to fetch the value of sales from location 10010 so that the CPU can operate on it, followed by

010000000 10011

to multiply by the contents of location 10011, or price, and then

110000001 10100

to store the result in location 10100, identified as revenue.

If you think about the process of coding a more complex and useful set of instructions in such series of zeros and ones, called machine code, it should be obvious why the process would at best be a very painful one. For one thing, the human user would really prefer not to have to worry about details such as fetching and storing in memory. Even if it were not possible to avoid such detail, there is also the problem that series of zeros and ones are not natural ways for humans to communicate. The mere task of typing all of the needed sequences is burdensome and it is the rare person indeed who can type many of them without making frequent errors. Errors in programs may make it impossible for the computer to proceed. Even worse, the errors may look to the computer like perfectly valid sets of instructions which it will execute. The problem is that the sequence will not be the one the user wanted and hence the results will not be what was desired.

This very simple example of a program in machine code or machine language should make very clear the enormous gulf between the way most human users think and the form in which instructions must be provided to computers. The entire history of the development of alternative systems for specifying computer programs (that is, of *computer languages*) can be thought of as an attempt to narrow that gulf. The first step along this path was a very simple one. People are very bad at typing, checking, and reading sequences of zeros and ones; they are somewhat better with strings of numbers that are not all ones and zeros. As the first aid in programming, designers realized that triples of zeros and ones could be recoded by single digits from 0 to 7. For example, 000 could be represented by 0,001 by 1,010 by 2, . . ., 111 by 7. Programmers could be allowed to provide their instructions in terms of the digits from 0 to 7; the machine could then automatically translate those digits into sequences of zeros and ones.

The next step in the development of programming languages involved a similar although more complex type of translation. If the computer could translate from 400 to the instruction to add (100000000), then it seemed perfectly reasonable for the computer to translate the letters ADD to 400 and from that to the instruction to add. There would be no creativity and no imagination in this translation process. The machine would not be able to deal with user errors, such as typing AAD instead of ADD. On the other hand, ADD was easier for most people to deal with than was 400, and it was clearly easier to proofread, so that the addition of mnemonic codes for basic machine operations was a big help to programmers. So was a related improvement in which users could declare only once that a particular location in memory would be given a particular alphabetic name throughout a computer program. For example, the user might declare that location 10010 was to be called SALES. Then rather than having to type 100000000 10010 to mean "add the contents of the memory word containing sales," the user could simply type ADD SALES and the machine would translate to machine code.

Computer languages such as one in which the user could type ADD SALES are called *assembly languages*. Their development greatly facilitated the task of computer programming. Assembly languages did not solve the problems of programming by any means, however. The sequence of instructions

```
FETCH  SALES
MULT   PRICE
STORE  REVENUE
```

is certainly easier to read than are the sequences of zeros and ones given earlier, but the picky detail in the assembly language code is still very unnatural for human users. Additional developments of computer languages have narrowed further the gap between computers and human users. Computer professionals have developed what are called *higher level languages* in which computer programs can be written. In many of these languages, the definition of revenue as sales times price would be written in a form such as

```
REVENUE = SALES * PRICE
```

Many higher level languages are in common use today. For numeric and scientific work the most common is FORTRAN. Other languages serving similar purposes are Algol, Basic, and PL/I. For business record-keeping, such as billing, another language, called COBOL, is very widely used. There are numerous other examples. With these languages, users are spared some of the pain that was inherent in machine-language programming, although by no means all of that pain has been eliminated. Spelling must still be perfect; computers do not recognize that SLAES is SALES with a typing error. Similarly, computer languages require commas and parentheses and other punctuation to be included exactly correctly. The user is spared some of the detail of assigning names to specific memory locations, yet s/he must still tell the machine to save ten words for sales figures if in fact s/he wants to consider ten periods of data.

Computer languages continue to evolve today and the newer languages become increasingly powerful. Yet, the gap between computer and human still exists. In fact, the existence of that gap is the basic motivation for this book. Developments in the field of computer languages can help narrow the gap from one side, but users and designers of computer programs must do the bulk of the work in translating from the normal, rather intuitive, and often somewhat fuzzy, way in which people think to the absolute specificity needed for the computer.

Before concluding this brief discussion of computers and computer programming, we now turn to a consideration of the changes that have occurred in computer availability and in the ease with which computers can be accessed and used. It is these changes that have increased enormously the potential for intelligent use of the computer in almost any field and which, therefore, provide some of the motivation for mastering the task of designing computer models.

Early computers were rare and expensive and the ways in which they were operated reflected this fact. The early computer centers (for use by communities such as businesses or universities) operated in what is called *batch processing* mode. In this mode, the expensive powerful computer was central and the efficient use of its time was the key management objective. Users wrote their programs and then keypunched them onto cards at equipment totally separate from the computer. They then fastened their decks, or sets of cards, with rubber bands and submitted them to a person who served as a dispatcher for the computer center. Many such decks or jobs would be collected to be input together, for efficiency. In fact, the decks of instructions and data were not input directly to the main computer at many computer centers. The main computer in the mid-1960s was likely to be a very powerful calculator that could add two numbers together in a few millionths of a second. It was also very expensive. Inputting information to such a computer from punched cards did not use the computer resource very efficiently and, as a result, many centers used a smaller, slower, but less expensive computer as a pre-processor. The pre-processor would read the decks for many users and would write the data and instructions onto a magnetic tape. Magnetic tape input on the main computer was much faster than was input from cards, so this pre-processing step enabled the main computer to read its instructions and data more quickly.

The magnetic tape would then be carried to the main computer, where the machine would read and try to execute the programs, one by one. It would provide output for the users, according to the instructions provided by the programs. Rather than print the output in a form suitable for people to read, the main computer would write its results on another magnetic tape, again to save its valuable time. The magnetic tape would then be carried to a smaller machine where the information on it would be transferred to printed output, most likely with a high-speed line printer. The printed output would be returned to the users, as would the decks of cards. Turnaround time, or the time between submitting a deck and receiving the results, might be several hours at a well-run batch center. During that time, a user's job would have consumed perhaps a few seconds of computer time—a few minutes at a maximum in most cases. The remainder of the turnaround time would have been used in the batching operations designed to ensure efficient machine utilization—the waiting for a full set of decks to arrive, the transfer to magnetic tape, the transfer to the main computer, the transfer from the output magnetic tape to line-printer output, the separation of the output for different users, and returning their output and their input decks to them.

Machine utilization was indeed very high. The needs of the user received considerably less attention. Waiting five hours or so for useful output was unpleasant enough. More often than not, users who were developing new programs did not find really useful output after the wait. Instead, they found a message that there had been something wrong with their deck—a missing comma perhaps. They then had to find the error, type corrections for their decks, resubmit and wait several more hours—perhaps just to discover yet another picky error in the program. There were other inconveniences. Programmers from those olden days usually have stories to tell about the day they were in the process of fixing the fifteenth missing or misplaced comma when they dropped their deck of punched cards on the floor and then had to spend several more days trying to get it back into the correct order.

Batch processing is still used today on many computers. In some cases in which programs involve particularly heavy computational burdens it still makes sense to work hard to make the most efficient use of the computer's power, even if users are inconvenienced. In many other situations, however, computers are operated in another mode, called *time-sharing*. Computer power has become less and less expensive, even though computers have become increasingly powerful. Many computers today can add two numbers in a fraction of a millionth of a second. Yet, a computer comparable in power to one that would have sold for a million dollars in 1965 might have sold for $25,000 in 1978. With computer costs reduced so markedly, users and designers find it sensible to worry less about the maximally efficient use of computer time and more about increasing the efficiency with which users can manage their time. Time-sharing is particularly effective at this task. The basic idea behind time-sharing involves the notion that the time scale of a computer (adding in a millionth of a second or less) and that of a person (taking several seconds to type instructions as to what should be added—and perhaps several minutes to decide what to type) are vastly different. As a result, a computer can give its attention, in small slots of time, to more than one user and still make each user feel as if s/he has all the computer attention s/he needs. In this mode, a number of different users communicate with the computer, each through his or her own terminal. Users input data and instructions through their respective terminals. The computer turns its attention from one user to the next, and the next, yet it is able to handle user requests so quickly, on the human scale, that most users feel as if they are receiving instantaneous reponses to their requests.

The contrast of time-sharing with batch processing is marked. In time-sharing, the user can obtain information about a missing comma (which, unfortunately, still must be found and fixed) in a minute or two rather than in hours. S/he can fix a whole series of minor program errors and get useful output in well under an hour. Clearly, time-sharing makes using the computer much more pleasant and efficient for people. It does not use the computer as efficiently as does batch processing, however. The computer may remain idle for periods of time in time-sharing. In addition, there is a large amount of monitoring work that must be done by the computer to keep the users straight, remember who needs attention next, and perform similar overhead tasks. It is the decreasing costs of computers and the increasing costs of the time of users that have made the trade-off implicit in time-sharing appropriate in many situations.

As we conclude this discussion of computers and computer programs, we turn briefly to the question of what changes are in process in the computer field. The basic design of a computer shown in Figure 1–1 still describes in broad conceptual form the design of modern computers. Specific designs are varied, with some computers today using several memories, others using several CPUs, some using what is called *firmware* in read-only memories—and many other combinations. From the point of view of the computer hardware designer, such variations are clearly very important, but for the designer of computer models, the details are really not crucial. What is important is to realize that the costs of all computer hardware components—CPUs, memories, and I/O devices—have been falling dramatically. Computers become more and more powerful, yet less and less costly. In addition, the range of computers available in the marketplace has increased. Machines may be faster or slower, more or less expensive, better for I/O convenience or better for heavy computation. Some handle only batch processing, but many can perform time-sharing or both types of operations. Many companies have their own computers, called "in-house machines," in large computer centers. Many firms own several computers. Often a group within a company buys a smaller computer for its own exclusive use, rather than use the main company facility. Some of these same firms, together with many companies that do not own their own hardware, buy time on a variable basis from vendors that sell computer time, often on time-shared machines. In such time-sharing services, users rent or buy terminals and then use telephone lines to provide the communication link between their terminals and the main computer, owned by the time-sharing firm. The computer keeps track of how much of its resources is used by each user account; users are billed accordingly.

Hence, computers have become more powerful and more widely available, so that more and more businesses and individual executives use them routinely. These trends will continue.

## III. SPECIFYING COMPUTER MODELS

Computer programs are explicit sets of totally unambiguous instructions telling computers what calculations to perform and what data to use. These sets of instructions are serial; in other words, they tell the computer exactly what actions to take in exactly what order. A number of different steps are involved in bridging the gap between the thought processes of a computer user and the final computer program that can provide helpful calculations. First, the potential computer user must begin to analyze and structure the problem s/he faces. For example, we might be trying to decide what to charge for a particular new product. In the initial step of our analysis, our thinking is likely to be relatively unstructured as we try to identify the important aspects of the problem: what are the possible decisions for price—how will potential customers respond to different price levels—how will different choices affect our financial results. At this stage we do not try to answer these questions, but merely attempt to make sure that we have scoped out the entire problem and identified the important parts. We might, for example, decide that we really have two related decisions to make—how much to charge and how much to spend on promotion. We might further decide that we must consider the sensitivity or response of demand to different possible prices and that we should consider the results over more than a single year of operation. This first part of the analysis might be called *basic case analysis.* It is the type of thinking that must be done in any decision situation, whether or not computer analysis later helps with the number work. In most problems the basic case analysis is the most difficult part of the work, requiring judgment and insights, and the basic analysis is clearly the work of a person rather than a machine.

Having performed some sound basic case analysis, we can next proceed to a decision on how much computer analysis, if any, we should use. For one thing, we must at this stage interject consideration of the capabilities and limitations of computer analysis. We might decide that we would like to have projected income statements (or pro forma income statements) forecasting the results of different sets of decisions and assumptions. The computer can easily provide us with such statements if we make explicit all of the assumptions we want it to use in their preparation. In fact, such *pro forma generators* are one of the most common types of deterministic computer models. We might also think that it would be nice to have the computer predict what demand will be at different price levels. On further thought, however, we should at least question seriously the ability of the machine to make such projections for us. Recall from the previous sections the totally explicit nature of a computer program. If we now think about all of the considerations that we would use ourselves in projecting demand, there is some question as to whether it makes sense to have the computer do the projections. Computer projections must be given by totally explicit, unambiguous rules. In forecasting for most products most people would think about an assortment of market influences and then would rather intuitively arrive at an estimate of demand for a particular price level. There are two possible ways to bridge the gap between the way people arrive at projections of demand and the way a computer would do so. One is for the computer user to provide the computer with a complete set of instructions for finding demand (such as: take 1 million units and subtract 10,000 units times the price charged). Notice how mechanical this rule is. It involves extremely strong assumptions. For example, this particular rule assumes that the difference in demand between prices of $20 and $21 (800,000 and 790,000 units, respectively) is exactly the same as the difference in demand between prices of $29 and $30 (710,000 and 700,000, respectively). Such simplistic rules are certainly not completely accurate and, in many cases, are not at all satisfactory approximations of the true situation.[4]

If we decide that we do not have the ability to express the price-demand relationship in explicit quantitative terms, we can bridge the gap between user and machine in the second available way. We can do the demand projections ourselves, in whatever way suits our thought processes, and then simply provide the machine with lists of the projections. Notice the distinction between the two methods: We treat the demand projection as a relationship of the model in the first case but as an input in the second. This example illustrates one of the most difficult types of trade-offs that must be made in designing computer models. On the one hand, the computer is very powerful and can perform calculations very quickly, so that we would like to have the machine do as much as possible of the analysis for us. On the other hand, the computer is extremely rigid, and any work that it does for us must be done according to rigid, explicit rules that we provide. We must decide what parts of a problem can be expressed in sufficiently precise quantitative form for computer analysis and what parts we would rather have performed by the slower but infinitely more creative human mind. In the example of pricing a new product, we might decide that our inputs must include price, demand, and promotion, reasoning that we are simply not able to make explicit for the computer the important linkages among those quantities. We might, on the other hand, decide that we are considerably more comfortable about specifying explicitly the cost structure of our manufacturing process and that the machine can figure on fixed costs of $1 million per year and variable costs of $10 per unit we make. Similarly, we might make explicit assumptions about other aspects of costs, such as selling costs. Notice that the process of deciding how to construct the various parts of our desired pro forma generator program is really very analogous to the process we would go through if we were to prepare pro forma statements by hand calculation. The only major difference is that we must think about the instructions at a level of detail suitable for the computer and we must decide which parts of the analysis the computer can in fact perform.

Having decided what parts of the problem can usefully be analyzed by computer, we can then proceed to specify the algorithm in more detail. As a first step, we will want to give the algorithm in outline terms, specifying inputs, relationships, and outputs. For the pricing problem, we might give the following specification of a pro forma generator.

---

[4] Notice also that this rule will predict negative demand for prices above $100. We might or might not want to instruct the computer to do some error checking and to reject prices outside of some sensible range of values.

A. Inputs (for each of five years)
   1. Price.
   2. Promotion.
   3. Demand.
B. Relationships (for each year)
   1. Revenue equals price times demand.
   2. Variable cost of goods equals ten times demand.
   3. Fixed cost equals $1 million.
   4. Selling costs equal promotion plus 5 percent of revenue.
   5. Total cost equals variable cost of goods plus fixed cost plus selling costs.
   6. Earnings before tax equal revenue minus total cost.
   7. Taxes equal 48 percent of earnings before tax.
   8. Earnings after tax equal earnings before tax minus taxes.
C. Outputs (for each year)
   1. Revenue.
   2. Total cost.
   3. Earnings before tax.
   4. Taxes.
   5. Earnings after tax.

The next step in the process of constructing a computer program will involve programming or coding our design. In other words, the general set of instructions given above must be translated into the exact form of some appropriate computer language. As the preceding section of this chapter should have suggested, the coding step involves a careful and picky translation process. It turns out, however, that the general instructions given above are not very far in content from actual computer language specification of the algorithm. As an example, the model defined above is written in Figure 1–2 in FORTRAN.[5] The second FORTRAN program (Figure 1–3) gives the same program listing; it also gives comments to explain what the different lines of the program mean. With the exception of bookkeeping types of detail (such as the statement to reserve needed memory locations), the general model specification and the FORTRAN are quite similar.

This book assumes that not all readers will be performing their own coding. Some will, but many others will not. The above simple example should suggest that most of the hard work in model specification involves the initial design choice and the initial specification of the design. Coding is not trivial, but it involves translation of a design rather than creation of the design itself. If you have a problem to analyze, you generally cannot let someone else do the design for you, or the resulting computer program may not provide the outputs you want, may request inputs in a form which you

[5] In FORTRAN, as in many computer languages, * means *multiply*.

**FIGURE 1–2**
FORTRAN program

```
      DIMENSION PRICE(5), PROMO(5), DEM(5),
         REV(5), VARCST(5), FIXCST(5), SELCST(5), TOTAL(5),
         EBT(5), TAX(5), EAT(5)
      READ(5,10) PRICE
 10   FORMAT(5G)
      READ(5,10) PROMO
      READ(5,10) DEM
      DO 20 I = 1,5
      REV(I) = PRICE(I) * DEM(I)
      VARCST(I) = 10. * DEM(I)
      FIXCST(I) = 1000000.
      SELCST(I) = PROMO(I) + .05 * REV(I)
      TOTAL(I) = VARCST(I) + FIXCST(I) + SELCST(I)
      EBT(I) = REV(I) - TOTAL(I)
      TAX(I) = .48 * EBT(I)
      EAT(I) = EBT(I) - TAX(I)
 20   CONTINUE
      WRITE(5,30) REV
 30   FORMAT('_REVENUE_', 5F12.0)
      WRITE(5,31) TOTAL
 31   FORMAT('_TOT_CST_', 5F12.0)
      WRITE(5,32) EBT
 32   FORMAT('_EBT_________', 5F12.0)
      WRITE(5,33) TAX
 33   FORMAT('_TAXES_______', 5F12.0)
      WRITE(5,34) EAT
 34   FORMAT ('_EAT_________', 5F12.0)
      END
```

cannot provide, or may include incorrect assumptions about relationships. Once you have specified the design, however, it is often possible to have someone else do the coding (and the worrying about getting the parentheses and commas just right).

Even if you do have coding help in creating computer programs, the process of specifying a computer program and then having it coded involves considerable effort. It is appropriate at this point to begin to consider the question of when that effort is worthwhile. In doing so, we can start by recalling the strengths of computers—their accuracy and speed. The corresponding disadvantages of computer use are the requirements for giving instructions as explicit, unambiguous serial sets of steps. A bit of reflection should suggest that computerization is indicated when the specification effort

**FIGURE 1–3**
Annotated FORTRAN program

First, we ask the computer to save memory space for five price figures, five promotion figures, etc.:

```
      DIMENSION PRICE(5), PROMO(5), DEM(5),
        REV(5), VARCST(5), FIXCST(5), SELCST(5),
        TOTAL(5), EBT(5), TAX(5), EAT(5)
```

Next, we tell the computer to input or read values for prices, promotion, and demand. (With a FORMAT statement, we provide some detail about what the input will look like):

```
      READ(5,10) PRICE
   10 FORMAT(5G)
      READ(5,10) PROMO
      READ(5,10) DEM
```

We ask the computer to consider years 1 through 5:

```
      DO 20 I = 1,5
```

For each year, we want revenue, costs, etc.:

```
      REV(I) = PRICE(I) * DEM(I)
      VARCST(I) = 10. * DEM(I)
      FIXCST(I) = 1000000.
      SELCST(I) = PROMO(I) + .05 * REV(I)
      TOTAL(I) = VARCST(I) + FIXCST(I) + SELCST(I)
      EBT(I) = REV(I) - TOTAL(I)
      TAX(I) = .48 * EBT(I)
      EAT(I) = EBT(I) - TAX(I)
```

We tell the computer to end the year-by-year calculations:

```
   20 CONTINUE
```

We ask for the output, using FORMAT statements to give details about just what form to use:

```
      WRITE(5,30) REV
   30 FORMAT ('_REVENUE_', 5F12.0)
      WRITE(5,31) TOTAL
   31 FORMAT ('_TOT_COST_', 5F12.0)
      WRITE(5,32) EBT
   32 FORMAT('_EBT__________', 5F12.0)
      WRITE(5,33) TAX
   33 FORMAT ('_TAXES______', 5F12.0)
      WRITE(5,34) EAT
   34 FORMAT ('_EAT__________', 5F12.0)
      END
```

is relatively low compared with the computational benefit. Each step in a process must be specified explicitly. The payoff comes when we plan to use (or execute) the same set of instructions many times. In such cases, the costs of specification are more than repaid by the subsequent repeated use. In our specific example above on pricing, this principle takes the following form: It would not make much sense to computerize our model if we wanted to analyze only one or two sets of inputs; we could do the calculations by hand in much less time than it would take to specify a model, have it programmed, and then use the program. If, on the other hand, we will use the program many times, to investigate different assumptions about price, promotion, and demand, then the trade-off between specification time and calculation time will at some point make it useful to have the algorithm programmed for a computer.

The general idea that we execute the same set of instructions many times is sometimes called *looping* and it is fundamental to the usefulness of computers. Looping can occur within a program; we can, for example, perform a basic set of payroll calculations for each of a large number of employees. Or, the repetition can occur when a program is run on many different occasions, presumably with different sets of inputs. In the pro forma model above we would likely have both forms of repetition. The program loops to perform basic financial calculations for each of five years on any one execution or run. In addition, we would want to make many different runs to consider different sets of inputs.

Before we end this introductory section on the design of deterministic models, it is worth stating explicitly a point that was covered to some extent implicitly above. When a user gives a particular set of inputs to a computer model, it is generally up to the user to make sure that the inputs make sense in the context of whatever problem is being analyzed. In the pricing problem, it is the user's job to make sure that a particular set of price, promotion, and demand figures makes sense. The computer program described above will work perfectly well on nonsensical inputs. For example, the user could give one set of inputs with high promotion expenditures providing low demand and, for the same set of prices, a second set of inputs with lower promotion expenditures and higher demand. The computer will not find this apparent error in logic. The sets of inputs that a user submits to a computer program will be called *scenarios.* The point we are emphasizing here is that it is the user's job to make sure that the input scenarios make sense. Sometimes computers are programmed to do some error-checking on inputs (and, for example, to check that prices are not negative), but most of the work in constructing interesting scenarios must be done by the user. We have just noted that much of the value of computer programs lies in their ability to be repetitive. For a pro forma generator, the value is that we can consider many different scenarios which have been selected by the human user because they are interesting to study.

To summarize, then, there are a series of steps involved in constructing even the simplest of computer programs. First, there must always be sound basic case analysis to determine what the problem is. Next, we must decide how much useful analysis can be done by machine. At that point, we can proceed in the third step to begin the explicit model design. As a fourth step we write or have written for us a computer program to perform the algorithm we have designed. Finally, we use the program, for alternative sets of interesting inputs (or scenarios), and then we interpret and use the results.

## IV. BLOCK DIAGRAMS FOR MODEL SPECIFICATION

One way to define or describe a model (or algorithm) is to specify in prose the inputs to the model, the relationships among those inputs, and the outputs of the model. In some cases such prose descriptions are very clear and are quite satisfactory as definitions. In other cases, however, prose descriptions quickly become confusing and, in particular, prose definitions are not ideal for describing how parts of a model fit together. Often, therefore, we use a part-graphic and part-prose description of a model or algorithm; this section discusses such descriptions (which are called *block diagrams* or *flowcharts*).

The basic idea in constructing a block diagram is to divide an algorithm or model into parts, to describe the parts (in prose and/or algebra) inside boxes of the diagram, and to use arrows to show how to proceed from one part of the algorithm to another (or, stated in terms of models, the arrows are used to show how the parts of the model fit together). As an extremely simple example, suppose that we want to construct an algorithm for calculating the end-of-month balance in a savings account. (We assume that no deposits except for the month's interest, and no withdrawals, are made during the month.) We would input (or start with) the beginning balance and the monthly interest rate. We would then multiply the starting balance by 1 plus the interest rate; this amount would be the ending balance. Finally, we would output the ending balance. This algorithm is, of course, too simple to gain much from a block diagram presentation, but for purposes of illustration we give a block diagram (Figure 1–4) for the process. In reading such a diagram, we simply begin at the START and follow the arrows to the END.

As noted above, the block diagram adds very little, if anything, to the clarity of the algorithm. If we change the program a bit, the diagram does a bit more good. First, we will introduce the idea of *branching,* or of *alternate paths* through the process. Suppose that the savings account is a minimum balance account and that no interest is paid if the balance dips below $100; in fact, suppose that the bank wants to send a warning to customers whose balances have dropped below the minimum allowed. The algorithm must now say that we add interest to an account only if the starting balance is

FIGURE 1–4

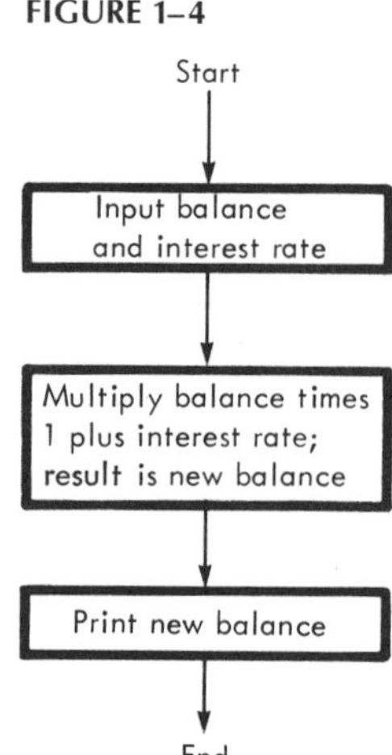


$100 or more; otherwise, we must print out a warning message. The block diagram in Figure 1–5 describes the new algorithm.

Figure 1–5 has two types of boxes. The first kind contains basic operations, such as inputting numbers, multiplying, or adding. (The first diagram, in Figure 1–4, contained only this type of box.) In Figure 1–5 there is also a

FIGURE 1–5

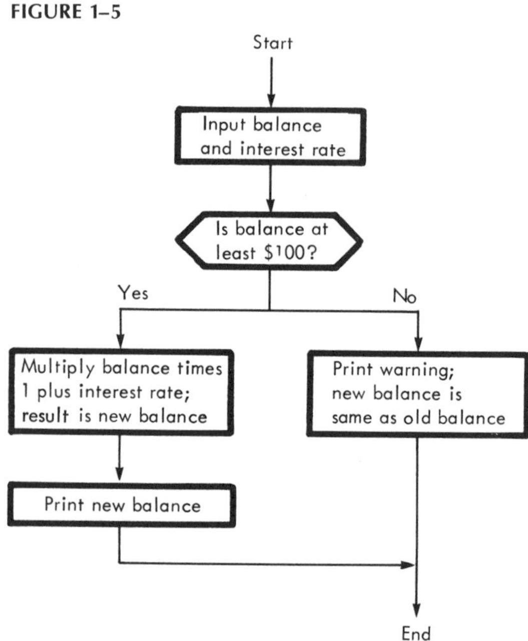

box which performs a comparison and then specifies that the algorithm is to proceed along different paths for different outcomes of that comparison. Thus, the *comparison* or *condition box* allows the algorithm to branch. (In terms of models, the comparison allows different relationships to be invoked for different conditions. If the balance is $100 or more, the new balance is the old balance times 1 plus the interest rate. If not, the relationship is that the new balance is the same as the old balance—and, moreover, that the account is issued a warning.) The flow through the diagram now depends on the outcome of the comparison.

The diagram in Figure 1–5 shows one other point about models and block diagramming. Note that the arrow from the warning box and the arrow from the calculate-new-balance box rejoin before the end of the diagram. Thus, block diagrams are not like decision trees, in which branches can never diverge and then rejoin.[6] In a block diagram or model, it is entirely proper (and, in fact, it is likely to be useful) to have paths diverge for part of the diagram, while different conditions are handled properly, and then to come back together again.

Next, we add another feature of block diagrams by adding a new dimension to the problem. Suppose that we want to calculate the ending balance for each of several accounts in the bank; in addition, we want to know the total interest paid. We assume that the interest rate is the same for each account but that the starting balances differ. We include the minimum-balance assumption from above. Also, we assume there will be no other deposits to or withdrawals from the accounts. The algorithm should now include instructions to take the accounts one at a time and calculate the interest and new balance for each. In addition, it should specify that a running sum should be kept of the total interest paid. In technical terms, we want the algorithm to loop through the accounts or, in other words, to repeat the same procedure over and over, once for each account. Figure 1–6 shows such a looping mechanism.

Note that the rate is input only once and that the interest counter is set to 0 only at the start. The loop is followed for each account. The diagram should be read to mean that only after the loop has been followed the specified number of times do we follow the bottom arrow out of the loop (to END). When we include a loop in an algorithm, it is extremely important to specify when the looping should stop. In computer jargon, such a specification is called a *stopping rule*. (Computers are very literal and not at all imaginative. If you don't tell them to stop, they won't, and they will simply continue to loop indefinitely.) Thus, the diagram in Figure 1–6 shows a flow of control that involves examining the first account and printing a warning or obtaining a new balance, then looping back to consider the next account, . . . and so on, continuing to loop until each account has been considered. After consid-

[6] See Chapter 2 and the Appendix.

**FIGURE 1–6**

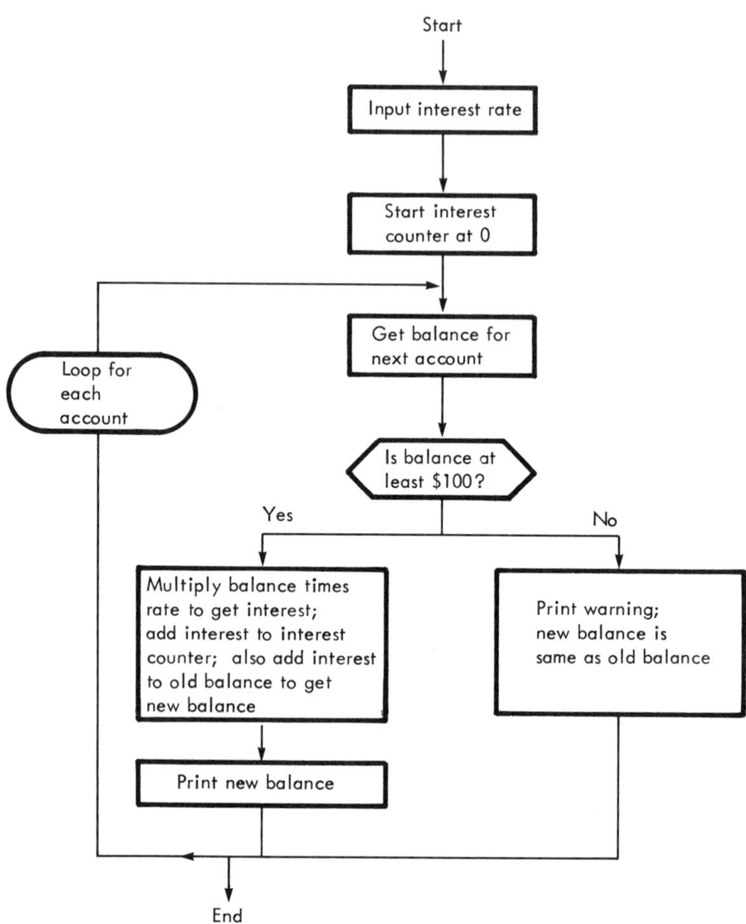


ering all the accounts, the algorithm will not follow the looping arrow but instead will take the arrow to END.

The way the steps of a block diagram are explained in the prose and/or algebra within the boxes is largely a matter of style (as often is the question of how much of the process to put in a single box). Often, it saves time and effort (and adds clarity) to use a bit of symbolism. For example, we might want to say, "Multiply the balance times the interest rate to get the interest," more concisely in symbols. To do so, we will use the symbol ← to mean "is defined as" or "becomes." Thus, INTEREST ← BALANCE * RATE would mean the same thing as the preceding prose. (Here we use the * for multiplication, as is common in computer languages.) Corresponding symbolism is also used when a quantity or variable is updated (or given a new value) in an algorithm. For example, BALANCE ← BALANCE + INTEREST means that the balance is updated to (or that it becomes) the previous balance plus the interest.[7]

Another convention which may help make diagrams clear involves subscripts. In the savings account algorithms, we are really talking about several different accounts and, hence, different starting balances. Rather than call each balance the same name (BALANCE), we may want to use $BALANCE_i$ to mean the balance of the $i$th account. The diagram in Figure 1–7 is equivalent to the one in Figure 1–6 except that it uses more formal notation.

**FIGURE 1–7**

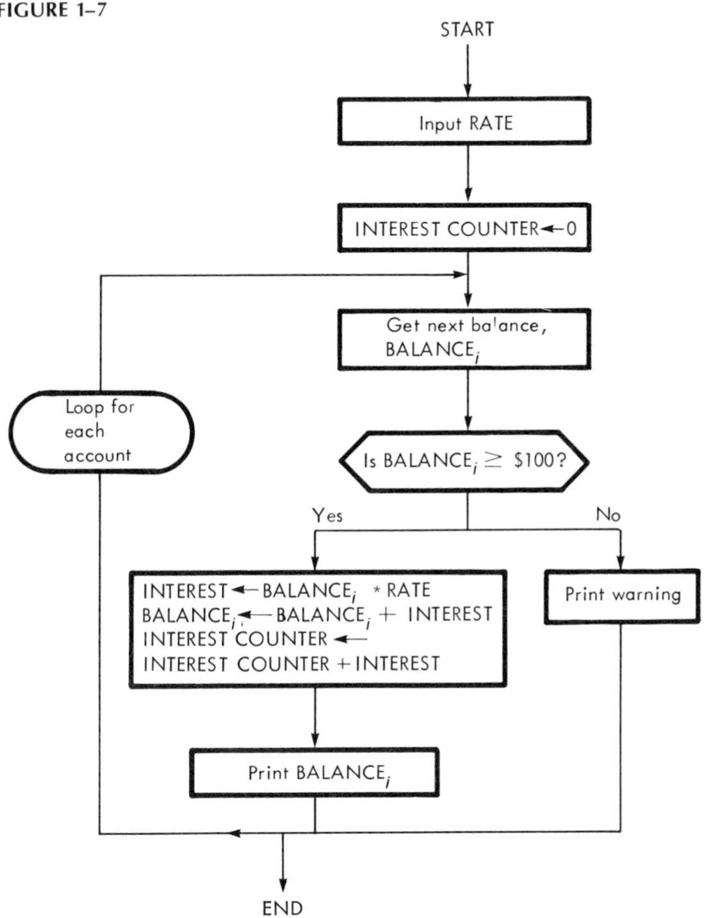


Note: where the response to the question is negative, $BALANCE_i$ is unchanged, so no statement is needed about $BALANCE_i$.

---

[7] A bit of description of how computers work may explain these conventions. Recall that the computer contains a CPU to perform various calculations and also memory cells to hold values. The arrow notation in the statement for BALANCE, for example, would be interpreted as: Add the current value of BALANCE and the value of INTEREST. Put the sum into the memory cell which holds the BALANCE.

By combination of operations boxes, comparison or condition boxes, and loops we can build up block diagrams to describe very complicated models. In particular, we can use many different comparisons to make the algorithms handle many special conditions. In addition, we can use numerous loops; in fact, we often want to use what are called nested loops (loops within loops). As an example, suppose that we want to expand the previous algorithm to calculate the ending balances and the total interest paid in each of six months. The diagram in Figure 1–8 describes the new process. If you follow

**FIGURE 1–8**

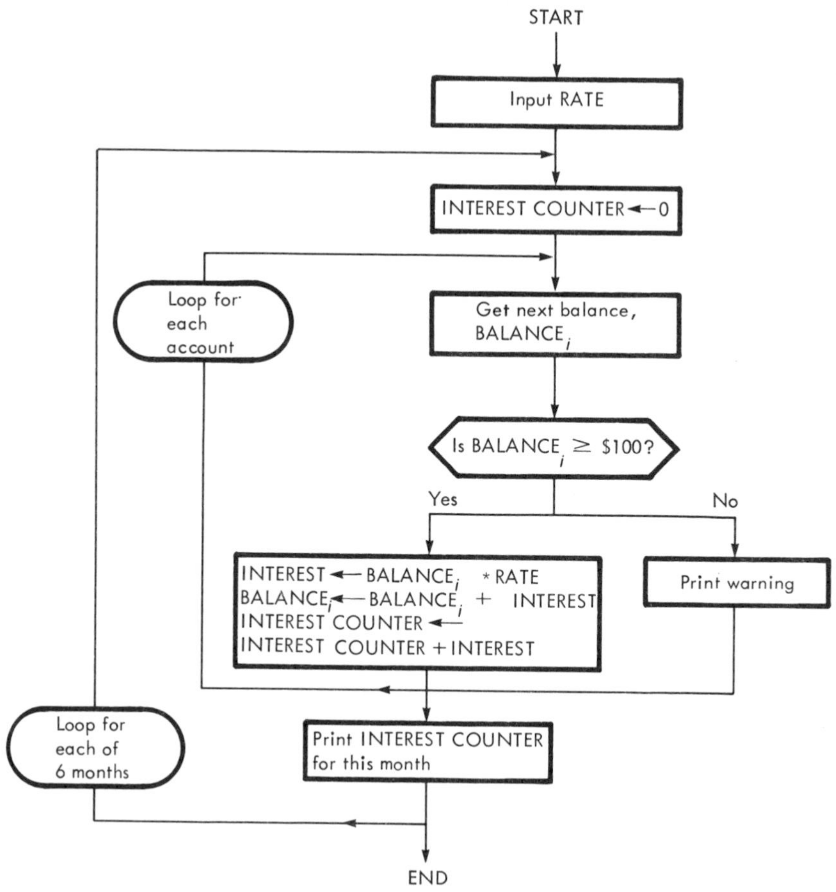


the arrows through that diagram, you will see that the outer loop is performed (or executed) once each month; the interest counter is reset to 0 at the start of each month. Within each month the inner loop is executed once for each account. Thus, the diagram says to consider each account for the first month (following the inner loop), to print the total interest for that month, then to go on to the second month (via the outer loop) and consider each account again (with the inner loop), and so on.

Block diagrams are thus a way to lay out the interrelationships in a model or algorithm, specifying the inputs, the relationships, and the outputs. The level of detail which should be included in such a diagram depends on several factors, including the complexity of the problem and the preference of the particular modeler involved. We will be using these diagrams as a way of specifying models in enough detail to give to a programmer to implement; consequently, in practice the level of detail which you should use will depend on the particular programmer with whom you are working. Often, you will have to give considerably more detail the first time you work with a specific individual than you will after working with the same person for some time. For one thing, you will begin to build up a repertoire of algorithms to use. For example, it is important to think through an algorithm for calculating net present value the first time you need one, but after that first time you and your programmer can assume that you both know how to calculate net present values and, hence,

| NPV ← net present value at the start the first year of the ten annual cash flows at 15 percent per year |
|---|

would be sufficient detail for your diagrams.

Finally, it is worth noting that there is not any set of truly universal conventions for constructing block diagrams.[8] Some people use square boxes for operations boxes and diamonds for comparison boxes; others use circles for some parts of the diagram; etc. We will take the attitude that rigid conventions are not needed or even particularly helpful for block diagramming; clarity and consistency within a specific diagram are considerably more important.

## V. TOP-DOWN PROGRAMMING, STRUCTURED PROGRAMMING, AND RELATED CONCEPTS

As you block out designs for increasingly large models and difficult problems, you soon discover that for larger designs it is not usually advisable to try to write down a model in one attempt, start to finish. Instead, most people find it easier and more natural to sketch the model in outline first and then to fill in details later. Often, we start with a consideration of what outputs we

[8] Various organizations, including the U.S. military and ANSI (a national standards group), have proposed standard conventions. Both the literature and common practice still use many different styles, however.

want and then back up to consider what relationships the model must contain and what inputs would be required. This section considers concepts called *top-down programming* and *structured programming,* which have been receiving considerable attention recently in the computer journals. While the computer scientists' discussions of these and related concepts focuses on the coding of computer programs, the concepts are also of interest to people who will be using the services of programmers—both because they are useful in the design of models and because they contain ideas which are helpful in managing programmers.

Top-down programming might also quite reasonably be called outlining.[9] Basically, the idea of top-down programming is that it is not good practice to try to write a computer program (or, by extension, to design the model which a program will later implement) from start to finish. Instead, the programmer or modeler would better block out a rather broad outline of the model, showing the major pieces and how they fit together. As a next step, s/he can proceed to fill in the parts in more detail. With large complicated models, the process might well take several steps, each one giving a more detailed description of the model. Recall that the specification of a model must contain a description of the inputs to the model, the relationships which form the heart of the model, and the outputs which the model will provide. Most people find that they cannot easily start specifying a model by listing all the inputs and then all of the quantities which must be initialized within the model. Instead, they find it preferable to begin some models by outlining the outputs section. Having done so, they then find it much easier to think through the relationships that will form the heart of the model; they specify the inputs and initialization steps later. Hence, in top-down programming, after a model has been blocked out in broad outline, it is often appropriate next to describe the outputs and then how the central parts of the model will work—and only then to go back to describe further the inputs and initialization. In other situations some people find it more natural to begin with the specification of the relationships of a model, delaying design of both output and input sections.

As an example of this concept, we will consider the design of a very simple model. Suppose that we wish to construct a payroll program for a small company that has not yet automated the payroll function. The program will be used for hourly employees who must fill out time cards each week, so that the company accounting department knows how many hours each employee worked, who took sick leave, who was on vacation, etc. In designing a model or algorithm for this problem, the first step might be a very broad outline, showing only that the model must be initialized, that it must then loop through calculations for each individual employee, finding, saving and

[9] Harlan D. Mills, "Top Down Programming in Large Systems," in *Debugging Techniques in Large Systems,* ed. R. Rustin (Englewood Cliffs, N.J.: Prentice-Hall, 1971), pp. 41–55.

**FIGURE 1–9**

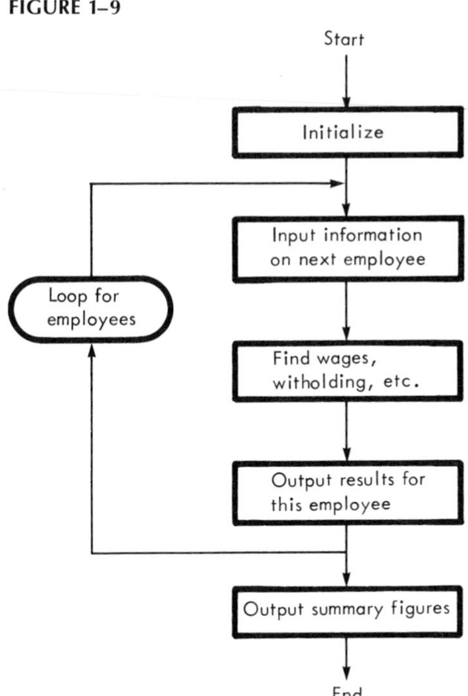


printing appropriate results. A schematic description of this broad outline is shown in Figure 1–9.

As suggested above, the next step is, most likely, to decide in more detail what outputs we want for each employee and what overall summary figures should be provided—in other words, to design the output portions of the model.

In describing the output portion we will be led naturally to consider what information must be calculated and, in addition, we will begin to identify the inputs that the model will require. Suppose that for each employee we want to output total wages for the week; FICA, or Social Security, tax to be withheld; federal income tax to be withheld; state income tax to be withheld; and net pay. We also want to know how many hours of vacation and how many hours of sick leave the employee has accumulated by the end of the week. The overall summaries should give totals for wages and for each type of withholding. In addition, we want to know how many hours of sick leave and how many hours of vacation time were taken by all employees during this week. Thus, we might expand the last two boxes of the model in Figure 1–9 to give the details shown in Figure 1–10.

At this point, it should be clear that we must include in the calculation portion of the model the rules for finding withholding amounts and the rules

FIGURE 1–10

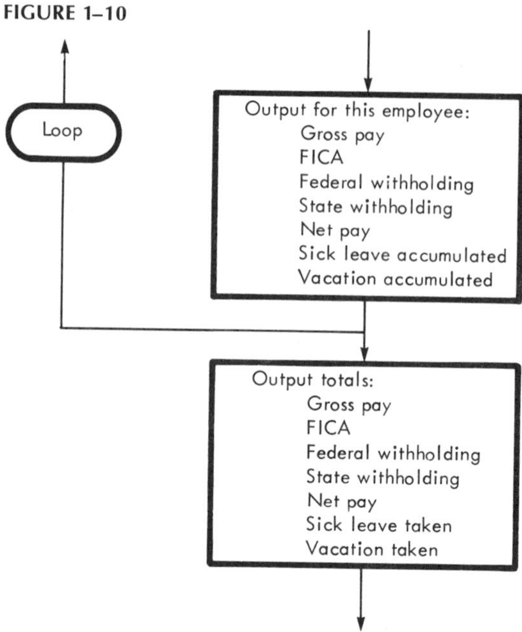


for accumulating vacation and sick leave. We must also know how much vacation and sick pay each employee had accumulated at the end of the previous week. We will want to keep running totals of wages, withholding, and related items; these totals should start at zero and should be increased, as appropriate, for each employee during our calculations. Notice in this process how the necessary relationships and inputs become clearer as we think about what outputs we want our program to provide. The next step in our design might be to flesh out the boxes in Figure 1–9 for initialization and for calculations for each employee. Suppose that each employee earns 2½ hours of vacation and 2 hours of sick leave each week. (Suppose that different employees earn different hourly wage rates.) The initialization and calculations boxes might be redrawn as shown in Figures 1–11 and 1–12.

FIGURE 1–11

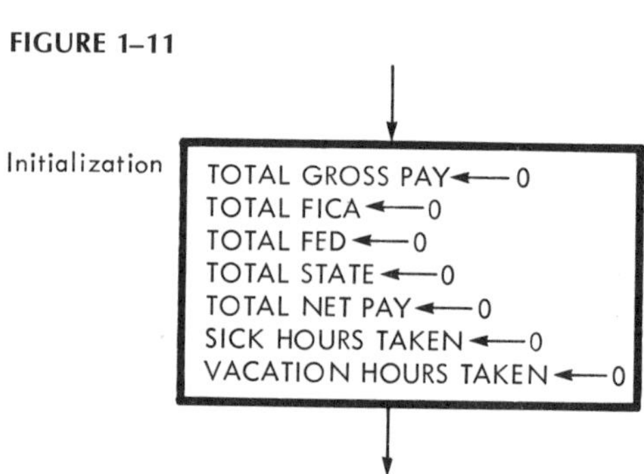

FIGURE 1–12

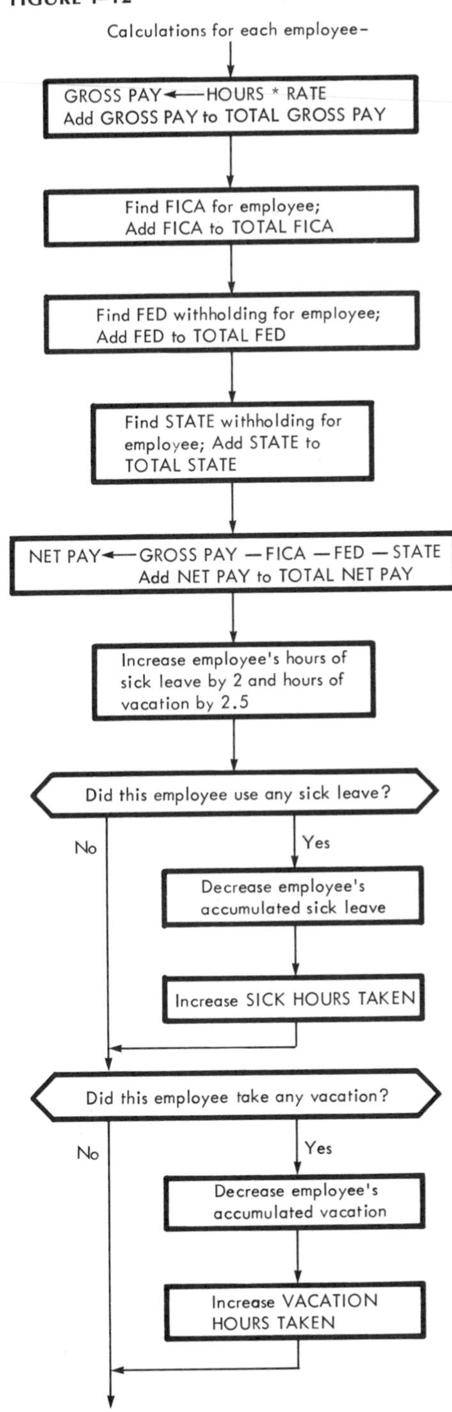
Calculations for each employee–
GROSS PAY ← HOURS * RATE
Add GROSS PAY to TOTAL GROSS PAY
Find FICA for employee;
Add FICA to TOTAL FICA
Find FED withholding for employee;
Add FED to TOTAL FED
Find STATE withholding for employee; Add STATE to TOTAL STATE
NET PAY ← GROSS PAY — FICA — FED — STATE
Add NET PAY to TOTAL NET PAY
Increase employee's hours of sick leave by 2 and hours of vacation by 2.5
Did this employee use any sick leave?
No
Yes
Decrease employee's accumulated sick leave
Increase SICK HOURS TAKEN
Did this employee take any vacation?
No
Yes
Decrease employee's accumulated vacation
Increase VACATION HOURS TAKEN

As we specified the calculations part of the model in Figure 1–12, it would become clear what inputs we needed. We will want HOURS worked and hourly RATE for each employee. We will also need to know how many hours of sick pay each employee took during the week and, as noted above, how many hours the employee had at the start of the week. We will need similar information about vacation time.

Even if we now assemble the output specifications from Figure 1–10, the initialization from Figure 1–11, the calculations from Figure 1–12, and a list of the inputs just given, we are still not finished. Before the design is complete we would have to specify in more detail how the computer should find FICA, FED, and STATE withholding amounts. In other words, the boxes for those calculations in Figure 1–12 are still just outlines and they must be filled out further. For the purposes of the discussion of this section, however, we will stop the model design here. It should be clear that for complex models it is not realistic to expect to be able to write the specification down in one process from start to finish. Instead, the payroll example should suggest the way in which we can start with a broad outline and then fill in one part at a time. Filling in one portion will generally help us to decide what must be done in other portions of the design.

A couple of additional points might be made about the concept of top-down design. First, for small models we might want to put all of the parts of our completed design together in a single diagram. With large models, however, it often gives a more readable description if the separate parts of the model are shown in broad outline in one diagram and are then described further in separate diagrams (which are *not* linked together in one large detailed description). Second, it may seem surprising that so simple a concept as this outline approach to design is one of the more fashionable topics in computer science today. Perhaps the reason is that there has been rather a lack of management in computer programming. Good programmers have been scarce and many managers have not had the familiarity with programming nor the confidence to manage programmers effectively. Partly as a consequence, programs have often just grown, without a structured design, and they often seem like patchwork. Hence, the idea that programs (and their design specifications) should be clearly presented in increasing levels of detail is viewed as a good management tool for more effective programming.

The related concept of structured programming has a similar origin.[10] While there is considerable debate in the computer science literature about just what the term means and doesn't mean, at least a partial explanation is that structured programming involves a clean, easy-to-follow structure for models and programs. The debates in the literature about structured programming have involved lengthy discussions of which constructs of which

[10] O. J. Dahl, E. W. Dijkstra, and C. A. R. Hoare, *Structured Programming* (London: Academic Press, 1972).

particular computer languages are good and bad, or allowed and not allowed in structured programs. The basic aim, however, is to obtain clear programs which are easier to read and easier to debug. This text will not discuss the concept of structured programming further except to mention that top-down programming can be thought of as a way to construct structured programs. Again, it may seem surprising that this simple (and reasonable) idea would be receiving large amounts of attention. The reason arose from some common practices in programming. Programmers who were under time pressure or who were unwilling to spend the time to clean up a program, or, in some cases, who enjoyed the creation of abstruse (and clever) code, have often created programs which are difficult to read and, unfortunately, difficult to check out (or debug, in the computer terminology).

A related concept, which concerns the management of the programming effort for very large models and programs, is called the *chief programmer team* concept.[11] This idea, which has been developed at IBM, involves an organized team effort for generating a working program. You might best think of the chief programmer team concept as a management tool to do top-down programming when a group of programmers is involved. In this approach, one chief programmer is in charge of the team effort. Once the program has been blocked out and the relations among the different parts of the program have been specified, the chief programmer assigns parts of the coding effort to various members of the team. The chief programmer continues to oversee the process and, in particular, to supervise the testing of the program. Finally, s/he is responsible for maintaining adequate documentation on the program so that at the end of the project there will be a complete description of the program and how it works. Again, the amount of attention being given this concept is explained by the problems which have arisen under more common programming practices. Often, in large programming efforts, many people work on different parts of a program but the relations among the parts have not been fully designed and specified. As a result, the parts do not fit together (for example, the writer of the second part of the model might expect one set of results from the first part, while the author of that first part provides a different set of results). In addition, often programs are not adequately explained (or documented) so that finding out just how a program works (in order to change or correct it) may be extremely difficult. The chief programmer team idea was devised to try to reduce these common problems; IBM reports that the concept has been extremely successful, increasing programmers' output significantly.

---

[11] Harlan D. Mills, "Chief Programmer Teams, Principles, and Procedures," IBM Federal Systems Division Report FSC 71-5108, Gaithersburg, Maryland, 1971; F. T. Baker, "Chief Programmer Team Management of Production Programming," *IBM Systems Journal*, vol. 11, no. 1 (1972), pp. 56–73; and Frederick P. Brooks, Jr., *The Mythical Man-Month: Essays on Software Engineering* (Reading, Mass.: Addison-Wesley, 1974).

## VI. ADDITIONAL ISSUES IN MODEL DESIGN

Even in the relatively simple deterministic models discussed in this chapter, there arise other difficult issues in model design. This section addresses three of those issues. These concerns are particularly important because they will remain important design issues in later chapters of the book, as we proceed to consider more complex models.

1. One basic decision involved in any model design concerns the question of where the models should be positioned on a scale from *special purpose* to *general purpose*. As an example, we will discuss the simple payroll model whose top-down design we sketched in the preceding section. Referring back to the figures in that section, you will see that the model involves some restrictive assumptions about the types of employees and the types of situations that it can and that it cannot handle. For example, the model handles only hourly wage earners. In addition, we have assumed a single hourly rate for any individual worker. Hence, we cannot calculate withholding for salaried workers in any straightforward way and, in addition, we have no provision to handle time-and-a-half pay for overtime. Certainly, we could, if we wished, modify the model to handle both situations. If we did so, both the input section of the model and the relationships section would have to become more complicated. In the relationships portions we would need to calculate gross pay differently for hourly and for salaried employees. In addition, we would need to know how many hours for an hourly worker were to be classified as regular time; hours worked in excess of that figure would be credited at a higher rate. In fact, the overtime calculations for some companies would be even more complicated. Some firms pay time-and-a-half for most overtime but double time for Sundays. If the firm for which we were constructing the model had such a system, we would have to know rules for identifying regular hours, time-and-a-half hours and Sunday hours. To provide such additional calculations in the relationships portion, we would require additional input information. We would, for example, need an indication for each employee as to whether the person was an hourly worker or a salaried one.

Further changes to our initial model might help make it more useful. We were not explicit in the preceding section about the details of the calculations of state withholding tax, but most readers probably automatically filled in some details about one withholding rate for workers at one pay level, another for workers who earned more than that level, etc. In fact, however, the model could usefully be made more general than this outline suggests. Many companies have employees who live in different states. For example, a firm in New York might have employees from New York, New Jersey, Pennsylvania, Connecticut, and perhaps other states. Each state would have different withholding rules and the firm would want its program to be sufficiently general to handle each employee correctly. The issue of just how general-purpose a model should be can be highlighted with this very simple example. In particular, we must ask when we should stop in adding to the model the capability to handle withholding for residents of different states. It is unlikely that the New York company, which we assume is small and has only one location, will have employees who live in California. Perhaps we could leave out the instructions for California residents. Similarly, we could convince ourselves to leave out many other states. In the current example, it may well be intelligent to build the program to handle only about a half dozen different states. If so, it will be much easier to construct the model to handle only six cases than it would to require it to handle all 50 states. Yet, notice that we have given up something, at least potentially, when we made such a choice. If Maryland is not one of the states we include and if for some reason an employee of the firm chooses to commute from Maryland, our program will not work for that employee.

As you think about this simple payroll program you should see the basic issue of general-purpose versus special-purpose programs. At one extreme, a program that handled only hourly workers who could not earn overtime and who lived in New York would be quite easy to design and build. At the other extreme, a program that handled many different payment arrangements for residents of any state would be considerably harder to design but would work for a wider range of inputs. Somewhere between these extremes is likely to be the appropriate level of generality for our hypothesized small local company. For a nationwide firm with many compensation arrangements, however, an appropriate choice would be considerably closer to the general-purpose end of the spectrum. For such a company the extra design time would be worthwhile because the extra program options would be used regularly. Thus, the choice of how special-purpose and how general-purpose a model should be is one that is closely linked to the details of the problem to be analyzed and to the ways in which the program will be used. The choice is properly one that should be made by the model designer, not by the coder who implements the design.

2. A second major design choice in modeling concerns the question of whether the model should simply perform calculations to explore sets of inputs provided by the user, with the user bearing all responsibility for finding a good sets of inputs and decisions, or whether, instead, the model should help select decisions. At the extreme, we could consider building what is called an *optimization model*. Such a model searches for the best or optimal set of decisions in some problem situation. To clarify this design issue it is useful to begin by repeating the type of model use that has been envisioned in the discussions to this point in the chapter. (This type of use assumes that we do not have an optimization model). As an example, consider the pro forma model considered earlier in the chapter for investigating choices of price and promotion for a new product. As we noted earlier, we decided that the model would not determine what levels of demand would

result from specific choices for price and promotion; instead, the user would be responsible for inputting reasonable scenarios, giving projections for price, promotion, and demand. A good decision maker would use this model to understand how the pro forma statement, summarizing the results, would be affected by different choices for price and promotion and for different possible results in terms of demand. S/he would make many different runs of the model, trying plausible scenarios. At the end of those runs, s/he should have a fairly good idea of how sensitive the results are to changes in assumptions about the input quantities. For this reason, this type of analysis, in which a user makes many changes in model inputs to determine how the results change, is called *sensitivity analysis.* Notice that we have assumed an intelligent user conducting the sensitivity analysis. For example, s/he does not usually change just one input number. Rather, users should be aware that a change in one part of a scenario is likely to result in changes in other parts. Thus, the user should consider the interrelated changes and only input scenarios that make sense. Having conducted such sensitivity analyses, the user must make a decision as to what to charge for the product and how much to put into promotion. In a more realistically complex pro forma model for this problem, there might be additional inputs, such as the commission to pay on sales, the price (reflecting the quality) of the raw material to be used, and other factors. Similarly, there would be other output measures, in addition to earnings after tax. We might want to look at cash flow, return on investment, and similar measures. The decision maker would use the model to determine the sensitivities of the various output measures to the assumptions of the inputs and to different available decisions. S/he would then have to choose a set of decisions that, in light of the computer results and of any other factors that had not been included explicitly in the program, seems appropriate. The computer program itself does not take part in this choice process. Its function is, instead, to help provide the human decision maker with the information on which to base a decision.

In an optimization model, by contrast, the machine is instructed to search for the best available decision. Thinking back to the earlier discussion of how literal and precise a computer is, we see immediately that an optimization model requires that the designer include complete explicit instructions on how to make a choice. In particular, the computer must generally be told how to reduce all of the effects of a set of decisions to a single measure of attractiveness or unattractiveness. In technical terms, we must specify a single *criterion* or *objective function.* Similarly, we must specify all of the relationships that constrain or limit the choices of decisions that the computer can consider. For example, in the pricing problem we would somehow have to tell the machine just how demand would decrease as we increased price, so that it could consider all of the ramifications of a price rise. Clearly, in most problems we are not able to provide the computer with a sufficiently explicit statement of objectives and constraints for an optimization model to be feasible. In other problems, however, optimization is in fact effective. Linear programming computer programs are a form of optimization model in which an objective function can be expressed as a linear function of certain decision variables (or quantities whose values can be decided by the decision maker). In addition, the constraints limiting the allowable values for the decision variables also take the form of linear expressions. Linear programming models have been used with great success in running oil refineries, for example, where they are used to determine what products should be made from the crude oil entering the refinery. In problems where an optimization model can capture the essence of the situation, such models are extremely powerful. In designing models, you will often want to consider whether optimization by the computer is appropriate; in many, although not all cases; you will decide that it is not feasible.[12]

3. A third issue which should be discussed at this point in the book concerns the question of how many of the details of basically numerical algorithms the nontechnical computer-user (or even a relatively technical user who is not a specialist in numerical procedures) must understand and help design. For example, suppose that you want the computer to sort 100 quantities into increasing order. Someone will have to provide a serial explicit set of machine instructions to perform a sorting algorithm, but in general you would be quite happy to assume that the definition of a correctly sorted sequence of numbers is clear to everyone involved and that a programmer can provide you with a sorting program or routine without your worrying about the details. In fact, on most computers, there are what are called *subprograms* or *subroutines,* which are pieces of computer code that can be used by other programs to perform general-purpose and clearly defined tasks. Similarly, in a technically oriented program a designer might want to instruct the computer to find the value of $X$ which, when plugged into the following algebraic expression, made the value of the expression as small as possible:

$$3x^2 - 10x + 2$$

Effective procedures for such numerical operations as finding the minimum or maximum of a function are the province of a specialty of computer science called numerical analysis. As a designer and user of computer programs you will want to know that such procedures exist but you will generally assume that if you need such a procedure you will either obtain one from the library of generally available subroutines on your computer or else that you will take the details of the procedure from a specialist, without worrying about them yourself.

---

[12] Among the useful references on optimization models are: Harvey M. Wagner, *Principles of Management Science,* 2d ed., (Englewood Cliffs, N.J.: Prentice-Hall, 1975) and George B. Dantzig, *Linear Programming and Extensions,* (Princeton, N.J.: Princeton University Press, 1963).

This last statement may seem at variance with the emphasis in this chapter on how important it is that the computer user or decision maker be closely involved in model design. In fact, there is not a conflict between this statement and earlier ones, but only because they differ in one very important respect. In a numerical procedure like maximization or in a quasi-numeric one like sorting you can give a complete definition of what you want a subprogram to accomplish for you. You do not really care very much how the subprogram accomplishes that goal. For example, you do not really care how the computer sorts your 100 numbers, as long as it does so correctly. Compare the situation in the payroll program design situation. There you do care how the program works, because you cannot be sure that the program is useful until you are sure that it contains the correct assumptions about overtime and other issues. The payroll problem is specific to a particular business situation. Hence, the design must match that situation. A sorting problem, on the other hand, is a general problem and a general-purpose program or subprogram can handle the calculations for many different users. Thus, in designing a model, we can use pieces that are general-purpose subprograms for accomplishing well-defined explicit tasks.[13] For those other parts of the model that must match our particular problem, however, we will generally have to do the design ourselves and will have to make sure that the design is properly chosen for the particular problem.

## VII. DESIGNING THE USER INTERFACE

The preceding portions of this chapter have described the use of models as involving repeated runs for interesting sets of inputs. It should be evident, therefore, that to be successful a model must be designed in such a way that the user is not subjected to undue pain in the input and output portions. For example, consider the output portion.

It is often wise to design a model for use in time-sharing mode. The idea is to let users make several runs in one short session at the computer terminal and thus to encourage them to make enough runs to investigate many sets of inputs. If we think about a pro forma generator that is being used in time-sharing mode, we might start to worry about the volume of output that would be generated. If the users were provided with several different financial statements for each set of inputs, they might get tired of waiting for their

---

[13] For an excellent discussion of sorting, searching, and many other computer procedures, the reader is referred to:

Donald E. Knuth, *The Art of Computer Programming* (Reading, Mass.: Addison-Wesley).

Volume 1: *Fundamental Algorithms,* 1968

Volume 2: *Semi-Numerical Algorithms,* 1969

Volume 3: *Sorting and Searching,* 1973.

There are many useful sources on numerical procedures, including Germund Dahlquist and Åke Björck, *Numerical Methods,* trans. Ned Anderson (Englewood Cliffs, N.J.: Prentice-Hall, 1974).

terminals to print all of the results. A likely outcome would be that they would make fewer runs of the model than would really be needed to investigate the model results. On the other hand, for at least some particularly important sets of inputs, the users will want to see detailed output and will be quite willing to wait while it is printed. How do we get around this problem? Often, by allowing the user choices of how much output to receive. For example, we might automatically print a short output summary for each set of inputs. We could then ask users if they wanted more detailed output. Only if they responded yes would we print more detailed reports.

A similar philosophy should be used to try to make the input portion of a model relatively easy to use. Again, the reasoning here is that programs become useful only if users try enough sets of inputs to understand the messages of the results; if the I/O portions of a program are unduly awkward, users are unlikely to make many runs. As an example, consider the choice of the level of detail the computer provides when it types a question asking a user in time-sharing mode for input information. Users who are relatively new to the program will need considerable information from the computer specifying what type of information to input and in what form the information is needed. For such users, it is useful to have the computer print detailed descriptions of how to proceed with the input. For more experienced users, however, repeated use will have taught them the required input conventions and they will rapidly become impatient as they sit at the terminal waiting for the computer to finish printing instructions that they already understand. Their impatience is likely to translate into an unwillingness to use the program or, at least, an unwillingness to make many runs. Again, this apparent conflict can be addressed through a two-stage approach. The computer should be capable of printing instructions of the sort needed by new users. On the other hand, the instructions should be printed only in response to some easy-to-use and easy-to-remember request. Thus, experienced users can skip the printing of the instructions by simply not requesting the information.

A particularly difficult issue in model design, from the standpoint of ease of use, concerns the large volume of input information that is often required. One fact that becomes obvious very quickly to users of most computer models is that the data requirements of many such models are large. Even for a very simple deterministic pro forma generator, the user must somehow provide the model with the means to project each line in the pro forma statement (revenues, various costs, interest, and so forth). As an example, suppose that we wish to prepare monthly pro forma cash flow statements for a particular product over the next five years. We will have to provide the model, in one way or another, with values for sales or revenues, costs, and other quantities for each month. If we make an initial run of the model and then wish to perform sensitivity analyses on some variable such as sales, we will have to input additional sets of numbers. To test various scenarios for sales we will have to provide the computer with 60 sales values, as well as other data, to define each scenario.

There are two major problems caused by the enormous data requirements of models. One is that it is difficult for users to assess meaningfully the large numbers of input values. Often, what happens is that users think carefully about some of the values and then become more careless about others, perhaps because of a lack of time. Also, the tedium involved in preparing a single scenario carefully is an impediment to the preparation of a sufficiently large number of alternative scenarios. Users often simply do not have enough time to spend preparing such vast amounts of input data. The second problem caused by data requirements is that, even if a user has constructed a good set of inputs for a model, transmitting those inputs to the computer (perhaps by typing them in at a computer terminal or else by some similar means) is in itself a tedious process. This burden involved in inputting alternative scenarios is another impediment to the consideration of enough possible input sets.

Because of these problems, it makes sense to try to construct models in such a way that users can input scenarios more easily, with fewer judgments required per scenario. We hope that such designs will encourage users to conduct meaningful numbers of analyses with the models. This section discusses one type of mechanism for reducing the data requirements of models to manageable proportions. As will be seen below, the methods involve a trade-off between generality of the model design and ease of use; one of the tasks for the model designer is to make these trade-offs wisely.

Basically, the idea here is that the model is built to include in it assumptions about general relationships among some of the needed data items. The user inputs only enough information to allow the model to infer the remaining needed values, using the relationships. To make this idea clearer, it will be useful to refer back to the example described just above in this section. Suppose that we want to prepare monthly cash budgets for a product for the next five years. Suppose that we are particularly concerned with various possible scenarios for sales levels and that we want to investigate the ability of our firm to meet its cash needs under different sales patterns. We will assume known fixed costs, known cost of goods as a percentage of sales, and so forth, so that our main concern is with sales levels. As noted above, it would require specifying 60 numbers to give the model a complete sales scenario the laborious way. Making up and typing in 60 numbers is a sufficiently unpleasant task that we can be almost sure that users will not run a great number of scenarios if we require lists of 60 numbers. On the other hand, if sales variation really is crucial, we must allow flexibility in assumptions of sales patterns. One possible compromise would be to let the user input five annual values only. If the model included a set of assumptions about how yearly sales could be divided among 12 months, the model could easily translate from 5 annual figures to 60 monthly ones. An alternative solution would be to let the user input 12 monthly figures for the first year but annual figures thereafter, with the model translating to monthly values from a set of assumed proportions. This solution would require more data than would the first one but it would allow more flexibility in modeling the first year and might be preferable if we felt that the first year would likely be the crucial one in terms of cash flow. It should be obvious that there are many possible compromises between volume of input per scenario and flexibility of inputs. The basic idea in making a choice is to trade off detail and flexibility in a manner appropriate to the particular problem at hand.

Another way of expressing some of the methods for easing the input problem involves what are called *functional forms.* The idea of these forms will be demonstrated with an extremely simple example, which very likely would not be an appropriate choice in our cash flow pro forma model. Once the principles have been illustrated with this simple example, we proceed to a brief survey of some of the possible functional forms that might make more sense for problems of that sort.

Suppose that we simplify the problem of specifying a set of monthly sales figures for our five-year analysis period by assuming that the monthly figures will fall precisely on a straight line, increasing or decreasing over time. Increasing straight line trends might look like any of the lines in Figure 1–13.

**FIGURE 1–13**

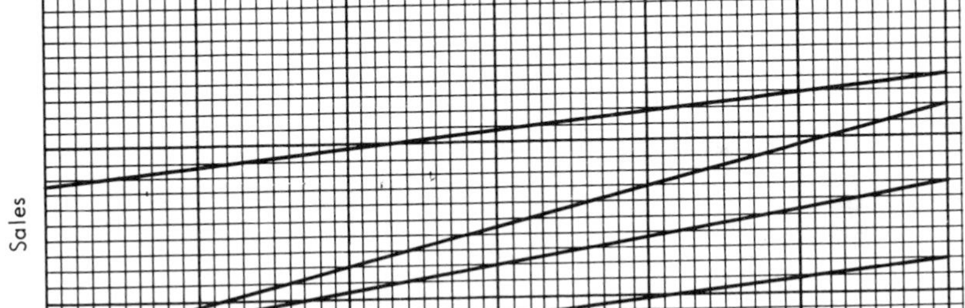

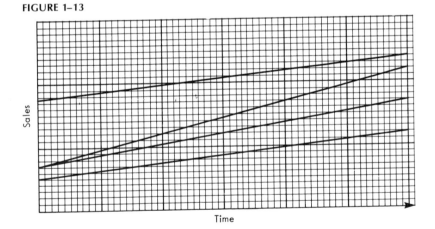


(or like any other line sloping upward toward the right). Decreasing straight line trends might look like any of the lines in Figure 1–14 (or like other downward sloping lines).

In specifying that sales will fall on a straight line when they are plotted against time (in months), we are saying that we are willing to assume an equation of the following form:

$$\text{Sales} = A + B * t$$

**FIGURE 1–14**

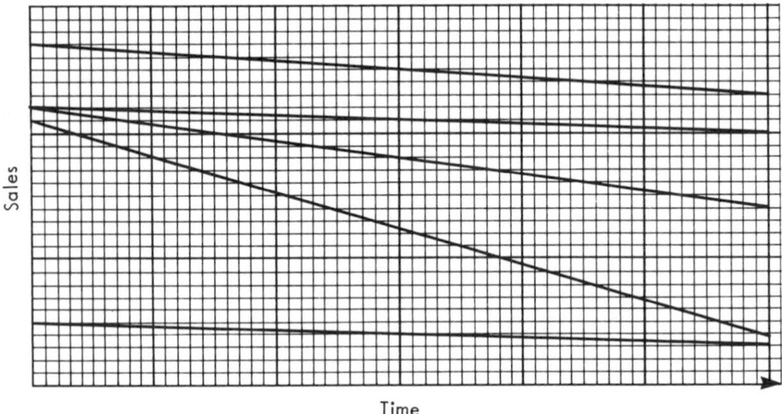


In this equation $t$ is the time in months (measured, perhaps, from the start of our five-year period) and $A$ and $B$ are constants which determine exactly which of the possible lines, such as those shown in Figures 1–13 and 1–14, we consider appropriate for a particular scenario. $A$ is called the intercept of the line (it is the value of sales when $t$ is 0) and $B$ is called the slope. In technical terms, the equation describes sales as a function of $t$; $t$ is called the *argument* of the function. The general equation written above is called a *functional form,* for it is a general form of equation that will be made specific when we select particular values for $A$ and $B$. $A$ and $B$ are called *parameters* of the function. Thus, parameters are quantities that appear as letters (variables) in the general form but that take specific constant values in any specific version of the equation. If, for example, we make $A = 15$ ($000) and $B = .1$ ($000), then the function for sales will be

$$\text{Sales} = 15 + .1 * t \qquad \text{(in \$000)}$$

and the sales scenario will be as shown in Figure 1–15.

Hence, if we are willing to assume a linear function for sales, then we can require the user to input only two numbers per scenario. If the user tells the model the values for $A$ and $B$, the computer can calculate the corresponding sales figure for each monthly period and can then proceed to produce the required pro formas.

In fact, in many cases we would not want to ask the user to specify $A$ and $B$ directly. We would often feel that users would not find it most natural to make judgments about functional parameters in exactly the way in which those parameters appear in the functional form. In the current example, $A$ is the sales level at time "zero" and $B$ is the monthly change in sales. Perhaps we feel that users of the model we are constructing would find it easier to

FIGURE 1–15

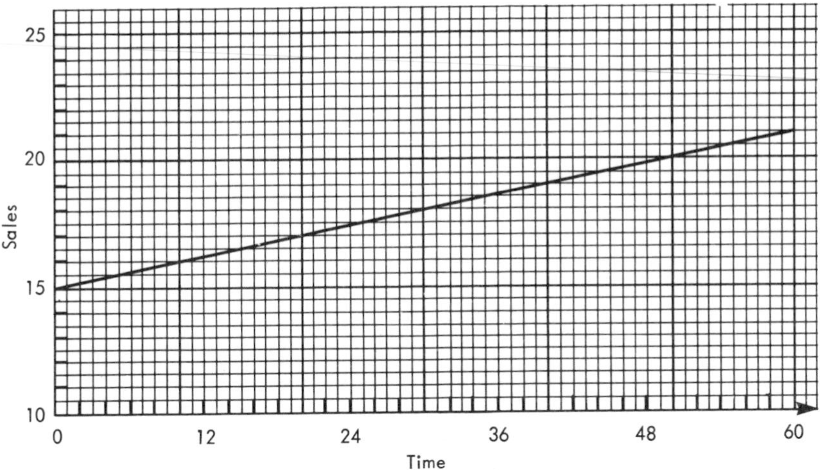


make sensible judgments about the sales at the end of year one (month 12) and the sales at the end of year 4 (month 48). Since any two points can be used to determine a straight line, there is no reason why the inputs could not be the sales levels for months 12 and 48 and the model could not then proceed to find the implied values for the parameters $A$ and $B$. Having found $A$ and $B$, it could proceed to prepare 60 monthly sales figures agreeing with the user's inputs.

To summarize, the idea of using functional forms in models is as follows. We select a general shape that we can assume for some set of numbers, such as the values of sales over time. Thus, we select a general functional form. To make that form specific enough to give the model a complete set of values for any one scenario, we require the user to input only enough judgments to find the parameters of our selected functional form. Often, to encourage frequent use of the model and to facilitate judgments, we have the user input information closely related to the parameters rather than the parameters themselves. In such cases the computer finds the parameters from the user's inputs. Once it has the parameter values, the computer can prepare a scenario. Another way of expressing the idea is to note that the functional form identifies what is often called a family of individual functions (they are related by having the same general functional form but differ because they correspond to different sets of parameters). When the user specifies a set of parameters, either directly or indirectly, a particular member of the family of forms has been identified and the computer can proceed to use that function to project values for the variable of interest. Use of a functional form involves two stages—the important step of choice of the general form and then the second step of defining a specific member of the family of forms by giving input points.

Straight lines are sometimes convenient functional forms to use in modeling but more often than not a straight line form does not really prove satisfactory. Often, however, we can find some other functional form that has a type of shape more in keeping with our assumptions about how a group of input values should behave. Figure 1–16 demonstrates a few of the types of forms

**FIGURE 1–16A**
Quadratic functions

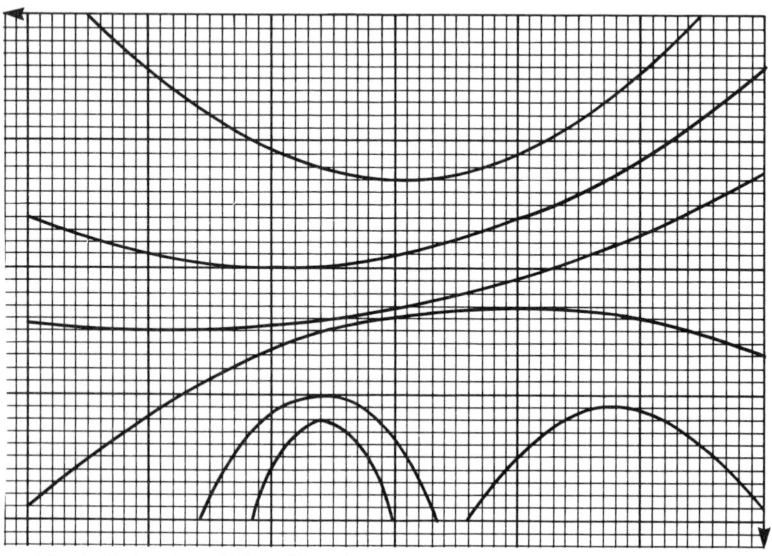

Quadratic functions $AX^2 + BX + C$.
$A$, $B$, and $C$ are parameters; $X$ is the argument.

that might be used. The first part of that figure shows various members of the family of quadratic functions. The second part shows a few bounded exponential functions, one of the families of functions that can be used to model behavior showing diminishing marginal returns. The third part of the figure shows examples of S-shaped curves that might be used to model sales of a product over the product life cycle.

Many other families of functions could be used in models. In general, the more complicated the shape of the form we want to use, the more parameters there will have to be in the selected family of forms and the more points the user will have to specify. In selecting a family of forms for use in a particular problem, the model designers will have to consider two aspects of their problems. They should first think about what general types of shapes are necessary; for example, they might consider how much flexibility in

**FIGURE 1–16B**
Bounded exponential functions

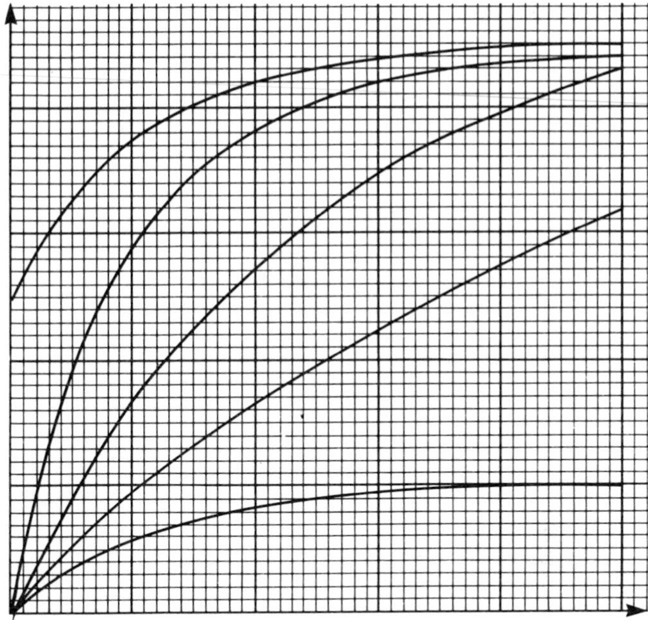

Bounded exponential forms

$$A(1 - e^{-BX}) + C$$

*A*, *B*, and *C* are parameters; *X* is the argument; *e* is the exponential constant (2.71828 . . . ).

**FIGURE 1–16C**
S-shaped curves

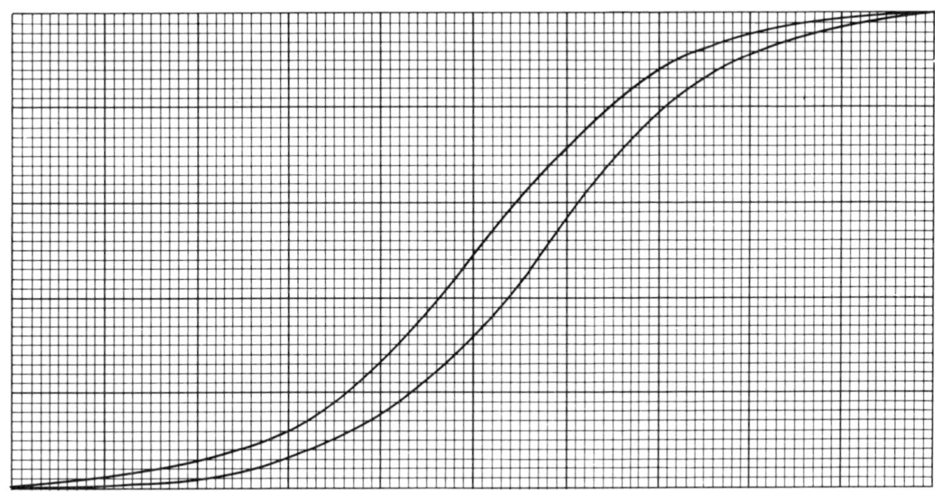

Logistic functions $A/(1 + Be^{-CX})$.
*A*, *B*, and *C* are parameters; *X* is the argument; e is the exponential constant (2.71828 . . . ).

shape they really need to model sales over time in a useful way and what types of shapes they will want to consider. Then, either selecting from a repertoire of shapes and functions they have at hand or occasionally with technical help, they can select particular families. The second aspect of the selection process involves the ability of the model user to make sensible judgments to allow the computer to find parameters for a particular function. Often, selecting a family of forms for use in a model will involve a compromise between generality (and complicated forms) and ease of assessment by users (and simpler forms requiring fewer user judgments to define a particular set of parameters and hence a particular member of the selected family). In many modeling situations, it is important that users feel that they can understand and accept the general type of form selected. This feeling of comfort is often necessary for users to make sound judgments in model use. Hence, simple functional forms have an additional advantage in terms of user comfort levels.

To summarize, families of functional forms are an extremely powerful tool for use in model building. Users can provide a limited number of inputs and the computer can use those inputs to find a particular member of the selected family. A scenario can be constructed with relatively little pain.

## VIII. USING EXISTING PROGRAMS VERSUS DESIGNING NEW ONES

As a summary of this chapter, and also because the question is an important one, we now turn to a consideration of when it is best to try to use an existing computer program to solve a problem and when, instead, it is worth the effort to design a new one for the problem at hand. (The issue arises, of course, only when there is a program available that might conceivably be useful for the current problem.) A useful way to address this question involves considering the steps in designing new programs and then contrasting them with the steps in using existing programs.

As has been discussed above, the first and crucial step in designing a computer model consists of what was called basic case analysis. In other words, we decide what the problem is, what the major decisions are, what factors will affect those decisions, and so forth. This step is fundamental to all the following steps and in general it must be performed by someone familiar with the problem rather than by a computer support person. Next, we must decide how much analysis can usefully be done by computer. In this phase we are concerned with the trade-off between the computer's speed and ability to perform accurate calculations on the one hand and the computer's requirement for unambiguous serial sets of instructions on the other. Much of the work in this step of the design process must be done by an individual who is very familiar with the problem rather than by a computer specialist. The third step involves specifying a model design in some form, such as a block diagram, that can be understood as the basis for computer coding. This step is often most successful if it is conducted using a top-down approach. Often, in practice, we find that the second and third steps are intermingled. We might make a preliminary decision as to what analysis could usefully be done by computer and then proceed to sketch a design. In that process, we would be led to make more detailed decisions as to just what analysis should be computerized. . . . Once the basic design is in place, it can be translated into machine language, or coded. As we have been repeating throughout the chapter, if the design step is complete, the coding step can be separated and can, if appropriate, be performed by a different person from the designer. Finally, the coded program should be tested and used. Most computer programs are not fully correct the first time around; they contain errors, called bugs. Thus, one of the most important tasks for the user of a program, regardless of who did the coding, is to test the program carefully. Often, this stage involves some hand checking of some of the computer results. It also often involves giving the program sets of inputs which are selected to help with the checking and correction (or debugging), even though the inputs are not sensible in the decision problem at hand. For example, we might tell a pro forma income statement program that sales will be zero, just to see what assumptions the program makes about which costs, revenues, and other quantities are dependent on sales levels and which are not. Only after such debugging runs have convinced us that the program seems to be correct would we proceed to input the scenarios we consider relevant for analyzing the problem we face. We would use the program repeatedly, performing sensitivity analyses on interesting parts of the input. Finally, we would proceed to use the results, together with any other important information, to make a decision. If we are using an optimization model, the computer suggests the best decision. In most cases, however, the computer program has simply allowed us to understand the situation more fully. The actual decision must be suggested by and also selected by the human user.

Perhaps surprisingly, the steps involved in using existing computer programs are not fundamentally very different from the list just discussed. The first basic step of case analysis is crucial in both situations. Similarly, in both cases the designer or user must also decide how much analysis could usefully be performed by machine. When there is an existing program that may be used, the third step becomes one of figuring out just what the program does, rather than a step of design as it is for new models. In investigating existing models, we often find it helpful to use the same types of tools we would use for new models. In particular, a top-down approach to figuring out a program is often very helpful. Similarly, block diagrams are often a convenient way of describing the operation of existing programs that we are investigating. Thus, for either new or existing models the third step will likely result in block diagrams of the program. For existing models, the next step entails deciding whether or not the program is useful for the current problem.

1.3. The internal rate of return of a series of cash flows is the discount rate (or rates) at which the net present value of the series is exactly zero. Design an algorithm that accepts as inputs a series of timed cash flows and a rate and outputs an indicator as to whether or not the input rate is an internal rate of return for that series of cash flows.

1.4. Design a model for keeping track of the amount of inventory on hand of a particular item. Inputs should be the starting inventory amount and also a list of transactions concerning that item. What specific details would be needed in the input? How would the model work?

1.5. Specify an algorithm for determining yearly depreciation under:
   *a*. The straight line method.
   *b*. The sum-of-the-years'-digits method.
   *c*. The double declining balance method.

1.6. Try to design an algorithm for the following problem. (Warning: this exercise is tricky.)

   Describe an algorithm that meets the following specifications:

   Inputs are starting debt and five annual sales figures. For the relationships section, assume that contribution or margin is 20 percent of sales. Interest for the year is 8 percent of the average of starting and ending debt. There are no other expenses, so that earnings before tax are the margin minus interest. The tax rate is 48 percent. During the year excess cash is used to pay off the debt, while cash deficits are met with additional debt financing. The total debt will not be paid off under any feasible scenario, so that it is unnecessary to consider other uses of cash. The model should output earnings after tax and year-end debt for each of the five years.

## case 1.1

# Spencer Department Stores

Robert Crawford, vice president of Spencer Department Stores, was evaluating the decision of whether or not to modernize the firm's main store in Windsor, Massachusetts, a suburb of Boston. The store was almost 30 years old and it looked both old-fashioned and crowded. Spencer executives felt that the store would provide more sales dollars for the company if it had a more modern, airy appearance. They also worried that failure to modernize might lead to an erosion of the existing business at the store. The question of modernization had become a top priority issue when a small piece of land next to the parking lot of the Windsor store had been put up for sale. Spencer had the opportunity to buy that land for $100,000 and to pave it for use as additional parking space. It could then afford to use some of the existing parking lot to build an addition to the store.

Spencer was a small successful chain of retail stores in the Boston area. The firm owned and operated three department stores which carried wide lines of medium-priced clothes, housewares, and small appliances. The firm's original store (and the store that was still the home of the chain) was the Windsor store. Executives felt that the image of that store was slipping in the eyes of its customers, mainly because of its physical appearance. For one thing, it was crowded. It had been built to accommodate a more narrow line of goods and when the firm had introduced a wider merchandise policy, it had been necessary to sandwich more departments and more displays into the limited space. After carefully considering the space issue, Mr. Crawford had concluded that it would be impossible to squeeze any more selling space out of the existing floor plan. He also felt strongly that the store could not afford to cut back the variety of items it offered for sale. Finally, he was convinced that the crowded conditions at Windsor created an image in the mind of the customer that was not sufficiently like the pleasant, quality image that the firm wanted to project.

A second related problem with the Windsor store was that it looked old-fashioned. It had been built in 1949 and it had the style of department stores built at that time. Mr. Crawford felt that a more modern appearance, with a more airy feeling, more light and a brighter tone would improve the atmosphere and boost sales at Windsor.

Spencer had investigated the costs of expanding the Windsor store several times, but executives had never carried out the expansions because they felt they could not afford to cut back the store's somewhat limited parking space. When the parcel of land adjacent to the existing parking area became available, they saw a very good opportunity to acquire the means to expand both the store and the parking lot at the same time. Accordingly, Mr. Crawford had proceeded to try to identify as exactly as possible the likely costs and benefits of acquiring the land and modernizing the store.

As noted above, the land would cost $100,000. The building expansion would cost an additional $4 million. Mr. Crawford felt that Spencer would be able to obtain a 30-year mortgage for $3 million. The mortgage would carry a 9 percent interest rate. It would be paid back in 60 semiannual payments of $145,363 each. The remainder of the funds would be borrowed in a note that would require payments of 4½ percent interest each six months on the balance outstanding during that period. In addition, Spencer would repay $110,000 of the principal each six months. For tax purposes the firm would depreciate the $4 million over 30 years, using the sum-of-the-years-digits method.

In investigating the issue of whether or not to expand, Mr. Crawford had also considered the impact which the new construction would have on the sales of the Windsor store. Without renovation, sales in the first half of 1977 would be approximately $4 million, while those in the second half would be $8 million. If the firm began construction, they would try to keep operation of the store as normal as possible but Mr. Crawford was quite sure that all of the construction activity and the disorganization that would inevitably result would hurt sales for 1977. By 1978 the renovation would have been completed and sales would increase over what they would have been in the old store. Exhibit 1 summarizes Mr. Crawford's best estimates of the incremental sales that the renovated store would provide in constant dollars, for each half-year. It also includes the depreciation schedule and the interest payments on the loans. The variable costs associated with the additional sales would be assumed to be 76 percent of the sales. Mr. Crawford wanted to calculate the internal rate of return that would be provided by the project. He was also concerned about what the impact on that return would be if some of his assumptions (particularly those for increased sales, and to a lesser extent, those for building costs) were wrong.

**EXHIBIT 1**

| Half year (1 = Feb.–July) (2 = Aug.–June) | Incremental sales ($000) | Depreciation | Interest on mortgage | Interest on note |
|---|---|---|---|---|
| 1977 | | | | |
| 1 . . . . . . . . . | $– 500 | $131,148 | $135,000 | $49,500 |
| 2 . . . . . . . . . | – 800 | 128,962 | 134,534 | 44,550 |
| 1978 | | | | |
| 1 . . . . . . . . . | 1,500 | 126,776 | 134,046 | 39,600 |
| 2 . . . . . . . . . | 3,000 | 124,590 | 133,537 | 34,650 |
| 1979 | | | | |
| 1 . . . . . . . . . | 2,000 | 122,404 | 133,005 | 29,700 |
| 2 . . . . . . . . . | 4,000 | 120,219 | 132,449 | 24,750 |
| 1980 | | | | |
| 1 . . . . . . . . . | 2,000 | 118,033 | 131,868 | 19,800 |
| 2 . . . . . . . . . | 4,000 | 115,847 | 131,260 | 14,850 |
| 1981 | | | | |
| 1 . . . . . . . . . | 2,000 | 113,661 | 130,626 | 9,900 |
| 2 . . . . . . . . . | 4,000 | 111,475 | 129,963 | 4,950 |
| 1982 | | | | |
| 1 . . . . . . . . . | 2,000 | 109,290 | 129,270 | 0 |
| 2 . . . . . . . . . | 4,000 | 107,104 | 128,545 | 0 |
| 1983 | | | | |
| 1 . . . . . . . . . | 2,000 | 104,918 | 127,789 | 0 |
| 2 . . . . . . . . . | 4,000 | 102,732 | 126,998 | 0 |
| 1984 | | | | |
| 1 . . . . . . . . . | 2,000 | 100,546 | 126,171 | 0 |
| 2 . . . . . . . . . | 4,000 | 98,361 | 125,308 | 0 |
| 1985 | | | | |
| 1 . . . . . . . . . | 2,000 | 96,175 | 124,405 | 0 |
| 2 . . . . . . . . . | 4,000 | 93,989 | 123,462 | 0 |
| 1986 | | | | |
| 1 . . . . . . . . . | 2,000 | 91,803 | 122,477 | 0 |
| 2 . . . . . . . . . | 4,000 | 89,617 | 121,447 | 0 |
| 1987 | | | | |
| 1 . . . . . . . . . | 2,000 | 87,432 | 120,370 | 0 |
| 2 . . . . . . . . . | 4,000 | 85,246 | 119,246 | 0 |
| 1988 | | | | |
| 1 . . . . . . . . . | 2,000 | 83,060 | 118,070 | 0 |
| 2 . . . . . . . . . | 4,000 | 80,874 | 116,842 | 0 |
| 1989 | | | | |
| 1 . . . . . . . . . | 2,000 | 78,689 | 115,559 | 0 |
| 2 . . . . . . . . . | 4,000 | 76,503 | 114,218 | 0 |
| 1990 | | | | |
| 1 . . . . . . . . . | 2,000 | 74,317 | 112,816 | 0 |
| 2 . . . . . . . . . | 4,000 | 72,131 | 111,352 | 0 |
| 1991 | | | | |
| 1 . . . . . . . . . | 2,000 | 69,945 | 109,821 | 0 |
| 2 . . . . . . . . . | 4,000 | 67,760 | 108,222 | 0 |
| 1992 | | | | |
| 1 . . . . . . . . . | 2,000 | 65,574 | 106,550 | 0 |
| 2 . . . . . . . . . | 4,000 | 63,388 | 104,804 | 0 |
| 1993 | | | | |
| 1 . . . . . . . . . | 2,000 | 61,202 | 102,979 | 0 |
| 2 . . . . . . . . . | 4,000 | 59,016 | 101,071 | 0 |

**EXHIBIT 1 (*continued*)**

| *Half year (1 = Feb.–July) (2 = Aug.–June)* | *Incremental sales ($000)* | *Depreciation* | *Interest on mortgage* | *Interest on note* |
|---|---|---|---|---|
| 1994 | | | | |
| 1 ......... | 2,000 | 56,831 | 99,078 | 0 |
| 2 ......... | 4,000 | 54,645 | 96,995 | 0 |
| 1995 | | | | |
| 1 ......... | 2,000 | 52,459 | 94,819 | 0 |
| 2 ......... | 4,000 | 50,273 | 92,544 | 0 |
| 1996 | | | | |
| 1 ......... | 2,000 | 48,087 | 90,167 | 0 |
| 2 ......... | 4,000 | 45,902 | 87,684 | 0 |
| 1997 | | | | |
| 1 ......... | 2,000 | 43,716 | 85,088 | 0 |
| 2 ......... | 4,000 | 41,530 | 82,376 | 0 |
| 1998 | | | | |
| 1 ......... | 2,000 | 39,344 | 79,541 | 0 |
| 2 ......... | 4,000 | 37,158 | 76,579 | 0 |
| 1999 | | | | |
| 1 ......... | 2,000 | 34,973 | 73,484 | 0 |
| 2 ......... | 4,000 | 32,787 | 70,249 | 0 |
| 2000 | | | | |
| 1 ......... | 2,000 | 30,601 | 66,869 | 0 |
| 2 ......... | 4,000 | 28,415 | 63,337 | 0 |
| 2001 | | | | |
| 1 ......... | 2,000 | 26,230 | 59,646 | 0 |
| 2 ......... | 4,000 | 24,044 | 55,789 | 0 |
| 2002 | | | | |
| 1 ......... | 2,000 | 21,858 | 51,758 | 0 |
| 2 ......... | 4,000 | 19,672 | 47,546 | 0 |
| 2003 | | | | |
| 1 ......... | 2,000 | 17,486 | 43,144 | 0 |
| 2 ......... | 4,000 | 15,301 | 38,544 | 0 |
| 2004 | | | | |
| 1 ......... | 2,000 | 13,115 | 33,737 | 0 |
| 2 ......... | 4,000 | 10,929 | 28,714 | 0 |
| 2005 | | | | |
| 1 ......... | 2,000 | 8,743 | 23,465 | 0 |
| 2 ......... | 4,000 | 6,557 | 17,979 | 0 |
| 2006 | | | | |
| 1 ......... | 2,000 | 4,372 | 12,247 | 0 |
| 2 ......... | 4,000 | 2,186 | 6,257 | 0 |

# case 1.2

# Franklin Property Trust

In 1977, six years after his graduation from Harvard Business School, Douglas Schair was reviewing all that he could of his school work on discounting and on inflation as he and Stanley Sclar, the two owners of the Franklin Property Trust, analyzed the question of whether they should sell one of the parcels of land owned by that company.

The Franklin Property Trust had been founded by Mr. Schair and Mr. Sclar in 1976. The firm was, however, the successor to an old company that had been very important in the history of the state of Maine. The origins of the company went back to the end of the 18th century, when Col. Moses Little of Newbury, Massachusetts, became interested in the sources of water power in the area of Lewiston, Maine. (Lewiston itself was incorporated in 1795). Little proceeded to acquire ownership of 8 of 14 towns in the area. Moses Little's son Josiah and Josiah's son Edward developed the family investment in 1836 by building the Great Androscoggin Falls Dam, Locks and Canal Company to exploit the power of the great falls of the Androscoggin River; in 1845 they changed the company's name to the Lewiston Water Power Company. In the middle of the 19th century a wealthy Bostonian named Benjamin Bates joined with a group of associates to buy out the interests of the Little family. Bates and his associates formed the Franklin Company; chartered on April 5, 1854, that company's stated purpose was to finance and construct new textile plants and to assist in raising funds for dams and waterways. The firm quickly became an important force in the industrialization of the Lewiston–Auburn area, an important owner and developer of water power, and an important landowner as well.

The "Report upon the affairs of the Franklin Company of Lewiston, read and adopted at the annual meeting of the stockholders, September 17, 1879, with accompanying exhibits" was one of the documents given to Mr. Schair and Mr. Sclar when they purchased the assets of the Franklin Company in 1976. The 1879 report described a large and powerful company. Franklin had built cotton mills in Lewiston and sold them to the Continental Mills, some of whose stock Franklin still owned. It also owned stock (valued in 1879 at a quarter of a million dollars) in the Lewiston Bleachery and Dye works, as well as controlling stock interest in the Union Water Company, which owned ponds, lakes and other water sources in the Lewiston area. In addition, the Franklin company owned real estate in Lewiston and Auburn valued at $750,000 at that time. The 1878 financial statements showed total assets of $1.5 million.

The 1879 annual report describes the Franklin Company as primarily "the great proprietor of land and water power at Lewiston" whose interest in mills and industry in general was one of developing users of water power. Hence, the report states that the proper strategy for Franklin was to help build and finance mills but then to sell those mills to be run by others. The water resources of the Franklin Company were considerable; the report notes:

> Absolute control of the water supply of the Androscoggin, including the storage of the Rangely lakes and the tributaries, was purchased and legally secured to the Union Water Power Company, with important rights of flowage, above the Errol dam, to the great benefit of the several companies associated in the Union Water Power Company, and of the City of Lewiston,—the latter corporation thereby securing a permanent and inexhaustible water supply for its citizens. . . .
>
> Previous to this arrangement the insufficiency of the natural flow of water in the Androscoggin river, to supply the necessary power required by existing mills and machinery at Lewiston, in periods of drought, had been repeatedly demonstrated.

In 1900 the Franklin Company still owned over 3,000 acres in Lewiston and Auburn. Between 1900 and 1976 Franklin had sold off most of its acreage so that in 1976 approximately 85 acres of real estate were all that remained. In 1976 Douglas Schair was a vice president of Insurance Investment Associates, specializing in mergers and acquisitions of insurance companies. He became aware of the Franklin Company through his father-in-law, an Auburn dentist who was one of the leading stockholders in Franklin. Mr. Schair joined with Stanley Sclar, a real estate investor from Maine, and made an offer to the Franklin Company's stockholders for the assets of the firm. At a stockholders' meeting on July 15, 1976, the required two-thirds vote approved the sale; the final purchase price was approximately $360,000. The property of the Franklin Company was divided by the owners among a number of entities, the principal one being Franklin Property Trust.

The real estate transferred to the Franklin Property Trust included the land under 123 houses and land under some of the streets of Lewiston. In addition, Messrs. Schair and Sclar acquired the land under the Canal National Bank in Lewiston. That property was being leased to the bank under the terms of a long-term lease that had been arranged by the Franklin Company and the bank. While the financial arrangements dissolving the Franklin Company were being arranged in 1976, the bank had approached that firm about the possibility of arranging to purchase the land. As the new owners of the land, Messrs. Schair and Sclar had to consider what the sale price would have to be for it to be attractive for them to sell the land to the bank.

Canal National Bank was owned by the Canal Corporation, which also owned other banks and a mortgage company in Maine. In September 1976, Canal Corporation had $230 million in assets; approximately 75 percent of that amount consisted of the assets of the Canal National Bank. The bank was headquartered in Portland; the Lewiston building was a branch office. Exhibit 1 shows the building.

**EXHIBIT 1**

Franklin Property Trust

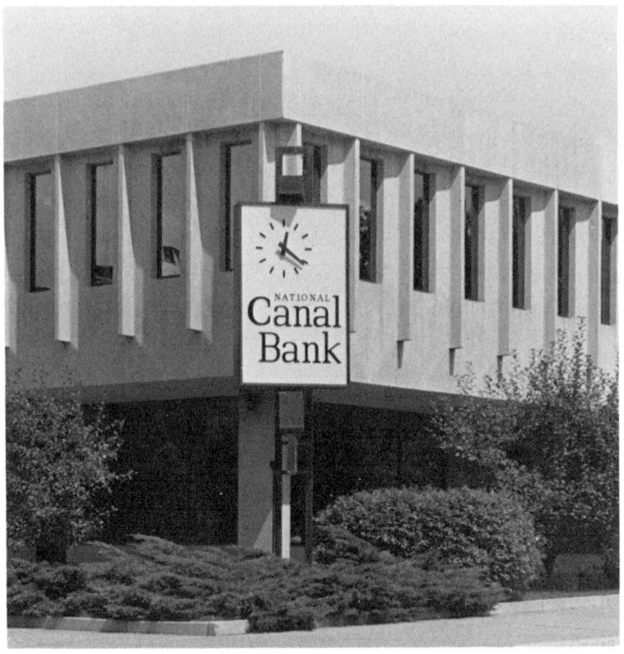


The original lease between the bank and the Franklin Company was signed in August 1966. The lease specified a rental price for the land of $6,000 per year, payable in equal monthly amounts, for 1966 through 1971. If the bank constructed a building on the site, the lease provided that the arrangement would be extended for 25 years (at the same $6,000 yearly cost) from the date on which the building permit was obtained. Canal National Bank did build a structure on the land, obtaining the building permit in October 1969. The lease provided further that at the end of such a 25-year period, the lessee would have the option to extend the lease for 25 more years. At the start of that period, a new monthly rental figure would be computed by adjusting the original $500 by the change in the Consumer Price Index (U.S. City Average, All Items) during the 25-year period. The lease payments would also be adjusted by the CPI at the start of the 6th, 11th, 16th, and 21st years of the lease extension. (If no such index were published during any part of the life of the lease, the agreement provided for the lessor and lessee to select a comparable index.) During the entire period of the lease, the bank was responsible for paying real estate taxes and insurance premiums. At the end of the lease period, both the land and the building would be the property of the lessor, Franklin Property Trust.

The parcel of land consisted of 26,000 square feet. At the time of the sale of the Franklin Company assets, $52,000 of the sale price had been allocated to that property. The book value of the bank building was approximately $600,000 at the time of the creation of the Franklin Property Trust.

## case 1.3

# The Upstate Canning Company, Inc.*

During the period following his graduation from a business school in 1950, Mr. Nelson Shields had attempted to prepare himself for the opportunity of becoming the manager and sole or part owner of a company with real growth possibilities. Because he lacked financial resources, he had sought employment which offered substantial immediate income as well as managerial experience which would be useful in later years. This search led him successively through positions in three distinctly different businesses, in each of which experience was largely concentrated in the sales and sales management areas. By 1956 he had accumulated personal savings of $15,000 which, added to some family money placed at his disposal, gave him an investment fund of $35,000.

At this point Mr. Shields had begun an active search for opportunities to purchase an existing business. In the course of the year he looked into about 25 possibilities which came to his attention. Some of these were quickly rejected; others involved the expenditure of considerable time and some money before a negative decision was reached. While looking for business possibilities, Shields also sought to develop contacts with business and professional people who might be induced to invest equity capital in an attractive opportunity, should one be found requiring more capital than he possessed. By the end of 1956, Mr. Shields was still investigating business leads, but with no real prospects in sight. Meanwhile, the pressure to settle on a business was increasing. Shields had given up employment in October in order to devote full time to his search, and he realized that he could not afford many months of unemployment without eating into the sum set aside for investment.

In February of 1957 a business broker called Shields to advise him that a small cannery had just come up for sale. The property consisted of two plants, equipped for the canning of fruits and vegetables, which were located close to the source of supply in rural towns in New York State. The business, known as the Upstate Canning Company, Inc., was owned and managed by

* This case was written by Gordon Donaldson.

Mr. A. C. Fordham. Mr. Fordham's health was uncertain and, at 55, he had decided to sell out because he had no relatives to take his place in the business. The broker urged Shields to investigate this opportunity because it looked as though it might fit his circumstances.

Mr. Shields immediately set out to learn what he could about the fruit and vegetable canning industry in general and this business in particular. The broker arranged a meeting with Mr. Fordham, and from this and subsequent meetings and telephone conversations, Mr. Shields assembled a picture of the business.

In general Mr. Fordham was very cooperative in providing the information requested from him. He was reluctant, however, to disclose the financial details of operations for the three years prior to 1956. During 1952 Fordham had brought in a general manager on a three-year employment contract as a means of easing himself out of the day-to-day responsibilities of the business. The new man had not worked out well, and sales and profits had suffered as a result. Upon the termination of this contract, Fordham had again assumed full management responsibilities, and results in 1956 improved substantially over those of 1953, 1954, and 1955. Fordham argued that these years were not representative of the earnings potential of the business and that 1956 should be taken as the most accurate measure of its possibilities. From what Shields had been able to find out about the business from other sources, he was inclined to accept Fordham's explanation and to base his estimates on the figures for 1956.

The physical plant of the business appeared to be in very good condition. The two buildings had been kept in excellent repair, and the canning equipment was modern. The combined plant and equipment had recently been appraised for insurance purposes, and their value had been placed at $200,000. Shields was assured that no major repairs would be necessary over the next few years.

Mr. Fordham had been accustomed to operating the plants only during the limited harvest season for the fruits and vegetables which he canned. The season lasted for four months, from July through October, with August and September normally accounting for two-thirds of the company's total production. At times Fordham had considered stretching out the production period with other canning operations, but he had never taken any action on the idea. During the 1956 season Upstate had produced canned fruits and vegetables with a total value of $850,000 (valued at Upstate's selling price). This production represented only about 50 percent of combined productive capacity of the plants during the production season. Excess capacity was attributed to the substantial expansion of facilities which had been undertaken to meet wartime demands.

The vegetables and fruits canned by Upstate were bought on a contract basis from farmers in the surrounding area; farmers were paid cash on delivery on the basis of prevailing market prices at the time of delivery. The quantities canned by Upstate varied to some extent with the crop conditions from year to year; normally output could be increased considerably, however, by noncontract purchases, if good marketing opportunities existed. The production process was almost entirely mechanical, and the towns and surrounding areas offered an ample supply of seasonal labor sufficiently skilled to perform the various operations in the plant. Labor was paid on a weekly basis.

The products of the Upstate Canning Company were marketed primarily under the Upstate brand through jobbers. It was the normal practice to sell the entire season's pack before the next canning season began, so that little inventory would be carried over from one year to the next. Sales tended to be concentrated during and immediately following the production period. Fordham indicated that about 50 percent of the pack would normally be sold by the end of the canning season (October) and 70 percent by the end of December. The balance of sales was customarily spread rather evenly over the remaining months through June.

Mr. Shields was particularly attracted by the marketing opportunities of the business. It was his impression that Fordham had not been aggressive in sales promotion—that much better use could be made of the company's productive capacity. Shields believed that he could greatly increase the scale of operations by undertaking an active but relatively inexpensive sales program. He had in mind direct sales to supermarket chains of both Upstate and private brands to be obtained largely through his own efforts with no significant increase in present selling costs.

Relying on these expectations, Shields prepared a five-year sales program (see Exhibit 1) which he planned to use as the basis of his estimates of profits

**EXHIBIT 1**
Planned sales volume, 1957–1962

| | |
|---|---|
| 1957–1958 .......... | $ 850,000 |
| 1958–1959 .......... | 1,050,000 |
| 1959–1960 .......... | 1,250,000 |
| 1960–1961 .......... | 1,450,000 |
| 1961–1962 .......... | 1,650,000 |

and working capital requirements. He was informed by Fordham that collections on accounts receivable caused little trouble in this business; bad debt losses were rare, and accounts were normally collected within 30 days. Shields expected that the planned expansion would not affect this collection period and might even improve it because he would be increasing direct sales to large accounts.

In examining the cost aspects of the business, Shields soon became aware of the high proportion of variable costs. The principal items were the fruits and vegetables and other ingredients, cans, and direct labor. As previously indicated, fruits and vegetables were bought on a cash basis, labor was paid weekly at fixed hourly rates, and cans and "other ingredients" were purchased on normal terms of 2%/10, net 30 days. The details of revenues and costs for 1956 are shown in Exhibits 2 and 3.

**EXHIBIT 2**

Income Statement
For Year Ended December 31, 1956
($000)

| | Amount | | Percent of sales |
|---|---|---|---|
| Sales (net after returns and allowances) | | $850 | 100 |
| Less: Cost of goods sold | | | |
| Beginning inventory, January 1, 1956 | $257 | | |
| Add: Cost of goods manufactured | 630 | | |
| | $887 | | |
| Less: Ending inventory, December 31, 1956 | 254 | 633 | 74 |
| Gross profit on sales | | $217 | |
| Less: Selling and administrative expense | | | |
| Selling and delivery | $ 64 | | 8 |
| Administrative and general (including salary to Fordham of $20,000) | 56 | 120 | 7 |
| Profit before taxes | | $ 97 | |
| Less: Federal income tax* | | 45 | 5 |
| Net profit after taxes | | $ 52 | 6 |

* Federal income tax is computed on the basis of 30 percent of the first $25,000 of taxable income plus 52 percent of income in excess of $25,000. For companies of this size the tax is payable in the succeeding fiscal year as follows: 50 percent on the 15th day of the third month following the end of the tax year and 50 percent on the 15th day of the sixth month following.

As negotiations proceeded it became evident that Fordham was anxious to sell the business as soon as possible. The new crop season was coming on, and Fordham felt that if he were to operate the business for another year, it would soon be necessary to sign contracts with farmers for the year's production. After three weeks, during which Shields was gathering and studying information and talking to bankers, can company officials, government agencies, and others, Fordham came forward with a specific proposal for the sale of the business (see Exhibit 4).

The plan anticipated that Shields would organize a new company and purchase certain Upstate assets; namely, its plant and equipment, a small amount of finished goods inventory, and the right to use the Upstate brand names. Current assets (other than the inventory mentioned above) and liabilities of the old company would not pass to the new company. It was apparent from the plan that Fordham had guessed that Shields had very limited resources and, accordingly, had provided for an installment purchase of Upstate assets through the gradual redemption of $300,000 of

**EXHIBIT 3**

Statement of Cost of Goods Manufactured
For Year Ended December 31, 1956
($000)

| | | Amount | Percent of total cost of goods manufactured |
|---|---|---|---|
| Direct costs | | | |
| Vegetables and fruit | $232 | | |
| Labor | 138 | | |
| Cans | 112 | | |
| Other ingredients | 36 | $518 | 82 |
| Variable overhead | | | |
| Fuel oil | $ 17 | | |
| Electricity and water | 7 | | |
| Factory supplies | 5 | | |
| Payroll taxes | 7 | | |
| Truck and auto expenses | 2 | | |
| Gas and oil | 5 | 43 | 7 |
| Fixed overhead | | | |
| Repairs and maintenance | $ 18 | | |
| Insurance | 12 | | |
| Property taxes | 10 | | |
| Depreciation—plant and equipment | 24 | | |
| Machinery rental | 5 | $ 69 | 11 |
| Total cost of goods manufactured | | $630 | 100 |

income bonds to be issued to Fordham. By this time Shields had become convinced that this business was sufficiently promising to justify a full and detailed study of Fordham's proposal.

Before accepting Fordham's proposal or making a counterproposal, it was necessary for Shields to determine how the new company was to be financed. His best lead for additional equity capital was a professional man who had indicated that he was prepared to invest as much as $100,000 if the right opportunity came along. This man was 50 years of age, and his investment goal appeared to be that of capital appreciation over the years rather than immediate income.

Shields was determined that the plan for the new company would include a means by which he could become the owner of 51 percent of the voting stock as soon as possible. More specifically, he hoped to obtain control within five years, and hence was intent on arranging a compensation plan for himself as manager which would enable him to accomplish this objective. Shields's plan, as tentatively formulated, provided for a basic salary of $15,000 plus 5 percent of profits before taxes; these figures took account of his estimate that roughly 60 percent of his annual income would be absorbed by living expenses and tax payments. His plan also included an option to buy enough additional shares—either new shares to be issued by

**EXHIBIT 4**

Initial Proposal by Mr. Fordham for the Purchase of Certain Assets of the Upstate Canning Company, Inc., by Mr. Shields and Associate(s)

1. New corporation to be formed with capitalization of $400,000 and with a capital structure as follows:
   *a.* $100,000 of Common Stock, $1.00 par, one vote per share, to be issued to Shields and associate(s) for $100,000 cash. Cash to be retained in new corporation.
   *b.* $300,000 of income bonds due June 30, 1967; 3 percent interest per annum payable semiannually (June 30 and December 31), if and when earned, cumulative, to be issued to Fordham in exchange for all plant and equipment of Upstate Canning Company, $50,000 of salable finished goods inventory and the right to use the brand names of the Upstate Canning Company. (Prior to the exchange, the Upstate Canning Company will be liquidated and the assets distributed to Fordham as sole owner.)
2. Repayment provisions of Income Bonds:
   *a.* Company to repurchase $50,000 of income bonds on or before June 30, 1958
   *b.* In succeeding years, company to repurchase income bonds, equivalent in par value to 50 percent of the net profit after taxes, provided that the amount in any year will be no less than $15,000. The $15,000 will be due June 30, and any balance within 30 days after the close of the fiscal year.
   *c.* Company to have the option of purchasing any amount of income bonds in excess of the minimum requirements according to a schedule of discounted prices as follows: in the first year at 80 percent of par; in the second year at 82½ percent of par; in the third year at 85 percent of par; and so on.
3. No fixed assets to be sold or encumbered in any way without the consent of the income bondholders.
4. Control of the company to be divided equally between the income bondholders and the common shareholders until the income bonds have been completely retired. Each group will elect two directors to a four-person board.
5. Fordham to act as Chairman of the Board and receive compensation for whatever time he spends on operating matters, beyond board meetings, on a basis to be determined in further negotiations.
6. Shields to act as president and general manager.
7. New company to be incorporated and assets of Upstate to be acquired on or about June 30, 1957. In the meantime, it is to be understood that Fordham and Shields will work together in negotiating contracts with farmers and arranging for an orderly transfer of ownership.

the company or outstanding shares held by his associate(s)—to raise Shields's holdings to 51 percent of all outstanding voting stock. It was clear, however, that the exact details of the final plan would have to be worked out with the other shareholder or shareholders before arrangements could be completed with Fordham.

As part of his program to assure an adequate supply of capital, Mr. Shields obtained an introduction, through a mutual friend, to one of the officers of a medium-sized bank in a nearby city. This officer indicated that it was the bank's normal policy to avoid substantial loans to new enterprises, but that exceptions were occasionally made where there was adequate security. Canning operations were important to the surrounding area, and he suggested that the bank might consider a secured loan to the new company if it looked promising on closer examination. From further conversation Shields concluded that the best possibility would be a loan of up to 75 percent of the cost of finished-goods inventory under a field warehousing arrangement. The cost of this kind of financing, including field warehousing expenses, which would not otherwise have been incurred, would be about 6 percent per annum. In addition to the bank loan Shields also believed that it might be possible to stretch the payment period on cans to 60 days without creating serious credit problems.

In considering his preliminary calculations, Shields planned to make a detailed study of the year 1957–58 and to use this study as a basis for approximating the necessary figures for the fiscal years 1958–59 through 1961–62. He had in mind a fiscal year beginning July 1.

Shields was aware that the next move was up to him. As he saw it, there were three obvious courses of action: (1) accept Fordham's proposal as presented; (2) reject the proposal and look for another business; (3) propose a compromise plan which would have a reasonable prospect of meeting the objectives of all interested parties.

## COMPUTER SUPPLEMENT

Program UPSTAT is a BASIC program for analysis of the case Upstate Canning Company, Inc. The program is a deterministic pro forma generator which will investigate the performance of the firm over a four-year time horizon under various sets of assumptions. This supplement discusses the assumptions incorporated into UPSTAT and includes instructions and sample protocols for running the program.

### Assumptions

Program UPSTAT will prepare yearly income statements for fiscal years 1958, 1959, 1960, and 1961 or will print cash budgets for one or more sets of four months between July 1957 and June 1961 (or will provide both types of output). The program requires the user to provide fixed and variable figures for cost of goods sold, for selling and delivery costs, and for administrative and general expenses. In addition, the program inputs information on the availability of bank financing (based on inventory) and on the amount which Mr. Shields will obtain from an outside investor. The program requires four (yearly) sales projections and also an input specifying the collection period for receivables.

UPSTAT assumes that production occurs in July ($1/6$ of the year's total), August ($1/3$), September ($1/3$), and October ($1/6$). It assumes that sales occur in each of the 12 months with $1/8$ of the fiscal year's total in each of July through October, with $1/10$ in each of November and December and with $1/20$ in each of January through June. Thus, all of the fiscal year's production is assumed sold during that year. Payments for sales are received either one or two months after the time of the sales (depending on the user's assumption about receivables).

The fixed and variable cost components are provided by the user. Of the fixed-cost-of-goods-sold figure, $24,000 is assumed to be depreciation (and, hence, does not appear in the cash budget segment). The cash fixed costs are then allocated to the months of the year in proportion to production in those months. Fruit and labor costs are assumed paid in the same months in which those inputs to the production process are used. Cans are paid for 60 days after use, while other variable components of the cost of goods are paid for one month after use. The program assumes that the proportions of each of these types of costs are the same as the fraction (of $561,000) represented by each of the types in Exhibit 3 of the case.

For selling and delivery costs and also for the general and administrative costs, the variable components are assumed to occur at the time of the sales (with $1/8$ in July, and so forth) while the fixed components are assumed evenly spread over the 12 months of the fiscal year. Taxes are paid in equal installments in September and December (for the previous fiscal year). Interest on the income bonds is paid at a yearly rate of 3 percent in equal installments in December and June.

The initial amount of the income bonds is $300,000. Fifty thousand dollars are retired in June 1958. After that first year, the amount retired is either $15,000 or half of after-tax earnings, whichever is larger. The minimum $15,000 for any fiscal year is paid on June 30 of that year; any required amount above $15,000 is paid the next month. The program does not consider early retirement of the bonds, although the agreement in the case does allow for such early payments.

Mr. Shields's salary is $15,000 per year. His bonus is 5 percent of operating income net of interest payments. The program assumes that Shields invests $35 thousand on June 30, 1957.

The program assumes that the availability of bank loans in any month depends on the level of inventory at the start of the month. It asks the user to specify the percentage of beginning inventory which is the maximum that the bank will lend. The cash budget outputs include information on cash needs and on available borrowing. The program does not, however, consider the cost of borrowing; the only interest payments considered are the interest payments on the income bonds. In addition, the program does not consider compensation of the outside investor.

The following protocol gives an example of the use of UPSTAT.

```
* .BASIC        At the monitor level, the user requests BASIC.

NEW OR OLD -- OLD            } The user asks BASIC to find the
OLD FILE NAME--UPSTAT        } existing program called UPSTAT.

READY          BASIC types READY to show that it is ready to
RUN            run; the user asks to begin.

BAS:UPSTAT       13:30            31-AUG-78
```

UPSTAT first requests the various cost figures:

```
VARIABLE COST OF GOODS SOLD AS A PERCENT OF SALES ?66
FIXED COST OF GOODS SOLD (THOUSANDS $) ?69

VARIABLE COST OF SELLING AND DELIVERY AS A PERCENT OF SALES ?4
FIXED COST OF SELLING AND DELIVERY (THOUSANDS $) ?30

VARIABLE COST OF ADMINISTRATIVE AND GENERAL AS A PERCENT OF SALES ?0
FIXED COST OF ADMINISTATIVE AND GENERAL (THOUSANDS $) ?51

                  FIXED COSTS    VARIABLE COSTS  } The program prints
GOODS SOLD        $ 69 (000)      66 % OF SALES  } out these initial
SELL/DELIVER      $ 30 (000)      4 % OF SALES   } assumptions to be sure
ADMINSTRATIVE     $ 51 (000)      0 % OF SALES   } they are OK.

ALL OK ?Y   The user approves the assumptions.

PERCENT OF BEGINNING INVENTORY THAT THE BANK WILL LOAN ?75
HOW MUCH DO YOU PLAN TO BORROW FROM THE OUTSIDE INVESTOR?
    TYPE '1' IF $0; TYPE '2' IF $65000; TYPE '3' IF $100000 ?2
```

The program allows only these three choices for the amount borrowed from the outside investor.

```
PROJECTED SALES FOR 4 YEARS (THOUSANDS OF DOLLARS)
 ?850,1050,1250,1450   The user gives four yearly sales
                       figures, separated by commas.
BANK WILL LOAN 75 % OF BEGINNING INVENTORY
YOU PLAN TO BORROW $ 65000 FROM OUTSIDE INVESTOR

                 PROJECTED SALES    The program prints out the
YEAR 1           $ 850 (000)        second batch of assumptions
YEAR 2           $ 1050 (000)       for checking.
YEAR 3           $ 1250 (000)
YEAR 4           $ 1450 (000)
ALL OK ?Y

ANALYSIS? TYPE '1' FOR INCOME STATEMENT,'2' FOR CASH BUDGET,'3' FOR BOTH
 ?3   The user requests both types of output
```

---

* In this protocol, the actual dialog is shown in typeface, with the parts that were typed by the user underlined to distinguish them from the parts that were printed by the computer. Explanatory comments have been added in handwriting.

Income statements

| | YEAR ENDING JUNE 30 | | | |
|---|---|---|---|---|
| | 1958 | 1959 | 1960 | 1961 |
| SALES | 850 | 1050 | 1250 | 1450 |
| VARIABLE COSTS | 595 | 735 | 875 | 1015 |
| FIXED COSTS | 150 | 150 | 150 | 150 |
| OPERATING INCOME | 105 | 165 | 225 | 285 |
| INTEREST | 9 | 8 | 6 | 5 |
| BONUS | 5 | 8 | 11 | 14 |
| PROFIT BEFORE TAX | 91 | 150 | 208 | 266 |
| PROFIT AFTER TAX | 49 | 77 | 105 | 133 |
| BOND PRINCIPAL (income bonds outstanding) | | | | |
| OPENING | 300 | 250 | 211 | 159 |
| REPAYMENT | 50 | 39 | 53 | 67 |
| CLOSING | 250 | 211 | 159 | 92 |
| Shields' compensation: | | | | |
| SALARY | 15 | 15 | 15 | 15 |
| BONUS | 5 | 8 | 11 | 14 |
| TOTAL INCOME | 20 | 23 | 26 | 29 |
| GRAND TOTAL | | | | 98 |

The program asks which months' cash budgets to give:

```
CHOOSE 4 MONTHS OF THE POSSIBLE 48 FOR WHICH YOU WANT DATA
FOR EXAMPLE: JULY,1957= 1,AUG,1957= 2,...JUNE,1958=12
             JULY,1958=13,AUG,1958=14,...JUNE,1959=24
             JULY,1959=25,AUG,1959=26,...JUNE,1960=36 ?1,2,3,4
ACCOUNTS RECEIVABLE TYPE '1' FOR 30  DAYS,'2' FOR 60 DAYS ?1
```

The user selects July–October 1957 and then specifies 30 days for receivables.

CASH BUDGET
(ARITHMETIC ERRORS DUE TO ROUNDING)

| MONTH NUMBER | 1 | 2 | 3 | 4 |
|---|---|---|---|---|
| MONTHLY SALES | 106 | 106 | 106 | 107 |
| CASH RECEIPTS | 0 | 106 | 106 | 106 |
| CASH OUTLAY | 80 | 163 | 194 | 144 |
| MATERIALS,LABOR,MFG,O.H. | 70 | 152 | 183 | 133 |
| SELLING AND DELIVERY | 7 | 7 | 7 | 7 |
| ADMINISTRATION / GENERAL | 4 | 4 | 4 | 4 |
| TAXES | 0 | 0 | 0 | 0 |
| INTEREST | 0 | 0 | 0 | 0 |
| BOND REPAYMENT | 0 | 0 | 0 | 0 |
| BONUS | 0 | 0 | 0 | 0 |
| MONTHLY CASH NEED | 80 | 57 | 88 | 38 |
| CUMULATIVE CASH NEED | 80 | 137 | 225 | 263 |

since July 1, 1957, before borrowing from the bank.

The maximum bank loan available is the percentage of inventory specified (above) by the user.

| MAXIMUM BANK LOAN | 38 | 57 | 156 | 254 |
|---|---|---|---|---|
| BEGINNING INVENTORY | 50 | 76 | 208 | 339 |
| + COST OF GOODS PRODUCED | 105 | 210 | 210 | 105 |
| - COST OF GOODS SOLD | 79 | 79 | 79 | 79 |
| ENDING INVENTORY | 76 | 208 | 339 | 365 |
| 75 % BEGINNING INVENTORY | 38 | 57 | 156 | 254 |
| CASH SURPLUS UTILIZING MAX LOAN | 57 | 20 | 30 | 91 |

(INCLUDES BANK BALANCE $ 100  6/30/57)

Thus, the program assumes Shields invests $35 thousand; for this run, the user assumed Shields borrowed $65 thousand. The cash surplus is the maximum bank loan plus the initial investment minus the cumulative cash need.

```
DO YOU WANT ADDITIONAL MONTHS PRINTED ?Y
```

The user asks to have budgets printed for additional months.

```
CHOOSE 4 MONTHS OF THE POSSIBLE 48 FOR WHICH YOU WANT DATA
FOR EXAMPLE: JULY,1957= 1,AUG,1957= 2,...JUNE,1958=12
             JULY,1958=13,AUG,1958=14,...JUNE,1959=24
             JULY,1959=25,AUG,1959=26,...JUNE,1960=36 ?5,6,7,8
ACCOUNTS RECEIVABLE TYPE '1' FOR 30 DAYS,'2' FOR 60 DAYS ?1
```

The user selects Nov. 1957 - Feb. 1958 and retains the 30-day assumption for receivables.

```
                  CASH BUDGET
        (ARITHMETIC ERRORS DUE TO ROUNDING)

MONTH NUMBER                         5         6         7         8
MONTHLY SALES                        85        85        43        43

CASH RECEIPTS                        107       85        85        43
CASH OUTLAY                          60        34        8         8
  MATERIALS,LABOR,MFG,O.H.           50        19        0         0
  SELLING AND DELIVERY               6         6         4         4
  ADMINISTRATION / GENERAL           4         4         4         4
  TAXES                              0         0         0         0
  INTEREST                           0         5         0         0
  BOND REPAYMENT                     0         0         0         0
  BONUS                              0         0         0         0
MONTHLY CASH NEED                   -47       -51       -77       -35
CUMULATIVE CASH NEED                 216       165       88        54

MAXIMUM BANK LOAN                    274       227       179       155
  BEGINNING INVENTORY                365       302       239       207
  + COST OF GOODS PRODUCED           0         0         0         0
  - COST OF GOODS SOLD               63        63        32        32
  ENDING INVENTORY                   302       239       207       175
 75 % BEGINNING INVENTORY            274       227       179       155
CASH SURPLUS UTILIZING MAX LOAN      158       162       191       202
    (INCLUDES BANK BALANCE $ 100  6/30/57)

DO YOU WANT ADDITIONAL MONTHS PRINTED ?N


TIME:  3.79 SECS.

READY
```

The user specifies no further months and the program ends this run of UPSTAT.
At this point, the user could, if s/he wished, change the assumptions by starting the program again and typing in a full set of them.

## case 1.4

# Quaker Oats Company Contract Bidding Program

In the spring of 1972, Quaker had developed a computerized system to calculate the square footage of corrugated linerboard to make their various sized containers for shipping products. A separate system also was developed to use this basic common denominator, the square footage of board, to evaluate easily and quickly the vendor's quotes received under a corporate bidding program for corrugated containers. In the spring of 1975, Quaker had also developed a computerized system to evaluate vendor's quotes received on the firm's needs for folding cartons (which were used to package products).

Early in 1976, work was started toward modifying and improving these systems to shorten the lead time necessary to analyze the bids to be received on contracts to be awarded effective July 1. The container systems were rewritten and blended into a single, unified system requiring substantially less vendor input and ensuring a higher degree of accuracy of results. The folding carton system was also revised to enable fast turnaround of vendor bid information received on punched cards.

The folding carton system was successfully used in analyzing and awarding business. The container system was not utilized because the firm did not open bidding in 1976 but instead renegotiated contracts with existing suppliers.

### Company background

Quaker Oats employed 25,000 people and achieved sales of $1,473,000 during the 1976 fiscal year. The majority of the sales came from the Grocery Products Area, which handled foods and pet foods sold worldwide through grocery channels. The Foods Division produced and sold hot cereals (Quaker Oats, Instant Quaker Oatmeal, and related products); ready-to-eat cereals (Life cereal, Cap'n Crunch, Quaker 100% Natural cereal); mixes, syrup, and corn products (Aunt Jemima Cornmeal and Grits, Pancake Mix, syrup, and related products); and frozen foods (Celeste Pizza and Aunt Jemima Frozen Waffles and French Toast). The Pet Foods Division sold Ken-L

Ration dog food and Puss'n Boots cat food in the United States and Canada, and other brands abroad.

Quaker's other major area was the Diversified Businesses Area, which included Fisher-Price Toys (pre-school toys), Marx Toys (toys and games), Needlecraft Division (yarn and needlecraft kits), Chemicals Division (agriculturally based specialty chemicals), Burry Division (institutional cooky sales), and the Restaurants Division (Magic Pan Restaurants).

The corporate purchasing function at Quaker Oats was in the operations part of the corporate staff. William Bales, the vice president for Purchasing, reported to Sam Flint, the vice president for Corporate Operations. The basic organization of the firm was a divisional one. The purchasing department's job was to buy those nonagricultural products that were used by more than one division. Agricultural products were handled separately, and products required by only one division were purchased directly by the divisions needing them. Much of the strength of the corporate purchasing group in obtaining favorable prices and good service lay in its ability to offer volume business to its vendors. Mr. Bales felt that suppliers knew that Quaker meant a lot of business to them and, moreover, that the company had a reputation for dealing fairly with its vendors. For example, when paper prices rose rapidly in the mid-1970s, Quaker had renegotiated some of the prices it was paying for paper products rather than insist that the suppliers bear the full brunt of the unexpected cost increases. The result of such policies was that Quaker felt its suppliers were loyal and could be counted on to help the firm if problems arose.

Another part of the corporate operations staff was the Operations Research group. In the late 1960s the firm had been organized on functional lines and the distribution function had included a Distribution Planning and Analysis Group, while the Information Services group had included an Operations Research Group. The OR group had been involved primarily in critical path analyses for the engineering departments and for new-product developments. In 1970 Quaker was reorganized into profit centers. At the same time the Operations Research group and the Distribution Planning and Analysis group were combined under corporate operations.

Mr. Flint, the vice president for Corporate Operations, explained that in setting up and managing the new OR group he and its director had tried to avoid some of the mistakes they felt were common in such departments. For one thing, he felt that operations research groups often made the error of assuming and maintaining control over the computer programs they wrote. At Quaker, on the other hand, the group would not undertake a project unless they had a full commitment from the group for whom the program was to be developed that that group, rather than OR, would be responsible for running the program once it had been completed. The result, according to Mr. Flint, was that users of the programs became involved in the projects and understood the programs better than would have been possible under alternative policies. Another principle of the OR group was that assignments to that group should not generally be permanent ones. Instead, the goal was for one or two members of the group (which had a total of only eight or ten members) to be shifted each year into one of the operating groups of the company. The OR group might hire technically trained graduates of business schools, might keep them for a few years, during which time they would work with operating groups and in the process learn about the company and its operation, and then might transfer them to one or another of the operating groups. The long-term result of such a policy would be that there would be people who understood and were receptive to operations research scattered through the company; these people would become users and sponsors of the OR group.

### Purchasing cartons and boxes—the manual system

Before 1976 the evaluation of bids from vendors for containers and folding cartons had required considerable amounts of time from several members of the purchasing staff. The evaluation of the bids for corrugated boxes alone might take three people three weeks to process, while the carton bids might take a similar amount of effort.

Bids were taken on corrugated boxes by plant and by box size and type. There would be 10 to 15 plants, with an average of perhaps 40 different boxes each to consider (although in some cases the total could go as high as 120 boxes); there might be 20 or more bidders on any one of these items. Contracts were let for one year at a time, although there would be many deliveries under each contract. So that the plant and divisional managers were aware of the cost factors that determined the final cost of a specified container, Quaker required costs on a basic regular slotted container (RSC) with a schedule of upcharges (increments) for extras. On corrugated boxes, the vendors were asked to bid for the various required sizes of a basic box which would be top or end loading, natural kraft, with one-color printing. In addition to the base charge a set-up charge would be made on orders below some minimum quantity specified by the vendor. Vendors supplied a price per thousand square feet of board which was applied to the square footage of each box. The square footage of each size box was calculated with a formula specified by Quaker. (There was some variability in the industry as to how square footage was measured; Quaker's formula calculated total surface area, including an allowance for a glue overlap at one corner and for the scoring necessary for each right angle to produce the box.) There were a number of different options that might be added to the basic container. Plant managers might want special coatings (for boxes that would hold frozen foods, for example), or they might want a different color box, or they might want dividers within the box, or they might want to order quantities less than the minimum specified by the vendor. As far as order quantity was concerned, the plant managers tended to want small order sizes; in general they had very limited space for inventories and, therefore, they preferred to have many small deliveries during the year rather than a smaller number of larger deliveries. Vendors would often include extra charges for small orders, however, and Mr. Bales wanted to make explicit the extra costs that would be incurred with small orders. His philosophy on the other possible upcharges was similar.

Exhibit 1 shows the form that was used for bids on corrugated boxes with the manual system. The vendor filled in the form and performed the cost per square foot and other calculations. The sheet then went to Quaker's purchasing department. There the numbers on the sheet were all rechecked and total contract cost (and variance from plan) were calculated in a laborious process. Errors were frequent. The company had tried to use temporary help to check the forms but the procedure had not worked satisfactorily and so the checking was done by the Quaker personnel, often working overtime during the period when bids were evaluated. Once the cost figures had been found the numbers were used in making decisions on suppliers for the coming year. Other factors included in those decisions were the quality of service provided by a vendor and also the desire of Quaker to deal with a relatively small number of suppliers so as to be able to provide volume business to its vendors.

The evaluation of bids from vendors of the printed cartons that would be used for packaging Quaker's products was similar although even more complicated. The corrugated boxes were used for shipping products and, hence, although they had to be strong, properly sized, and so forth, their appearance was not particularly important because they would not be seen by the consumer. The cartons, on the other hand, were the packages seen by consumers and their appearance was therefore very important. Quaker set particularly high standards for the printing of the cartons. They insisted on sharp pictures with clear colors. In addition, they tried to ensure as much consistency in color as possible, so that the colors on different packages of a particular product would match as closely as possible.

The basic philosophy for the evaluation of bids on cartons was like that for corrugated boxes. Vendors were asked to provide information on both fixed and variable costs. There were two types of printing process that might be used—lithograph and rotogravure. In general, gravure was more consistent in terms of color and also less expensive for longer runs (that is, larger numbers of cartons printed at the same time); lithograph was less expensive for shorter runs. For the gravure process a cylinder had to be prepared for each color of a carton design; for vendors bidding such a process, Quaker asked for an additional figure for cylinder cost, so that product managers would understand the costs of design changes. Often the firm would use whichever process was less expensive, but managers might sometimes specify one process or the other and the cost information would give com-

**EXHIBIT 1**

March 1975

CORRUGATED QUOTATION

TO: THE QUAKER OATS COMPANY
ATTENTION: W. A. Bales - Director, Corporate Purchasing

BY: FIRM NAME ______

SIGNED ______ DATE ______

The prices and upcharges listed below are firm for the period July 1, 1975 through December 31, 1975. The January 1 through June 30, 1976 period is to be negotiated as outlined in Quaker's letter of March 17, 1975.

QUAKER PLANT ______

The minimum order quantity for this plant is ______
(See alternate minimum below).

All prices are basis:

1. One color printing with average ink coverage.
2. R.S.C. unless specified - glue joint.
3. Corrugating medium 26# .009 Semi-Chem - Regular Adhesive.
4. Unitized or baled - NOT string tied or bundled.
5. Sq. Ft. basis area formula:
   2 lengths + 2 widths +2 3/8" X 1 Width + 1 Depth + 1" ÷ 144 - (This is the only acceptable formula)

the type of material to be used for the middle layer of the three-layer (corrugated) box material.

(2lengths + 2widths + 2 3/8") * (width + depth + 1") gives area in square inches, including overlapping to allow gluing the sides and also including the flaps at the opening end of the box.
Dividing the figure by 144 converts it to square feet.

**EXHIBIT 1 (*continued*)**

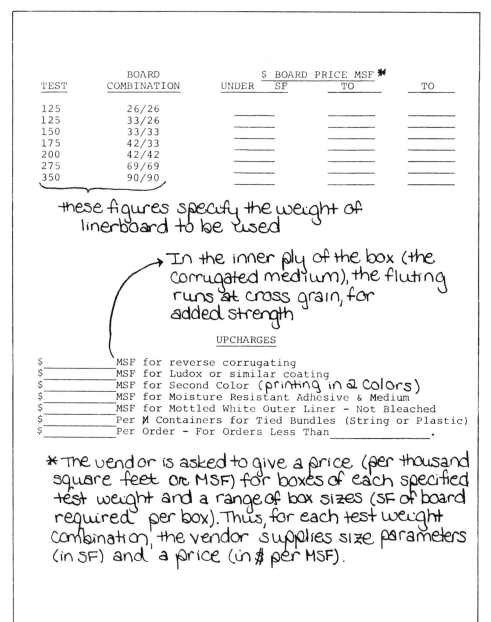

| TEST | BOARD COMBINATION | $ BOARD PRICE MSF * UNDER SF | TO | TO |
|---|---|---|---|---|
| 125 | 26/26 | ______ | ______ | ______ |
| 125 | 33/26 | ______ | ______ | ______ |
| 150 | 33/33 | ______ | ______ | ______ |
| 175 | 42/33 | ______ | ______ | ______ |
| 200 | 42/42 | ______ | ______ | ______ |
| 275 | 69/69 | ______ | ______ | ______ |
| 350 | 90/90 | ______ | ______ | ______ |

these figures specify the weight of linerboard to be used

In the inner ply of the box (the corrugated medium), the fluting runs at cross grain, for added strength

UPCHARGES

$__________ MSF for reverse corrugating
$__________ MSF for Ludox or similar coating
$__________ MSF for Second Color (printing in 2 Colors)
$__________ MSF for Moisture Resistant Adhesive & Medium
$__________ MSF for Mottled White Outer Liner - Not Bleached
$__________ Per M Containers for Tied Bundles (String or Plastic)
$__________ Per Order - For Orders Less Than __________.

* The vendor is asked to give a price (per thousand square feet or MSF) for boxes of each specified test weight and a range of box sizes (SF of board required per box). Thus, for each test weight combination, the vendor supplies size parameters (in SF) and a price (in $ per MSF).

VENDOR: AJAX BOX Co. VENDOR PLANT: CHICAGO, ILL QUAKER PLAN

| "P" CODE NUMBER "V" | LENGTH (inches/sixteenths) | WIDTH (inches/sixteenths) | DEPTH (inches/sixteenths) | "P" SQ. FT./BOX | "P" ANN. VOL. M CONT. | "P" NORMAL RELEASE QUANT., M CONT. | TEST WEIGHT | FLUTE | $ PER MSF | 2ND COLOR PER MSF | BL. OUTR. LNR. PER MSF | MTLD. WHITE OUTR. LNR. UNBL. PER MSF | OUTER COATING PER MSF (LUDOX) | MOIST. RES. MED. PER MSF | REVERSE CORR. PER MSF | "V" TOTAL | |
|---|---|---|---|---|---|---|---|---|---|---|---|---|---|---|---|---|---|
| 1 | 2 | 3 | 4 | 5 | 6 | 7 | 8 | 9 | 10 | 11 | 12 | 13 | 14 | 15 | 16 | 17 | 18 |
| 830 | 17/14 | 11/15 | 4/7 | 7.479 | 157 | 15 | 175 | B | | | | | x | | | | |
| 905 | " | " | " | " | 276 | 15 | 175 | B | | | | | x | | | | |
| 912 | " | " | " | " | 329 | 15 | 175 | B | | | | | x | | | | |
| 913 | " | " | " | " | 62 | 5 | 175 | B | | | | | x | | | | |
| | | | | | | | | | | | | | | | | | |
| 900 | 17/14 | 11/13 | 8/13 | 8.847 | 166 | 8 | 200 | B | | 2" GAP TOP | | | x | | | | |
| 901 | " | " | " | " | 801 | 8 | 200 | B | | " | " | " | x | | | | |
| 908 | " | " | " | " | 145 | 7 | 200 | B | | " | " | " | x | | | | |
| 915 | " | " | " | " | 61 | 7 | 200 | B | | " | " | " | x | | | | |
| | | | | | | | | | | | | | | | | | |
| 909 | 12/0 | 6/12 | 21/2 | 7.993 | 587 | 10 | 350 | C | | | | | x | | x | | |
| 918 | " | " | " | " | 611 | 10 | 350 | C | | | | | x | | x | | |
| 921 | " | " | " | " | 476 | 10 | 350 | C | | | | | x | | x | | |

Total volume for year (column 6)

Amount to be delivered at a time (column 7)

Please enter the appropriate price per MSF for the size and test weight of each box in column #10.

Enter your upcharges in columns #11 through #16 if applicable as indicated by an "x" and enter in column #17, the total of columns #10 through #16.

Enter your upcharge for less than minimum orders for this plant in column #18.

parative information (in those cases in which the vendor chose to bid both processes), again so that the Quaker managers would understand the costs of their choices.

The bids for cartons were taken on a divisional basis rather than on a plant basis. Thus, a bid might cover a year's supply of cartons for Life cereal or some other Quaker product. Actually, the bids often involved more than one product at a time. The reason was that the printing presses, whether gravure or litho, accepted only specific sizes of paper. In an attempt to reduce waste and therefore to save money, Quaker in some cases specified groups of cartons that could be printed in a single run. The combinations were chosen so as to use efficiently one of the standard printing press or paper sizes. Vendors might bid such products in combinations if they wanted to; they could, however, still bid the cartons individually, instead.

As was true for box bids, the carton bids required several weeks of the time of several Quaker employees for evaluation and checking. Once the number work had been completed, the decisions on suppliers would be made. Cost was an important consideration in this process, as were the quality of the graphics provided by a vendor, the quality of service, and the Quaker policy of using a relatively small number of suppliers so as to be an important factor in the business of its suppliers.

## Computerized contract bidding programs

The manual system for evaluation of bids involved several problems. For one thing, as noted above, the volume of calculations that had to be performed was burdensome (and the work was dull). In addition, the need for manual evaluation of bids took time. For example, under the old system the bids for cartons would be required by April 1 so that a decision could be made by mid-June on suppliers for the year starting July 1. Mr. Bales felt that the result was that Quaker bore the vendors' hedging costs for the three-month period between the submission of bids and the start of the contract year. In other words, he felt that bidders built cushions into their bids to allow for possible cost changes during the delay period. If bids could be processed more quickly so that bids could be submitted later, Mr. Bales felt that the vendors would be able to figure their costs more closely and, therefore, that Quaker would save money.

Accordingly, during the winter of 1975–76 Mr. Bales asked John Lauger and Bonnie Spinasanta, members of his group who had been involved in the tedious clerical work of bid evaluation, to work with Arthur Horberg, a member of the Operations Research group, to streamline and improve the existing computerized system for evaluation of bids. They began work on the program for the evaluation of bids on corrugated boxes. When it was decided that the boxes would not be bid competitively during 1976 but that instead contracts would be renegotiated with the previous year's suppliers, they shifted their attention to the existing program for the evaluation of bids on folding cartons. That program was improved and used for bids for the year starting July 1, 1976. The corrugated box program was also finished; it was planned that the program would be used for competitive bids on boxes in 1977.

The program for bids on cartons mechanized what had previously been done by hand. The various divisions of the company submitted information on their estimated requirements for cartons during the year, on the costs for those cartons that had been built into their yearly plans, and on the prices they were currently paying for the items. This information was fed into the computer and saved in a file for use in evaluating vendors. Exhibit 2 shows the requirements for a fictitious Quaker Division as they would be given to the vendors. Each bidder was asked to fill in a form of the type shown in Exhibit 3. Vendors were then instructed to have the information on the form keypunched (in a specific format) and then to submit to Quaker the resulting deck of cards. These cards were read into the computer. The machine used the bidder's information together with the divisional requirements to calculate the costs of various cartons from that bidder. The possibility of using combination runs complicated these cost determinations. When combinations were bid by a vendor, the program allocated the cost of the combination run among the different items in the run proportionately (in terms of numbers of cartons). The result of this step of the analysis was an output sheet showing the cost of using the particular vendor, together with the planned and current costs for the various cartons. The vendor portion of that sheet was xeroxed and sent to the vendor. The information on the sheet was retained in a file within the computer for later use in ranking vendors on the basis of cost. Exhibit 4 gives an example of the output provided for a single vendor.

The bids of all vendors were evaluated individually, and with the results retained within the computer, were analyzed by another computer program called the ranker. For each item being bid, this program listed the top seven bidders, in order of decreasing cost (provided, of course, that there were that many bidders). For each bidder other than the one ranked first for the item, the program calculated and printed the percentage additional cost that would be incurred by Quaker if it chose that bidder instead of the lowest cost bidder. In addition, the ranker provided some summary information describing the overall performance of the different bidders. At the bottom of the report printed by the ranker, the program listed for each bidder the number of cost dollars on items for which that bidder ranked first (that is, had lowest costs), the number of bid dollars on which that bidder ranked second, etc. Exhibit 5 gives an example of the type of output obtained from the ranker. (The figures in that exhibit have been disguised so that the exhibit does not give any actual information on the relative attractiveness of real bids on any product.)

**EXHIBIT 2**

THE QUAKER OATS COMPANY

D I V I S I O N A L   R E Q U I R E M E N T S

CORPORATE CONTRACT

FOLDING CARTONS, TRAYS, PRINTED CARDS, ETC.

EFFECTIVE PERIOD: 10-01-76 TO 10-02-76

DIVISION: FOODS

Code # for carton

Plant(s) requiring this carton

Yearly requirements in thousands of cartons

Number of print runs per year

| LINE NO. | CODE | PRODUCT | NO. COLORS | VARNISH | PROCESS | LOCATION | REQMNT/M | NO. RUNS |
|---|---|---|---|---|---|---|---|---|
| 1001 | 122 | 10-OZ INST OATS | 6 | | LITHO | CEDAR RAPIDS IA | 7500 | 4 |
| 1002 | | | | | | SHIREMANSTOWN PA | 5300 | |
| 1003 | | | | | | ST JOSEPH MO | 3500 | |
| THE FOLLOWING 2 CODES MAY BE RUN IN COMBINATION | | | | | | | | |
| 1004 | 125 | 12-OZ R SPCE OAT | 6 | | LITHO | ST JOSEPH MO | 6300 | 4 |
| 1005 | 127 | 13-OZ C SPCE OAT | 6 | | LITHO | CEDAR RAPIDS IA | 6100 | 4 |
| 1006 | 129 | 10-OZ APL ON OAT | 6 | | LITHO | ST JOSEPH MO | 9500 | 4 |
| 1007 | | | | | | DANVILLE IL | 5300 | |
| 1008 | 131 | 12-OZ MPL BN OAT | 6 | | LITHO | CEDAR RAPIDS IA | 8500 | 4 |
| 1009 | | | | | | DANVILLE IL | 2900 | |

these two cartons may be combined in a single run; they are currently being run together

May be combined

**EXHIBIT 3**

**The Quaker Oats Company**

CORPORATE CONTRACT PROGRAM

Folding Cartons, Trays, Printed Cards, Etc.

QUAKER DIVISION: ______ PAGE ______ OF ______

VENDOR QUOTATION SHEET

KEY PUNCH INSTRUCTIONS: PUNCH ON STANDARD (SIZE 7.375" BY 3.250") KEY PUNCH CARDS. ALL FIELDS ARE TO BE VERIFIED, LEFT JUSTIFIED. ALL ENTRIES TO END IN DECIMAL. USE NO COMMAS AS DELINEATORS. COLUMNS WITHIN FIELDS ARE INDICATED BELOW. ONE "HEADER CARD" FOR EACH DIVISION. ONE "HASH TOTAL" CARD FOR EACH DIVISION. KEEP DIVISIONS SEPARATE.

HEADER CARD, ENTER VENDOR NAME: 1 2 3 4 5 6 7 8 9 10 11 12 13 14 15 16 17 18 19 20 21 22 23 24 25

| LINE NUMBER | DELIVERED PRICE PER THOUSAND $ | BID FOR ROTO-GRAVURE PRINTING: ONE-TIME CYLINDER COST | BID FOR ROTO-GRAVURE PRINTING: MAKE/READY PER RUN | FOR OFFSET-LITHO PRINTING: PLATE & MAKE READY PER RUN |
|---|---|---|---|---|
| 1 2 3 4 5 | 6 7 8 9 10 11 12 13 | 14 15 16 17 18 19 20 21 22 23 | 24 25 26 27 28 29 30 31 | 32 33 34 35 36 37 38 39 40 41 |
| | costs per thousand cartons | set-up costs | | |
| | | Gravure | | Litho |

when vendors chose to run combinations of cartons, as allowed in the DIVISIONAL REQUIREMENTS from Quaker, they were supposed to enter only one set-up cost line per combination.

⋮ ⋮

HASH TOTAL CARD → 9 9 9 9 . ENTER TOTALS BELOW ONLY ON LAST PAGE FOR THIS DIVISION:

QO-2035

The output of the ranker, together with the individual bidder reports, were given to Mr. Bales. He and his staff, working with the people from the divisions for which the cartons were being purchased, would select vendors for the year.

The carton program was used successfully in evaluating bids for the year

**EXHIBIT 4**

AJAX FOLDING BOX CO    HOODS    09/13/76    C04335/FODOUT

Handwritten annotations: "Company submitting bid"; "Carton code"; "Quaker plant"; "Prices for next 6 months and 12 months"; "Bid (EST) cost, planned cost and amount currently being paid—all excluding plate & make ready (set-up) costs"; "Plate and make ready costs—bid, planned & current"; "Total costs—bid, variance from plan, variance from current cost"; "These columns would not be shown to the"

| CODE | PLANT | 6MO CONTR PRICE | 12MO EST PRICE | EXCLUDING P & MR: EST CONTR COST | PLAN COST | CUR COST | EST CONTR P & MR | PLAN P&MR | CUR P&MR | INCLUDING P & MR: EST CONTR COST | EST CONTR VARIANCE FROM PLAN | EST CONTR VARIANCE FROM CUR |
|---|---|---|---|---|---|---|---|---|---|---|---|---|
| | CRA | 37.28 | 37.28 | 279600. | 224850. | 191250. | | | | | | |
| 122 | TOTAL | | | 279600. | 224850. | 191250. | 3994. | 13200. | 12000. | 283594. | -45544. | -80344 |
| | SHI | 36.93 | 36.93 | 195729. | 185394. | 160325. | | | | | | |
| 122 | TOTAL | | | 195729. | 185394. | 160325. | 2822. | 0. | 0. | 198551. | -13157. | -38226. |
| | SJO | 37.77 | 37.77 | 132195. | 115430. | 101430. | | | | | | |
| 122 | TOTAL | | | 132195. | 115430. | 101430. | 1864. | 0. | 0. | 134059. | -18629. | -32629. |
| | SJO | 36.74 | 36.74 | 231462. | 207774. | 188874. | | | | | | |
| 125 | TOTAL | | | 231462. | 207774. | 188874. | 3082. | 6706. | 6097. | 234544. | -20064. | -39573. |
| | CRA | 36.25 | 36.25 | 221125. | 182878. | 158478. | | | | | | |
| 127 | TOTAL | | | 221125. | 182878. | 158478. | 2984. | 6494. | 5903. | 224109. | -34738. | -59728. |
| | SJO | 36.74 | 36.74 | 349030. | 313310. | 284810. | | | | | | |
| 129 | TOTAL | | | 349030. | 313310. | 284810. | 3894. | 13200. | 12000. | 352924. | -26414. | -56114. |
| | DAN | 35.60 | 35.60 | 188680. | 158894. | 153594. | | | | | | |
| 129 | TOTAL | | | 188680. | 158894. | 153594. | 2173. | 0. | 0. | 190853. | -31959. | -37259. |
| | CRA | 36.25 | 36.25 | 308125. | 280330. | 246330. | | | | | | |
| 131 | TOTAL | | | 308125. | 280330. | 246330. | 4523. | 13200. | 12000. | 312648. | -19118. | -54318. |
| | DAN | 35.60 | 35.60 | 103240. | 86942. | 75342. | | | | | | |
| 131 | TOTAL | | | 103240. | 86942. | 75342. | 1543. | 0. | 0. | 104783. | -17841. | -29441. |
| DIVISION | TOTAL | | | 2009186. | 1755802. | 1560433. | 26880. | 52800. | 48000. | 2036066. | -227464. | -427633. |

**EXHIBIT 5**

```
                              RANKED VENDORS FOR PLANT/DIVISION FOODS

CODE      PLAN                                                       ****** VENDORS ******

(PERCENT PENALTY SHOWN IN PARENTHESES. )
                   AMERICAN CAR   NATIONAL CAR   RIVAL CARTON   SOVEREIGN CA   PARAGON FOLD   AJAX FOLDING   EXCELSIOR CA
 122     538874. 543555. ( 0. ) 548535. ( 0.9) 568578. ( 4.6) 573612. ( 5.5) 587908. ( 8.2) 616204. (13.4) 631621. (16.2)
                   AMERICAN CAR   NATIONAL CAR   RIVAL CARTON   SOVEREIGN CA   PARAGON FOLD   AJAX FOLDING   EXCELSIOR CA
 125     214480. 199019. ( 0. ) 204348. ( 2.7) 216848. ( 9.0) 220656. (10.9) 227916. (14.5) 234544. (17.9) 242163. (21.7)
                   AMERICAN CAR   NATIONAL CAR   RIVAL CARTON   SOVEREIGN CA   PARAGON FOLD   AJAX FOLDING   EXCELSIOR CA
 127     189372. 188309. ( 0. ) 198409. ( 5.4) 206792. ( 9.8) 209748. (11.4) 217630. (15.6) 224109. (19.0) 230266. (22.3)
                   NATIONAL CAR   AMERICAN CAR   RIVAL CARTON   SOVEREIGN CA   PARAGON FOLD   AJAX FOLDING   EXCELSIOR CA
 129     485404. 457253. ( 0. ) 465828. ( 1.9) 501183. ( 9.6) 511016. (11.8) 513228. (12.2) 543777. (18.9) 564369. (23.4)
                   AMERICAN CAR   NATIONAL CAR   SOVEREIGN CA   RIVAL CARTON   PARAGON FOLD   AJAX FOLDING   EXCELSIOR CA
 131     380472. 356696. ( 0. ) 356783. ( 0.0) 391713. ( 9.8) 394949. (10.7) 397488. (11.4) 417432. (17.0) 430898. (20.8)

TOTAL    1808602.      1744832.       1773903.       1885114.       1909981.       1944170.       2036066.       2099316.
```

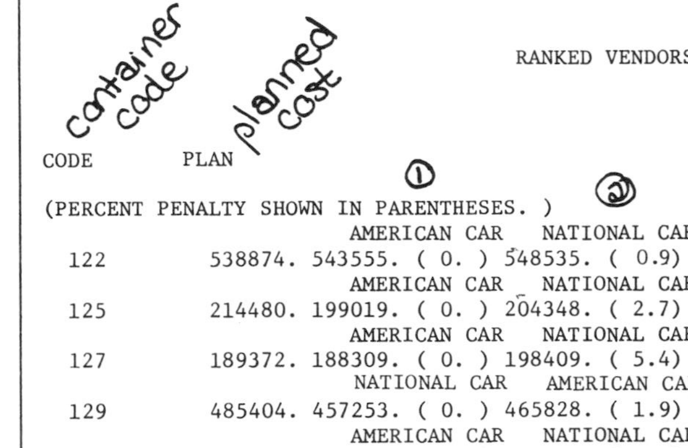

① The name of the first ranked (least cost) company for each carton, with the $ cost if that company is used
② The name of the second-ranked company, its dollar cost, and the % penalty (extra cost) that would be incurred if the second company were used instead of the first.

**EXHIBIT 5** *(continued)*

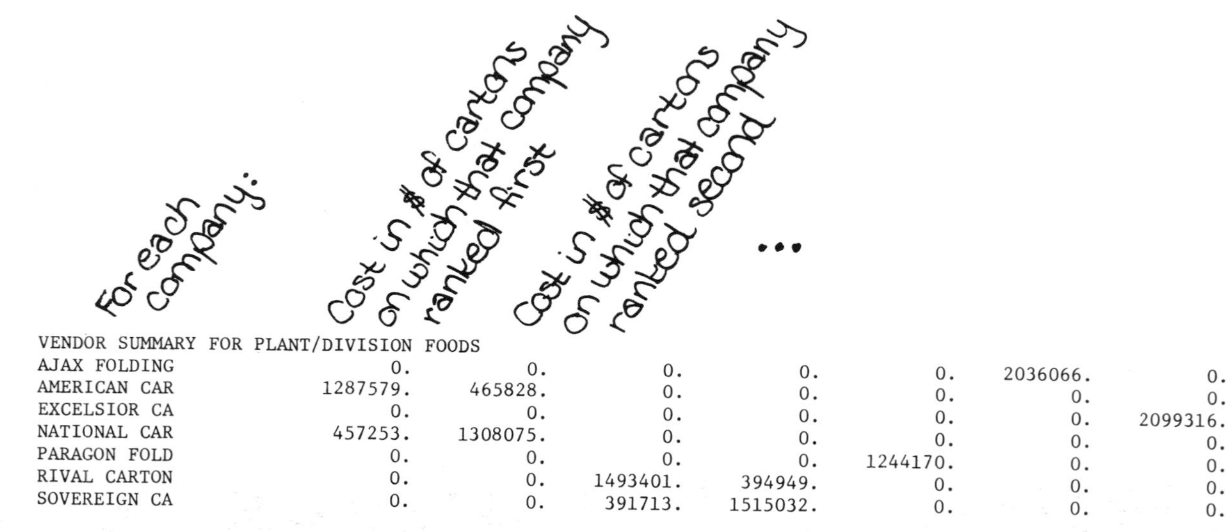


VENDOR SUMMARY FOR PLANT/DIVISION FOODS

| | | | | | | | |
|---|---|---|---|---|---|---|---|
| AJAX FOLDING | 0. | 0. | 0. | 0. | 0. | 2036066. | 0. |
| AMERICAN CAR | 1287579. | 465828. | 0. | 0. | 0. | 0. | 0. |
| EXCELSIOR CA | 0. | 0. | 0. | 0. | 0. | 0. | 2099316. |
| NATIONAL CAR | 457253. | 1308075. | 0. | 0. | 0. | 0. | 0. |
| PARAGON FOLD | 0. | 0. | 0. | 0. | 1244170. | 0. | 0. |
| RIVAL CARTON | 0. | 0. | 1493401. | 394949. | 0. | 0. | 0. |
| SOVEREIGN CA | 0. | 0. | 391713. | 1515032. | 0. | 0. | 0. |

starting July 1, 1976, although there were a few bugs that had to be solved in the process. One particular problem was that Quaker had not specified the quality of computer cards that they would require for the bid information. As a result, some of the bid information came in on cards that were rejected by the company's card-reading equipment and had to be repunched. This problem would be solved in 1977 by the specification of a minimum quality (in terms of weight) for the cards. Other problems arose in debugging the computer program but these problems too were solved and the program evaluated the bids successfully.

The corrugated-box contract evaluation program was very similar to the carton program. The individual plants provided information on requirements and on planned and current costs for the program. This information was used to generate the computer "plant requirements" schedule that was sent to vendors. Exhibit 6 shows such a schedule. Exhibit 7 shows the input sheets sent to the bidders to be filled in with their quotes. For the corrugated program the bidders were not asked to keypunch the cards; the punching was to be done at Quaker. The input sheets included much the same basic information that had been included under the manual system. Bidders were not asked to perform the calculations to find the square footage per box; instead, they simply provided the costs per MSF and the computer did the area calculations and computed the cost per thousand containers. The plant requirement information was combined with the information on the bid sheets to provide bidder cost detail of the type shown in Exhibit 8. The bidder portion of those sheets (but not the planned and current figures) were xeroxed and sent to the vendors for verification. The information for each bidder was also retained within the computer for later evaluation with the ranker. After all of the bidders had been analyzed, the information was processed by the ranker, in the same process used for carton bids. Exhibit 9 shows an example of output from the ranker for bids on corrugated boxes. (Again, the data are fictitious and so the exhibit does not contain useful information about the relative ranking of Quaker's suppliers on any actual products.)

## Future of the contract bid programs

The performance of the carton bid program in 1976 had been a big improvement over the earlier system, Mr. Bales felt. The hand number-pushing had been greatly reduced. The bidders had also had to do less number work, and they found the computer-generated summary sheets useful. The corrugated box program promised to be equally successful when used in 1977. Mr. Bales wondered what more useful analysis could be done by computer in evaluating bids and also how the information from the bid programs could be incorporated into Quaker's planning processes.

**EXHIBIT 6**

THE QUAKER OATS COMPANY

- CORRUGATED CONTRACT -

PLANT REQUIREMENTS

(F-76)

UPCHARGES:
A = SECOND COLOR
B = BLEACHED OUTER LINER
C = MOTTLED WHITE OUTER LINER
D = MOISTURE RESISTANT MEDIUM
E = REVERSE CORRUGATED
F = DIAGONAL SCORING
G = TWO INCH GAP TOP
H = TWO INCH GAP TOP AND BOTTOM
I = TAPED JOINTS
J = LUDOX OR SIMILAR COATING
K = WAREHOUSING

QUAKER PLANT: QUAKERLAND MINIMUM ORDER: 5000 DEDUCTION ON ORDERS OVER: 7000 TIED BUNDLES: NO

PLANT CODE 9010

- CONTAINER SPECIFICATIONS -

| CODE NUMBER | DIMENSIONS (INCHES) LENGTH WIDTH DEPTH | SQUARE FEET | TEST | FLUTE | VOLUME REQUIREMENTS ANNUAL/M | RELEASE/M | UPCHARGES APPLICABLE ONLY IF X A | B | C | D | E | F | G | H | I | J | K |
|---|---|---|---|---|---|---|---|---|---|---|---|---|---|---|---|---|---|
| 130 | 17/14 11/15 4/ 7 | 7.479 | 175 | B | 125. | 15. | | | | | | | | | | X | |
| 205 | 17/14 11/15 4/ 7 | 7.479 | 175 | B | 175. | 15. | | | | | | | | | | X | |
| 212 | 17/14 11/15 4/ 7 | 7.479 | 175 | B | 360. | 15. | | | | | | | | | | X | |
| 213 | 17/14 11/15 4/ 7 | 7.479 | 175 | B | 90. | 15. | | | | | | | | | | X | |
| 200 | 17/14 11/13 8/13 | 8.847 | 200 | B | 150. | 8. | | | | | | | X | | | X | |
| 201 | 17/14 11/13 8/13 | 8.417 | 200 | B | 1300. | 8. | | | | | | | | X | | X | |
| 208 | 17/14 11/13 8/13 | 8.847 | 200 | B | 150. | 7. | | | | | | | X | | | X | |
| 215 | 17/14 11/13 8/13 | 8.417 | 200 | B | 50. | 7. | | | | | | | | X | | X | |
| 202 | 17/14 11/14 8/13 | 9.319 | 200 | B | 20. | 4. | | | | | | | | | | X | |
| 206 | 13/11 10/ 3 11/ 1 | 7.743 | 200 | B | 1000. | 20. | | | | | | X | | | | X | |
| 209 | 12/ 0 6/12 21/ 2 | 7.993 | 350 | C | 1000. | 10. | | | | | | X | | | | X | |
| 218 | 12/ 0 6/12 21/ 2 | 7.993 | 350 | C | 1200. | 10. | | | | | | X | | | | X | |
| 221 | 12/ 0 6/12 21/ 2 | 7.993 | 350 | C | 500. | 10. | | | | | | X | | | | X | |
| 216 | 9/ 9 6/12 23/ 8 | 7.597 | 275 | C | 1000. | 7. | | | | | | X | | | | X | |

code for box; dimensions (inches + sixteenths); SF; test weight; flute type; annual volume (thousand boxes); # of boxes (thousands) per release

- DIVIDER SPECIFICATION PER PIECE -

| | | | | | | NO. PIECES PER CONTNR |
|---|---|---|---|---|---|---|
| 209 | 6/10 20/ 1 | 0.924 | 350 | 2000. | 20. | 2 |
| 218 | 6/10 20/ 1 | 0.924 | 350 | 2400. | 20. | 2 |
| 221 | 6/10 20/ 1 | 0.924 | 350 | 1000. | 20. | 2 |
| 216 | 6/10 14/ 4 | 0.653 | 275 | 3000. | 21. | 3 |

**EXHIBIT 7**

CORPORATE CONTAINER CONTRACT

VENDOR QUOTATION SHEET - SIDE 1

Your quotation is to be entered on Side 2 of this form. Refer to the attached letter for your assigned vendor number. The Plant Requirements form will show the assigned Quaker Plant number.

In completing Section C of the Quotation Sheet, note that you may use from one to four parameters. The following is an example of how to indicate your parameters, if you were to use two parameters:

FROM [3.000] SF TO [5.500] SF FROM [5.500] SF TO [12.000] SF

All pricing inserted in the first column (per test weight) would be applied to containers from 3.000 SF to 5.499 SF. Prices entered in the second column would be applied to containers from 5.000 SF to 11.999 SF. In this example, 3.000 SF would be considered a minimum size container that you could run. Any containers 2.999 SF and under would not be bid on. Likewise, any containers 12.000 SF and over would not be bid on, as 11.999 SF would be considered a maximum container that you could run.

The board combination for each test weight is as follows:

| Board Combination | Test Weight |
|---|---|
| 26/26 | B125 (B=Balanced Board) |
| 33/26 | 125 |
| 33/33 | 150 |
| 42/33 | 175 |
| 42/42 | 200 |
| 69/69 | 275 |
| 90/90 | 350 |

Our formula for computing RSC square footage is:

2 Lengths + 2 Widths + 2 3/8" X 1 Width + 1 Depth + 1 ÷ 144.
(This is the only acceptable formula.)

All MSF prices are basis:

1. F.O.B. delivery point, mixed truckloads.
2. Printed one color with lead free inks, average ink coverage.
3. RSC unless specified - Glued joint.
4. Corrugating medium 26# .009 semi-chem, regular adhesive.
5. Unitized or baled packing; maximum height 42" per unit loaded two-high in trailer.

Upon completion of your quotation, return the quotation sheets to The Quaker Oats Company, Corporate Purchasing, Merchandise Mart Plaza, Chicago, IL. 60654

**EXHIBIT 7 (*continued*)**

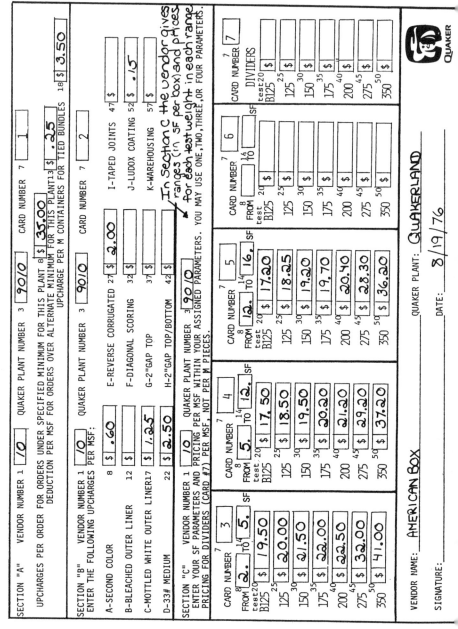

SECTION "A" VENDOR NUMBER 1 [10] QUAKER PLANT NUMBER 3 [9010] CARD NUMBER 7 [1]

UPCHARGES PER ORDER FOR ORDERS UNDER SPECIFIED MINIMUM FOR THIS PLANT 8 $ 35.00

DEDUCTION PER MSF FOR ORDERS OVER ALTERNATE MINIMUM FOR THIS PLANT 13 $ .25

UPCHARGE PER M CONTAINERS FOR TIED BUNDLES 18 $ 3.50

SECTION "B" VENDOR NUMBER 1 [10] QUAKER PLANT NUMBER 3 [9010] CARD NUMBER 7 [2]

ENTER THE FOLLOWING UPCHARGES PER MSF:

| | | | | | | | |
|---|---|---|---|---|---|---|---|
| A-SECOND COLOR | 8 $ .60 | E-REVERSE CORRUGATED | 27 $ 2.00 | I-TAPED JOINTS | 47 $ | | |
| B-BLEACHED OUTER LINER | 12 $ | F-DIAGONAL SCORING | 32 $ | J-LUDOX COATING | 52 $ .15 | | |
| C-MOTTLED WHITE OUTER LINER | 17 $ 1.25 | G-2"GAP TOP | 37 $ | K-WAREHOUSING | 57 $ | | |
| D-33# MEDIUM | 22 $ 2.50 | H-2"GAP TOP/BOTTOM | 42 $ | | | | |

In Section C the vendor gives ranges (in SF per box) and prices for each test weight in each range.

SECTION "C" VENDOR NUMBER 1 [10] QUAKER PLANT NUMBER 3 [9010]

ENTER YOUR SF PARAMETERS AND PRICING PER MSF WITHIN YOUR ASSIGNED PARAMETERS. YOU MAY USE ONE, TWO, THREE, OR FOUR PARAMETERS.
PRICING FOR DIVIDERS (CARD #7) PER MSF, NOT PER M PIECES.

| | CARD NUMBER 7 [3] | CARD NUMBER 7 [4] | CARD NUMBER 7 [5] | CARD NUMBER 7 [6] | CARD NUMBER 7 [7] |
|---|---|---|---|---|---|
| | FROM 8 [2.] TO 14 [5.] SF | FROM 8 [5.] TO 14 [12.] SF | FROM 8 [12.] TO 14 [16.] SF | FROM 8 [ ] TO 14 [ ] SF | DIVIDERS |
| test B125 | 20 $ 19.50 | 20 $ 17.50 | 20 $ 17.20 | 20 $ | 20 $ |
| 125 | 25 $ 20.00 | 25 $ 18.50 | 25 $ 18.25 | 25 $ | 25 $ |
| 150 | 30 $ 21.50 | 30 $ 19.50 | 30 $ 19.20 | 30 $ | 30 $ |
| 175 | 35 $ 22.00 | 35 $ 20.20 | 35 $ 19.70 | 35 $ | 35 $ |
| 200 | 40 $ 22.50 | 40 $ 21.20 | 40 $ 20.40 | 40 $ | 40 $ |
| 275 | 45 $ 32.00 | 45 $ 29.20 | 45 $ 28.30 | 45 $ | 45 $ |
| 350 | 50 $ 41.00 | 50 $ 37.20 | 50 $ 36.20 | 50 $ | 50 $ |

VENDOR NAME: AMERICAN BOX QUAKER PLANT: QUAKERLAND

SIGNATURE: ____________ DATE: 8/19/76

**EXHIBIT 8**

PLANT ****** QUAKERLAND ******

AMERICAN BOX CO

******CONTAINER COST DETAIL******

| CODE | SQFT/ BOX | PER MSF | ANN VL MCONTR | ANN VL MSQFT | COST/ MCONTR | CONTRACT DOLLARS | PLAN DOLLARS | VARIANCE DOLLARS |
|---|---|---|---|---|---|---|---|---|
| code for box | | cost per MSF | annual volume (boxes) | annual volume (MSF) | cost/thousand boxes | cost for year | planned cost | variance |
| 130 | 7.479 | 20.10 | 125.00 | 934.9 | 150.33 | 18791.25 | 19375.00 | 584. |
| 205 | 7.479 | 20.10 | 175.00 | 1308.8 | 150.33 | 26307.75 | 27125.00 | 817. |
| 212 | 7.479 | 20.10 | 360.00 | 2692.4 | 150.33 | 54118.80 | 55800.00 | 1681. |
| 213 | 7.479 | 20.10 | 90.00 | 673.1 | 150.33 | 13529.70 | 13950.00 | 420. |
| 200 | 8.847 | 21.10 | 150.00 | 1327.1 | 186.67 | 28000.50 | 29250.00 | 1250. |
| 201 | 8.417 | 21.10 | 1300.00 | 10942.1 | 177.60 | 230880.00 | 253500.00 | 22620. |
| 208 | 8.847 | 21.10 | 150.00 | 1327.1 | 186.67 | 28000.50 | 27750.00 | -251. |
| 215 | 8.417 | 21.10 | 50.00 | 420.9 | 177.60 | 8880.00 | 9000.00 | 120. |
| 202 | 9.319 | 21.35 | 20.00 | 186.4 | 198.96 | 4154.20 | 3900.00 | -254. |
| 206 | 7.743 | 21.10 | 1000.00 | 7743.0 | 163.38 | 163380.00 | 145000.00 | -18380. |
| 209 | 9.841 | 38.83 | 1000.00 | 9841.0 | 382.13 | 382130.00 | 290000.00 | -92130. |
| 218 | 9.841 | 38.83 | 1200.00 | 11809.2 | 382.13 | 458556.00 | 348000.00 | -110556. |
| 221 | 9.841 | 38.83 | 500.00 | 4920.5 | 382.13 | 191065.00 | 145000.00 | -46065. |
| 216 | 9.556 | 30.58 | 1000.00 | 9556.0 | 292.22 | 292220.00 | 300000.00 | 7780. |
| TOTAL | | | 7120.00 | 63682.5 | 266.86 | 1900013.70 | 1667650.00 | -232364. |

these columns do NOT go to the vendor

******** AVERAGE $/MSF = 29.84 ********

COST SAVINGS BY ORDERING 5. )M OR MORE = $ 175.00
(UPCHARGE - 35.00 )

**EXHIBIT 9**

```
                                                      RANKED VENDORS FOR PLANT/DIVISION QUAKERLAND

CODE(1)     PLAN                                                             ******VENDORS******
(PERCENT PENALTY SHOWN IN PARENTHESES. )(2)   (3)
                      NATIONAL CON   EXCELSIOR PA   AMIERCAN BOX   PARAGON CORR   AJAX MFG COR     • • •
 130         19375.  18184. ( 0. )  18651. ( 2.6)  18791. ( 3.3)  19165. ( 5.4)  19866. ( 9.3)
                      NATIONAL CON   EXCELSIOR PA   AMERICAN BOX   PARAGON CORR   AJAX MFG COR
 205         27125.  25457. ( 0. )  26112. ( 2.6)  26308. ( 3.3)  26831. ( 5.4)  27813. ( 9.3)
                      NATIONAL CON   EXCELSIOR PA   AMERICAN BOX   PARAGON CORR   AJAX MFG COR
 212         55800.  52369. ( 0. )  53716. ( 2.6)  54119. ( 3.3)  55195. ( 5.4)  57215. ( 9.3)
                      NATIONAL CON   EXCELSIOR PA   AMERICAN BOX   PARAGON CORR   AJAX MFG COR
 213         13950.  13092. ( 0. )  13429. ( 2.6)  13530. ( 3.3)  13799. ( 5.4)  14304. ( 9.3)
                      NATIONAL CON   EXCELSIOR PA   AMERICAN BOX   PARAGON CORR   AJAX MFG COR
 200         29250.  26144. ( 0. )  26807. ( 2.5)  28001. ( 7.1)  28532. ( 9.1)  28863. (10.4)
                      NATIONAL CON   EXCELSIOR PA   AMERICAN BOX   PARAGON CORR   AJAX MFG COR
 201        253500. 215553.   0. ) 221026. ( 2.5) 230880. ( 7.1) 235261. ( 9.1) 237991. (10.4)
                      NATIONAL CON   EXCELSIOR PA   AMERICAN BOX   PARAGON CORR   AJAX MFG COR
 208         27750.  26144. ( 0. )  26807. ( 2.5)  28001. ( 7.1)  28532.(  9.1)  28863. (10.4)
                      NATIONAL CON   EXCELSIOR PA   AMERICAN BOX   PARAGON CORR   AJAX MFG COR
 215          9000.   8291. ( 0. )   8501. ( 2.5)   8880. ( 7.1)   9049. ( 9.1)   9154. (10.4)
                      NATIONAL CON   EXCELSIOR PA   PARAGON CORR   AMERICAN BOX   RIVAL BOXBOA
 202          3900.   3797. ( 0. )   3915. ( 3.1)   4107. ( 8.2)   4154. ( 9.4)   4257. (12.1)
                      NATIONAL CON   EXCELSIOR PA   AMERICAN BOX   PARAGON CORR   AJAX MFG COR
 206        145000. 152540. ( 0. ) 156410. ( 2.5) 163380. ( 7.1) 166470. ( 9.1) 168410. (10.4)
                      AJAX MFG COR   PARAGON CORR   AMERICAN BOX   EXCELSIOR PA   RIVAL BOXBOA
 209        290000. 299460. ( 0. ) 304780. ( 1.8) 382130. (27.6) 391870. (30.9) 392750. (31.2)
                      AJAX MFG COR   PARAGON CORR   AMERICAN BOX   EXCELSIOR PA   RIVAL BOXBOA
 218        348000. 359352. ( 0. ) 365736. ( 1.8) 458556.( 27.6) 470244. (30.9) 471300. (31.2)
                      AJAX MFG COR   PARAGON CORR   AMERICAN BOX   EXCELSIOR PA   RIVAL BOXBOA
 221        145000. 149730. ( 0. ) 152390. ( 1.8) 191065. (27.6) 195935. (30.9) 196375. (31.2)
                      PARAGON CORR   AJAX MFG COR   AMERICAN BOX   RIVAL BOXBOA   EXCELSIOR PA     • • •
 216        300000. 250560. ( 0. ) 266990. ( 6.6) 292220. (16.6) 303020. (20.9) 326150. (30.2)

TOTAL      1667650.      1600672.       1645268.       1899967.       1948056.       1983310.      • • •
```

VENDOR SUMMARY FOR PLANT/DIVISION QUAKERLAND

| | ④ | ⑤ | | | |
|---|---|---|---|---|---|
| AMERICAN BOX | 0. | 0. | 1895860. | 4154. | 0. |
| EXCELSIOR PA | 0. | 555372. | 0. | 1058049. | 326150. |
| PARAGON CORR | 250560. | 822906. | 4107. | 582833. | 0. |
| RIVAL BOXBOA | 0. | 0. | 0. | 303020. | 1064682. |
| AJAX MFG COR | 808542. | 266990. | 0. | 0. | 592478. |
| NATIONAL CON | 541570. | 0. | 0. | 0. | 0. |

① Container code

② The name of the first ranked (least cost) company for each container, with the $ cost if that company is used.

③ The name of the second-ranked company, its dollar cost, and the % penalty (extra cost) incurred if the second company were used instead of the first.
(Normally, the top 7 companies would be listed)

④ Cost in $ of containers on which that company ranked first

⑤ Cost in $ of containers on which that company ranked second

# case 1.5

# McKinsey & Company FINPLAN

McKinsey & Company is an international consulting firm which concentrates on the development and implementation of business strategies and the resolution of strategic issues in all functional management areas. Particularly in strategic planning and merger and acquisition work, consultants frequently need to prepare pro forma financial statements projecting the impact of alternative strategies or business decisions. In 1972, McKinsey developed a generalized financial projection model, designed to be readily adaptable to many different client situations and to allow consultants to carry out basic analysis using financial information in far less time than was possible in the past. This model, called FINPLAN, has since been used successfully with well over 150 clients. This case contains a description of a subset of the design features of FINPLAN.

## Overview of FINPLAN

FINPLAN is basically a sophisticated, deterministic pro forma generator, with a strong emphasis on realistic and appropriately detailed modeling of the financial policy implications of management decisions. In broad outline, FINPLAN is designed to accept inputs consisting of information on income statement and balance sheet items from the past and also assumptions about the future performance of some of those items. The model traces through the accounting implications of the assumptions and provides the user with output information on income statements, balance sheets, important financial ratios, sources and application of funds, and other related items.

One major design decision was that the model should allow different levels of detail in the inputs (and outputs). For example, users can if they wish give a single series of values for gross sales in successive years. On the other hand, users who want to consider more detail with respect to sales information can provide history and yearly projections for sales broken down into various categories (by product line, perhaps); the model will then automatically find the total sales.

Another design decision was that the model would have built into it the ability to perform the accounting calculations that would be needed to project the financial statements forward; the user would not have to specify the accounting equations. Because the model includes the accounting principles, it allows the user to consider a more detailed and correct financial picture of a firm than would be feasible with a model that required the user to give the equations. Users provide information about future sales, costs, and related quantities; they also specify the policies that are to be followed on such issues as dividends, financing instruments, etc. The model translates such user assumptions into future financial statements, using accepted accounting principles to do so. It carries out whatever policies the user has specified about such issues as raising required financing.

The design makes available to the users an assortment of different methods for forecasting values of important variables. They can specify actual values, such as yearly sales figures. Alternatively, they can specify changes in important variables, such as yearly percentage changes in sales. In other cases, users can tie one set of values to another—cost of goods sold as a percentage of sales, for example, with the percentage allowed to vary from one year to the next. Finally, users can even use linear regression to fit a trend to values of some variable and then extrapolate that trend to produce forecasts.

As far as outputs are concerned, FINPLAN allows the user a variety of options, so that a particular user can select an appropriate level of detail. The model is capable of printing out a variety of financial statements, in whole or in part, at the request of the user.

Finally, the design of FINPLAN provides for easily performed sensitivity analyses because such analyses are considered central to the usefulness of the model. If only one set of figures were to be analyzed for a particular project, the number work could be done by hand. It is only when users want to consider alternative sets of assumptions about the future that the number pushing becomes sufficiently burdensome to justify use of a computerized model. Hence, the model was designed so as to facilitate sensitivity analyses. This consideration meant that the user should not have to input a full set of assumptions for each run of the model. Instead, the computer retains a set of input assumptions and allows the user to change only one or a small number of the assumptions and then easily to obtain results.

### The input section of FINPLAN

The model automatically applies accounting rules to the inputs provided by the user. The input format must contain values for variables (such as sales) and also information on *which* variables are sales, which involve fixed assets, etc. To serve this purpose, FINPLAN uses a system of numbered lines for inputs. For example, sales figures for successive past and future periods constitute one (or more) input lines. The line numbers identify the variables. Line 10 is interpreted to be gross sales. The user provides information on line 10 that allows the model to forecast sales for the future; the program then treats those figures according to the accounting rules for sales. Similarly, line 40 contains marketing expenses for each year, while lines 230 and 240 are equipment and depreciation for equipment, respectively.

In order to allow users to consider different levels of detail for the firms they are analyzing, the design includes what are called split lines. For example, a user who wants to consider only a single gross sales figure for each year provides information about gross sales on line 10 of the inputs for the model. Another user who wants to consider sales broken down by category instead lists sales projections by category on lines 1 through 9 or on a subset of those lines. The model knows (from the line numbers) that lines 1 through 9 correspond to partial sales figures. It will automatically add the results to find line 10, gross sales, and will then have both the partial figures and the totals for later use (in calculating cost of goods sold, for example). The model allows use of split lines for most of the input variables; the general convention chosen was that the major line numbers, corresponding to totals for various categories such as sales, would all end in 0 (10, 20, 30, and so forth). For any line which can be split, the nine line numbers immediately preceding the total line number are interpreted as breakdowns of the total. For example, because line 40 is marketing expense, lines 31 through 39 are interpreted as components of marketing expense. Users do not have to use all input lines; they specify only enough lines to provide the program with the information it needs to give the desired level of detail on outputs.

For each line that a user does decide to use, s/he provides both historical and future information. For almost all lines that are used, the value for at least one historical period is required, although more information can be included. The historical information provides the model with the starting condition of the balance sheet and other financial statements. Only those variables, such as yield on marketable securities, whose future values are required but whose past values will not be needed to construct pro formas, are exempt from this requirement.

In order to forecast the input lines into the future, to provide the basis for the pro forma calculations, users select from among a set of forecasting options. To allow flexibility in forecasting, FINPLAN provides a range of forecasting options:

1. The user can forecast a particular line by giving a set of percentages specifying the change from the previous value for that line. For example, if the most recent historical sales figure were $20,000,000 and the forecast instructions specified percentage changes of .05, .04, . . . the future sales values would be calculated by the model as $21,000,000, $21,840,000, . . .
2. The user can forecast a particular line by listing the actual amounts. For example, s/he might give $8000000, $8100000, $8500000, $8300000, . . . as the entries for sales.
3. The user can forecast some lines as percentages of sales or sales compo-

nents. Cost of goods would likely be forecast in this way, for example. The user would simply list a series of fractions, one for each future period; the model would apply those fractions to the sales figures in the corresponding periods.

4. The user can forecast a line by giving a series of dollar changes (increases or decreases) for that line. The model would start with the last historical value for the line. It would then apply the first dollar change to find the first future value. To that value it would apply the second specified change to find the second future value, . . . .
5. The user can specify that the values for a particular line should be percentages of the values of another line (the line whose number is 10 less than that of the line being forecast with this option). This option is useful for lines such as interest on long-term debt (line 450), which can be forecast as a fraction of long-term debt (line 440).
6. The user has available a number of special options for particular input lines. For example, dividends can be given through a series of payout ratios (one for each period) or else they can be given as actual dividend-per-share figures, in dollars.
7. The user can forecast a line of values by fitting one of three forms of regression equation to the past values of that line. For this option, of course, the user would have to provide several past values for the variable (or line); up to ten past values are allowed. The program can handle linear regressions of the form.

$$\text{Next value} = a + b * \text{Current value}$$

or it can handle the following two forms of multiplicative models:

$$\text{Next value} = a * (b)^{\text{Current value}}$$

$$\text{Next value} = a * (\text{Current value})^{b}$$

8. Finally, the user has available additional options for tying the values on one line of input to the values on almost any other line in the model. One choice is to forecast a line as a series of percentages of another line; for example, inventories might be calculated as a percentage of cost of goods sold in each period. Another choice is to keep a running balance for the line, adding to it in each period a specified percentage of some other line; a balance sheet item such as investment in a subsidiary, which accumulates from year-to-year, might be handled through this option. (Option 5, by contrast, requires that the values on one line be tied to the values on the line whose number is exactly 10 smaller.)

The line-linkage options allow the user to define additional accounting-type links among the financial statements. For example, a user might tie payroll taxes payable on the balance sheet to wages on the income statement. These line-linkage options also give the FINPLAN user great flexibility in terms of what units to use in the analysis. As noted at the outset, FINPLAN is primarily a generator of forecast financial statements and, accordingly, financial calculations were built into the logic of the model. In some situations, however, it is extremely useful for managers to think in economic (or physical) units as well as in financial terms; for example, a user might want to build up projections in terms of units of output. Line linkages allow such modeling. For example, direct labor cost can be forecast as the product of the following elements: number of units sold, current labor cost per unit, an index of wage rate increases, and an index of labor productivity. Linking variables together in this manner allows the user to test the sensitivity of a single factor such as labor productivity by changing the values of that variable *only*. The model, not the user, then traces the impact of the changes through to the dollar values for direct labor cost. When such types of analysis are accomplished through the line-linkage options, corresponding output information can then be obtained with some of the flexible nonstandard output options described below.

In addition to the forecasting information given in the forms just described, the user must input information about what debt-equity policy the firm should be assumed to follow in the future. The user must specify how the model should allocate excess cash in a period or, on the other hand, what it should do if the firm needs additional financing. As will be noted again below, the question of how the user should specify such financial policy decisions was a difficult design problem.

In specifying the forecasting information, the user gives enough data to allow the model to forecast for a number of future periods; the user can select any number of forecast periods up to 25.

**The output section of FINPLAN**

Once the user has given the necessary starting financial information and the information needed to forecast for the desired number of periods, the model proceeds to run out the pro forma statements into the future; the calculation part of the model will be discussed briefly below. The next interaction that the user has with the model is with the output portion. As noted above, the model was designed to be used by different people who wanted different levels of detail in their output. In addition, an individual user might want a different level of detail on a base case run of the model than would be appropriate on subsequent runs for conducting sensitivity analyses. Consequently, FINPLAN includes a range of different possible standard output statements and, in addition, allows the user to select all or part of any of these statements. Thus a user can request an entire statement as output or can request only a subset of the lines in that report. Finally, users can also design their own output statements if the standard financial statements do not present the output information in a convenient format.

The design of the output section was facilitated by the fact that the model would be run on high-speed terminals which printed 120 characters per second. (A standard teletype, by comparison, prints only 10 characters per second; other terminals, such as DECwriters, print 30 characters per second.) The high speed of the terminals made it practical to expect that users would wait during the printing of detailed output information when that information was important to them.

The standard output options that were finally selected for use in FINPLAN are as follows:

1. Complete income statement, EPS summary, balance sheet, ratios and measures of performance, and capital structure planning report.
2. Complete income statement and EPS summary.
3. Complete balance sheet.
4. Ratios and measures of performance, and capital structure planning.
5. Complete income statements, EPS summary, and balance sheet.
6. Short versions of option 1, containing only selected lines.
7. Merger information summary (for the use of the model to handle mergers and acquisitions).
8. Statement of sources and applications of funds.
9. Individual lines of output. For this option, the user would refer to a listing of the possible output lines, by number, and would specify the numbers of the desired lines.
10. Individual groups of lines whose numbers are listed on a separate file (to save repeated typing of the same line numbers on different runs).
11. Income statement as a percentage of sales.
12. Balance sheet as a percentage of total assets.
13. Balance sheet as a percentage of sales.

Options 9 and 10 give the user flexibility in selecting whichever output lines are of interest in a particular application. Other capabilities of FINPLAN allow the user to define appropriate output reports to describe the results of an analysis that has been conducted in terms of physical units rather than in financial terms. These features can be used in cases in which the user wants to specify a set of ratios and measures of performance that are different from the standard set incorporated into the model. To define such a set of output measures, the user would specify the desired ratios and summaries in terms of standard line numbers; the program would then compute and print the information.

FINPLAN also allows flexibility with regard to the names used for entries on the output. The program contains a standard set of names for output lines and for ratios, but the user can provide an alternative set of names. This capability allows the user to put onto the output whatever terms are used by the particular client firm that is being analyzed.

## Capabilities of FINPLAN

Because FINPLAN is intended as a general tool for use in financial analysis, it requires a broad range of capabilities in the internal (accounting equation) design. First, of course, the model must be able to handle the accounting details for a simple one-division firm. In addition, users want to consider multi-division firms. FINPLAN therefore has the abilities to accept inputs for the individual divisions of such a firm, to forecast the divisional results, and then to consolidate those results to give corporate reports. In performing the consolidation, FINPLAN does not merely add the business units together but rather gives the user the option to consider intracompany transfers of goods and services and also investments. Based on such inputs, the model automatically handles consolidation.

Other options involve mergers and acquisitions, since much of the original impetus for FINPLAN was the need for a tool for such analyses. The user specifies forecast information for both firms involved in a merger or acquisition and also makes policy decisions about how the merger or acquisition should be financed. FINPLAN then automatically provides pro formas for the combined business entity following APB opinions 16 and 17, which give detailed procedures for acquisitions using pooling of interests or purchase of assets accounting.

Yet another set of capabilities allows FINPLAN to handle convertible and callable securities. Determination of prices and times for conversions is intended to simulate rational investor behavior. The prices and times are therefore determined not by direct user inputs but rather by the model as it projects the financial positions of the firm.

Other capabilities built into the model involve choices of financing instruments. The user specifies the financing policy of a firm, giving decisions on how to raise additional funds or, on the other hand, how to apply excess funds. The model then carries out the policy directives of the user. Actually, two sets of reports are available. The first are what are called *unbalanced* reports; they show the cash deficit or surplus in each year, before the user's assumptions about financial policy have been used to close what is called the "financing gap." Then, the model applies that policy and prepares the balanced set of statements (the *balanced* reports), which are the ones normally printed for the user.

For each of these modes of operation of FINPLAN, the basic design policy was to follow as closely as possible the user's thought process rather than to impose a rigid model structure. As a result the input forms were designed to allow for a widely varying set of input assumptions and degrees of detail. For each possible option the form for the input information had to allow the user to specify reasonably realistic policies and, at the same time, had to be tractable for FINPLAN to handle through its automatic accounting equation procedures.

Working with whatever combination of data and options the user has chosen, FINPLAN projects financial results by applying appropriate accounting principles. In doing so, the model incorporates policy decisions, such as debt-equity or treatment-of-merger decisions, which the user has specified. It will always enforce internal consistency on the data and will produce fully balanced statements.

## Using FINPLAN

The general procedure for use of the model involves starting with specially designed input sheets. A portion of one input sheet is shown in Exhibit 1. For each line of input to be considered on a particular run, the user circles one of the allowable input options. Options 1–5 correspond to the first five options listed in the section above on input design. Options 6–10 are special input options for various lines. Options 11, 12, and 13 are the three regression options. Finally, to give a line as a percentage of another line, the user crosses out the suggested list of options and instead writes 2xxx where xxx is the number of the other line to be used in the calculations. Similarly, 4xxx gives forecasts involving a running balance and additions that are percentages of line xxx.

After specifying the option number, the user gives the needed information for each period. For option 2 (actual amounts), the user simply lists a value for each period. For option 1 (changes from the previous value), the user gives a series of percentage changes, expressed as decimals.

Other lines on the input forms allow the user to specify assumptions about policy decisions. In addition, s/he would specify the number of periods to forecast, the type of output desired, and other needed information. Further, the user would specify what changes were to be made in the basic assumptions in conducting sensitivity analyses. (Although decisions on sensitivity analyses would usually be delayed until results had been obtained for the base case.) Exhibit 2 gives an annotated example of part of a list of input assumptions in the form that FINPLAN requires. The user inputs the information and then responds to a series of questions about time frame, etc., and the computer produces pro formas.

After running the first set of assumptions and providing output on them, the model asks the person at the terminal to specify any sensitivity analyses to be performed. Such analyses really involve changing one or more of the input lines and then reanalyzing the problem under the altered assumptions. The model offers repeated sensitivity analyses until the user asks to end the run of FINPLAN.

Exhibit 3 shows some of the types of output that are provided by FINPLAN.

EXHIBIT 1

| FINPLAN | STANDARD INPUT |
|---|---|

## I — INCOME STATEMENT

➡ *See balance sheet for depreciation, dividends, minority interests, deferred taxes, and interest*

| LINE | PLANNING VARIABLE | OPTION (circle one) | VALUE IN PERIOD 1 | 2 | 3 | 4 | 5 | 6 | 7 | ••• |
|---|---|---|---|---|---|---|---|---|---|---|
| ENTER: Either gross sales as line 10, or as the product of lines 10 and 980, or as the product of lines 10, 980, and 990* | | | | | | | | | | |
| 10 | Gross sales | 1 2 4 | | | | | | | | ••• |
| 980 | — | 1 2 4 | | | | | | | | |
| 990 | — — | 1 2 4 | | | | | | | | |
| 800 | Discounts and allowances | 1 2 3 4 | | | | | | | | |
| 30 | Cost of goods sold I** | 1 2 3 4 | | | | | | | | |
| 630 | Cost of goods sold II** | 1 2 3 4 | | | | | | | | |
| 640 | Cost of goods sold III** | 1 2 3 4 | | | | | | | | |
| 40 | Marketing expense | 1 2 3 4 | | | | | | | | |
| 50 | Selling cost | 1 2 3 4 | | | | | | | | |
| 60 | Research & development | 1 2 3 4 | | | | | | | | |
| 70 | General & administrative | 1 2 3 4 | | | | | | | | |
| 20 | Other income and interest income | 1 2 3 4 | | | | | | | | ••• |

**EXHIBIT 2**
Partial listing of inputs

```
10 11,6,500,1000,1500,2000,2500,3000
```

↑ line 10 gives gross sales
Option 11 specifies that linear regression be used for forecasting
The user then gives the number of historical periods to be used in fitting the regression equation (6) and the historical sales values (500, 1000, 1500, 2000, 2500, 3000)

```
30 3,1290,.44,.44,.44,.44,.44,.44,.44
40 3,900,.3,.3,.3,.3,.3,.3,.3
50 3,60,.02,.02,.02,.02,.02,.02
```

↑↑ for lines 30 (cost of goods sold), 40 (marketing expense) and 50 (selling cost), the user selects option 3, which provides for forecasting these items as percentages of sales. For each line, the user gives one historical (dollar) figure followed by a series of future fractions (of sales)

```
70 4,100,15,15,15,15,15,15,15
```

↑ For line 70 (G+A) the user selects option 4 (actual dollar changes). Thus, the historical value was 100. The first forecast value will be 15 higher (or 115); the next forecast will be 130; ....

**EXHIBIT 2 (*continued*)**

```
80 2,5,5,5,5,5,5,5,5,5,5
```

For line 80 (extraordinary item, after taxes) the user selects option 2 and gives the actual dollar amounts for one historical period followed by a series of future periods.

```
90 4,130,10,10,10,10,10,10
120 1,100,.1,.1,.1,.1,.1,.1
```

Cash (line 90) is given, via option 4, as one historical value (130) and a series of dollar changes (increases of 10 in each period)

Line 120 (marketable securities) is forecast with option 1. 100 is the historical value. In each future period, securities are to be increased 10% over the previous period. Thus, the future values are 110, 121, ....

```
130 5,,.08,.08,.08,.08,.08,.08,.08
```

With option 5 the user gives yield on marketable securities (line 130) as a series of fractions of the values on the line with number 10 smaller (that is, marketable securities on line 120). (The second comma after the 5 indicates that the historical value has been omitted, as it may be for line 130.)

**EXHIBIT 3**

Sample output (the user has asked for output for one historical period, 1975, and for three future periods)

INCOME STATEMENT

| | 1975 | 1976 | 1977 | 1978 |
|---|---|---|---|---|
| 10 SALES | 3000.00 | 3500.00 | 4000.00 | 4500.00 |
| 1* NET SALES | 3000.00 | 3500.00 | 4000.00 | 4500.00 |
| 30 COST OF GOODS SOLD | 1290.00 | 1540.00 | 1760.00 | 1980.00 |
| 2* GROSS PROFIT | 1710.00 | 1960.00 | 2240.00 | 2520.00 |
| 40 MARKETING | 900.00 | 1050.00 | 1200.00 | 1350.00 |
| 50 SELLING COST | 60.00 | 70.00 | 80.00 | 90.00 |
| 70 GENERAL & ADMINISTR. | 100.00 | 115.00 | 130.00 | 145.00 |
| 3* OTH. OPERATING COSTS | 1060.00 | 1235.00 | 1410.00 | 1585.00 |
| 4* TOT. OPERATING COSTS | 2350.00 | 2775.00 | 3170.00 | 3565.00 |
| 220 DEPREC. BUILDINGS | 100.00 | 135.00 | 155.00 | 170.00 |
| 240 DEPREC. EQUIPMENT | 10.00 | 10.00 | 10.00 | 10.00 |
| 5* TOTAL COSTS | 2460.00 | 2920.00 | 3335.00 | 3745.00 |
| 11 INV. INCOME | 4.50 | 0. | 0. | 0. |
| 19 INTEREST INCOME | 0. | 8.80 | 9.68 | 10.65 |
| 20 TOT. OTHER INCOME | 4.50 | 8.80 | 9.68 | 10.65 |
| 6* PROFIT BEF INT & TAX | 544.50 | 588.80 | 674.68 | 765.65 |
| 830 INTEREST EXPENSE | 51.00 | 84.36 | 96.96 | 96.76 |
| 7* PROFIT BEFORE TAXES | 493.50 | 504.44 | 577.72 | 668.89 |
| 618 FEDERAL INCOME TAX | 234.38 | 230.03 | 263.44 | 305.01 |
| 619 DEFERRED FED. TAXES | 12.34 | 12.11 | 13.87 | 16.05 |
| 620 TOTAL TAXES | 246.72 | 242.13 | 277.31 | 321.07 |
| 6* PROFIT AFTER TAXES | 246.78 | 262.31 | 300.41 | 347.82 |
| 80 EXTR. GAIN OR LOSS | 5.00 | 5.00 | 5.00 | 5.00 |
| 9* TOTAL EARNINGS | 251.78 | 267.31 | 305.41 | 352.82 |
| 780 MINORITY INTEREST | 53.46 | 53.46 | 61.08 | 70.56 |
| 350 GOODWILL AMORTIZAT'N | 4.00 | 3.00 | 3.00 | 3.00 |
| 10* EARNINGS TO COMMON | 189.32 | 205.85 | 236.33 | 274.26 |
| 602 COMMON DIVIDENDS | 81.93 | 100.00 | 130.00 | 160.00 |

**EXHIBIT 3 (*continued*)**

| | | | | | |
|---|---|---|---|---|---|
| 11* | RETAINED EARNINGS | 112.39 | 110.85 | 111.33 | 119.26 |

EPS - VALUES

| | | | | | |
|---|---|---|---|---|---|
| 12* | EPS (PRELIM/COMMON) | 1.89 | 2.06 | 2.36 | 2.74 |
| 13* | PRIMARY EPS | 1.80 | 2.00 | 2.30 | 2.67 |
| 14* | PRIMARY AFT EXT ITEM | 1.85 | 2.04 | 2.34 | 2.72 |

BALANCE SHEET (ASSETS)

| | | 1975 | 1976 | 1977 | 1978 |
|---|---|---|---|---|---|
| 90 | CASH | 130.00 | 140.00 | 150.00 | 160.00 |
| 120 | MARKET. SECURITIES | 100.00 | 110.00 | 121.00 | 133.10 |
| 140 | ACCOUNTS RECEIVABLE | 220.00 | 210.00 | 240.00 | 270.00 |
| 150 | INVENTORIES | 630.00 | 700.00 | 800.00 | 900.00 |
| 15* | CURRENT ASSETS | 1080.00 | 1160.00 | 1311.00 | 1463.10 |
| 210 | BUILDINGS | 2200.00 | 2700.00 | 3100.00 | 3400.00 |
| 261 | ACC. DEPR. BUILDINGS | 580.00 | 715.00 | 870.00 | 1040.00 |
| 262 | NET BUILDINGS | 1620.00 | 1985.00 | 2230.00 | 2360.00 |
| 230 | EQUIPMENT | 200.00 | 210.00 | 220.00 | 230.00 |
| 263 | ACC. DEPR. EQUIPMENT | 20.00 | 30.00 | 40.00 | 50.00 |
| 244 | NET EQUIPMENT | 180.00 | 180.00 | 180.00 | 180.00 |
| 59* | GROSS FIXED ASSETS | 2400.00 | 2910.00 | 3320.00 | 3630.00 |
| 270 | ACC. DEPRECIATION | 600.00 | 745.00 | 910.00 | 1090.00 |
| 16* | NET FIXED ASSETS | 1800.00 | 2165.00 | 2410.00 | 2540.00 |
| 300 | L-T INVESTMENT | 180.00 | 198.00 | 217.80 | 239.58 |
| 340 | GOODWILL | 60.00 | 57.00 | 54.00 | 51.00 |
| 17* | OTHER ASSETS | 240.00 | 255.00 | 271.80 | 290.58 |
| 18* | TOTAL ASSETS | 3120.00 | 3580.00 | 3992.80 | 4293.68 |

**EXHIBIT 3 (*concluded*)**

BALANCE SHEET (LIABILITIES)

| | | 1975 | 1976 | 1977 | 1978 |
|---|---|---|---|---|---|
| 360 | SHORT-TERM NOTES | 200.00 | 200.00 | 200.00 | 200.00 |
| 380 | CURR. PORTION LTD. | 50.00 | 60.00 | 75.00 | 85.00 |
| 400 | ACCOUNTS PAYABLE | 210.00 | 350.00 | 400.00 | 450.00 |
| 420 | OTHER CURRENT L.#1 | 40.00 | 50.00 | 60.00 | 70.00 |
| 430 | ACCRUED TAXES | 150.00 | 175.00 | 200.00 | 225.00 |
| | | ------- | ------- | ------- | ------- |
| 19* | CURRENT LIABILITIES | 650.00 | 835.00 | 935.00 | 1030.00 |
| 440 | LONG-TERM NOTES | 340.00 | 340.00 | 340.00 | 340.00 |
| 460 | STR. DEBENTURES | 300.00 | 275.00 | 250.00 | 225.00 |
| 471 | 6.5% CONV. DEBENTURE | 100.00 | 90.00 | 80.00 | 70.00 |
| 480 | DEBENTURES (TOTAL) | 100.00 | 90.00 | 80.00 | 70.00 |
| 500 | OTH. LONG-TERM DEBT | 90.00 | 213.08 | 362.60 | 384.11 |
| | | ------- | ------- | ------- | ------- |
| 20* | LONG-TERM DEBT | 830.00 | 918.08 | 1032.60 | 1019.11 |
| 410 | DEFERRED LIABILITIES | 30.00 | 40.50 | 52.50 | 66.00 |
| | | ------- | ------- | ------- | -------- |
| 21* | TOTAL LIABILITIES | 1510.00 | 1793.58 | 2020.10 | 2115.11 |
| 820 | DEFERRED TAXES | 250.00 | 262.11 | 275.97 | 292.03 |
| 570 | MINORITY INTEREST | 100.00 | 153.46 | 214.54 | 285.11 |
| 520 | EQUITY RESERVES | 10.00 | 10.00 | 10.00 | 10.00 |
| | | ------- | ------- | ------- | ------- |
| 601 | COMMON AT PAR | 100.00 | 100.00 | 100.00 | 100.00 |
| 605 | PAID-IN SURPLUS | 250.00 | 250.00 | 250.00 | 250.00 |
| 606 | RETAINED EARNINGS | 900.00 | 1010.85 | 1122.18 | 1241.44 |
| | | ------- | -------- | -------- | -------- |
| 23* | COMMON EQUITY | 1250.00 | 1360.85 | 1472.18 | 1591.44 |
| | | -------- | -------- | -------- | -------- |
| 24* | SHAREHOLDERS' EQUITY | 1360.00 | 1524.31 | 1696.72 | 1886.55 |
| | | -------- | -------- | -------- | -------- |
| 25* | LIABILITIES & EQUITY | 3120.00 | 3580.00 | 3992.80 | 4293.68 |

# case 1.6

# Applied Decision Systems New-Product Planning System

NEWPROD (New-Product Planning System) is a computer model for use in planning and monitoring new-product introductions of consumer package goods. The system was developed by Applied Decision Systems of Wellesley, Massachusetts, and has been used by a number of important marketers of consumer products.

Applied Decision Systems (ADS) was founded in 1969 by Stanely Buchin (a specialist in decision analysis and other quantitative methods who had previously been a faculty member of Harvard Business School) and other HBS faculty members. ADS was a consulting firm that provided its clients with seminars and consulting help in the areas of planning, forececasting, and using decision analysis. In one of the early seminars given by ADS, Dr. Buchin had taught managers from a well-known consumer goods marketer about modeling trial and repeat behavior of consumers, about the use of probabilities in modeling, and about related ideas. After that seminar the client company had become interested in the development and use of a computer model incorporating some of the concepts that had been covered. ADS proceeded to develop such a model, eventually producing NEWPROD. The model had been used by that first client company and, by 1977, it had also been used in analyzing new product launches of other consumer goods.

In 1975 ADS was acquired by the firm Temple, Barker and Sloane, Inc., a management and economic consulting firm. It continued its operations as a division of TBS, with Stan Buchin continuing to act as president of ADS. With approximately 12 professional employees, ADS offered consulting services in decision analysis and forecasting and related fields. NEWPROD was one of the computer packages that were available to its clients, who could either run the model on their in-house computers or could use it through a time-sharing computer service firm.

Basically, the idea of NEWPROD was to combine a model of consumer behavior in first trying and in then making repeat purchases of a consumer good with a model of trade inventory behavior to produce a summary of factory shipments of a new product. NEWPROD produced detailed information for the first year of the planning period, giving output for each of the first 13 four-week periods. After that first year, the model provided output for each of four more years, but on an annual basis only. The program output projected shipments, trial and repeat purchases, and inventory positions of retailers. In its basic form NEWPROD did not translate those sales, shipments, and inventory figures into financial pro formas for the manufacturer but in essentially all actual applications NEWPROD was modified to produce pro formas based on the model's results.

## QFC's international frozen entrées

As an example of the use of NEWPROD this case considers the planned introduction of a new line of frozen main courses by Quality Food Company, a major consumer package goods marketer.[1] QFC produced and sold a wide variety of food items and it was a highly respected firm with considerable marketing power in supermarket channels. In 1976 QFC had begun testing the concept of a line of frozen foods. The new products would include only the entrée for a main meal (and, hence, would be very different from TV-dinner products). They would be marketed as aids for the consumer who needed help with meal preparation yet was unwilling to use complete frozen meals. The new entrées would be presented as a quality product worthy of use by discriminating consumers who served good food. This image would be enhanced by the international, even gourmet, quality of some of the offerings in the line. Included would be Swedish meatballs, Italian lasagna, German sauerbraten, Polish cabbage rolls, and similar ethnic dishes. Packages of these products would retail for just under two dollars. The entrées would be sold by QFC's existing sales force to supermarkets. They would, of course, require space in the frozen food chests of those stores.

Early tests of the new line gave QFC very encouraging results. In focus group discussions of the new product concept, consumers were favorable to it. A typical consumer responded that s/he did not have the time to prepare meals from scratch every day and yet that s/he was unwilling to eat inferior pre-packaged meals. The idea of a pre-prepared frozen entrée of high quality to be accompanied by separately prepared bread or rice or vegetables seemed a good compromise between convenience and high quality food. The QFC product development lab proceeded to develop recipes for a series of entrées. The recipes were tested on panels of company employees and a few of them were modified slightly on the basis of employee reactions. By the end of 1976 the new product planners at QFC were satisfied with the formulations of the international entrées. In addition, they had prepared one

---

[1] Both QFC and its international frozen entrées are entirely fictitious. They have been devised, however, to provide a typical example of the use of NEWPROD.

of the firm's factories to manufacture the items for use in a market test in 1977.

Test marketing was conducted starting in February 1977. Three cities were used in these tests. In each, results were monitored closely, with inventories taken at the retail outlets every two weeks to measure the sales of the products and with interviews and consumer diary techniques used to try to separate trial (or first time) purchases from repeat purchases.[2] The test market results were satisfactory and QFC management had decided to go ahead with a national launch of the line in 1978. QFC planners felt that the target for the entrées consisted of about one quarter of the households in the United States. In 1978 they estimated that sales of frozen main course products would run at about 70 million units. Over the five-year planning horizon they were using, they expected the fraction of households using this product category to grow somewhat. If the new line performed as they hoped it would, they expected to attain a market share of approximately one third by the end of the planning period.

As will be described in more detail below in the section on model inputs, the concept tests and the test market results had given QFC managers considerable information on likely trial and repeat behavior by consumers. They also felt that they had a reasonably good idea of how much changes in the level of awareness of their products would change the trial rates for them. The one major decision remaining before the start of the national roll-out of the international entrées concerned the level of advertising expenditure that should be used. Two separate advertising plans were being considered, one including a relatively high level of advertising expenditure and the other involving only a moderate expenditure level. The QFC managers felt that they could make some educated guesses about the difference in levels of awareness that would result from the alternate advertising programs, and they were even willing to estimate the resulting trial rates, but they had not yet converted these estimates of awareness into their implications for sales of the new line. QFC was working with the consulting firm of ADS to use the new-product planning model to investigate those sales implications, in order to choose one of the two advertising plans being considered. They would also use NEWPROD during the national roll-out to monitor the performance of the line.

The specific model inputs selected by QFC managers to analyze the international entrées and the outputs provided to them by NEWPROD will

---

[2] In the test markets (and in this case) trial purchase is defined as the purchase by a particular consumer for the first time of any international entrée. If a consumer buys a specific item in the line for the first time after having bought some other item in the line earlier, the purchase is called a repeat purchase, not a trial. Thus, if one consumer buys lasagna one week and then buys cabbage rolls two weeks later and if these two purchases are that consumer's first purchases from the line, the lasagna is a trial purchase, while the cabbage rolls are a repeat purchase.

be described below, after the general outline of the model has been discussed.

## NEWPROD's model of consumer behavior

In modeling consumer behavior for package goods, NEWPROD considered three main factors. First was the effective household base (or pool of potential customers). Second was the trial purchase behavior of households in the potential pool and third was the behavior of trial purchasers with respect to repeat purchases.

In determining the effective household base, NEWPROD began with the total household population of the United States (or, in general, of whatever was assumed to be the relevant market area). The user provided five annual figures for total number of households. Several factors were then used to adjust the total figures. First, NEWPROD required the user to provide five annual figures for the fractions of households that purchased the general product category containing the new product being analyzed. Multiplying these fractions by the corresponding total household values, NEWPROD was able to calculate the target market for the new product, in households.

Two other types of adjustments were made to obtain the effective household base. The first involved consumer awareness of the new product. Users supplied five annual figures specifying the fractions of the target market households that were aware of the new product; these fractions were summary measures of advertising effectiveness. Users also specified how many unaware households (those comprising what the model called the awareness gap) were lost as consumers. The idea here was that at least a few consumers who had not been reached by the advertising campaign might, nevertheless, purchase the product when they saw it in the market. Hence, the model did not automatically assume that all unaware consumers represented lost sales potential.

The second type of adjustment involved distribution of the new product. Users specified five annual figures and also 13 additional figures, one for each of the four-week periods during the first year, giving the fractions of retail outlets (on a volume basis) stocking the product. The model also required five annual figures for the fractions of the distribution gaps (the differences between 1.0 and the distribution levels) representing lost sales potential. The idea in this adjustment was that some consumers who were especially interested in the new product might actively seek that product in alternative outlets if the places they normally shopped did not have it in stock. Hence, in some situations not all of the distribution gap would result in lost sales potential.

For each four-week period during the first year and for each of four full years thereafter, NEWPROD combined the information on total market potential with the information on distribution and on awareness to give the effective household base.[3] Trial purchase rates were then expressed in terms of these base figures.

Rather than requiring users to specify trial rates for the 13 first-year and four remaining yearly intervals, NEWPROD instead assumed that the cumulative trial rate (as a fraction of potential) would follow the general (exponential) shape shown in Exhibit 1.[4] It therefore required the user to give only enough information to allow it unambiguously to determine a particular function of this general shape.

**EXHIBIT 1**

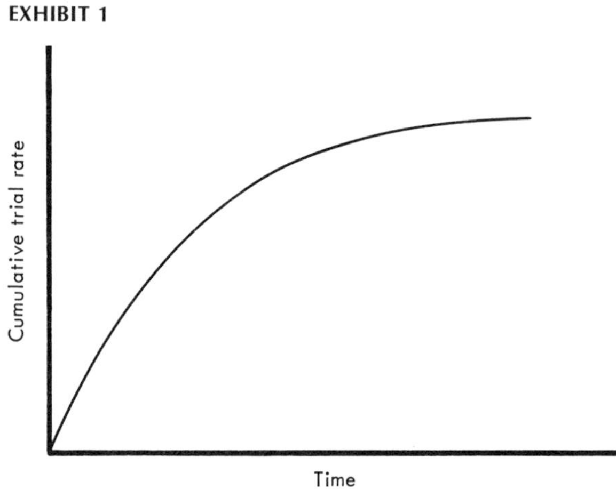


In particular, NEWPROD requested two numbers to determine the curve for cumulative trial. First was the total fraction of the effective base households that would have tried the product by the end of the second year. In addition, NEWPROD asked what part of that second-year cumulative trial level would have been achieved by the end of the first year. With these two

---

[3] The effective household base was defined as total household population * fraction purchasing this category from retail outlets *

(1.0 − potential lost via awareness) * (1.0 − potential lost via distribution).

In this formula,

potential lost via awareness = (1.0 − fraction aware)
* fraction of awareness gap representing lost sales

and

potential lost via distribution = (1.0 − fraction distribution)
* fraction of distribution gap representing lost sales.

[4] Through observation of the actual trial rates for several dozen consumer products, the NEWPROD designers at ADS has become convinced that the exponential curve form was representative of trial rate patterns.

numbers, NEWPROD determined the trial function, as explained in the appendix [at end of case]. It then found cumulative trial figures for all reporting periods from this function. To find the actual number of triers during a period, NEWPROD could convert the cumulative trial fractions to cumulative numbers of triers (by multiplying by the effective household bases). It could then subtract the cumulative number of triers in one period from the cumulative number in the following period to find the actual number of triers during the later period.

NEWPROD also considered the number of repeat purchases in each period (four-week periods during the first year and annual periods thereafter). For this purpose, it allowed the user to define what it called repeat groups of consumers. Repeat groups might differ according to how frequently their members bought the product or how many packages their members purchased at one time. NEWPROD asked users to specify what percentages of trial purchasers joined each of these repeat groups immediately after trial. Usually, these percentages would not total 100 percent, so that some triers of the product would be assumed not to purchase it again. For each repeat group, the user provided the interval, in weeks, between successive purchases and also the number of packages of the product purchased by an individual in that repeat group at one time.

In modeling the behavior of these repeat groups over time, NEWPROD did not assume that consumer re-purchase behavior remained static. For most products, it was observed that repeat levels decrease over time. If 20 percent of the triers of a particular product start out as heavy users immediately after trial, it is most likely that appreciably less than 20 percent of the triers will remain heavy users a year or two later. In order to model this type of behavior, NEWPROD needed to know not only the fraction of triers who fell into a particular repeat group after trial but also the fractions of that same group of triers who fell into that same repeat group two periods after trial, three periods after trial, and so on. In the same spirit as that in which cumulative trial information was handled, NEWPROD modeled the behavior of repeat groups over time by assuming a general (decaying exponential) form, as shown in Exhibit 2, and required the user to give only enough information to allow it to select a specific curve with this general shape. For each repeat group, NEWPROD required only (1) the initial repeat rate (after trial) as a fraction of the total number of triers; (2) what is called the ongoing repeat rate, also expressed as a fraction of the total number of triers; and (3) the number of purchase cycles that would be needed for that repeat group to reach the ongoing rate. With this information NEWPROD could fit the repeat rate function, as described in the appendix, and could trace out over time the repeat sales generated by any group of trial purchasers.

NEWPROD required a few additional data items to allow it to forecast retail sales and shares. It required the user to specify the total market in units for each of the five years so that it could calculate market shares for the user's

EXHIBIT 2

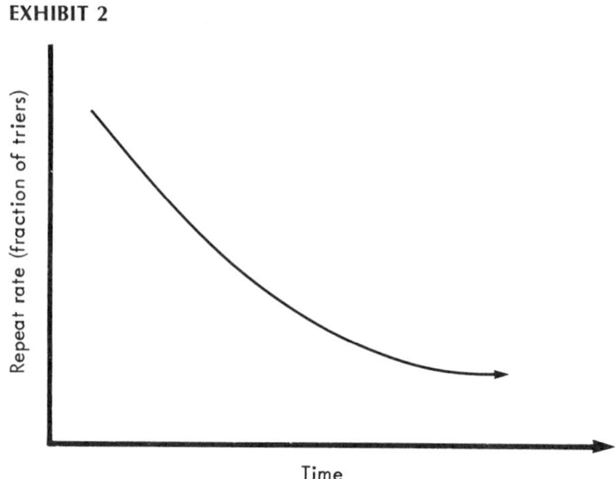


company. NEWPROD allowed the user to consider up to three different package sizes (small, medium, and large) for the product. It requested the user to specify the fraction of trial volume for each of the sizes and also the fraction of repeat volume in each size. (The fractions of repeat volume in the three sizes were assumed to be the same for all repeat groups.)

## NEWPROD's model of competitive behavior

Because new product introductions are often followed by competitive introductions, NEWPROD's designers included a section for modeling competitive product sales. Users could specify the time period in which competitive retail sales started. They also specified a cumulative trial function and a repeat rate function for the competitor (much as they had specified these functions for their own product). Users gave the number of packages per trier, packages per repeat interval and length of the repeat interval for the competitor. NEWPROD allowed only one repeat group and one package size for the competitor. Finally, NEWPROD required as an input the fraction of the competitor's volume that was taken from the user-company's sales.

## NEWPROD's model of trade inventory behavior

NEWPROD's designers felt that it was important to include in the system a mechanism for modeling trade inventories during the first few months of sales of a new product. They felt that when a powerful consumer marketer first brought a new product to the market, the trade would tend to rely on the manufacturing firm for advice on how much of the product to stock. The trade knew that the manufacturer had more information about the new product than did the trade; moreover, they felt they could count on the manufacturer to take back any inventories that turned out to be extra. At first, the manufacturer's sales force would be pushing the new product. After a product had been on the market for a few months, however, retailers would adjust their stocks to whatever they considered was an appropriate ratio to sales for the product.

To model trade inventories, NEWPROD requested the user to give the time period in which the sell-in would start and also the total sell-in volume of each package size. This volume would be distributed over five four-week periods, starting at the specified time, in proportions given by the user. Trade inventory behavior after the sell-in was determined from five percentages, giving the year-end trade inventories in relation to retail sales. Adjustments to inventories were made smoothly to move from the level at the end of the sell-in to the desired level at the end of the first year.

### Other inputs

This case is concerned with the use of NEWPROD for deterministic modeling. It should at least be noted, however, that NEWPROD allowed probabilistic modeling as well. Users could specify probability distributions for input quantities, giving pairs of values and probabilities for discrete uncertainties or giving pairs of values and cumulative probabilities for continuous ones. They could also, if they wished, specify a normal distribution for an input.

### Inputs for the QFC International Entrées

Exhibit 3 contains a detailed listing of the inputs selected for analyzing QFC's new international entrées under each of the two possible advertising programs. The two sets of inputs differ only as to their assumptions about the awareness levels during the first few years of the product's life. Both assume a single package size (small). They assume that there will not be a competitive product entry. In each, the total market starts at 70 million units of frozen entrées and grows to 85 million by the end of the fifth year. This increase in total category sales comes from an increase in the number of households in the United States (from 68 million to 72 million) and also from an increase in the fraction of households purchasing products in the general category (from 25 percent to 31 percent).

QFC managers felt that they could achieve a cumulative trial rate of 20 percent of the effective household base by the end of the first year. (Recall that this base was determined from the number of households that purchased items in the category, the distribution fractions, and the awareness rates.) They felt that 40 percent trial would be achieved by the end of the second year.

As for repeat groups, the planners found it useful to think of three groups,

**EXHIBIT 3**

New product planning system (model inputs for the international entrees)

*Data on distribution, awareness, population base:

```
REM DATAFILE FOR THE NEW PRODUCT TRIAL/REPEAT MODEL
REM COPYRIGHT JAN, 1974, APPLIED DECISIONS SYSTEMS, WELLESLEY, MASS.
REM 1978  1979  1980  1981  1982
```

← The labels for the 5 years

```
REM ************************ DISTRIBUTION/POP BASE
3 "DISTRIBUTION YR END LARGE SIZE (% OF TARGET POP)"
.85 4*1.0
```

← The five annual distribution fractions are .85, 1.0, 1.0, 1.0, 1.0

```
8 "DISTRIBUTION PERIODS 1-13"
.1  .2  .28  .34  .4  .46  .52  .58  .64  .7  .75  .8  .85
```

← Distribution fractions for the first 13 four-week periods

```
48 "% DISTN GAP REPRESENTING LOST SALES"
5*1.0
```

← All potential consumers not reached by distribution are lost sales

```
49 "% AWARENESS"
.65  .75  .85  .93  1.0
```

← Awareness rates (annual) for the lower advertising and promotion campaign. For the higher expenditure campaign, the values are .8, .9, .95, 1.0, 1.0

```
50 "% AWARENESS GAP REPRESENTING LOST SALES"
5*90%
```

← Only 90% of potential customers not reached by advertising are in fact lost sales

```
4 "HHOLD POPULATION (000S)"
68000 69000 70000 71000 72000
```

← Total US households for each of the five years

```
23 "FRAC OF HHOLDS WHO PURCH CATEGORY FROM RETAIL STORE"
.25  .26  .27  .29  .31
```

← fractions of households purchasing items in this category

```
6 "FIRST PERIOD OF RETAIL SALES"
1
7 "UNITS PER CASE"
5*1
```

Data on trial and repeat:

```
REM ************************ TRIAL/REPEAT DETAIL
9 "CUMULATIVE TRIAL AT END OF SECOND PRODUCT YEAR"
40%
```

← 40% trial after two years

* In this protocol, the dialogue is shown in typeface, with the parts that were typed by the user underlined to distinguish them from the parts that were printed by the computer. Explanatory comments have been added in handwriting.

**EXHIBIT 3 (*continued*)**

```
10 "YEAR 1 TRIAL AS % OF YEAR 2"
50%
```
← half of that (20% trial) is achieved in the first year

```
11 "UNITS PER TRIER"
1.0
```
Each trier buys one package

```
5 "NUMBER OF REPEAT GROUPS"
3
16 "PURCHASE INTERVAL/GROUP IN WEEKS"
12 8 4
12 "INITIAL REPEAT RATE (% OF TRIAL"
30% 20% 25%
13 "REPEAT RATE (PC OF TRIAL) ON GOING"
10% 10% 15%
14 "PURCH INTERVALS TILL ON-GOING REPEAT LEVEL"
4 5 6
15 "PACKAGES PER REPEAT PURCHASE INTERVAL"
1 1 1
```

There are three repeat groups:

| | light users | medium users | heavy users |
|---|---|---|---|
| Interval between successive purchases (weeks) | 12 | 8 | 4 |
| Initial % of triers in this group | 30 | 20 | 25 |
| "On-going" % of triers in this group | 10 | 10 | 15 |
| Number of purchase intervals it takes to reach the ongoing rate | 4 | 5 | 6 |
| Packages per repeat purchase | 1 | 1 | 1 |

Data on sizes:

```
REM ******** SIZE SHARES (MED=MEDIUM,SML=SMALL, LARGE=BALANCE)
37 "MED % OF TOTAL TRIAL VOLUME"
 00%
52 "MED % OF TOTAL REPEAT VOLUME"
 00%
51 "SML % OF TOTAL TRIAL VOLUME"
100%
53 "SML % REPEAT VOLUME"
100%
```
QFC will sell only one size package

**EXHIBIT 3 (*concluded*)**

Data on the total category and on trade behavior;

```
REM******************TOTAL CATEGORY SIZE / TRADE INVENTORY INPU
21 "TOTAL MARKET  (000S UNITS)"
70000  72500  76000  80000  85000
```

← The total category is 70 million units the first year... 85 million the fifth

```
22"YEAR-END TRADE INV. (% OF RETAIL SALES)"
5*10%
```

← Retailers try to maintain inventories for this type of product at 10% of annual sales

```
55 "START PERIOD# OF TRADE SELL-IN"
1
```

← Sell-in starts the first period

```
58 "SELL-IN% FOR 1ST 5 PERIODS OF PROD LIFE"
20%  30%  20%  15%  15%
54 "SELL-IN QUANTITY (000 UNITS)"
1500
45"% SELL-IN QTY (SMALL,MEDIUM,LARGE)"
100% 2*0
```

Sell-in involves 1.5 million packages (all small size, the only one available). Of this amount, 20% is shipped in the first four-week interval, 30% in the second, ..., 15% in the fifth.

Data on competitive entry:

```
REM COMPETITIVE PRODUCT ENTRY ******************
REM WITH SAME NUMBER OF REPEAT GORUPS AND PURCHASE INTERVALS
56 "FISCAL PERIOD OF COMPETITIVE RETAIL SALES"
0
66 "% COMP VOLUME TAKEN FROM CAMPANYS PROD SALES"
0
59 "COMP CUMULATIVE TRIAL AT END OF 2ND PROD YEAR"
0
60 "YR1 TRIAL AS % OF YR2 - COMP"
0
61 "UNITS PER TRIER - COMP"
0
62 "INITIAL REPEAT RATE (% OF TRIAL) - COMP"
0
63 "ON-GOING REPEAT RATE (% OF TRIAL) - COMP"
0
64 "PURCH INTERVALS TILL ON-GOING REPEAT LEVEL - COMP"
0
65 "PACKAGES PER REPEAT PURCHASE INTERVAL - COMP"
0
```

QFC planners assume there will not be a competitive entry.

representing light, medium, and heavy users. Light users would purchase one international entrée every 12 weeks; they would initially be 30 percent of triers but after a year only 10 percent of triers would remain light users. Medium users would purchase an international entrée every 8 weeks; initially 20 percent of the triers would fall in this group, but in the long run only 10 percent would. Finally, heavy users would purchase an entree every 4 weeks; they would be 25 percent of triers initially and 15 percent after about six months.

In both analyses, distribution was assumed to grow to approximately 50 percent in the first six months, to 85 percent by the end of the first year and to 100 percent by the end of the second year. QFC would sell 1.5 million units to the trade during the sell-in period; after that period, retail inventories would be adjusted to 10 percent of the annual sales.

As stated above, the two advertising proposals were assumed to differ only in terms of the awareness levels they achieved in the target market segment. The campaign involving high advertising and promotion expenditures would, it was estimated, achieve 80 percent awareness by the end of the first year and 100 percent awareness after five years. The medium advertising and promotion campaign would achieve only 65 percent awareness in the first year but it would also reach all target customers within five years.

### NEWPROD's outputs

NEWPROD produced two basic reports when it was run in deterministic mode. The first was a monthly summary of consumption, shipments, and inventory movements during each of the four-week periods in the first year. Users could select any of the following lines of output in this first report:

1. Consumption.
    *a.* Total.
    *b.* Consumption of small size.
    *c.* Consumption of medium size.
    *d.* Consumption of large size.
2. Shipments.
    *a.* Total.
    *b.* Small size.
    *c.* Medium size.
    *d.* Large size.
3. Inventory change.
4. Trial sales volume.
5. Repeat sales volume.
6. Percent cumulative trial.
7. Percent distribution.

The second report provided an annual summary of activity for each of the first five years. At the user's option, it could include information on:

**EXHIBIT 4**

New product planning system (output reports for medium advertising and promotion)

INTERNATIONAL FROZEN ENTREES

DETAIL FOR THE FIRST YEAR 1978

PERIOD=4 WEEKS FIGURES IN THOUSANDS

| | PER 1<br>1/28 | PER 2<br>2/25 | PER 3<br>3/25 | PER 4<br>4/22 | PER 5<br>5/20 | PER 6<br>6/17 | PER 7<br>7/25 | PER 8<br>8/12 | PER 9<br>8/9 | PER10<br>9/7 | PER11<br>10/4 | PER12<br>12/2 | PER13<br>12/30 |
|---|---|---|---|---|---|---|---|---|---|---|---|---|---|
| TOTAL CONSUMPTION | 24.2 | 57.9 | 103 | 158 | 203 | 239 | 305 | 344 | 398 | 456 | 508 | 543 | 618 |
| INVENTORY CHANGE | 300 | 358 | 208 | 133 | 133 | -92.0 | -92.0 | -92.0 | -92.0 | -92.0 | -92.0 | -92.0 | -92.0 |
| TOTAL SHIPMENTS | 324 | 416 | 311 | 291 | 336 | 147 | 213 | 252 | 306 | 364 | 416 | 451 | 526 |
| TRIAL/REPEAT DETAIL | | | | | | | | | | | | | |
| CUMULATIVE TRIAL | 2.08% | 4.04% | 5.91% | 7.68% | 9.36% | 10.9% | 12.5% | 13.9% | 15.2% | 16.5% | 17.7% | 18.9% | 20.0% |
| TRIAL VOLUME | 24.2 | 45.8 | 60.9 | 70.1 | 78.2 | 85.2 | 91.3 | 96.6 | 101 | 105 | 106 | 108 | 108 |
| REPEAT VOLUME | .000 | 12.1 | 42.6 | 87.5 | 125 | 154 | 214 | 247 | 297 | 351 | 402 | 435 | 510 |
| DISTRIBUTION | 9.99% | 20.0% | 28.0% | 34.0% | 40.0% | 46.0% | 52.0% | 58.0% | 64.0% | 70.0% | 75.0% | 80.0% | 85.0% |

INTERNATIONAL FROZEN ENTREES

PLANNING YEARS 1978–1982

FIGURES IN THOUSANDS

| | 1978 | 1979 | 1980 | 1981 | 1982 |
|---|---|---|---|---|---|
| TOTAL CONSUMPTION | 3959 | 12742 | 17320 | 21822 | 25721 |
| TOTAL CATEGORY SIZE | 70000 | 72500 | 76000 | 80000 | 85000 |
| MARKET SHARE | 5.7% | 18% | 23% | 27% | 30% |
| INVENTORY CHANGE | 396 | 878 | 458 | 450 | 390 |
| TOTAL SHIPMENTS | 4355 | 13621 | 17777 | 22272 | 26111 |

**EXHIBIT 5**
New product planning system (output reports for high advertising and promotion)

INTERNATIONAL FROZEN ENTREES

DETAIL FOR THE FIRST YEAR 1978
PERIOD=4 WEEKS FIGURES IN THOUSANDS

| | PER 1 1/28 | PER 2 2/25 | PER 3 3/25 | PER 4 4/22 | PER 5 5/20 | PER 6 6/17 | PER 7 7/15 | PER 8 8/12 | PER 9 8/9 | PER10 9/7 | PER11 10/4 | PER12 12/2 | PER13 12/30 |
|---|---|---|---|---|---|---|---|---|---|---|---|---|---|
| TOTAL CONSUMPTION | 28.9 | 69.3 | 124 | 189 | 244 | 286 | 365 | 411 | 477 | 546 | 609 | 650 | 740 |
| INVENTORY CHANGE | 300 | 364 | 214 | 139 | 139 | -85.5 | -85.5 | -85.5 | -85.5 | -85.5 | -85.5 | -85.5 | -85.5 |
| TOTAL SHIPMENTS | 329 | 434 | 338 | 328 | 383 | 200 | 280 | 326 | 391 | 461 | 523 | 564 | 655 |
| TRIAL/REPEAT DETAIL | | | | | | | | | | | | | |
| CUMULATIVE TRIAL | 2.08% | 4.04% | 5.91% | 7.68% | 9.36% | 10.9% | 12.5% | 13.9% | 15.2% | 16.5% | 17.7% | 18.9% | 20.0% |
| TRIAL VOLUME | 28.9 | 54.9 | 72.8 | 83.9 | 93.6 | 102 | 109 | 116 | 121 | 125 | 127 | 129 | 130 |
| REPEAT VOLUME | -.000 | 14.5 | 51.0 | 105 | 150 | 184 | 256 | 296 | 356 | 421 | 481 | 521 | 610 |
| DISTRIBUTION | 9.99% | 20.0% | 28.0% | 34.0% | 40.0% | 46.0% | 52.0% | 58.0% | 64.0% | 70.0% | 75.0% | 80.0% | 85.0% |

INTERNATIONAL FROZEN ENTREES

PLANNING YEARS 1978–1982
FIGURES IN THOUSANDS

| | 1978 | 1979 | 1980 | 1981 | 1982 |
|---|---|---|---|---|---|
| TOTAL CONSUMPTION | 4739 | 14962 | 19122 | 23289 | 25721 |
| TOTAL CATEGORY SIZE | 70000 | 72500 | 76000 | 80000 | 85000 |
| MARKET SHARE | 6.8% | 21% | 25% | 29% | 30% |
| INVENTORY CHANGE | 474 | 1022 | 416 | 417 | 243 |
| TOTAL SHIPMENTS | 5213 | 15984 | 19538 | 23706 | 25965 |

1. Consumption (total and/or broken down by size).
2. Shipments (total and/or by size).
3. Inventory change.
4. Percent distribution.
5. Total category size (in units).
6. Market share (in terms of units).

When NEWPROD was used in probabilistic mode it would produce risk profiles summarizing the values taken by one or more of these output variables, as specified by the user.

Exhibit 4 contains the output reports produced by NEWPROD with the assumptions of the medium advertising and promotion campaign. Exhibit 5 contains the corresponding reports for the high advertising and promotion choice.

## APPENDIX

### I. Cumulative trial function

NEWPROD used user inputs to determine a function of the form

$$y = a(1 - e^{-bt})$$

for the cumulative trial function. Here $y$ is cumulative trial (as a fraction of the effective household base), $e$ is the constant 2.1718 . . . (the base of the natural logarithms), and $t$ is time measured in four-week intervals so that $t$ is 13 at the end of the first year and 65 at the end of the fifth. Values of $a$ and $b$ were determined as follows. The user specified two inputs.

$I2$ is the trial at the end of year 2 (when $t$ is 26).

$f1$ is the fraction of $I2$ that is the cumulative trial at the end of year 1 (when $t$ is 13).

Hence, NEWPROD could find $I1$, the cumulative trial at the end of year 1 (when $t$ is 13) by multiplying $f1 * I2$. Then, NEWPROD could set up the following two equations:

$$I1 = a(1 - e^{-13b})$$

$$I2 = a(1 - e^{-26b})$$

Since $I1$ and $I2$ are inputs given by the user (known numbers), NEWPROD could solve these two equations for the two unknowns, $a$ and $b$.

### II. Repeat rate function

NEWPROD used input values to determine a function of the form

$$y = b + (a - b)e^{-gt}$$

for the repeat rate (as a fraction of triers) for a particular repeat group. In this equation $y$ is the repeat rate, e is a constant (the base of the natural logarithms), $t$ is the number of repeat intervals starting from $t = 0$ at the first repurchase time for this particular group. Values of $b$ and $g$ were determined from user inputs. The user specified three inputs.

- $a$ is the initial repeat rate.
- $R$ is what the program called the ongoing repeat rate. (In fact, the real long-term repeat rate is $b$.)
- $C$ is the number of repeat intervals needed to reach $R$.

To find $b$ and $g$, NEWPROD assumed that $y$ equaled $R$ after $C$ periods (when $t$ equaled $C - 1$). It assumed that $b$ was almost equal to $R (b = .99R)$. Then it solved the following equation for $g$:

$$R = b + (a - b)e^{-(C-1)g}$$

chapter 2

# PROBABILISTIC MODELS

## O. INTRODUCTION

In the previous chapter we discussed deterministic models as aids in decision making. In general, we make decisions today which we hope will lead to future outcomes that are favorable to us. In doing so, we must think about what the outcomes of our actions are likely to be. If we could predict the future with certainty, then, in principle at least, our decision making problems would be straightforward. Looking into the future, we would determine what would be the consequences of the various decisions we could make and we would then select that action (or set of actions) whose consequences we liked best. Unfortunately, of course, we cannot know the future with certainty. Our problem therefore becomes one of making the best possible decisions for the future in light of our uncertainty about what that future will be. The deterministic models of the preceding chapter help in decision making under conditions involving uncertainty, but they do so without really expressly addressing or modeling the uncertainty. For example, users who are trying to make a decision about what price to charge for a new product should clearly be aware of the uncertainty in the demand for their new product; they should also be aware that the demand is most likely closely tied to the price they decide to charge, with higher demand for lower prices and vice versa. In building a deterministic model we do not model and express their uncertainty explicitly, however. Instead, we envisioned a mode of use in which the model users ran many sets of inputs through a deterministic model in order to determine the sensitivity of the results to differences in inputs. In such a way they would explore the sensitivity of the results to changes in their assumptions about demand. Good model usage would require that users spend more time investigating the results of changing those inputs which were in their opinions most uncertain, so in a sense the concept of uncertainty enters into the use of deterministic models, but such models do not contain explicit statements about the input uncertainties. Similarly, the intelligent use of the output of a deterministic model does involve some concept of uncertainty but does not involve any explicit statement or measurement of uncertainty. Faced with model output for many different scenarios, decision makers must choose their actions in ways which seem intelligent in light of the results indicated by the output. In weighing the output and arriving at decisions, users must consider how likely or unlikely are the different scenarios that were used to generate the different sets of outputs. Notice that the model does not provide any clues as to these relative likelihoods of different results; the model simply generates a set of outputs for each set of inputs provided by the user, regardless of how likely that set of inputs is in reality or in the judgment of the user.

In this chapter we proceed to a consideration of *probablistic models.* In such models the uncertainties involved in decision problems are considered explicitly in the model inputs, in the relationships, and in the outputs. First, we discuss probabilities themselves. Next, we consider decision trees as a useful mechanism for structuring problems involving uncertainties. We are then prepared to consider the design and use of probabilistic computer models. As the reader will undoubtedly already have guessed, there are trade-offs that must be considered in deciding whether a probabilistic model should be built in any given situation. Probabilistic models are in general harder to build than are deterministic ones, yet in some decision problems they give superior information to the user. Therefore, in this and the following chapters we will have to consider both the problems and the advantages of probabilistic modeling as compared with deterministic modeling.

## I. PROBABILITIES

Before we try to build computer models incorporating probabilities, it is important to review the basic concepts of *probabilities* themselves. Most people have an intuitive feeling that probabilities refer to such things as the toss of a coin or the roll of a die, but in this book we are not using probabilities in that sense, to mean long-run frequencies. Instead, we use probabilities as a language to express an individual's beliefs about the relative likelihoods of various outcomes of uncertainties.[1] They express quantitatively the personal judgment of a decision maker about the future outcomes

---

[1] For discussions of probabilities of this sort see: Howard Raiffa, *Decision Analysis* (Reading, Mass.: Addison-Wesley, 1968), and Robert Schlaifer, *Analysis of Decisions under Uncertainty* (New York: McGraw-Hill, 1969).

Many texts on probability and statistics discuss the long-run-frequency type of probabilities. Particularly good is: William Feller, *An Introduction to Probability Theory and Its Applications,* vols. 1 and 2 (New York: John Wiley & Sons, 1950 and 1966).

of specified uncertainties. For example, suppose that we are concerned with the total demand in the United States for electric power next year. That total demand will be a single number, so it does not involve any concept of repetition and long-run frequency (as does the outcome of rolling a die, for example). Yet, the power demand is clearly uncertain today; we cannot forecast it precisely. We would use a probability distribution, as described below, to express how certain or uncertain we are about what demand will be in the next year.

This section will not consider in detail how to determine probabilities that express our uncertainty about future events. The Appendix (on decision analysis) contains a brief description of one of the methods available for helping decision makers to express their uncertainty in the form of probabilities. The point to be stressed here is that probabilities reflect the judgment of individuals about uncertainties.

In this introduction to the concepts of probabilities we begin by considering what we will call *few-valued uncertain quantities* (or few-valued UQs). Such a UQ is one which will result in one of only a small number of possible outcomes. For example, suppose we face a problem in which one uncertainty is the price that our competitor will charge. Notice that this price is in fact an uncertainty to us. It is a decision for the competitor, but since we cannot decide what the price will be it is an uncertainty from our point of view. Suppose that because of industry conventions we are certain that the price will be some multiple of $0.25. Suppose further that we are essentially certain that the competitor will not charge more than $3.00 nor less than $2.25. If so, then the uncertainty of competitor's price has only four possible outcomes, in our estimation: price can be $2.25, $2.50, $2.75, or $3.00. The UQ for competitor's price is few-valued. In another situation, by comparison, there might not be such industry-wide conventions about pricing in even multiples and we might think it possible that the competitor would charge any amount between $5.00 and $7.50 for some other product. The UQ for price for the second product would be considered *many-valued* rather than few-valued. We will consider many-valued UQs later in the section.

In defining UQs and the probabilities describing them, we must first think about all of the outcomes that a particular UQ could have. In determining possible outcomes, we follow two rules. First, the outcomes should be *mutually exclusive*—that is, they should be defined clearly in such a way that only one of the possible outcomes can occur at a time. In the first pricing UQ above, we define outcomes of $2.25, $2.50, $2.75, and $3.00. We do not define outcomes of "$2.75 or more" and "$2.75 or less," for example, because those two "outcomes" are not mutually exclusive—the price of $2.75 falls in both categories. The second rule is that the outcomes be *collectively exhaustive*. In other words, they should be defined in such a way that one or another of them must occur.

After we have identified a set of mutually exclusive and collectively exhaustive outcomes for some uncertain quantity, we can proceed to determine a probability distribution for the UQ. A probability distribution for the possible outcomes of some uncertainty is a quantitative statement of the likelihoods assigned to each possible outcome. In assigning probabilities to the outcomes, you are distributing a set of weights among those possible events in a way which reflects your judgments about their relative likelihoods. Thus, if one possible outcome is twice as likely, in your estimation, as is another outcome, then you assign a probability to the first which is twice the probability which you assign to the second. There are two common ways of presenting a probability distribution: the probability mass function and the cumulative distribution function. Both types of functions will be described below.

For many uncertainties (or uncertain quantities) it makes sense to talk about the likelihood that the actual event or outcome is exactly equal to a particular value. A *probability mass function* assigns to each possible outcome the likelihood which the decision maker attaches to having exactly that outcome occur. For example, consider a low-volume item sold by a small hardware store. The retailer might have 12 of the items in stock and might be trying to predict next week's sales. If no further items will be received by the store that week, then sales will not exceed 12. The retailer can probably think intelligently about the likelihoods of various sales figures which do not exceed 12; after some careful thought s/he might assign the weights given in Table 2–1. Note that those weights are all between 0 and 1 and that they sum to 1.0; they are therefore a proper probability mass function.

Probability mass functions are sometimes presented in graphical form. The mass function for sales given in Table 2–1 is shown in Figure 2–1. By

**TABLE 2–1**
Probability mass function for sales

| *Number of units sold* | *Probability* |
|---|---|
| 0 | .10 |
| 1 | .15 |
| 2 | .15 |
| 3 | .12 |
| 4 | .10 |
| 5 | .10 |
| 6 | .08 |
| 7 | .07 |
| 8 | .05 |
| 9 | .03 |
| 10 | .02 |
| 11 | .02 |
| 12 | .01 |
| | 1.00 |

**FIGURE 2–1**

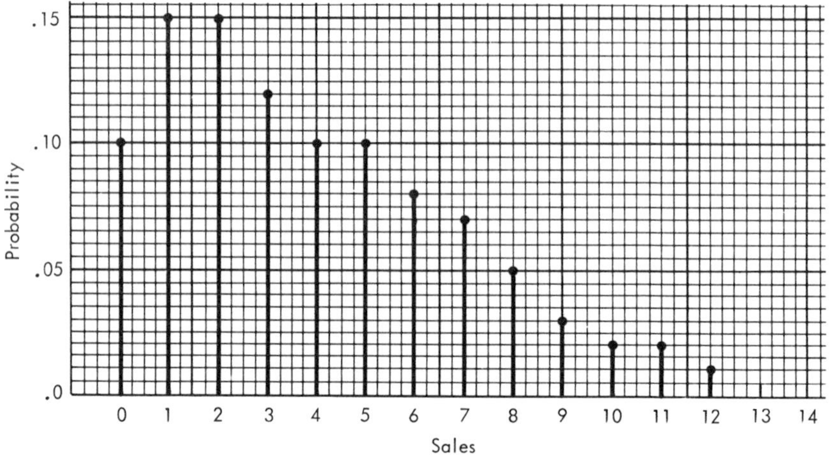


custom, the Y-axis (the vertical axis) in a graph of a probability function gives the probability values while the X-axis (the horizontal axis) gives the possible values of the UQ (or uncertain quantity). A probability mass function has the value zero for values of the uncertain quantity which the decision maker considers impossible. Thus, for example, the graph in Figure 2–1 is zero at 1.5 and 13 units for sales. In fact, the function is zero everywhere except for the integers from 0 through 12, and so the graph below is simply a row of vertical lines at these integers. The height of each line is proportional to the probability assigned to that particular sales value.

Frequently, instead of talking about the probability that an uncertain quantity will assume a particular value exactly, we talk instead about the probability that the UQ will be less than or equal to a specific value (that it will not exceed that value). The *cumulative distribution function* assigns to each value the probability that that value will not be exceeded.[2] For example, in the probability mass function in Table 2–1, the retailer has said that there is a .1 chance that sales will be 0 and a .15 chance that sales will be 1. S/he could also have said that there was a .25 probability that sales would not be more than 1 (because sales not more than 1 means sales must be 0 or 1). Thus, the cumulative distribution function, which gives the probabilities that the UQ will not exceed the various possible values, can easily be constructed from the probability mass function. To find the value assigned by the cumulative function to a specific value, simply add up the values as-

[2] It makes just as much sense to talk instead about the probabilities that the UQ will *not be less than* specified values but it is conventional to discuss probabilities of *not exceeding* specified values instead.

signed by the probability mass function to all values not exceeding the specific value. The cumulative distribution function corresponding to the distribution given in Table 2–1 is shown in Table 2–2. Notice, for example, that the cumulative probability for sales of 4 units is .62, which is simply the sum of the individual probability mass values for 0, 1, 2, 3 and 4 units (or .10 + .15 + .15 + .12 + .10 = .62).

**TABLE 2–2**
Cumulative distribution function for sales

| *Number of units sold* | *Cumulative probability* |
|---|---|
| 0 | .10 |
| 1 | .25 |
| 2 | .40 |
| 3 | .52 |
| 4 | .62 |
| 5 | .72 |
| 6 | .80 |
| 7 | .87 |
| 8 | .92 |
| 9 | .95 |
| 10 | .97 |
| 11 | .99 |
| 12 | 1.00 |

Cumulative distribution functions are often presented in graphical form. By convention, such graphs have the cumulative probability values on the vertical axis and have the possible values of the UQ on the horizontal axis. Such a graph for the distribution in Table 2–2 is shown in Figure 2–2. Notice that the cumulative distribution function is non-zero for every number above 0. Even for a value which is impossible (such as 1.5) it still makes sense to ask for the probability that that number will not be exceeded. (For example, 1.5 will not be exceeded if sales are 0 or 1, and the probability of one or the other of those outcomes is .25). Similarly, even though sales could not be 13, the probability is 1.0 (certainty) that sales will not exceed that value.

As shown above, we can use the probability mass function to obtain the cumulative distribution function. It is also possible to go in the reverse direction and use a cumulative distribution function to find the corresponding probability mass function. If you recall how cumulative probabilities are calculated from mass probabilities (by adding a set of probabilities) it should be clear that the difference between the cumulative probability at 5 and that at 4 is simply the mass probability that sales are exactly 5 (which is the value of the probability mass function at 5). Similarly, the cumulative probability at

**FIGURE 2–2**

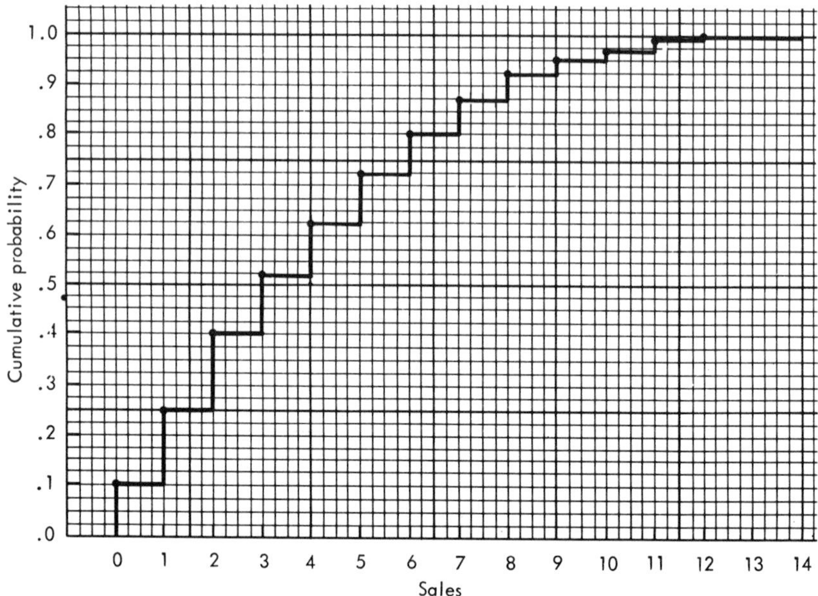


7 minus the cumulative probability at 6 is the value of the probability mass function at 7, or .07.

The examples above have concerned few-valued UQs only. The concepts we have introduced for few-valued UQs are not completely appropriate for many-valued uncertainties. To see why, suppose that a meteorologist is trying to forecast the likely amounts of rain which will fall in a particular area over the next three months. There are a very large number of possible outcomes for this uncertainty. For example, the rainfall might be 1.00347528 inches. In fact, there are an essentially infinite number of possible outcomes. (Even if we limit our discussion to numbers with no more than 5 decimal places, there are still a very large number of possible outcomes.) The meterologist will find it virtually impossible to assign probability mass values to individual rainfall values in an intelligent way.

The problem in this situation is that the uncertain quantity (inches of rain in the next three months) is continuous; that is, it can take any value between 0 and some large amount. Because there are an essentially infinite number of outcomes, the probability that the UQ will take a specific value exactly is very small indeed. Thus, it does not make sense to talk about the probabilities of specific outcomes. Instead, we talk in terms of the probabilities that the UQ will take values in different ranges (such as the range between 0 and 1 inches, or the range of values which are greater than 1 but not larger than 2). Very often we use the probabilities for the ranges of values not greater than specified numbers (such as the probability of no more than 3 inches of rain or the probability of no more than 5 inches of rain); these numbers are simply cumulative probabilities. Thus, for continuous uncertain quantities we often use cumulative distribution functions to describe a decision maker's belief about the possible outcomes. The meterologist might, for example, give the cumulative probability function in Figure 2–3.

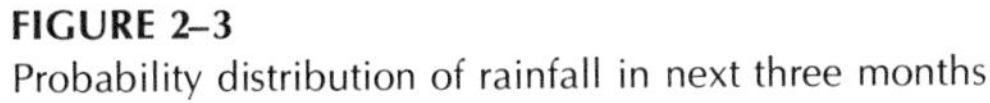

**FIGURE 2–3**
Probability distribution of rainfall in next three months

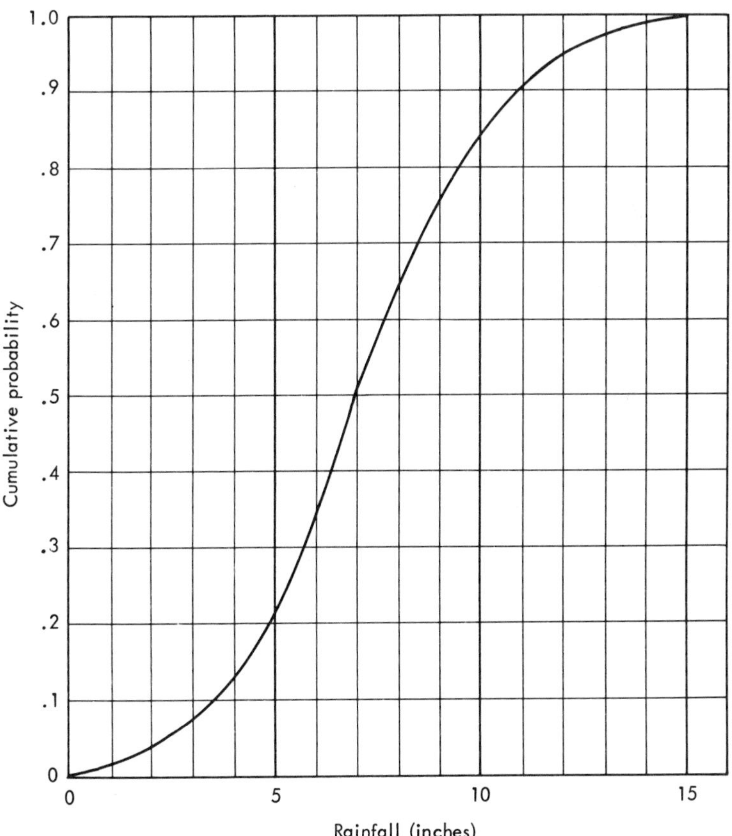


Figure 2–3 shows that the probability that rain will not exceed 11 is .91 while the probability that it will not exceed 9 is .75. Thus, the probability that rain will be between these two values can be calculated (using logic similar to that we used in moving between a cumulative function and a probability mass function above) as .91 − .75 or .16. Cumulative distribution functions have the property that their graphs rise more steeply above ranges of values which are more likely to occur than above ranges which are

less likely. For example, notice that the curve in Figure 2–3 rises more steeply over the range between 7 and 9 (which has probability .24) than it does over the range from 9 to 11 (which has probability .16).

It is also possible to construct and graph an analog of a probability mass function for a continuous UQ: such a function is called a probability density function. We will not consider probability density functions in detail, because in the future we will use cumulative distribution functions almost exclusively for continuous UQs, for two reasons. It turns out in practice that such functions are easier for decision makers to determine (either judgmentally or from historical data) than are probability density functions. In addition, the cumulative curves are better suited for use in the techniques which we will consider in this book.

The preceding discussion introduced the distribution function for an uncertain quantity which was in fact essentially continuous (ANY number of inches of rain—such as 3.342594—could in fact occur). In practice, we often encounter quantities which are not in fact continuous. For example, consider the sales of quarts of milk by a supermarket during one week. The store sells hundreds of quarts. Surely it sells an integral number of quarts (not 652.2 for example), yet the decision maker usually will not be able to think intelligently about the probability that sales will exactly equal some specified value, such as 425 quarts. Instead, it will generally be much more natural to make judgments about cumulative probabilities, such as the likelihood that sales will not exceed 500 quarts. This type of uncertain quantity, which can assume many different values but which is not strictly continuous, is called a many-valued UQ. In assessing probability distributions for such UQs, we generally treat them as if they were continuous and we deal with cumulative distribution curves for them just as we did for the truly continuous rainfall example above.

The probability mass functions and cumulative distribution functions discussed above provide rather complete descriptions of probability distributions. Frequently, instead of or in addition to these functions, we find it useful to have various summaries of the properties of a probability distribution. The most commonly used summary of a distribution is the *mean* or expected value. The mean is calculated from a probability mass function as follows: for each outcome, multiply the value (the outcome) by its probability. Add all of the products; the mean is the resulting sum. Table 2–3 shows how to calculate the mean of the probability distribution in Table 2–1.[3]

[3] The mean is the average value of the UQ, with the probabilities used as weights. You calculate it as you would any other weighted average: first you take a sum of weights times values. Then you would normally divide by the sum of the weights; but because the probabilities sum to 1.0, this step is unnecessary in calculating a mean from a probability distribution.

**TABLE 2–3**
Calculating the mean of the distribution in Table 1

| *Value* | *Probability* | *Value * Probability* |
|---|---|---|
| 0 | .10 | .0 |
| 1 | .15 | .15 |
| 2 | .15 | .30 |
| 3 | .12 | .36 |
| 4 | .10 | .40 |
| 5 | .10 | .50 |
| 6 | .08 | .48 |
| 7 | .07 | .49 |
| 8 | .05 | .40 |
| 9 | .03 | .27 |
| 10 | .02 | .20 |
| 11 | .02 | .22 |
| 12 | .01 | .12 |
| Mean | | 3.89 |

A second summary measure of a probability distribution is the *mode,* which is defined as the most likely value of the uncertain quantity. In the distribution in Table 2–1, there are two values which have the highest probabilities (1 and 2 each have probability .15). We say that that distribution has two modes (or is bi-modal). Similarly, a distribution may have more than two modes.

A third commonly used measure is the *median,* which can be read easily from the cumulative graph of the distribution (Figure 2–2). To find the median, start on the probability (vertical) axis at .5. Move straight across, parallel to the X-axis, until you hit the distribution curve; then read straight down until you hit the horizontal axis at some value. That value is the median. Using this procedure in Figure 2–2, we would find that the median is 3.

Verbal definitions of the median that are correct for few-valued as well as for many-valued UQs tend to be rather awkward. For a continuous UQ, the median is the value for which it is true that: there is exactly a .5 probability of that value or a smaller one. For few-valued UQs, the definition of a median must be generalized to be the value for which it is true that (1) there is at least a .5 probability of that value or a smaller one, and (2) there is at least a .5 probability of that value or greater. In less precise but less awkward terms, the median can be thought of as the middle value on the cumulative distribution curve.

Actually, the median is just a special example of a class of measures called *fractiles.* The median is the .5 fractile; other fractiles are also read from the cumulative graph. For example, to find the .4 fractile, start at .4 on the vertical axis, move across to the curve and then straight down; the value at which you hit the horizontal axis is the .4 fractile.

**FIGURE 2–4**

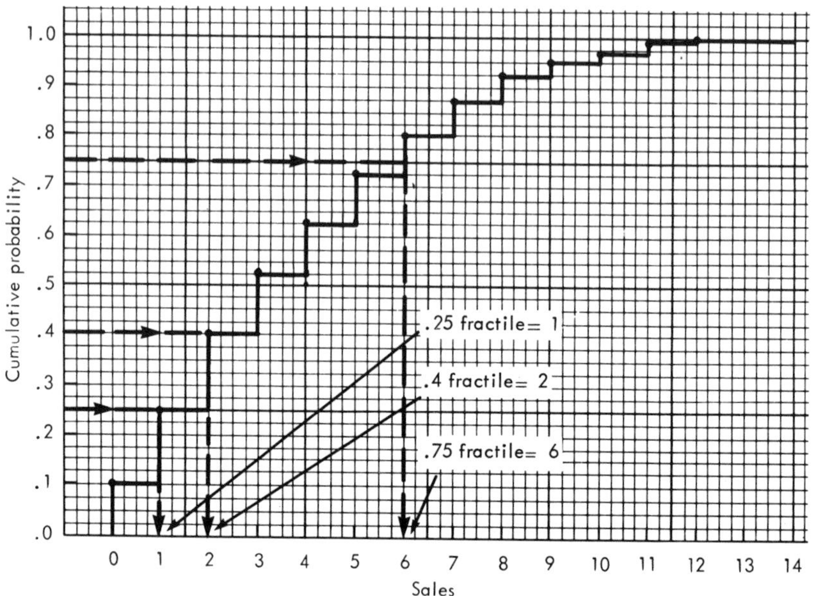


Similarly, you could calculate the .25 or the .75 or other fractiles. Figure 2–4 shows how to find several fractiles for the distribution also shown in Figure 2–2.

All three of the summary measures we have considered so far are in some sense measures of typical or central values from probability distributions. Accordingly, they are called measures of central tendency. Another characteristic of a probability distribution with which we are frequently concerned is the extent to which the values assigned appreciable levels of probability are similar to one another; in other words, we ask to what extent the likely values are different from one another. There are additional measures which summarize probability distributions and focus on the spreads of those distributions.

To see why the measures of central tendency do not completely describe the interesting properties of a distribution, consider the mean as an example. Table 2–4 gives probability mass functions for four different uncertain quantities. Each of these UQ's has a mean of 3, but the UQs are far from identical. For example, the range of possible values (or the difference between the highest and lowest values) is 4 for the first UQ and 20 for the fourth. Even though they have the same mean, these two distributions show very different amounts of *spread*. Hence, we would like another summary statistic for probability distributions to use in describing how spread out the possible values of the UQ are. One such measure is the difference between the highest and the

**TABLE 2–4**

| *UQ1* | | *UQ2* | | *UQ3* | | *UQ4* | |
|---|---|---|---|---|---|---|---|
| *Value* | *Probability* | *Value* | *Probability* | *Value* | *Probability* | *Value* | *Probability* |
| 1 ...... | .2 | −15 ...... | .2 | 1 ...... | .6 | 1 ...... | .9 |
| 2 ...... | .2 | −10 ...... | .2 | 6 ...... | .4 | 21 ...... | .1 |
| 3 ...... | .2 | 3 ...... | .2 | | | | |
| 4 ...... | .2 | 16 ...... | .2 | | | | |
| 5 ...... | .2 | 21 ...... | .2 | | | | |

lowest possible values, or the range. In many cases, however, we prefer not to concentrate on the range (which is made much larger by extreme values of the UQ regardless of whether those values are in fact also extremely unlikely, although still possible) but rather to use a measure which considers both how spread out and how likely are the various possible values. Two summary statistics which serve this purpose are the variance and the closely related standard deviation.

The *variance* of a probability distribution is the expected value (or, the weighted average, with probabilities used as weights) of the square of the differences between the UQ values and their mean. An example of how to calculate a variance should make this definition a bit clearer. The first UQ defined in Table 2–4 is used in Table 2–5 to show how to calculate a variance. The variance for the third UQ is shown in the second part of the table. Similarly, the variances of the remaining UQ in Table 2–4 can be

**TABLE 2–5**

| *Value* | *Probability* | *Difference between value and mean* | *Difference squared* |
|---|---|---|---|
| 1 .......... | .2 | 1 − 3 = −2 | 4 |
| 2 .......... | .2 | 2 − 3 = −1 | 1 |
| 3 .......... | .2 | 3 − 3 = 0 | 0 |
| 4 .......... | .2 | 4 − 3 = 1 | 1 |
| 5 .......... | .2 | 5 − 3 = 2 | 4 |

Note: Weighted average of differences = the variance = .2(4) + .2(1) + .2(0) + .2(1) + .2(4) = 2.

| *Value* | *Probability* | *Difference from mean* | *Difference squared* |
|---|---|---|---|
| 1 .......... | .6 | 1 − 3 = −2 | 4 |
| 6 .......... | .4 | 6 − 3 = 3 | 9 |

Note: Variance = .6(4) + .4(9) = 6.

calculated as 197.2 and 36, respectively. Thus, while those UQs have the same mean, they have quite different variances.

The variance of an uncertain quantity is measured in units which are the square of the units of the UQ itself; if, for example, the UQ is measured in dollars, then the variance is in dollars squared. It is not natural to think in such squared units and, for that reason, we generally use another measure of spread, called the *standard deviation,* which has the same units as the UQ itself. The standard deviation of a distribution is simply the square root of the variance of that distribution. If, for example, the UQ is measured in dollars, then the standard deviation is measured in dollars, too.

The best intuitive definition of the standard deviation is that it is the average distance to the mean of values of the UQ, where the probabilities are used as weights. In reality, however, variance and standard deviation are not very intuitive concepts. It is probably best to think of them as *relative* concepts which are particularly useful for comparing two distributions: A UQ with a higher standard deviation than another is more spread out than is the other.

Finally, we note that although we have used only discrete uncertain quantities in this description of the variance and standard deviation, those measures are also well defined (and have the same general meaning) for continuous UQs. The methods of calculating these statistics for continuous UQs will not be discussed here.

Thus, probability distributions can be described by a collection of summary statistics. Some, such as the mean, median, and mode, are primarily measures of what is called location or central tendency—where, in general, the distribution is. Others, such as the variance and the standard deviation, measure the spread of the possible values of the UQ. The larger the variance (or standard deviation), the greater is the spread.

As we proceed with this chapter's discussion of designing probabilistic computer models, we will use many of the basic concepts introduced in this section. In particular, probability mass functions, cumulative distribution functions, fractiles, means, and standard deviations are important in probabilistic modeling. Throughout our discussion we assume that the decision maker who is using a model provides distributions expressing uncertainty and we do not consider in most cases how those distributions were obtained. The Appendix text on decision analysis considers briefly how a decision maker might assess probability distributions—for both few-valued and many-valued UQs.

## II. DECISION TREES FOR DESCRIBING PROBLEMS INVOLVING UNCERTAINTY

Having considered how probabilities are used to express quantitatively our judgments about uncertain quantities and, in addition, how probability distributions can usefully be described, we now proceed to consider how we can structure, describe, and model decision problems involving UQs.

In this section we introduce *decision trees* as a useful method of describing decision problems involving probabilities and we provide a brief description of decision trees. Readers who have not been exposed to the concepts of decision trees before will find it important to read the Appendix material on decision analysis before they proceed with the remainder of the chapter.

In describing decision problems with decision trees, we consider two types of problem components: *act nodes* and *event nodes.* Act nodes represent those parts of the problem where the decision maker has complete control: the decision maker can choose which of various alternatives to take. Event nodes, on the other hand, represent uncertainties, or parts of the decision problems over which the decision maker does not have control. In describing a problem through a decision tree, the basic idea is to decompose the overall problem into a series of parts. Each part is either an act node or an event node. At an act node we identify each of the possible actions that the decision maker could choose to take; at an event node we identify a mutually exclusive and collectively exhaustive set of possible outcomes for the uncertainty. The decision tree is a graphic representation of a sequence of act nodes and event nodes. As a matter of convention, an act node is shown as a square with one branch leading from it for each possible action; similarly, an event node is shown as a circle with a branch for each of the possible outcomes.

One extremely important point about decision trees is that they are specific to individual decision makers. For one thing, the definition of what is an act node and what is an event node depends on the point of view of the diagram. From our point of view the price which our competitor will charge for a new product is an event because we cannot determine that price; from the competitor's point of view, on the other hand, the same price is an act. Similarly, the sequencing of the act nodes and event nodes in a decision tree should reflect the timing in the problem from the point of view of the decision maker for whom the diagram is being constructed. In particular, the act nodes and event nodes are sequenced in the time order in which acts must be chosen and in which the outcomes of uncertainties are learned by the relevant decision maker.

As an example of a decision tree for a specific decision problem, suppose that you are planning to produce a specialty souvenir to be sold as part of your state's centennial celebration. You must make a decision very soon about what type of machinery to buy to use in manufacturing the item. Because you expect the souvenir to sell during a single year only, we have chosen a single year for your planning horizon. There are two major uncertainties in the problem: the market which will exist for the item and whether or not a competitor will enter the field. Suppose that as a first approximation you are willing to assume that demand will be either 100,000 or 80,000 or 50,000 (with probabilities .4, .3, and .3, respectively). In addition, you feel that there is a 25 percent chance that there will be competition. If a competitor does enter the market, you will have the option of spending $10,000 on a promotion campaign. The campaign would not affect the total market size but would only affect your share. (Hence, if there is no competition you will certainly not promote.) Even with competition and without the campaign you believe you will get 70 percent of the market because of the high quality and attractiveness of your product; with the promotion campaign you feel you can increase your market share to 85 percent. Standard equipment costs $31,000 and gives a contribution margin (revenue minus variable production cost) of 75¢ per item. Alternatively, you could buy automated equipment at a higher cost of $50,000 and a higher contribution margin of $1 per item. Because the automated machine wears out somewhat faster than does the standard one, we assume that their salvage values at the end of the year will be equal and we decide to ignore the salvage values in the analysis of the decision.

There are two act nodes in this problem: the decision on machinery and the decision on whether or not to promote. There are two event nodes: the size of the total market and the presence or absence of competition. Suppose that you must decide on the machinery almost immediately but that you can delay the promotion decision until you know whether or not there will be competition. From your point of view as the decision maker, the sequence is: choose machinery, learn about competition, choose whether or not to promote, learn about demand. A decision tree for this simplified problem is shown in Figure 2–5.

One way in which the decision tree is unrealistic is that it assumes only three possible levels of demand. In reality, of course, you probably think many demand levels are possible. In other words, demand is most likely a many-valued UQ. When continuous or many-valued UQs arise in decision trees, they are depicted by what are called *event fans*. The revised tree in Figure 2–6 shows the demand fork from Figure 2–5 replaced by a more realistic demand fan.

After structuring a problem by drawing a decision tree, we must consider the consequences of following various paths through the tree. As the decision problem unfolds over time, we will follow one or another of those paths. At any point in the tree, everything "behind" us has already happened (that is, the decision maker has made the decisions and learned the outcomes of the events) and everything in front of us lies in the future. When we reach the end of a path, we can evaluate the overall results. In analyzing a decision tree, we take trips through the tree in our imagination and consider the values of possible paths. By convention, we put the value of taking a particular path through the tree at the end of the path. Such values are called *endpoint values*. In some problems it is possible to identify a single criterion

FIGURE 2–5

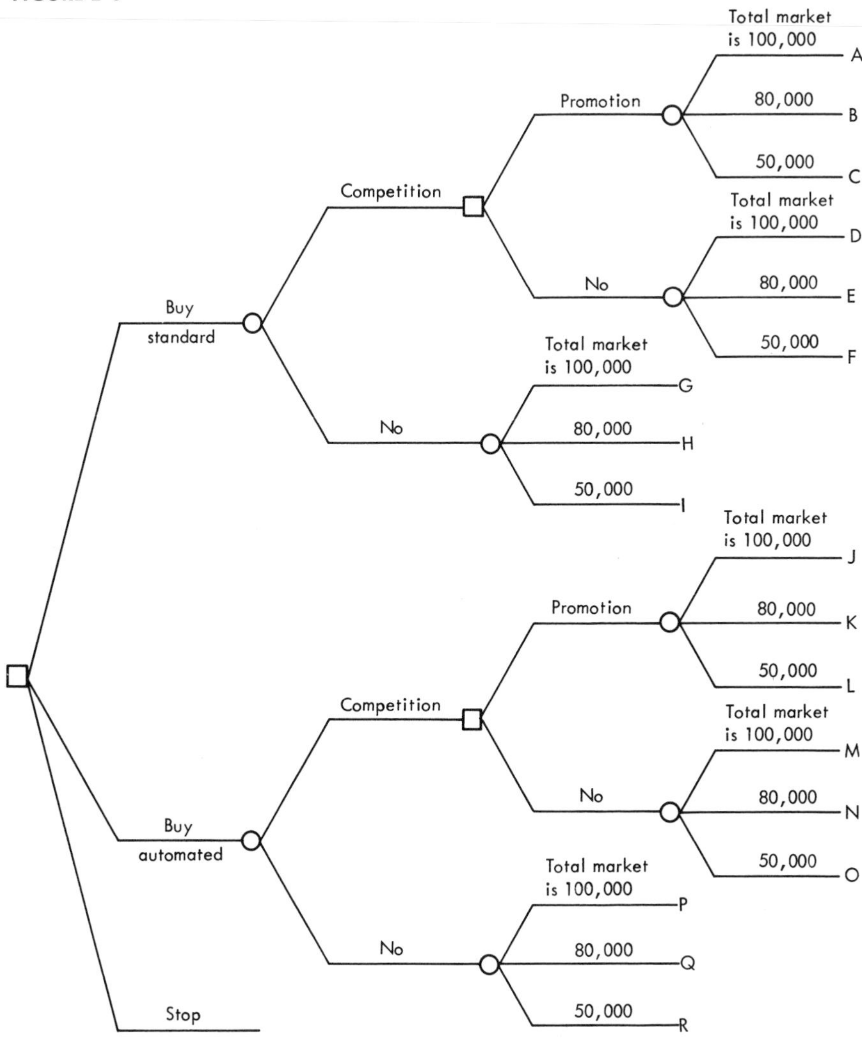


for judging the relative attractiveness of different endpoints of a tree. In other problems, several important dimensions characterize each endpoint. For example, in some problems we might consider profit after tax for a single year a satisfactory criterion for summarizing each endpoint. In other problems we might find it important to consider profit after tax, cash flow, market share, and capital investment as four important dimensions of each endpoint position.

In many decision analyses we use the concept of expected value to analyze a decision tree. For such analyses we generally use a single criterion

**FIGURE 2–6**

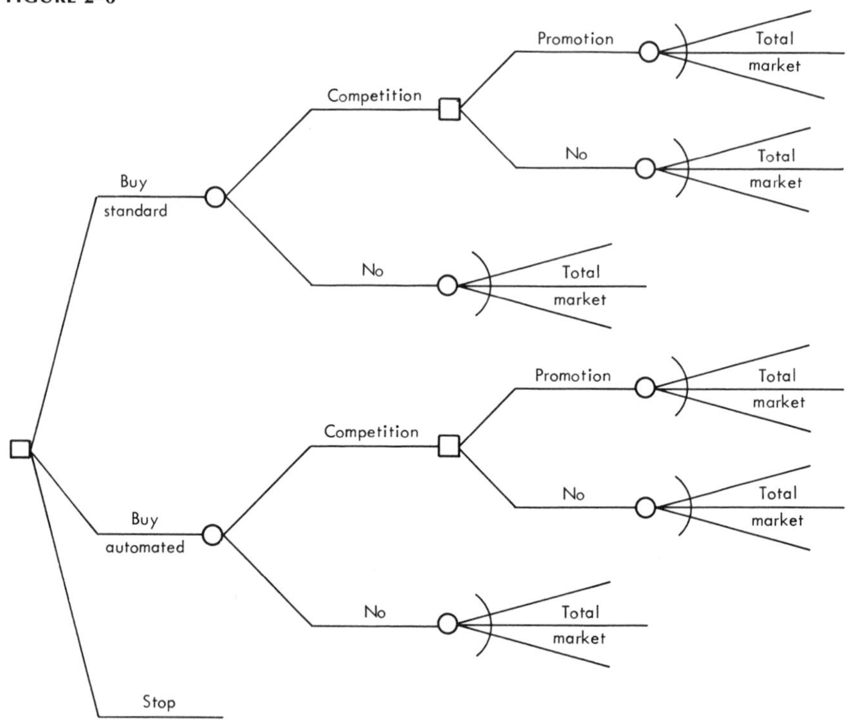


only and we assume that the decision maker is willing to play the averages when faced with uncertainties.[4] In other problems, however, the decision maker is not willing to play the averages, often because the risks involved are unacceptably large. In such cases, we analyze decision trees through mechanisms that describe the range of possible outcomes that could result from a particular set of actions by the decision maker. In addition, we want to describe not only the range of outcomes but also the relative likelihoods of different criterion values within that range. If profit after tax for one year is our criterion, for example, we might want to know the range of possible values for profit and the relative likelihoods of different subranges within that range. One very useful mechanism for describing such results is called a *risk profile.* In a risk profile we focus on a single *strategy,* or set of action choices for the decision maker. There is therefore a separate risk profile associated with each complete set of action choices available to the decision maker. For the specified strategy the risk profile lists all of the possible outcomes, in

[4] See the Appendix for further details. The Appendix also contains an analysis of the decision problem described in Figure 2–5.

terms of the criterion we are using to evaluate endpoints, together with the probabilities of those outcomes. Thinking back to the previous section, you will realize that the precise form of a risk profile depends on whether there are a few or many possible results in terms of our criterion. For a few-valued situation the risk profile takes the form of a probability mass function or of a cumulative mass function. For example, Table 2–6 gives a risk profile for the strategy: buy standard equipment and do not promote even if there is competition (from the problem in Figure 2.5).

**TABLE 2–6**

| *Result* | *Probability* |
|---|---|
| $44,000 | .3 |
| 29,000 | .225 |
| 21,500 | .1 |
| 11,000 | .075 |
| 6,500 | .225 |
| −4,750 | .075 |

**FIGURE 2–7**

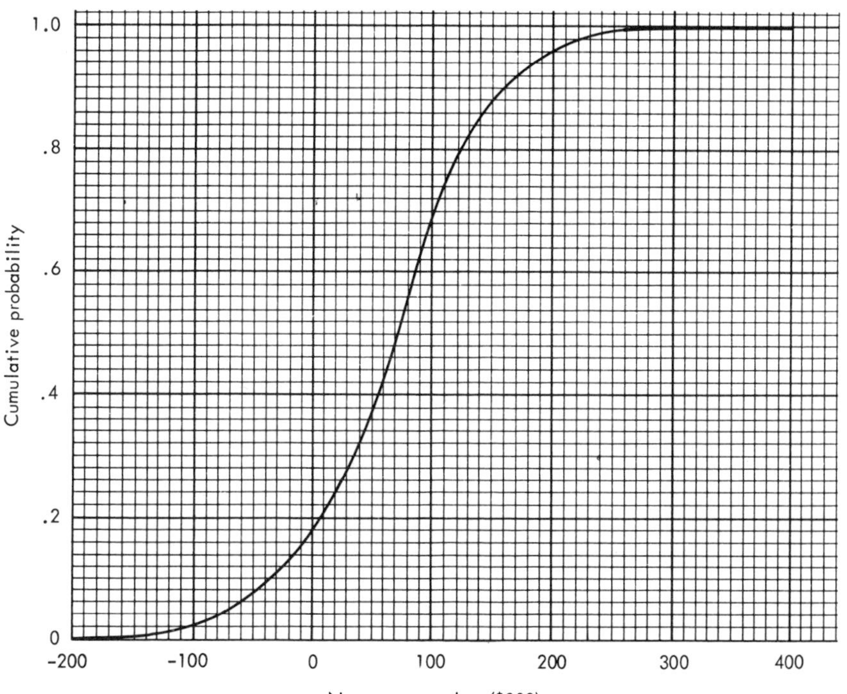

When there are many possible outcomes of a particular strategy, the risk profile is generally shown as a cumulative distribution function. For example, in a new product introduction we might evaluate endpoints as the net present values (or discounted present values) at 15 percent of the cash flows generated over the next ten years. The risk profile for a particular strategy in this problem might look like the cumulative distribution function in Figure 2–7.

## III. SIMULATION MODELS AND DECISION TREES

Having covered the basics of decision trees and probabilities, we can now consider the relationship between decision trees and the deterministic computer models we discussed in the preceding chapter. In this chapter we will be concerned almost exclusively with what would be called *deterministic simulation models* and *probabilistic simulation models.* In the previous chapter we briefly covered optimization models and we also considered briefly the ability of the computer to analyze and solve sets of mathematical equations (or what would be called analytic models). In this chapter, however, we will be concerned with the main type of computer model discussed in Chapter 1; that is, we will consider simulation models, in which the computer follows through a series of steps in some process (such as the construction of a pro forma income statement or the calculation of ending balances for savings accounts) and in which the machine does not attempt to optimize any criterion function.

If we try to relate the decision trees of the preceding section with the deterministic models of the preceding chapter, we find that the decision tree concept is useful for some but not all of the deterministic models considered. First, consider the model sketched in Chapter 1 for performing the interest calculations for savings accounts for a bank. That model might best be characterized as a retrospective number-cruncher. It mechanizes some of the drudgery needed to perform the accounting for a savings bank. The model does not involve any concept of probability, even implicitly. In fact, if a bank used such a model to find interest amounts and ending balances, the calculations would be performed at the end of a month or other period, when all of the deposits and withdrawals were known because they had already occurred. A computer program of this sort is simply a numerical aid in performing calculations about events that have already happened; hence, the concept of probability does not enter into such models. As the preceding section explained, the essence of decision trees is that they lay out in a time sequence a series of act nodes and event nodes reflecting a decision problem that must be analyzed in the face of uncertainty. These decision trees have nothing to add to the structuring of problems such as the construction of a savings account calculation program and we will not try to use them for such situations. The payroll program sketched in the preceding chapter is another example of a computer model whose main function is to perform the number work needed in the accounting for events that have already occurred; decision trees would not be useful in structuring that problem, either.

There were problems in the preceding chapter in which decision trees would help, however. We discussed the construction of a pro forma generator to help in decisions about price and promotion for a new product. In that type of situation we are clearly making decisions for an uncertain future. For example, we might feel that our major decisions are the price and the promotion levels and that the main uncertainties in our problem are the price that our main competitor will charge, the overall market size, and the market share we will obtain. We might then structure the problem as shown in the decision tree in Figure 2–8. In that figure, the decision nodes are

**FIGURE 2–8**

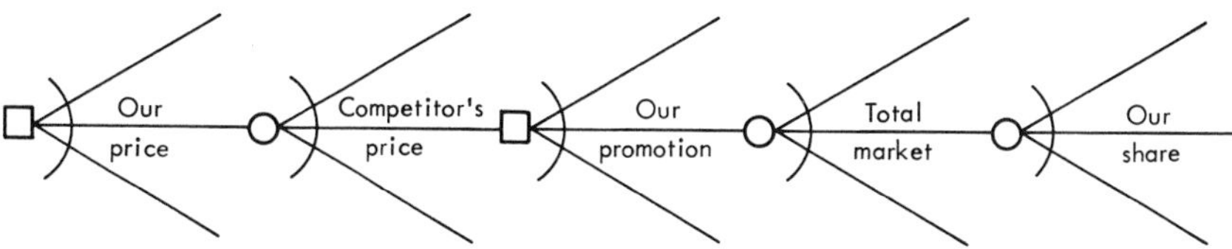


shown as decision fans, reflecting the fact that there are many possible decisions for price and many possible choices for promotion. The tree assumes that we can delay our promotion decision until after we know the competitor's price, but that we must make our decision on price before learning the outcome of any of the uncertainties.

If you now think back to the type of deterministic pro forma generator we might have constructed in the previous chapter and try to relate such a model to the decision tree in Figure 2–8, you will recognize that the deterministic model contains no statement of probabilities. Rather, such a model would accept a complete scenario as input and would then produce a pro forma statement based on that scenario. In the language of decision trees, the deterministic model requires that the user specify a single path through the decision tree, in the form of the input scenario. The model then proceeds to perform numerical calculations to investigate the results of taking that path through the tree. The output describing those results is likely to be an entire pro forma statement. We can think of such a deterministic model as an endpoint calculator for the tree in the problem. The endpoints are described by entire pro formas rather than by single criterion values as they were in decision trees earlier in this chapter.

Even in cases such as this example in which we propose to construct only a deterministic model, it is often useful to constrct a decision tree as one step in structuring the problem. The preceding chapter emphasized the idea that the basic case analysis of a problem is crucial to the successful analysis of the problem and to the construction of any computer aids to help with that analysis. Because decision trees are one formalism for thinking carefully through the different parts of a decision problem, they are often very helpful in the basic problem analysis. Having drawn a decision tree for a large problem, we generally would not attempt to solve or analyze the tree by hand. Rather, in some cases we would construct a simple deterministic model to investigate individual endpoints of the tree, where it would be the job of the model user to specify which endpoints to consider by giving input scenarios. In other cases, we might proceed to try to build computer models to consider probabilities explicitly in some of the ways to be described in the remainder of this chapter and in later chapters.

Before proceeding to discuss methods for building probabilistic simulation models, we now use the context of decision trees for a bit longer in order to present some of the motivations for proceeding to probabilistic models. Decision analysis indicates that in analyzing decision problems under uncertainty we should consider two aspects of different endpoints. First, we must consider the attractiveness or unattractiveness to us of being at various endpoints of a decision tree. Second, we must also consider the likelihood of ever actually reaching each of those endpoints. We would worry considerably less about unattractive outcomes that were extremely unlikely to occur than we would about bad results that had substantial probabilities of happening. When we use a deterministic computer model to help evaluate the results of taking particular paths through a decision tree, we do not provide any quantitative measure of the likelihood of each set of results. The user prepares a set of inputs and is presented with the results corresponding to that scenario; s/he then prepares another set of inputs and receives the corresponding results, and so on. An intelligent user of such a model will weigh the relative probabilities of the different results in the process of arriving at a decision on what actions to take in a problem, but the computer model does not help with that weighing. Rather, we assume that the decision maker somehow judgmentally incorporates the probabilities into the decision process. To do so is not easy. Often, we find that individuals are much more able to provide judgments about individual specific uncertainties or event nodes in a problem than they are able to provide meaningful assessments of the likelihoods of entire scenarios. One argument in favor of building probabilities into a computer model is that doing so allows the user to make judgments about the individual parts of a problem without requiring him or her to judge the likelihoods of entire scenarios. Given sufficient information about the probabilities of the parts, the computer can find the probability of an entire scenario.

Another argument in favor of probabilistic modeling becomes important in large decision problems described by large decision trees. Most real decision problems involve many different parts; further, most of the uncertainties we encounter in real problems are many-valued rather than few-valued. The number of endpoints that must be considered in order to provide useful analyses of such problems is large. In the decision tree in Figure 2–8 there are three event fans shown. Suppose that we decided to approximate each of those event fans by only ten representative values or bracket medians.[5] Suppose, in addition, that we decided to consider only ten possible decisions on price and only ten possible promotion levels. If we then counted the endpoints of the resultant tree, we would find one endpoint for each combination of our price, competitor's price, our promotion, total market, and our market share. We would count $10^5$ or 100,000 endpoints. Moreover, in arriving at an estimate of 100,000 endpoints to consider, we made rather strong simplifying assumptions. Ten representative values for each of our event fans may not be enough. In particular, if we are especially concerned with possible extreme outcomes (such as extremely bad outcomes), we will likely not find 10 values sufficient to approximate the distributions. For the analysis of most decision problems, we would use 25 or 50 values to approximate each event fan. The resultant number of endpoints in the decision tree would increase accordingly.

In some decision trees of moderate complexity, we might decide that there were too many endpoints for hand calculation and analysis of the tree but that a computer program could be constructed to analyze the tree completely, much as we would have analyzed the tree by hand had it been smaller. In other words, we could construct a computer model to consider all endpoints and probabilities in the tree, to average out at event nodes and to fold back at decision nodes. In addition, if we were concerned with risk as well as with expected values, we could have the computer program construct risk profiles for us for different available strategies. Designing a computer program for these purposes would simply amount to specifying in a serial and unambiguous set of steps the instructions needed to perform the types of calculations described in the Appendix for the analysis of decision trees.

In most problems, however, the option of having the computer perform the same calculations we would have performed by hand is not feasible. The discussion of the number of endpoints in Figure 2–8 suggests why. Even in as simple a problem as is diagrammed in that figure, the number of endpoints becomes very large if we include a sufficient number of representative values for each of the fans. In most problems, there are considerably more fans than there are in Figure 2–8, so that the size of the decision problem and the number of endpoints are even larger. While the computer can perform calculations enormously much faster than human analysts can, even the number-crunching capabilities of the computer will be exceeded by the size of many realistic decision trees. Therefore, we must devise some way other than

[5] See the Appendix.

extensive analysis of all end positions and probabilities for the analysis of large trees.

The most common way of handling the problem of dealing with extremely messy decision trees in which we cannot consider each individual endpoint is to consider only a sample of endpoints from the tree. In fact, the mode of using computer models that we discussed in the last chapter is one way of implementing this strategy; in that mode, the human computer user selects endpoints by specifying inputs scenarios and the computer analyzes those endpoints. It is also possible to have the computer select the sample endpoints to be considered, however. Many probabilistic computer models can be thought of as procedures for sampling endpoints of decision trees.

When we design computer programs to select scenarios for analysis, we usually have the computer choose only the portions of the scenarios corresponding to event nodes in the decision tree describing our problem. For the remainder of the scenario, consisting of the actions chosen at act nodes, we usually have the computer-user specify the decisions to take. A set of instructions on how to choose at all of the act nodes in a problem is called a complete *strategy* for the problem. Thus, the usual method of probabilistic computer analysis of decision trees is to have the human computer-user specify a strategy and then to have the computer sample from the distributions for all of the uncertainties in the problem. A specific user-defined strategy is combined with one set of computer-generated outcomes for the event nodes to provide a complete scenario for the problem. The results of that scenario are evaluated by the computer. Then, the computer typically selects other values for the UQs in the problem, combines them with the same user-specified strategy to form another scenario and evaluates the second scenario. The machine proceeds in that way to consider many different scenarios for the same strategy. It then provides the user with a description of the results and then is ready to proceed to consider another strategy. In broad outline, the most common type of probabilistic model is shown schematically in Figure 2–9. There are other approaches to probabilistic modeling, including some in which the computer generates some or all of the strategies to be considered, but the type shown in Figure 2–9 is far more usual and is the type on which we will focus.

Some reflection on the general outline given in Figure 2–9 should suggest the major problems and issues that arise in probabilistic modeling. We must decide what constitutes a strategy in a decision problem, so that the user can specify a complete strategy for computer analysis. We must also instruct the computer on how to construct the event portions of the scenarios. In particular, we must make sure that the resultant scenarios make sense. In the simple problem outline in Figure 2–8, it is very likely that the values of the three UQs are related to one another. If our competitor charges a high price, then our market share is apt to be higher than it would be if the competing price were low, all other things being equal. Somehow, we must incorporate

FIGURE 2–9

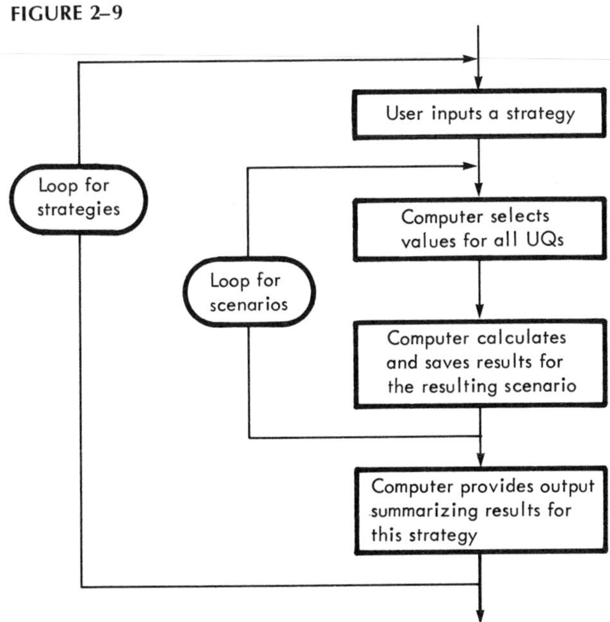


judgments such as this one into the computer procedure for generating scenarios. A third issue arising in probabilistic modeling concerns the evaluation of endpoints. We must decide how to summarize the results of different trips through the decision tree. Further, we must find efficient and effective ways of summarizing for the human computer-user the results of many such trips through the tree. In the next section we begin the discussion of these modeling issues as we consider risk analysis models, one of the most widely used types of probabilistic models.

## IV. RISK ANALYSIS MODELS[6]

In order to introduce risk analysis models, we will consider a very simple example of a decision problem for which such a model is appropriate. Suppose that the management of a firm is trying to decide whether or not to introduce a proposed new product. If it were introduced, initially, the product would sell for $4 per unit. The firm's planning horizon is ten years. Equipment to make the product would cost $10,000. The manager of the firm feels that the sales of the product would be essentially constant over the ten-year period, although the exact sales level which would be achieved is

[6] Important articles in risk analysis are David B. Hertz, "Risk Analysis in Capital Investment," *Harvard Business Review,* January–February 1964, pp. 95–106, and David B. Hertz, "Investment Policies that Pay Off," *Harvard Business Review,* January–February 1968, pp. 96–108.

unknown before introduction. Variable production costs would start at $2 per unit. Selling prices would rise 5 percent a year, while costs would rise at a 7 percent rate. The company would depreciate the new equipment on a straight-line basis over ten years. The product would require working capital equal to 10 percent of sales. The criterion for measuring performance is net present value of after-tax cash flows at the firm's hurdle rate of 15 percent. The manager of the firm has given a probabilistic forecast of the sales level for the new product, in the form of a cumulative distribution function.

In designing a model to help analyze this decision problem, we can start with a decision-tree representation of the situation. Because we have assumed that we know all important factors except sales, the decision tree takes the very simple form shown in Figure 2–10.

**FIGURE 2–10**

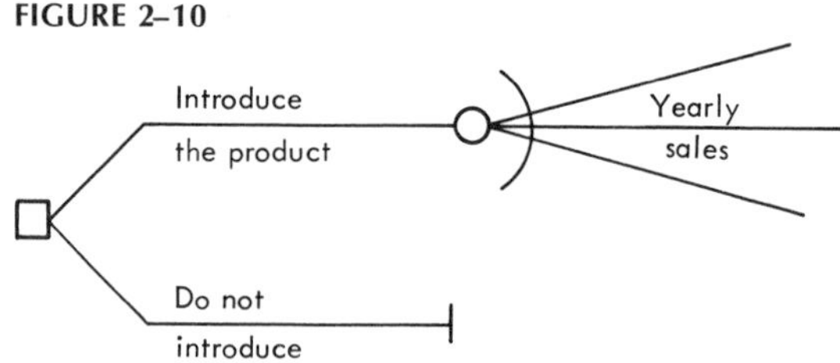


There are really only two major strategies in this problem: one is to introduce the new product and the other is not to introduce it. If we don't introduce, we will wind up with the current status quo. If we do introduce, we face an uncertain future. While this particular problem is too simple to require computer analysis (for there is only one event fan in the problem and, thus, we could simply evaluate each of a representative set of endpoints), we will proceed with the design of a model for illustrative purposes. The model's aim will be to investigate the possible results of the introduction of the product. Referring to the schematic of probabilistic models in Figure 2–9, we find first of all that for our simple new-product problem there is no need to include the outer loop for strategies; the only strategy we have defined, other than the one of doing nothing, is to introduce the product. Thus, the overall design for a model might look like Figure 2–11.

Each trip around the loop in the figure corresponds to one sample trip through the decision tree. Each such trip is called a *trial*.

The next step in our design process might be to fill in more details in the portion of the model represented by the two center boxes in Figure 2–11. We might then obtain the partial block diagram in Figure 2–12.

Next, we might specify more precisely how to calculate the profit, cash flow, and other quantities mentioned above. In addition, it should now be clear that we must initialize the price and cost figures for each scenario or trial, since price should start at $4 and cost at $2. Further, we will need a tax

FIGURE 2–11

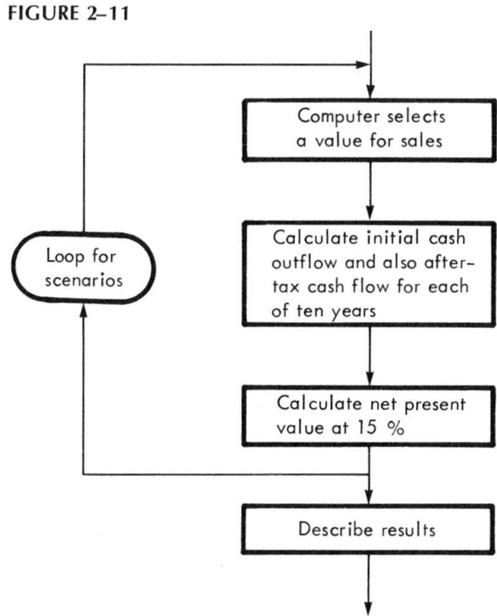


FIGURE 2–12

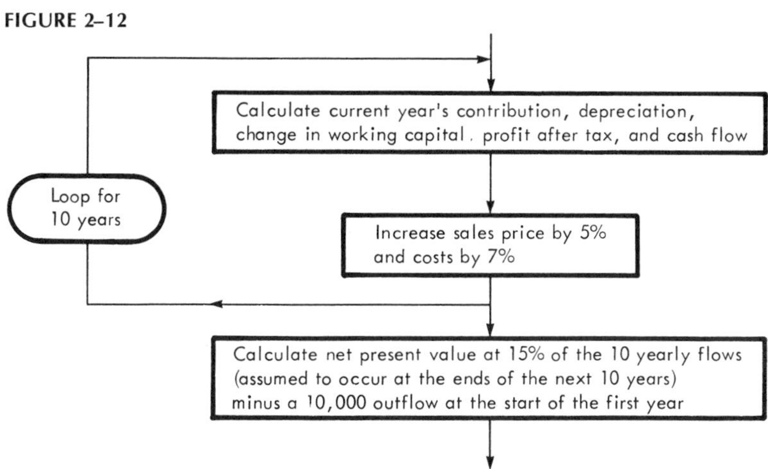


rate (which might be an input or might be assumed in the relationships of the model). Suppose that we decide to make the tax rate and also the salvage value of the equipment after ten years inputs to the model. Proceeding in this way, we can flesh out the sketchy description given in Figure 2–11 to obtain a more complete block diagram. We might arrive at the diagram shown in Figure 2–13.

**FIGURE 2–13**

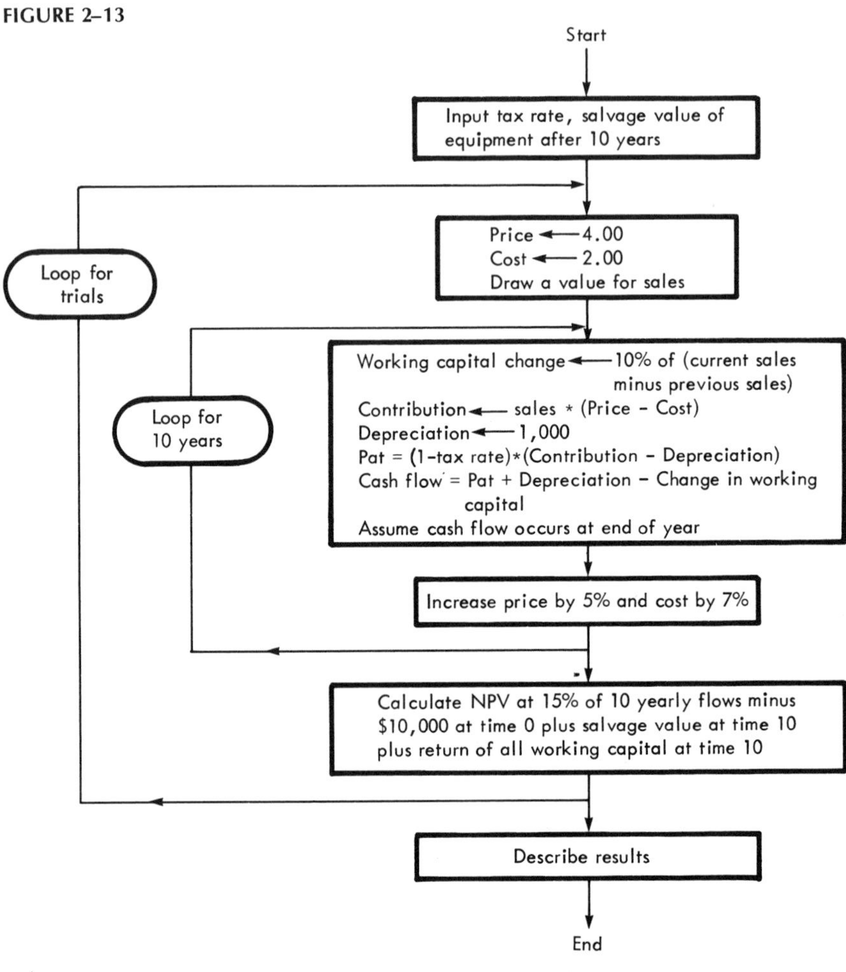


A few more points in this model design should be clarified before we go on to use this model as the basis for a more general discussion of risk analysis models. First, we have not been specific about the way in which the computer is to select a value for yearly sales on each trial. We know that we want the process to accord, in some sense, with the manager's judgments about what sales are likely to be, but we have not yet been precise about what it means for the process to do so. The fan in Figure 2–10 suggests that the manager's assessed distribution for sales is many-valued. In fact, let us assume that we have a cumulative distribution function for yearly sales. We then argue that a selection procedure for sales values is acceptable, in that it agrees with the manager's judgments, if for each range of possible values it is true that: the probability that the procedure will select a value in that range is the same as the probability the manager said should be assigned to values in that range. For example, the manager has said that there is a .1 chance of a value less than or equal to the .1 fractile. Accordingly, our selection procedure should select a value from that range with probability .1. Similarly, the manager has assigned a .1 probability to the values between the .1 and the .2 fractiles; our procedure should have one chance in ten of selecting such a value.

One very useful method of designing a selection procedure to use in drawing values at random in accord with a specified distribution involves the idea of representative values or bracket medians.[7] If we decide to use 50 representative values, for example, we divide the total range of possible values for the UQ described by the distribution into 50 equally likely ranges. The range between the .00 and .02 fractiles is one such range, that between the .02 and .04 fractiles is another, that between the .04 and .06 fractiles is a third, and so on. We now identify one representative value for each range; a good candidate is the center of the range, in a probability sense. Thus, we would take the .01 fractile for the first range, the .03 fractile for the representative of the second range, and so on. As will be explained further in the next section, computers generally have included in their libraries of subprograms algorithms for selecting one of a set of different numbers at random, where each number is to be assigned the same chance of selection. In our selection procedure with 50 representative values, we would ask the computer to select at random a number between 1 and 50, inclusive. We would use that number to decide which of our 50 ranges to use, and we would select the UQ value associated with that range. If, for example, the random number indicated 2, we would select the representative of the second range (or the .03 fractile of the original distribution). Notice what we have done with this procedure. The computer has the capability to select one of a set of numbers at random, provided that it is just as likely to select one as it is to select another of those values. Our distribution function for the UQ in the problem assigned different probabilities to different values of the UQ. We used fractiles of the distribution to help us define equally likely ranges of values of the UQ, we defined a single representative for each such range, and we could then use the random number capabilities of the machine to select one representative value. The resulting selection process will accord with the beliefs of the decision maker, as expressed by the original distribution. (The more mechanical details of this procedure, including the question of how the computer obtains random numbers and how we convey to it the representative values to be used, will be covered in the next section.)

The reader may at this point be wondering why we don't simply use all representative values of the UQ in the problem. In the simple problem under discussion, we could do so, and, in fact, we could do all of the necessary

[7] See the Appendix.

calculations by hand without excessive pain. Recall, however, that this simple problem is being used for illustrative purposes and that in reality probabilistic models are used when there are simply too many endpoints to consider each one. In such problems, we must sample from the representative values because we cannot consider them all.

A second point in the diagram that requires some further discussion concerns the last box in the diagram, in which the model is supposed to provide useful output describing the results of the new product introduction. The way the example problem was structured, there was only one number used to describe the results of each trial; the single criterion was the net present value at 15 percent of the after-tax cash flows. At the end of the loop for trials, the computer will have calculated and kept one such number per scenario. If we told it to consider 100 different scenarios, it would have 100 net present values. Because the selection procedure for the uncertainty in the problem, as sketched above, gives representative scenarios (or scenarios that accord with the manager's judgments), the resulting net present values can be considered representative results, in light of the manager's beliefs. In fact, it is useful to think of those values as describing a distribution of possible results. Each of the individual values constitutes $^{1}/_{100}$ of our results; hence, we say each value has a frequency of .01. These frequency values are analogous to probability mass values. In providing output for the user of the model, we can use many of the techniques available for describing probability distributions. We are likely to want to see the mean and standard deviation of the individual values. In addition, we can think of the computer's constructing a cumulative curve with the values. If we have 100 output results (from 100 trials), we first have the machine sort them into increasing order. We then construct (or at least think of constructing) a graph in which we plot the individual values against the cumulative frequencies or, in other words, the portions of our set of values which did not exceed those individual values. Thus, the smallest of the results would have a cumulative frequency of .01, the next smallest would have .02, and so on. A plot of the cumulative frequency curve would look something like Figure 2–14. Notice that the graph in that figure is very like the smooth cumulative distribution curve, giving a risk profile, in Figure 2–7. The only difference is that the cumulative frequency curve is not entirely smooth. In practice, when we consider many different scenarios, we ignore the slight lack of smoothness and plot the cumulative frequency curve as if it were smooth. The curve would be called a risk profile, giving the distribution of results (in this case, net present values at 15 percent for the specified strategy of introducing the new product.)

In addition to a graph such as that in Figure 2–14, we can provide summary information based on the graph. In particular, we are often interested in particular fractiles of the distribution. We might, for example, print the .01; .1; .25; .5; .75; .9; and .99 fractiles to give the user an idea of the nature of the distribution. (A few more technical details about handling

**FIGURE 2–14**

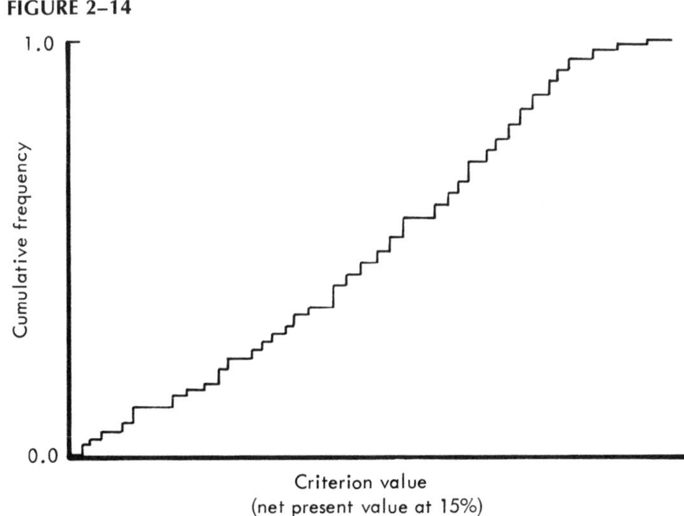


output distributions within computers will be discussed in the following section.)

In moving from this simple example of a probabilistic model to a more general consideration of risk analysis, we start by describing the basic operation of the model we have just designed in a slightly different way. The cash flow calculations at the heart of the model are really just like the pro forma calculations that we might have defined for a deterministic analyzer for this problem. Hence, we might describe this model as a deterministic pro forma generator embedded in a loop which draws scenarios at random. The structure is shown in Figure 2–15. In fact, that figure can be considered a general schematic of a risk analysis model. It shows a deterministic pro forma generator whose input scenarios are selected by the computer, in accord with distributions provided by the user.

While the design in Figure 2–15 is typical of most risk analysis models actually built, for many problems it could be improved. In particular, notice that the design makes the same assumption about strategies that we made in analyzing the simple example problem earlier in this section. It assumes that the only strategy to be analyzed is one of introducing the product, carrying out the project, or, in general, performing whatever actions are being considered. As a result, there is no loop shown in the figure for considering various possible strategies. In fact, however, even in the very simple example described earlier, real strategies are apt to be a bit more complicated. If the results of the introduction are bad enough in the first year or two, most firms would at least consider dropping the product. They would not automatically proceed with a losing product for a full ten years. It might therefore be better for us to define strategy in the model to include a specification of a cut-off

FIGURE 2–15

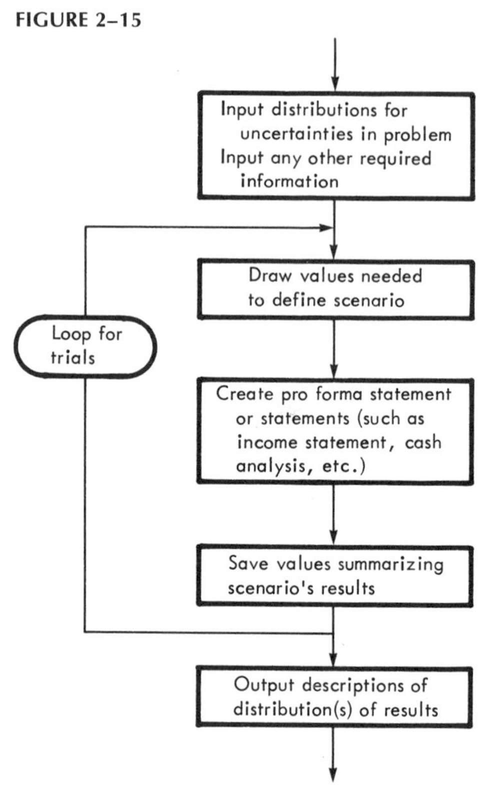


level of earnings in the first year (or years). If earnings were lower than the cutoff, the model would discontinue the project. We would have to add to the model specification instructions on what financial values to assign upon such liquidation. If we made this change in the model in Figure 2–13, we would have to add a portion to the model showing the input of a strategy. The main portion of the model would then construct a distribution of results if that strategy were followed; the distribution would be called a risk profile for the particular strategy. Such cutoff or stopping rules could be used to improve many risk analysis models in practice.

The portion of Figure 2–15 in which values are drawn on each trial to define a scenario is a very simple statement covering one of the most difficult areas in risk analysis (or any probabilistic) modeling. In the simple model defined earlier in the section, there was only one uncertain value needed per trial. We assumed that only sales level was uncertain; in addition, we assumed that the same sales level would prevail in each of the ten years of our analysis, so that there was only a single figure needed to define a scenario. Most problems, of course, are considerably more complex. In Figure 2–8, for example, there are three event fans shown. Even if our planning horizon is only a single year, we would need three values, drawn from appropriate distributions, to define a scenario. What makes this aspect of risk analysis and other probabilistic modeling so difficult is the fact that in many situations we cannot simply assume that the model will be satisfactory if we draw a value for each uncertainty without considering the values taken by the other UQs. In the problem sketched in Figure 2–8 we cannot simply draw a value for competitor's price from one distribution and then, entirely independently, draw a value for our market share from another distribution. The reason is that our share is related to competitor's price. If we knew the competitor's price we would change our assessment of the likely values for our share. We would generally not be able to determine our share precisely from the competitor's price, but knowledge of that price would reduce somewhat our uncertainty about our own share. If the computer is to draw scenarios for us automatically, it must consider such linkages among the UQs in our problem. Put into technical terms, this point says that the computer must somehow be made to consider the *correlations* or *dependencies* among the uncertain quantities in the problem. If we believe that, other things being equal, a high price from the competitor will lead to a higher share for ourselves, then the process by which the computer draws scenarios should reflect such a relationship. Many risk analysis models in practice do not adequately consider correlations among the uncertainties they model. In fact, the improper definition of strategies and the improper modeling of correlations among uncertainties are probably the most common technical errors in probabilistic models. The correlation issue turns out to be a rather difficult one, and much of the remainder of this chapter, as well as a good portion of the next one, addresses handling it. Before we consider specific methods for considering correlations or dependencies in models, however, we must consider the mechanics of handling and sampling from distributions within computers; that topic is considered in the following section.

Thus, the scenario generation portion of a risk analysis model is more complex than is the corresponding part of a deterministic pro forma generator. In the deterministic models, we envisioned a user providing the computer with complete sensible scenarios. In a risk analysis model, two types of problems arise because the computer is generating the uncertain portions of the scenarios. For one thing, as noted above, the values drawn for the UQs must be related in sensible ways. The relationships are not provided by the judgment and intuition of the user in constructing each individual scenario, as they would be in a deterministic model. Instead, they must be specified in model rules. The second problem, that with strategy specification, stems from the fact that the computer will analyze many different scenarios and then provide only a summary of the results. In a deterministic model, the user would likely be provided with an entire pro forma statement for each input scenario. If the model simply ran the figures out for ten years, there would be little problem, even if the results were consistently bad. The human user would take one look at the bad results and would conclude that, faced with one or two years that bad, the firm would have discontinued the project. The reason that we were led to incorporate a cutoff level for results in the probabilistic model is that the computer will be generating and then summarizing the results for each trial automatically, without human intervention and examination of each complete set of results. We do not want an unrealistically bad case to distort the summary picture presented to us.

In fact, because the computer will run through a large number of trials automatically in a risk analysis model, we must give some additional attention to the design of the output portion of the model. In the deterministic pro forma generators of the previous chapter, we thought it perfectly reasonable to output a pro forma statement for each input scenario. A user who considered 20 or 30 different scenarios would have to input each scenario separately and would receive an output statement corresponding to each set of inputs. In the risk analysis models of Figures 2–13 or 2–15, there is available all the information needed to construct a pro forma statement for each scenario. It is extremely unlikely, however, that we would ever want to do so. If the model considered only 100 trials, for example, we would bury the user in 100 pro forma statements. Moreover, those statements would correspond to scenarios drawn by the computer rather than to scenarios selected by the user as being particularly interesting. If we were analyzing a larger problem and considered 1,000 trials instead of 100, the option of outputting a full pro forma for each scenario would become ludicrous. Instead, we need to select a small number of values summarizing the information for each trial. In the example modeled above we used only net present value as the summary of each set of results. In another problem we might elect to save net present value, maximum yearly cash requirement, and market share as the three summary measures for each trial. The output portion of the model could then provide descriptions of the distributions for each of these three summaries. Thus, in going from a deterministic model to a probabilistic one, we facilitate the consideration of larger numbers of scenarios, because much of those scenarios will be drawn by the computer from relevant probability distributions. In doing so, however, we must be careful about designing the output portion of the model. We should save information on the important summaries of each trial and give the user access to each of the resultant distributions. We should not, however, make the volume of output unmanageable.

## V. HANDLING PROBABILITIES

Before we proceed with the discussion of difficult technical issues such as dependencies, we now turn to consider more basic questions of how computers can be instructed to deal with probabilities. In this section we first address the questions of how procedures for handling probabilities can be expressed in unambiguous sets of instructions that would be clear to people; in the later part of the section we discuss a few additional considerations that arise in implementing such algorithms on computers.

For the initial discussion in this section, as an example of structuring and conducting simulation studies, we will consider the following very simple example (which is really too simple to require simulation but which will serve nonetheless as an illustration):

> A manufacturer has just received a rush order from an important customer. The manufacturer is anxious to fill the order quickly and is worrying about a particular component needed for making the ordered parts. S/he is expecting an order of 1,000 components in three days, well in time for use. A normal batch of these components contains many rejects. The probability distribution of good parts in a batch of 1,000 is shown in Figure 2–16. Reordering from

**FIGURE 2–16**

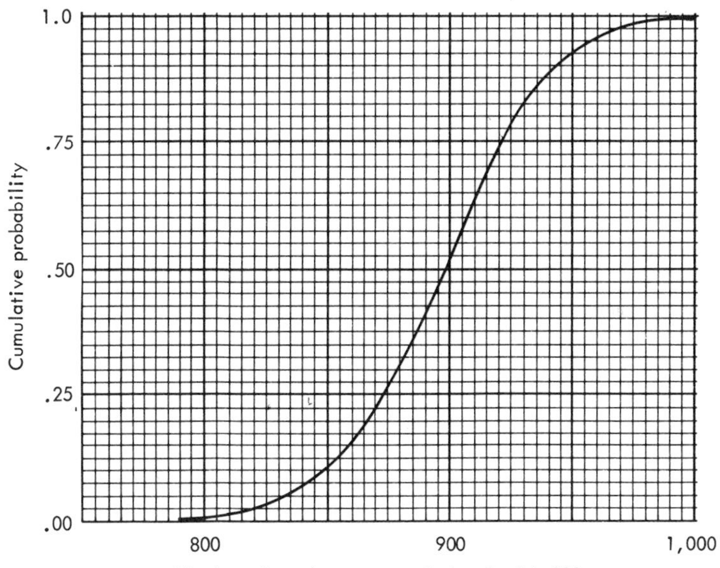


> normal channels in time for use on the rush job will be impossible and the manufacturer is worried about the possibility that s/he will have fewer than the 900 components needed for the job. Consequently s/he is considering ordering more components from a supplier who provides more reliable parts at higher prices. The manufacturer will have to pay $50 for each component ordered from the alternate supplier. The fraction of good components obtained in a batch from that supplier has the probability distribution shown in Figure 2–17.
>
> The manufacturer faces the additional problem that the delivery time for the more reliable parts is uncertain. S/he has assigned the probability mass function given in Table 2–7 to the number of working days until the parts are delivered if

FIGURE 2–17

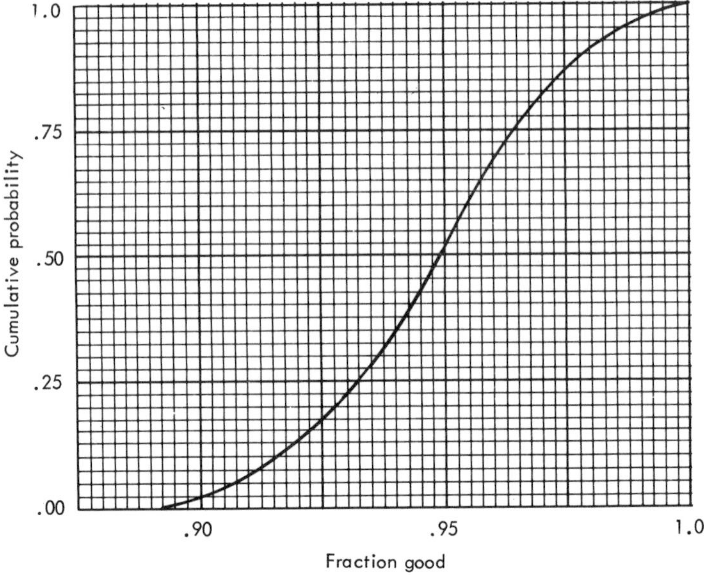


they are ordered now. The parts will be required in the production process at the end of four working days. If the required 900 good parts have not arrived at that time, the manufacturer will hae to have parts reworked in-house to make up the deficiency. Reworking would invole a substantial cost of $150 per item reworked. Finally, the manufacturer has decided to use a criterion of the cost of obtaining the 900 good components; s/he has decided that any extra good components left in inventory should be valued at $35 each.

TABLE 2–7

| *Number of working days* | *Probability* |
|---|---|
| 3 | .25 |
| 4 | .5 |
| 5 | .15 |
| 6 | .10 |

To apply simulation analysis to this problem we first set up a decision tree as shown in Figure 2–18. Next, we decide how to evaluate the endpoints. The decision maker has chosen a cost criterion. Hence we can figure the costs at any endpoint:

FIGURE 2–18

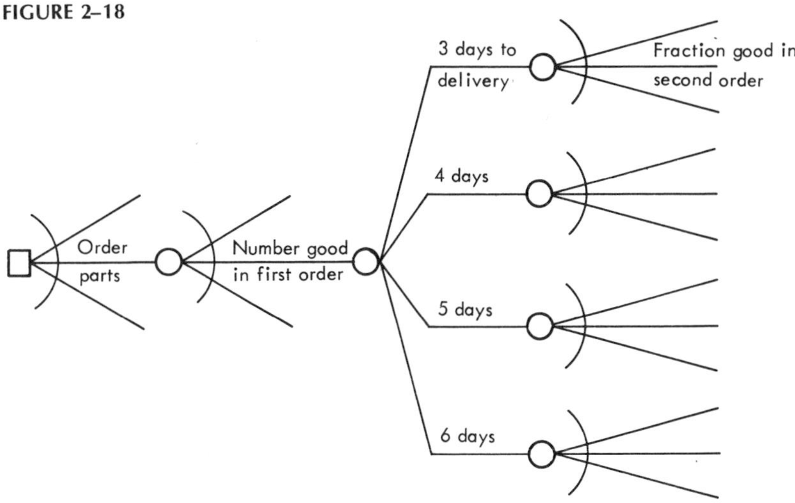


1. There is a $50 cost for each item ordered now.
2. Once the total number of good items available at the end of day 4 is known we can calculate the extra reworking cost of $150 for each item (if any) short (of 900).
3. Extra good components are worth $35 each; we can subtract $35 from the total cost figure for each extra good component.

A block diagram of a Monte Carlo (or probabilistic) simulation model to analyze this problem is shown in outline in Figure 2–19.

The model shown in Figure 2–19 is not the same type of pro forma–based model discussed in the previous section and described in Figure 2–15. It does, however, follow the general outline for probabilistic simulation models given in Figure 2–9. In order to complete the algorithm in Figure 2–19, we must fill in a few more details. We must specify how many trials the model should conduct; perhaps 1,000 would be a reasonable choice. We must also give a bit more detail in the output box. For example, we could instruct the computer to calculate the mean and standard deviation of the cost figures (and provide details saying how to do so). We might also request the computer to sort the cost figures into increasing order and then to output the 1st, 10th, 50th, 100th, 200th, 300th, 400th, 500th, 600th, 700th, 800th, 900th, 950th, 990th, and last of those values, to give us a good idea of what the output distribution would look like.

Finally, we must specify the procedure to be used in selecting values for each trial from the distributions in Figures 2–16 and 2–17 and in Table 2–7. In order to devise a procedure for random selection from a specified probability distribution, we use what is called a *sequence of random numbers*. In

**FIGURE 2–19**

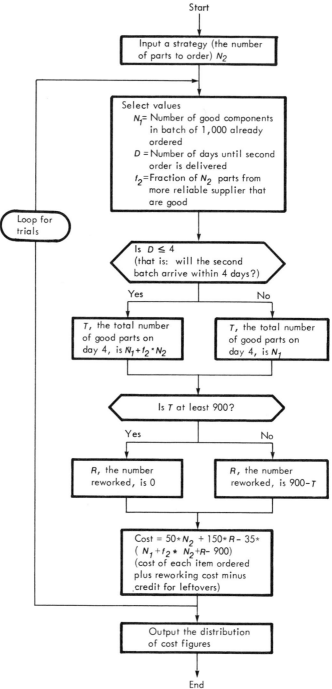

Start

Input a strategy (the number of parts to order) $N_2$

Select values
$N_1$ = Number of good components in batch of 1,000 already ordered
$D$ = Number of days until second order is delivered
$f_2$ = Fraction of $N_2$ parts from more reliable supplier that are good

Loop for trials

Is $D \leq 4$
(that is: will the second batch arrive within 4 days?)

Yes: $T$, the total number of good parts on day 4, is $N_1 + f_2 * N_2$

No: $T$, the total number of good parts on day 4, is $N_1$

Is $T$ at least 900?

Yes: $R$, the number reworked, is 0

No: $R$, the number reworked, is $900 - T$

Cost = $50 * N_2 + 150 * R - 35 * (N_1 + f_2 * N_2 + R - 900)$
(cost of each item ordered plus reworking cost minus credit for leftovers)

Output the distribution of cost figures

End

particular, we will consider sequences of random numbers in which each number is between 0 and 1.0; random sequences within those limits are the most common types of random number sequences on computers. Most people have intuitive notions of random sequences that involve the concepts of repetition and chance. For example, if we rolled a single die repeatedly, and if each roll were fair and the die were fair to begin with, we might consider the results of the rolls to be a random sequence, each member of which was either 1, 2, 3, 4, 5, or 6. Perhaps an even better example of sequences that we would consider random would come from radioactive decay in nature. If we set up a scintillation counter to monitor the emissions of particles from some radioactive material, the resultant counts could be converted into a random sequence of numbers.

When we are presented with a very long sequence of numbers and asked to decide whether that sequence should be considered random, however, we must use some concept of randomness different fron such intuitive notions. In defining such a concept and devising tests for randomness, we ask whether or not there are discernible patterns in the sequence. For example, we ask whether members of the range of values from 0.0 to 0.1 are exactly as likely to occur in the sequence as are members of the range of values from 0.1 to 0.2, and whether the range from 0.2 to 0.3 is also equally likely, and so on. If we have a sufficiently long sequence of numbers (perhaps an infinitely long one) then exactly $1/10$ of the numbers should come from the range from 0.0 to 0.1, exactly $1/10$ should be betewen 0.1 and 0.2, and so on. One part of the definition of randomness that we will use requires this condition. This single condition is not sufficient, however; for example, the sequence .05, .15, .25, .35, .45, .55, .65, .75, .85, .95, .05, .15, .25, .35, .45, .55, .65, .75, .85, .95, .05, .15, .25, .35, .45, .55, .65, .75, .85, .95, .05, .15, .25, .35, .45, .55, . . . satisfies that condition; yet it is hardly random. Thus, we expand our definition in two ways. For one thing, we want the sequence to include many different fractions. Therefore, we require for every subrange of length $f$ in the total interval between 0.0 and 0.1, that essentially a fraction $f$ of an infinitely long sequence come from that range in order for the sequence to be considered random. Similarly, we wish to rule out regular patterns such as that in the sequence given above. To do so, we require that for any subsequence that can be defined from the original sequence without involving in its definition the values taken by the sequence, we find that the subsequence satisfies the rules for a random sequence. What this rather awkward definition means is the following. We can define a subsequence consisting of the first, eleventh, twenty-first, thirty-first, and, in general, every tenth member of the original sequence in a way that allows someone to identify the members of the subsequence by their positions in the original sequence rather than by their values; therefore, the subsequence so defined is required to be random. On the other hand, the subsequence defined as all numbers in the original sequence between 0.0 and 0.1 cannot be identified without examining the values from the original sequence, as opposed to just their positions. Hence, such a subsequence need not (and, in fact, cannot) be random. When we consider how to determine randomness on an operational basis in a sequence of finite rather than infinite length, there are a few complications introduced, but the flavor of the above discussion carries over. Basically, a sequence is random if all subranges of the same length in the allowable range are equally likely to occur and if there is not a regular pattern in the sequence or in any of the subsequences that can be defined on the basis of position alone. We will return briefly later on to the question of how computers, which are deterministic machines by nature, can give us random numbers. For the time being, however, we will assume that we have available a sequence of random numbers between 0.0 and 1.0.[8]

In defining procedures for use in selecting values from distributions, we will use a sequence of random fractions. We will consider two procedures, one for distributions of few-valued UQs and the other for distributions representing many-valued uncertainties. First, consider the few-valued UQ in Table 2–7 for number of days to delivery. In using random numbers to select paths at event nodes in trials of a simulation model, we must be sure that we can expect to select paths with the same probabilities that the decision maker assigns to the outcomes represented by those paths. For days to delivery, we should select the outcome 3 days with probability .25, the outcome 4 days with probability .5, etc. To set up a procedure for selecting a value for days to delivery, we must set up some way of drawing random numbers from our sequence and assocating .25 of the numbers with 3 days, and so forth. Recall that the fraction of values in our sequence that lie in a subrange (of the total range from 0.0 to 1.0) of length $f$ is just that fraction $f$. For example, the chance of a value between .25 and .6 is the length of the subrange or .35. Therefore, all we need to do is to set up a rule associating numbers in one subrange of length .25 with 3 days, those in another separate subrange of length .5 with 4 days, and so on. One possible assignment procedure is shown in Table 2–8.

**TABLE 2–8**

| *Number of working days* | *Probability* | *Random numbers* |
|---|---|---|
| 3 . . . . . . . . . . . | .25 | Less than .25 |
| 4 . . . . . . . . . . . | .5 | At least .25 but less than .75 |
| 5 . . . . . . . . . . . | .15 | At least .75 but less than .9 |
| 6 . . . . . . . . . . . | .10 | At least .9 |

[8] For an excellent, more technical, discussion of pseudorandom numbers see Donald E. Knuth, *The Art of Computer Programming, Volume 2: Semi-Numerical Algorithms* (Reading, Mass.: Addison-Wesley, 1969).

The instructions for selecting a value from the distribution in Table 2–7 then become: take the next value from the sequence of random numbers, and identify the range, from among those listed in Table 2–8, containing that random number. The days to delivery for the current trial is the number of days listed next to the identified subrange in Table 2–8. This procedure generalizes to handle any few-valued uncertainty. We set up a correspondence between values of the UQ and subranges of the range between 0 and 1. Assuming, as we have been, that we have available a sequence of random numbers, the selection procedure is to define a value of the UQ by taking the next random number and to assign to the UQ whichever of its values is associated with the subrange containing that particular number from the random sequence.

For continuous or many-valued uncertainties we use a different procedure for choosing paths at event nodes. For such uncertainties we use random numbers to select fractiles from the cumulative distributions for the UQs. For example, consider the selection of a value from the distribution in Figure 2–16 for the number of good components in the first order. We take the next random number from our sequence; suppose that number is .58, to two decimal places. We would then read the .58 fractile from the distribution, finding 906 as the value. This value is assigned to the number of good parts and, in our trial, or trip through the decision tree, we would follow the path for 906 good parts from the corresponding event fan.

To see why this sampling procedure works consider the following: For a particular event fan (such as number good in the first batch) consider 100 bracket medians to represent the quantity. Recall that we defined bracket medians in such a way that each was the representative of an equally likely range of values for the UQ. The 100 bracket medians correspond, strictly speaking, to the .005, .015, .025, . . . , .985, and .995 fractiles of the UQ. For simplicity (and because there is very little difference between the .000 and the .005 fractiles or between the .250 and the .255) we use the .00, .01, .02, . . . , .98, and .99 fractiles instead of the true bracket medians. These fractiles are taken as representatives of equally like ranges of the UQ. Hence, we want a sampling procedure which is equally likely to select any one of these fractiles. Because all two-place decimal fractions are equally likely in the random sequence, if we use such a fraction to select one of these 100 fractiles (which are almost bracket medians) we will select these values with equal probabilities (and we will be sampling the UQ in accord with its probability distribution).

To conclude the discussion of the model described in Figure 2–19, we can consider how that model would operate on a few trials. We begin by choosing a strategy for the model to consider. Suppose we identify the strategy of ordering 20 parts now. (This decision is in fact a strategy; it tells us what to do at each decision node in the tree. In more complicated problems strategies can be much more complicated and can often involve instructions contingent on events which have occurred earlier in the tree.)

We next proceed to conduct trials and to collect results for that strategy. Suppose that our first three random numbers are .45, .29, and .67. We take the .45 fractile of the first UQ to find out that there are 895 good components in the first batch. The .29 is translated to give four workings days until delivery of the second batch; thus, that batch will arrive in time to be useful.

The .67 fractile of the fraction-good distribution tells us that the second batch has .958 good or (20)(.958) = 19 good parts. There are then 895 + 19 = 914 good parts in all. Thus, for the first trial of the strategy order 20 we find costs of 50(20) or $1,000 for ordering the second batch and a total of 914 good parts. Therefore, the manufacturer must rework no parts (for a cost of $0). The cost for ordering the second batch and for reworking is $1,000. There are 14 extra good parts, each of which is a $35 credit against costs. Total cost is thus $1,000 − 490 = $510. We save this result of the first trial.

We now use three more random numbers to take another trip through the tree (another trial). If the numbers are .22, .80, and .95, the fractiles are 870 good parts in the first batch and .985 good of the 20 (or 20 good components) in the second. Unfortunately, however, the second batch arrives after five working days, and is not available for use on the rush order. Therefore, 30 items (900 − 870) must be reworked, even though 20 good parts will be in inventory after the second order arrives. Total costs for this trial are $1,000 for the 20 items plus 150(30) = 4,500 for reworking minus 20(35) = 700 for extra components, for a total of $4,800. Proceeding in this way we can conduct many trials and build up a distribution for the costs associated with ordering 20 items from the more reliable manufacturer.

Finally, we can use an entirely analogous procedure to investigate (through many simulation trials) other strategies, such as ordering 30 or ordering 50. The results will be a set of probability distributions for costs— one distribution for each strategy. The simulation model does not select among these strategies (and their accompanying distributions); it merely summarizes the probabilistic results of the choices. The manager must then select one of the strategies for adoption.

Two important technical points can be made on the basis of this example problem. The first concerns the relationship among the different values drawn for the three uncertainties on any one trial. We assumed implicitly in the procedures given above that there was no relationship among those three values. In other words, we drew a value for the number of days until delivery from the distribution for that uncertainty without any consideration of what fraction of good components we drew for the first batch on that trial. Similarly, we assumed there was no relationship between the days to delivery and the fraction good from the more reliable supplier. In technical probability terms, we say that we have assumed that the three uncertain quantities are *independent* of one another. The distribution we would assign to any one of them conditional on (with knowledge of) a particular value for any of the others is exactly the same distribution we would have assigned to the first UQ without any such knowledge of the values of the others. Such independence is not always an appropriate assumption; as we noted earlier, dependencies are very common in probabilistic modeling and they are often difficult to handle satisfactorily. Our current procedures assume no dependencies.

The second technical point concerns a concept called *blocking*. The description of how we would operate the model suggests that we would consider, in turn, each of at least several possible strategies. For each strategy we would have the model consider many different trials, with each trial defined by a set of values for all of the UQs in the problem. When we proceeded to compare the output distributions for the different strategies, we might worry that one strategy looked better than another because it had the "luck" to be assigned a particularly favorable set of scenarios on its trials. Strictly speaking, if we ran a very large number of trials for each strategy, we would not have to worry about one strategy's looking good because of the luck of the draw rather than because it really was good. In actual modeling, however, we generally do not know precisely how many trials is enough. Further, while each trial for our simple example problem in this section is very easy to carry out and would require very little computer time, for many real models trials are considerably more complicated and we do not have the computer resources available to conduct extremely large numbers of them. Hence, we worry about making efficient use of results obtained by more limited numbers of trials. When we block our runs of a computer model, we require that each strategy we evaluate be subjected to exactly the same luck, in the form of values for the UQs. In other words, the UQ values on the first trial with one strategy are required to be exactly the same as the UQ values on the first trial with the second strategy, and with the third strategy, and so on. One way to achieve this purpose is to select the random numbers only for the trials associated with the first strategy. We use the random numbers to evaluate that strategy and we also save the random numbers, in the same in order in which we use them, for later reuse. In evaluating the next strategy we use this saved sequence of numbers rather than a new set of random values. By blocking the model operation in this way, we ensure that each strategy faces the same outcomes for the uncertain events. Thus, any differences in results for the different strategies can be ascribed to differences in the efficacy of those strategies rather than to differences in luck in the course of the simulation.

To complete this section, we now turn to a few additional points about how the procedures we have just described can be handled within computers. The procedures are well defined, but there are a few details necessary to translate them successfully for machine implementation. It turns out in practice that computer programmers generally have only limited, if any, experience with handling probabilities. For that reason, it is at present advisable for you to be able to specify just how probabilities are to be treated, in even more detail than that given above, even if you are acting as a designer only, with someone else coding your model design.

For few-valued UQs, the procedures above are quite adequate for representing and handling distributions. We generally deal with probability mass functions for such UQs. To input such a distribution to the computer we would simply provide a list of possible values for the UQ, together with a list of the corresponding probabilities. Suppose the values were $v_1, v_2, \ldots, v_{10}$, and the corresponding probabilities were $p_1, p_2, \ldots, p_{10}$. To define a rule for assigning values to the UQ on different trials, based on random numbers, we form the cumulative frequencies $c_1, c_2, \ldots, c_{10}$. These cumulative frequencies are defined as follows:

$$
\begin{aligned}
c_1 &= p_1 \\
c_2 &= p_1 + p_2 \\
c_3 &= p_1 + p_2 + p_3 \\
&\;\;\vdots \\
c_{10} &= p_1 + p_2 + p_3 + p_4 + p_5 + p_6 + p_7 + p_8 + p_9 + p_{10}
\end{aligned}
$$

The assignment rule is then to select a random number, as explained further below. Locate the first of the cumulative frequencies which is larger than the random number. The corresponding value of the UQ is selected for the current trial.

For many-valued UQs a bit more translation is needed because we naturally describe distributions for such UQs in terms of graphs and we draw values by reading fractiles from those graphs. Computers do not deal easily with graphs, so we face a potential problem. The problem is easily solved, however, if we notice that in the procedures described above for taking values from a cumulative distribution function for a continuous UQ we really only dealt with a set of representative values (or bracket medians) for the UQ. The random numbers we drew told us which of the representative values to use on any particular trial. In inputting such distributions to computers and in manipulating the distributions within the machines we can dispense with the graphs, which are more natural for people to use, and we can instead simply deal with lists of representative values. Because such representatives are selected from equally likely ranges, we can assume that each of them has the same probability and we do not have to input a list of probabilities as well as a list of values. Once we have input such a list of values, we use random numbers to select one of them. If we have 100 values, we can take a random fraction, multiply it by 100, and take the representative value whose index or position in the input list is given by the resulting value. (To make this procedure work precisely, we may have to take the next larger integer, so that fractions from 0.00 to .00999 are interpreted as indicating the first representative value, and so forth.) If, instead, we have only 50 representatives, we could multiply the random fractions by 50, take the next larger integer for each resulting product, and use the integer to indicate which representative value to choose.

This procedure for handling many-valued UQs is extremely general and, therefore, it is often an appropriate one to use in modeling. The procedure does, however, require that the user input a rather long list of representative values to define a particular distribution with any precision. In some cases, models use a shortcut for reducing input which is analogous to the idea of functional forms discussed in Chapter 1. The model assumes that the distribution is one of some particular family of analytical distributions. A common example is the normal distribution whose density functions (analogous to probability mass functions for few-valued UQs) are familiar bell-shaped curves. Having assumed a particular family, the model requires as input only enough information from the user to define one individual member of the family. For the normal distribution, only two numbers, the mean and standard deviation, are required. The use of such families of analytic distributions clearly cuts down the amount of input required rather dramatically. The disadvantage of using such a family, however, is that the user may not be aware of all of the implications of having such a choice built into the model. In the normal family, for example, all of the members are symmetric and unimodal. In other words, values near the mean are most likely and values farther and farther from the mean become less and less likely. Moreover, a range of values a particular distance above the mean is exactly as likely as a range of values that same distance below the mean. For many UQs in practice the decision maker believes that such symmetry is not appropriate because values above the mean show more spread than values below the mean, or vice versa. In situations in which it does not seem absolutely safe to assume a particular type or particular types of distributions, the option of requiring the input of lists of representative values is always available as a relatively safer choice.

The discussion above has considered the procedures for describing distributions of results in the output sections of models. If we have a set of values, one from each trial, it is easy to instruct the computer to calculate the mean or the standard deviation of those numbers. In addition, if we have the model sort the numbers into increasing order, it is easy to instruct the machine to output specific ones of those values that are (essentially) specific fractiles of the output distribution.

A final point to consider in implementing the simplest probabilistic models in detail concerns the random numbers that are at the core of the procedures we have devised. Since most computer libraries come complete with what are called random number generators, even programmers do not have to produce code to give random numbers between 0.0 and 1.0. Instead, a coder can call on the random number subroutine to provide the next number in a sequence whenever one is needed. Most of these random number generators are designed to facilitate blocking. Some allow the user to specify a number, called a seed, to help start the generation process. By giving the same seed and requesting the start of a fresh sequence for each strategy, users can accomplish blocking. Other generators always start at the same place in a sequence when a program is first started. For such generators, blocking can be accomplished by requiring that the program be started fresh for each strategy.

Even though we usually do not have to worry about how the random numbers are generated on a computer, it is worth a bit of discussion to explain the process, mainly because it seems unnatural to most people that computers, which are fundamentally deterministic machines, can generate random sequences. In fact, the value of a computer is that it does exactly what it is told. The machine behaves in random fashion only when it is malfunctioning. Yet, we want the computer to generate random sequences of numbers. This apparent contradiction is solved, in computer science, by the definition of what are called pseudorandom sequences. A pseudorandom sequence is a series of numbers that can be calculated by the computer in a well-defined algorithm consisting of a serial, unambiguous, totally explicit, set of instructions. Hence, it is really a deterministic algorithm and the resultant sequence is deterministic to anyone who knows the procedure used to generate it. The clue to the usefulness of such sequences, however, is that they *appear* random to anyone who is not familiar with the particular generation algorithm used. Presented with such a good sequence of pseudorandom numbers, we could apply the various tests of randomness described in this section, and the sequence would pass. Therefore, for modeling purposes we can use the sequence as if it consists of random numbers.

The specific procedures used to generate satisfactory sequences are beyond the scope of this discussion.[9] They depend on the particular characteristics of the computers on which they are used and, especially, on the number of zeros and ones in the representation of a number on those computers. One example of such a procedure that was used in the past involves multiplication of a number by itself. After the multiplication, the middle portion of the result is used as the next pseudorandom number. The middle portion is also used in the next computation, where it is in turn multiplied by itself. The middle portion of the new result is extracted, and so on. The choice of a number to use to start this process depends on the characteristics of the machine being used. (In fact, other procedures are today considered far superior to this one.) It will suffice for our purposes to assume that random number sequences are available as needed and that the procedures for generating them can provide blocking when appropriate.

---

[9] For further details, see Knuth, vol. 2, (*Semi-Numerical Algorithms*).

## VI. MODELING IN STAGES

The preceding discussion most likely seems to suggest that deterministic modeling and probabilistic modeling are alternative ways to tackle the same problem. In practice, however, the two types of models are often successive rather than alternative tools. For a realistically large problem, we may sketch a decision tree of the problem and then have some trouble if we try to build a probabilistic model directly. If the tree contains a large number of event fans, we may find it advisable to include in a probabilistic model an explicit consideration of only the most important uncertainties. Yet, if we try to build a model of a reasonably complicated situation involving uncertainty, we will almost always find that at the start of our modeling effort we are not at all sure which uncertainties are important and should be incorporated explicitly into the model and which uncertain quantities can be treated as if they were known. We can try to follow the principle that we should devote more attention to those parts of the model (and those uncertainties) which have significant impacts on the results of our decisions (however we decide to measure those results). Unfortunately, as a rule, we do not understand the problem thoroughly enough at the start of model-building to be able to guess which uncertainties fit this description. In fact, often one of the most important results of the modeling effort is to give a better understanding of the relative importance of the different uncertainties in the problem. Consequently, it is often unwise to try to design a single model incorporating all of the most important aspects of a problem. Instead, it is often preferable to build a sequence of models, with each model incorporating the insights which have been gained from building and experimenting with the previous versions.

Often, the first step in modeling is to build a simple deterministic model of a problem, a model which does not consider the uncertainties at all. For example, if we are studying the possible introduction of a new product, we might build a deterministic pro forma generator which accepted as inputs values for yearly sales, selling prices, costs, and other relevant factors. The model would assume that those input values were known with certainty and would run out a series of pro formas on the basis of the inputs. You will recognize this first step in modeling as one which is often taken in analyzing business decisions. Often, managers investigate the results of possible decisions under what they consider the most likely values of the various uncertainties in the problem. What differentiates the approach described here from such most-likely-outcome analysis is that we suggest using the deterministic analysis as a first step only. (Actual analyses too often stop with that first step.)

The second step in the modeling process would be to perform sensitivity analysis on some of the input values which were assumed to be known with certainty in the first step. To determine the candidates for sensitivity analysis, we should ask ourselves the following questions:

1. Which of the values that were assumed known in the first version of the model are in fact uncertain? In practice, almost any number is at least somewhat uncertain. For example, Congress might change the corporate tax law and so the tax rate we use in our calculations is not absolutely fixed. On the other hand, we do not want to consider every input value as unknown. Therefore, we might better rephrase this question to ask which of the many values assumed in the initial deterministic model are marked by a significant degree of uncertainty in our judgment. On the basis of that criterion, we would very likely ignore uncertainty about the tax rate but not ignore uncertainty about the sales which our new product would achieve.

2. For which of the uncertainties identified in the first step is it true that the actual value assumed by that uncertain quantity has a significant impact on the results of the possible decisions? If, for example, we measure the results of the new-product introduction by the net present value (at 12 percent) of the after-tax cash flows from the project over the next ten years, then we would ask ourselves at this step which uncertainties had a significant impact on the net present value results and which uncertainties were not as important. To answer this second question, we will often want to vary one of the uncertain quantities and rerun the deterministic model to see whether the change has made a significant change in the results. We might then try another run to determine the impact of a change in another of the uncertain quantities. As a rule, in this process we would investigate the uncertainties one or perhaps a few at a time; we would not investigate the results of changing all of the uncertainties simultaneously.[10] Hence, this sensitivity analysis stage of the modeling would not explore fully the joint effects of the uncertainties in the model. The sensitivity analysis phase should, on the other hand, give some insight into the effects of the individual uncertainties and, in many cases, might give some ideas for refining the model to consider in more detail the parts of the model which seem important. (For example, we might decide that costs and the growth of costs seem particularly important and so we might redesign the model to consider explicitly several types of costs or different ways of accounting for costs.)

Once we have constructed a deterministic model and used sensitivity analysis to reach some tentative conclusions about which uncertainties are important, we can proceed to build a probabilistic version of the model. Rather than consider all of the many uncertainties which we might have thought of at the start of the modeling process, we can build into the probabilistic version of the model only those uncertainties which we have iden-

[10] Although you might want to consider all combinations of a representative set of values (perhaps 10 or 50) for each uncertainty, the computational effort in such an approach is usually forbidding (and, moreover, it would be difficult to interpret the results of such large numbers of runs with differing individual probabilities of occurrence).

tified as being important. The probabilistic version of the model can then provide probability distributions of the results of following different possible strategies and, thus, information on which to base a choice of strategy. In addition, the probabilistic version can provide insights into the likely values of obtaining additional information on some of the uncertainties in the problem.

The relative emphasis placed on each of the modeling stages in any individual problem situation will in general depend on the nature of the problem. For a situation in which we are constructing a pro forma generator, to be followed by a risk analysis model, we are likely to find it important to spend considerable time on the deterministic model and its output. For one thing, the complete pro forma statements that can be provided by the deterministic model are apt to be understandable and worthwhile. They are also important in checking out or debugging the program. The calculations involved in producing a pro forma statement are complex and it is extremely likely that the program will not work exactly correctly on the first few tries. The user can best decide whether the model is correct in cases in which detailed information on input and output is available; an output pro forma, along with a list of the input assumptions, gives the appropriate level of detail in many problems. In the probabilistic risk analysis model corresponding to such a deterministic pro forma generator, recall that the model saves only a few summary numbers from each trial. It is almost impossible to check out such a program by looking at the probabilistic results alone, without checking some of the pro formas in detail.

In some cases for which a deterministic pro forma generator is the first model, it may well turn out that the deterministic model should also be the last model built, because it has provided sufficient information through its outputs. Suppose, for example, that we try a set of reasonable scenarios in the deterministic model. The different scenarios will surely lead to different detailed results, but in some cases they may all indicate the same decision or decisions as appropriate. For example, if we evaluate a new-product introduction, different scenarios may lead to different levels of financial and market success, but if all really realistic scenarios suggest that our best strategy is to introduce the new product, there is likely little need to proceed to a probabilistic model for considering large numbers of additional scenarios. Only if the few scenarios we study with the deterministic model suggest different strategies should we proceed to build a probabilistic model to help weigh the probabilities of the different possible scenarios to allow us to arrive at a choice of strategy that is appropriate in the face of the uncertain future.

In many other problems, uncertainties are more central in the natural structuring of the problems than they are in the pro forma types of models. For example, consider an inventory control problem. A typical inventory management problem involves decisions on when and how much to order of many different items that are kept in stock. For our discussion here, first consider only one such part or item. In deciding how much and how often to reorder, we must somehow balance several different considerations. On the one hand, there are costs associated with maintaining stock in inventory. Even for nonperishable items, inventory is costly because it ties up the money that has been spent to purchase the inventoried items. On the other hand, too low an inventory level can also be risky because it exposes us to potential stockouts, in which we cannot provide customers with the items they want. Such stockouts may result in loss of the current orders; they may also result in loss of future business because customers may try to find more reliable suppliers. Similarly, there is a trade-off in deciding how often to reorder. Frequent reordering allows us to maintain lower inventory levels and thus to tie up less money in the inventory. On the other hand, less frequent reordering reduces the bother and expense involved in placing an order, arranging for delivery, handling the bill, and similar tasks. Uncertainty lies at the heart of such an inventory problem. If, as is the case in most situations, demand for an inventoried item is uncertain, with more demand at some times than at others, the unevenness in demand requires us to worry more about stockouts than we would if demand were known and predictable. With predictable demand and predictable lead times for the delivery of new items, we could always ensure that we would have enough stock on hand to meet all customer demand. The uncertainty in demand is what causes the potential for stockouts.

If we wanted to build a model to evaluate different inventory strategies, in the form of reorder times and amounts, in detail, then in order to obtain accurate results we would have to build a probabilistic model. Given assessments for the demand UQ, we could test each inventory strategy under many different trials and construct an output distribution or output distributions summarizing the performance of that strategy. Deterministic calculations, based perhaps on the mean demand level, are simply unable to capture the essence of an inventory problem. Such a problem might therefore be considered *inherently probabilistic*.

Yet, although the really accurate modeling of an inventory problem would require the use of probabilities in almost all cases, many real inventory decisions are made without full-blown probabilistic modeling. Moreover, in many situations the decision not to build a full probabilistic model is a wise one. Modeling takes time and effort; even running the resulting program and evaluating the output takes considerable time. Often an inventory manager must run an inventory in which there are a very large number of different parts, no one of which accounts for a very significant part of the business. The prototypical example of this type of inventory is a hardware distributor. Detailed modeling of the thousands of different items is simply not sensible. Instead, it makes considerably more sense to use shortcuts to arrive at stocking decisions efficiently. One such shortcut is the economic order quantity model, in which demand is assumed to be known and constant. Under this clearly unrealistic assumption, the costs of stocking are compared with the costs of reordering to decide how often and how much to reorder.[11] Even though most inventory managers know that the EOQ assumptions do not hold for their problems, some find it a satisfactory approximation which gives the stocking decision on each individual item about the right amount of attention. Another shortcut for solving inventory problems is the critical fractile model. This approach has the advantage that it does explicitly consider the uncertainty in demand. It assumes that the inventory manager faces the same constant cost per unit stocked unnecessarily and that in addition there is one constant per unit cost for each unit that was demanded but not available. These costs are called the cost of overage and the cost of underage, respectively. In addition, the critical fractile model assumes that the manager makes one order per period of analysis. Under these assumptions, the best stocking level for each item can be found through a simple procedure of reading one of the fractiles from the distribution for demand.[12] In problems in which the critical fractile assumptions actually hold, it is of course advisable to apply the model. Even in other situations, however, the model is often used in inventory decisions. Managers often feel that the assumptions are not a bad approximation of reality and that the stocking decisions indicated by the critical fractile model are good enough. Those decisions are very easy to determine and are often made automatically by computer. The alternative method of full probabilistic modeling would in many cases give a more accurate analysis of each stocking decision, but often those decisions are too small and too numerous for the detailed modeling to make sense.

Thus, the nature of the particular problem we are trying to analyze will often be central in our decisions on what kinds of modeling to do. Analytic models such as the critical fractile model are used either when they are completely appropriate, because all of their assumptions hold, or else when they are close enough approximations to reality and the problem at hand does not merit further analysis. Specially designed simulation models are built when the shortcuts do not apply and the problems are important enough to warrant the effort of model construction. We usually begin with deterministic modeling, although the amount of emphasis placed on the deterministic phase will likely depend on the nature of the problem. For

[11] When the unit price is the same regardless of the quantity ordered, the economic order quantity (EOQ), or amount to order at one time, is

$$\sqrt{\frac{2 * (\text{annual usage in units}) * (\text{dollar cost of ordering})}{(\text{cost per item ordered}) * (\text{cost of capital})}}$$

[12] In particular, the model says that the best level of supply is the $C_u/(C_u + C_o)$ fractile of the demand distribution where $C_u$ is the cost of underage and $C_o$ the cost of overage.

inherently probabilistic problems, we may proceed almost immediately to probabilistic modeling. For other problems, we may use a deterministic model extensively and plan to build a probabilistic version only if the runs of the deterministic version have not made it clear what actions we should take.

## VII. MODELING PROBLEMS: STRATEGIES AND DEPENDENCIES

We mentioned earlier in the chapter that perhaps the two most frequent and serious problems in probabilistic modeling concern strategies and dependencies. The problems with strategies arise because in probabilistic modeling the user must be able to specify a complete strategy without knowing the results or outcomes of the uncertainties in the problem. In other words, the strategy statement must be general enough for it to make sense for the computer to apply that statement regardless of the outcomes of the events defining any one trial. In reality, the strategies we follow in decision situations often are at least partially dependent on the outcomes of uncertainties. We might discontinue a new product if first-year sales are not at least half a million units, for example. Or, we might make the amount of money we spend on promotion of a product conditional on the sales results we achieve during the first year. Because in a probabilistic model the computer takes many different trips through the decision tree without user intervention, the strategy input by the user must be a complete set of instructions, or a road map of which way to go at each decision node within the tree. Often, models are designed with insufficient provisions for allowing users to input rich and realistic strategies. There is not really a technical solution to this problem; the best we can do is to emphasize that it is important and that it requires the attention of the model designer who is closely familiar with the real-world problem being modeled. More creative designers and managers will often see more interesting options for actions in any particular decision problem. The argument here should suggest that as far as possible such creativity should also be applied in deciding what will constitute a strategy in a probabilistic model. Designers also have to consider the mechanics of inputting strategies to their models; the user must be able to specify a complete strategy relatively easily in the input portion of the model.

On the topic of dependencies, there are considerably more technical results available to help with the solution of the modeling problem. As suggested earlier, one of the most important and difficult tasks for the decision maker and modeler is to identify the dependencies among the various parts of a problem. Doing so is crucial in probabilistic modeling because the computer will be constructing scenarios through random selection from appropriate probability distributions. Dependencies in the problem must be reflected in dependencies in this selection process. In this section and in much of the next chapter we consider techniques for building dependencies into models. Before we address that topic, however, we first discuss briefly the effects that dependencies can have in models; the introductory discussion should serve as motivation for the discussion of specific techniques that follow.

As an example, suppose that we want to build a risk analysis model for a proposed new-product introduction. To keep the example simple, we assume that the product's life will be exactly five years, that costs and prices are known precisely, that there will be no inflation, and that taxes can safely be ignored; in fact, the only uncertainties we will consider will be the sales levels in each of the five years. Suppose that the contribution on the product will be $1 per unit and that essentially all production costs will be variable. Suppose that the company considering the introduction has a hurdle rate of 12 percent and that we will use net present value at 12 percent of the five yearly contribution figures as our criterion. As a first step, we can depict the problem with a decision diagram as shown in Figure 2–20. The endpoints in that diagram will be net present values of the five-year stream of contributions. Suppose that the company is not willing to act on the basis of expected monetary values alone, and, therefore, that they would like to have a risk profile or distribution of the possible net present values which might occur.

**FIGURE 2–20**

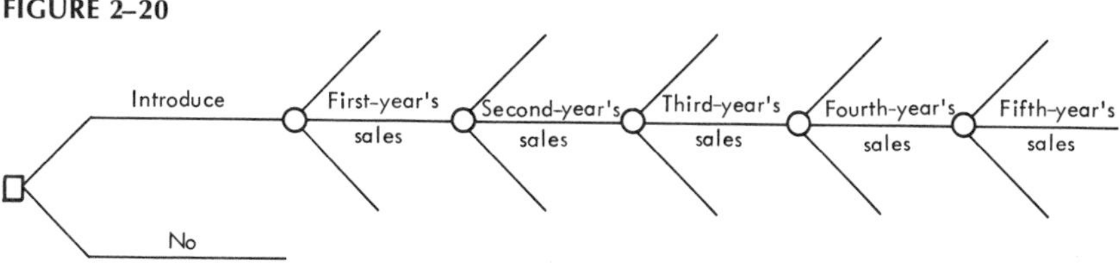


The simplest assumption to make in analyzing this problem is that the sales levels in successive years are independent of one another. If, at the extreme, we assume the same distribution for sales in each of the five years, then we can conduct trials of a simulation model for the problem by drawing five values, independently, from the same distribution for each trial. For example, if we assumed the single distribution for sales given in Figure 2–21 and if on the first trial we drew random numbers of .20, .74, .61, .33, and .11, the five sales figures would be $82,700, $111,000, $103,400, $89,600, and $76,500, and the net present value at the start of the first year of the contribution (at 12 percent and at $1 per item) would be $336,300.

We could repeat the process for a large number of trials and obtain the distribution of net present values given in Figure 2–22 (which was, in fact, obtained from a simulation program for the problem).

If instead we believed that the individual years had different distributions for sales we might still be willing to assume that the values in successive years were independent: that is, we might be willing to assume that regard-

FIGURE 2–21

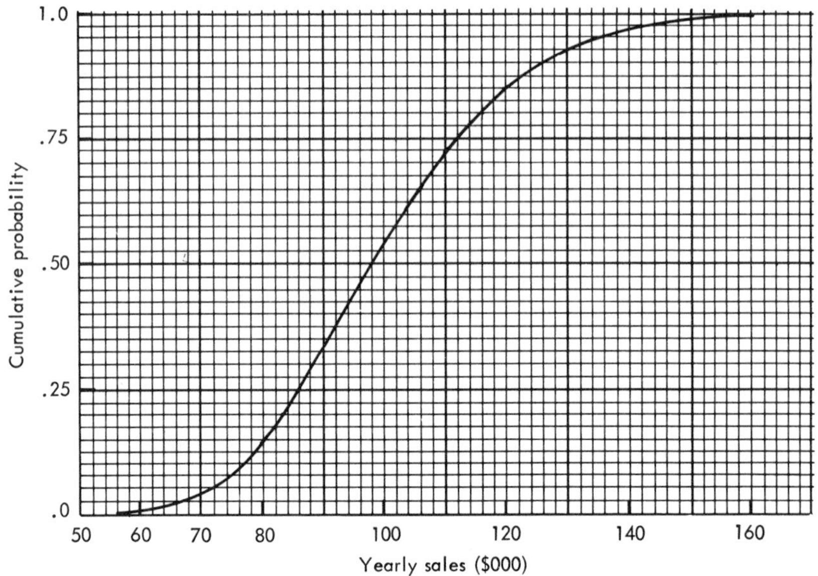


FIGURE 2–22

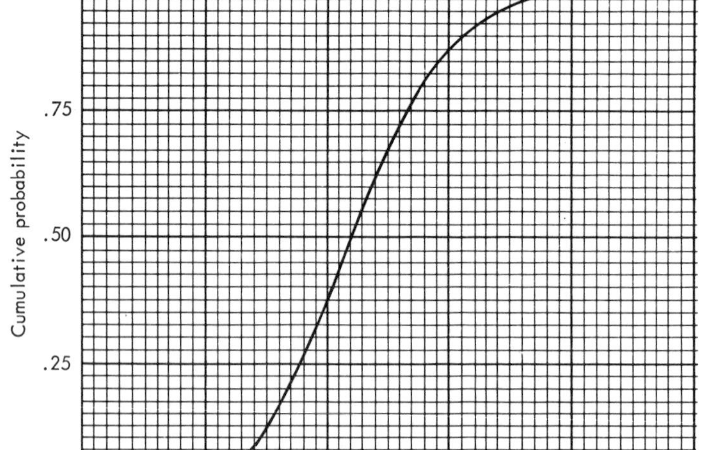

less of whether the first year's sales were high, medium, or low for their distribution, we would not alter our feelings about what the sales might be in the second year, that knowing the second year's sales number (or knowing the sales for the first and second years) would not alter our beliefs about the third year, and so forth. If we were willing to make those rather substantial assumptions, then the problem would be only slightly complicated. We would have to assess five distributions—one for sales in the first year, one for sales in the second year, . . . , and one for sales in the fifth year. Once we had accomplished the assessment task, the trials could be conducted much as were the trials in the first, simpler example with a single distribution: the only difference would be that we would draw one value from each distribution rather than five from a single distribution.

The problem with this approach, of course, is that we often are unwilling to make independence assumptions, at least about what we feel are the most important uncertainties in a model. It may be true in special situations, but it hardly seems likely that sales of a product will be entirely uncorrelated from year to year. At the opposite extreme to the independence assumption is the assumption that sales are completely determined by the first year's value. Under this assumption we would draw only a single sales figure per trial and we would then use that sales level for each of the five years. The distribution for sales in Figure 2–21 and this assumption result in the distribution for net present values shown in Figure 2–23.

Notice that the distribution in Figure 2–23 is considerably more spread out than is the one in Figure 2–22. The reason is that to a large extent in the model behind Figure 2–22 good years are likely to be balanced by bad years (and vice versa) in any five-year sequence. In Figure 2–23, for which only one

**FIGURE 2–23**

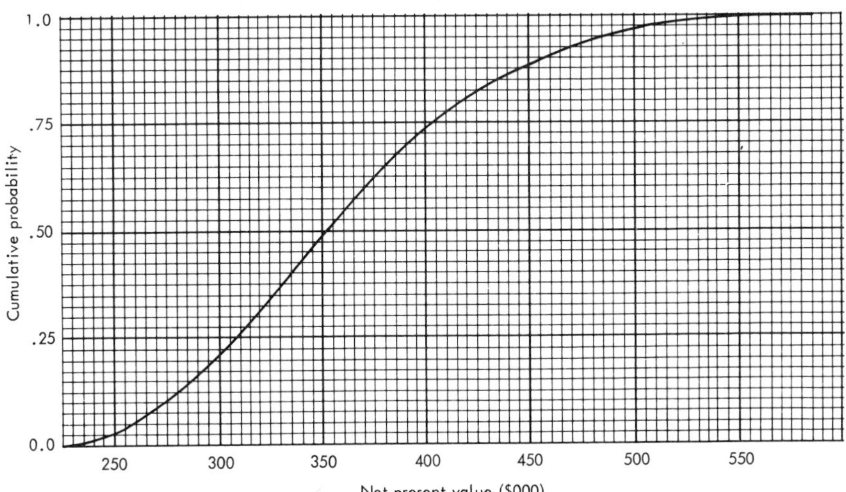

sales value is drawn at random for each five-year sequence, there will be no balance of good and bad years in a single sequence and, consequently, the five-year net present values on different trials will be more spread out.

Again, it was not at all difficult to design a model incorporating the assumption of total interdependence of yearly sales figures. The problem is that this assumption is usually no more satisfactory than was the original independence assumption. In most situations we feel that knowing the sales level in a particular year gives us partial but not complete information on the likely sales level the next year.

One obvious way to attempt to solve this problem of dependencies is to use the concept of conditional probabilities. In other words, we assume that the distribution for the second year's sales should be different for different levels of first year's sales. The second-year distributions should be conditional on the values taken by the first UQ. In the current example, we might take ten representative values (or bracket medians) from the distribution for the sales in the first year. For each bracket median we would assess a distribution of second-year's sales. If the brackets for sales from Figure 2–21 were $71,000; $80,000; $86,000; $91,000; $95,500; $100,500; $106,000; $112,000; $120,000; and $136,000, we might assess the distribution in Figure 2–24A for second-year sales following first-year sales of $71,000 and the distribution in Figure 2–24B for the distribution of sales in the second year following first-year sales of $80,000 . . . .

**FIGURE 2–24A**

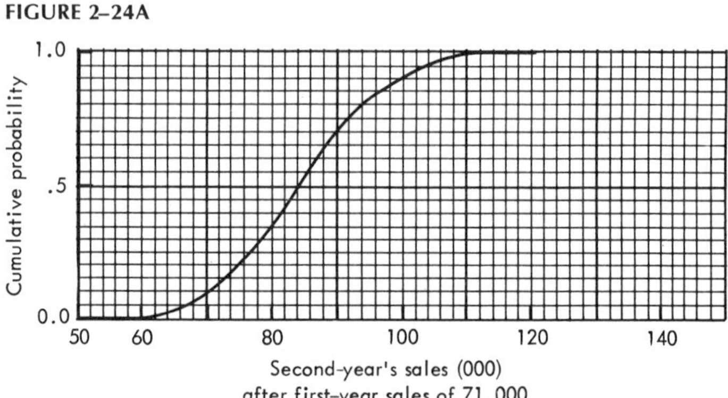


After assessing ten conditional distributions for second-year sales, we could proceed to represent each of those distributions by ten bracket medians and then proceed to assess a conditional distribution for third-year sales for each of those 100 brackets. Continuing in this manner we could in theory (though hardly in practice) assess conditional distributions for the remaining years. This approach might be called the brute force method. It is certainly extremely general in that it allows the user to build many kinds of interrelationships into the models. The problem, of course, is that the as-

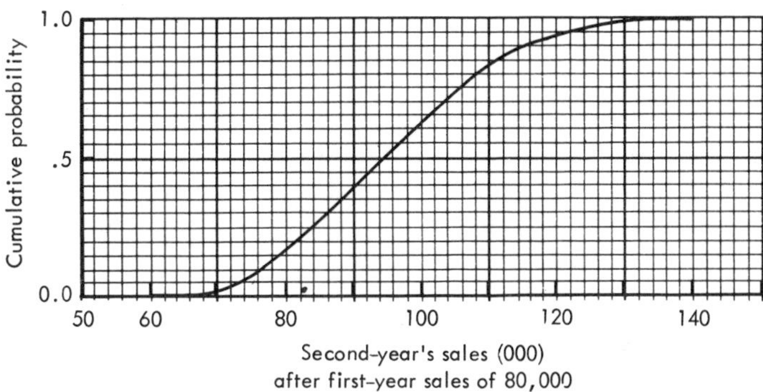


sessment task is not feasible. There are far too many distributions to assess and we would undoubtedly find that we could not even think sensibly about all of those distributions. Hence, the task which we discuss in this book is the problem of building dependencies into models in ways which are sufficiently flexible to be useful but, at the same time, not so difficult to use that they are impractical.

In problems where it is possible to do so, perhaps the easiest way to build interrelationships into a model is to reformulate the uncertainties in the problem in such a way that we are in fact reasonably comfortable in assuming independence. In the risk analysis problem under discussion, we might conceivably be willing to assume that the *sales levels* from year to year are related but that the *changes* in sales from year to year can safely be considered independent. Thus, we might envision a value for first year's sales drawn from the distribution in Figure 2–21 and then four values for sales changes (for the second through the fifth years) drawn independently from the distribution in Figure 2–25. The particular distribution shown in that figure allows only relatively small changes in sales from year to year. We

**FIGURE 2–25**

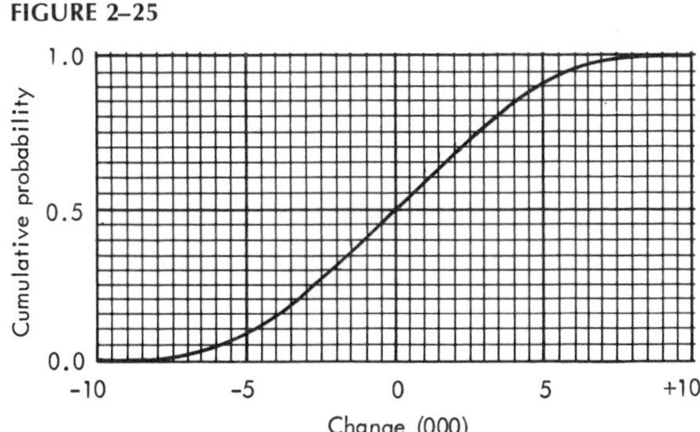

could, of course, have used a more spread out distribution function to allow more substantial annual sales changes.

A simulation model for this new set of assumptions is quite simple. For each trial we draw a value for the sales in the first year and then four values for changes; on the first trial the random numbers might be .67, .22, .45, .91, and .83. These figures would translate into five sales figures of $107,000; $104,000; $103,500; $108,500; and $112,500. Finally, the five sales figures would give a net present value for the trial of 384,902. After running many trials of this model, we could obtain the risk profile shown in Figure 2–26.

**FIGURE 2–26**

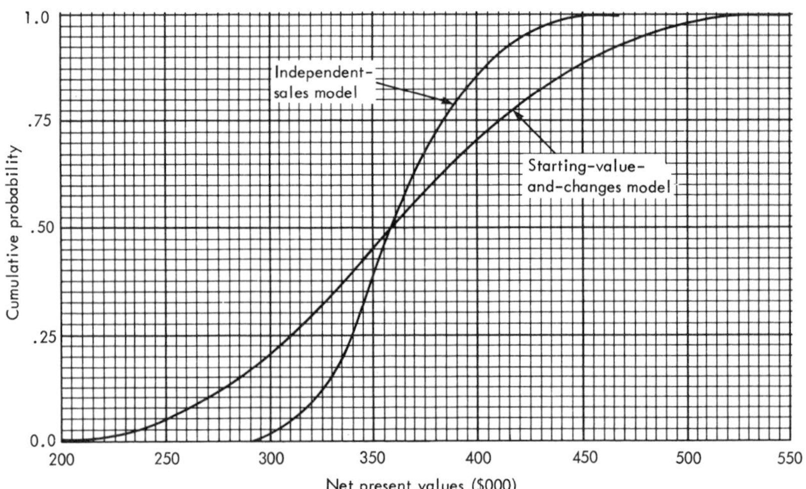


It can be shown that the mean or expected net present value for this formulation of the model is exactly the same as the expected net present value for the original problem (the risk profile for which is also shown in the figure). It is evident, however, that the spreads of the two distributions are quite different. The assumption of independent sales for successive years gives a tighter risk profile (that is, less risk). Basically, what is happening is that in the original model it is quite likely that good years and bad years will balance out over a five-year history and, hence, that the total results will reflect some good and some bad luck. When we build dependence into the sequence of sales values, on the other hand, we are assuming that it is more likely, although not absolutely certain, that bad years will follow bad years and good years will follow good years. (Once we have drawn a low value for initial sales, it will take several healthy year-to-year changes to bring sales to a favorable level.) Thus, the five-year histories are more likely to reflect consistently good periods or consistently bad ones; as a result, the range of possible net present values is greater than it is under the independence assumption.

Another type of procedure for building correlation into models involves a modification of the starting value and changes procedure discussed above (and for which some results are given in Figure 2–26). In that model we assumed that the value for next year was obtained by taking this year's value as a starting point and then adding a change. In the example above, we assumed that the distribution of changes had a median of zero so that we could think of the distribution for the next year as centered about the current value. In some cases we are sure that the value for the next year is influenced by the current value but we are not quite willing to shift our distribution for the next year quite as far as to center it on the current value. Instead, we may feel that the median estimate for the next year should instead be a compromise between some overall mean (or median) and the current year's value. Suppose that the mean of the original distribution is $100,000 and suppose that on a particular trial we draw a value of $80,000 for the first year. We might then take $90,000, which is halfway between the two values, as the median of our distribution for the second year. If we then added in the uncertainty described by Figure 2–25, we would obtain the distribution shown in Figure 2–27A for the second year's sales level. Suppose we drew a value of $92,000 (from that distribution) for the second year's sales. We could then construct the distribution for the third year by centering it at $96,000 (which is midway between the original mean of $100,000 and the second-year value for this trial) and then adding in the uncertainty from Figure 2–25. The result is shown in Figure 2–27B.

**FIGURE 2–27A**

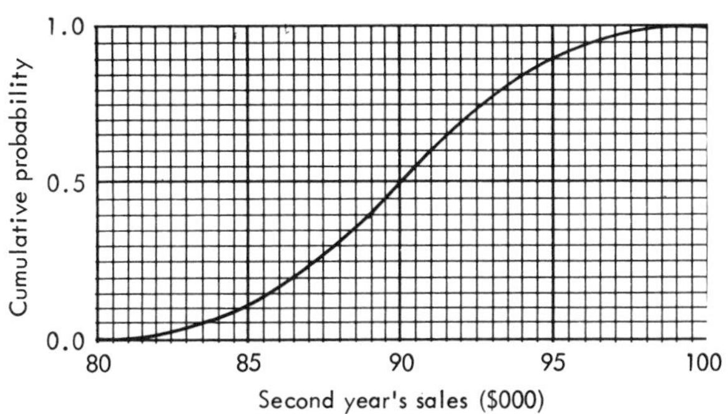


Proceeding in this way we could draw the remaining values for this trial. Figure 2–28 gives the results, in terms of risk profiles, for the model which assumed independence of changes and for the current model. Figure 2–29 gives the results for mechanisms similar to the current one, but with adjustments of different fractions of the difference between the current value and the overall median. The closer the adjustment is to the current value, the

FIGURE 2–27B

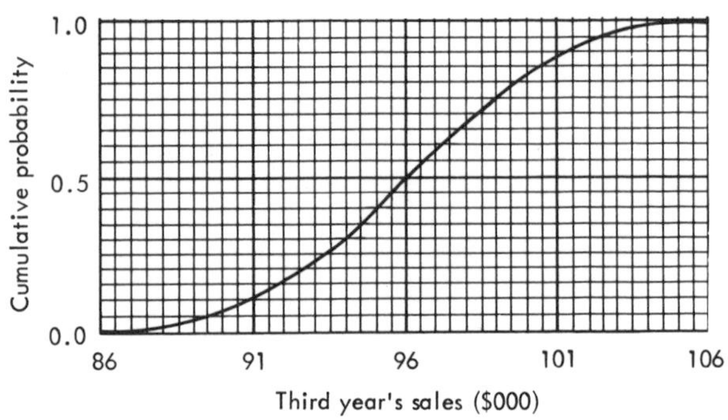


FIGURE 2–28

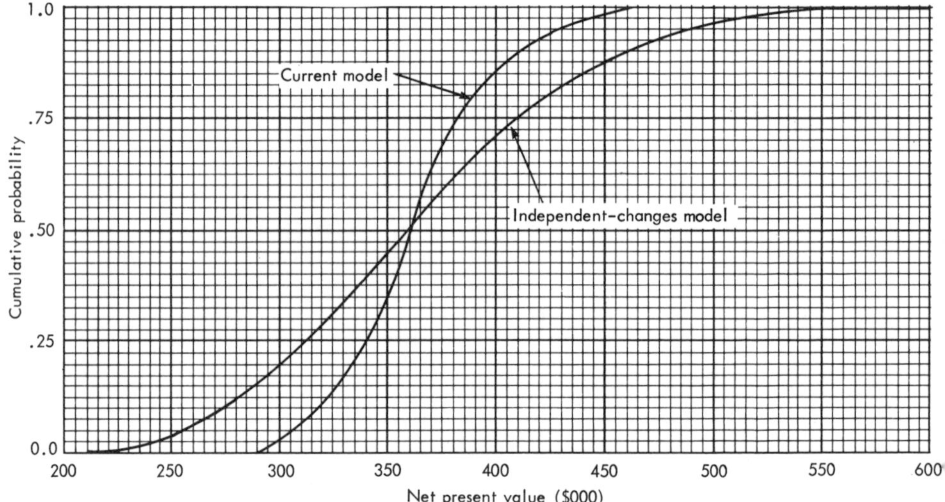


more carryover or correlation there is between successive values (and the more variable is the resulting distribution of net present values).

The type of mechanism which has just been described can be made more general. We could, for example, adjust by different fractions for high values and for low values of sales. In this example and in general the problem is apt to be one of being able to assess (meaningfully) the values which are needed to specify the model; in this case, we would have to say just what fraction to use for adjusting each possible sales level. It seems unlikely that we could give meaningful assessments for a complex model of this type.

In summary, interrelationships can be very important in determining the results of decisions made under uncertainty. The different models in this section have given distinctly different results in terms of risk. For example, if

FIGURE 2–29

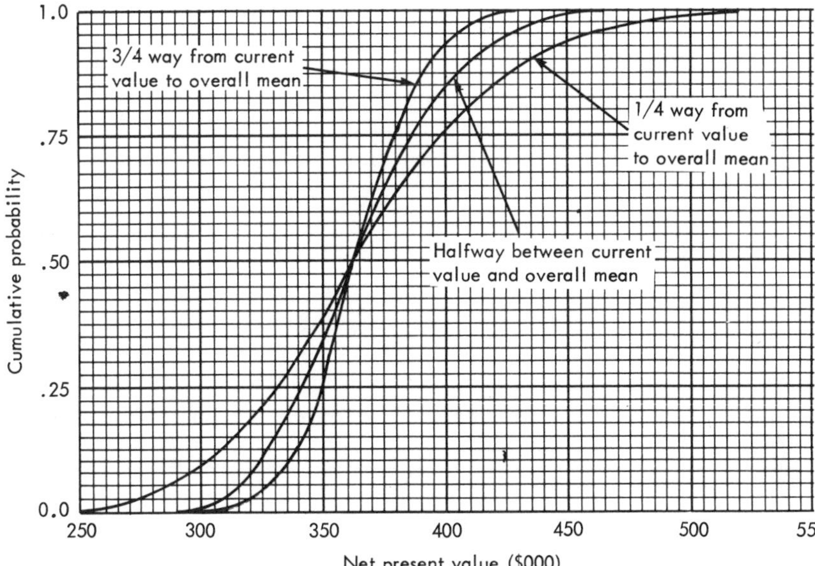


we believed the model whose results are shown in Figure 2–26 labeled starting-value-and-changes model, then we would greatly underestimate the variability of the potential results of the new-product introduction if we used the original model with independent sales levels instead. On the other hand, it is often very difficult to specify what form interrelationships should take; assessment rapidly becomes impossible as we build complex models. In addition, fitting the relationships to past data is also difficult in general for complex models (most especially when data are relatively scarce). Consequently, the task is to identify those interrelationships which seem to be most important and to build them into models in ways which make assessment of the required inputs practical. It is important to try to consider all of the *important* interrelationships (because not doing so may greatly underestimate the variability of results) but it is also important not to try to capture *all* interrelationships (or the assessments would be impractical). The techniques described in this section sometimes allow us to handle dependencies satisfactorily. Other techniques will be described in the following chapter. It should be clear, however, that dependencies remain a difficult modeling issue. Identifying the important dependencies in a problem is hard. It is also hard to find ways to handle dependencies that are at the same time satisfactorily realistic for the problem at hand and also well enough designed, in terms of input information required, that they are practical to use.

To conclude this section, we should note that we sometimes encounter situations in modeling in which we are sure that there are important interrelationships among the parts of a model but we are simply unable to specify any reasonable form for those interrelationships. A good example is probably the behavior of inflation rates in the 70s and 80s. Most people believe that the inflation rate in one year is related to the rate in the next year. In constructing risk profiles for this period we will regularly feel that inflation must be considered. On the other hand, it is very hard to imagine many people feeling comfortable about specifying how inflation rates are related to one another over time. (A favorite topic in the press of late has been the inability of the economics profession to predict such behavior.) One possible solution for this problem is not to try to build the interrelationships into the model—but not to build in false independence assumptions, either. Instead, we might ask the model's users (who may be ourselves) to give a scenario for inflation (i.e., a list of rates to be assumed in the years of the analysis) for each run of the model. For each such deterministic inflation scenario, we could run many trials, sampling all of the other uncertainties (some of which might well be linked to the inflation) and could then produce a distribution of results. We could then input another inflation scenario and investigate its consequences. . . . Thus, we would be using a deterministic modeling type of approach for the inflation patterns and probabilistic modeling techniques to handle the remaining uncertainties. The attractiveness of this approach is that it spares us from trying to specify interrelationships which we feel totally unable to assess (but which we believe are important). Its disadvantage is that it does not tell us how likely any of the inflation scenarios is; we must somehow consider for ourselves both the results of the different inflation scenarios and the probabilities which we assign to those scenarios. On balance, the deterministic scenario approach is worth considering when we believe we would get more useful information from the model if we used that approach than if we had built in formal interrelationships which we did not really believe or understand.

## EXERCISES

2.1. Design an algorithm that accepts as input the definition of a probability mass function for a few-valued UQ and prepares as output a listing of the cumulative distribution function of the UQ.

2.2. Design an algorithm that accepts as input the definition of a cumulative distribution function of a few-valued UQ and prepares as output a listing of the probability mass function of the UQ.

2.3. Design an algorithm that accepts as input the definition of the probability mass function of a few-valued UQ and outputs the mean and standard deviation of that UQ.

2.4. Describe as an algorithm the procedure for inputting a probability mass function of a few-valued UQ and for drawing values at random from that distribution.

2.5. Design a model that will input distributions for demand for some product; there will be a separate distribution for each day of the week (Monday through Saturday). The model should calculate the distribution of weekly demand. First, assume that demand on one day in a particular week can be assumed independent of demand on the other days during that week. Then, imagine that such independence assumptions are not warranted. How might you reformulate the problem to take account of the fact that some weeks show generally strong demand while other weeks show weaker demand, although there is, at the same time, a day-to-day pattern typical within weeks?

2.6. Give designs for programs that could give output required to construct Figures 2–22, 2–23, 2–26, 2–28, and 2–29 in the chapter.

2.7. (For computer programmers) Give programs to implement:

*a*. The risk analysis model in section IV (see Figure 2–13).

*b*. The manufacturer's ordering-decision model in section V (see Figure 2–19).

# case 2.1

# Green Cap and Closure Company (A), (B), (C)

## GREEN CAP AND CLOSURE COMPANY (A)

On December 11, 1967, the executive committee of the Green Cap and Closure Company met to discuss the possible introduction of a new plastic-lined cap for the ale-bottling industry. Mr. Harrison E. White, the new-products manager, met with the committee in an advisory capacity.

Green was a medium-sized firm which produced and marketed bottle caps and closures for the food and beverage processing industry. The 35-year-old company was the third largest cap and closure producer in the United States, with estimated 1967 sales of $25 million, or about 10 percent of the total cap and closure market.

### The cap and closure industry

The largest cap and closure producer in 1967 was the Roberts Cap Company with 40 percent of the market; next were the Montgomery Manufacturing Company (30 percent) and Green (10 percent). Fifteen smaller companies accounted for the remaining 20 percent of the market.

Caps and closures were classified as either standard or special. For a cap or closure to be considered standard it had to be used on standard capping equipment for standardized containers or bottles filled with contents which did not react with the standard cap materials. If any of these conditions were not met, the cap or closure was considered a special item.

The standard cap market was characterized by high volume and low profits. For example, in 1966 these items had constituted 70 percent of Green's unit volume but only 50 percent of dollar sales and 20 percent of net profits. The standard cap purchasers were extremely price conscious. Moreover, entry into the market was very easy; in fact, all that was needed to sell standard caps was a cap punch and a salesperson.

The special caps market was split between two types of companies:

innovators and copiers. The innovators spent considerable time and money learning about the requirements of their customers and designing new products to meet those requirements. To carry on this product innovation successfully required an experienced technical staff and large amounts of capital. Green estimated that it took an average of three years and $250,000 in research and development for each new product developed. On the other hand, copying a special product required no investment in research and development and a minimum of sales engineering activity.

To compensate for this difference in investment, the customer was usually willing to pay a somewhat higher price to the firm which had developed a product to the customer's specifications. This customer loyalty was not sufficient, however, to allow the innovator to charge arbitrarily high prices. Therefore, in introducing a new product, an innovator tried to set a price which was low enough to discourage copiers from undercutting and entering the market. (Even for the rare patentable cap or closure, the innovator avoided excessively high profit margins because they would encourage other companies to do research and development to bring out improved competitive products.)

**Green's new ale cap**

The executive committee was discussing an ale bottle cap with a new plastic liner on which the company had already spent $235,000 for research and sales engineering (of which $100,000 would be capitalized at the end of 1967).

The impetus for starting the research effort on this cap had been the introduction by the Roberts Company in 1964 of a new ale cap which had been such an improvement over Green's old ale cap that it had reduced Green's sales to the ale industry almost to zero. The executive committee had decided at that time that copying Roberts' cap would not be profitable and so had started a development program for a cap of their own.

Mr. White, the new-products manager, believed that Roberts had not done any development work on ale caps over the past three years. Moreover, particularly because Roberts and Green had dominated the ale market for some time, Mr. White felt it was extremely unlikely that any of the other cap and closure companies would try to break into the ale-cap market with developments of their own. He recommended that if the executive committee did decide to introduce the new product, the price be set at $235 per thousand dozen, the same price that Roberts charged for its ale cap. He felt that a lower price would be interpreted by Roberts as a break from the usual pattern of competing in the special closures field on the basis of product features rather than price and he worried that Roberts might retaliate by cutting prices on other products. A price higher than $235, on the other hand, would attract copiers.

## Market for the new product

Mr. White estimated that total industry sales for 1967 would total 9,700 thousand dozen and he forecast 1968 sales at 10,000 thousand dozen. He believed that the cap was good enough to capture about 70 percent of the market:

**White:** Of course, even though we've worked with the customers and think we know what they want, introducing a new product is still a bit risky. We can't be sure that the customers will buy—although the degree of customer acceptance is pretty well established by the end of the first year after introduction. That first year there is some delay in customer acceptance, but there are also customers who try the cap once and don't adopt it, so the 70 percent figure is probably good for the first year, too.

**Lindstrom:** A 70 percent market share certainly sounds attractive, but for how long do you think we can keep it?

**White:** The thing that worries me most is that, as unlikely as it sounds right now, the market for our cap might disappear completely. I understand that several of the chemical companies are trying to develop a plastic bottle with a break-off top. So far they've been unsuccessful because the prolonged contact with the plastic affects the taste of the ale, but they may be able to overcome that problem one of these days. I'm sure the market will disappear, one way or another, within 10 years or so.

**Lindstrom:** I appreciate the problems of predicting the time of obsolescence, but that's certainly not our problem. Surely, if we were to get the 70 percent share which you predict, Harrison, you wouldn't expect the competition just to sit on their hands and do nothing about it would you?

**White:** Certainly not. I think the $235 price will protect us pretty well from copiers, but there is still Roberts to worry about. I think that what they do will depend on how successful we are. If we do achieve a 70 percent share—and remember, that figure's just my best guess and by no means a certainty—I estimate that Roberts would have a competing product on the market in five years. If we had a bust, with only 20 percent of the market on this new product, I wouldn't expect them to enter the market with a new product for ten years (if the market lasts that long). And, of course, if we take the whole market now, you can be sure that Roberts will go to work on a new cap immediately—and I'd guess they'd have one on the market in two years. Again, I'm not certain about these figures; I could be off by a year or two in either direction.

Another thing about a new Roberts product is that we aren't sure how good it would be and, therefore, what fraction of our share it would take away. I'd bet even money that we'd keep 35 percent or so of our original share—although we might keep as much as 85 percent of what we started with or we might lose the whole market.

Also, remember that the total market for ale caps is likely to keep growing over the next ten years—or as long as the market lasts. Our planning people predict about 1.8 percent growth per year, but they admit that growth could conceivably be less than 1 percent or even as high as 5 percent.

**Production equipment for the new cap**

Mr. Lindstrom next called on Mr. Jonathan Morgan, the factory manager, to discuss the production of the new product. Mr. Morgan reported that the only equipment on the market which would be capable of producing and packaging the new ale cap was a Gordon Model K semiautomatic cap punch. Some modification of the machine would be necessary for production of the new cap, but then no other equipment would be required to make or package the new product. The total cost of the equipment, including delivery, installation and modification, would be $280,000.

The Gordon machine could produce and package eight million dozens of caps a year if operated eight hours per day, including an allowance for expected breakdowns. (This schedule amounted to 2,000 regular hours per year.) The machine required a team of four men, each of whom would be paid $2.50 per hour. Mr. Morgan believed that the machine operators could be moved to other jobs when they were not needed for ale-cap manufacture. He also said that although the factory used overtime only infrequently, there was no reason why overtime couldn't be used to increase the workday to 12 hours, allowing a maximum total yearly production of 12 million dozen caps. He was certain that, even if the maximum overtime were used for machine operation, the other work on the caps (primarily inspection and packaging) could be done during the normal working day. Workers were paid time and a half for overtime.

The cost accounting department had provided the following factory cost estimate (per thousand dozen) for caps produced on the Gordon machine at its capacity speed:

| | | |
|---|---|---|
| Direct materials | | $180.00 |
| Direct labor: | | |
| Gordon machine operation | $2.50 | |
| Other (primarily inspection and packaging) | 2.00 | |
| Total direct labor | | 4.50 |
| Overhead: 100% of direct labor | | 4.50 |
| Total factory cost | | $189.00 |

Mr. Morgan reported that the purchasing department had told him that these cost estimates assumed Green would be able to take full advantage of quantity discounts on some of the raw materials for the caps. If sales were to fall below 5 million dozen per year, the discounts would not be available and materials costs would increase to $183 per thousand dozen.

When asked about maintenance expenses for the Gordon machine, Mr. Morgan estimated that $6,000 would be required yearly for maintenance labor and $10,000 would be required for maintenance materials and molds, assuming production of 8 million dozen. Of these amounts, $2,000 for labor and $2,000 for materials were fixed and the remaining sums were variable with production.

The 100 percent overhead rate was based on the relationship of overhead costs to direct labor costs in 1967. Exhibit A–1 gives the breakdown of these overhead costs for 1967, including a classification of the costs by the accounting department. Mr. Morgan presented the committee with the overhead budget he had prepared for 1968 (Exhibit A–2).

In 1967, the company was using a 10 percent of sales figure for research, selling and administrative expenses; of this amount, 4 percent of the selling price was paid in sales commissions.

**EXHIBIT A–1**

Breakdown of overhead expense for year ending December 31, 1967

| | *Amount (000)* | *Classification* |
|---|---|---|
| Supervision | $ 700 | Variable |
| Indirect labor | 300 | Variable |
| Maintenance labor | 500 | Semivariable |
| Unemployment compensation, social security, pensions | 1,300 | Variable |
| Maintenance materials and molds | 700 | Semivariable |
| Supplies, heat, light, and power | 800 | Variable |
| Depreciation | 700 | Fixed |
| Total overhead expense | $5,000 | |

**EXHIBIT A–2**

Budget of overhead expenses for 1968

| *Class of expense* | *Budgeted amount at expected level of production for factory (all products)* | *Additional amount for each $100 of direct labor* | *Budgeted amount at expected level of production for factory* | *Additional amount for each thousand dozen caps* |
|---|---|---|---|---|
| Supervision | $ 700,000 | $14 | | |
| Indirect labor | 300,000 | 6 | | |
| Unemployement compensation, etc. | 1,300,000* | 24 | | |
| Supplies, heat, light and power | | | $800,000 | $4.00 |
| Depreciation | | | 700,000 | 0 |
| Maintenance labor | | | 500,000 | 0.50 |
| Maintenance materials and molds | | | 700,000 | 1.00 |

* 20 percent of total labor (direct labor, indirect labor, supervision, and sales commissions).

**EXHIBIT A–3**

GREEN CAP & CLOSURE COMPANY (A)
Projected Balance Sheet
As of December 31, 1967
(000)

| | | | |
|---|---|---|---|
| *Assets* | | | |
| Cash and marketable securities | | $2,500 | |
| Accounts receivable | | 2,500 | |
| Inventories | | 5,000 | |
| Total current assets | | | $10,000 |
| Land | | $ 500 | |
| Buildings, machinery, and equipment—cost | $9,500 | | |
| Less: reserve for depreciation | 5,000 | | |
| Buildings, machinery, and equipment—net | | 4,500 | |
| Development expenses | | 500 | |
| | | | 5,500 |
| Total Assets | | | $15,500 |
| *Liabilities and Net Worth* | | | |
| Notes payable | | $ 500 | |
| Accounts payable | | 1,000 | |
| Other accruals | | 1,000 | |
| Total current liabilities | | | $ 2,500 |
| Long-term bonds | | | 2,500 |
| Total liabilities | | | $ 5,000 |
| Common stock | | $2,500 | |
| Retained earnings | | 8,000 | |
| Total net worth | | | 10,500 |
| Total Liabilities and Net Worth | | | $15,500 |

Green used the sum-of-the-years-digits method for depreciation; it was required to depreciate equipment over no less than seven years. The Gordon machine would have a physical life of at least ten years, but once modified to produce the new cap, it would not be useful for any other purposes and, in fact, it was not expected to have a salvage value in excess of the cost of dismantling and removing it.

Finally, Mr. Jones, the treasurer, reminded the committee that new products or expanded production of old ones required additional working capital. He estimated that working capital would have to be 20 percent of sales, an amount which he felt should be considered as part of the investment. He added that the company used a 15 percent (after taxes) hurdle rate on its investments for the next ten-year planning period and that it used a 48 percent tax rate in its investment calculations.

**EXHIBIT A–4**

GREEN CAP & CLOSURE COMPANY (A)
Projected Income Statement
For Year Ending December 31, 1967
(000)

| | | |
|---|---|---|
| Net Sales | | $25,000 |
| Cost of goods sold: | | |
| Beginning inventories | $ 4,500 | |
| Plus: Materials purchases | 10,000 | |
| Direct labor | 5,000 | |
| Overhead expense | 5,000 | |
| | $24,500 | |
| Less: Ending inventories | 5,000 | |
| Cost of goods sold | | 19,500 |
| Gross profit | | $ 5,500 |
| Research, selling, administrative and interest expenses: | | |
| Research expense | 250 | |
| Sales expense | 1,340 | |
| Administrative expense | 730 | |
| Interest expense | 180 | |
| Total research, selling, administrative and interest expenses | | 2,500 |
| Net profits before taxes | | $ 3,000 |
| Taxes | | 1,500 |
| Net profit after taxes | | $ 1,500 |
| Dividends declared | | 500 |
| Net addition to retained earnings | | $ 1,000 |

## GREEN CAP AND CLOSURE COMPANY (B)

To help the executive committee of the Green Cap and Closure Company decide on whether to introduce a new plastic-lined cap for the ale bottling industry, Mr. Harrison White, the new-products manager, had engaged a consultant to develop a mathematical model of the problem. After listening to the discussion at the executive committee meeting on December 11, the consultant had suggested Monte Carlo simulation on a computer as an appropriate way to analyze the problem. Working with the accounting department and with Mr. Morgan, the factory manager, he had prepared the summary of accounting information given in Exhibit B–1. He had then had a long meeting with Mr. White to discuss the uncertainties which were relevant for the decision. Exhibit B–2 is an informal memo from the consultant to his staff, summarizing the results of his meeting with Mr. White.

*Initial Market Share*

White believes the share will certainly be between 20 percent and 100 percent, with a fifty-fifty chance of its exceeding 70%. His .25 and .75 fractiles are about 55 percent and 83 percent.

**EXHIBIT B–1**
Summary of costs (per thousand dozen caps)

| | | |
|---|---|---|
| 1. | Selling price | $235.00 |
| 2. | Sales commissions (4%) | 9.40 |
| 3. | Gordon machine operation— | |
| | regular time (up to 8,000 thousand) | 2.50 |
| | overtime | 3.75 |
| 4. | Other direct labor | 2.00 |
| 5. | Supervision (14% of total labor) | 0.63 |
| 6. | Indirect labor (6% of total labor) | 0.27 |
| 7. | Maintenance labor (plus $2,000/year fixed) | 0.50 |
| 8. | Unemployment compensation, etc. (20% of items 2–7): | |
| 9. | Direct materials | |
| | Less than 5,000 dozen | 183.00 |
| | More than 5,000 dozen | 180.00 |
| 10. | Supplies, heat, light, etc. | 4.00 |
| 11. | Maintenance materials (plus $2,000/year fixed) | 1.00 |

**EXHIBIT B–2**

Memorandum to Staff

We have identified the major sources of uncertainty in this problem as:

1. Initial market share.
2. Years to obsolescence.
3. Years before a new product is introduced by Roberts.
4. Fraction of initial share kept by Green after Roberts introduces a new product.
5. Growth of the market.

*Years to Obsolescence*

We'll assume that the market will disappear after between four and ten years. White and I hammered out the following probabilities:

| *Last year before obsolescence* | *Probability* |
|---|---|
| 5 | .10 |
| 6 | .15 |
| 7 | .25 |
| 8 | .25 |
| 9 | .15 |
| 10 | .10 |

*Years Before New Roberts Product*

We assessed this quantity in stages. First, White gave me his best guess for the years to competition as a function of Green's original share—the graph below shows the relationship. (To make this accounting easier, we'll want to round to an integral number of years.)

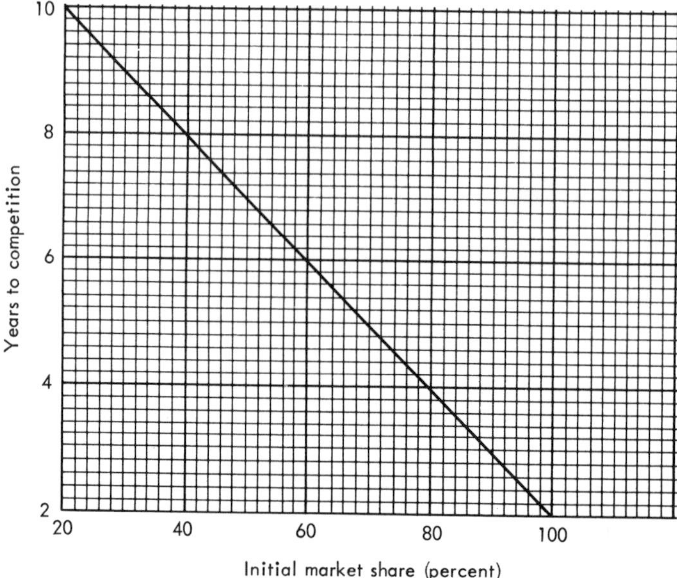


I've decided to use the above graph to get the median number of years to competition (five years for a 70 percent share, for example) and then to make a distribution by adding the following uncertainty:*

| *Error in median estimate (in years)* | *Probability* |
|---|---|
| −2 | .10 |
| −1 | .15 |
| 0 | .50 |
| 1 | .15 |
| 2 | .10 |

Thus, as an example, an initial share of 70 percent gives a median of five years and the following distribution:

| *Years* | *Probability* |
|---|---|
| 3 | .10 |
| 4 | .15 |
| 5 | .50 |
| 6 | .15 |
| 7 | .10 |

* An error of −1 means that the actual years-to-competition are 1 *fewer* than the median estimate.

*Fraction Kept by Green*

White's range runs from 0 percent to 85 percent with a median of 35 percent. His .25 and .75 fractiles are 20 percent and 52 percent. (Thus, if Green starts with 70 percent, White's median estimate is that they will keep 35 percent of that initial amount or 24.5 percent of the total market.) He believes that Green's new share will be established in the first year the new Roberts product is on the market.

*Growth in the Total Market*

White gave me a median of 1.8 percent growth per year, with a range of .5 percent to 5.5 percent; his .25 and .75 fractiles are 1.3 percent and 2.5 percent. I'm really not too happy about assuming a constant growth rate for the next 10 years, but White has told me that growth is likely to be reasonably level (barring obsolescence) and that he really can't assess anything more accurate than a level rate.

The following graphs give the three continuous distributions.

**EXHIBIT B–2**

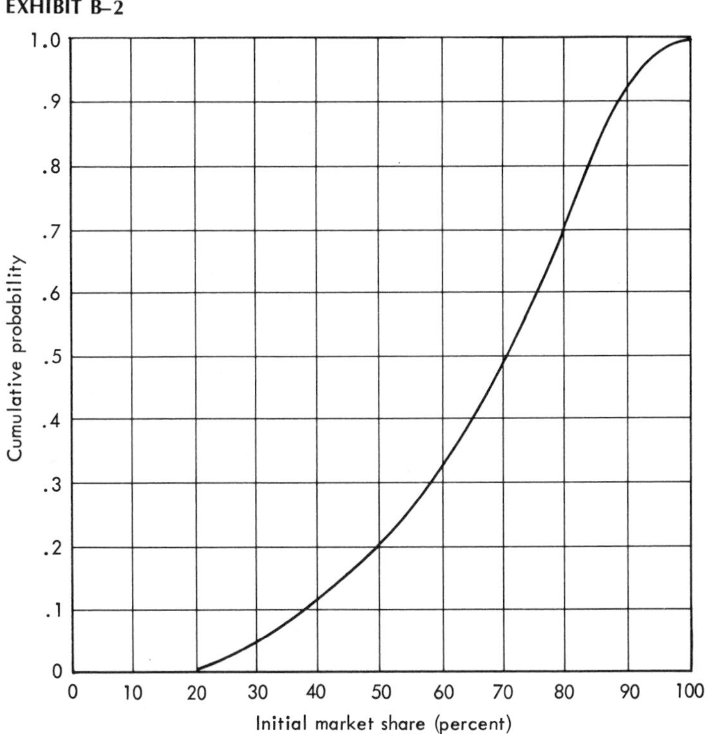

**EXHIBIT B–2 (*continued*)**

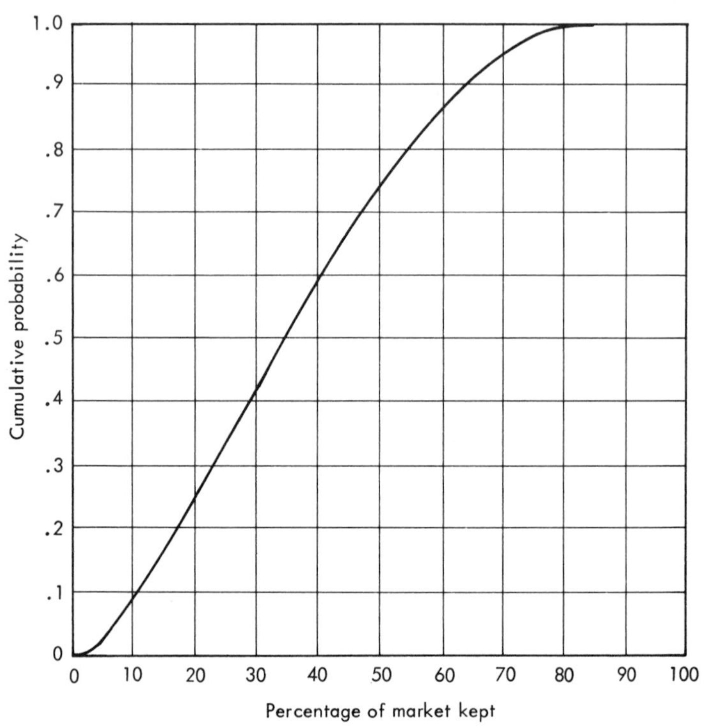

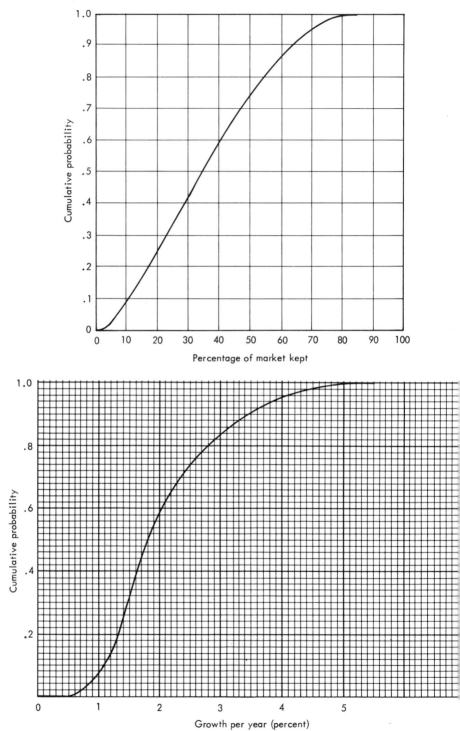


1.0
.8
.6
.4
.2
Cumulative probability
0
1
2
3
4
5
Growth per year (percent)

## GREEN CAP AND CLOSURE COMPANY (C)

This case describes the results of the computer simulation of Green Cap and Closure's decision on the new ale cap. Exhibit C–1 gives detailed output for one trial. Exhibit C–2 gives the risk profile obtained by running 500 trials.

### Explanation of exhibit C–1

1. Costs and revenues are given in Exhibit B–1 of the (B) case.
2. Contribution margin = sales revenue − total costs.
3. Profit before = contribution margin − depreciation
4. Total working capital = 20 percent of sales; change in working capital is the addition or the reduction in the amount needed in a given year to bring working capital to 20 percent of sales.
5. In calculating NPV, it is assumed that changes in working capital occur at the *start* of the indicated year while profits are spread evenly through the indicated year.

**EXHIBIT C–1**

Computer output for one trial

Computer Output for One Trial

| YEAR NUMBER | 1 | 2 | 3 | 4 | 5 | 6 | 7 | 8 | 9 | 10 |
|---|---|---|---|---|---|---|---|---|---|---|
| SALES (THOUS DOZEN) | 7286 | 7348 | 7411 | 7475 | 7539 | 4177 | 4212 | 4248 | 4285 | 4321 |
| SALES ( $) | 1712210 | 1726780 | 1741585 | 1756625 | 1771665 | 981595 | 989820 | 998280 | 1006975 | 1015435 |
| | | | | | | | | | | |
| SALES COMMISSIONS | 68488 | 69071 | 69663 | 70264 | 70866 | 39263 | 39592 | 39931 | 40278 | 40617 |
| GORDON MACHINE OPER | 18215 | 18370 | 18527 | 18687 | 18847 | 10442 | 10530 | 10620 | 10712 | 10802 |
| OTHER DIRECT LABOR | 14572 | 14696 | 14822 | 14950 | 15078 | 8354 | 8424 | 8496 | 8570 | 8642 |
| SUPERVISION | 4590 | 4629 | 4668 | 4709 | 4749 | 2631 | 2653 | 2676 | 2699 | 2722 |
| INDIRECT LABOR | 1967 | 1983 | 2000 | 2018 | 2035 | 1127 | 1137 | 1146 | 1156 | 1166 |
| MAINTENANCE LABOR | 5643 | 5674 | 5705 | 5737 | 5769 | 4088 | 4106 | 4124 | 4142 | 4160 |
| TOTAL LABOR | 113475 | 114424 | 115388 | 116367 | 117346 | 65908 | 66443 | 66994 | 67560 | 68111 |
| UNEMP COMP ETC | 22695 | 22884 | 23077 | 23273 | 23469 | 13181 | 13288 | 13398 | 13512 | 13622 |
| DIRECT MATERIALS | 1311480 | 1322640 | 1333980 | 1345500 | 1357020 | 764391 | 770796 | 777384 | 784155 | 790743 |
| SUPPLIES HEAT ETC | 29144 | 29392 | 29644 | 29900 | 30156 | 16708 | 16848 | 16992 | 17140 | 17284 |
| MAINTENANCE MATRLS | 9286 | 9348 | 9411 | 9475 | 9539 | 6177 | 6212 | 6248 | 6285 | 6321 |
| GENERAL DEPN | 0 | 0 | 0 | 0 | 0 | 0 | 0 | 0 | 0 | 0 |
| TOTAL COSTS | 1486080 | 1498689 | 1511500 | 1524516 | 1537531 | 866365 | 873588 | 881017 | 888652 | 896081 |
| | | | | | | | | | | |
| CONTRIBUTION MARGIN | 226129 | 228090 | 230084 | 232109 | 234133 | 115229 | 116231 | 117262 | 118322 | 119353 |
| EQUIP DEPRECIATION | 70000 | 60000 | 50000 | 40000 | 30000 | 20000 | 10000 | 0 | 0 | 0 |
| PROFIT BEFORE TAX | 156129 | 168090 | 180084 | 192109 | 204133 | 95229 | 106231 | 117262 | 118322 | 119353 |
| TAXES | 74941 | 80683 | 86440 | 92212 | 97984 | 45710 | 50991 | 56286 | 56794 | 57289 |
| PROFIT AFTER TAX | 81187 | 87407 | 93643 | 99896 | 106149 | 49519 | 55240 | 60976 | 61527 | 62063 |
| | | | | | | | | | | |
| PAT + DEPREC | 151187 | 147407 | 143643 | 139896 | 136149 | 69519 | 65240 | 60976 | 61527 | 62063 |
| | | | | | | | | | | |
| TOTAL WORKING CAP | 342442 | 345356 | 348317 | 351325 | 354333 | 196319 | 197964 | 199656 | 201395 | 203087 |
| | | | | | | | | | | |
| CHANGE WORKING CAP | 342442 | 2914 | 2961 | 3008 | 3008 | -158014 | 1645 | 1692 | 1739 | 1692 |

```
ORIGINAL MARKET SHARE   0.729
YEARLY MARKET GROWTH    0.009
YEARS BEFORE COMPETITION   5
FRACTION OF SHARE KEPT  0.549
YEARS BEFORE OBSOLESCENCE 10
NPV AT 15. 0/0          131093
```

DISTRIBUTION OF NET PRESENT VALUES AT 15 0/0:

**EXHIBIT C–2**
Risk profile

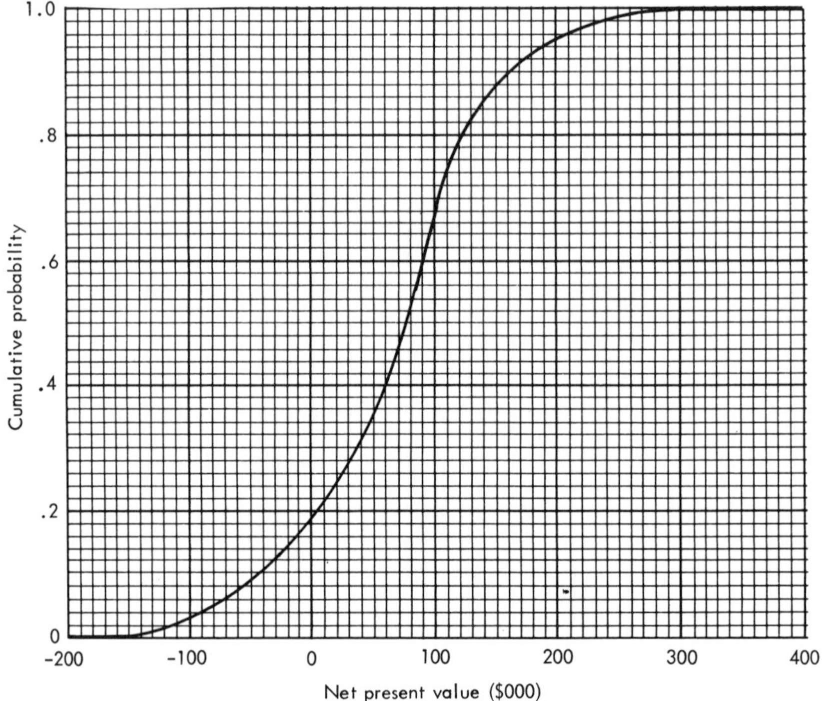

## case 2.2

# Hudson Chemical Company of Canada Limited* with Computer Supplement

Hudson Chemical Company of Canada Limited began to manufacture a product brand-named "Aqua-Pur" early in 1963. Aqua-Pur was a chemical agent used as part of the softening process for commercial boiler feed water. Of immediate importance to the company's executives was the problem of establishing a pricing policy. The company was at a severe competitive disadvantage, as their competition was an established firm which had enjoyed a virtual monopoly in the industry over the past 20 years. The general manager knew that the establishment of a sound pricing policy would be instrumental in determining the company's success in entering the Canadian market.

Hudson Chemical Company of Canada Limited was a wholly owned subsidiary of the Hudson Chemical Company Incorporated, a large U.S. chemical firm with annual sales in excess of $500 million. The company, in addition to its eight plants in the United States, operated subsidiary firms in seven countries, including Canada. On a consolidated basis Hudson's total assets were reported at just under $300 million. For some time the company had been noted for its excellent research and development facilities which were thought by many to account for its spectacular growth over the past 20 years. As a result of this research, Hudson had followed a policy of wide diversification within the chemical industry.

Hudson's largest foreign operation was in Canada where Hudson Chemical Company of Canada reported sales of almost $10 million a year. This firm operated one plant in Montreal but distributed its products nationally. The sales organization was divided into six product groups, each with a product manager and from two to five specialized salespeople. In 1963, the water-treatment product group was relatively small, although the company felt it had a great potential. In addition to Aqua-Pur, the group handled a chemical

 It was written by D. S. R. Leighton and J. D. Pearson.

fungus control for industrial water treatment and two other products, both of which represented relatively small volumes.

Most industrial concerns operated their own boiler plants and were continually facing the problems of treating boiler feed water. In hard water areas the problem was acute, as the chemicals within the water formed a sediment inside both pipes and tanks. Eventually this sediment clogged the system and often forced a program of costly replacement. To overcome this, many firms installed water-softening devices on their boiler systems. Water softening was simply a chemical process which removed the hardening chemicals from the water before it was fed into the boiler.

In the early 1940s Chicago Chemical Company developed a compound to be used in conjunction with the regular water-softening chemicals. This product did not in itself soften the water but rather dispersed the water-softening compounds, thus lengthening their economical life. It provided not only a saving in water-softening chemicals but also a reduction in the time and effort required to continually regenerate the softeners. Chicago Chemical patented the product in both United States and Canada under the name of Purafax.

Chicago Chemical was a relatively small firm specializing in certain water-treatment chemicals. The company did not manufacture or sell water-softening chemicals as such. Trade sources reported that 70 percent of its business was in the sale of Purafax, while the remainder was made up of a variety of small-volume items such as a slime-control agent and a fungi-control chemical. The company's consolidated statements for 1961 showed sales of $75 million and total assets of $40 million.

Since 1951 Hudson Chemical Company had been working on a compound that would compete with Purafax. By 1957, a satisfactory compound had been developed, but to market it would have violated Chicago Chemical's patent rights. By 1961, however, these patent rights would terminate. Thus Hudson continued work on the product. During this period, two major findings were made. First, it was found that the major raw material in the compound could be extracted from brewer's spent grain. From the brewer's standpoint, this was waste material and could therefore be purchased by Hudson very cheaply. Second, Hudson developed an additive for the dispersing compound which would reduce rust formation in the boiler system. A number of the company officers felt this would be an excellent feature when the product was introduced into the market, particularly as Chicago Chemical's Purafax did not contain a rust-reducing agent. It was believed that with these refinements Aqua-Pur could readily compete with Purafax.

Tests with Aqua-Pur indicated the proper formula for addition to softening chemicals was one gallon of Aqua-Pur for every seven gallons of water-softening chemical. Use of Aqua-Pur would reduce the amount of softening chemical required to do an equivalent job by 35 percent. Water-softening chemicals cost about 50 cents a gallon and a firm operating a boiler might use anywhere from $100 to $50,000 worth of softening chemicals a year. The company realized Aqua-Pur would be of interest primarily to firms using between $10,000 and $50,000 worth of softening chemical, but that this range included most of the large production plants in the country. An example of savings in the use of softening chemical by use of Aqua-Pur for a firm not now using Purafax and initially using $20,000 worth of chemical follows:

| | *Before Aqua-Pur* | *With Aqua-Pur* |
|---|---|---|
| Gallons of Softening Chemical | 40,000 | 26,000 |
| Aqua-Pur | 0 | 3,715 |

In late 1962 a decision was made to introduce Aqua-Pur to the Canadian market. The basis for this decision was a study conducted by the market research department which estimated Canadian sales of Purafax in 1961 at the equivalent of approximately 6 million gallons (of Aqua-Pur), or $4,500,000 f.o.b. the Chicago Chemical plant.[1] A geographical breakdown of these figures is given in Exhibit 1. The report noted that Chicago had concentrated its efforts in the largest plants and had made few attempts to develop the smaller customers currently consuming $10,000 to $20,000 worth of softening chemical annually. It was the researchers' opinion that the potential might be at least twice current Purafax sales, particularly if a considerable cut in prices could be achieved.

**EXHIBIT 1**
**Canadian market—1961 (in gallons)**

| | |
|---|---|
| British Columbia | 900,000 |
| Alberta | 900,000 |
| Saskatchewan | 100,000 |
| Manitoba | 400,000 |
| Ontario | 2,000,000 |
| Quebec | 1,300,000 |
| Maritimes | 400,000 |
| Total | 6,000,000 |

In preparation for the new product the company had hired two new salespeople who were experienced in the water-treatment field, and were considering hiring additional sales help. It was decided that the product would be most efficiently handled through distributors, at least until the product be-

[1] Purafax was a powder; for ease of comparison the case will deal with it in terms of equivalent gallons of Aqua-Pur.

came established in the market. The salespeople would be responsible for training distributor personnel, providing technical assistance to the distributor and missionary work at the customer level. In addition, a man was brought in from the American company to act as product sales manager and to be directly responsible to the general manager of Hudson Chemical Company Limited of Canada. Mr. Roberts, the new product sales manager, had several years' experience in both the development and sale of Aqua-Pur in the United States and was therefore considered a valuable asset to the Canadian company.

Immediately upon his arrival, Mr. Roberts was called in by Mr. Morton, the general manager, and together they started to plan a marketing program for the new product. The first problem was to arrange for tests on the product by independent laboratories in each locality. Until such a time as a favourable report had been received from these laboratories, few customers could be interested in the new product. The company salespeople and the distributor's salespeople would have to contact both company purchasing agents and boiler or stationary engineers to make a sale. The latter had proved to be most influential from the company's experience in the United States.

Based on their experience in the United States, it was decided that the distributor would have to install a dispenser and storage tank in the client's plant. The total cost of each installation ranged between $400 and $500. While some distributors considered this to be a definite problem, others realized the advantages it provided. There would be a sense of permanence in the supplier-customer relationship when such a physical installation had been made. The distributor would also have to service the installation and provide continuous technical assistance at a cost of from $200 to $500 a year or more, depending in part upon the size of the account.

By May 1963, the company's plans to enter the Canadian market with Aqua-Pur were well launched. Several pilot runs had been put through the plant and a number of independent laboratory tests had been conducted. The results of these tests had been most satisfactory and would act as certification to the company's claim that the performance of their product was equal to, if not better than, that of Chicago Chemical's Purafax. As the product was introduced in each local market, however, additional tests would have to be conducted by local laboratories. The company did not anticipate any problems in this regard. Although price had not been mentioned, the company had obtained favourable reactions from a number of distributors after a series of informal meetings.

The more Mr. Morton and Mr. Roberts studied the situation, the more they realized the importance of establishing a sound pricing policy at the outset. Both executives felt that this would be the deciding factor in determining the success of the venture. As a basis from which to start, Mr. Roberts suggested that serious study be given to each of the basic pricing alternatives open to them.

Before considering the alternatives individually, Mr. Morton instructed the accountant to analyze the costs of the new product. The accountant presented the following facts:

1. The cost of direct labour, packaging, and raw materials amounted to 45 cents per gallon.
2. It was estimated that the new product should absorb $40,000 of general administrative overhead and $20,000 of general factory overhead per annum.
3. Grouped under fixed expenses were the following items:
   a. A new 10,000-square-foot addition to the existing plant had just been added at an average cost of $8 per square foot.
   b. The new machinery for the process had cost $70,000 installed.
   c. Early in June a new salesperson had been hired which brought the sales force complement to three, excluding the new product manager, Mr. Roberts. Each salesperson cost the company an estimated $15,000 per year, including salary, expenses, and fringe benefits.
   d. Two laboratory personnel had been added, one of whom doubled as a plant supervisor for the new process, at an estimated $12,000 each.
   e. Mr. Roberts' salary plus expenses was calculated at $20,000 per year.

Mr. Roberts noted that the present machinery and plant had a capacity to produce 1,200,000 gallons per year, and that an additional investment of approximately $50,000 could double this capacity.

Given these financial facts, the two executives started their analysis of three alternatives:

1. Mr. Morton suggested that they first consider the pros and cons of simply meeting their competitor's prices. He noted that some changes would be necessary inasmuch as Aqua-Pur was in liquid form while Purafax was a powdered substance. However a gallon equivalent to the pound-price basis would be all that was required. By converting Chicago Chemical's price list from pounds to gallons, it was calculated that Hudson Chemical would receive an average price of 76 cents per gallon for its product f.o.b. the Montreal plant. Average freight costs would be about 20 cents a gallon and distributor margins about 40 cents a gallon, giving an estimated consumer price of $1.36 a gallon. This price would likely vary somewhat from customer to customer depending on size, location, competitive circumstances, and distributor pricing policies but overall was roughly equivalent to delivered prices for Purafax. Mr. Roberts stated that he believed this alternative would be the most suitable. First, because of its obvious simplicity it would be easy to explain to potential customers and, second, he did not feel the company knew the market sufficiently well either to judge the effect of a premium price on the consumer or to estimate what competitive retaliation

might result should they cut the price. Although Mr. Morton did agree that it was the alternative involving the least risk, he believed there were strong arguments for another alternative.

2. As a second alternative, Mr. Morton suggested that a price lower than Chicago Chemical's might be the best method of getting an initial foothold in the market. He noted that although they could expect some retaliation from Chicago, even a short lag would be of great assistance in getting established and, in addition, a lower price might tend to enlarge the total market. It could quite conceivably make the product of interest to potential users who currently considered it too expensive. Mr. Roberts agreed that this was quite possible and that operating margins at the existing price level were sufficiently large to permit the reduction. However, he noted that to reduce prices would incur the wrath of the softener chemical companies as it would mean further inroads into their sales. In other words, more firms would use Aqua-Pur to increase the life of normal softener chemicals. Mr. Roberts attached considerable importance to this point, as the firms producing softening chemicals were for the most part large and could quite conceivably influence the consumer against Aqua-Pur. Mr. Morton on the other hand questioned the importance of this threat. He believed that the consumer would not be influenced even if the chemical companies launched a campaign against Aqua-Pur.

3. The final alternative that the company considered was that of a premium price. Neither executive was particularly impressed with this possibility but they did recognize some of its merits. In the first place, the rust preventative included in Aqua-Pur gave them an advantage over Purafax. They could price just below what a combination of Purafax and a recognized rust preventative would cost the consumer. A premium price would mean even higher margins and, as a consequence, a lower volume would be sufficient to cover the overhead. This had much to recommend it because, for some time at least, the large Quebec and Ontario markets would be most difficult to enter.

Both Mr. Roberts and Mr. Morton knew that there were other factors that should be studied in each alternative. They also knew, however, that a decision had to be reached quickly if they were to get under way during 1963.

## Computer Supplement

Program HUDSN is a deterministic pro forma generator for use with the case Hudson Chemical Company of Canada, Limited. (In the protocol, all responses typed by the user have been underlined.) The following protocol shows how the program can be run.

* .R HUDSN ← At the monitor level, the user asks to run program HUDSN

Program HUDSN follows the convention that questions are initially asked in very terse form. If the user does not understand the brief question, s/he can ask for more information by typing a question mark.

```
HUDSON PRICES: ?
GIVE A PRICE TO BE CHARGED FOR AQUA PUR IN EACH OF UP TO
 10 YEARS.
HUDSON PRICES: 1.26 1.26 1.36
```

← Request for elaboration.

← when the user does not give 10 yearly values for prices or for any of the other quantities requested below, the program assumes that the last value given by the user is repeated for each of the remaining years. Hence, in this case, the program assumes that the prices are: 1.26, 1.26, 1.36, 1.36, 1.36, 1.36, 1.36, 1.36, 1.36, 1.36

```
DISTRIBUTOR MARGINS ($): ?
GIVE THE DISTRIBUTORS' MARGINS, IN $, FOR EACH OF UP TO
 10 YEARS.
DISTRIBUTOR MARGINS ($): .37 .37 .40
HUDSON SHARES: ?
GIVE HUDSON'S MARKET SHARES (AS FRACTIONS OF TOTAL AQUA-PUR EQUIVALENT
 UNITS) FOR EACH OF UP TO 10 YEARS.
HUDSON SHARES: .100 .150 .1667 .200
NUMBER OF YEARS: 5
```

← the program will use .40 for years 3–10

← pro formas are available for up to 10 years.

NOTE: the program starts with the following assumptions–

1. Variable costs (including transportation) are \$.65/gallon in each year.
2. Fixed costs are \$149 (000) each year.
3. Market size is 6000 (000) Aqua-Pur equivalent gallons each year.

As shown later, the user CAN alter these assumptions.

| | | | | | |
|---|---|---|---|---|---|
| UNIT SALES | 600. | 900. | 1000. | 1200. | 1200. |
| REVENUE | 756. | 1134. | 1360. | 1632. | 1632. |
| VAR (+ TRANS) COSTS | 390. | 585. | 650. | 780. | 780. |
| DISTR MARGINS | 222. | 333. | 400. | 480. | 480. |
| CONTR MARGIN | 144. | 216. | 310. | 372. | 372. |
| FIXED COSTS | 149. | 149. | 149. | 149. | 149. |
| EBT | -5. | 67. | 161. | 223. | 223. |

* In this protocol, the actual dialog is shown in typeface, with the parts that were typed by the user underlined to distinguish them from the parts that were printed by the computer. Explanatory comments have been added in handwriting.

```
OPTION? ?  ← request for elaboration
AVAILABLE OPTIONS:
 1  CHANGE PRICES
 2  CHANGE DISTRIBUTOR MARGINS
 3  CHANGE HUDSON SHARES
 4  CHANGE MARKET SIZES
 5  CHANGE FIXED COSTS
 6  CHANGE VARIABLE COSTS
 7  RUN PRO FORMAS
 $  STOP
OPTION? 4
MARKET SIZES (ØØØ'S): ?
GIVE THE MARKET SIZE (ØØØ'S OF GALLONS) FOR  EACH OF
 UP TO 1Ø YEARS.
MARKET SIZES (ØØØ'S): 12ØØØ.  ← The user changes the market size to 12000(000) each year
OPTION? 7
NUMBER OF YEARS: 4

UNIT SALES               12ØØ.   18ØØ.   2ØØØ.   24ØØ.
REVENUE                  1512.   2268.   2721.   3264.
VAR (+ TRANS) COSTS       78Ø.   117Ø.   13ØØ.   156Ø.
DISTR MARGINS             444.    666.    8ØØ.    96Ø.
CONTR MARGIN              288.    432.    62Ø.    744.
FIXED COSTS               149.    149.    149.    149.
EBT                       139.    283.    471.    595.

OPTION? 5  ← Changing fixed costs
FIXED COSTS: ?
GIVE THE FIXED COSTS (THOUSANDS OF $) FOR EACH OF UP TO 1Ø YEARS.
FIXED COSTS: 2ØØ. 165. 149.
OPTION? 6  ← Changing variable costs
VARIABLE COSTS: ?
GIVE THE VARIABLE COSTS PER GALLON ($) FOR EACH OF UP TO
 1Ø YEARS.
VARIABLE COSTS: .7Ø .68 .65 .65
OPTION? 7
NUMBER OF YEARS: 3

UNIT SALES               12ØØ.   18ØØ.   2ØØØ.
REVENUE                  1512.   2268.   2721.
VAR (+ TRANS) COSTS       84Ø.   1224.   13ØØ.
DISTR MARGINS             444.    666.    8ØØ.
CONTR MARGIN              228.    378.    62Ø.
FIXED COSTS               2ØØ.    165.    149.
EBT                        28.    213.    471.

OPTION? $  ← Request to end this run of HUDSN

EXIT
```

NOTE: within any run of HUDSN, the program keeps the changes in assumptions given by the user (until the user changes any of those values). Each time the program is run, however, HUDSN starts with the assumptions (on market size, fixed costs and variable costs) listed on the protocol (handwritten) above – and it asks for prices, margins and shares.

# case 2.3

# Eastern Insurance Company

Arthur Bramble, a vice president with the Eastern Insurance Company, was trying to decide whether Eastern should invest in a proposed new town outside of Atlanta, Georgia. Eastern had been approached about the deal by Jones and Kimmel, a firm of real estate developers who were anxious to try to develop the town, which would be called Adamsville. The developers needed a financial partner for the venture and thought Eastern would be a good choice.

## Background information

The concept of developing new towns away from existing cities was suggested by Ebenezer Howard, an English court clerk, in a book called *Garden Cities of Tomorrow,* which was published in 1898. The book was Howard's answer to the problem of congestion in London; in it he suggested that entirely new towns should be developed outside the city. The towns would include both residences and businesses, so that they would not simply be residential communities, whose workers commuted elsewhere to work, but would instead be relatively self-contained communities in which people would find work, homes, and recreational opportunities.

Working with Howard's idea in mind, developer Alexander M. Bing decided in 1929 to build a new town called Radburn, New Jersey, 15 miles from Manhattan. Bing planned the town for 25,000 people but never completed his design because the stock market crash withered his lines of credit. (In the early 1970s, 2,300 people lived in 200 apartments and 500 private houses in Radburn.) Howard's idea was also behind the funding by the Roosevelt administration of three "green belt" towns. In the long run, these towns were not successful in erecting buffer zones between their town lines and the nearby urban areas; as a result, they became part of the general urban sprawl.

Howard's new-town concept found new proponents in the early 1960s. Chief among these were Robert Simon, a New York real-estate man who began the development of Reston, Virginia, and James Rouse, whose company built the city of Columbia, Maryland. The developers and public alike looked to these new towns as a way to halt the urban spread of the Baltimore-Washington area. Both of the towns were privately financed and developed. They differ from conventional subdivision communities in that they contain industrial areas (and, hence, jobs). They were intended for a cross section of people of different income levels, and they were planned as a whole, with town centers and free space included. Both towns have single family homes, apartments, professional buildings, and light industry.

Despite optimistic starts, both Reston and Columbia suffered serious setbacks. Gulf Oil had loaned Robert Simon $15 million to start Reston; when sales lagged and the project became seriously overextended financially, Gulf wrote off $7 million of its original investment, replaced Simon with a Gulf executive and invested another $35 million. Gulf did, however, continue to work from Reston's master plan. By 1971 Reston was able to arrange its own financing.

James Rouse borrowed $25 million from Connecticut General Life Insurance Company in 1963 to buy land for Columbia. Other private investors later joined the project, so that by early 1975 the total investment was about $100 million. Inflation, high interest rates, and the sagging housing market of the early 1970s forced Rouse to cancel plans for developing other new towns and, in addition, put financial pressure on Columbia. In 1974 Rouse had concluded that privately developed towns required more than a decade to establish and that there was so much uncertainty about their ultimate viability that, he felt, they were dead for the foreseeable future in the United States.

There were, nevertheless, many new towns under development in the United States at that time. In this country the development of new towns has been done primarily by private industry, although the government has provided some funding for the projects. The backers of these towns have been insurance companies, banks, and large companies which wanted to invest in real estate. (In Europe, on the other hand, new towns were more likely to be developed with governments doing the planning and private companies carrying out those plans.)

**The proposed town at Adamsville**

The Adamsville development was planned as a large, mixed-use development on a 5,000-acre site in the country near Atlanta. Plans called for the developer to make necessary improvements on the land and then to sell individual lots for housing, industry, and commercial use. The development would be carried out under a land-use plan for the entire site which, among other things, earmarked part of the land as greenbelt (or open space). Individuals and groups who purchased lots would have to clear their building plans with a town planning commission which would try to ensure the development of an aesthetically attractive community. Plans called for sale of land for 15,500 housing units, consisting of single family lots (at three per acre), condominums or townhouses (at seven per acre), and apartments (with 15 apartments per acre). In addition, the project would include 750 acres for industry and 232.5 acres for commercial use (stores, restaurants, and so forth). The remainder of the land would be open space which would be turned over to the town government in installments as the residential, industrial, and commercial lots were sold. (For example, when half of the acreage intended for sale had been sold, half of the greenbelt land would have been turned over.) The project would also include what were called amenities and off-lot improvements; these included swimming pools, park and picnic areas, and a golf course. The amenities were important in the marketing plans for the community; the developers would argue that one of the chief advantages of a planned community was that it could include such attractions.

Mr. Bramble and his staff had completed some preliminary negotiations with the developers and, as a result, the basic form of the financial arrangements had been agreed upon. The developer would provide an initial $6 million in equity; that money would be used as part of the down payment for the land. (The site would be purchased for $30 million, with $9 million down and the remainder covered by a mortgage at 7.5 percent interest, with interest plus $3 million in principal to be repaid each year until the mortgage had been paid off.) The developer would also provide management services for the project. If Eastern agreed to become the financial partner, it would provide an initial $10 million in subordinated debt (at 9.5 percent interest). It would also be responsible for raising (or providing itself) whatever additional funding was necessary for the project; Bramble felt that the interest rate for additional money would likely be about 6 percent above the inflation rate in any year. Once the project reached the break-even point (and all debt had been paid off), the cash it generated would be paid out as dividends, half to the developer and half to the investor. Bramble knew that Eastern's hurdle rate was 12 percent, so that the project's returns should be analyzed using that discount factor.

### The market study

Development of Adamsville would take about 15 or 20 years to complete, so that planning involved a long time frame. Especially for that reason, Eastern and also Jones and Kimmel had felt it important to commission a careful market study of the project. Bramble had received the results of the study and felt considerable confidence in them. The analysis had been based on the initial assumptions about market mix, revenues, and costs which are shown in Table 1. The appraisal firm which had prepared the study had provided the sales projections given in Table 2 for the three residential types (single family, condominium, and apartment) and for industrial acreage. Rather than prepare a separate schedule for sales of commercial land, they

**TABLE 1**
Initial assumptions

| | *Single family* | *Condo-minium* | *Apart-ment* | *Indus-trial* | *Commer-cial* |
|---|---|---|---|---|---|
| Initial selling price | $10,000 | $3,500 | $1,800 | $40,000 | $40,000 |
| Initial development costs (lot-related) | $ 5,000 | $2,200 | $1,000 | $13,000 | $13,000 |
| Acres/unit | 1/3 | 1/7 | 1/15 | 1 | 1 |
| Total units planned | 5,000 | 7,500 | 3,000 | 750 | 232.5 |

**TABLE 2**
Sales projections

| *Year* | *Sales of single family lots (number of lots)* | *Condominiums (units)* | *Apartments (units)* | *Industrial acreage* |
|---|---|---|---|---|
| 1 | — | 150 | 300 | 10 |
| 2 | 150 | 300 | 300 | 20 |
| 3 | 200 | 400 | 400 | 30 |
| 4 | 250 | 550 | 500 | 40 |
| 5 | 300 | 600 | 250 | 50 |
| 6 | 400 | 600 | 250 | 60 |
| 7 | 400 | 600 | 250 | 60 |
| 8 | 400 | 600 | 250 | 60 |
| 9 | 400 | 600 | 100 | 60 |
| 10 | 500 | 600 | 100 | 60 |
| 11 | 500 | 500 | 100 | 60 |
| 12 | 500 | 500 | 100 | 60 |
| 13 | 600 | 500 | 100 | 60 |
| 14 | 200 | 400 | — | 60 |
| 15 | 150 | 300 | — | 60 |
| 16 | 50 | 300 | — | — |
| 17 | — | — | — | — |
| 18 | — | — | — | — |
| 19 | — | — | — | — |
| 20 | — | — | — | — |

had suggested the assumption that 15 acres of commercial property would be sold for each 1,000 housing units of any of the three types; this assumption seemed reasonable because the customers for the stores and other establishments would, for the most part, be residents of the new town.

In addition, the market study gave a schedule of spending for amenities and off-site improvements; it assumed that those expenditures would be made during the first nine years of the project. Table 3 gives the projected amenities and improvements spending figures (in constant dollars). Further, the study assumed that the general and administrative expenses (G & A) for

**TABLE 3**
Amenities and G & A

| Year | *Amenities and improvements (constant dollars)* | *Fixed component of G & A (constant dollars)* |
|---|---|---|
| 1 | 2,000,000 | 500,000 |
| 2 | 3,000,000 | 500,000 |
| 3 | 3,000,000 | 500,000 |
| 4 | 3,000,000 | 500,000 |
| 5 | 2,000,000 | 500,000 |
| 6 | 2,000,000 | 500,000 |
| 7 | 2,000,000 | 500,000 |
| 8 | 2,000,000 | 500,000 |
| 9 | 1,000,000 | 500,000 |
| 10 | — | 400,000 |
| 11 | — | 400,000 |
| 12 | — | 400,000 |
| 13 | — | 400,000 |
| 14 | — | 400,000 |
| 15 | — | 200,000 |
| 16 | — | 200,000 |
| 17 | — | 200,000 |
| 18 | — | — |
| 19 | — | — |
| 20 | — | — |

the project would involve both fixed and variable components. The fixed components are given (in terms of constant dollars) in Table 3. The variable components were estimated to be 4 percent of sales. Selling and promotion were assumed variable and were taken to be 7 percent of sales.

Another factor discussed in the market study was what was called the value inflator. This factor expressed the underlying growth in value of the lots in the town that was expected to occur over time. Basically, the idea was that the prices which the partners could obtain for the lots would increase not merely at the inflation rate but at a higher rate, reflecting an increase in inherent value (or constant-dollar value) of the property. The study argued that in the prosperous and growing Atlanta area, property in the country would show such an increase in basic value. The market study assumed that the prices which could be obtained for the lots at Adamsville would grow at the inflation rate compounded by a value inflator rate of about 6 percent. Hence, in a single year in which inflation was 8 percent, the prices would increase by 8 * 1.06 percent.

As noted above, Mr. Bramble felt considerable confidence in the general outline of the market study but, nonetheless, in an investment of this size he felt it important to consider more than a single set of projections. Among the issues which he felt would be important for the outcome of the project was the future pattern of inflation and the extent to which various costs and revenues would grow with inflation. Accordingly, he had hired two consultants to provide further analysis of the Adamsville project and of the risk exposure which Eastern would face if it decided to enter the deal.

## The consultants' analysis

After a careful study of the work that had already been done and, in particular, of the market study, the consultants proceeded to pin down some additional assumptions that would be needed to model the deal in more detail. They found that the inventory policy for the project would be to develop in any given year a number of lots in each category equal to the maximum of the current year's sales of that category and the projection (from the market study) of the next year's sales of that type. As far as payments were concerned, they assumed that the project would receive 20 percent of the purchase price of a lot at the time of sale; 50 percent of the price would come in at the end of the first year and 15 percent would be received at the ends of each of the next two years. At the end of each year the project would receive 8 percent interest on the outstanding balances on sales of lots. Real estate taxes for the property would be $125 per acre (in constant dollars); the partners would have to pay taxes both on acreage that was destined for sales as lots and on whatever greenbelt acreage was still under their control.

In talking with Mr. Bramble about the model that they were building, the consultants found that he had considerable faith in the market study and wanted the model to be based on that document. He was, however, amenable (and, in fact, anxious) to question some of the assumptions of numbers in the study. Accordingly, the consultants decided to use the figures from the study (given in Tables 1, 2, and 3) as a basis for the model and to have Mr. Bramble give them adjustments for those estimates rather than to have him describe his uncertainty about prices, costs, and other factors directly. Further, they were able to identify the main uncertainities which seemed to them and to Bramble to require consideration. First was the pattern of inflation rates that would occur over the 20-year history of the project. Eastern executives wanted to be able to give a specific inflation pattern and to see what the results of the project would be under that pattern. In doing so, they would have to make some assumptions about how the different types of costs and revenues would grow with inflation. Mr. Bramble felt that the economy was in the midst of adjusting to higher inflation levels, and he felt that it would be a number of years before the behavior of prices and wages settled down into a new pattern. He said that he thought of the adjustments to inflation in terms of three stages. The first would involve considerable differences in the way various cost and price components. responded to inflation. In the second stage business people would be learning to live with new inflation levels and the effects of the inflation would be less disruptive, while in the last stage the higher inflation levels that he thought were inevitable would be an accepted part of the economy. Bramble suggested that the first and second stages might take four and six years, respectively. Accordingly, he and the consultants tried to specify the factors by which the different cost components would grow with inflation. They decided, for example, that the lot-related costs would grow at 1.3 times the inflation rate in the first period, 1.25 times inflation in the transition period and at 1.2 times inflation after that. Table 4

**TABLE 4**
Growth factors (with inflation)

| | *Years 1–4* | *Years 5–10* | *Years 11–20* |
|---|---|---|---|
| Amenities | 1.3 | 1.15 | 1.0 |
| Lot-related costs | 1.3 | 1.25 | 1.2 |
| Fixed G & A | 1.0 | 1.2 | 1.25 |

gives the factors which were chosen for amenities, lot-related costs, and fixed G & A. Bramble was willing to assume that real estate taxes would grow at the same rate as inflation in all three stages.

Bramble was not able to assign a corresponding set of three numbers for the value inflator (the growth of intrinsic value of the lots). Instead, the consultants decided to make this factor one of the input factors required for a particular run of the model. In addition, they decided that the inflation growth factors for amenities and lot-related costs did not reflect adequately the uncertainty about those costs; they wanted to include in the inputs for any run of the model two factors, one for each of these cost categories. The initial cost schedule would be raised or lowered by these factors and the growth with inflation would then be applied to the adjusted schedules. Finally, they felt that the inputs for a given model run should also include factors by which the sales projections from the market study would be scaled up or down. The factors would change the sales figures for the various years of the project. If the sales in a particular category, such as apartments, were scaled down by some factor, the model would assume that the full number of units would eventually be sold but that they would be sold later in the life of the project than had been anticipated. Four sales-adjustment factors would be used, with one each for single family lots, condominiums, apartments, and industrial acreage.

## case 2.4

# Marsh & McLennan (A) and (B)*

## MARSH & McLENNAN (A)

Marsh & McLennan are international insurance brokers and employee benefit consultants.[1] The firm is an independent contractor remunerated on a commission or fee basis. Its principal function is to assist its clients in placing risks in the insurance market at conditions and premiums equitable to both insured and insurer, as well as to provide consulting, actuarial, and communication services for its clients' employee benefit plans. Marsh & McLennan's services are primarily purchased by corporate and institutional organizations who require specialized and professional counsel to assess their exposures to risk and to fulfill their insurance and employee benefit requirements.

### Aircraft insurance

Early in 1969, in preparation for the renewal of coverage for a three-year policy term, Marsh & McLennan began reviewing the insurance program for one of its clients, Eastern Airlines, Inc.

Aircraft insurance received little attention until after World War I. There were no special forms to cover aviation risks, and the few policies that were issued made use of the ordinary fire and automobile forms. Initially, underwriting was characterized by a considerable element of trial and error. The volume of business was small, and values in a single risk were great. Experience upon which to predict rates was lacking. Early insurers charged high premiums, imposed heavy deductibles, and used some complicated policy conditions.

For a considerable period, insurance companies were organized into un-

* This case was written by Howard Pifer and Paul A. Vatter.

[1] From the *Marsh & McLennan Story:* "The responsibility of the [insurance] broker is to provide for his client, through quality service by technical, administrative, and executive personnel, an expert appraisal of his insurance requirements, development of custom-made policy conditions to provide proper insurance protection, and the purchase of such coverage in the insurance markets of the world. Additionally, the broker provides during the policy term technical advice and assistance on a continuing basis to assist the client with all related problems."

derwriting syndicates to handle the growing volume of aircraft business. Such syndicates still account for a substantial part of the business, especially the protection for the large airline transportation and aircraft manufacturing companies.

At first glance, the aircraft coverages seem to parallel the familiar automobile coverages. Each is divided into two classifications: direct loss and liability coverages. However, compared with automobile risks, aircraft insurance involves huge sums for each accident, and direct loss insurance, depreciation, and obsolescence become important factors.

## Hull insurance

The specific insurance policy under study by Marsh & McLennan was hull insurance for Eastern's entire jet fleet.[2] Premiums for aircraft hull insurance are frequently determined in a retrospective fashion and are based on the amount of losses during the coverage period. There is an upper limit on the premium amount which transfers some risk to the insurer, but generally the insurer is directly reimbursed for losses paid under the contract. There are many alternative reimbursement formulas, giving the insurer varying margins

**EXHIBIT A–1**
Eastern Airlines jet fleet (January 1, 1969)

| | | *Book value* | | *Insured value* | |
|---|---|---|---|---|---|
| *Aircraft* | *No.* | *Plane value* | *Fleet value* | *Plane value* | *Fleet value* |
| DC-8-61 . . . . . . . . | 17 | $ 8,709,000 | $148,053,000 | $ 9,000,000 | $153,000,000 |
| DC-8-63 . . . . . . . . | 2 | 11,100,000 | 22,200,000 | 11,300,000 | 22,600,000 |
| | 19 | | $170,253,000 | | $175,600,000 |
| DC-9-14 . . . . . . . . | 15 | 3,310,000 | 49,650,000 | 3,400,000 | 51,000,000 |
| DC-9-21 . . . . . . . . | 14 | 2,772,000 | 38,808,000 | 3,000,000 | 42,000,000 |
| DC-9-3 . . . . . . . . . | 62 | 3,825,000 | 237,150,000 | 3,900,000 | 241,800,000 |
| DC-9-31 . . . . . . . . | 5 | 3,825,000 | 19,125,000 | 3,900,000 | 19,500,000 |
| | 96 | | $344,733,000 | | $354,300,000 |
| 720 . . . . . . . . . . . . | 15 | 2,455,000 | 36,825,000 | 3,200,000 | 48,000,000 |
| | 15 | | $ 36,825,000 | | $ 48,000,000 |
| 727 . . . . . . . . . . . . | 50 | 3,854,000 | 192,700,000 | 4,200,000 | 210,000,000 |
| 727-225 . . . . . . . . | 1 | 6,092,225 | 6,092,225 | 6,200,000 | 6,200,000 |
| 727-QC . . . . . . . . . | 17 | 5,710,000 | 97,070,000 | 5,900,000 | 100,300,000 |
| 727-QC . . . . . . . . . | 8 | 5,710,000 | 45,680,000 | 5,900,000 | 47,200,000 |
| | 76 | | $341,680,000 | | $363,700,000 |
| Totals . . . . . . | 206 | | $896,353,225 | | $941,600,000 |

[2] See Exhibit A–1 for schedule of aircraft.

for expense and risk premiums, but Eastern was considering only two hull insurance proposals submitted by Associated Aviation Underwriters. A third alternative, self-insurance, was not being considered by Eastern at this time.

1. Loss Conversion Plan—Eastern had been utilizing a Loss Conversion formula. Under this plan, annual premiums are equal to 135 percent of all losses incurred within that year, subject to a maximum annual rate of $1.05 and a minimum rate of $.50 per $100 insured value. With this method of premium calculation, an incentive credit equaling 10 percent of total three-year premiums in excess of total three-year losses is given the insured if the plan runs for the full three-year term.
2. Profit Commission Plan—John Lawton, Marsh & McLennan's Account Executive, suggested that Eastern modify its insurance program to utilize a cumulative three-year Profit Commission method of calculation. Annual premiums under this plan equal losses plus $.25 per $100 insured, subject to a maximum annual premium of one percent of insured value. The incentive credit refunded at the end of the policy was equivalent to the excess, if any, of (*a*) premiums paid over (*b*) total losses plus $.20 per $100 value per year.

When the Profit Commission plan was suggested to Mr. Peter Mullen, Eastern's Director—Insurance, he expressed some concern that it could be more expensive than the Loss Conversion plan. He pointed out that Eastern had 206 jet aircraft with a total fleet value of nearly one billion dollars and an average value of $4.6 million per aircraft. If the assumption is made that one "average aircraft" is lost each year, the Loss Conversion plan would produce significant savings when compared to the Profit Commission plan. In addition, of the 206 aircraft in the Eastern jet fleet, all but two were presently valued at amounts which, in the event of loss, would produce lower costs under the Loss Conversion plan.

Mr. Lawton thought there were other factors that should be considered. Mr. Mullen was correct in pointing out that Eastern's annual insurance premium could be less under the Loss Conversion plan providing losses were "average." However, the alternative Profit Commission plan would cost less if there were no losses or if two or more losses occurred in a given year. Considering various possible combinations of losses over a three-year term, the Profit Commission plan produced a lower cost in eight out of ten sample adjustments. See Exhibit A–2 for the sample adjustments submitted to Eastern.

In order to prepare for an upcoming conference with Mr. Mullen and other Eastern executives, Mr. Lawton asked a Marsh & McLennan actuary, Charles Porter, to evaluate the relative merits of the two alternative plans and to prepare his recommendations prior to the meeting.

**EXHIBIT A–2**
Eastern Airlines hull insurance comparison of costs based on catastrophic losses (estimated fleet value $1,000,000,000)

| Losses | Loss conversion plan | Profit commission plan |
|---|---|---|
| 1. $1,000,000 | $ 5,000,000 | $ 3,500,000 |
| 2. 1,000,000 | 5,000,000 | 3,500,000 |
| 3. 1,000,000 | 5,000,000 | 3,500,000 |
| Total (3,000,000) | $15,000,000 | $10,500,000 |
| Incentive credit | 1,200,000 | 1,500,000 |
| Net cost | $13,800,000 | $ 9,000,000 |
| 1. 1,000,000 | 5,000,000 | 3,500,000 |
| 2. 1,000,000 | 5,000,000 | 3,500,000 |
| 3. 6,000,000 | 8,100,000 | 8,500,000 |
| Total (8,000,000) | $18,100,000 | $15,500,000 |
| Incentive credit | 1,010,000 | 1,500,000 |
| Net cost | $17,090,000 | $14,000,000 |
| 1. 1,000,000 | 5,000,000 | 3,500,000 |
| 2. 6,000,000 | 8,100,000 | 8,500,000 |
| 3. 6,000,000 | 8,100,000 | 8,500,000 |
| Total (13,000,000) | $21,200,000 | $20,500,000 |
| Incentive credit | 820,000 | 1,500,000 |
| Net cost | $20,380,000 | $19,000,000 |
| 1. 6,000,000 | 8,100,000 | 8,500,000 |
| 2. 6,000,000 | 8,100,000 | 8,500,000 |
| 3. 6,000,000 | 8,100,000 | 8,500,000 |
| Total (18,000,000) | $24,300,000 | $25,500,000 |
| Incentive credit | 630,000 | 1,500,000 |
| Net cost | $23,670,000 | $24,000,000 |
| 1. 1,000,000 | 5,000,000 | 3,500,000 |
| 2. 1,000,000 | 5,000,000 | 3,500,000 |
| 3. 11,000,000 | 10,500,000 | 10,000,000 |
| Total (13,000,000) | $21,500,000 | $17,000,000 |
| Incentive credit | 850,000 | 0 |
| Net cost | $20,650,000 | $17,000,000 |
| 1. 1,000,000 | 5,000,000 | 3,500,000 |
| 2. 6,000,000 | 8,100,000 | 8,500,000 |
| 3. 11,000,000 | 10,500,000 | 10,000,000 |
| Total (18,000,000) | $23,600,000 | $22,000,000 |
| Incentive credit | 560,000 | 0 |
| Net cost | $23,040,000 | $22,000,000 |
| 1. 1,000,000 | 5,000,000 | 3,500,000 |
| 2. 11,000,000 | 10,500,000 | 10,000,000 |
| 3. 11,000,000 | 10,500,000 | 10,000,000 |
| Total (23,000,000) | $26,000,000 | $23,500,000 |
| Incentive credit | 300,000 | 0 |
| Net cost | $25,700,000 | $23,500,000 |

**EXHIBIT A–2 (*continued*)**

| *Losses* | *Loss conversion plan* | *Profit commission plan* |
|---|---|---|
| 1. 6,000,000 | 8,100,000 | 8,500,000 |
| 2. 6,000,000 | 8,100,000 | 8,500,000 |
| 3. 11,000,000 | 10,500,000 | 10,000,000 |
| Total (23,000,000) | $26,700,000 | $27,000,000 |
| Incentive credit | 370,000 | 0 |
| Net cost | $26,330,000 | $27,000,000 |
| 1. 6,000,000 | 8,100,000 | 8,500,000 |
| 2. 11,000,000 | 10,500,000 | 10,000,000 |
| 3. 11,000,000 | 10,500,000 | 10,000,000 |
| Total (28,000,000) | $29,100,000 | $28,500,000 |
| Incentive credit | 110,000 | 0 |
| Net cost | $28,990,000 | $28,500,000 |
| 1. 11,000,000 | 10,500,000 | 10,000,000 |
| 2. 11,000,000 | 10,500,000 | 10,000,000 |
| 3. 11,000,000 | 10,500,000 | 10,000,000 |
| Total (33,000,000) | $31,500,000 | $30,000,000 |
| Incentive credit | 0 | 0 |
| Net cost | $31,500,000 | $30,000,000 |

## Additional information

A variety of industry-wide statistics was available. Losses could be studied in detail as to type of aircraft, cause of loss, or related to the number of flights, revenue miles, flying hours, etc. In an attempt to estimate the probability that an aircraft would be lost in the course of a calendar year, Mr. Porter had found a research report of the FAA. This statistical survey had shown that the accident rate per cruise hour was essentially identical for all types of aircraft. To adjust for increased exposure during takeoff and landing, 3.7 hours of cruising were added for each flight. Thus, a flight between New York and San Francisco (flight time 6 hours) would be equivalent to 9.7 hours of cruising; whreas a flight between New York and Boston (flight time 45 minutes), although only one eighth as long in terms of flight time, would be equivalent to 4.45 hours of cruising.

To determine the "equivalent hours" of exposure for all jets flown by domestic trunk carriers, Mr. Porter found detailed data for both 1967 and 1968. During that period of time 15,660,000 "equivalent hours" were recorded with total losses of jet aircraft numbering ten. While Eastern's recent experience had been much better, data relating solely to Eastern would be too scanty to provide a meaningful basis. In addition to total losses, partial hull damage (minor aircraft damage on a landing or take-off) may be estimated from Eastern's experience as $500,000 to $1 million per year.

Information on future fleet expansion and flight schedules was not firm;

but for the purposes of his analysis, Mr. Porter was told to base his evaluation of alternative plans upon the current fleet size (Exhibit A–1) and an annual estimate of 10,060 "equivalent hours" per jet. The recent congestion along the eastern seaboard would eliminate any possibility of significantly higher utilization.

Armed with these data, Mr. Porter prepared to make his evaluation of the two plans.

## MARSH & McLENNAN (B)

Charles Porter, an actuary on Marsh & McLennan's staff, decided to prepare a computer-based Monte Carlo simulation of the two alternative hull insurance plans. His objectives were to simulate the net costs of both insurance plans over the next three years, to compare these costs to determine which plan would be best for Eastern, and to ascertain whether either or both plans would provide effective protection against the excessive losses that could occur with no insurance at all.

After reviewing the information available to him, Mr. Porter constructed a computer program to simulate the possible three-year histories of aircraft losses. He reasoned that the actual losses in any one year would consist of both partial hull damage and possible total losses due to aircraft crashes. He assumed that the losses due to partial hull damage would be equally distributed between a minimum of $500,000 and a maximum of $1 million per year. He further assumed that the probability of a total loss would be the same for any aircraft in any one year, and approximately equal to the "equivalent hours" flown per year times the probability of a crash in any one "equivalent hour" based upon historical records of the FAA. He thereby determined that the probability of losing any one aircraft in a given year was approximately .006424 (10,060 hours times 10 ÷ 15,660,000 crashes per hour). Using these two assumptions, he structured a computer simulation program which, for each of the next three years, generated a sequence of random numbers: one to simulate the amount of partial hull damage and one random number for each of the 206 aircraft to determine if that plane would "crash." The program then added the insured values of each aircraft which "crashed" plus the partial hull damage to obtain the combined losses for each year. These yearly losses were used to determine the insurance premiums under each plan in each year, the total premiums for the three years, the combined losses for the three years, and finally the net cost after incentive of each plan for the three-year period. These basic computations formed the basis of one simulation trial. The program was instructed to run for 200 trials, and then to offer printouts of the distributions of:

1. The net three-year cost of the Loss Conversion Plan.
2. The net three-year cost of the Profit Commission Plan.

3. The combined losses during the three-year period (which would be the actual cost with no insurance plan).
4. The net three-year cost of the Loss Conversion Plan minus the net three-year cost of the Profit Commission Plan.

In addition, the program was instructed to compute and print out the number of runs (out of 200) when the Loss Conversion Plan yielded a lower net cost than the Profit Commission Plan, and the number of runs when each plan yielded a lower three-year cost than the actual three-year losses.

After checking the simulation program for validity, Porter produced the simulation results shown in Exhibit B–1. He observed that the average costs

**EXHIBIT B–1**

Simulation results for 200 trials (costs are net 3-year values in millions) (the yearly probability of a total loss is .006424 per plane)

| | *Loss conversion* | *Profit commission* | *Actual losses* | *Loss conversion minus profit commission* |
|---|---|---|---|---|
| Mean | 22.078 | 20.881 | 20.501 | 1.196 |
| Standard deviation | 4.030 | 4.721 | 9.104 | 1.431 |
| Fractiles: | | | | |
| .001 | 12.91 | 7.60 | 1.96 | −1.76 |
| .01 | 12.99 | 7.79 | 2.25 | −1.56 |
| .1 | 16.93 | 15.16 | 9.94 | − .95 |
| .25 | 19.50 | 18.77 | 13.87 | .25 |
| .5 | 21.79 | 21.67 | 20.02 | 1.18 |
| .75 | 24.61 | 24.80 | 26.44 | 2.20 |
| .9 | 27.98 | 27.42 | 32.10 | 3.02 |
| .99 | 29.63 | 28.22 | 45.30 | 5.11 |
| .999 | 29.66 | 28.25 | 48.98 | 5.31 |

LOSS CONVERSION LESS THAN PROFIT COMMISSION IN 41 OF 200 TRIALS.
LOSS CONVERSION LESS THAN ACTUAL LOSSES IN 64 OF 200 TRIALS.
PROFIT COMMISSION LESS THAN ACTUAL LOSSES IN 72 OF 200 TRIALS.

of the Profit Commission Plan appeared to be less than the Loss Conversion Plan, but the standard deviation of these costs was greater. In addition, the output indicated that on 159 out of 200 runs the Profit Commission Plan yielded lower net costs. This section of the output also indicated that the Loss Conversion costs were less than the actual losses on only 64 out of 200 runs, and the Profit Commission costs were less than the actual losses on only 72 of the 200 runs.

Mr. Porter wanted to make sure that he had not obtained misleading results by only using 200 trials. He therefore ran the entire simulation program again four more times using a different sequence of random numbers each time. The results of these additional runs were compiled and compared to the original results in Exhibit B–2 (only means and standard deviations are compared for the sake of brevity). Porter wanted to use these results to verify whether a run with only 200 trials could be used as a valid tool for decision making.

Finally, Porter was worried about his assumption that the FAA research data could be used as an accurate determination of the probability of a total

**EXHIBIT B–2**
Four additional runs with 200 trials using different sequences of random numbers (means and standard deviations in millions of dollars)

| | *Loss conversion* | *Profit commission* | *Actual losses* |
|---|---|---|---|
| *Run 2* | | | |
| Mean | 22.004 | 20.944 | 20.469 |
| Standard deviation | 4.268 | 4.830 | 9.416 |
| *Run 3* | | | |
| Mean | 21.506 | 20.285 | 19.622 |
| Standard deviation | 4.195 | 4.837 | 9.583 |
| *Run 4* | | | |
| Mean | 22.294 | 21.237 | 20.744 |
| Standard deviation | 4.315 | 4.960 | 9.471 |
| *Run 5* | | | |
| Mean | 21.795 | 20.627 | 19.906 |
| Standard deviation | 4.307 | 5.070 | 10.271 |

*RUN 2:* LOSS CONVERSION LESS THAN PROFIT COMMISSION IN 38 OF 200 TRIALS.
LOSS CONVERSION LESS THAN ACTUAL LOSSES IN 67 OF 200 TRIALS.
PROFIT COMMISSION LESS THAN ACTUAL LOSSES IN 72 OF 200 TRIALS.

*RUN 3:* LOSS CONVERSION LESS THAN PROFIT COMMISSION IN 34 OF 200 TRIALS.
LOSS CONVERSION LESS THAN ACTUAL LOSSES IN 62 OF 200 TRIALS.
PROFIT COMMISSION LESS THAN ACTUAL LOSSES IN 71 OF 200 TRIALS.

*RUN 4:* LOSS CONVERSION LESS THAN PROFIT COMMISSION IN 47 OF 200 TRIALS.
LOSS CONVERSION LESS THAN ACTUAL LOSSES IN 65 OF 200 TRIALS.
PROFIT COMMISSION LESS THAN ACTUAL LOSSES IN 74 OF 200 TRIALS.

*RUN 5:* LOSS CONVERSION LESS THAN PROFIT COMMISSION IN 45 OF 200 TRIALS.
LOSS CONVERSION LESS THAN ACTUAL LOSSES IN 55 OF 200 TRIALS.
PROFIT COMMISSION LESS THAN ACTUAL LOSSES IN 74 OF 200 TRIALS.

loss. Suppose, for example, that the future probability of a crash was significantly less than the relative frequency recorded in 1967 and 1968 because of newly installed radar tracking equipment on many airport approach paths. Or suppose that this probability had increased since 1967 and 1968 because of the greatly increased congestion of major airfields and continued obsolescence of the fleet. Because of these possibilities, Porter decided to produce two more simulation runs, one with the yearly probability of a total loss increased by a factor of 1.50 to .009636 and one with this probability de-

**EXHIBIT B–3**

Simulation results for different values of the yearly probability of a total loss

| | *Loss conversion* | *Profit commission* | *Actual losses* | *Loss conversion minus profit commission* |
|---|---|---|---|---|
| *Part A* | | | | |
| Mean | 17.937 | 15.644 | 11.494 | 2.293 |
| Standard deviation | 3.678 | 4.999 | 6.938 | 1.730 |
| Fractiles: | | | | |
| .001 | 12.89 | 7.47 | 1.82 | −1.82 |
| .01 | 12.90 | 7.51 | 1.86 | −1.58 |
| .1 | 12.99 | 7.92 | 2.26 | .28 |
| .25 | 14.76 | 11.78 | 6.14 | .95 |
| .5 | 18.36 | 15.63 | 10.80 | 2.62 |
| .75 | 20.27 | 19.41 | 15.49 | 3.21 |
| .9 | 23.61 | 21.94 | 20.79 | 5.02 |
| .99 | 28.27 | 27.51 | 32.53 | 5.38 |
| .999 | 28.41 | 27.69 | 39.19 | 5.42 |
| *Part B* | | | | |
| Mean | 25.025 | 23.954 | 29.425 | 1.047 |
| Standard deviation | 3.487 | 3.708 | 10.972 | 1.226 |
| Fractiles: | | | | |
| .001 | 12.94 | 7.62 | 2.05 | −1.63 |
| .01 | 15.42 | 14.61 | 8.95 | −1.51 |
| .1 | 20.40 | 19.57 | 16.55 | .79 |
| .25 | 23.04 | 21.82 | 22.25 | .19 |
| .5 | 24.80 | 24.84 | 28.64 | 1.27 |
| .75 | 28.49 | 27.63 | 36.43 | 2.12 |
| .9 | 29.58 | 28.16 | 43.45 | 2.59 |
| .99 | 29.65 | 28.24 | 59.24 | 3.83 |
| .999 | 29.66 | 28.25 | 60.29 | 5.31 |

*PART A:* PROBABILITY DECREASED TO .003212.
LOSS CONVERSION LESS THAN PROFIT COMMISSION IN 16 OF 200 TRIALS.
LOSS CONVERSION LESS THAN ACTUAL LOSSES IN 11 OF 200 TRIALS.
PROFIT COMMISSION LESS THAN ACTUAL LOSSES IN 15 OF 200 TRIALS.

*PART B:* PROBABILITY INCREASED TO .009636.
LOSS CONVERSION LESS THAN PROFIT COMMISSION IN 37 OF 200 TRIALS.
LOSS CONVERSION LESS THAN ACTUAL LOSSES IN 126 OF 200 TRIALS.
PROFIT COMMISSION LESS THAN ACTUAL LOSSES IN 141 OF 200 TRIALS.

creased by a factor of .50 to .003212. He decided to use the same sequence of random numbers that was used for the first simulation (Exhibit B–1) for the sake of comparison. The results of these last two simulation runs are presented in Exhibit B–3.

Armed with this collection of simulation results, Mr. Porter returned to his office to formulate his final recommendations for an insurance plan.

## case 2.5

# Crimmins Distribution Company*

Emily Hillyer was trying to determine an inventory control policy for the Crimmins Distribution Company, a major wholesaler of hardware in the Cincinnati area. In particular, she wanted to start with stock item No. 5302 and to set an inventory control strategy of the following kind. At the end of each business day a clerk would calculate the number of gross of the part which were on hand and also the number of gross which were on order from the factory. In addition, he would find the number of customer backorders (customer orders which were waiting to be filled). He would then calculate the quantity on hand plus the quantity due in from the factory minus quantity due out (to fill backorders); this net amount was called the "status" of the inventory item. Hillyer wanted to chose two numbers, $R$ and $S$, for the product to determine the inventory strategy. The rule adopted would be to order whenever the status of the item fell below $R$, which would be the reorder point. The number ordered would be the amount required to raise the status to $S$ (it would be $S$ minus the current status).

In analyzing the problem, Hillyer wanted to assume that if a customer's order could not be filled immediately it would not be cancelled but, instead, the customer would allow Crimmins to place the order on backorder and to fill it when stock arrived from the manufacturer. To reduce expense and confusion in the shipping and billing departments, no partial shipments were made.

Despite the fact that customers did allow backordering, Hillyer knew that failure to fill an order immediately increased the chance that the customer would later transfer all of his or her business to another wholesaler. This risk seemed so serious that she decided that she should consider explicitly the loss of goodwill involved in backordering. She felt that in order to avoid holding a customer order for $N$ units on backorder for $D$ days, she would be willing to pay a premium to the manufacturer for immediate delivery (were that possible) of up to $N$ times $f(D)$ where $f(D)$ was the function given in Exhibit 1. Such instantaneous deliveries were not possible, but by thinking about them Hillyer was able to quantify the goodwill costs of backorders.

---

* Adapted from Robert Schlaifer *Analysis of Decisions under Uncertainty* (New York: McGraw-Hill, 1969).

**EXHIBIT 1**

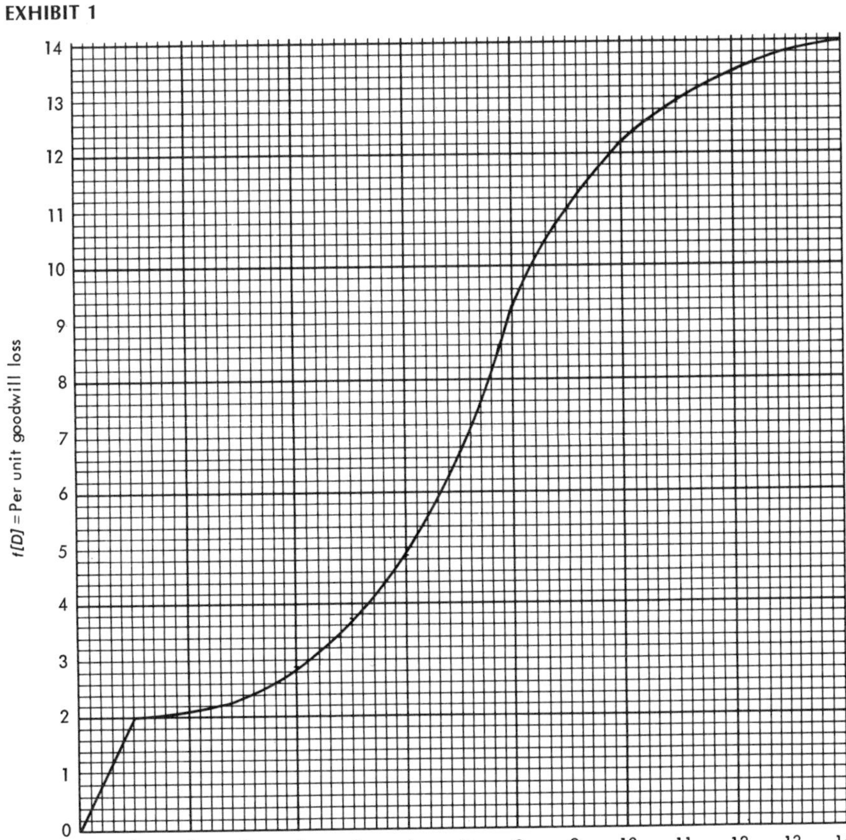


For use in her analysis, Hillyer had assessed a distribution for the number of customer orders received on any of 260 working days in the coming year (as given in Table 1) and also a distribution for the number of units of the product in an individual customer order (Table 2). Moreover, she was willing to assume that the number of orders on a given day and the number of items in any of those orders were independent of each other and of the past history of numbers and sizes of orders. Factory lead time was another uncertainty which had to be considered in setting a policy; the distribution in Table 3 seemed appropriate for factory lead times. In addition Hillyer would assume that the distribution in that table would hold for each order during the year.

The new inventory policy would go into effect the next morning (February 20). At the close of business on February 19, there were 20 units on hand, no backorders, and no factory orders outstanding.

**TABLE 1**
Distribution of number of customer orders received in one day

| *Number of orders* | *Probability* |
|---|---|
| 0 | .15 |
| 1 | .35 |
| 2 | .25 |
| 3 | .15 |
| 4 | .10 |

**TABLE 2**
Distribution of number of units (gross) demanded in one customer order

| *Number (of gross)* | *Probability* |
|---|---|
| 1 | .06 |
| 2 | .11 |
| 3 | .15 |
| 4 | .18 |
| 5 | .15 |
| 6 | .12 |
| 7 | .10 |
| 8 | .07 |
| 9 | .04 |
| 10 | .02 |

**TABLE 3**
Distribution of factory lead time in working days

| *Number of days* | *Probability* |
|---|---|
| 4 | .00 |
| 5 | .05 |
| 6 | .10 |
| 7 | .20 |
| 8 | .30 |
| 9 | .20 |
| 10 | .10 |
| 11 | .05 |

chapter 3

# ADDITIONAL TOPICS ON PROBABILISTIC MODELING

## O. INTRODUCTION

This chapter continues the discussion of probabilistic modeling from the preceding chapter. The first part of the chapter introduces additional methods for handling dependencies among the uncertainties in probabilistic modeling. We first consider the use of functional forms in probabilistic models. Chapter 1 introduced those forms as very powerful tools for facilitating the input portions of deterministic models. In the current chapter we show that such forms are also very useful in probabilistic modeling, both for facilitating input in general and for incorporating dependencies into scenarios. In section I of this chapter we also generalize one of the methods introduced in Chapter 2 for handling dependencies. We suggest the possibility of considering the values of one UQ to be decomposable into two parts. One part is assumed to be a deterministic function of the values taken by other UQs. The second part is assumed peculiar to the first UQ and not to be related at all to the values taken by other uncertainties. Creative and careful thinking in determining the exact definitions of such decompositions can often produce very satisfactory ways of building dependencies into models.

Next, we consider some special topics in probabilistic modeling. Section II introduces Markov models, giving an introduction to some of the concepts in the theory of Markov processes and then showing how Markov models can provide yet another method for handling dependencies within probabilistic models. In Section III we turn to a consideration of waiting lines or queues. Queues are inherently probabilistic situations about which computer models can often provide useful information. We introduce the basic concepts of queueing theory in Section III and then proceed to consider some of the useful insights into the behavior of waiting lines that are provided by that theory. Finally, we discuss methods for building simulation models of queues.

## I. ADDITIONAL METHODS FOR HANDLING DEPENDENCIES

The previous chapter established the potential importance of considering the important dependencies among the uncertainties in a probabilistic model. It also suggested the difficulty involved in handling dependencies satisfactorily. Because of the importance and difficulty of dealing with dependencies, it is useful to have available a whole selection of techniques for building such interrelationships into computer models. With a selection of tools available, a model designer is more likely to find some method that is a sufficiently close approximation to reality to be acceptable and at the same time is a procedure for which the relevant users and decision makers can provide sensible estimates of the required input distributions and other required input information. In this section we discuss two very general and powerful techniques for handling dependencies.

The first new method involves the idea of functional forms. Such forms were introduced in Chapter 1 in the discussion of methods for facilitating input of different scenarios to deterministic models. Recall that in the earlier discussion we considered the problem of inputting a set of numbers such as a series of sales levels over time. Rather than make the model-user specify a long string of values for each scenario, we suggested incorporating into a model a particular general functional form, such as a linear function, a quadratic, or a bounded exponential. Such a general form includes quantities, called parameters, that appear as letters (or variables) in the general form but that must be made equal to specific numeric values before a specific version of the general form can be used in the model. Rather than having to specify all of the individual values for sales, for example, the user of a model with such a general form is required only to specify the parameters of the form. We suggested further in Chapter 1 that it is often useful not to require the user to specify the parameters directly. Instead, users may find it more natural to think about values taken by the sales function in a scenario at specific points in time, such as at the end of the 6th, 12th, and 18th months of the period being modeled. The input requirements of such a model can be so designed that the user inputs just enough information, in some convenient form, for the computer to determine the parameters of the functional form. The machine then uses the resulting specific function to determine values for one scenario.

One of the results of using functional forms in defining scenarios in deterministic models is that series of numbers, such as successive monthly sales figures, are related to one another over time. In fact, such relationships are a form of dependency within scenarios, albeit scenarios of deterministic models. It should not be surprising, therefore, that the same concepts are useful in building dependencies, especially dependencies over time, into probabilistic models. Often, we believe that we know in general, although not in all specific details, how some series of numbers will behave in the future. In planning to manufacture some new product, for example, we may believe that the amount of labor needed to produce each individual item will exhibit a learning-curve type of behavior, decreasing regularly over time. We may feel very uncertain, however, about exactly what the labor requirements will be, either at the start of the production period or later, after learning has taken place. Hence, labor costs are uncertainties, in our view.

The techniques of the previous chapter are not well-suited for modeling this learning type of behavior in probabilistic modeling. Certainly an independence assumption would be inappropriate for successive labor costs. Such an assumption would allow the costs to fluctuate widely and we expect instead that costs will follow a smoothly decreasing pattern. Similarly, a starting-value-and-changes approach would likely not be entirely satisfactory. We expect costs to decrease, so that a changes model would certainly not be satisfactory if we assigned nonzero probability to positive changes in costs. Even if we used only negative changes (or cost decreases) in a starting-value-and-changes approach, we might not find the results acceptable. Such an approach would allow an erratic pattern in the sizes of changes, with a small change being followed by a large one and then another even smaller one, for example. The theory of learning in production processes suggests, to the contrary, that changes in costs form a decreasing sequence over time, with the largest absolute change first, the next largest second, and so on. The starting-value-and-changes approach, as we have described it, will not produce such behavior over time. Similarly, the technique described in the previous chapter for using a compromise between some overall distribution and the current value of a sequence to form the distribution for the next value in the sequence will not work, for the same types of reasons that the starting-value-and-changes approach is unsatisfactory.

Instead of using any of the previous techniques, which are not fully appropriate, it is very reasonable instead to use a general functional form to impose on the sequences of values we draw for labor costs over time the type of shape we believe those sequences should follow. One common way to express learning types of behavior is through the following type of equation:

$$Y = A * X^{-B}$$

Here $Y$ is the cost of the current individual item. $A$ is a constant, sometimes called the cost of the first item produced. $X$ is the total number of items produced to date, often called the cumulative production amount. $B$ is another constant. In modeling the uncertain sequence of production costs in a probabilistic model, we can use this functional form, assuming that the two parameters $A$ and $B$ are uncertain. For this particular form, we may want to ask the model-user to specify a distribution for the parameter $A$ directly, because it may seem reasonable to make judgments directly about the cost of the first regular production item.[1] For the parameter $B$, another approach is likely to be preferable. We may want to ask the user to provide information in a slightly different form than is needed to identify the parameters of the functional form directly. $B$ is closely related to a more intuitive value that is a fundamental to the learning curve concept. The basic idea of the learning curve is that every time cumulative output doubles, the cost per unit is reduced to a constant fraction of the cost before the doubling. Suppose we called the constant fraction (often called the learning parameter) $\lambda$. The learning curve idea is that if the cost of the $N$th unit is $C$, that of the $(2N)$th unit will be $\lambda C$, that of the $(4N)$th unit will be $\lambda^2 C$, and so on. $\lambda$ is a more intuitive quantity than $B$. Therefore, we may ask the user to assess a distribution for $\lambda$; the model can translate from any particular value of $\lambda$ to the corresponding value of $B$. In fact, $B$ is equal to minus the logarithm to the base 2 of $\lambda$.[2] For example, if we take $\lambda$ equal to .75, we find that $B$ is approximately $-.42$. The cost of the 4th item is 75 percent of that of the second when $\lambda$ is .75; similarly, the cost of the 8th unit is 75 percent that of the 4th, and so on.

A model can use the input distributions for $A$ and for $\lambda$ easily to form needed portions of scenarios for trials. On each trial the model would select at random, in the way described in the preceding chapter, values for $A$ and for $\lambda$. We could assume that those values were independent of one another, so that the selection process would be straightforward. From the value of $\lambda$ we would find the implied value of $B$. Once we had values for the parameters $A$ and $B$, we would have a well-defined specific function from the general family. The computer could use that specific function to find values for cost on each of the units produced on the current trial. After completing that trial, it would draw values for $A$ and $\lambda$, find $B$, and then use those values to determine the specific function and then the cost values for the next trial. This procedure is entirely analogous to the one we used with functional forms except that we draw values to determine specific functions from probability distributions rather than take such values as user inputs. As was also true in deterministic modeling with functional forms, we sometimes ask users to provide information about quantities (such as $\lambda$) that are related to parameters (such as $B$) rather than about the parameters themselves.

In probabilistic modeling with functional forms, a bit of extra care is sometimes needed to ensure that the functions are well-defined once values have been determined for the parameters. As an example, suppose we choose to model sales levels over time by using an increasing bounded exponential. We might want to ask the user for judgments about sales levels

---

[1] In practice, however, determining or thinking about $A$ is not always easy.

[2] Alternatively, $B$ can be found as $-\log \lambda/\log 2$ where both the logarithms can be taken to the base 10 or else both can be taken to the base e.

at two points in time rather than to ask for direct judgments about the parameters. We must be careful, however, about the precise input distributions we require. If we asked for one distribution for sales at some specified time and for another distribution for sales at some specified later time, the computer could conceivably draw values on one trial so that the later sales level was smaller than the earlier one. But such behavior is impossible under our assumption of an increasing bounded exponential. Instead, we should ask the user for somewhat different forms of assessments in order to ensure that our assumption of functional form will make sense for any combination of values that could possibly be drawn on a particular trial. A good choice is to ask for input assessments of (1) the distribution of possible sales levels at the first time and (2) the distribution for sales at the second time as a percentage of those at the first, with the requirement that the percentages be more than 100 percent. A pair of values drawn from these two distributions can be used to define an increasing bounded exponential function.

The potential power of functional forms in probabilistic modeling should be obvious. There are many different families of forms that can be used. The fact that we can often accept input distributions for quantities we find more natural to consider and that we can then use those input distributions to find specific parameter values needed to use the functional forms makes this technique particularly useful in probabilistic modeling.

The second general technique we discuss in this section is related to the suggestion in the previous chapter that it is sometimes possible to reformulate a probabilistic modeling problem in terms of UQs that we can reasonably comfortably assume to be independent. The starting-values-and-changes example was one instance of that type of approach. Even if we were unwilling to assume that successive sales levels were independent of one another, we might be willing to assume that successive changes were independent. Modeling the behavior of sales in terms of a starting level and changes would then be a reformulation that allowed us to assume independence among the new UQs we had defined.

In other situations, we can generalize this approach and consider the possibility of decomposing an uncertainty into two (or even more) parts, one of which is directly tied to the values of other uncertainties and the other of which is independent of the others. As an example, suppose that we are constructing a risk analysis model for one division of a company. Suppose that the division sells a laboratory instrument and, in addition, sells supplies appropriate for use with that instrument. Suppose, in addition, that the supplies can also be used on the instruments made by competing firms. The division we are studying has a superior quality line of supplies so that essentially all purchasers of its instruments buy its supplies as well. A typical user buys 105 gallons of supplies per year. Both the sales of instruments and the sales of supplies are uncertain and should be considered within the risk analysis model. Clearly, sales of supplies are linked to sales of instruments;

the two sets of values are dependent. A natural way to handle the dependency in this situation is to consider the uncertain quantity for supply sales in any year to consist of two parts. In technical terms, we will decompose the UQ for supply sales into two parts. One part will be supply sales for instruments made by the same firm. Since we know past sales of instruments, if we assume 105 gallons per instrument, we can determine this portion of supply sales as soon as we have determined a value for current instrument sales. A good approximation might be to assume 105 gallons for each instrument sold in any of the five years preceding the current one, plus 52.5 gallons (or half a year's usage) for each instrument sold during the current year. We might then consider the supplies sold for use on competing machines to be entirely separate and we could then draw values for those sales from an appropriate distribution. If we assumed that sales for use on other equipment were independent of instrument sales, the selection procedure would be straightforward. Moreover, once we have decomposed the UQ for supply sales, that independence assumption seems quite reasonable.

This decomposition procedure can be made more complex. We might decompose one UQ into parts depending on several other UQs plus a part specific to the UQ under consideration. Or, we could introduce some uncertainty into the portion of one UQ that was linked to another UQ. In the instruments and supplies example, we might assume that the fraction of owners of the division's instruments who also purchased its supplies was uncertain; we could build into the model a distribution or distributions for that fraction. As long as we assumed that the fraction, the instrument sales themselves, and the supply sales to users of competing instruments were independent, the modeling procedure would remain easy to implement.

Again, it should be obvious that the idea of decomposition is a powerful one in probabilistic modeling. Creative and careful use of decomposition can help make models both reasonably realistic and reasonably easy to use.

## II. MARKOV PROCESSES

Markov processes are a special type of stochastic (or random) process for which the behavior of the process in one period depends in a very special way on the past history of the process. Such processes are of interest in themselves because they provide a useful framework and vocabulary for considering many situations involving uncertainty. Markov processes are also of interest in our discussion of computer models because they provide another method for incorporating complex dependencies into models. This section will first give one simple example of a Markov model (one for analyzing the reliability and maintenance of a machine). It will then use this and other small examples to introduce some definitions in the theory of Markov processes. Finally, it will show how Markov processes can be used to build interrelationships over time into simulation models.

First, consider the problem of a machine which is subject to breakdowns. When the machine stops working properly it is repaired and then returned to service. Repairs take at least one day. Suppose that we believe that if the machine is working at the start of a particular day the probability is 1/10 that it will break during that day, *regardless* of the past history of reliability. In addition, suppose that we believe that if the machine is broken (and hence being repaired) at the start of a day, there is a 3 in 4 chance that the repairs will be completed that day but a 1 in 4 chance that the machine will still be in the repair shop at the start of the next day; notice that we have made the strong assumption that the probability of staying in the shop does not depend on how much time the machine has already spent in the shop. For this very simple problem we can think of the machine (or, in Markov process terminology, the *system*) as being in one of two conditions (or *states*); either the machine is working or it is in the shop. We can diagram the process as shown in Figure 3–1, with one node for each possible state and with arrows between the states labeled with the probabilities of moving between those states. Those probabilities are called *state transition probabilities*.

**FIGURE 3–1**

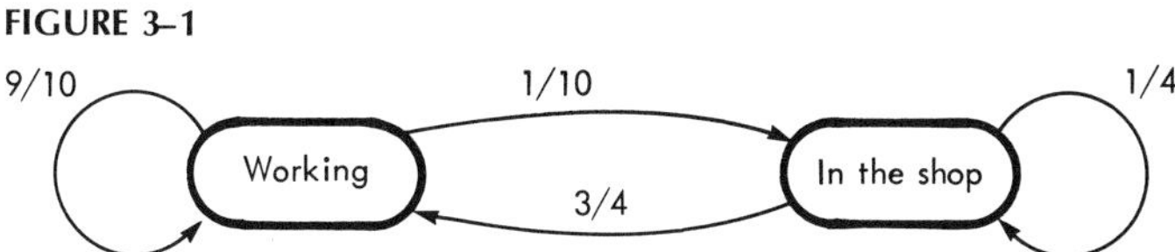


Implicit in the formulation in Figure 3–1 are the basic properties of a Markov model. We have identified a unit of time, here a day.[3] We have also identified the possible states of the system (working, or in the shop). We assume that once each time period the system follows one of the arrows in the diagram. (Note that the arrow may lead back to the same state. Thus, if we start a day in the working state we will either take the arrow back to the working state or else take the arrow to the shop.) We have made the strong assumption (called the *Markov assumption*) that the probability of a particular transition during any given day depends on the state at the start of the day but does *not* depend on any other aspect of the history of the process. Thus, if we know that the machine has been working for ten days (before which it was in the shop), we assume the same 1/10 probability of a breakdown as we do if the machine has been out of the shop for only five days.

Very simple Markov models like this one have several uses. For one thing, they provide a conceptual framework for thinking about the process. For another, the considerable theory of Markov processes allows us to solve for interesting properties of the process. In the (overly) simplified repair example

[3] In the general theory of Markov processes the time intervals need not all have the same length. We will not consider such complications.

above, we can calculate that the long-run probability that the machine will be in the shop on a particular day is 2/17.[4]

Most people would consider the above repair model far too simple to be a reasonable approximation of reality. It seems considerably more reasonable to assume that the probability of a breakdown depends on the time that the machine has spent since the last breakdown. Suppose that we think some more about this particular machine and decide that the probabilities of breakdown for the first two days out of the shop vary (we might think of this interval as a shakedown period during which we find out whether the repairs were in fact successful); suppose that after that two-day interval we think that the probability of a breakdown is the same for each day. Now we can model the system with some additional states. We will still use the interval of a day, but in order to describe (in probabilistic terms) the future behavior of the system, we will need to keep track of whether the machine has been out of the shop 0, 1, 2, 3 or more days. Hence, we might draw the diagram shown in Figure 3–2. Note from that diagram that it does not have to be possible in a Markov process to move from each state to each other state in a single move. For example, we cannot move immediately from working-first-day to working-three-or-more-days. We often leave out the arrows corresponding to impossible transitions.

Some more complicated calculations (which will not be repeated here)

---

[4] That value can be derived as follows. Suppose $p_w$ is the long-run probability that the machine is working and that $p_s$ is the long-run probability that it is in the shop. Since we assume there are only two possible states, the probabilities of those states must add to 1.0

$$p_w + p_s = 1$$

If $p_s$ is a stable long-run probability, then it must be the probability of the machine's being in the shop on *each* day. In particular, if $p_s$ is the probability for the shop on one day, it must be the probability of the machine's being in the shop and the next day as well. There are two different paths the machine could have followed to arrive in the shop on the second day. It could have spent the first day in the shop and then remained in the shop. Alternatively, it could have spent the first day in working condition but then traveled to the shop the second day. The probability of the first of these combinations of events is $p_s * (1/4)$, or the probability of being in the shop times the probability of staying in the shop at least one more day. Similarly, the chance of the second combination is $p_w * (1/10)$, or the probability of working on one day times the probability of changing from working to shop on a single day. The total probability of being in the shop on the second day is the sum of these two terms, or

$$p_s = p_s/4 + p_w/10.$$

An entirely analogous argument allows us to express the long-run probability of the machine's working as the sum of two parts:

$$p_w = (9/10) * p_w + (3/4) * p_s.$$

To find the values of $p_w$ and $p_s$ we need only solve these two equations, subject to the restriction that the two probabilities sum to 1. The answers are:

$$p_w = 15/17 \text{ and } p_s = 2/17.$$

FIGURE 3–2

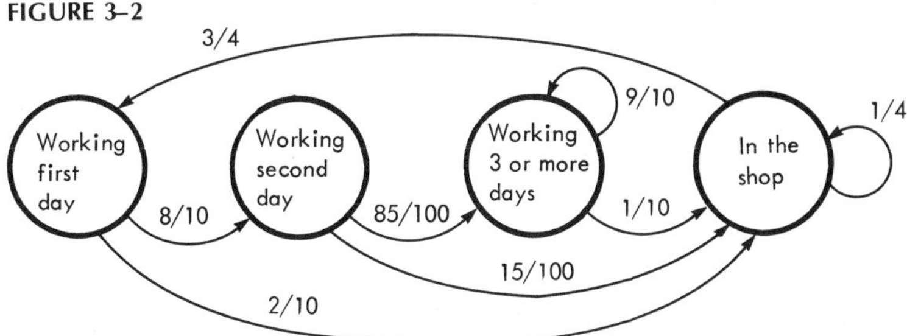


can be used to find the long-run probability that the machine is in the shop. This value turns out to be about .134.[5]

Before we proceed to consider how Markov models can be used in simulation models, it is worthwhile to consider some of the special properties of Markov process. First, we will return to the original repair model (in Figure 3–1), but we will add the possibility that after the machine goes into the shop it is found that the machine cannot be repaired and that it must be discarded. We can draw the diagram shown in Figure 3–3. Notice that once the machine reaches the non-repairable state it stays there; that state is called a *trapping* or *absorbing* state. (In a Markov model for the cash status of a business, we might want (or be forced) to consider the trapping state of bankruptcy; once we reach that state we stay in it.)

FIGURE 3–3

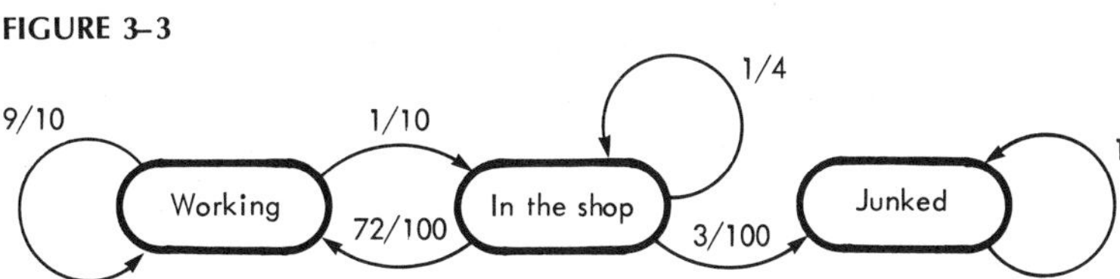


Other interesting questions about Markov models concern the long-run probabilities of being in particular states. We often wonder whether the system will settle down into a stable (or equilibrium) pattern, with the probabilities of being in different states being the same in successive periods. (For a particular history of the process, of course, we will be in exactly one state at each time. This question about long-run or *steady state probabilities* is

---

[5] Suppose the long-run probabilities are called $p_{w1}$ (for working first day), $p_{w2}$, $p_{w3}$, and $p_s$ (for in the shop). The equations to be solved are:

$$p_{w1} = (3/4) * p_s$$
$$p_{w2} = (8/10) * p_{w1}$$
$$p_{w3} = (85/100) * p_{w2} + (9/10) * p_{w3}$$
$$p_s = (1/10) * p_{w3} + (15/100) * p_{w2} + (2/10) * p_{w1} + (1/4) * p_s$$
$$p_{w1} + p_{w2} + p_{w3} + p_s = 1$$

concerned not with a single well-defined history but rather with the probabilities which we should ascribe to being in different states if we didn't know the particular history.) For example, consider an inventory system which we are certain will contain 0, 1, 2, or 3 units on hand. Suppose further that we have decided on transition probabilities as shown in Figure 3–4; our

**FIGURE 3–4**

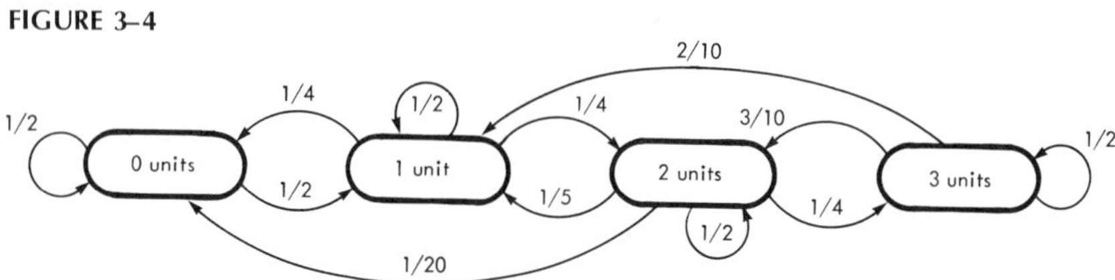


time interval is one day per transition. We can now ask for the long-run chance that the inventory will contain two units, no units, one unit, etc. For this particular problem, calculations give the steady-state probabilities as 16/74 for no units, 28/74 for one unit, 20/74 for two, and 10/74 for three.[6]

Other interesting properties of Markov processes are what are called *first passage times* or *recurrence times*. The expected first passage time from one state to another is the expected length of the time interval for moving from the first state to the second. In the inventory example, we might ask for the expected time which it will take to move from an inventory of 3 to an inventory of 0. We might, for example, move from 3 to 1 and then to 0; the length of this path is two time units and its probability of occurrence is $2/10 \times 1/4$, or .05. Similarly, we could consider other possible paths—their lengths and their probabilities—to find the average or expected number of intervals to move from 3 to 0. (Fortunately, there are efficient ways to find the expected passage times for Markov processes.) Sometimes we are interested in the expected length of the interval between one occurrence of a particular state and the next occurrence of that state. For example, if we start a day with no inventory we might want to know the expected number of days until we have no inventory again. This expected time to return to the same state is called an expected recurrence time.

Other interesting values are what are called *n-step transition probabilities*. For example, in the first repair example above, we know that if we start in the working state then after one day the chances are 9/10 that the machine will

---

[6] Let $p_0$, $p_1$, $p_2$ and $p_3$ denote the long-run probabilities of 0, 1, 2, and 3 units in inventory, respectively. The equations to be solved are:

$$
\begin{aligned}
p_0 + p_1 + p_2 + p_3 &= 1 \\
p_0 &= (1/2) * p_0 + (1/4) * p_1 + (1/20) * p_2 \\
p_1 &= (1/2) * p_0 + (1/2) * p_1 + (1/5) * p_2 + (2/10) * p_3 \\
p_2 &= (1/4) * p_1 + (1/2) * p_2 + (3/10) * p_3 \\
p_3 &= (1/4) * p_2 + (1/2) * p_3
\end{aligned}
$$

again be in the working state and 1/10 that it will be in the shop state. We might next ask: If we start the current day in the working state what are the probabilities of the different states two days from now? To find those probabilities we can consider all of the paths which we could follow over the two-day period and the probabilities of those paths. We could be in the working state on the next day and also on the second day; the probability for that path is 81/100. We could go to the shop on the first move and then return to the working state; the probability of this sequence is 1/10 × 3/4 or 3/40. Similarly, the probability of going to the shop and staying there a second day is 1/40. Finally, the probability of staying in the working state on the first day and then going to the shop the second day is 9/100. We can now add up the probabilities of all of the two-day paths which start in working and end in working; this value (of 81/100 plus 3/40, or 88.5 percent) is the probability of being in the working state two days after starting in the working state. Similarly, the two-step transition probability from working to shop is 9/100 plus 1/40, or 11.5 percent. In an analogous way we could find transition probabilities for longer intervals (called *higher order transition probabilities*) or we could find transition probabilities for the other (shop) state.

Fortunately, the theory of Markov processes offers some efficient ways of finding higher order transition probabilities and steady-state probabilities. This section is intended to introduce the concepts, not to explain such calculations, so those methods will not be discussed here. Instead, we suggest that Markov models be thought of as a useful way of describing certain situations (those for which we are willing to make the Markov assumption that the probabilities of transitions to different states on the next step depend only on the current state of the system, not on the previous history).[7]

We next turn to the use of Markov processes within simulation models. We have emphasized the idea that one of the most difficult problems in designing probabilistic models concerns dependencies among the uncertainties in the problems we are analyzing. Markov models offer a flexible technique for building dependencies, including complex dependencies, into models.

In order to have an example to use in this discussion, suppose that we must decide whether or not to introduce a new product and that we want to build a risk analysis model to help in evaluating the decision. We assume that the life of the new product will be five years and, therefore, use that planning horizon. Suppose that the only important uncertainty in the problem is the series of prices for the next five years for the principal raw material we will be using. Our sales of the product would be fixed by contract and the

[7] For further information on analytic results for Markov processes see Frederick S. Hillier and Gerald J. Lieberman, *Introduction to Operations Research* (San Francisco: Holden-Day, 1967) and William Feller, *An Introduction to Probability Theory and Its Applications,* vols.1 and 2 (New York: John Wiley & Sons, 1950 and 1966).

**FIGURE 3–5**

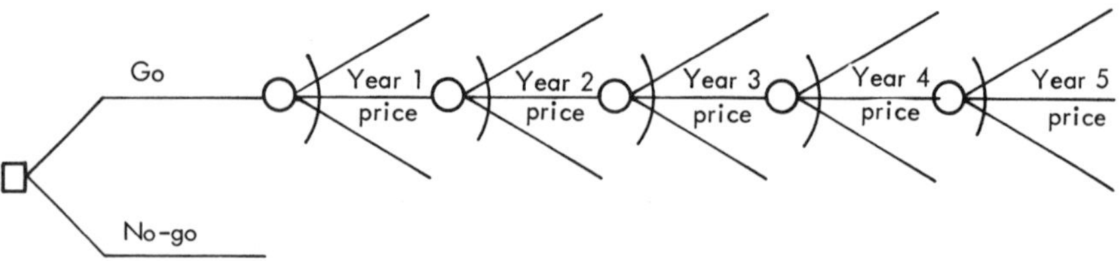


other costs are assumed quite accurately known. We might diagram the problem as shown in Figure 3–5.

Suppose that we have identified all of the relevant costs and revenues and have decided how to value the possible endpoints of the tree. Our next step is to find probability distributions for the fans for raw materials prices in the tree. As we have argued earlier, if we believed that those prices were independent from year to year, then the job would be relatively easy. We would simply draw values independently from five different price distributions (or even from a single distribution, if it seemed appropriate to do so). It is highly unlikely, however, that we actually believe that the successive price levels are independent or that independence would be a satisfactory approximation of reality. We assume instead that the price in one year is dependent, to some extent, on preceding prices. We have argued earlier that the brute force method of assessing large numbers of conditional distributions is likely to be impractical, although it could certainly handle the problem in theory. Because the method we will discuss can be considered a simplification of the brute force method, we nevertheless show how the brute force method might work in the current problem. With that method we assess many different conditional distributions to build dependence into the model. For example, suppose that we assessed a distribution for the first price and then took ten representative values (probably bracket medians) from that distribution. For each value, we could assess a conditional distribution for price the second year, *given* that particular first-year price. Suppose that the ten first-year prices were $10.00, 10.35, 10.60, 10.75, 10.85, 10.95, 11.05, 11.20, 11.45, and 11.80. Then we might assess the distribution in Figure 3–6 for second-year prices conditional on a first-year price of $10.00.

For a first-year price of $10.35 we might choose the distribution in Figure 3–7, which suggests higher prices than we gave for the conditional distribution corresponding to the lowest first-year price. We could similarly give a conditional distribution corresponding to each of the representative values for first-year price. If we now redraw Figure 3–5 to show what we have just done, the result will be as shown in Figure 3–8. The first event fan has been replaced by a ten-branched event fork. At the end of each of the ten branches is an event fan for second-year price. We assume that those ten distributions are different from one another, reflecting dependence between first- and

FIGURE 3–6

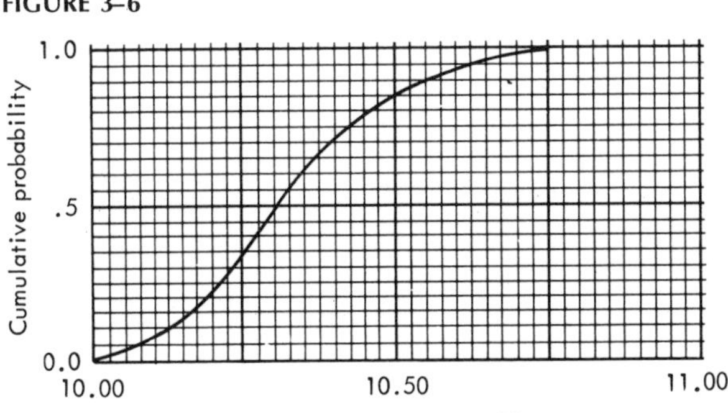


FIGURE 3–7

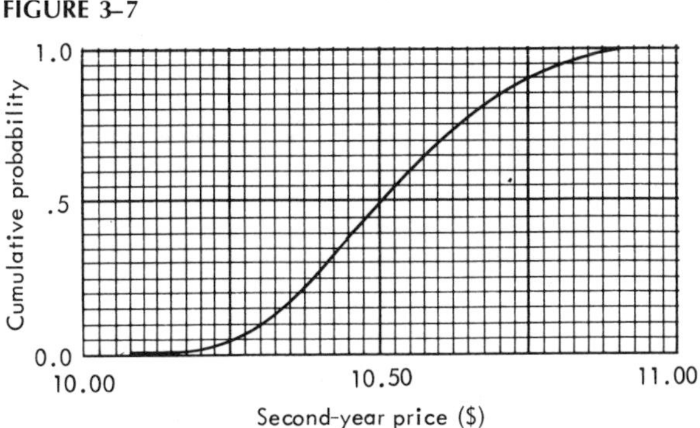


second-year prices. The fans for the remaining years have not yet been considered.

The next steps in the brute force approach would involve approximating each of the event fans for second-year price by ten representative values. The topmost such fan corresponds to the distribution in Figure 3–6. We might approximate it by the bracket medians: $10.05, 10.18, 10.22, 10.25, 10.28, 10.32, 10.36, 10.42, 10.50, and 10.65. Similarly, the second fan from the top in the column of fans for second-year prices corresponds to the distribution in Figure 3–7. Representative values would be: $10.28, 10.34, 10.39, 10.43, 10.48, 10.52, 10.58, 10.63, 10.70, and 10.78. If we replaced each second-year fan by its own set of representative values, we would have 100 branches at that level of the tree. At the end of each such branch would be three more event fans, one each for price in the third, fourth, and fifth years. We would then proceed to assess distributions for third-year price for each of the 100 combinations of first- and second-year prices. For example, we would assess one distribution for third-year price conditional on a first-year price of $10.00 followed by a second-year price of $10.05, another for a first-year price of $10.00 followed by a second-year price of $10.18, and so

**FIGURE 3–8**

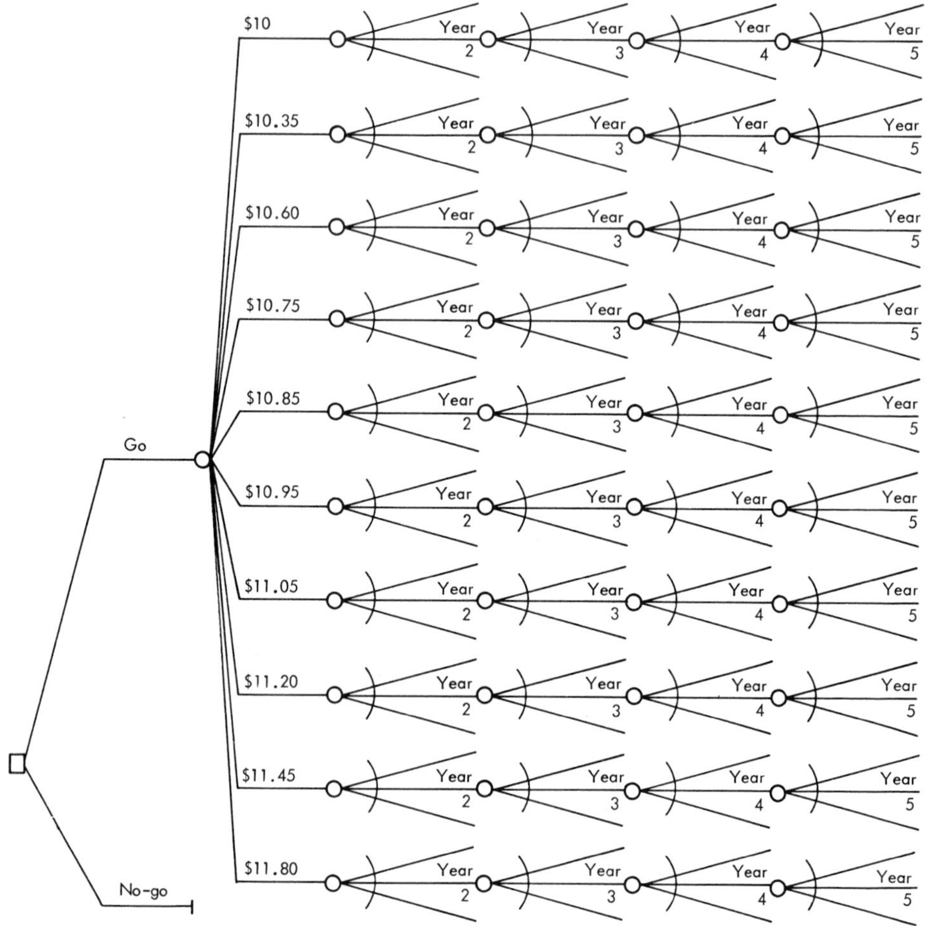


on. Having (theoretically, anyway) assessed all 100 required distributions, we could approximate each one by ten representatives, thus giving 1,000 different combinations of first-, second-, and third-year prices. For each such combination we would assess a conditional distribution for fourth-year price. Finally, we would approximate those 1,000 distributions by ten representatives each and would then have 10,000 combinations of first-, second-, third-, and fourth-year prices. We would assess a distribution for each such combination and would have completed the assessment process. It should be clear that the brute force method is essentially impossible. The assessment job is impractical.

Notice that in the brute force method as described above, the price distribution for one of the later years is conditional on the entire price history up to that point. In the third year, for example, we consider both the first-year price and the second-year price that have already been assumed to occur when we assess distributions for third-year price. Similarly, distributions for fourth-year prices are assessed conditional on specific prices in each of the preceding three years. In fact, we most likely believe that the price in the third year does depend on both preceding prices and that, similarly, the fifth-year price depends on the entire preceding sequence of prices. It is this assumption of dependence on the entire preceding history, however, that makes the numbers of required assessments explode with 10, 100, 1,000 and 10,000 assessments required at successive stages of the tree. Consequently, even though we usually believe that one value in a sequence depends on the entire preceding history, we often find it useful for practicality's sake to make the very powerful Markov assumption. In other words, we assume that the entire history of the process at any one time in the sequence can be summarized by the current price at the time, for purposes of considering dependencies.

In the simple risk analysis example under consideration, we would not assess 10,000 different fifth-year distributions. Instead, we would have to assess only ten distributions for what might be called following prices; these distributions would give probabilities of different prices in one year conditional on various specific prices the previous year. In addition, we would also have to assess one distribution for prices in the first year. The following discussion shows in more detail how a Markov assumption could be used in the problem. We start by considering more aspects of the price behavior we expect. Suppose, for example, that we believe that if we start the first year with low prices we are relatively *unsure* that prices will remain low the second year but that if we start with a high price we are very likely to face high prices the next year. Thus, we believe that the likelihoods of different price changes in a year depend on the price level at the start of that year. Suppose, however, that we think that the changes in a year depend only on the level at the start of that year, not on the previous history of prices. For example, to consider possible changes in the third year we need to know only the level at the start of that year, not what happened in the first year. (In other words, all that we need to know about the effects of the first year is summarized in the price level reached in the second year.) Note that we have made a Markov assumption for the process. If we think of the possible price levels as states, then we assume that the probabilities of state transitions (price changes) during any year depend only on the state (price level) at the start of that year.

We could formulate a procedure for modeling price behavior, with a Markov assumption, in terms of cumulative distribution functions of the sort shown in Figures 3–6 and 3–7. It turns out to be more convenient, however, to use a slightly different, though related, method for describing price behavior.

**TABLE 3–1**

| | *Ending state (and price)* | | | | | | | | | |
|---|---|---|---|---|---|---|---|---|---|---|
| | *1* (10.00) | *2* (10.35) | *3* (10.60) | *4* (10.75) | *5* (10.85) | *6* (10.95) | *7* (11.05) | *8* (11.20) | *9* (11.45) | *10* (11.80) |
| *1 (10.00)* | .15 | .35 | .25 | .15 | .10 | 0.0 | 0.0 | 0.0 | 0.0 | 0.0 |
| *2 (10.35)* | .10 | .30 | .20 | .20 | .10 | .05 | .05 | 0.0 | 0.0 | 0.0 |
| *3 (10.60)* | .10 | .15 | .25 | .20 | .15 | .10 | .05 | 0.0 | 0.0 | 0.0 |
| *4 (10.75)* | 0.0 | .15 | .20 | .25 | .20 | .10 | .05 | .05 | 0.0 | 0.0 |
| *5 (10.85)* | 0.0 | .10 | .10 | .15 | .30 | .15 | .10 | .10 | 0.0 | 0.0 |
| *6 (10.95)* | 0.0 | 0.0 | 0.0 | .15 | .20 | .30 | .20 | .15 | 0.0 | 0.0 |
| *7 (11.05)* | 0.0 | 0.0 | 0.0 | 0.0 | 0.0 | .20 | .30 | .30 | .20 | 0.0 |
| *8 (11.20)* | 0.0 | 0.0 | 0.0 | 0.0 | 0.0 | 0.0 | .25 | .30 | .25 | .20 |
| *9 (11.45)* | 0.0 | 0.0 | 0.0 | 0.0 | 0.0 | 0.0 | 0.0 | .30 | .40 | .30 |
| *10 (11.80)* | 0.0 | 0.0 | 0.0 | 0.0 | 0.0 | 0.0 | 0.0 | 0.0 | 0.0 | 1.0 |

It is customary to describe Markov processes with small (or finite) numbers of possible states by what are called *state transition matrices.* These matrices are really tables with one line or row for each possible state of the system. In the first row, we give the probability of transition in a single interval from the first state to the first state, then the probability of a single-step transition from the first to the second, then the probability for a move from the first to the third, and so forth. In the second row we give the probabilities of transitions from the second state to other possible states, and so forth. For example, we might give the matrix in Table 3–1 for the price problem under discussion.

Each row in a table of transition probabilities is really just a probability mass function. More specifically, it is the probability mass function for the next state conditional on a particular current state. For example, the first row of the table can be translated into the probability mass function in Table 3–2, which gives probabilities for each of the ten states to follow a year in which the system was in the first state or, in other words, to follow a price of $10.00.

**TABLE 3–2**

| *Next price* | *Probability* |
|---|---|
| 10.00 | .15 |
| 10.35 | .35 |
| 10.60 | .25 |
| 10.75 | .15 |
| 10.85 | .10 |
| Any other price | .00 |

Consulting Table 3–1 we find that if we start in state 3 (a 10.60 price) the probabilities of transition are .10 for a $10.00 next price; .15 for $10.35, .25 for another $10.60; .20 for $10.75; .15 for $10.85; .10 for $10.95; and .05 for $11.05. Similarly, we find that state 10 is what is called a *trapping state* (or an absorbing state); once prices reach the highest price we are certain that they will stay there. Notice that in general the matrix implies noticeably more persistence (or stickiness) at the lower right than at the upper left. In other words, the high prices at the lower right have following prices very much like, if not exactly equal to, themselves. The lower prices, shown at the upper left of the matrix, have much wider ranges of possible followers.

The transition matrix can also be used to determine two-stage or higher transition probabilities. For example, we find that the two-stage transition probability from state 1 to state 10 is 0 (it is impossible to reach state 10 from state 1 in two steps) but that we could *eventually* move from state 1 to state 10.[8]

Notice what we have gained by introducing this Markov model. In order to include price movements in our model we must assess the transition probabilities in the matrix in Table 3–1 (and we must also specify the probabilities of the price levels for the first year—i.e., the initial state). The job is more complicated than that of giving five independent distributions or of giving one initial distribution and distributions for changes, but we have already decided that those simpler alternatives do not adequately reflect the complexities of the interrelationships. On the other hand, specifying the matrix is considerably simpler than giving the horrendous number of different conditional distributions discussed above.

As mentioned above, we must also give the probabilities of what are called starting or initial states. In our problem these would be the first-year price levels. Suppose, as we have assumed, that each of the ten prices ($10.00, 10.35, 10.60, 10.75, 10.85, 10.95, 11.05, 11.20, 11.45, and 11.80) has a 1/10 chance of being the initial price. A trial of the model would then be conducted as follows. We would first draw a value from this distribution for initial price, using the method for few-valued UQs described in the previous chapter. Suppose we select an initial state corresponding to a price of $10.35 (state 2). Recall that the planning horizon is five years so we must consider four more years for this trial. To find a second-year price, we start by selecting the row corresponding to the first year's price (row 2). We would use the probabilities in the second row of the transition matrix to guide our selection of the next price. For example, we should select a price of $10.00 with probability .10; a price of $10.35 with probability .3; and so forth. Again, we would use the method from the preceding chapter for handling few-valued UQ's. Suppose we selected $10.75, or state 4. For the third year, we would then use this price to tell us what row of the table to use; the third price should be selected from row 4 of the matrix. Proceeding in this way, we would construct an entire five-year price history for use in one trial. After evaluating the results of that history and saving appropriate summary measures, we would proceed to the next trial. We would draw another value from the distribution for starting price and then would use the transition matrix for random selection of the following prices.

In some Markov models we are concerned with the long-run steady-state behavior of the system (as discussed in the earlier examples).[9] In this particular example we are instead concerned with the short-run or transient behavior over the next five years, given the appropriate probabilities for initial

---

[8] Two-stage or higher transition probabilities can be found by matrix multiplication. If we denote the original matrix in Table 3–1 by $P$, the two-step probabilities are given by the matrix $P^2$, the three-step probabilities by $P^3$, and so on.

[9] Technical aside: Suppose $P$ is the known transition matrix and $\pi$ is the vector of steady-state

states. We have used a Markov model as an efficient way of building complex relationships into our description of price changes. It has served to build dependencies into a probabilistic simulation model.

## III. QUEUES

Many decisions in management involve providing facilities or planning schedules in ways to reduce or avoid losses (in time, money, etc.) caused by delays. The theory of *queues* or waiting lines provides information on delays in systems involving uncertainty and, hence, provides insights which can be useful in scheduling and in facilities planning. This section will introduce some of the terminology from queueing theory. We will then proceed to discuss some of the general properties of waiting lines which are observed in queueing analyses, to give the reader some intuitive understanding of the behavior of queues. Next, we will discuss briefly the types of problems for which the theory provides explicit answers (through analytic techniques rather than simulation) and the types of problems for which there are no existing general answers (so that simulation of a particular situation becomes appropriate). Finally, we will consider techniques for building simulation models of queues.

The general outline of a queueing system might be given as shown in Figure 3–9. The general model involves some pool or *population* from which

**FIGURE 3–9**

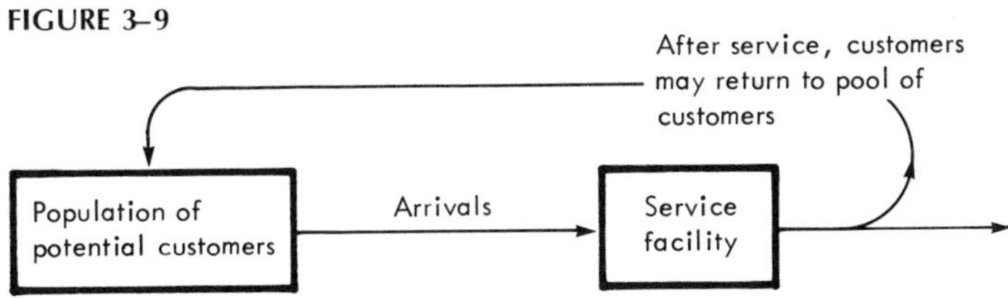


individual items arrive at a *service facility*. The population may consist of people or it may consist of inanimate objects (such as orders for parts). Regardless of whether the population is in fact human, the individuals arriving at the service facility are often called *customers* or, merely *arrivals*. The customers come to the service facility to receive a specified *service* (humans might arrive at a barber shop to have their hair cut; orders arrive at a warehouse to be filled). After receiving the service, the customer leaves the service facility; he, she, or it may return at some time in the future for further

---

probabilities whose values we want to determine. $\pi$ can be found by solving the matrix equation

$$\pi P = \pi$$

subject to the condition that the sum of the entries in $\pi$ be 1.

service. The capacity of the service facility is assumed limited and, hence, an arriving customer may have to wait for service. Queueing analysis is usually aimed at the questions of how many customers will have to wait, how long they will have to wait, how long the waiting line will be, and what can be done about those problems.

One very typical example of a queueing system is a checkout counter in a supermarket. The arrivals are the customers who have selected their purchases and want to pay for them and leave. Another example is the set of toll booths on a turnpike or at a bridge or tunnel. Here the individual customers are drivers (or cars) and the "service" is collection of the toll. Another example is the emergency room of a hospital. Customers are people arriving to obtain medical help; service consists of emergency treatment, and, after the treatment, customers are either released or sent to other parts of the hospital. As should be obvious from these examples, the relative importance of the time that customers spend waiting varies from one queueing system to another. At the checkout counter of a supermarket, customers generally expect to wait at least a short period, although they may become dissatisfied (and perhaps take their business elsewhere in the future) if they feel that the waits are excessive. In the emergency room, on the other hand, even relatively brief waits could be critical and the design and operation of the facility must aim at avoiding delays.

Each part of the general description in Figure 3–9 can be described in more detail; in doing so, we will introduce some more of the terminology from queueing theory. First, consider the population from which the arrivals come. The *population* may be *infinite* (or at least very large) or else it may be *finite* (or relatively small). The distinction can be important. For example, consider the problem of maintenance on five drilling machines in a factory. Suppose that the repair shop of the plant handles those machines and many other jobs as well. If we are interested in the requirement for service for those five machines only, we can consider a queueing system in which an arrival is a call for service. (In this case the serviceperson may come to the machine rather than vice versa, so we note that arrivals in the queueing model need not involve a physical move by the customer.) Once a call comes in, the repair shop sends out someone to fix the machine. Suppose that no machines are being repaired on a Monday. We can think about (and hopefully say something specific about) the probabilities that one or two or three . . . or five machines will require repair during that day. If, on the other hand, we start another day with two machines already being serviced, then we would most likely change considerably our probability assessments for the number that will *enter* service during the day; for one thing, there are only three working machines at the start of the day which could break down and hence enter service. Thus, for small populations, the probabilities of various numbers of arrivals may well depend on how many members of the population are in the service facility, if only because the number inside limits the number outside (the potential arrivals). On the other hand, consider an appliance repair service in a major city. Customers call for service and the repair people go out on service calls to repair refrigerators and freezers. It is technically true that a refrigerator for which a call has already come in will generally not give another service call on the same day, and, hence, for a larger number of units being repaired or awaiting repairs we may find slightly lower probabilities for a large number of new calls. On the other hand, it is very likely true that the number of units being repaired or waiting for service is quite small relative to the population of appliances which could require service (all appliances in the city, perhaps). Hence, we usually ignore the limiting effects on arrivals of the number in service or awaiting service when the population is very large. As will be discussed below, the distribution of arrivals *may* still be related to the number in service (both may be high in summer, for example), but the relation does *not* arise because the number in service has significantly limited the number of potential arrivals.

Even though, as just explained, for large or infinite populations we usually assume that the number of potential *arrivals* is not limited by the number who have already requested service, we may not be willing to assume that the behavior of a customer after requesting service is independent of the state of the system. For example, suppose that you go into a store to buy one or two items. You arrive at the checkout counter and find long lines at all of the registers. You may decide to wait or you may decide that the one or two items are not that important after all and, therefore, you may leave. When a customer arrives for service but then leaves because the line is too long, s/he is said to *balk*. Balking is important in some waiting line problems and not in others. When balking is a problem, the manager may want to study the question of which customers are apt to balk and then adjust the service facility accordingly. In supermarkets, for example, it may be that customers who are buying many items will put up with moderate waits because they feel that supermarket prices are lower than prices at small neighborhood stores (where the wait would be shorter) and they believe that the savings on a shopping cart full of purchases justify the wait. The customer who wants only one or two items may be more likely to pay the premium at the smaller store; the premium is unlikely to add up to a large amount on only one or two items and hence the wait in the supermarket seems less worth while. Thus, it should not be surprising that many supermarket managers have installed express lines for customers with small numbers of items. These lines are meant to reduce the waiting times for such customers to a point which many of them find acceptable.

As mentioned briefly above, even for large populations for which the number of customers receiving or awaiting service does not limit the population of *potential* arrivals in any significant way, it is often still true that the number of *actual* arrivals and the number receiving or awaiting service are related. At the toll booths on a major bridge, the number in line may be quite large during the morning and evening rush hours, and in addition, the rate of arrivals may be high at those times. Thus, if we knew that there was a substantial waiting line at the tolls, we would be inclined to guess that arrivals would also be high during the next hour or so, at least.

We next turn to a discussion of the service facility in the general queueing model. In the standard terminology, the number waiting or in service is called the *state of the system*. Hence, if one customer were being served and two were waiting for service, the system would be said to be in state three. Similarly, the number in the service facility is usually defined as the state (the number waiting plus the number being served). Hence, if we refine the diagram in Figure 3–9, we might obtain Figure 3–10, which shows a waiting line and also a service portion within the service facility.

**FIGURE 3–10**

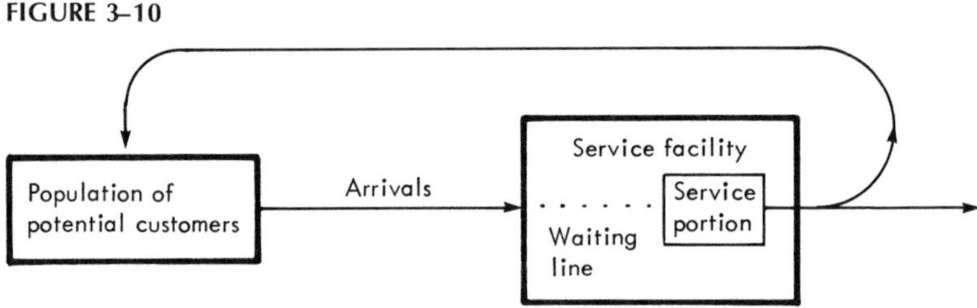


Once customers have arrived at the facility and joined the line (rather than having balked and left), we must consider the order in which to serve them. One very common rule is first-come-first-served; under this rule arriving customers are taken into the facility from the head of the line. Supermarkets and toll booths generally operate on a FIFO basis. In a hospital emergency room, on the other hand, if the medical staff is under time pressure, its members will try to see the cases who require immediate attention first; hence, they assign priorities to the arrivals and treat the higher priority patients first. In other queues it might be possible that the jobs that promise to require the shortest service times are taken first or, alternatively, that the shortest jobs are delayed. Thus, there are a wide range of rules that can be used to determine which of the customers in a waiting line is to be served next. The rule used in any particular queueing system is called the *queue discipline* for the system.

If we now turn to the actual service portion of the queueing system, we can differentiate various systems according to how many different servers there are. For example, in a supermarket we can count the number of different checkout stations. For the toll booths on a turnpike, we can count the number of different booths. Each server is called a *channel;* one of the important descriptions of a queueing system is the number of channels it contains. Moreover, increasing (or decreasing) the number of channels in a system is one of the important decisions open to a manager in trying to

FIGURE 3–11

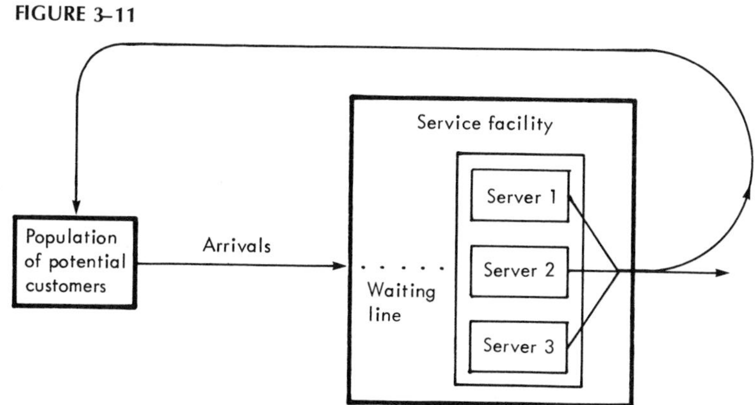


improve performance of the system. Figure 3–11 shows a three-channel facility.[10]

As mentioned above, the important characteristics of the performance of a system include the amounts of time that individual customers must spend waiting for service. We are often concerned with the average waiting time (per customer) and the average length of the waiting line. In addition, we must frequently consider the entire distribution of waiting times.[11] For example, in a supermarket we may feel that an average wait of two minutes for checkout is acceptable. At the same time, if we find that the individual waiting times (which give an average of two minutes) are greatly varied, with many customers waiting no time at all and with a significant number of others waiting eight and ten minutes, we may decide that the distribution of times is not acceptable even though the average seems reasonable.

In trying to understand and manage queues, it is important to consider the other side of the picture as well. Each channel in a service facility costs money. Hence, a manager must try to balance the waiting times for the system against the costs of providing additional service channels (to reduce the waits). In many queueing problems, managers face capital budgeting problems, with the choice of spending money now for more facilities in order to reduce future waiting times or of leaving the status quo and the existing pattern of waits. In other cases, they may be able to change the queue discipline to reduce future waiting times and either increase or reduce future costs of operation.

---

[10] Notice that the figure assumes that there is a single waiting line, even though there are three servers. The *next* customer (according to the chosen queue discipline) is presumed assigned to the first available server. The question of whether there should be a single waiting line (or whether each server should have a separate line) will be discussed later in this section.

[11] The literature is not consistent as to whether waiting time does or does not include service time. The usual definition, which will be followed here, is that "waiting time" is the time between a customer's entering and leaving the service facility (that is, it includes service time).

In modeling a queueing system in order to decide how to manage it or whether to expand (or contract) it, we must know the characteristics of the arrival pattern, the characteristics of the service facility, and any other information on balking, queue discipline, and costs. The arrivals are often described in terms of probability distribution(s) for the number of arrivals during individual periods (such as days or hours). The number of arrivals during a particular time interval may depend on the number of customers in the system (the state of the system) at the start of that interval, as stated above. In other cases, the number of arrivals during an interval is assumed to depend only on the length of the interval, not on the past history of the system.

A second very common way of describing the distribution(s) for the number of arrivals is by giving a distribution for what are called the *interarrival times,* or the times between arrivals of successive customers. When the model is formulated in this way, it is generally assumed that the distribution of interarrival times does not depend on the number of customers in the system. In addition, a very common assumption is that the interarrival times do not depend on any other aspects of the history of the process.[12]

In describing the service portion of a queueing system, we usually give distribution(s) for the service times for individual customers. As was true for the numbers of arrivals, the service times may or may not depend on the number of customers in the system. (That is, we may feel that the same distribution of service times holds regardless of how many customers are waiting. In other situations we believe that the servers speed up the service process when there is a long line. In still other cases, we may feel that the servers become flustered when there is a long line (or, perhaps, that the waiting customers get in the way of the servers) so that the service times actually increase when the line is long. In any of these cases, we usually feel that there is some distribution of service times (individual customers do not require the same amounts of time) but that the general characteristics of the distribution of times may or may not change for different states of the system.

Having introduced many of the definitions from queueing theory,[13] we will turn now to a consideration of some of the general results that emerge from the study of waiting lines. As a simple example, we will consider a queueing system in which the pattern of arrivals and the distribution of service times both are independent of the state of the system. We will assume that the interarrival times come from the probability distribution shown in Figure 3–12. In addition we will assume the distribution for service times

---

[12] In many situations in practice, interarrival times *are* related to the state of the system. In some situations, there are different distributions for interarrival times in different seasons (on different days of the week . . .).

[13] It is worth noting as a technical aside that many queueing models are in fact classed as Markov processes. The Markov processes we have discussed have involved discrete time intervals and discrete states. Queues, on the other hand, often involve discrete states (numbers in the queueing system) but continuous time (since distributions for interarrival times are usually continuous).

**FIGURE 3–12**

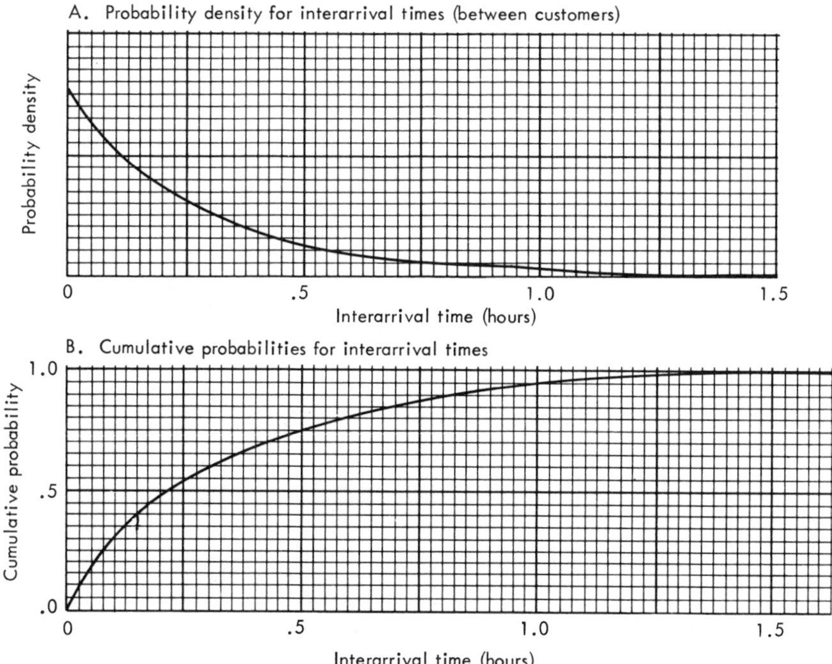


given in Figure 3–13. We will assume that there is no balking (customers will wait indefinitely for service) and that the queue discipline is first-in-first-served. Finally, we will assume to start with that there is only one server in the system. While these assumptions are quite specialized, it turns out that the general insights we will draw from this specific queueing problem can be generalized to many other cases.

Suppose that we are measuring time in hours. One of the important numbers describing the queueing system is the average rate of arrivals (in this case, the average rate per hour); almost invariably in queueing theory this quantity is called $\lambda$. In the example above it turns out the $\lambda$ is 3. If we know that there are an average of three arrivals per hour, then we can see that the corresponding time between arrivals (called the average interarrival time) is ⅓ hour. Another important quantity is the average service rate; in the distribution in Figure 3–13 the service facility is able to handle customers at an average rate of four per hour. Again almost invariably, the average rate for service that the facility could supply (if there were a steady supply of customers) is called $\mu$. In this example, $\mu$ is 4.

If we form the ratio of $\lambda$ to $\mu$ we find what is called the *utilization factor* for the system, almost always denoted $\rho$. In the current example $\rho$ is ¾ so that, on the average, ¾ of the potential capacity of the service facility is in fact used.

**FIGURE 3–13**

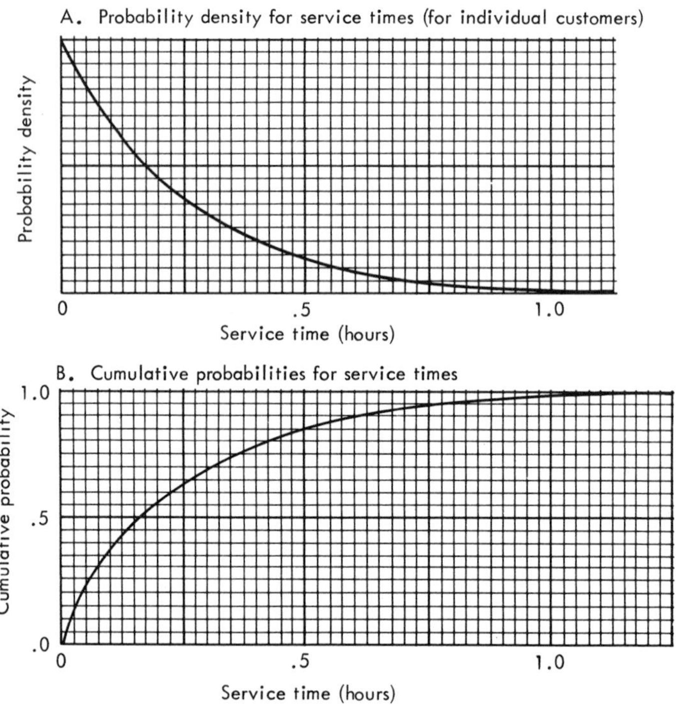


The first and most basic insight into queueing systems concerns the relation between $\rho$ and the quality of service (as measured by the waiting times) of the system. If we could schedule arrivals and service times at our convenience, then there would be no problem (beyond careful scheduling) in achieving a utilization factor of 1. Hence, in a deterministic queueing system, careful scheduling can achieve full utilization with no waiting lines. For systems marked by uncertainty, the situation changes markedly. In our example system, it may seem at first that there is one and a third times as much capacity as is needed to provide service. Hence, we might argue that there should be no waiting time. The problem with this argument is that arrivals and service times are both uncertain. In fact there will often be waiting in this system. In intuitive terms, the problem is that spare service time cannot be saved for use when the system becomes busy. The system will experience some slack times and some busy times. During the slack times the service facility will sit vacant; during the busy times the customers will have to wait. Once the system gets behind it becomes very difficult to catch up. To see the extreme importance of this effect, consider Figures 3–14A and 3–14B. Those figures give a plot of average waiting time versus $\rho$ for queues like the one in our example. In the figures we have assumed that the distribution of interar-

**FIGURE 3–14A**
Average waiting time per customer ($\lambda = 3$; $\rho$ from .3 to 1.0)

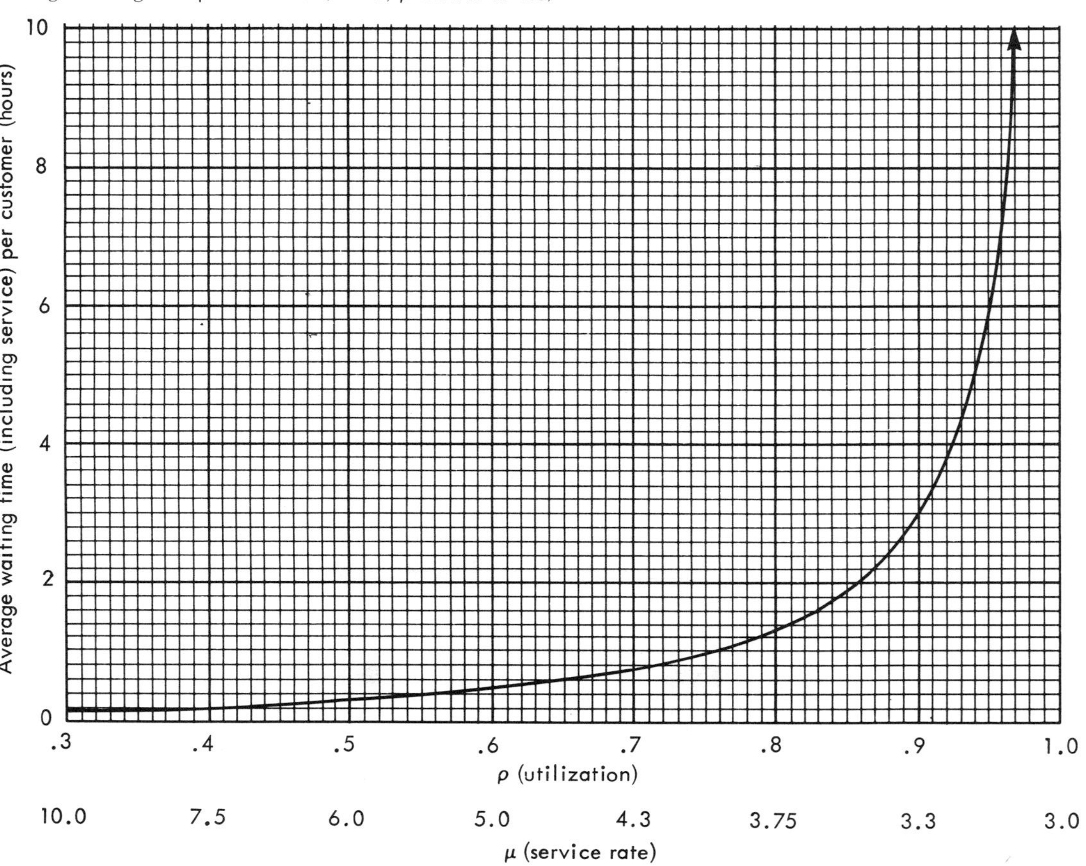

**FIGURE 3–14B**
Average total waiting time (including service) per customer and average service time per customer ($\lambda = 3$; $\rho$ from .3 to .9)

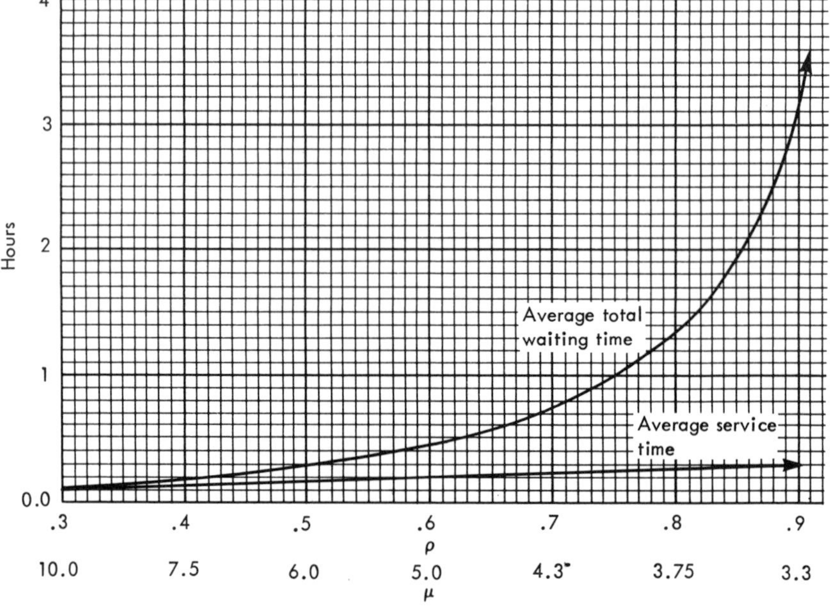


rival times remains the one we gave in Figure 3–12 (with $\lambda = 3$) but that the distribution of service times varies. We assume the same general type of distribution as in Figure 3–13, but we consider service rates ranging from three per hour to ten per hour (and, hence, values of $\rho$ ranging from .3 to 1).

What should be most striking about Figures 3–14A and 3–14B is the very sharp increase in the expected waiting time as the utilization of the service facility approaches 1. In fact, it can be shown that the waiting line will increase without bound as $\rho$ approaches 1 for a system marked by uncertainty. These figures should also be read to mean that the change in performance achieved when the system is adjusted so that the utilization moves away from 1 is considerable for the first changes (and less important for a queue that is already operating with a good margin).

To develop this point further, we can consider the distribution of waiting times for individual customers in our initial example (with $\lambda = 3$ and $\mu = 4$) with one server and the distribution of waiting times that would be obtained if a second server were added. Those distributions are given in Figure 3–15. Notice that there will occasionally be some time spent in line before service even if the second server is added; on the other hand, the customers will generally wait less often and for shorter periods if the facility is expanded.

**FIGURE 3–15**

A. Total waiting times per customer ($\lambda = 3$; $\mu = 4$)

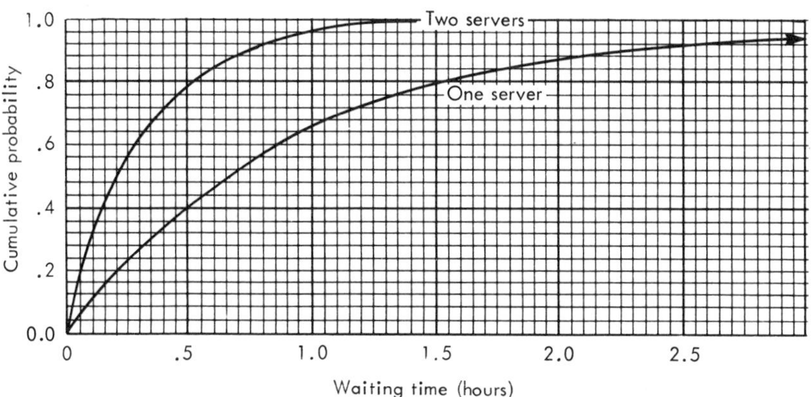


B. Waiting times minus service times ($\lambda = 3$; $\mu = 4$)

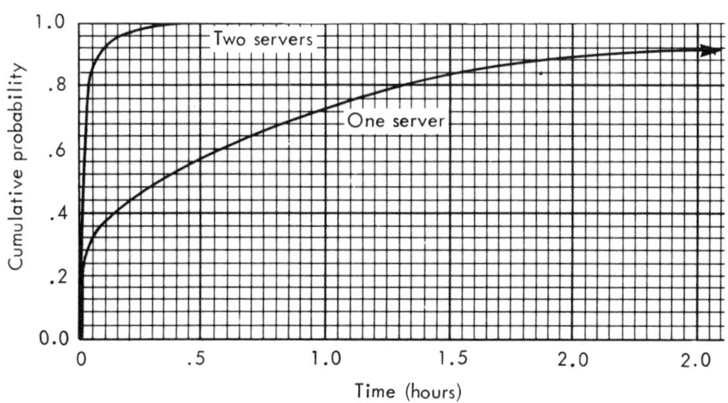


Another general insight that can be obtained for queueing systems concerns the variability of service times. Suppose that we feel that we cannot change the variability of arrival times for the system in our example, and moreover, that we cannot increase the number of servers above 1. Even so, it turns out that it is in our interest to consider reducing the variability of the individual service times. In particular, if we could somehow ensure that each customer received exactly the same service time (¼ hour in our example) we could cut the average waiting time *in half*. Thus, a manager who cannot change the arrival patterns can still often gain substantial benefits by altering the characteristics of service times.

Next, we turn to the question of multi-channel queues and, in particular to the question of whether there should be a single waiting line (with the next customer going to the next available server) or whether instead each server should have a separate line of its own. Consider interarrival and service distributions like those in Figures 3–12 and 3–13 but with $\mu = 4$ (for *each* of two servers) and with $\lambda = 6$. Suppose that we consider two possibilities for waiting lines; the first involves a single line (but two servers) for the system. In the second plan, assume that there are two separate entrances to the facility and that each entrance experiences arrivals at half the overall rate. One entrance, with its own waiting line, is for the first server; the second entrance and its line are for the second server. Figure 3–16 shows the differences in the distributions of waiting times obtained.

**FIGURE 3–16**

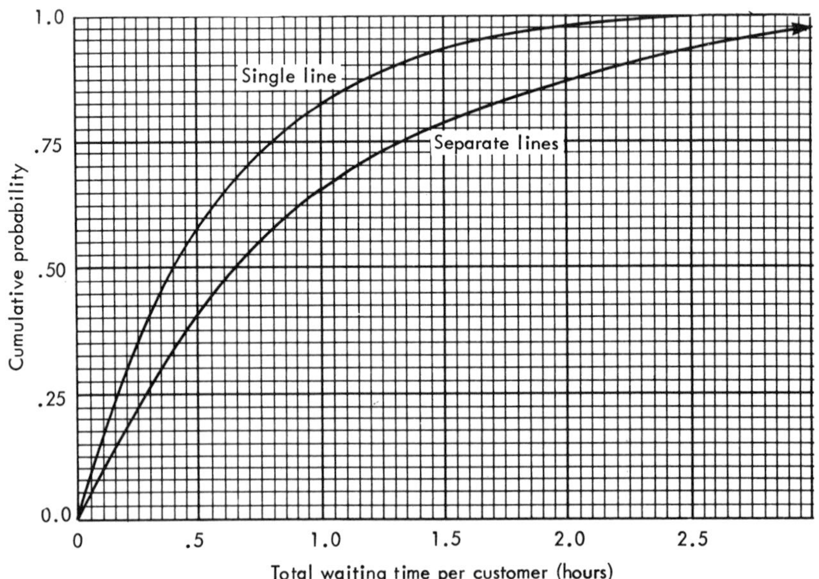


The figure shows that a single line gives a better performance in terms of waiting times than does a system with two separate lines. The reason should be relatively intuitive; if we maintain separate lines then the first server may be idle (having finished with a succession of relatively short jobs) while the second server is busy and a line of customers wait for attention from the server. Hence, pooling of facilities (with a common waiting line) will always reduce waiting times, providing of course that pooling is feasible. If we think of a supermarket, we probably conclude that a single waiting line is not physically feasible (such a line would likely stretch up one aisle and down another . . .) and hence, that the additional waiting time caused by having individual lines for the different checkout stations must be tolerated. (In addition, customers will try to shift to shorter lines and so some of the benefits of pooling will be achieved anyway.) In other cases, a single line may be feasible and worthwhile.

Finally, we return to the question of whether the service and arrival patterns depend on the state of the system. As an example, assume one channel, suppose that the arrival pattern remains the same as the one we have been considering, with $\lambda = 3$, but suppose that the single server works faster when there is a line. In particular, we assume the same general type of distribution as in Figure 3–13 but we assume that the average service rate is related to the number in the queue as shown in Table 3–3 below. Under these assumptions, the distribution of waiting times is found as shown in Figure 3–17.

**TABLE 3–3**

| *Number in system when customer starts service* | *$\mu$ for that customer* |
|---|---|
| 0, 1 | 4 |
| 2, 3, or 4 | 5 |
| 5 or more | 6 |

**FIGURE 3–17**

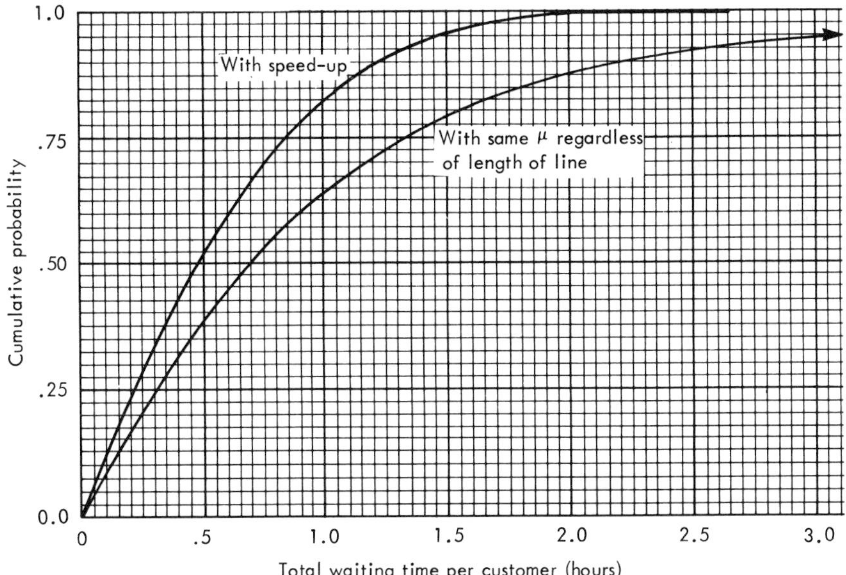


If, on the other hand, the service becomes slower when the queue is long, we might assume that the average service rate is related to the length of the line as shown in Table 3–4. In that case, the distribution of waiting times is the one in Figure 3–18. Comparing Figures 3–15, 3–17, and 3–18 shows that

**TABLE 3–4**

| *Number in system when customer starts service* | *$\mu$ for that customer* |
|---|---|
| 0, 1 | 4 |
| 2, 3, or 4 | 3.75 |
| 5 or more | 3.5 |

the response of the service facility to a heavy work load can be important in determining waiting times and line lengths. Similarly, we could show that the effects of line lengths on arrivals (or interarrival times) can also be significant.

Having drawn some general insights into queues, we now turn to a brief consideration of the types of analytic results that are provided by queueing theory. The distinction here is between analytic results (situations in which a general mathematical proof can be used to derive properties of certain types of queues) and problems which cannot currently be solved analytically and, hence, must be investigated by simulation. There are available a number of general results about queues. Most of these results assume a special distribution for the number of arrivals to the system (during a particular period) called the Poisson distribution. For this distribution, the number of arrivals in an interval does not depend on the state of the system nor on the length of time since the last arrival; instead, the probability of a particular number of arrivals during a given time interval depends only on the length of the interval and on the average arrival rate, $\lambda$. This set of assumptions turns out to be

**FIGURE 3–18**

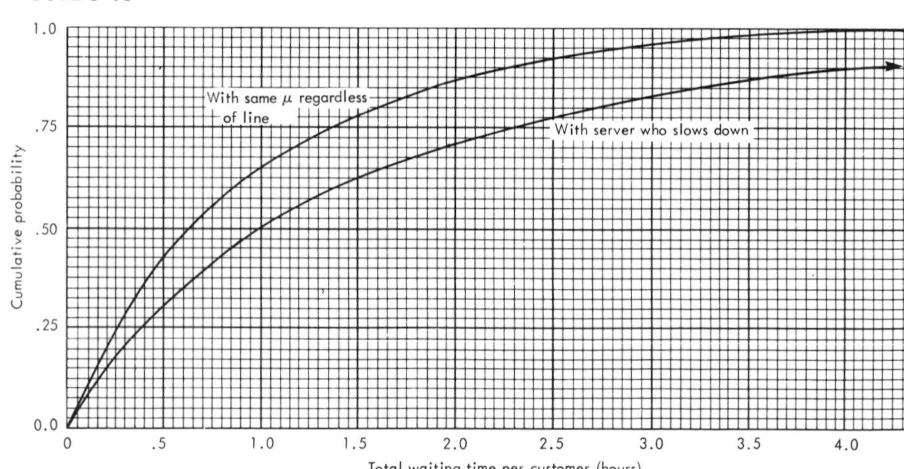

more generally applicable than it seems at first, but the fact remains that the assumptions are restrictive. Much of the theory also considers cases in which the service times follow the same general form of distribution (with a different rate) as do the interarrival times. (For a Poisson distribution for the number of arrivals during a particular interval it can be proven that the interarrival times follow what is called an exponential distribution. Much of queueing theory concerns exponential interarrival times and exponential service times.) In addition, there are results for different numbers of channels or servers.[14]

Another important consideration in discussing the available analytic results is the distinction between what are called transient and steady-state behavior. Most of the theory concerns what is called *steady state behavior,* the behavior of the system when it has been operating (under the *same* probability distributions) for such a long time that the effects of the condition it started in are no longer noticeable. The important phrase in this definition is "under the same probability distributions." If we think of a toll booth at a turnpike entrance next to a large factory, one of the first things that occurs to us is that the characteristics of arrivals and service times may differ at different times of the day. Hence, if we are most concerned with the busy periods at the ends of the shifts in the factory, we are concerned with the behavior of the system during periods that will almost certainly have started with essentially no line. Hence, we are interested in the build-up from an empty state. It may well be that we do not care about steady-state behavior, for the system may not settle into a steady state by the end of the peak periods. Instead, we are interested in the transient or short-term behavior for the busy periods.

When a queueing problem arises for which there is no analytic solution (as is most often the case) we have two general alternatives. The first is to approximate the problem by one of the problems that can be solved directly and then use the solution to that second problem. The other alternative is to build a simulation model with the characteristics of the particular problem at hand and then to operate the model to observe the behavior of the system under various management decisions. Especially before computers became available, the first approach was often taken. More recently it has become sufficiently simple to simulate the conditions of individual problems that the risks of tailoring the problem to the solution (rather than vice versa) can often be avoided. As always, of course, the modeler must decide which aspects of the problem must be considered and which can safely be ignored. Arrivals, service patterns, balking, queue discipline, the effects of the state on arrivals or on service should all be considered for possible inclusion. Once the difficult decisions have been made on which factors are important enough to

[14] For further discussion of queues see: Russell L. Ackoff and Maurice W. Sasieni, *Fundamentals of Operations Research* (New York: John Wiley & Sons, 1968); Frederick S. Hillier and Gerald J. Lieberman, *Introduction to Operations Research* (San Francisco: Holden-Day, 1967); and Harvey M. Wagner, *Principles of Management Science,* 2d ed. (Englewood Cliffs, N.J.: Prentice-Hall, 1975).

include, and once the relevant distributions and relationships (such as any relationship between service time and line length) have been made explicit, modeling a queueing system is relatively straightforward.

There are a few techniques that facilitate modeling of queueing systems with probabilistic simulations; we now turn to a discussion of such techniques. The preceding material has mentioned the fact that distributions for interarrival times and distributions for service times are usually used for the probabilistic portions of queueing models. Moreover, it is extremely common to use exponential distributions for both interarrival and service times if those times are uncertain. There are two reasons for the use of exponential distributions. One is that those distributions are suited for use in analytical queueing models, where the steady-state results are derived through mathematical manipulation of formulas rather than through simulation. As has been stated above, before the widespread availability of powerful computers, the analytic results were essentially all that were available in queueing and related problems. While the computer has made those analytic results less crucially important, such results are still widely studied and used in queueing. In part, they are used because they should be or, in other words, because they provide satisfactory approximations of situations under consideration. In many other cases, however, analytic results are used more from habit than anything else and they do not adequately capture the essence of the problems being analyzed. The second reason for using the exponential distributions should, today, be the more important one. In empirical studies of many systems involving queues, those distributions turn out to be close to the patterns actually observed.

The mathematics of the exponential distribution are particularly easy to apply in computer simulation studies. The discussion in Chapter 2 indicated that in using probability distributions in computer models we generally must either input a list of representative values or else must input the parameters of some particular probability distribution so that the computer can find a set of representative values. Members of the exponential family of distributions have only one parameter. They have shapes like those in Figures 3–12 and 3–13. The parameter defining a specific member of the family gives the average rate of occurrences per time period; for interarrival times the parameter would be $\lambda$, while for service times it would be $\mu$. Once the parameter has been given, we can easily find fractiles of the resulting specific distribution. Suppose we call the parameter $\alpha$. Then if $f$ is a fraction between zero and one and if $X$ is the $f$-fractile of the exponential distribution, then[15]

$$X = -(1/\alpha) \log (1 - f)$$

[15] Here the "log" is the natural logarithm or the log to the base e. It is the natural logarithm that is available as a library subprogram on essentially all computer systems.

To use an exponential distribution with parameter $\alpha$ in a computer simulation, we would simply have the computer construct a set of representative values, such as the .005, .015, .025, .035, . . . , .985, .995 fractiles of the distribution.

Another technical concept that is extremely useful in modeling queueing systems involves the idea of *event-sequenced* as opposed to time-sequenced models. The first way many people think to build a simulation model would follow this general pattern:

> Set up a clock to keep track of time. It could, for example, look at the queueing system every .01 hour. Set up a list of waiting customers and start the list empty. Find the arrival time of the first customer (by adding a randomly selected interarrival time to time 0, or the start of the trial). Then proceed one time period at a time. For each time period, check whether the clock has reached the arrival time of the next customer. If so, immediately find the arrival time of the following customer by drawing an interarrival time and adding it to the arrival time of the customer who has just arrived. Then put the current arrival in line (perhaps at the head of the line if no one else was waiting).[16] Now, regardless of whether a customer has just arrived, check whether the service facility is free. The facility starts the trial empty. Whenever a customer is admitted to the service facility for service draw a value for the service time and use that value plus the current clock reading to determine when the facility will next be free. A customer is admitted to the facility whenever there is a customer in line and, at the same time, the server is free. If there is no customer or if the facility is busy, go on to the next time period. Whenever a customer is admitted for service, calculate a waiting time by subtracting the time at which the customer arrived from the time at which the same customer will complete service.[17]

This type of procedure is quite capable of providing a model of the behavior of the queue. If a few additional details are filled in, trials of such models will provide lists of waiting times, and those waiting times can be summarized for output. The idea in this model design is to examine the system in successive time intervals; hence, it is called a *time-sequenced* model. Its feasibility depends on the ability of computer models to maintain lists, in this case, lists of waiting customers and their arrival times.

---

The formula above is derived as follows. The density function for the exponential is $\alpha e^{-\alpha t}$. To find the $f$-fractile, we solve the equation

$$\int_0^x \alpha e^{-\alpha t} dt = f.$$

[16] A correct procedure is in fact a bit more complicated at this point. We must consider the possibility of more than one arrival per (.01 hour) interval. The problem can be solved if we modify these instructions and continue to add customers to the queue until we reach a customer whose arrival time is in the next period or later.

[17] Recall that we define waiting time to include service time.

A somewhat different approach to modeling a queueing system turns out to be easier in practice, although many people do not find it as easy to understand as the time-sequenced approach. In this alternative method, called event-sequenced modeling, we are able to examine the queueing system, not at regular time intervals, such as every .01 hour, but, instead, only at the times of important occurrences or events; hence the name "event-sequenced." In queueing models we generally examine the system at the arrival times of successive customers only. The trick in this approach is that we can find both the arrival and departure (and waiting) times for a customer, upon arrival, provided that we know the departure time of the preceding customer. The procedure for drawing interarrival times and using them to find arrival times is straightforward. Similarly, we draw a service time for each customer upon arrival. Now, assume that the queue starts empty. The first customer arrives, is served immediately, and leaves. That customer's departure times is his or her service time plus the arrival time. Thus, we can easily find the first departure time.

Now, assume that we are somewhere in the middle of a trial and that we have just found the arrival time for the next customer; we have also drawn that customer's service time. Suppose that we know the departure time for the preceding customer. Then we can find the departure for the current customer as follows. If the preceding customer departed before the current one arrived, the new customer is served immediately upon arrival. The new departure time is then just the customer's arrival time plus the service time. If, on the other hand, the current customer arrives before the preceding one has left, the current customer must wait in line until the previous one leaves. The current customer enters the service facility at the time the preceding one departs and remains in the facility for the service time we have drawn. Thus, that customer's departure time is the previous departure time plus the current service time. Proceeding in this way, we can find the departure time for each customer. As soon as we have a customer's departure time we can find the corresponding waiting time by subtracting the arrival time from the departure time.

This event-sequenced approach turns out to be easier to implement than the time-sequenced approach. We do not have the complication posed by multiple arrivals during one time interval and we do not have to keep a list of waiting customers. Event-sequencing is a powerful tool in modeling queues.

## EXERCISES

3.1. Assume that a manufacturing facility will be making ten items per month of a new product. The managers of the plant expect production costs to follow a learning curve. They are uncertain about the initial cost per item and also about the rate of cost reduction (or learning). They are trying to build a risk analysis model for the new product. As one preliminary step, they would like to know how much variability there is in their estimates of costs after 12 months. Construct an algorithm that accepts inputs of the distributions for initial cost and for the learning rate and that finds the implied distribution of costs after a full year.

3.2. Construct an algorithm for determining a distribution of total supply sales in the instruments-and-supplies example described in section I.

3.3. Assume that the Markov matrix in Table 3–1 is the appropriate representation of the uncertainty about price in a simple risk analysis example. (Each of the ten prices $10.00, 10.35, 10.60, 10.75, 10.85, 10.95, 11.05, 11.20, 11.45, and 11.80 is equally likely to be the first price.) Variable cost is $8 per item sold. Yearly sales are fixed by contract at 10,000. Fixed costs are $27,000 per year. The planning horizon is seven years. Ignore inflation. The criterion is net present value at 12 percent of earnings before tax. Construct an algorithm to find risk profiles for the problem.

3.4. Assume that you have available a description of the distribution of interarrival times for some queueing problem. Describe an algorithm that will use that distribution, on a particular trial of some larger model, to construct a list of the arrival times of successive customers. Assume that the distribution is given in terms of hours and that one trial should consist of 12 hours of arrivals.

3.5. Design a queueing model in which the interarrival times are uncertain but the service times are not. There is a single server. Inputs should be the distribution of interarrival times and the single (constant) service time per customer. The model should run trials of one day (12 hours) each and should find the distribution of waiting times (across all trials).

# case 3.1

# LAB Products, Inc.

In November 1976, LAB Products, Inc., was considering the question of whether or not to begin producing a new item in its line of nutrient media for use in laboratory cultures. Rebecca Miller, the product manager for nutrient-medium and related products, and Roger Gold, an accountant and computer specialist for the firm, had assembled as much as possible of the relevant information about the new product, and the next task was for them to use that information to investigate the likely returns and risks that would accompany an introduction.

## Company background

LAB Products had been founded in 1948 in Woburn, Massachusetts. It produced equipment for use in biological and chemical laboratories, including items in several different product lines. One line included specialty lab glassware. Another contained specimens of particular bacteria for lab use. Still another was the line of laboratory animals, including white mice and similar animals. The company also sold chemical and biochemical products for laboratory use.

The line managed by Ms. Miller consisted of products that served as the nutritive medium for growing bacteria in culture in the laboratory. The medium would be placed in the bottom of a petri dish (a round dish made of glass or a similar material, with a matching round lid). The medium would be sterilized and would then be innoculated with a sample of the chosen bacterium or some substance whose bacterial content was to be investigated by allowing the bacteria to grow and multiply in the rich medium. The dish would be covered and placed at a temperature suitable for bacterial growth. The plate would be checked daily or even more frequently to monitor the growth. Later, some of the bacteria might be removed from the dish for use in further tests or experiments.

In 1975 LAB Products had sales of $50 million. It distributed its products throughout the United States, using distributors of laboratory goods as its principal channel.

### The new product

The new medium under consideration would be called Nutra-pure if it were made by LAB Products. Ms. Miller knew that the type of medium of which Nutra-pure would be an example was a considerable improvement over earlier products for a small set of specialized tests that were being used increasingly in hospital and other medical laboratories. She also knew that the discovery of the principle behind the new product had been accomplished by an industry leader, a chemical company that had begun to market its version of the product. The process for making such media was not patentable, although it was a bit difficult from a production point of view. LAB Products was certain that other firms would enter the market and that Nutra-pure would be a small factor in the total market for any feasible production level. They felt that customers would view Nutra-pure and its competitors as commodities, so that LAB Products and the other firms in the market would have to meet prevailing prices or else they would be uncompetitive. On the other hand, LAB Products was sufficiently well established that it was reasonable to assume that the firm would be able to sell all of its production of Nutra-pure if its price were competitive. Thus, Ms. Miller was willing to assume that LAB Products would be able to sell any of the feasible production quantities under consideration, although the firm would have to do so at the prevailing market prices.

### Analysis of the new product

In order to consider the likely risks and returns which would accompany a new-product introduction, Ms. Miller had begun to work with Mr. Gold, who was knowledgeable both in the accounting practices of the firm and also in the use of computers. They had decided to construct a computer program to analyze the possible results of the new product introduction over the firm's ten-year planning horizon. Accordingly, they ran some pro forma projections for deterministic scenarios for the performance of the new product. On the basis of those preliminary results, they felt that they were ready to try to construct a probabilistic model for analyzing the risks involved in the introduction.

In particular, Ms. Miller and Mr. Gold had identified what they felt were the major uncertainties in determining the results which LAB Products would realize from the new product. As stated above, Ms. Miller felt that the firm would be able to sell all of its output of Nutra-pure for any of the production levels being considered, but that LAB Products would have to meet the prevailing market price. Hence, sales would be assumed equal to production in each year considered, but prices would be treated as uncertain.

In discussing how prices would behave over the ten-year planning period, Ms. Miller and Mr. Gold realized that there were several assumptions that would have to be built into their model. For one thing, it was clear to them that prices could not be considered to fluctuate randomly, nor, on the other hand, would they remain stable over the period. Instead, prices likely would be determined by a combination of market factors that would produce some pattern of price levels. The pattern would not be entirely random, for there would be correlation between successive price levels, but the pattern would contain what would look like random elements as well as systematic ones. The planners considered the possibility of designing the model to select a starting price level and then to select nine price changes, from some distribution for price changes, under the assumption that the price *changes* (though not the levels) would be independent. This possible solution to the problem of modeling price behavior was rejected because Ms. Miller felt that the price changes could not be considered to be independent of the price level in the preceding year. She felt that a low price in a year would likely reflect relatively weak overall acceptance of the new type of medium and that conditions similar to the conditions causing the low price in one year would very likely occur in the following year. On the other hand, a high price in one year might be followed by another year with a high price or might be followed by a somewhat lower price. Thus, the tendency for one low price to be followed by another low price would be considerably stronger than would be the tendency for a high price to follow another high price.

A second major source of uncertainty concerned the level of production that would be achieved by the new production line LAB Products would install if it chose to make the new product. The total capacity of the production line would be 1,000,000 pounds per year. The yield of salable product would change over time as the operation of the line improved. Hence, Ms. Miller viewed the output of the LAB Products production line as uncertain. It seemed appropriate to consider two aspects of the uncertainty. One unknown factor was the eventual yield level that would be reached by the line when it had achieved mature operation, perhaps a few years after it began to work. The second factor was the rate at which that ultimate production level would be reached. LAB Products usually found that their production lines exhibited learning-curve types of behavior with regard to costs and other measures of performance. It seemed reasonable to assume that the Nutrapure line would exhibit a similar type of behavior with regard to acceptable output. Mr. Gold suggsted that LAB Products often found in examining past results that it was useful to determine the length of time during which a production line achieved some overall level of cost reduction after its introduction (i.e., the time its production process took to reach a limit of efficiency). It was then often possible to find some shorter period, such as a year or 18 months or more, so that half of the eventual cost reduction was achieved during the first period of that shorter length, an additional quarter of the reduction was achieved during the second shorter period of the same length, an eighth was achieved during the third such period, and so on. He felt that these observations from past experience might provide the basis for modeling the rates of production of salable Nutra-pure that would be achieved over time.

Other quantities which would be considered as uncertain in the model were the capital expenditure that would be required to build the new production line and also the maintenance (repair and replacement costs) that would be incurred in following years. Fixed costs and variable costs were not known, although the planners felt that once they had identified the relevant items of fixed and variable costs they could assess single distributions for each of these two types of costs, with the same two distributions to be used in each of the years of the analysis.

Managers at LAB Products had used computerized pro forma generators for years and recently they had begun to use probabilistic computer models. Accordingly, a risk analysis (or probabilistic simulation) model of the new-product introduction would be understandable to Ms. Miller and the other decision makers at the firm.

case 3.2

# Great Western Steel Corporation*

The Great Western Steel Corporation operated a dock at a port on the West Coast of the United States at which it unloaded iron ore coming by ship from Venezuela. The dock had facilities for unloading two ships at one time. The ships were all of about the same size and type. The time required to unload a ship was at least one 24-hour day, but on occasion equipment breakdowns would result in longer unloading times as shown in Exhibit 1. Labor was readily available. When there was no ship to unload, the company did not pay for a crew's time. On the other hand, the company could go on a three-shift, 7-day basis when required by the number of ship arrivals.

**EXHIBIT 1**
Unloading times

| *Hours* | *Percentage of ships* |
|---|---|
| *24* | *4* |
| *25* | *9* |
| *26* | *18* |
| *27* | *13* |
| *28* | *10* |
| *29* | *5* |
| *30* | *4* |
| *31* | *4* |
| *32* | *6* |
| *33* | *8* |
| *34* | *11* |
| *35* | *6* |
| *36* | *2* |

This arrangement had worked out very well for several years. The ships radioed their arrival enough in advance so that a crew was always ready when a berth became available. Not infrequently an arriving ship found both

* This case is based on a problem contained in Robert Schaifer's book, *Probability and Statistics for Business Decisions* (New York: McGraw-Hill, 1959). It was adapted to its present form by Basil A. Kalymon.

of the dock positions occupied and had to wait before being unloaded, but it was very rarely that the delay amounted to more than a few hours. In September 1975, however, management became concerned about the fact that the approaching completion of its new steel mill would increase ore requirements and therefore ship arrivals. About 500 shiploads of ore would be required per year instead of the previous 250, and management was afraid the ships, for which the company paid a charter rate of $1,400 a day, would sometimes have to wait a very considerable amount of time before being unloaded.

A study had been made of the possibility of making the arrivals more regular, but it appeared that the variety of conditions encountered during the voyage made this impossible. (Ships could, of course, be instructed to proceed at slow speed when normal speed would have led to arrivals producing congestion in the harbor.) A study of past records showed that ships arrived completely unpredictably; equally often at all hours and on all days throughout the year with no apparent pattern. Exhibit 2 indicates the work-

**EXHIBIT 2**
Worksheet

| *Time of arrival* | *Time spent unloading* | *Berth #1* | | *Berth #2* | |
|---|---|---|---|---|---|
| | | *Time in* | *Time out* | *Time in* | *Time out* |
| | | | | | |

sheet used in gathering observations on arrivals and dock utilization. From past observations, the best estimate for the time between arrivals of ships with the increased traffic was thought to be as shown in Exhibit 3, where the mean value of the distribution is, of course, equal to 365 ÷ 500 = .73 days.

A study was then made of the possibility of extending the dock or of building a new dock nearby. The study showed that, using the most economical location available, the company would be obliged to spend about $1.3 million to build a one-berth dock and install all necessary equipment such as

**EXHIBIT 3**

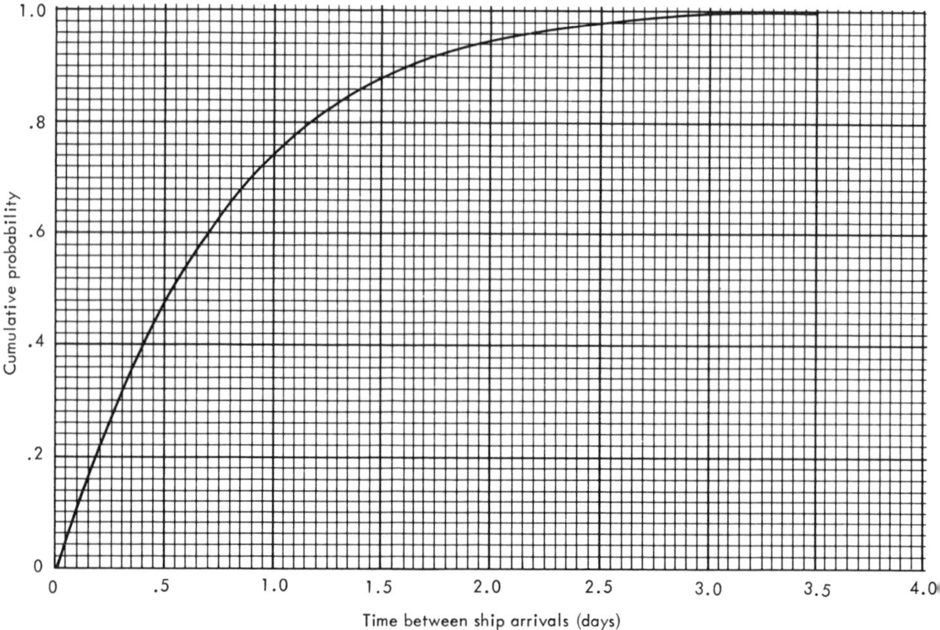


cranes, rail spurs, etc. Maintenance of the new facilities would cost about $28,000 a year; operating expenses could be neglected because they depended on the number of ships arriving and not on the number of berths available—no premium was paid to dock crews for working nights or holidays. The life of the proposed new facilities was estimated at 25 years, and the company's policy was to make no investments which did not earn 15 percent on the investment after taxes. The construction of the dock and installation of the facilities could not be completed by the time the new mill was in operation unless it was begun almost immediately.

## case 3.3

# Exercises on Queues

### EXERCISE 1: National Cranberry Cooperative* *with Computer Supplement*

A cranberry growers' cooperative has been experiencing delays at its main receiving plant. Trucks arrive at the plant carrying loads of cranberries. Some of the berries have been dry-harvested while others have been harvested by an alternate, wet, process in which the bogs are flooded to float ripe berries to the surface. There is separate storage space .for "wet" and for "dry" berries. The wet berries must be dried before further processing; at the moment, the plant has three dryers with capacities of 200 barrels (bbls) per hour each. Both wet and dry berries eventually reach the separators that grade them by size; the capacity of the separators is 1,200 bbls/hour. At the current time, the separator speed is the main constraint on processing speed after berries have left the dryers. Thus, the process flow for the plant can be thought of as shown in Exhibit 1.

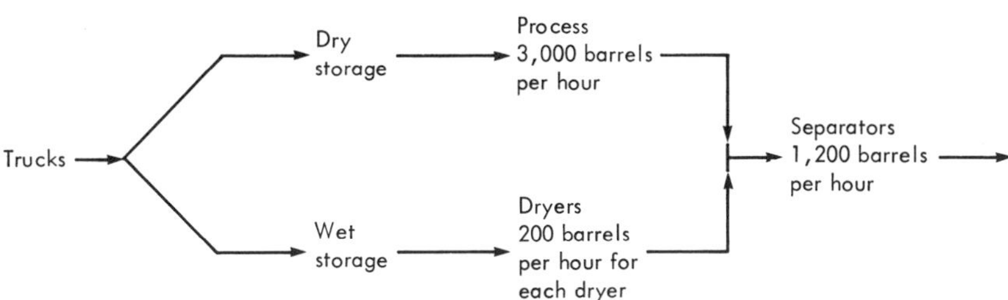


Assume that the owners of the cooperative are particularly concerned with the time they may have to spend waiting in line to unload their trucks and therefore that you want to construct a model to examine the distribution of waiting times under various policies. Assume that there are no problems with dry berries and that you will model *only* those parts of the process that

* This exercise is adapted from the case *National Cranberry Cooperative* (9-675-014), copyright 1974 by the President and Fellows of Harvard College.

involve *wet* berries. Wet berries are currently 70 percent of berry deliveries. A typical truckload of berries contains 75 barrels. Trucks start arriving at the plant at 7 A.M. and continue arriving for 11 hours. The receiving dock opens at 7 A.M. In the past, the actual processing has started at 3 P.M. on less busy days and at 11 A.M. on more busy ones. On a moderate day there might be 140 truckloads of wet berries; on a busy day there might be 185 such loads.

The cooperative is considering two options in terms of capital investment for decreasing the delays at the plant. They are considering increasing the amount of storage capacity available to hold wet berries awaiting processing; there are currently 3,200 barrels of holding bin capacity for wet berries. Alternatively or in addition, the managers of the cooperative are considering adding another dryer to the plant. Each dryer can process 200 barrels per hour.

The appended computer supplement shows a run of a program for analyzing this problem. Block out the design that seems to be incorporated into that program. For your analysis, assume that the drying process is a continuous, rather than a batch, process, and answer these questions:

1. What information would you need to decide what inputs to give to the model to evaluate the cooperative's investment decisions?
2. To investigate other interesting options?
3. Where would you get that information?

## COMPUTER SUPPLEMENT

Program NCRAN is a computer program for use in analyzing the case National Cranberry Cooperative. NCRAN considers arrivals and processing of wet berries *only*. It accepts as inputs information about the capacity of critical parts of the processing line for wet berries as well as information about the number and pattern of truck arrivals to the cooperative. Specifically, the program requires inputs on:

1. Processing capacity: the user must give the total bin capacity available for handling wet berries (in barrels); the total capacity of the dryers in barrels per hour (with three dryers this figure would be 600, for example); and the hourly amount of separator capacity available for wet berries (this quantity would be 840 if 70 percent of the separator time were used each hour for wet berries). The program does not specifically consider other potential bottlenecks although users can view the input for separator rate as representing the processing rate for the most binding type of capacity other than dryers and bins.
2. Processing time: the user must specify the time of day at which processing starts; for example, 7 means 7 o'clock A.M., 9 means 9 A.M., 13 means 1 P.M., etc.

3. Arrivals of trucks carrying wet berries: truck arrivals are assumed to occur during 11 hours, with or without a one-hour break at noon, depending on the user's inputs. Thus, with the noon break, arrivals occur from 7 to 12 and then from 13 (1 P.M.) to 19 (or 7 P.M.), while without a break the arrivals occur between 7 and 18. Arrivals can be assumed to be uniform (or evenly spread throughout the 11 hours). Alternatively, arrivals can be assumed random (in which case the program makes the very common assumption in queueing analyses of interarrival times distributed according to the exponential probability distribution). Users who assume uniform arrivals are asked to specify the total number of trucks (per day) that arrive. Users who elect random arrivals are asked for the average number of trucks that arrive during each hour. (The average number of trucks per hour need not be an integer.) For either method of specifying truck arrivals, no more than 500 trucks per day can be considered. The program assumes that there is no variability in the load of cranberries per truck but, instead, that there are exactly 75 barrels in each truck. It ignores dry-berry delivery and processing. It also assumes that unloading a truck takes no time.
4. Finally, the user specifies how many trials should be run. Each trial consists of a one-day simulation of arrival and processing. With uniform arrivals, of course, only one trial would be used (for there is no variability in the daily pattern). With random arrivals the user may request from 1 to 200 trials.

NCRAN provides output information on the hour of the day at which processing is finished, on the total waiting time per day (trial), on the number of trucks that must wait during any trial, on the fraction of trucks (from all trials) that must wait to be unloaded, and on the distribution (among all trials) of the waiting times for individual trucks. The following protocol shows sample runs of NCRAN. In the protocol, responses typed by the user have been underlined.

## First run of NCRAN:*

```
.R NCRAN
```
← At the monitor level, the user requests program NCRAN

```
WET BINS,DRYERS,SEPARATOR: ?
```
← Request for elaboration

```
WET HOLDING BIN CAPACITY (BARRELS), DRYER CAPACITY (BARRELS/HOUR),
 SEPARATOR CAPACITY AVAILABLE FOR WET BERRIES (BARRELS/HOUR)
WET BINS,DRYERS,SEPARATOR: 3200.,600.,840.
```

Thus, the user assumes 3200 barrels of holding bin capacity for wet berries, dryer capacity of 600 bbls/hour, and separator capacity of 840 bbls/hour.

```
HOUR AT WHICH PROCESSING STARTS? 7.
IS THERE A NOON BREAK IN TRUCK ARRIVALS? Y
```

Processing starts at 7 AM and there is a noon break in truck arrivals (not in processing; processing is assumed to continue without a break from the specified starting time until the trucks have all been unloaded and the bins are empty)

```
RANDOM ARRIVALS(1) OR UNIFORM ARRIVALS(2)? 2
TOTAL NUMBER OF TRUCKS: 168
```

When the user chooses uniform arrivals, the program asks for the total number of trucks for the day (that number may not exceed 500)

```
NUMBER OF TRIALS? ?
SPECIFY NUMBER OF TRIALS, WHICH MUST BE BETWEEN 1 AND 200
NUMBER OF TRIALS? 1
```

With uniform arrivals, only 1 trial should be considered.

```
HOUR PROCESSING FINISHES: 28.07
 TOTAL WAITING TIME (HOURS): 118.88
 NUMBER OF TRUCKS HAVING TO WAIT:   63
```

The program summarizes the day's results: Processing ended at 28.07 hours (that is, at about 4 the next morning)
There were 118.9 hours spent waiting by a total of 63 trucks.

---

* In this protocol, the actual dialog is shown in typeface, with the parts that were typed by the user underlined to distinguish them from the parts that were printed by the computer. Explanatory comments have been added in handwriting.

Next, the program describes the distribution of waiting times of the individual trucks:

```
FRACTION NOT WAITING:  0.6250 ← 62.5% of the trucks did
DISTRIBUTION OF WAITING TIMES:        not wait
```

(Distribution of waiting times for those trucks that did wait ONLY)

```
PRINTOUT? ? ← Request for information
AVAILABLE PRINTOUTS:
   1  SUMMARY STATISTICS OF THE DISTRIBUTION
   2  NINE STANDARD FRACTILES
   3  CUMULATIVE PROBABILITIES OF SPECIFIED VALUES
   4  VALUES WITH SPECIFIED CUMULATIVE PROBABILITIES (FRACTILES)
   5  GRAPH OF THE MASS FUNCTION
   6  GRAPH OF THE CUMULATIVE FUNCTION
   7  GRAPH OF PROBABILITY OF MORE THAN X
   8  COMPLETE LISTING OF THE CUMULATIVE FUNCTION
   $  NO FURTHER PRINTOUT

 PRINTOUT? 1 ← summary statistics
 MEAN    =     1.887
 STD DEV =     1.091

 PRINTOUT? 2 ← standard fractiles
 FRACTILES
  .001    .01     .1     .25     .5     .75     .9     .99    .999
   56     111    405    963    1876   2788   3346   3689   3744
*  DEC.PT -3

 PRINTOUT? $ ← No further description wanted

 EXIT ← End of this run of NCRAN
```

* The DEC PT entry says to move the decimals; -3 means 3 places left. Thus, the .5 fractile is 1.876.

Second run of NCRAN:

```
.R NCRAN

WET BINS,DRYERS,SEPARATOR: 3200.,800.,840. ← on this run, the user
                                   assumes there are 4 dryers
                                   (200 bbl/hour each)
HOUR AT WHICH PROCESSING STARTS? 7.
IS THERE A NOON BREAK IN TRUCK ARRIVALS? Y
RANDOM ARRIVALS(1) OR UNIFORM ARRIVALS(2)? 1
AVERAGE TRUCKS/HOUR: 15
```

With random arrivals, the program requires the average number of arrivals per hour.

```
NUMBER OF TRIALS? 100
```

With random arrivals and multiple trials, the program offers descriptions of the distributions of processing summaries:

```
DISTRIBUTION OF THE TIME AT WHICH PROCESSING ENDS
PRINTOUT? 1
MEAN    =     23.409
STD DEV =      0.662
```

← the mean is about 11:25 PM

```
PRINTOUT? 2
FRACTILES
 .001    .01     .1    .25     .5    .75     .9    .99   .999
 2165   2269   2299   2304   2309   2374   2439   2579   2583
DEC.PT -2

PRINTOUT? $
```

← No further description of this output measure.

Distribution of the total waiting time for all trucks in one day (or trial):

```
DISTRIBUTION OF TOTAL WAITING TIME (HOURS)
PRINTOUT? 1
MEAN    =     11.335
STD DEV =     23.216

PRINTOUT? 2
FRACTILES
 .001    .01     .1    .25     .5    .75     .9    .99   .999
    0      0      3      8     19    104    341   1467   1480
DEC.PT -1

PRINTOUT? $
```

Distribution of the number of trucks having to wait on any day:

```
DISTRIBUTION OF NUMBER OF TRUCKS HAVING TO WAIT
PRINTOUT? 1
MEAN    =     14.120
STD DEV =     19.842

PRINTOUT? 2
FRACTILES
 .001    .01     .1    .25     .5    .75     .9    .99   .999
    4     45    103    129    173   2106   4628   8811   8891
DEC.PT -2

PRINTOUT? $
```

Next, the program considers the distribution of individual trucks' waiting times across all trials (in this case, for the 100 days simulated):

```
FRACTION NOT WAITING:  0.9158
```

← 91.58 % of all trucks did not wait at all

```
DISTRIBUTION OF WAITING TIMES:
PRINTOUT? 1
MEAN    =     0.766
STD DEV =     0.813
```

← For the remaining trucks (which did have to wait), this is the distribution of individual waiting times

```
PRINTOUT? 2
FRACTILES
 .001    .01     .1    .25     .5    .75     .9    .99   .999
   51     60    148    324    623   1090   1607   2941   9822
DEC.PT -3

PRINTOUT? $

EXIT
```

## EXERCISE 2: Planning a Restaurant

You have decided to go into business and to open a restaurant. You are busily involved in planning the new venture. One of the first important decisions you must make is how large each part of your establishment (bar and lounge area, dining area, and kitchen) should be. For the time being, you are assuming that you will hire enough staff so that your operations will not face bottlenecks because of lack of staff. Also, you are assuming that you can decide on the kitchen size after you decide on the space for the lounge and that for the dining area. (You are constructing a new building so that there are no significant limitations on the sizes you can choose for the three areas.) Thus, you have decided to tackle first the decision on how large a bar and lounge and how large a dining area to have. Your decision will rest on a trade-off between the costs of construction and the costs you will incur if patrons have to wait for service.

*a*. First assume that all customers have identical distributions for times for service in the lounge and identical distributions for times for service in the dining room. Block out the general design of a model that would allow you to investigate the impact various decisions on size of rooms would have on the waiting times your customers would experience.

*b*. Now consider a more realistic version of the problem. What changes would you have to make in the model in (*a*) to obtain useful results? Block out the outline of a model for evaluating decisions on room sizes that is both useful and usable.

## case 3.4

# Paine, Webber, Jackson & Curtis, Inc.: Portfolio Dynamics

In 1974 and 1975 the brokerage firm of Paine, Webber, Jackson and Curtis developed and then introduced to the market a system called Portfolio Dynamics for evaluation of investment portfolios. The basic idea of Portfolio Dynamics was to market the theory of the stock market that had been developed by Markowitz, Sharpe, Lintner, and others and to use that theory as a tool in providing highly professional brokerage services to Paine Webber's retail customers. By 1976 the system had been introduced nationwide and was increasingly successful in attracting clients to Paine Webber.

### Company background

Paine Webber was founded in 1879 in Boston as a retail brokerage firm; thus it was one of the oldest brokerage houses in existence in the United States. The firm continued to emphasize its retail operations, providing services to the public through 134 branch offices and perhaps 2,000 salespeople. In the mid-1970s the firm was the fifth largest retail brokerage company. In addition to its retail business, Paine Webber had approximately $30 million in institutional investment business. Further, the firm was a major investment banker.

As a brokerage house, Paine Webber was conservative by style. Surveys showed that its clients tended to be older, more conservative, and more affluent than were the customers of other brokers such as Merrill Lynch. The Paine Webber brokers also tended to be older and more affluent than the brokers at other firms; Paine Webber tried to hire brokers with some business experience (such as work in sales for Xerox or IBM, for example), while many of the other firms were willing to hire people straight from college or, at least, with less experience.

### Customer surveys

In 1968, 1970, and 1972 Paine Webber had conducted surveys of some of its clients in order to learn more about the characteristics and opinions of its customers. What emerged from those surveys was a picture of the more important Paine Webber customers, the relatively small fraction of the accounts which provided the majority of the firm's revenues. These people, according to the surveys, were not interested in stock brokers who would try to make them rich—they already were relatively affluent. Instead, the customers were concerned with preservation of their capital; they wanted a broker who would keep them from becoming poor.[1] In addition, the surveys, together with other work on the stock market, showed a deep and, perhaps, growing distrust of Wall Street. Individual investors felt that the large institutions had great advantages over the individual and that the institutions had access to far better information and to better tools to aid them in investing their money. There was suspicion that brokers tended to buy and sell stock more than was wise in an effort to increase their commissions (a process called churning) and that individual investors did not fare well, in general, in the market.

In part in response to those surveys, Paine Webber had begun to investigate new techniques for use in its retail business. Another impetus to the effort came from the prospect of negotiated commissions which, Paine Webber felt, would require them to provide clear evidence of superior service if they were not to lose business to discount brokers. As Robert Dunwoody, who in 1976 was senior vice president for marketing, explained, "The thrust of Wall Street for 250 years has been to pick winners . . . even though the general track record has been quite poor." That is, the broker's aim was to identify individual stocks that would earn high returns for its purchasers. Paine Webber's management had concluded that picking "winners" simply did not work. Instead, they wanted to provide a different way of looking at and managing investment. In the process, they wanted to provide a more professional image for their brokers and to make their individual investors feel that they were receiving service comparable to that obtained by the institutional investors. Further, they wanted to differentiate their product so that they would have a strong position when competitive commissions were introduced.

As it happened, the director of research at Paine Webber at the time had previously been a senior officer of Standard and Poor's econometrics unit and was familiar with the capital market theory that had been developed by economists since the late 1950s. Mr. Dunwoody and others at Paine Webber began to study that theory, consulting with some of the theoreticians who had developed it, and surveying its uses. They found, for example, that Wells Fargo was using the concepts of the theory in managing its investments. As they became more comfortable with the ideas behind portfolio theory, they

[1] Later advertising by Paine Webber, aimed at such customers, would quote Will Rogers: " 'Most people are more interested in the return of their capital than the return on their capital.' "

began to feel that it could be the basis for a new approach to retail investment services.

## Portfolio theory

Over the past 20 years Markowitz, Sharpe, Lintner, and others had developed a rigorous theory of portfolios. This section describes some of the basic ideas of that theory, on which the Paine Webber executives planned to construct an investment service. Portfolio theory considers the different types of risk that are involved in investing in the stock market. The theory suggests that the risks be broken down into several main categories. The movements of a particular stock reflect, to varying degrees, movements of the stock market in general (as measured, perhaps, by the S&P 500 index or some similar measure), conditions in the particular industry to which the firm belongs, and conditions and events peculiar to the firm itself. For example, the price of the stock of Mobil Oil Corporation moves up and down, to some extent, with the market averages. In addition, that price is affected by conditions in the petroleum industry. Finally, the price is affected by conditions at Mobil itself—quality of management, decisions on dividends, and other issues. The traditional method of looking for winners on the stock market was aimed at finding companies that would have positive industry and firm influences on their stock prices. Portfolio theory, on the other hand, suggested considering all three influences and, most importantly, their relations to one another. First, the theory suggested measuring the degree to which changes in the price of a particular stock reflected changes in the market itself. For this purpose, investigators looked at the premium which a stock paid over some risk-free rate (such as the rate on Treasury bills) and compared that premium to the premium paid by the market, on average (measured, perhaps, through one or more market indices).[2] Running a regression of the premium for the particular stock on that for the market as a whole would give a coefficient, generally called beta, for the market rate premium (the explanatory variable). This value was called the beta of the particular stock. It showed how closely the stock could be expected to follow the market (in an expected value sense, only, it is important to note). Thus, a beta of 1 suggested that an increase in the market would be reflected exactly (in expectation) in a like increase in the stock; if the market premium went up 10 percent, the stock's premium would be expected to do likewise. Similarly, if the market premium decreased 5 percent, the stock's premium would be expected to do the same, on average. For stocks with betas greater than 1.0, the market changes would be amplified in the stock's changes. If the stock had a beta of 1.5, then a 10 percent increase for the market would correspond in expectation to a 15 percent increase in the stock, while a 5

[2] The stock's return was the amount the investor earned by holding the stock for one period.

percent market decrease would correspond to a 7.5 percent decrease for the stock. On the other hand, a stock with a beta of .8 would tend to dampen changes in the market. For such a stock, a 10 percent market change would correspond in expectation to an 8 percent increase for the stock, while a 5 percent decrease for the market would mean an average 4 percent decrease for the stock. Hence, other things being equal, high beta stocks could be considered riskier than low beta stocks. The high betas gave better returns when times were good but they produced bigger losses when times were bad.

Actually, the basic value of portfolio theory was in measuring betas for portfolios rather than for individual stocks. The theory argued that investors diversify in the stock market because they want to reduce their risks. Hence, an important measure for them was the extent to which they could diversify away their risks. To the extent that an individual stock moved with the market, the risk associated with that stock could not be diversified away, the theory argued. Instead, only the remaining risks, those associated with industry and company, could be diversified away. Hence, the beta for a stock or portfolio was sometimes called its systematic or undiversifiable risk.

Another measure of the uncertainty about a stock's price considered in portfolio theory is the variability of the individual stock's short-term fluctuations, often called the volatility of the stock. In other terms, the volatility can be thought of as the deviations from the regression line of stock premium versus market premium for a particular stock; hence, it could be measured by the residual standard deviation of the regression line. To illustrate these terms, consider Exhibit 1.

The line for the market in the figure shows a very simple pattern of changes in the overall market (premium). The expected stock price line shows the expected price for the individual stock, given the illustrated pattern of the market. This particular stock has a beta of .9 and so somewhat

**EXHIBIT 1**

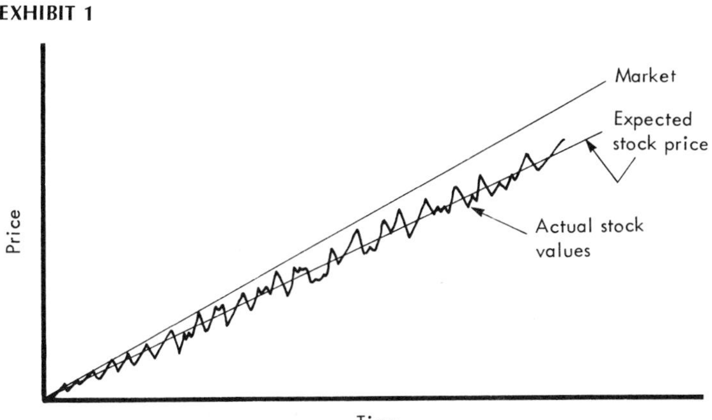

understates the market. The irregular line labeled "actual stock values" gives the actual prices (premiums) for the stock. As would be expected for any real-world regression line, the actual values show some deviations around the regression line. The stock's volatility is a measure of those deviations.

The argument of portfolio theory was that the individual movements of a stock could be diversified away; hence, the uncertainty associated with the volatility of a stock was sometimes called unsystematic risk. That risk could be removed by proper diversification of a portfolio. Studies had shown that perhaps one third of the price movements of individual stocks could be attributed to the characteristics of the particular stock, about an eighth could be ascribed to the industry, and the remainder (just over half) to the market.

In June of 1974 Paine Webber began implementation of a project, called Portfolio Dynamics, that would include portfolio theory as a tool for investment planning. The idea was to teach brokers and, through them, customers about portfolio theory and then use a computerized system to provide analyses of portfolios, using that theory. Marketing of the new system would stress that it used objective data (i.e., values fitted by statistical methods) rather than the hunches of individual brokers and that it would give individual investors access to one of the tools used by the larger institutional investors.

## Portfolio dynamics

Portfolio Dynamics was developed during the second half of 1974 and was tried on a pilot basis during September and October of that year. It was introduced at the end of 1974 and the start of 1975. By mid-1976 the system was well established at Paine Webber, handling perhaps 350 requests for analysis on any given day.

The basic operation of Portfolio Dynamics was as follows: a Paine Webber broker would enter information about the portfolio of a particular investor. (The different ways in which information could be input are discussed below.) The information would be transmitted to New York, to the firm's main computer center. Paine Webber had considerable computer power (two IBM system 370 model 155 computers in operation and a model 158 testing in mid-1976, for example). The computers were used primarily for record-keeping and for sending messages back and forth to branch offices and to stock exchanges. The requests for analyses would be stored until the end of the working day. At 5 or 6 P.M., Paine Webber would receive a computer tape giving information on stock prices and related information for that day. Using that information, together with additional information stored within the computer, the Portfolio Dynamics programs would analyze each of the requests in the middle of the night. The results would be sent out over the firm's communications lines starting at about 2 or 3 A.M. and would be waiting for the stockbrokers at the branch offices in the morning.

Exhibit 2 shows an annotated example of the data input sheet for a Port-

**EXHIBIT 2**

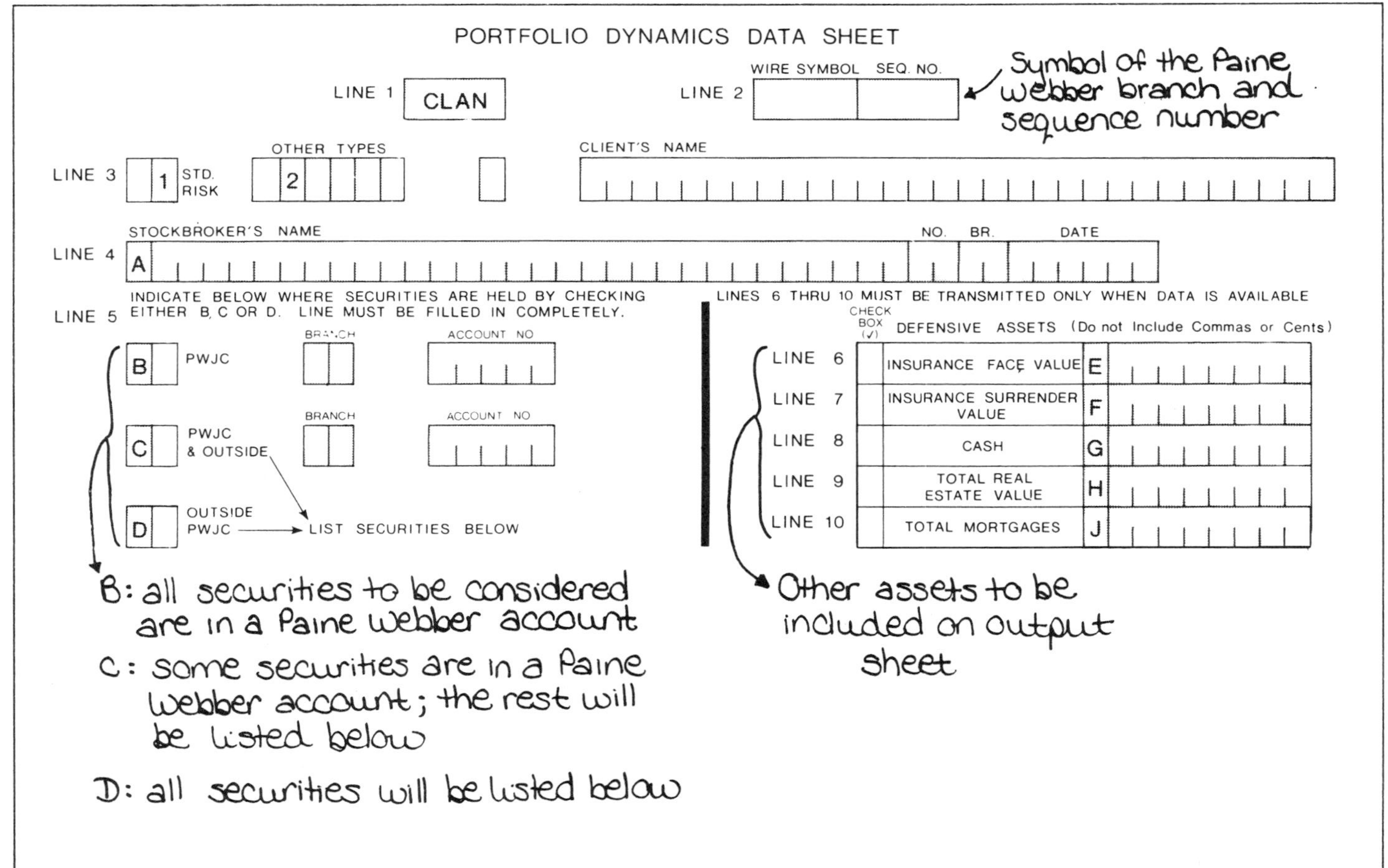

PORTFOLIO DYNAMICS DATA SHEET

LINE 1 CLAN

LINE 2 WIRE SYMBOL SEQ. NO.



LINE 3 1 STD. RISK  OTHER TYPES 2  CLIENT'S NAME

LINE 4 A STOCKBROKER'S NAME  NO. BR. DATE

LINE 5 INDICATE BELOW WHERE SECURITIES ARE HELD BY CHECKING EITHER B, C OR D. LINE MUST BE FILLED IN COMPLETELY.

B PWJC  BRANCH  ACCOUNT NO

C PWJC & OUTSIDE  BRANCH  ACCOUNT NO

D OUTSIDE PWJC → LIST SECURITIES BELOW

B: all securities to be considered are in a Paine webber account
C: some securities are in a Paine webber account; the rest will be listed below
D: all securities will be listed below



LINES 6 THRU 10 MUST BE TRANSMITTED ONLY WHEN DATA IS AVAILABLE

| | CHECK BOX (✓) | DEFENSIVE ASSETS (Do not Include Commas or Cents) | | |
|---|---|---|---|---|
| LINE 6 | | INSURANCE FACE VALUE | E | |
| LINE 7 | | INSURANCE SURRENDER VALUE | F | |
| LINE 8 | | CASH | G | |
| LINE 9 | | TOTAL REAL ESTATE VALUE | H | |
| LINE 10 | | TOTAL MORTGAGES | J | |

**EXHIBIT 2** *(continued)*

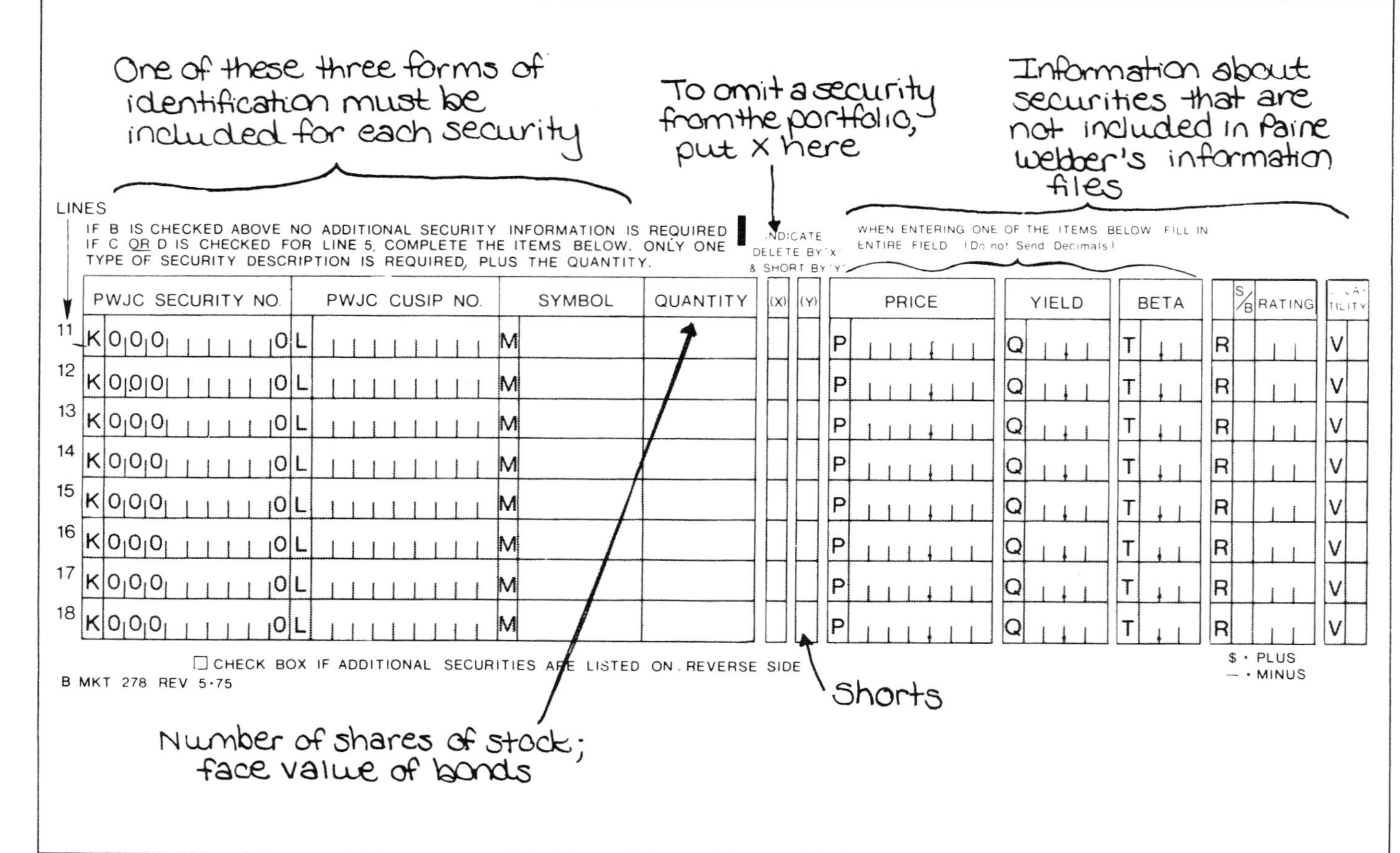

One of these three forms of identification must be included for each security

To omit a security from the portfolio, put X here

Information about securities that are not included in Paine Webber's information files

LINES

IF B IS CHECKED ABOVE NO ADDITIONAL SECURITY INFORMATION IS REQUIRED
IF C OR D IS CHECKED FOR LINE 5, COMPLETE THE ITEMS BELOW. ONLY ONE TYPE OF SECURITY DESCRIPTION IS REQUIRED, PLUS THE QUANTITY.

INDICATE DELETE BY 'X' & SHORT BY 'Y'

WHEN ENTERING ONE OF THE ITEMS BELOW FILL IN ENTIRE FIELD (Do not Send Decimals)

| LINES | PWJC SECURITY NO. | PWJC CUSIP NO. | SYMBOL | QUANTITY | (X) | (Y) | PRICE | YIELD | BETA | S/B | RATING | TILITY |
|---|---|---|---|---|---|---|---|---|---|---|---|---|
| 11 | K000 0 | L | M | | | | P | Q | T | R | | V |
| 12 | K000 0 | L | M | | | | P | Q | T | R | | V |
| 13 | K000 0 | L | M | | | | P | Q | T | R | | V |
| 14 | K000 0 | L | M | | | | P | Q | T | R | | V |
| 15 | K000 0 | L | M | | | | P | Q | T | R | | V |
| 16 | K000 0 | L | M | | | | P | Q | T | R | | V |
| 17 | K000 0 | L | M | | | | P | Q | T | R | | V |
| 18 | K000 0 | L | M | | | | P | Q | T | R | | V |

☐ CHECK BOX IF ADDITIONAL SECURITIES ARE LISTED ON REVERSE SIDE

B MKT 278 REV 5·75

\$ · PLUS
— · MINUS

Shorts

Number of shares of stock; face value of bonds

folio Dynamics request. The broker could simply list the account number for an existing customer and the computer would pick up the required information about the holdings of the account from files kept in New York. Alternatively, the system would allow the broker to start with the existing account status (from the master files) and to make changes indicated on the form; this feature allowed the broker to present "before" and "after" pictures of proposed changes in a portfolio or to consider additional stocks owned by the client but handled by a different broker. Finally, the broker could list all securities for people who did not have Paine Webber accounts; this feature was particularly important for selling ("prospecting," as it was called). In addition, the form had entries for the individual's other holdings (insurance, and so forth) so that his or her entire financial picture could be summarized on one page. The entry form allowed listing stocks by internal Paine Webber number, by CUSIP (or standard street) number, or by symbol. The program had available the information to translate among the three codes.

Once the broker filled out a form, s/he gave it to a wire operator who sent the information to New York. When processing began during the night, the program would first retrieve the information on the accounts, if so requested, and would make any necessary translations to Paine Webber numbers for securities. It would then look up in its files information on each security: beta, volatility, price, and so forth, on a stock issue; yield, coupon rate, and related quantities for a bond. The beta and volatility figures (for stocks only) were purchased by Paine Webber from another company. New values were computed each month. At such times, the computer files were updated and, in addition, the Paine Webber brokers were each provided with a new "Beta Book" listing the stocks, in alphabetical order, with their betas and volatilities and also listing the stocks in order of decreasing beta (as an aid in planning changes in portfolios).

The betas were calculated by running regressions of weekly changes in stock price (not premium) against corresponding changes in the S&P 500. Both types of changes were expressed as percentages. Actually, the system did not use the actual change values but instead used 12-month moving averages of the values in order to smooth away some of the variability. Fifty-two weeks of values were used in determining the betas.

For the volatilities, the system used 26 weeks of data for each stock. First it found the difference between the weekly high and the weekly low for a stock. It then found the average of these differences (all of which would be positive, by definition) and then it found the average deviation of the difference from the mean difference (that is, for each week it found the deviation, defined as the difference between that week's high minus low and the average high minus low for the stock. It then averaged the deviations). Finally, it took the ratio of the average deviation to the mean and used this figure as a measure of volatility. The following may explain the reasoning. A stock can show substantial changes in price and yet not be volatile; as an example consider the price movements shown in Exhibit 3.

**EXHIBIT 3**

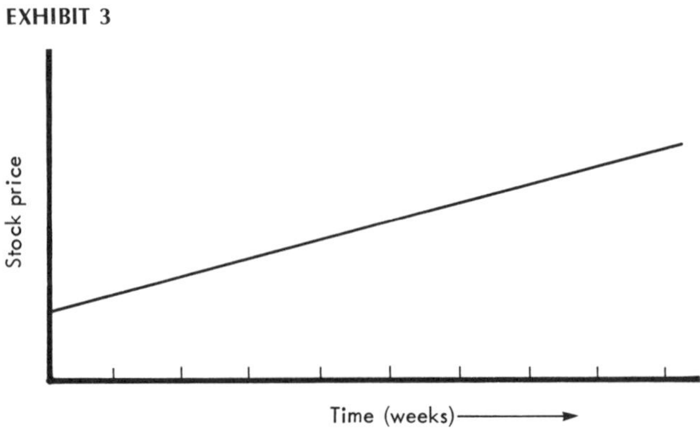


Exhibit 3 shows a change every week but the changes (and also the differences between the high and low values, which in this case are the same as the changes) are all exactly the same. The same thing would be true if the stock price were linearly decreasing rather than linearly increasing. Thus, changes in price do not imply volatility; only irregular changes do so. The differences between high and low are one measure of the changes in price. Hence, the amount of spread in these values is a measure of volatility. Further, we are probably interested in the relation between the magnitude of this spread and the overall size of the changes. An average spread of one or two dollars is more significant for a stock with small changes, on average, than it is for one with larger changes. For that reason, the ratio of average deviation of high minus low to overall average of high minus low was used to measure volatility.

After volatilities were calculated for each of the stocks, the Portfolio Dynamics program proceeded to classify the top 25 percent as high volatility issues, the bottom 25 percent as low volatility and the remainder as medium volatility.

Finally, the program calculated what it called the overall beta for the portfolio. This figure was meant to measure the extent to which the portfolio as a whole mirrored market changes. Portfolio Dynamics calculated a weighted average of the individual stock betas, with the amounts of money invested in the different stocks used as weights. This value was given as the beta of the portfolio.

Exhibit 4 shows an annotated example of the output of a Portfolio Dynamics review.

## Introduction of portfolio dynamics

The introduction of Portfolio Dynamics provided a major challenge for Paine Webber. First, the stockbrokers had to be convinced of the usefulness

**EXHIBIT 4**

OFFICE - PD ZZ00019 PAINE WEBBER JACKSON & CURTIS INC.

REQUESTED BY - 00 MARKETING DATE - 8/29/78

CLIENT ANALYSIS FOR

INDIVIDUAL INVESTOR

The client's name would normally go here

Stocks are listed by volatility category:

| CATEGORY HIGH VOLATILITY | VALUE | YIELD | RAT. | BETA |
|---|---|---|---|---|
| 100 GENL DYNAMICS CORP. | 8700 | NA | B | 1.24 |
| 100 HELENE CURITS INDUST | 988 | NA | B- | 1.37 |
| 100 LIMITED STORES INC. | 1513 | .5 | B+ | 1.08 |

VALUE gives the total value of the stock as of the date of the report

YIELD is the quarterly dividend (for the latest quarter) multiplied by four to give a yearly figure and then divided by the stock price and expressed as a percentage.

RAT is a quality rating

BETA is the individual stock's beta

---------TOTAL-------- 11201 AVG. YIELD- .07
DIV. INCOME- 8
PERCENTAGE- 5.

AVG YIELD gives the average percentage yield for the category

DIV. INCOME is the income in dollars for this category (that is, the average yield in percent times the total dollars invested in the category)

PERCENTAGE is the percentage of the total portfolio in this category

| CATEGORY MEDIUM VOLATILITY | VALUE | YIELD | RAT. | BETA |
|---|---|---|---|---|
| 100 BLACK AND DECKER MFG CO | 2075 | 2.8 | A+ | 1.27 |
| 100 COMMUNICATNS SATELLITE | 4825 | 4.1 | A- | 1.15 |
| 100 DOW JONES AND CO | 3875 | 3.4 | B+ | .80 |
| 100 EASTMAN KODAK | 6463 | 3.8 | A+ | 1.29 |
| 100 INTL ALUMINUM CORP | 1775 | 2.8 | B+ | 1.28 |
| 100 MASS MUTUAL MTG & RLTY INV | 1488 | 8.6 | NR | .95 |
| 100 NATL DATA CORP | 1294 | 1.5 | B | 1.55 |
| 100 PAN AMER WORLD AIR | 838 | NA | C | 1.20 |

---------TOTAL----------- 22633 AVG. YIELD- 3.71
DIV. INCOME- 840
PERCENTAGE- 11.

| CATEGORY LOW VOLATILITY | VALUE | YIELD | RAT. | BETA |
|---|---|---|---|---|
| 100 AMER CYANAMID CO | 3125 | 4.8 | A | .86 |
| 100 AMER HOME PRODUCTS | 3138 | 4.1 | A+ | 1.08 |
| 100 BAXTER TRAVENOL LABS INC | 4813 | .8 | A+ | 1.19 |
| 100 CENTL TEL & UTIL CORP | 2575 | 6.5 | A | .70 |
| 100 EL PASO ELECTRIC CO | 1106 | 9.4 | A | .63 |
| 100 FLORIDA PWR & LT CO | 2850 | 7.2 | A | 1.10 |
| 100 FORD MOTOR CO. COM | 4538 | 7.9 | A- | 1.16 |
| 100 GENL TEL & ELECTRONICS | 3038 | 8.1 | A | .84 |

---------TOTAL---------- 25183 AVG. YIELD- 5.59
DIV. INCOME- 1408
PERCENTAGE- 12.

**EXHIBIT 4 (*continued*)**

Short positions are listed separately and are not included in calculating the portfolio value of beta:

| SHORTS | VALUE | YIELD | RAT. | BETA |
|---|---|---|---|---|
| 3 CALL ALLIED CHEMCIAL CRP DUE 01 79 35 | 1650- | NA | NR | .00 |
| 3 CALL ABBOTT LABS DUE 02 79 40 | 675- | NA | NR | .00 |
| 3 CALL BAXTER TRAVENOL LAB DUE 11 78 35 | 3975- | NA | NR | .00 |
| ----------TOTAL------- | 6300* | AVG. YIELD- | | .00 |
| | | INCOME- | | |
| | | PERCENTAGE- | | 100. |

of shorts, only ← PERCENTAGE

BONDS:

| DEFENSIVE - RATED BAA OR BETTER | VALUE | YIELD | RAT. | BETA |
|---|---|---|---|---|
| 1000 AMER TEL&TEL 8 3.4 00 NEW DUE 5 15 2000 | 1019 | 8.5 | AAA | .00 |
| 1000 COMWLTH EDISON 3 1/4 82 DUE 7 1 82 | 865 | 3.7 | AAA | .00 |
| 1000 PAC GAS ELEC 3 3/4 78 DUE 12 1 78 | 987 | 3.8 | AA | .00 |
| 10000 CALIF 3 1/2 78 SCH BLDG DUE 9 1 78 | 10000 | 3.5 | AAA | .00 |
| 10000 MASS 310 81 COMW DUE 4 1 81 | 9500 | 3.2 | BAA | .00 |
| 10000 TEXAS 6 1/2 90 TPKE AU DUE 01 01 90 HOUSTON SHP CHANNEL BR REV | 10500 | 6.1 | A | .00 |
| 10000 US TSY BOND 4.2500% DUE 08/15/92 DTD 08/15/71 FC 02/15/72 | 7719 | 5.5 | AAA | .00 |
| 10000 US TSY BOND 8.2500% DUE 05/15/05 DTD 05/15/75 FC 11/15/75 | 9856 | 8.3 | AAA | .00 |
| -------OTHER--------------- | | | | |
| 1000 BOSTON EDISON 9 3/8 2000 DUE 6 1 2000 | 1008 | NA | NR | .00 |
| | ------- | | | |
| -----------TOTAL---------- | 61154 | AVG. YIELD- | | 5.58 |
| | | INT. INCOME- | | 3417 |
| | | PERCENTAGE- | | 31. |

Other bonds (BA or weaker) would be given here.
YIELD for bonds is the yearly coupon interest divided by the current price and expressed as a percentage.
BETAS are not used for bonds.

| PREFERRED AND CONVERTIBLE PREFERRED | VALUE | YIELD | RAT. | BETA |
|---|---|---|---|---|
| 100 AMER BAKERIES CO 5 CV PR | 8300 | 6.0 | NR | .00 |
| 100 BURLINGTON NTHN 285 CVPR | 4500 | 6.3 | NR | .00 |
| 100 GENL INSTRUMENT 3 CVPR A | 3900 | 7.6 | NR | .00 |
| 100 GULF & WSTN IND 3875CVPR C | 7663 | 5.0 | BB | .00 |
| 100 PENN ELEC CO 1172 PR J | 11000 | 10.6 | NR | .00 |
| 100 PUBLIC SVC COLO 715 PR | 7775 | 9.1 | AA | .00 |
| 100 STD OIL OHIO 4 PR B | 10000 | 4.0 | NR | .00 |
| 100 UNION ELEC CO 7 44 PR | 8075 | 9.2 | BBB | .00 |
| | ---------- | | | |
| ------------TOTAL---------- | 61213 | AVG. YIELD- | | 7.35 |
| | | INCOME- | | 4503 |
| | | PERCENTAGE- | | 31. |

**EXHIBIT 4** (*concluded*)

Mutual funds, with their betas:

| FUNDS | VALUE | YIELD | RAT. | BETA |
|---|---|---|---|---|
| 100 OPPENHEIMER OPTION INCOME FUND | 2383 | 2.1 | NR | .00 |
| 100 PUTNAM GROWTH FUND | 1169 | 3.5 | NR | .00 |
| | --------- | | | |
| ------------TOTAL---------- | 3552 | AVG. YIELD- | | 2.61 |
| | | INCOME- | | 93 |
| | | PERCENTAGE- | | 1. |

Rights, warrants, etc:

| RGTS,WTS,W.I.I AND UNITS | VALUE | YIELD | RAT. | BETA |
|---|---|---|---|---|
| 100 WTS AMER AIRLINES 84 EXPIRE 4 1 84 | 750 | NA | NR | .00 |
| 100 WTS MC DONOUGH CO | 4150 | NA | NR | .00 |
| 100 WTS PENN DIXIE INDUST EXP 5 1 83 | 113 | NA | NR | .00 |
| | --------- | | | |
| ------------TOTAL---------- | 5013 | AVG. YIELD- | | .00 |
| | | INCOME- | | |
| | | PERCENTAGE- | | 2. |

Options:

| OPTIONS | VALUE | YIELD | RAT. | BETA |
|---|---|---|---|---|
| 3 CALL EASTMAN KODAK DUE 01 79 50 | 4763 | NA | NR | .00 |
| 3 CALL AMER HOME PROD DUE 04 79 35 | 356 | NA | NR | .00 |
| 3 CALL GENL TEL ELEC DUE 04 79 30 | 656 | NA | NR | .00 |
| | -------- | | | |
| -----------TOTAL----------- | 5775 | AVG. YIELD- | | .00 |
| | | INCOME- | | |
| | | PERCENTAGE- | | 2. |

| ------TOTAL------- | LONG | SHORT | CLOSE OF | 08/28/78 |
|---|---|---|---|---|
| PORTFOLIO VALUE ($) | 195,724 | 6,300 | DJIA | 884.88 |
| YIELD DOLLARS | 10,269 | NA | S&P 500 | 103.96 |
| AVG YIELD (percent) | 5.20 | NA | | |
| PORTFOLIO BETA | 1.10 | ****** | | |

↳ This PORTFOLIO BETA is calculated using only long positions. The sum of the products of betas of the individual stocks times the values in those stocks is formed:

(beta for stock 1) * (value in stock 1)
+ (beta for stock 2) * (value in stock 2) + ···

(Mutual funds are also included)
Then, the sum is divided by the total of the value of all stocks and mutual funds.

+INSURANCE FACE VALUE
+INSURANCE SURRENDER
CASH
TOTAL REAL EST. VALUE
TOTAL MORTGAGES

} Other assets listed on the data sheet would be listed here.

PRICES WERE OBTAINED FROM STANDARD FINANCIAL SOURCES WE BELIEVE TO BE RELIABLE BUT WE CAN NOT GUARANTEE THEIR ACCURACY

+ THE MUNICIPAL BOND PRICES SHOWN ABOVE DO NOT NECESSARILY REFLECT THE LAST SALE. PLEASE CONTACT YOUR PAINE WEBBER BROKER FOR THE MOST RECENT PRICE.

of the new tool. Then, the brokers had to sell the clients on what was really a very sophisticated type of analysis. In addition, it was necessary to train the operations people who would handle the transmission of requests on the Paine Webber communications network.

Paine Webber had a training operation as part of its organization. The small training group consisted of people who had been successful brokers and who were being moved into management positions; a one- or two-year stint in the training department was often a step on the route into management. In 1974 the group was headed by David Koehler, a former minister who had become a broker for Paine Webber and had been successful for them. He had three other former brokers on his staff. The training group itself was first trained in an intensive three-day session in New York. The evening before the last day of that session the trainers were assigned the task of designing a program for presenting Portfolio Dynamics to the brokers. The next morning, after a rather long night, they presented a program for doing so.

As a first step, Paine Webber's Methods and Procedures Department prepared written instructions for the operations people for use of the system. After a pilot test of the procedures and some rewriting, the operations people throughout the country were trained, largely under the direction of Margo Allen, who at that time was a systems analyst with Paine Webber's EDP department (but by 1976 had become assistant vice president of marketing).

Once the operations staff had been trained, Mr. Koehler and the other trainers began a grueling set of visits to all of the branch offices. At each branch they introduced the new product by first attacking what they thought of as the attitudinal problems head on. Drawing on some of their own experience as brokers and working in small groups (where discussions could be freer) they tried to get agreement on the idea that trying to pick winners really was not a satisfactory system. Once the attitudinal problem had been handled, they could start to provide information on the new system. They explained beta as the tendency of a stock to underestimate or overestimate the market (and suggested that the beta of the portfolio as a whole, not the individual betas, was most important). They also explained volatility as a measure of variability, using figures like Exhibit 1 in the process. Further, they tried to get the brokers to run some of their important clients' portfolios through the system during the session; the feedback from the output the next morning was very effective.

Some of the brokers were resistant but others were very receptive. One of the problems was that some brokers were afraid of the lower turnover rates that would occur with a conservatively managed portfolio under Portfolio Dynamics. Mr. Dunwoody, the head of marketing, explained that he attacked those worries by using the following equation:

$$\left\{\begin{matrix}\text{commission}\\ \text{earned}\end{matrix}\right\} = \left\{\begin{matrix}\text{amount of}\\ \text{assets}\\ \text{managed}\end{matrix}\right\} \times \left\{\begin{matrix}\text{velocity with}\\ \text{which holdings}\\ \text{were changed}\end{matrix}\right\} \times \left\{\begin{matrix}\text{commission}\\ \text{rate}\end{matrix}\right\}$$

He suggested that Wall Street had been emphasizing velocity but that such a course was suicidal. Instead, he suggested that, using Portfolio Dynamics, Paine Webber brokers could increase the amount of assets under their control. The idea was to select a beta and choose volatility levels that were consistent with the individual investor's desires for management of a portfolio. If the investor believed that the portfolio was being managed as conservatively (or not) as s/he wished, the broker should be able to manage more of the assets, not just the money set aside for speculation. In addition, of course, the portfolio concept only made sense when applied to a description of the entire portfolio. (It was partly for that reason that the system allowed inclusion of other stocks even for Paine Webber accounts; many large investors used more than one broker.) Thus, Portfolio Dynamics was meant to leave the same (or increase) commissions earned by increasing the amounts of assets managed, while decreasing velocity.

Marketing of the new system stressed that it was based on objective information rather than on the hunches of brokers and, in addition, that it gave the average investor access to some of the techniques used by the institutions. Exhibit 5 shows some of the letters used. The program proved successful. As a few brokers tried the system and found it worked, particularly for bringing in new clients, the success stories spread and other brokers tried it. The tool was extremely effective in attracting the type of affluent and conservative customer that Paine Webber wanted; in 1976 its success as a prospecting tool had been greater than its success for management of existing accounts. The techniques had also been incorporated into some of Paine Webber's packages for large accounts (such as a program called Alpha Accounts for large individual portfolios). Analysis of a portfolio by Portfolio Dynamics was provided free of charge to Paine Webber's customers, who were urged to have analyses run about every three months after the initial period during which they adjusted their portfolios to the beta levels they wanted (and, in the process, used more frequent analyses). In addition, the offer of a free analysis was used as a sales tool to attract new customers.

The idea of the designers of Portfolio Dynamics for the use of a tool in managing individual portfolios was as follows. First, the broker and customer would review the starting portfolio to see whether it was consistent with the customer's stated investment objectives. In particular, they would consider the proportions of money invested in the different volatility categories, the ratings, the overall yield, and the portfolio beta. In addition they would consider the degree of diversification in the portfolio; Paine Webber suggested that a portfolio contain stocks in at least eight different companies spread among at least five unrelated industries. Usually, there would be some changes needed to make the portfolio conform to the customer's objectives. The broker would help select the changes to be made and would use Portfolio Dynamics analyses to evaluate the effects of the changes before making them.

Once the portfolio had been brought into line with the customer's wishes,

**EXHIBIT 5 (*continued*)**

Established 1879 · Members New York Stock Exchange, Inc. and other Principal Exchanges
140 Broadway, New York, N.Y. 10005 (212) 437-2121

November 14, 1974

Dear :

YOU TOLD US WHAT YOU WANTED - NOW SEE WHAT WE HAVE DONE!

"What do you want?" we asked investors like yourself in recent surveys. Here is what you told us:

1. You want access to the same professional investment tools used by large institutional investors.

2. You want more facts about the structure and quality of your portfolio.

3. You want precise and timely risk evaluation information regarding your assets.

4. You want these facts presented so clearly that independent self-analysis is possible.

So, we took your advice. We worked until we found a way to bring professional investment techniques, formerly available only to institutions, to you, the individual investor. We call it PORTFOLIO DYNAMICS. It offers you a factual analysis showing:

The investment quality of your portfolio,
The degree of risk to which you are exposed,
The income you currently receive, stock by stock.

These are the tools that help major investors make decisions - tools that, until now, were not generally available to the individual investor. Now these tools are brought to you by Paine Webber's PORTFOLIO DYNAMICS, in a personalized form designed to help you improve your investment performance.

To receive this outstanding new tool, you need only be ready with your list of securities at hand. In a few days I will telephone you for the needed information.

Sincerely,

**EXHIBIT 5 (*concluded*)**

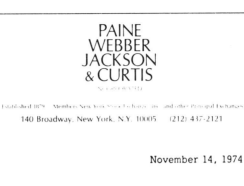

Established 1879   Members New York Stock Exchange, Inc. and other Principal Exchanges

140 Broadway, New York, N.Y. 10005   (212) 437-2121

November 14, 1974

Dear :

What will happen to <u>your</u> portfolio . . .

if the market goes up 10%?

if the market goes down 10%

For many years, large Institutional investors have used sophisticated techniques to help answer these questions and to initiate intelligent investment decisions. Now, Paine Webber is happy to announce that these same techniques are being made available to you.

Called PORTFOLIO DYNAMICS, this exciting new service is available to help answer these and many other questions you may have about your portfolio. It is an accurate, factual presentation of your investments in a form that will clearly aid you in choosing investment opportunities.

PORTFOLIO DYNAMICS is offered to you without cost or obligation. Try it for yourself - in a few days I will call you for the needed information.

Sincerely,

Paine Webber suggested occasional (perhaps quarterly) reviews. In that period betas or volatilities or yields or other characteristics of individual stocks might change and the portfolio might require changes again. Sometimes the customer's objectives would change and the portfolio would require corresponding changes. In some situations customers might want to revise their portfolios in light of their beliefs about what was going to happen to the market. Customers who expected the market to rise might want to increase the overall betas of their portfolios to increase the expected responses of the portfolios to the change, while customers who expected a drop in the market level might want to decrease their betas.

Thus, Portfolio Dynamics was viewed as a tool for bringing a portfolio into line with a customer's objectives and then for monitoring the portfolio. Its designers believed that the frequency of trading would be considerably lower for portfolios managed with Portfolio Dynamics than was the norm on Wall Street.

### The future of portfolio dynamics

In 1976 the Paine Webber executives had to decide what if any improvements to add to the Portfolio Dynamics system. They also had to decide what the effect would be on their marketing strategy of the new index funds (mutual funds that offered investors a mix of stocks that essentially mirrored one of the market indices, such as the S&P 500). Finally, they had to decide how to continue to increase the acceptance of the system and what competitive responses to it were likely to be.

chapter 4

# DESIGNING AND USING LARGE-SCALE MODELS

In designing large-scale computer models or in using existing large models, we balance and trade off many of the considerations discussed in the preceding three chapters. In the current very brief chapter we tie together some of the important concepts from the preceding chapters and, in addition, add a few more suggestions for successful model development and use.

Probably the most fundamental decision in designing or using models concerns the level of modeling that is appropriate in any particular problem. Chapter 1 stressed the idea that any modeling project must start with a careful analysis or conceptualization of the problem situation. Chapter 1 called this stage the basic case analysis and noted that it is a crucial step whether we are planning to design a new model are whether, instead, we want to use some existing model to analyze our problem. After that basic analysis we proceed to decide how much analysis can usefully be done by computer. The discussions of Chapters 2 and 3 have suggested several considerations for inclusion in this step. In Chapter 2 we discussed the types of quick approximations that are available for making decisions for inventory stocking levels; in particular, we considered the EOQ and the critical fractile models. In Chapter 3 we mentioned the analytic results in queueing theory, many of which were derived in pre-computer days and some of which are used in queueing problems today. In deciding what type of analysis to do in a specific problem we must trade off the costs of building and using a model that is specially designed for the current problem against the costs of using other quick and dirty approximations. The decision on whether to use shortcut methods will depend not only on the improvement that we would expect to gain from more detailed and realistic modeling but also on the additional cost of such modeling. If an existing analytic solution provides a good enough approximation to our problem, we should use it and avoid the expense of additional modeling. The question of what constitutes a good approximation is a difficult one and involves the judgment of a knowledgeable decision maker or designer.

If the stakes and risks in a particular problem are large, we will generally want a more carefully custom-tailored analysis than would be adequate for more minor decisions. Hence, many inventory systems use economic order quantity (EOQ) or the critical fractile model for large numbers of small parts, no one of which is individually very important to the business. The assumptions of those approximations do not hold exactly, but the methods give useful results, anyway, and the cost of more detailed modeling for large numbers of parts would be prohibitive. If, on the other hand, we must decide on the stocking level for some very important material for a production process, and if the assumptions of EOQ and critical fractile do not really hold, then more detailed modeling of the specific situation may well be appropriate. Similarly, if the analytic steady-state results of classical queueing theory gave us useful and sufficient information in analyzing some particular problem, we would use those results. Only for problems that are important and for which the assumptions of the traditional theory do not apply would we build queueing models that could handle such considerations as server slowdown under stress.

The considerable literature on operations research and management science contain much useful discussion of analytic results for queues, Markov processes, and other systems. Those results are not repeated here, not because they should not be considered in analyzing real problems but rather because the discussions are available elsewhere. This book has concentrated instead on the art of designing models for cases in which the analytic results (or, even, a few calculations on the back of an envelope) do not provide adequate information. Because computers are relatively new, there has been little written to guide design in such cases. In addition, the lack of instruction in model design stems in part from the fact that designing simulation models is so problem-specific a process or art that the best we can offer is suggestions, not real rules.

Once we have decided to proceed with computer modeling in a specific problem, we must either begin to design a new model or must evaluate an existing one. In designing models from scratch the preceding discussion has suggested that a series of stages is often appropriate. In most, although not all problems, we start with a deterministic model and perform sensitivity analyses with it. At that point, only if the indicated actions are not clear on the basis of the deterministic runs do we consider proceeding to a probabilistic model. In other cases, the problems we are considering are more inherently probabilistic. In a queueing problem, for example, the uneven pattern of arrivals and, perhaps, service times, is what causes the problem. In such situations, it does not make sense to perform analyses without considering such unevenness. Usually, we use probabilistic modeling for that purpose and, in inherently probabilistic situations, the probabilistic model would be emphasized or, often, would be the only one built.

The preceding chapters have suggested some of the aspects of model design that are crucial in determining whether models are in fact useful. The user interface, or the input and output portions of the models, are extremely important in both deterministic and probabilistic modeling. Functional forms provide one useful way of facilitating input. Another mechanism involves building an entire set of base case assumptions into a model and then asking the user to specify only changes in those assumptions. In a complicated pro forma program, for example, users will likely find it burdensome to be required to input entire complex scenarios; on the other hand, if the model is to be useful, its users must consider many such scenarios. A possible solution is to build into the model one base case scenario and, in addition, to build into the model the capability for the user to change any part or parts of the basic set of assumptions. If users are conscientious and really do make appropriate changes for sensitivity runs, this design choice can make the model considerably easier to use.

The discussions of deterministic and probabilistic modeling showed that in deterministic modeling the user is responsible for constructing interesting scenarios for evaluation, while in probabilistic models the computer constructs scenarios according to user instruction and model assumptions. Once the model has been designed, scenario construction is easy with probabilistic models, but the process of design is considerably more difficult for such models. Of special difficulty are the questions of how to specify strategies and of how to handle dependencies. As suggested earlier, errors in handling dependencies or in defining strategies are probably the most common types of errors made in probabilistic modeling in practice. In handling these modeling issues we face trade-offs, as always. The models must be sufficiently realistic that their results provide useful information for analyzing the real-world situation, yet they must be sufficiently simple that users can provide the input information required and can understand the results provided in the output.

The process of using existing model is, as suggested in Chapter 1, parallel to that of designing from scratch. Rather than produce a new design we must discover the design of the existing model from whatever documentation we have on that model. We must then decide if the model is adequate for our purposes. In this stage the same issues of ease of input, specification of strategies, handling of dependencies, and the like arise as arise in model design from scratch. If the existing model is satisfactory on the relevant issues, then we can proceed to use it as we would a model we had specially designed. If not, we must consider either modifying the existing design or else starting from scratch.

Once a model has been designed and built, or obtained from some existing source, and, in addition, once the model has been checked out to make sure that it works as intended, the user must run the model on interesting inputs to provide insights for the decision problem under analysis. We have not specified many details for this model-use process except to say that the user must be certain to make enough runs of the model to come to understand the problem and the available options. A concept called *screening* is sometimes very useful in model use. In fact, the concept enters into the design process as well, as described below.

In using simulation models (deterministic or probabilistic) to aid in selecting decisions, the general procedure is that the user specifies interesting possible decisions (or strategies) and the model investigates each decision, providing the user with a summary of the results that might occur with that decision. In problems in which there are many possible decisions and, especially, when strategies are complicated and/or expensive to investigate, the problem of which strategies to consider is a difficult one. The user cannot just ask the machine to consider all possible strategies and so the user must be involved in selecting candidates. Often, however, the user starts the modeling process with a very imperfect understanding of the results of different strategies (indeed, this imperfect knowledge was usually the motivation for modeling in the first place), and so selecting candidates is not easy for the user.

In some situations, a series of models can be used in a screening process to help search for interesting strategies without straining impossibly the user's ability to help. Basically, the idea is to use a simple model to screen a large number of alternative strategies and then to subject only those options that "pass" the initial screen to more thorough examinations with a more thorough (and more expensive) model. An example of screening can be seen in the way the Internal Revenue Service selects from the millions of income tax forms it receives the returns to be audited. The IRS subjects returns to a relatively simple (though closely guarded) computer program that checks for conditions that are likely to be associated with problem returns. The IRS is extremely reluctant to provide the public with information on what these conditions are, but we can guess that unusually large deductions in one category or another might be an example. The computerized check (the screening procedure) is fast and relatively inexpensive. Once the screening procedure has been used to screen a large majority of returns out of further consideration, a far more time-consuming and expensive human audit can be applied to the returns that remain under consideration; if the screen is effective, this reduced pool should contain many of the problem returns. This IRS example should suggest some of the qualities of a good screen and some of the potential problems with screening. The screen should be a satisfactorily good surrogate for the actual problem or model; for the IRS the problem conditions should be satisfactorily good indicators of problem returns. Note that we do not require—and probably think it very unlikely—that the screen give exactly the results that a more thorough investigation would give. A screen for selecting good decisions may pass bad alternatives and it may screen out good ones. The first problem is usually less serious, for bad options will be weeded out later in the analysis; the problem of having the screen reject good plans is considerably more serious. That second type of problem cannot be avoided in many situations. The IRS undoubtedly knows that some problem (even fraudulent) returns will slip through its screen and avoid audit. Surely the agency tries to reduce the number of returns in this category, but the prohibitive expense of a complete audit makes some kind of screening necessary and hence allows the potential for such errors.

Thus, it should be obvious that the use of more than one model can often be an efficient way to look for good decisions. The first model can be rather crude; it can serve to weed out uninteresting options. That model should be easy to run on a large number of decisions. Strategies that survive that first screen can be investigated with a second more thorough (and more expensive) model which will give more detailed information. In some cases, it might be useful to have the second model also be only a screen for a third and even more complicated model. The advantage of this approach is that it allows a relatively quick consideration of many possible decisions, so that more time and effort can be spent on strategies which seem promising. The disadvantage is that in investigating potential decisions with a relatively simplistic model we run the risk of distorting the problem too much and, hence, of rejecting options that a more detailed model would show as attractive. Thus, the selection of good screens is itself part of the rather difficult art of good modeling.

Another suggestion for successful modeling in large difficult problems involves both the concept of modeling in stages and also a concept like that of screening. As has just been noted, we often start the analysis of a problem with relatively little understanding of what are the important uncertainties and what are the important decisions. We may decide to build a model in large part because of this lack of understanding. In many real situations, we do not build a model without collecting information that we feel will improve our understanding of the problem and hence allow us to build a better model. For example, if we are studying the possible introduction of a new product we might find it useful to collect data from the past on the performances of other products that we feel are in some sense comparable to the new one, in the periods following their introductions. Even though we often feel that past data can not be used directly in predicting the future (because of differences in the products or because of differences in economic conditions at the times they were introduced, for example), nevertheless we may find the past data extremely useful in prompting our understanding of the current problem, by suggesting differences as well as similarities to us. The problem with data collection and analysis is that those activities can be costly in terms of money and, especially, time. The collection tends to be considerably more costly than does the analysis in most cases. At the start of a modeling exercise we often do not feel that we understand the problem well enough to make difficult decisions about committing resources to the collection of additional information, yet we know that such information is potentially very valuable to use. A useful procedure to follow in such situations is to build a series of models, using the results obtained from the first one to help decide what further information would be valuable. If we then collect additional information we can use it to refine the first model. The output of the new model may then suggest still further data collection, and so on. This concept of an iterative procedure in which a model helps suggest what information to collect and the information then helps in refining the model is so useful that we turn in the final chapter of the book to a brief consideration of data and of methods for analyzing data.

In concluding this brief chapter on overall design considerations it is worth repeating a point that has been made in passing in the preceding text. The computer simulation models we have been discussing are designed for specific decision problems and they embody the judgments of specific decision makers. Whether or not such models are useful will depend in large part on two things. First, the models will be more or less useful according to whether or not the designers did or did not have adequate understandings of the situations being modeled and of the major issues in model design. Second, the usefulness of models will depend on whether they have been made easy enough to use for the decision makers to use them well. In particular, models should require input information in forms that are relatively easy (or, to be realistic, the term might better be relatively less painful) for the users of those models to provide. Similarly, output should be provided in forms that the users find most useful. A related point can be made about the level of complexity that can and should be built into models. Model outputs are only as good as the combined model designs and model inputs, and it is important that users understand those facts. There is still some tendency for people to be snowed by impressive computer output, often with the unfortunate result that they put inappropriate faith in tentative output information. My own solution to this problem when I help design models that others will use, is to insist that the models contain nothing that the users do not understand and, moreover, that through its input and output procedures, the model make clear to the user how firmly the results are based on user inputs and assumptions. A slightly less fancy model, whose output the user properly questions, is far more useful in the end than an elaborate model that the user does not understand and might, unfortunately, believe.

## case 4.1

# Clarke's Markets Incorporated with Risk Analysis Supplement*

In the spring of 1971 Mr. John Steele, vice president of administration and controller for Clarke's Markets Incorporated, was concerned with what recommendations he should make to top management regarding adoption of the use of risk analysis for evaluating investment projects. Although the company currently had a well-established set of procedures for evaluating capital investment projects based on return on investment, these did not involve the explicit consideration of uncertainty. Mr. Steele was well aware that several other companies had recently adopted risk analysis techniques in order to obtain a more complete analysis of proposed projects. One of the staff specialists working for Mr. Steele had developed such a model for the company's in-house computer system and was anxious to have it adopted as part of corporate policy for evaluating investments. However, there were several questions that Mr. Steele felt should be answered before taking any steps toward corporate-wide adoption.

The remainder of this case describes the nature of corporate activity at Clarke's Markets, the management style used in running the company, and the types of investment decisions that frequently must be made. In addition, some brief comments on the risk analysis model that has been developed and the circumstances relating to its adoption at Clarke's are included. (The details of this particular model are described in a separate section, the Risk Analysis Supplement.)

### Operation of Clarke's Markets Incorporated

Clarke's is engaged primarily in the retailing of food products and other articles for personal and household use in the Southern California area (mainly Los Angeles and the surrounding suburbs). The company conducts its retailing operations through three types of outlets. Retail food stores (generally large supermarkets), so-called convenience stores (smaller, compact, self-service food stores with early opening and late closing hours), and self-

* This case and the supplement were written by Steven C. Wheelwright.

service discount department stores. For the fiscal year ending April 1, 1970, sales through all three types of outlets totaled $720 million. The vast majority of these sales were through the supermarket stores, with less than 15 percent coming through the other two types of retail outlets.

The retail supermarkets operated by Clarke's are operated under the "Clarke" trade name in the greater Los Angeles area. The company currently has 276 such stores, ranging in size from 12,000 square feet of floor space to 26,000 square feet. During the past fiscal year, nine new supermarkets were opened and five older stores were closed. Plans for the current year are to open 14 new supermarekts. Of the supermarkets currently operated by Clarke's, 105 of them are fully owned (land and building) and the remainder are located in leased facilities.

Table 1 indicates the number of Clarke's supermarkets in operation at the end of each of the last five fiscal years.

**TABLE 1**
Operation of Clarke's Markets retail food stores*

| Year | Stores opened | Stores closed | Ending number | Ending area (000 sq. ft.) |
|---|---|---|---|---|
| 1966 | 15 | 21 | 255 | 3,682 |
| 1967 | 11 | 7 | 259 | 3,923 |
| 1968 | 17 | 8 | 268 | 4,179 |
| 1969 | 10 | 6 | 272 | 4,266 |
| 1970 | 9 | 5 | 276 | 4,325 |

* The Supermarket Institute classifies as "modern supermarkets" retail food stores whose sales exceed $1 million annually. On this basis all but nine of Clarke's chain of food stores qualify as modern supermarkets.

Although Clarke's Markets have been operating in the greater L.A. area for 35 years, it has only been in the last decade that they have significantly increased their market share from the 10 to 12 percent level experienced in the 40s and 50s. During the 60s they have continually increased that share to its present level of 27 percent. Management anticipates that this will continue to increase to perhaps 35 percent, but will not rise much above that level.

In 1968 Clarke's began the development of so-called convenience stores in the metropolitan Los Angeles area. These stores, which average about 2,500 square feet in size, are operated under franchise agreements with independent operators. The company currently has 15 of these stores which have been built in the last two years and anticipates building an additional 11 such stores this next year. The decision to enter this type of retail outlet was based largely on management's feelings that substantial opportunity existed in that area which was not being met in any organized fashion by other major competitors. To date, management has been very satisfied with the performance of these convenience stores.

Because of the company's long experience in retail food operations, they have developed a number of processing facilities to further integrate their operation. Presently about 8 percent of the volume of sales coming from their convenience stores and supermarkets represents products actually manufactured, processed, and/or packaged at Clarke's central facilities. The principal processing operations include blending, roasting, grinding, and packaging of coffee and tea; the preparation and packaging of cosmetics; the baking, slicing, and packaging of bread, buns, doughnuts and pastries; the processing of fluid milk and fluid milk products; and the processing of sausage-type meats. These processing operations have been expanded considerably in the last few years and management anticipates a continued expansion in that area.

The final area of Clarke's operations is in self-service department stores. The company has ten such stores located in greater Los Angeles, all of which are adjacent to one of their supermarket facilities. These discount department stores vary in size from 60,000 to 120,000 square feet and all of them were built in the last seven years. One new department store is scheduled to be opened during 1971.

## Management at Clarke's Markets

Clarke's has long prided itself on the entrepreneurial spirit of its individual managers. Top management clearly attributes the company's successes in the past decade to the innovations suggested by middle managers and to their acceptance of responsibility for their portion of the operation. Physically, the management operations of the company are largely centralized in the Anaheim area with only the individual store managers and those working directly for them located throughout the greater L.A. area. This physical centralization has made it possible for the company to be much more decentralized in decision-making responsibility than many of its competitors, and yet still achieve the economies available through efficient coordination among stores and functional areas.

The operations of the company are divided into six main areas, each headed by a senior vice president. These areas are Information Systems and Data Processing, Marketing (largely market research and information gathering), Finance, Production, Administration and Control, and Operations. The majority of the management personnel are located in the operations area. These people have responsibilities for individual store performance as well as for performance of each of the three main categories of retail outlets. In many respects the other five areas operate largely as staff support to the operations. Top management is well aware of the fact that the actual operations of the stores are what determine the success or failure of the *whole* company. Thus considerable emphasis is given to meeting the needs of the operations people.

In many cases the lines of authority connecting the various operating units and the support staffs are not well defined. However, the performance measures used for evaluating individual managers are well defined. Thus, managers are free to work directly with any other support group or operation in the company if they think it will help them better meet their objectives. As a result of this organization and the type of people that the company has hired over the past several years, there is an extremely cooperative spirit among the individual managers and very much the feeling that they are part of a winning team.

## Investment decisions at Clarke's Markets

Wherever it has been feasible, individual operating units at Clarke's have been organized as profit centers. Even many of the production processes are managed in this fashion, using internally agreed-upon transfer prices in order to come up with a profit figure for each period for each operation. The performance criteria used in evaluating such profit centers are gross profit (total dollars of profit for a given period) and return on investment. As a consequence virtually all of the members of Clarke's management understand the computations involved in return on investment and profit and feel very comfortable with the accounting operations that underlie these.

The existing procedures for evaluating new investments in the company vary somewhat, depending on the particular area in question. However, generally the investment proposal originates within a particular management group and is then presented to the executive committee of the company which consists of the president and senior vice presidents. Frequently, several of the managers concerned with the project will attend the committee meeting where that project is being reviewed. The types of decisions made by the executive committee are usually either of a policy nature or focused on recommending the best alternative way to carry out a proposed project. Very few of the projects that are proposed to the committee are turned down completely.

An example might help to illustrate how investment decisions are presently handled. In mid-1970 one of the directives coming from the executive committee was that the company desired to further develop its production and manufacturing operations in support of its retail food sales. As a result the management directly responsible for bakery production and bakery marketing developed a proposal for expanding bakery production operations. When this proposal was presented to the executive committee the majority of the discussion centered on alternative ways in which this expansion might be carried out. Subsequently the committee decided, with the aid of middle management, which approach to the expansion would be followed. There was never any serious doubt that the expansion would be undertaken.

The infrequent rejection of investment proposals is probably due to two factors. One is the close communication within management and thus the substantial agreement on the general policies of the firm and the direction in which it wishes to move. Second is the fact that the entrepreneurial spirit of the individual managers probably leads them to eliminate most of the unsatisfactory projects before ever making any proposals to the executive committee.

The mechanics involved in the current system for project evaluation focus on the development of a set of pro forma income and cash flow statements for that project for the next several years; from these projections a return-on-investment figure is computed. Much of the discussion in the executive committee and in meetings that precede the project's formal review centers on factors that might possibly alter the actual return on investment that the company will realize if it undertakes the project.

In some areas of the company where similar projects are continually being evaluated, very systematic procedures for doing the necessary analysis have been developed. This is the case in the evaluation of new supermarkets. The marketing group, in conjunction with the senior operations people, will generally identify each year several dozen possible locations for new stores. Each of these locations is analyzed in order to determine the potential sales revenue and the costs that could be expected if that location were developed. The marketing group then takes this information and, using a time-sharing model, they make several deterministic projections of return on investment based on different assumptions about that location. (*No* probabilities are included in this model.) The computer model used for this analysis was developed by someone in the marketing group and it is maintained by them. Frequently included in the presentation to the executive committee for a new store location will be the printout from this computer model. The model itself is straightforward and really just a high-speed calculator for running out projections made by management.

Many of the other operating groups at Clarke's Markets have less well-defined techniques for doing preliminary evaluations of investment projects. However, in all cases these managers present to the executive committee a set of projections regarding cash flows, profits over the next several periods (often 10–20 years), and the return on investment that they think can be expected.

### Support for computer-based models at Clarke's Markets

During the past few years the company has greatly expanded its use of the computer. While the majority of these applications involve routine data processing such as order handling, billing, transportation scheduling, and accounting operations, there have also been a number of applications to management problems. Unfortunately, with the rapid expansion of the company and the growth of data processing applications during the past year, management users of the computer have been less than satisfied with the service they have been receiving. As a consequence, a number of these managers have had their programs adapted so that they can now be used on a time-sharing system offered by a local service bureau.

The batch-processing computer operations of the company are headed by Jerry Harper, Vice President of Information Systems. Included under his direction are a number of programmers and computer operators but only a few systems analysts. Most of the work done by this group is the running and maintaining of programs and systems already implemented within the company and the programming of new projects *after* they have been clearly identified and defined by a management group. As an example of how a new batch-processing application might be developed, one might consider a new production system initially identified and defined by someone working directly for the production manager. Once it was fully designed, it would then be turned over to the information systems group for programming, debugging, and regular running. This procedure seems to have worked fairly well in the past in that almost all systems completed by MIS in the last few years are currently being used by those for whom they were intended. However, Mr. Harper realizes that such an approach overlooks many useful systems that might have been recognized had a more unified planning approach been used.

In addition to the support for information systems, programming, and computer operations given by Mr. Harper's area, another staff group is often involved in the early identification and definition of new computer-based systems. This group comes under John Steele, the vice president for administration and control. Mr. Steele's general responsibilities include not only accounting and management reporting but also management development and the development of new management techniques within the firm. It was one of Mr. Steele's people, Rod Johnson, who introduced the use of time-sharing to many of the managers in the company. The extensive use of time-sharing at Clarke's is something in which Mr. Steele takes considerable pride. Currently the company has four time-sharing terminals that are in almost constant use. These are paid for by the individual managers who use them (that is, by their departments). The supervision and coordination of time-sharing usage is under the direction of Mr. Rod Johnson. (Mr. Harper only gets involved with the in-house batch-processing computer and those operations performed on it.)

It is not unusual for managers, while having lunch with Mr. Steele, to mention an area of their decision-making where they feel some substantial improvements could be made. In response to such suggestions Mr. Steele will often have Rod Johnson visit with the manager and with a member of the manager's staff and work with them in identifying the potential application and development of a computer model. (This was in fact the procedure by which the new-store-location, return-on-investment model was developed.) While most of the models developed in recent months in this manner have ended up on time-sharing, Rod Johnson has gotten involved in a number of batch-processing applications as well.

In his search for areas in which he might substantially improve decision making, Mr. Steele has recently been considering the adoption of a return-on-investment model based on the technique of risk analysis. Over the past year he has had an operations researcher on his staff working full time on development of such a model that could be used in evaluating a wide range of investment projects at Clarke's. However, to date there are only a couple of people in addition to Mr. Steele, Rod Johnson, and the OR specialist who are aware that this development has been going on. The risk analysis model is almost completely debugged on the firm's batch-processing computer now, and Mr. Steele feels he must take some time to determine whether or not this particular risk analysis model is an appropriate starting point for adopting such techniques at Clarke's and for determining how he should go about evaluating this. He is also concerned about the specific benefits that will be realized if this model is used in place of existing procedures such as the deterministic time-sharing model for new-store evaluation. Finally, he is anxious to design a plan for introduction that will consider the educational problems, the operating procedures, and the documentation that will be needed to achieve successful implementation.

## RISK ANALYSIS SUPPLEMENT

In the spring of 1971, Mr. John Steele, vice president of administration and controller of Clarke's Markets Incorporated, was in the process of evaluating a recently developed risk analysis model for use in analysis of investment projects at Clarke's Markets. To aid him in this evaluation, he had asked Dale Goodson, the Operations Researcher who had spent the past year developing this model, to write up an explanation of the general concepts underlying risk analysis, the characteristics of the computer program that Mr. Goodson had developed for use on the batch-processing system at Clarke's, and some of the requirements that Mr. Goodson envisioned in getting it adopted by management.

This supplement contains the information which Mr. Goodson put together in response to Mr. Steele's request. In turning it over to Mr. Steele, Mr. Goodson pointed out that this write-up was not intended for general distribution to all of the members of management at Clarke's. Rather, this was simply a starting point for Mr. Steele so that he could assess what steps should be taken in evaluating this project and designing its implementation for the organization.

## The general concept of risk analysis

One of the most important types of decisions which the management of a corporation such as Clarke's Markets must make involves the allocation of financial resources to individual investments projects. To aid in this allocation process, several evaluation techniques can be applied. The most common approaches include the calculation of one or more performance measures such as (*a*) the payback period, (*b*) the net present value (discounted cash flow), and (*c*) the internal rate of return.

A simple model for applying any of these evaluation techniques to an investment project requires information on several factors. These include:

1. Required investment (in dollars per time period).
2. Market size (in dollars per time period).
3. Market share (as a percent of market size for each period).
4. Variable costs (as a percent of sales revenue per period).
5. Fixed costs (in dollars per period).
6. Useful project life (in number of time periods).
7. Residual value of the investment at the end of its useful life (in dollars).

Using these seven factors, one can calculate the total revenue per period, the total cost per period, the net cash flows per period, and the net income for each of the periods in the project's life. These results can then be used to determine the payback period, the internal rate of return, and the net present value (given some discount rate) as measures of the investment's attractiveness.

Historically, most investment evaluation models like those described above have been based on deterministic values (that is, the most likely values) for each of the relevant factors. However, in practice one can usually only estimate the expected outcome within a range of possible values. Thus by simply using a single, most likely value for each factor, the risk or uncertainty concerning the outcome of that factor is obscured in the analysis.

The risk analysis (or Monte Carlo simulation) approach overcomes this limitation of only being able to use a single value for each factor by allowing use of a range of values for each factor. The user of such an approach might input a low, most likely, and high value for each of the important factors. Using Monte Carlo methods of simulation, the model could then compute a distribution of possible cash flows and their associated rates of return for the investment project.

The real advantage of the risk analysis approach can best be demonstrated through an example. Suppose that a firm is considering investment in either

Project X or Project Y, and that use of the deterministic model in evaluating these two projects has indicated an expected rate of return for Project X of 10 percent and for Project Y of 13 percent. Now, using the risk analysis approach, suppose the following results are obtained:

| *Project X: probability of return less than or equal to R* | *R (percent)* | *Project Y: probability of return less than or equal to R* |
|---|---|---|
| .0 | 0 | .05 |
| .0 | 2 | .1 |
| .0 | 4 | .15 |
| .0 | 6 | .2 |
| .25 | 8 | .3 |
| .50 | 10 | .4 |
| .75 | 12 | .47 |
| 1.0 | 14 | .6 |
| 1.0 | 16 | .7 |
| 1.0 | 18 | .9 |
| 1.0 | 20 | 1.0 |

From this example, it can be seen that what appeared to be results clearly in favor of Project Y (based only on the deterministic evaluation) now leaves some doubt as to which project is most attractive, because of the much greater uncertainty that is associated with Project Y than with Project X.

Two things have made the risk analysis approach[1] appealing to managers who have used it:

1. Certainly in every case it is a more descriptive statement of the opportunities, and in some cases it may reverse the decision.
2. This is not a difficult technique to use, since much of the information needed is already available or readily accessible, and the validity of the principles involved has, for the most part, already been proved in other applications.

### The BRISK model

During the past year an efficient and accurate computer program has been developed and debugged for use on the Clarke's Market in-house batch-processing computer. While this model has not yet been tested on an actual investment project being considered by the company, it has been tested on sample data and technically it appears to be working very well.

While this specific risk analysis model is based on the general concepts

[1] The theoretical basis of this approach has been described by David Hertz, *Harvard Business Review*, January 1964, pp. 95–106.

outlined in the previous section, it is much broader in scope and more flexible than most such models. Essentially, the model is designed to take a series of cash flows and compute such things as the payback period, return on investment, and net present value. In using the program the user can specify any number of cash flow variables that may be desired. Thus, instead of having a single variable represent revenues, it is possible to have several variables representing various components of revenues (cash inflows). Similarly, cash outflows, or costs and expenses, can be represented either by a single variable or again by several variables.

The two types of information that must be supplied in order to use the BRISK program relate to project identification and variable identification. The first type of information includes the project title, the name or number of the alternative being considered under that project title, and the starting and ending dates for the life of that project. This information is printed out at the heading of all results so that the user can easily identify which project and which alternative the results apply to.

The variable identification information that is needed relates to the specific variables that the user wants to define as making up cash inflows and cash outflows. There are three kinds of variables which can be defined. The first is a *simulated variable*. These are variables (representing, for example, variable cost items, investments, or revenue items) for which management is uncertain of their future values. For these variables the user inputs a range of values by specifying five points in that range and the probability of each of those five value's occurring. Thus, if a simulated variable were sales in the first time period, five different levels of possible sales would have to be specified. Once the values for the first period of any variable have been specified, the user can specify the percentage change in this variable from period to period, and the starting and ending dates for which this variable has an impact on the project. Thus one might specify first period sales revenues, the expected rate of growth in those revenues in each subsequent period, and the number of periods for which those revenues would be realized.

The second kind of variable that can be specified is referred to as a *tied variable*. These are factors whose value is "tied" to a simulated variable. That is, their values depend on the value of a specific simulated variable. For a tied variable the user must specify the simulated variable to which it is tied, the constant portion of the value of the tied variable, and the variable portion of the tied variable (as a percent of the simulated variable). Thus a cost variable might be specified as being tied to sales revenue. The value of this cost variable would consist of some constant fixed portion plus a percent of the sales revenue. Again, with such variables the user must specify the starting and ending periods for which that tied variable affects the project and the percent change occurring in this variable from period to period.

The final kind of variable that can be specified is a *nonsimulated* variable.

These are variables that have a single value. An example would be a cost whose value is predictable and independent of the level of activity of the project. Here the user could specify the starting value for that cost variable, the percent change per period, and the periods through which this variable affects the project.

Based on discussions with various management personnel at Clarke's, this range of possible definitions for variables seems to cover all of the ways in which managers commonly think of expense and revenue items being related. One of the reasons for designing the model with this range of capabilities was to minimize the amount of information the manager actually has to supply in using this program to evaluate a specific project. Thus, rather than having to specify the variable cost for each individual period as the dollar amount, the manager can simply specify the starting dollar amount (in the first period) and the percent by which this changes each period. It is hoped this will allow the manager to think of the inputs to this model in terms very similar to those presently used, and thus minimize the amount of adjustment that managers must make in thinking about investment possibilities.

To give a better idea of some of the detailed characteristics of this batch version of the risk analysis model, as compared to other general descriptions with which you may be familiar, the four sections of the BRISK program are briefly described below.

*I. Section 100*

This section checks the input data to make sure it is in the proper format and will fit with later dimension statements within the program. This section also makes some checks on the appropriateness of the actual values being entered.

*II. Section 200*

This is the main computational section of the program. The following six steps are carried out in this section:

*a.* A value is determined for each simulated variable. This is done by selecting a random number and determining the variable value, based on the probability distribution that the user input for that variable, that corresponds to that random number. The program then checks the starting date for this particular simulated variable and places the calculated value in a table of cash flows in the appropriate period. Each succeeding period value is then calculated using the fixed percentage change provided by the user and the initial period's simulated value. Thus, a table is built up having as rows each variable and as columns the period to which that variable applies. The individual entries in the table represent the value of that variable for that period.

*b.* The value of each tied variable is determined. No new random numbers are used at this point. Rather the value of each tied variable is determined directly from the value of the simulated variable to which it is tied and the other information supplied by the manager.

*c*. The values of the nonsimulated variables are determined. This step takes the starting value for the nonsimulated variable as it was input by the manager and calculates its value for each of the succeeding periods for which it is a factor.

(At the end of these three steps a table of values for each period and each variable has been developed. This table is for a single trial or single simulation for the project.)

*d*. Calculation of the return on investment. Using the table of values generated in the first three steps, the net cash flows for each period in the life of the project are computed. The return on investment for this set of cash flows is then calculated. (This gives what is commonly referred to as the internal rate of return.)

*e*. A table of return-on-investment values is developed. At this point, the first four steps above are repeated by the program one hundred times. Thus the result is one hundred values of the internal rate of return. A statistical test is then run on the mean of these calculations to determine if an appropriate number of trials has been carried out. If it has, the program then proceeds to step *f*. If more trials are needed, steps *a* through *d* are repeated an additional one hundred times.

*f*. Ranking the return-on-investment figures. All of the internal rate of return values in the table developed in step e are ranked and this ranking is made available to the next section of the program.

*III. Section 300*

This segment of the program provides the capability of adjusting the return-on-investment values calculated by the program, to take account of the risk preferences of the decision maker. Inclusion of such preference considerations in the program will probably not be needed initially and can be skipped over at this point. Later on, however, management at Clarke's may want to make explicit consideration of their attitudes toward risk.

*IV. Section 400*

This concluding section of the program calculates the *expected* return on investment and prints that value. This is done by fitting a curve to the ranked values of the internal rate of return and integrating over that curve. Thus the final printout is the expected return on investment for the project.

At this point, the project description input by the user is also printed. Other print options could be added, but that has not yet been done. Presumably, such things as a risk profile (showing the range of possible return-on-investment outcomes for the project), the average cash flows per period, and the payback for the project might be desired by management.

**Requirements for using BRISK at Clarke's Markets**

In order to make widespread use of this risk analysis program, it will be necessary to develop a set of procedures for defining projects and identifying the information that is needed for running the model. One way in which this might be done would be to first develop a form (work sheet) that could serve as a check list and as a place for writing down the information that is needed for using the model on a specific project (that is, the project identification and the definition of individual variables and their values). The administrative staff might then have one individual serve as a clearing house for using the program by getting data processing to punch the data in the appropriate format and run the BRISK program. It is probably realistic to assume a one-week turnaround time from when the information form is completed and when the results are available from the computer program. When managers see the risk analysis results for their projects, they may then want to have a couple of alternative sets of information (reflecting altered assumptions) evaluated for that same project. Turnaround time for any such follow-up run would probably be about three days.

Although the managers at Clarke's Markets are not familiar with the use of probabilities in their day-to-day operations, there should not be much trouble in getting them to supply the required information in probability form. They have often commented in their use of existing deterministic models that most variables could better be represented by a range of possible values. Because the BRISK model allows them to supply such a range of values, it will most likely be welcomed by managers as a way to express the uncertainties of which they are already well aware. Once the model is being used effectively, there are several additions that can be made to it. (Many of these have already been identified in another memo.) These additions include such things as the use of risk preferences and development of more accurate techniques for handling the probability distributions and for computing the expected value of the return on investment.

case 4.2

# Industrial National Bank—Trust Department (A)

Jack Nichols, manager of Trust Operations at Industrial National Bank, was considering what changes, if any, to recommend for the schedules of fees which the trust department charged its customers. When banks managed (or helped manage) assets for customers under trust and related arrangements, the fees were usually based in large part on the market value of the assets (generally securities) in the accounts; INB's fee schedule, which had been adopted in 1971, was based primarily on market value. Unfortunately, the declining stock market in 1974 had seriously affected the values of the trust assets and, accordingly, INB's trust fees had dropped over 15 percent, from $3,296,000 in 1973 to $2,786,000 in 1974. Mr. Nichols wondered whether some alternate schedule, partly based on market values but also based on the income generated by the accounts and perhaps on the various services which INB performed for those accounts, might be preferable; he was aware that expenses of the trust department had been rising continually since 1971, the time of the last fee change, and he felt that trust accounts should pay for the services which they consumed.

## Industrial National Bank

Industrial National Bank (or INB) was chartered in 1791 as the Providence Bank and, hence, was one of the oldest banks in the United States. In 1974 INB was the third largest bank in New England; it was a major subsidiary of the Industrial National Corporation, a financial services corporation. In addition to INB, the parent company had subsidiaries involved in mortgage banking, leasing, factoring, consumer finance, appraising (of real estate and equipment) and data processing. The consolidated balance sheet showed over $2 billion in assets in 1974.

INB had its main office in Providence, Rhode Island; it also had 48 branch offices throughout the state. The bank engaged in general commercial banking on a local and national (and international) basis. Its major activities included commercial lending, home loan mortgages, construction financing, credit card operations, consumer loans, trading of government and municipal securities, and trust and investment. In 1974 INB had $1.7 billion in assets and showed a net income of $12.2 million.

## Trusts

For many centuries, reliable or trustworthy individuals (and especially officials of local religious institutions) have acted as agents on behalf of others in administering property. As demand for such trust relationships grew, countries enacted laws to strengthen the agreements and to aid in administering trusts. When business in general became more complicated and more specialized, it became more and more difficult to find qualified individuals who were willing to act as trustees. In addition, of course, a trust agreement with an individual trustee was limited in time to the trustee's life span. Consequently, special trust institutions and also trust departments in savings and commercial banks were developed to provide trust services. These organizations had the advantages of continuity (they were not limited to the life span of an individual), of access to credit, and of general business experience.

Trust departments usually perform both trust services (in which the trustee has some legal rights and some autonomy in dealing with the property held) and agency services (in which the agent acts only in behalf of and subject to the control of the individual or group owning the property). The distinction between trust and agency functions is one of the degree of control and autonomy held by the trustee or agent. At one extreme, in some trusts the trustee makes all decisions about buying and selling property and, thus, assumes full responsibility for managing that property in the interests of the principal. At the other extreme, a trust department may act as an agent for individuals who keep all decision making about their investments in their own hands but rely on the agent to carry out the administrative details. In common use, the terms "trust department" and "trust services" often are used to include both trust and agency functions.

Trust and agency services are divided into two main groups: personal trusts and corporate trusts. Generally, only banks in large metropolitan areas have corporate trust departments. Fees for corporate trust services are highly competitive and profit margins are generally low; banks offer these services mainly to attract and keep corporate customers (whose demand deposits are very important to the banks) and, in general, to be able to offer full lines of banking services. Personal trust services are considerably more lucrative for trust departments; they include estate management, management of property for living individuals, and various agency relationships. In addition, trust departments often offer estate planning and investment counseling services, frequently without charge. Banks often use those services as a way to introduce customers to the other functions provided by their trust departments.

### Trust services at INB

INB classified its trust accounts into nine groups. Estates accounts, the first group, were ones in which the bank acted as executor or administrator of an individual's estate. (In an executorship the bank was acting under the instructions of the individual's will; when an individual died without a will, a court might appoint the bank to act as an administrator, carrying out many functions of an executor.) The executor's job was to collect and manage the assets of the estate, to pay off liabilities, and then to value and to distribute the remaining assets in accord with the will (or, if there were none, in accord with relevant law). These duties could include anything from stopping magazine subscriptions to selling major assets or to managing a family business until the estate had been settled. Fees for executorships were usually expressed as a percentage of the total assets administered, with the percentage declining as the size of the estate increased.

Three other types of personal accounts accounted for almost 60 percent of INB's trust revenues. The first of these three groups consisted of testamentary trusts, or arrangements in which the bank first acted as executor of an estate and then continued to manage the estate over the long term in the interests of the beneficiaries of the will. INB's marketing literature on trusts explained that in the past such testamentary arrangements had often been intended to tie up property under terms of a rigid will, safeguarding it for distant generations. More recently, the motivation for testamentary trust relationships had more likely been a concern by the testator (or maker of the will) to protect the interests or his or her immediate family. As INB's sales literature pointed out, such trusts not only provided for professional management of assets but also could help in reducing estate taxes.

A second group of personal accounts consisted of living trusts, or trust agreements with individuals for the management of their assets while they were still alive. Such trusts were often set up by individuals who feared physical or mental incapacity and wanted to ensure that their affairs would continue to be managed effectively. In addition, such trusts helped to provide privacy and to avoid probate (and some estate taxes). In other cases, living trusts were set up to relieve the principals of the details of handling their financial affairs or else to segregate a portion of their assets for specific purposes. Living trusts were managed in light of the trust-maker's personal investment goals (and such consideration of individual goals was a major selling point for the trust arrangement as opposed to other investment possibilities). In both the testamentary and living trust arrangements, the trustees held legal rights to the property and usually had wide latitude in managing the property (except that they might not manage the trust property for their own benefit). The exact degree of control held by the trustee varied from agreement to agreement, with the bank holding virtually complete control in some trusts (taking charge of all investment decisions and then paying out interest, and perhaps principal, as directed by the will or agreement) but with the trust department managing other accounts in closer conjunction with the trust maker.

The third group of personal trusts consisted of agency accounts, in which the customer maintained full ownership of the assets and the bank offered investment advice and also performed the paper work and administrative tasks associated with the investments. The actual investment decisions were often made by the bank, although for some of the accounts the bank had to obtain the customer's approval for each investment. The bank carried out the investment decisions and had physical custody of the securities in the account.

While executorships lasted only until the estates were settled, trusts and agencies often lasted many years. Testamentary trusts could not be terminated except by court order, but living trusts and agencies were usually revocable at the customer's option. Fees for the longer-lived trusts were generally paid quarterly and were based on some combination of principal managed, income generated, and activities performed.

A final class of personal accounts at INB contained custody accounts, in which the customers retained complete control over their investments and did not even receive advice from the bank's investment analysts. In such accounts, INB merely maintained physical custody of the securities and carried out the administrative details at the direction of the customers. Custody accounts generated approximately 10 percent of trust revenues.

INB grouped its corporate accounts into two classes. For accounts in the first class (called corporate trusts), the bank might act as a trustee for a bond issue. In that capacity, it would represent the bondholders as a group, performing functions which no individual bondholder would want to take on individually; for example, the bank would check to see that the corporation issuing the bonds was complying with any covenants in the bond agreement. In addition, the trust department would pay out interest to the bondholders. In other corporate accounts the bank would act as the legally-required registrar for a stock issue; under such arrangements, INB's job was to guard against overissuance of the stock. In yet other accounts the bank would act as transfer agent for a corporation, handling transfers of stock, maintaining stockholder records, and performing related duties such as mailing out corporate reports or dividends to current stockholders. For other corporations, INB might act as a paying agent, disbursing dividends, interest and/or principal payments.

The second class of corporate accounts consisted of pension and profit-sharing accounts. Corporations established these accounts to segregate employee funds from all other corporate funds. The bank's responsibilities in these accounts could range from those of a custodian to those of a trustee.

Finally, INB had two other classes of accounts, one a special group of agency accounts which were managed by a subsidiary (and, hence, were considered a separate group) and also a category of house accounts and miscellaneous accounts.

In addition to the (nine) classes of accounts described above, INB offered six common trust funds. These were trust funds which operated much like mutual funds; by offering six different common trust funds, INB was able to offer the smaller investor a range of objectives, with some funds emphasizing growth and others emphasizing income, for example. Because the bank incurred less expense in administering a single group account than it did in managing many smaller accounts, it offered customers substantial reductions from normal trust fees for investing in the common funds. In addition, the minimum fee for the common trust funds was considerably smaller than the minimum for a regular trust account.

Altogether, the trust department at INB managed approximately 3,300 accounts ranging in size from $5,000 to $50 million. The total value of the accounts was just under a billion dollars.

INB's trust department consisted of six divisions: the Estate Department, Investment Management, Investment Research, the Pension Department, and the largest two divisions, the Personal Trust and New Business Department and the Operations group. (Corporate accounts other than pension accounts were managed by a separate department). Exhibit 1 gives an orga-

**EXHIBIT 1**
Organization of the trust department

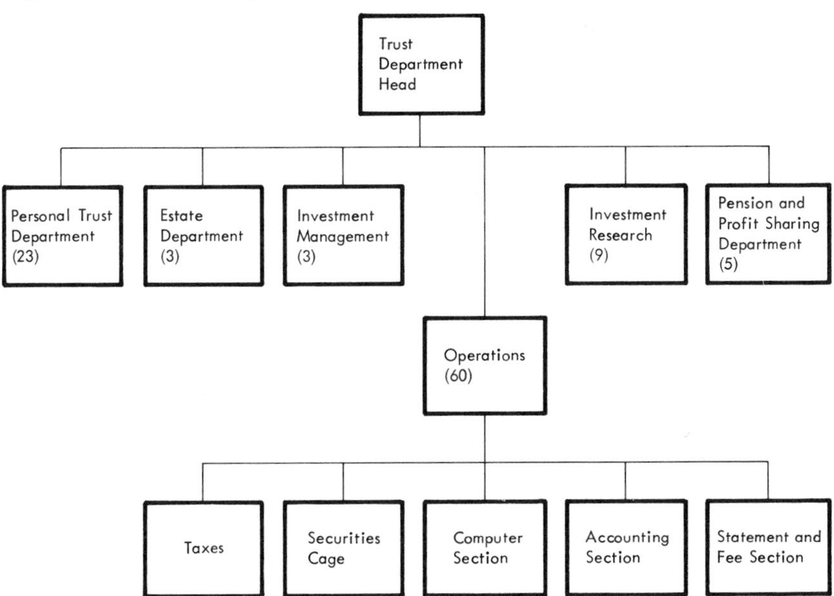


Numbers in parentheses indicate the number of key personnel in each area.

nization chart of the trust department. The personal trust division was responsible for the sales function of introducing new customers to the trust services of the bank (new business development), for making decisions to buy and sell securities for the personal trust accounts (through the personal trust investment section) and for maintaining liason between the customer and the bank (through the administrative section). The Operations Department, which with 60 people was the largest part of the trust department, handled the administrative details of the trust business, including processing of securities, safekeeping securities, bookkeeping, preparing tax returns, and collecting fees.

## Trust department fee schedules

In establishing fee schedules for their services, trust departments generally used a combination of market fees (or fees based on the market value of the assets under management), income fees (or fees based on the dividends and interest generated by the account), and sometimes activity fees (or fees based on the specific services performed for the account). Fees based on market value were typically expressed as percentages of the principal. Often the banks used one percentage for amounts up to a certain break point, another percentage for amounts over the first break and up to a second break, and so forth. Thus, a bank might charge .6 percent on the first $200,000 of market value; .4 percent on the next $300,000; .35 percent on the next $1 million; and .25 percent on the next $3 million. Similarly, income fees might involve different rates below and above a given break (or several given breaks) in income level. In setting a fee schedule, the banks had to select not only the percentages for market value and income fees but also the break points, if any, which were to be used for each type of fees.

In addition to market value and income fees, a bank might want to charge for the activities performed for a particular trust account. For example, the bank might charge a fixed amount each time it furnished a customer with a statement summarizing the status of his or her account. In many cases, at least some of the possible activities were furnished without charge; in other cases, an account might be entitled to a specified number of free activities of some particular type and might be charged only if it required more than the allowable free number. In addition, either the charge or the free allowance for various activities might vary with the size of the account, with larger accounts paying less or else allowed more free activities than smaller ones.

There were numerous activities for which the trust department could charge. For example, activities for which INB kept records included: receiving and depositing any of several types of income in an account (dividend collection, bond interest collection, note interest collection, rental income collection); buying or receiving various types of assets for the account (purchase of a security, acquisition of a security but not as a result of a buy or sell, deposit of cash into the account); selling or disposing of assets for the account (sale of a security, disposal of a security but not as a sale, transfer of cash from the account). In addition, the trust department might pay bills for the customer, it might prepare a statement showing the market value of an account and listing the transactions performed for that account, it might prepare a tax letter for the customer's accountant to use in preparing a tax return, or it might prepare the customer's tax return. In addition, there were other activities performed for the pension trusts, including making monthly payments to retirees.

In general, it seemed appropriate to charge different classes of accounts according to different schedules for activities. For example, because a trust department usually had a high level of control over the activity of personal trust accounts, the bank determined when to buy or sell securities or to conduct other activities for those accounts. Hence, it was inappropriate to charge the customer for most activities; only bill paying and statements or reviews (which described the state of the account) were activities whose numbers were determined by the customer and, hence, were appropriate for charges. In custody accounts, on the other hand, the bank performed only the administrative tasks and all decisions were made by the customer; hence, it was appropriate to charge those accounts for all transactions.

Finally, there were special conditions of accounts which might call for special fees. The bank might charge extra if customers wanted to be consulted by the bank on each investment decision. (It was customary to make a single charge for the stipulation in a trust agreement that the bank would obtain approval for investments; the charge generally did not depend on how many investments were made.)

In order to limit the number of small, unprofitable accounts, a bank might charge a minimum fee; the customer would have to pay this minimum amount, regardless of the activity or performance of the account. To encourage smaller accounts to invest in a common trust fund (which required less individual attention than a regular account) banks often charged lower minimum fees for accounts invested solely in common trust funds; in addition, the banks often offered such accounts discounts from the regular fee schedules.

Exhibit 2 shows the fee schedules for personal trust accounts used by INB and by several of its competitors. Exhibit 3 shows the calculation of the fees which would be charged to a few hypothetical accounts under a typical fee schedule.

## Analyzing fee changes

According to Jack Nichols of INB, "Changing fee schedules is one of the most significant decisions for Trust Department earnings. Many trust departments have assigned senior accountants for periods lasting over a year to

**EXHIBIT 2**

Personal trust fee schedules (see explanation at bottom of table)

| Fees | INB | First National Bank of Boston | Hospital Trust | New England Merchants | Shawmut | State Street |
|---|---|---|---|---|---|---|
| Market value fees* | \$6/1,000 \$200,000<br>\$4/1,000 \$300,000<br>\$3.50/1,000 \$1,000,000<br>\$2.50/1,000 \$3,000,000 | \$4/1,000 \$200,000<br>\$3/1,000 \$300,000<br>\$2/1,000 \$500,000<br>\$1/1,000 Balance | \$4/1,000 \$50,000<br>\$3/1,000 \$150,000<br>\$2/1,000 \$300,000<br>\$1/1,000 \$2,500,000<br>\$.50/1,000 Balance | \$5/1,000 \$100,000<br>\$4/1,000 \$100,000<br>\$3/1,000 \$100,000<br>\$2/1,000 \$200,000<br>\$1/1,000 Balance | \$4/1,000 \$200,000<br>\$3/1,000 \$300,000<br>\$2/1,000 \$500,000<br>\$1/1,000 \$2,500,000 | \$3/1,000 \$200,000<br>\$2/1,000 \$300,000<br>\$1/1,000 Balance |
| Income fees† | None | Flat 6% | 5% \$75,000<br>4% Balance | Flat 5% | 6% \$50,000<br>5% \$50,000<br>4% \$50,000<br>3% Balance | 6% \$50,000<br>5% Balance |
| Activity fees‡ | None | \$150 for consultation | None | \$150 for consultation | \$150 for consultation | \$150 for consultation |
| Minimum fees | \$500 | \$750 | \$500 | \$600 | \$640 | \$600 |
| Fee discounts offered to common trust fund accounts | 35% | None | 30% | 25% | 20% | 30% |
| Common trust fund minimums | \$150 | \$300 | \$200 | \$250 | \$250 | \$250 |

* The second column of numbers represents break-level increments. For example, INB's fee schedule would be read: 0.6% on the first \$200,000 of market value; 0.4% on the next \$300,000 (that is, all amounts between \$200,000 and \$500,000); 0.35% on the next \$1,000,000 (\$500,000–\$1,500,000); and 0.25% on the next \$3,000,000 (1,500,000–\$4,500,000).

† As with market value fees, the second column of numbers represents break-level increments.

‡ Consultation means the requirement that the bank obtain the customer's approval for investment decisions. The fee is a yearly charge (regardless of how many investments are actually made).

**EXHIBIT 3**
Calculation of personal trust fees

Suppose a trust department has the following fee schedule:

*Market Value Fees*

| | |
|---|---|
| \$5/1000 | \$200,000 |
| \$3/1000 | \$300,000 |
| \$2/1000 | \$500,000 |
| \$1/1000 | Balance |

*Income Fees*
Flat 5%

*Activity Fees*
\$150 for consultation (a yearly fee)
\$50/statement in excess of four per year

*Minimum Fee*
\$500

*Fee Discount Offered to Common Trust Fund Accounts*
35%

*Common Trust Fund Minimum*
\$200

*Example 1:* A hypothetical account has a market value of \$250,000 and produces income of \$8,125. During the year, there were six statements. The trust agreement required the customer's approval for each investment. The following fees would be charged:

*Market Value Fees*
.005(\$200,000) + .003(\$50,000) = \$1,150.00

*Income Fees*
.05(\$8,125) = \$406.25

*Activity Fees*
2(\$50) for the 5th and 6th statements = \$100.00
(there is no charge for the first four statements)
\$150 for the consultation requirement = \$150.00

Total \$1,806.25

*Example 2:* A hypothetical account has a market value of \$50,000 and produces income of \$1,600. During the year, there were four statements. Consultation was not required. The following fees would be charged:

*Market Value Fees*
.005(\$50,000) = \$250.00

*Income Fees*
.05(\$1,600) = \$80.00

*Activity Fees*
None

Total \$330.00

*But,* since this amount is less than the minimum fee, \$500.00 would be charged.

**Exhibit 3 (*continued*)**

*Example 3:* A hypothetical common trust fund account has a market value of $80,000 and produces income of $3,600. During the year, there were four statements. Consultation was not required. The following fees would be charged:

| | | |
|---|---|---|
| *Market Value Fees* | | |
| .005($80,000) | = | $400.00 |
| *Income Fees* | | |
| .05($3,600) | = | $180.00 |
| Total | | $580.00 |

Applying the common trust fund discount yields

$580 − .35($580) = $377.00

determine the 'what if's' of moving to a new fee schedule." He wondered if it would be possible for INB to use the computer to shorten this process and to eliminate much of the uncertainty in changing fees.

In analyzing possible fee changes, Nichols felt that there were three major considerations. First of all, he wanted to match revenues with costs. Each activity had a direct expense (consisting primarily of computer time and of labor). For cost analyses, the overhead was allocated proportionately. A recent study of the costs and revenues associated with the different classes and sizes of accounts at INB had shown that there were some groups for which revenues did not cover the costs of servicing those accounts. The second consideration in setting fees involved the risks to INB in periods of poor market conditions. A typical account included a mix of fixed-income and equity holdings, and, hence, its market value did not swing as widely as did the Dow Jones or other market indices. It was still true that overall performance did tend to follow the Dow Jones Industrial Average (though the extremes were dampened). Mr. Nichols wanted to find a fee schedule which would weather a variety of market conditions. Finally, he felt that fee selection should include consideration of the sensitivity of different market segments to fee increases. Although market research had indicated that the market for trust services was relatively price insensitive, he knew that excessive fee increases would cause the loss of some accounts. In addition, because of differences in income and in activities used, different accounts would react differently to changes in the fee schedule. For example, an overall increase in trust fees of 15 percent might result in only a 3 percent increase for some accounts and as much as a 27 percent increase for others. A new schedule should minimize the numbers of excessive or inadequate increases.

As a first step, Mr. Nichols had set up a file of all of the INB trust accounts. For each account, the file included information about type (from the list of nine classes discussed above), market value, income, activities of each type performed for the account, and any other conditions which might be the basis for fees (for example, it recorded whether an account was invested entirely in common trust funds).[1] To start with, Nichols wanted to set up a computer model which would let him investigate the first two considerations in setting up a fee schedule: matching revenues and costs (for specific account groups) and also designing a schedule which would be satisfactory (in terms of total fees taken by INB) under different market conditions. The variance in changes which the fee schedule would make in the fees for individual accounts (and the resulting potential losses of accounts) would be considered in detail later in the analysis.

[1] There were over 30 different activities and conditions which could be present.

case 4.3

# Industrial National Bank—Trust Department (B)

In mid-1975, Jack Nichols, the manager of trust operations for Industrial National Bank (INB), was studying the problem of the fee schedules which the bank charged its trust customers.[1] Briefly stated, INB's problem was to select a fee schedule for its Personal Trust accounts[2] (1) which would perform satisfactorily under changing stock market conditions, (2) which would match fees to the bank with costs of managing the accounts, and (3) which would be acceptable to most of the bank's trust customers.

On July 29, 1975, in a memo to the president of the bank, Mr. Nichols summarized some of the results that were emerging from his study of fee schedules:

> We believe that the 1971 fee schedule now in effect was set with little attention to performance at market levels such as we have now. As a result, it did not protect our downside risk in a falling market as did several of our competitors' schedules. Consequently, while the Dow averaged 200 points lower in 1974, our Personal Trust fees dropped $300,000 . . .
>
> . . . In the New England area we noted widely differing fee schedules. Our market surveys indicate that Personal Trust customers do not generally shop price. Recently, a Boston bank instituted a 40 percent increase for accounts up to $1 million. All of these facts lead us to believe this is a price *in*sensitive market.
>
> In completing cost studies of 1973 and 1974, we have found our margins generally weak for small accounts . . .
>
> Our analysis of the competition and our costs indicate that we can and should (1) raise prices to reap higher revenues while remaining competitive with our neighbors and (2) raise prices to improve margins on specific unprofitable account sizes.

The results discussed in this memo were based on the analysis which Mr. Nichols had performed using two computer programs for investigating fee schedules. Those programs are described in the remainder of this case. In

[1] See Case 4.2, "Industrial National Bank—Trust Department (A)."

[2] Class 2—Testamentary Trusts, Class 3—Living Trusts, and Class 4—Agency Accounts.

designing and using the programs, Mr. Nichols's aims had been to meet his three criteria for a good fee schedule as listed above.

## Defining fee schedules

In designing a program to analyze fee schedules, Mr. Nichols had first considered the question of how a fee schedule would be defined. He wanted a program which could be used to study any of the bank's nine classes of accounts, ranging from personal trusts to pension funds. As discussed in INB (A), fees for trust accounts were based on some combination of fees based on market value (or "market fees"), fees based on the income (in dividends, interest, and so forth) generated by the account ("income fees"), and fees for the different services which the bank might perform for the account ("activity fees"). In addition, there was usually a minimum fee per account; there generally were also reductions from the normal fee schedule for accounts which were invested solely in common trust funds.

*Market fees* would be defined in terms of breakpoints or levels and of rates to be charged at the various levels. The programs would have to be told how many market levels to consider, what dollar amounts would be the breaks between adjacent levels, and what percent of market value to charge accounts falling into each of the size levels.

*Income fees* were similarly defined in terms of levels and rates. In order to figure income fees, the programs would have to know the number of income levels to consider, the dollar amounts at which to make the breaks between adjacent levels, and the fractions of income which would be taken as fees in each income level.

Deciding on how to define *activity charges* was somewhat more difficult. Mr. Nichols first determined the list of services (such as purchasing a security or collecting bond interest) which the bank might perform for an account. His list had to include the activities appropriate for each of the nine classes of accounts, even though some of the activities applied to only some of the classes. For example, he included the activity of making a payment to a pensioner, although that activity applied only to the trust accounts which organizations had established for their pension funds. In addition to the list of activities, Mr. Nichols included a list of *conditions* which might describe an account. For example, one such condition was called "directed"; an account marked for this condition was one for which the bank had to deal with a particular broker chosen by the customer. For activities, the bank kept track of how many times it performed a service for a customer. Conditions, on the other hand, were characteristics which either were or were not present in an account; charges for conditions were similarly present or absent in the account's fee and those charges did not depend on a count of a number of services. Exhibit 1 of this case gives a list of the activities and conditions which could be included in fee schedules.

**EXHIBIT 1**
Activities and conditions for trust accounts

Activities and conditions are given in the same order used in the simulation program.

DIVIDEND COLLECTION—The bank receives a dividend check and deposits the check (as income) to the account.

REGISTERED BOND INTEREST—The bank receives interest on a registered bond (one for which the company keeps a record of the owner and then mails the interest automatically) and deposits the money to the account.

COUPON INTEREST—The bank presents a coupon and deposits the resulting bond interest to the account.

FIXED FEE—A condition. This field shows the actual amount of fixed fee. When there is a fixed fee for an account, that fixed amount is charged (regardless of the fee schedule).

NOTE INTEREST—The bank collects interest on a promissory note and deposits the money to the trust account.

RENT INCOME—The bank collects income from the customer's real estate holdings and credits the customer's account.

CONSULTATION—A condition indicating that the customer must be consulted before the bank buys or sells stock.

OWN NAME—A condition. Securities are registered in the customer's name rather than the bank's name.

DIRECTED—A condition indicating that the bank is to deal with a broker selected by the customer.

REVIEW—The bank issues a listing of the assets of the account.

COMMON TRUST ONLY—A condition indicating that the account is invested only in common trust funds.

NON-CASH DELIVERY—The bank sends a stock or bond to someone without receiving payment.

DATA PROCESSING GENERAL DELIVERY—The computer automatically transfers a stock or bond from an account.

INVESTMENT CERTIFICATE—Buy or sell of a CD (or deposit to or withdrawal from a time savings account).

SECURITY PURCHASE—Purchase of a stock or bond for an account.

ASSET ACQUISITION—The bank receives a stock or bond for an account but not as the result of a purchase or sale.

WITHDRAW CERTIFICATE—A stock certificate is withdrawn for examination, transfer, name change, etc.

SECURITY SALE—Sale of a stock or bond from an account.

ASSET DISPOSITION—An asset of the account is disposed of but not as the result of a buy or sell.

PRINCIPAL CASH RECEIVED—A straight cash deposit is made to the account.

CASH TRANSFER—Cash is transferred from the account.

INCOME DISTRIBUTION—The bank pays out income from the account.

BILL PAYING—The bank pays bills for the customer.

FEE COLLECTION—The bank collects its fee.

STATEMENT—The bank issues a list of all of the assets in an account and also a detailed list of each purchase or sale for that account.

PREPARE 1041—The bank prepares a tax return.

TAX LETTER—The bank sends an official letter for the customer (or an accountant) to use in preparing a tax return.

PENSION DEPARTMENT—PRINCIPAL CASH RECEIVED—A cash deposit is made to a pension account.

PENSION DEPARTMENT—BENEFIT PAYMENT—The pension department sends a benefit check to a retiree.

PENSION DEPARTMENT—RETURN PAYMENT—A pension department benefit check is returned.

PENSION DEPARTMENT—RETURN OF CONTRIBUTION—The contributions to the pension fund made by an employee are paid to the employee when s/he leaves the employer.

PENSION DEPARTMENT—MISCELLANEOUS PAYMENT—Other payments from a pension account.

DATA PROCESSING CASH TRANSFER—The computer automatically transfers cash from one account to another.

ISSUES—The number of different stock and bond issues held by an account (the number of companies, not the number of shares).

The precise form of charges for activities and conditions could be quite complicated, involving different numbers of free activities of a specific type for accounts at some market or income levels and other numbers of free activities at other levels. In designing the programs to study schedules, Mr. Nichols decided to allow differences in free activities for different market levels only. Further, he decided to allow only two groups of accounts by size for this purpose (that is, one break level). Thus, the programs would have to know which activities were to be charged and, for each such activity, the market level break and the numbers of free activities above and below that level.

In addition to deciding how fee schedules would be defined, Mr. Nichols had assembled a computer file of information on INB's existing accounts. For each account, the file contained a code number, the market value of the account as of a specified date, the income which the account had produced during the previous year, and the number of each type of activity which had been performed for the account (and information about whether different conditions were present in the account).

**Fee schedule response to market conditions—the simulation model**

At that point, Mr. Nichols was ready to build a deterministic simulation model to investigate the fees which INB would earn under various fee schedules and various assumptions about market value and income. Working with an experienced programmer, he constructed such a model. The program for the model either accepted a saved definition of a fee schedule (which the user had previously defined and saved) or else led the user through a series of questions for defining a schedule (giving market breaks and rates, income breaks and rates, activities with breaks and numbers and also a minimum fee for each account). The program also requested a minimum fee for accounts invested only in common trust funds and a discount to be applied to fees for such accounts.

In addition to specifying a fee schedule, the user of this program gave information about the accounts which were to be considered. The program allowed the user to consider all accounts in a particular file or, alternatively, to consider only accounts in certain of the bank's nine classes or else only accounts in specified categories by market value.

Finally, the program required information about the assumptions which the user wanted to make about market value and income. As mentioned above, the files of information on INB's accounts included figures for market values as of some particular date. In using the program, the user was asked to give that value of the Dow Jones Industrial Average (from the time that the accounts were valued). In addition, the program asked for the Dow average at the time the fees under the new schedule were to be calculated. To adjust from the original to the new Dow level, the program made increases or decreases in value which were strictly proportional to the change in the Dow. For example, if a particular account had a market value of $100,000 in the original data file and if the user stated that the file had been valued when the Dow was 750, and if the program was told to figure the fees with a Dow of 600, then it would simply reduce all market values by 20 percent, or (750 − 600)/750. Once the user had given the Dow at the time the file was valued and also the Dow to be used for the simulation of fee-taking, the program used the same proportional adjustment factor for every account in the file; thus, it assumed that the change in market value for each account was exactly proportional to the change in the Dow.

As stated above, the data file of information on accounts also contained the amount of income generated by each account in the previous year. In running the program, the user was offered two options for specifying income which would be subjected to the new fee schedule. The first option was simply to assume that the new income would be the same as the income in the data file; that is, that regardless of whether a new market level was used income levels would remain the same. Mr. Nichols knew that income for the trust accounts was relatively insensitive to market level and so he felt that this first option was often a reasonable one. On the other hand, he also knew that there were some changes in income as the market went through sizable changes in value. Accordingly, he included in the program another option which allowed the user to specify a fraction defining income as a percentage of market value. On a particular run of the program the same yield fraction would be used for each account in the data file. For example, assuming a yield of 4.5 percent would mean that if the market value for an account (at the Dow specified for the simulation of fee-taking) was $200,000 then the income for that account would be taken as $9,000 (rather than whatever income level was listed in the data file). On the basis of an analysis of INB's past history of market values and yields (with some extrapolation), Mr. Nichols had decided to use the following combinations of market levels and yields for his initial analyses.

| | | | | | |
|---|---|---|---|---|---|
| Dow Jones Industrial Average . . . . . . . . | 500 | 600 | 750 | 900 | 1100 |
| Yield (percent) . . . . . . . . . . . . . . . . . . . . . | 6.5 | 5.5 | 4.5 | 3.5 | 3.0 |

In determining the fees which would be taken under various fee schedules, the program assumed that the numbers and types of activities used by an account would be the same as the historical numbers given in the data file (that is, that those numbers did not depend on market or income levels).

The computer appendix of this case shows an example of the use of the simulation program applied to a sample of 274 personal trust accounts. As shown in that appendix, the program printed out a summary of market fees, income fees, activity (and condition) fees, minimum fees, and total fees for each class of accounts. In addition, the program gave the total fees taken under the fee schedule being considered.

With this program, Mr. Nichols was able to consider the first two of his design objectives: satisfactory performance for different market conditions and satisfactory matching of revenues and costs. For the first objective, he subjected the bank's accounts to different market and income assumptions (from the table above). In doing so, he studied INB's current schedule, its competitors' schedules, and also proposed new schedules for INB. To consider the problem of matching revenues and costs, Mr. Nichols used the program option which allowed him to select accounts by size (market value). He subjected different groups of accounts to proposed fee schedules in order to see how much each group would generate in fees. Comparing this information with the results of a detailed cost analysis of the bank's operation of accounts of different types and sizes allowed him to determine whether particular schedules satisfactorily matched fees and costs to the bank.

### The impacts of changes on different accounts

The third concern which Mr. Nichols had to consider in setting a new fee schedule was the impact that a change would have on the bank's trust business. The bank had conducted an in-house survey of 160 trust accounts and on the basis of this survey and of other information, Mr. Nichols felt that the trust market was not particularly price sensitive. Personal trust customers were often wealthy individuals who were shopping for effective money management more than for low fees; they found a manager who could provide better portfolio performance well worth a premium in price. On the other hand, Mr. Nichols felt that there was some limit to the size of fee increase which customers would accept. He felt that losses of accounts were most likely at the time of a change in fees; once a new fee schedule was established, losses of accounts were much less likely. On the basis of the bank's experience in 1971, at the time of its last fee change, and also on the basis of an analysis of recent moves by competitors, Mr. Nichols concluded that an overall increase of 20–30 percent might be acceptable for small accounts (less than $125,000 in market value). For accounts with market values between $125,000 and $400,000 he felt that a 15–20 percent increase was more appropriate, while for the large accounts (over $400,000) he wanted to keep the increase under 10 percent.

It was technically possible to consider the changes for different account groups with the main simulation program described above, by running the program once for each proposed fee schedule and each account size. For example, with six fee schedules and five groups of accounts there would be 30 runs of the program. When changing market conditions were added, more runs were needed. This procedure was time-consuming for the user and also consumed computer time at considerable expense.

In order to cut down on time and expense, Mr. Nichols decided to construct another "mini-simulation" program which would be used as a screen for new schedules. Basically, the idea was to use a fast analysis of a very small number of hypothetical accounts to do a preliminary analysis of possible fee schedules. Only those schedules which looked most promising on the basis of the preliminary screening would be subjected to a more exhaustive analysis with a full simulation using the bank's entire account base. Accordingly, Mr. Nichols constructed a very small data file of hypothetical accounts (with market values in multiples of $50,000); he included only one account in each size category. In addition to the information contained in the standard larger data files, he put into the small data file the fees which INB would charge those accounts under its current fee schedule. The mini-simulator operated much like the main simulator (except that it did not allow the user to use the existing income but instead required a yield assumption). The program output the fees under some proposed fee schedule for the hypothetical accounts and also gave the percentage changes from existing fees which those new fees represented. Thus, the mini-simulator gave a quick way to screen for excessive and inadequate fee changes. The program was inexpensive to run relative to the main simulation program.

Although the mini-simulator worked well for a single assumed yield (income as a percentage of market value), Mr. Nichols realized that because it only accepted a single yield assumption, it did not properly examine the range of increases or decreases that a prospective schedule would cause. For example, the average yield for accounts $200,000 to $400,000 was approximately 5.6 percent when the Dow Jones Industrial Average was at 600. However these accounts actually had a range of yields from below 2 percent to above 9 percent. Only 40 percent of the accounts had yields within one percent of the 5.6 percent average. Of the remainder, 30 percent had yields below 4.6 percent and 30 percent had yields above 6.6 percent. Part of the reason was that different accounts were managed differently, with some emphasizing income and others emphasizing growth. Since the distribution of yield would greatly affect the price increase for each account, Nichols realized that he would have to examine the distribution of price increases for each market segment before deciding on a final fee schedule. In addition, he knew that all of his analysis so far had been based on deterministic simulation programs. It seemed appropriate to consider the probabilities of losing various accounts and the impacts which such possible losses would have on the bank.

COMPUTER APPENDIX (begins on the following page)

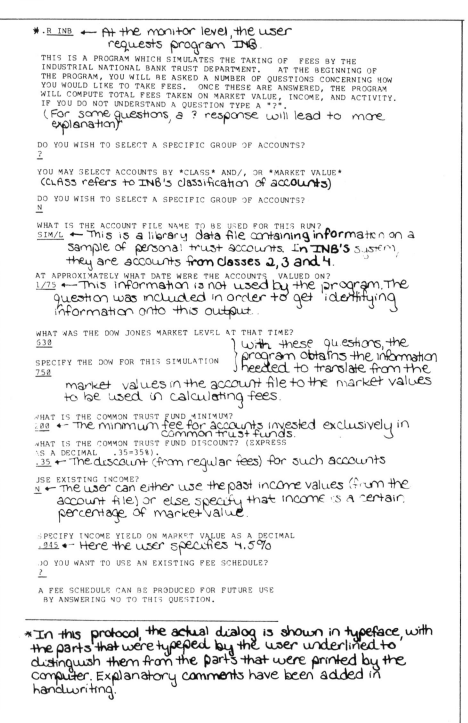

*.R INB ← At the monitor level, the user requests program INB.

THIS IS A PROGRAM WHICH SIMULATES THE TAKING OF FEES BY THE INDUSTRIAL NATIONAL BANK TRUST DEPARTMENT. AT THE BEGINNING OF THE PROGRAM, YOU WILL BE ASKED A NUMBER OF QUESTIONS CONCERNING HOW YOU WOULD LIKE TO TAKE FEES. ONCE THESE ARE ANSWERED, THE PROGRAM WILL COMPUTE TOTAL FEES TAKEN ON MARKET VALUE, INCOME, AND ACTIVITY. IF YOU DO NOT UNDERSTAND A QUESTION TYPE A "?".

(For some questions, a ? response will lead to more explanation)

DO YOU WISH TO SELECT A SPECIFIC GROUP OF ACCOUNTS?
?

YOU MAY SELECT ACCOUNTS BY *CLASS* AND/, OR *MARKET VALUE*
(CLASS refers to INB's classification of accounts)

DO YOU WISH TO SELECT A SPECIFIC GROUP OF ACCOUNTS?
N

WHAT IS THE ACCOUNT FILE NAME TO BE USED FOR THIS RUN?
SIM/L ← This is a library data file containing information on a sample of personal trust accounts. In INB'S system, they are accounts from classes 2, 3 and 4.

AT APPROXIMATELY WHAT DATE WERE THE ACCOUNTS VALUED ON?
1/75 ← This information is not used by the program. The question was included in order to get identifying information onto this output.

WHAT WAS THE DOW JONES MARKET LEVEL AT THAT TIME?
630

SPECIFY THE DOW FOR THIS SIMULATION
750

} With these questions, the program obtains the information needed to translate from the market values in the account file to the market values to be used in calculating fees.

WHAT IS THE COMMON TRUST FUND MINIMUM?
200 ← The minimum fee for accounts invested exclusively in common trust funds.

WHAT IS THE COMMON TRUST FUND DISCOUNT? (EXPRESS AS A DECIMAL .35=35%).
.35 ← The discount (from regular fees) for such accounts

USE EXISTING INCOME?
N ← The user can either use the past income values (from the account file) or else specify that income is a certain percentage of market value.

SPECIFY INCOME YIELD ON MARKET VALUE AS A DECIMAL
.045 ← Here the user specifies 4.5%

DO YOU WANT TO USE AN EXISTING FEE SCHEDULE?
?

A FEE SCHEDULE CAN BE PRODUCED FOR FUTURE USE BY ANSWERING NO TO THIS QUESTION.

---

*In this protocol, the actual dialog is shown in typeface, with the parts that were typeped by the user underlined to distinguish them from the parts that were printed by the computer. Explanatory comments have been added in handwriting.

```
DO YOU WANT TO USE AN EXISTING FEE SCHEDULE?
N ← The user will define a fee schedule, not use an existing one.

SPECIFY MINIMUM FEE PER ACCOUNT
500 ← Minimum fee for accounts not invested exclusively
      in common trust funds.
DO YOU WISH TO CHARGE A FEE ON THE MARKET VALUE?
?

YOU MAY SPECIFY UP TO 8 LEVELS FOR WHICH YOU WILL
 CHARGE SPECIFIC FEES BY GIVING DOLLAR AMOUNT BREAKS FOR EACH  LEVEL EXC
EPT THE LAST.  FOR EXAMPLE, YOU SPECIFY 3 LEVELS.  THE COMPUTER THAN ASK
S:  MARKET VALUE FOR LEVEL 1?
LEVEL 2?

IF YOU HAD SPECIFIED, SAY,
LEVEL 1 -50,000
LEVEL 2 - 100,000
THE PROGRAM WOULD  CONSIDER ALL ACCOUNTS WITH HOLDINGS VALUED
 BELOW 50,000 AS LEVEL 1 AND ACCOUNTS 50,000-100,000
AS LEVEL 2  AND ACCOUNTS OVER 100,000 AS LEVEL 3.
 NOTE THAT YOU DO NOT SUPPLY THE LAST LEVEL.  THE PROGRAM
AUTOMATICALLY ASSIGNS VALUES ABOVE YOUR LAST MARKET VALUE
IN THIS CASE, LEVEL 3.  YOU MAY SPECIFY UP TO 7 MARKET
VALUES FOR A TOTAL OF 8 LEVELS TO BE USED FOR MARKET FEES.
DO YOU WISH TO CHARGE A FEE ON THE MARKET VALUE?
Y

NUMBER OF LEVELS?
4

UPPER BOUND MARKET VALUE FOR LEVEL   1
200000

UPPER BOUND MARKET VALUE FOR LEVEL   2
500000

UPPER BOUND MARKET VALUE FOR LEVEL   3
1000000

FEE TO CHARGE AT LEVEL  1
.005

FEE TO CHARGE AT LEVEL  2
.003

FEE TO CHARGE AT LEVEL  3
.002

FEE TO CHARGE AT LEVEL  4
.001


YOUR SCHEDULE OF MARKET FEES NOW READS:

 .00500 TIMES AMOUNTS UP TO $  200000.00  (LEVEL 1)
 .00300 ON $  200000.00 TO $  500000.00
 .00200 ON $  500000.00 TO $ 1000000.00
 .00100 OVER $ 1000000.00
IS THIS CORRECT?
Y
```

The user specifies 4 levels and gives breaks between levels.

IMPORTANT NOTE: The program requires the user to give the upper bounds (for all but the last level). The common way of describing fee schedules (and the one used in the INB (A) case) gives the step size between levels instead.

The user gives the fees to be charged at each level.

Verification of the market fees.

In the terminology of the (A) case, the schedule being defined here for market fees would instead be described:

| | |
|---|---|
| 5/1000 | 200,000 |
| 3/1000 | 300,000 |
| 2/1000 | 500,000 |
| 1/1000 | Balance |

This line reads: $3 per $1000 for the next $300,000 (that is, for amounts between $200,000 and $500,000)

```
WANT INCOME FEE?
?

DO YOU WANT TO CHARGE A FEE ON THE INCOME GENERATED BY THE ACCOUNT?
Y

NUMBER OF INCOME LEVELS?
?

YOU MAY SPECIFY FROM 1 TO 8 LEVELS AT WHICH INCOME WILL BE
TAKEN.  A FINAL INCOME LEVEL WILL BE ALL THE AMOUNTS
ABOVE THE LAST LEVEL YOU SPECIFY

NUMBER OF INCOME LEVELS?
1

FEE TO CHARGE AT LEVEL  1
.05
```

The program allows up to 7 income breaks. Here, the user wants the same fraction, regardless of income level.

```
YOUR SCHEDULE OF INCOME FEES NOW READS:
 .05000 TIMES THE ENTIRE AMOUNT
IS THIS CORRECT?
Y
```

Verification of income fees

```
DO YOU WANT AN ACTIVITY CHARGE?
?

YOU WILL BE ABLE TO CHARGE FOR UP TO 5 ACTIVITIES
YOU GET 1 MARKET LEVEL BREAK FOR EACH ACTIVITY.  YOU
MUST THEN SPECIFY HOW MANY ACTIVITIES TO SUPPLY FREE TO
ACCOUNTS ABOVE THE MARKET LEVEL, AND HOW MANY TO GIVE
AWAY FREE BELOW THE MARKET LEVEL BREAK
DO YOU WANT AN ACTIVITY CHARGE?
Y

WHICH ACTIVITIES WILL BE CHARGED?
?

LIST ON 1 LINE THE ACTIVITIES YOU WISH TO CHARGE

 1  DIV COLLEC
 2  REG BOND I
 3  COUPON I
 4  FIXED FEE
 5  NOTE I
 6  RENT INCOM
 8  CNSLT ACCT
 9  OWN  NAME
10  DIRECTED
11  REVIEWS
12  CTS ONLY
13  N-CSH DEL
14  DP GEN DEL
15  INVST CERT
16  SECUR PUR
17  ASSET ACQ
18  WITHD CERT
19  SECUR SALE
20  ASSET DISP
21  PRIN CSH R
22  CASH TRANS
23  INC DISTRB
24  BILL PAYNG
25  FEE COLLEC
26  STATEMENT
27  PREP 1041
28  TAX LETTER
29  PPS PCSH R
30  PPS BEN PY
31  PPS RTN PY
32  PPS RTN CN
33  PPS MISC P
34  DP CSH TRN
35  ISSUES
DO YOU WANT AN ACTIVITY CHARGE?
Y
```

The activities (including on-off conditions) are explained in Exhibit 1.

```
WHICH ACTIVITIES WILL BE CHARGED?
8,26

PRICE FOR CNSLT ACCT?
150

PRICE FOR STATEMENT ?
50


MARKET LEVEL FOR ACTIVITY  8?
0

# OF ACTIVITIES TO GIVE BELOW THIS LEVEL?
0

ACTIVITIES FREE ABOVE THIS LEVEL?
0


MARKET LEVEL FOR ACTIVITY 26?
0

# OF ACTIVITIES TO GIVE BELOW THIS LEVEL?
4

ACTIVITIES FREE ABOVE THIS LEVEL?
4


YOUR ACTIVITY FEE SCHEDULE NOW LOOKS LIKE THIS:

   ACTIVITY   PRICE      MARKET       NO FREE       NO FREE
                         LEVEL        FOR A/C"S     FOR A/C"S
                                      BELOW BREAK   ABOVE BREAK

-----------------------------------------------------------
   8          150.00       0            0             0
  26           50.00       0            4             4
IS THIS CORRECT?
Y

SPECIFY A FILE NAME UP TO 5 CHARACTERS IN LENGTH  FOR THIS FEE SCHEDULE.
INBA

YOUR FEE SCHEDULE INBA  IS NOW READY TO RUN WITH  ACCOUNT FILE SIM
TODAYS"S DATE 13-Oct-78
ACCOUNT FILE USED: SIM
FEE SCHEDULE INBA
DO YOU WANT TO DISPLAY THE FEE SCHEDULE?
N
```

Handwritten annotations:

- (beside PRICE FOR CNSLT ACCT?) Consultation is an ON/OFF condition
- (beside activity 8 prompts) Consultation will incur a charge, regardless of market level
- (beside activity 26 prompts) Four free statements regardless of market level.
- (above fee schedule) Verification of activity fees.
- (beside INBA) ← The program will save the fee schedule definition.
- (beside N) ← The program offers to display the fee schedule.

The program applies the schedule to the accounts in the data file & prints a summary of the results:

| CLASS | NUMBER OF ACCOUNTS | MARKET FEES TAKEN | INCOME FEES TAKEN | ACTIVITY FEES TAKEN | MINIMUM FEES TAKEN | TOTAL FEES TAKEN |
|---|---|---|---|---|---|---|
| 0 | 0. | 0.00 | 0.00 | 0.00 | 0.00 | 0.00 |
| 1 | 0. | 0.00 | 0.00 | 0.00 | 0.00 | 0.00 |
| 2 | 82. | 38159.22 | 21722.20 | 17900.00 | 14290.00 | 92071.42 |
| 3 | 130. | 77539.37 | 65991.36 | 20100.00 | 21490.00 | 185120.72 |
| 4 | 62. | 34583.07 | 25062.28 | 13550.00 | 13000.00 | 86195.35 |
| 5 | 0. | 0.00 | 0.00 | 0.00 | 0.00 | 0.00 |
| 6 | 0. | 0.00 | 0.00 | 0.00 | 0.00 | 0.00 |
| 7 | 0. | 0.00 | 0.00 | 0.00 | 0.00 | 0.00 |
| 8 | 0. | 0.00 | 0.00 | 0.00 | 0.00 | 0.00 |
| 9 | 0. | 0.00 | 0.00 | 0.00 | 0.00 | 0.00 |
| | 274. | 150281.66 | 112775.83 | 51550.00 | 48780.00 | 363387.50 |

ACTIVITIES

| CLASS | 8 | 26 | | | | TOTAL |
|---|---|---|---|---|---|---|
| 0 | 0.00 | 0.00 | 0.00 | 0.00 | 0.00 | 0.00 |
| 1 | 0.00 | 0.00 | 0.00 | 0.00 | 0.00 | 0.00 |
| 2 | 2850.00 | 15050.00 | 0.00 | 0.00 | 0.00 | 17900.00 |
| 3 | 5250.00 | 14850.00 | 0.00 | 0.00 | 0.00 | 20100.00 |
| 4 | 4350.00 | 9200.00 | 0.00 | 0.00 | 0.00 | 13550.00 |
| 5 | 0.00 | 0.00 | 0.00 | 0.00 | 0.00 | 0.00 |
| 6 | 0.00 | 0.00 | 0.00 | 0.00 | 0.00 | 0.00 |
| 7 | 0.00 | 0.00 | 0.00 | 0.00 | 0.00 | 0.00 |
| 8 | 0.00 | 0.00 | 0.00 | 0.00 | 0.00 | 0.00 |
| 9 | 0.00 | 0.00 | 0.00 | 0.00 | 0.00 | 0.00 |
| TOTAL | 12450.00 | 39100.00 | 0.00 | 0.00 | 0.00 | 51550.00 |

EXIT ← The program then exits to the monitor

.R INB ← The user requests a second run...

THIS IS A PROGRAM WHICH SIMULATES THE TAKING OF FEES BY THE
INDUSTRIAL NATI^O and interrupts the introduction

DO YOU WISH TO SELECT A SPECIFIC GROUP OF ACCOUNTS?
N

WHAT IS THE ACCOUNT FILE NAME TO BE USED FOR THIS RUN?
SIM/L ← The same account file used above

AT APPROXIMATELY WHAT DATE WERE THE ACCOUNTS VALUED ON?
1/75

WHAT WAS THE DOW JONES MARKET LEVEL AT THAT TIME?
630

SPECIFY THE DOW FOR THIS SIMULATION
600 ← The second run will use a different value for the Dow.

WHAT IS THE COMMON TRUST FUND MINIMUM?
200

WHAT IS THE COMMON TRUST FUND DISCOUNT? (EXPRESS
AS A DECIMAL .35=35%).
.35

USE EXISTING INCOME?
N

SPECIFY INCOME YIELD ON MARKET VALUE AS A DECIMAL
.055 ← The user also changes the income assumption.

DO YOU WANT TO USE AN EXISTING FEE SCHEDULE?
Y

WHAT IS THE FILE NAME FOR THE EXISTING SCHEDULE?
INBA

The user requests the fee schedule that was defined and saved above

DO YOU WANT TO DISPLAY THE FEES?
N

The program applies the fee schedule to the accounts under the new market and income assumptions.

| CLASS | NUMBER OF ACCOUNTS | MARKET FEES TAKEN | INCOME FEES TAKEN | ACTIVITY FEES TAKEN | MINIMUM FEES TAKEN | TOTAL FEES TAKEN |
|---|---|---|---|---|---|---|
| 0 | 0. | 0.00 | 0.00 | 0.00 | 0.00 | 0.00 |
| 1 | 0. | 0.00 | 0.00 | 0.00 | 0.00 | 0.00 |
| 2 | 82. | 31761.18 | 21031.82 | 17550.00 | 15290.00 | 85633.00 |
| 3 | 130. | 64138.35 | 64175.24 | 20100.00 | 22490.00 | 170903.59 |
| 4 | 62. | 28937.53 | 24175.68 | 13050.00 | 14500.00 | 80663.21 |
| 5 | 0. | 0.00 | 0.00 | 0.00 | 0.00 | 0.00 |
| 6 | 0. | 0.00 | 0.00 | 0.00 | 0.00 | 0.00 |
| 7 | 0. | 0.00 | 0.00 | 0.00 | 0.00 | 0.00 |
| 8 | 0. | 0.00 | 0.00 | 0.00 | 0.00 | 0.00 |
| 9 | 0. | 0.00 | 0.00 | 0.00 | 0.00 | 0.00 |
| | 274. | 124837.06 | 109382.74 | 50700.00 | 52280.00 | 337199.80 |

ACTIVITIES

| CLASS | 8 | 26 | | | | TOTAL |
|---|---|---|---|---|---|---|
| 0 | 0.00 | 0.00 | 0.00 | 0.00 | 0.00 | 0.00 |
| 1 | 0.00 | 0.00 | 0.00 | 0.00 | 0.00 | 0.00 |
| 2 | 2850.00 | 14700.00 | 0.00 | 0.00 | 0.00 | 17550.00 |
| 3 | 5250.00 | 14850.00 | 0.00 | 0.00 | 0.00 | 20100.00 |
| 4 | 4050.00 | 9000.00 | 0.00 | 0.00 | 0.00 | 13050.00 |
| 5 | 0.00 | 0.00 | 0.00 | 0.00 | 0.00 | 0.00 |
| 6 | 0.00 | 0.00 | 0.00 | 0.00 | 0.00 | 0.00 |
| 7 | 0.00 | 0.00 | 0.00 | 0.00 | 0.00 | 0.00 |
| 8 | 0.00 | 0.00 | 0.00 | 0.00 | 0.00 | 0.00 |
| 9 | 0.00 | 0.00 | 0.00 | 0.00 | 0.00 | 0.00 |
| TOTAL | 12150.00 | 38550.00 | 0.00 | 0.00 | 0.00 | 50700.00 |

EXIT

## case 4.4

# Xerox Corporation—the 9200

In September 1974, Xerox Corporation formally entered a new segment of the copier and duplicator market by introducing its model 9200, a powerful integrated duplicating system combining functions normally performed by several different machines. Before the formal introduction, Xerox had placed more than 20 test models of the machine in the Chicago area (on special pre-introduction pricing schedules). After the introduction, Xerox faced the problems of maintaining these pilot accounts (once they were converted to the regular pricing schedule) and of generating more accounts. These tasks were complicated by the fact that, at first analysis, the Xerox pricing schedule seemed to imply a higher per copy cost than could be obtained with competing equipment, such as the AM 4250 from Addressograph-Multigraph.

### Company background

Xerox Corporation began in Rochester, New York, in 1906 as the Haloid Company, a manufacturer and marketer of sensitized photographic paper. Shortly after World War II the company acquired the rights to the basic patents for xerography, a new electrostatic-photographic copying process developed by Chester Carlson. It took until 1960 to incorporate that process successfully into the Xerox 914, the first fully automatic dry copier and the basis for Xerox's remarkable growth. In 1959 the firm's revenues were less than $35 million, while in 1974 they reached a record of $3.58 billion (with $331 million in profits).

In 1974 Xerox was selling copy/duplicators with many advanced features. Various of their machines could collate automatically, copy on both sides of the paper, or copy color, for example. In addition, Xerox had expanded its operations internationally and had entered several new product areas, such as electronic typewriters, facsimile devices (equipment for transmitting documents over telephone lines), xeroradiographic equipment (for printing X-ray pictures on paper rather than film), textbooks, and other learning materials. Most of the Xerox products had been developed internally by what in 1974 was called the Business and Product Development Group. That group, which was responsible for developing the 9200, will be discussed in more detail below.

### The reproduction market

The entire reproduction market is divided into three segments: copying, copying/duplicating, and duplicating. In those market segments individual jobs are described by the number of originals per job, by run length (or number of copies per original), and by total impressions or copies per job (which is the product of the two previous measures). The three market segments are defined in terms of these measures and in terms of monthly volume (total number of copies made).

The copying market segment includes monthly volumes of up to 25,000 copies and run lengths on the order of 10 or less. Copying machines are designed for casual secretarial use when a few copies must be made quickly and conveniently. These machines do not require a skilled operator and their speed generally ranges from 10 to 15 copies per minute.

In contrast, duplicating systems operate at speeds up to 150 copies per minute and generally produce superior copy quality. In the past, duplicating has most often been accomplished by offset lithography, which uses a metal, plastic, or paper plate (or master) prepared from the original document. The master is placed on an offset press which then inks the master, transfers the image from the master to a roll or "blanket," and then transfers the image again from the roll to paper; the inking and transfer process then repeats. Duplicating systems can handle monthly volumes of up to 250,000 copies per one-shift operation, depending on job complexity; they are generally used for runs of more than 25 copies per original. Such systems require skilled operators; they are found in large in-house printing centers in companies and in commercial printing establishments.

Copy/duplicating lies between the other two market segments and involves speeds of roughly 40 to 60 copies per minute and monthly volumes between 20,000 and 75,000 impressions. Copy/duplicators (or high-speed copiers) are large console-type machines; they are usually located so as to serve a large number of offices and they may be attended by semi-skilled operators.

In 1974, Xerox's greatest strength lay in the copying and copy-duplicating market segments, which amounted to 30 billion impressions annually in the United States. With the 9200, Xerox expanded further into the duplicating market segment, estimated at perhaps 300 billion impressions per year. At the time, that market segment was dominated by A. B. Dick Company and Addressograph-Multigraph.

### The 9200

The primary marketing targets for the Xerox 9200 were the more than 50,000 central reproduction departments (or CRDs) found in most large companies and government agencies. The duplicating department at Harvard Business School is an example of a CRD; that department is described in the appendix of this case.

The 9200 was an integrated system, designed to do a job that was generally done piecemeal by several different machines. According to Raymond A. Hay, then an executive vice president of Xerox, "We're not replacing an offset printing press but [instead we're replacing all the equipment for] an entire printing process with one complete integrated reproduction center."[1] The 9200 was intended to replace offset presses, copiers, spirit duplicators, machines for preparing masters and also either manual or automatic collating systems.

In using the 9200, the operator placed the original documents in the ADH (automatic document handler) and then proceeded to set the controls for the job; the machine offered a wide variety of control options and Xerox people referred to setting the controls as "programming" the job. Suppose, for example, that a job required 300 copies of a 35-page document. The 9200 automatically would take one original at a time and, for the first pass, make 25 copies of each of the 35 pages. The machine would collate these copies automatically (as it made them) in a set of 25 sorter bins at the output end of the machine. Once the first 25 copies had been made, the machine would automatically cycle through the originals again, filling a second set of 25 bins. In the meantime, the operator would be emptying the first set of bins, which contained the first 25 complete copies of the document. When the machine had finished filling the second tier of bins, it would shine a light down the first row of bins. If the light beam reached a sensor at the opposite end of the row, the 9200 would know that the bins had been emptied and it would proceed to fill those bins with the 51st through 75th copies while the operator took copies 26 through 50 from the second set of bins. On the other hand, if the machine sensed that the first tier of bins was not empty, it would wait for the operator to finish emptying those bins before proceeding to make more copies. The process would continue until the machine had made the requested number of copies. The capability of the machine to continue to make copies (in batches of 25 complete copies of the document) without ever having to stop, unless the operator had not emptied the sorter bins, was called "limitless sorting" or "infinite collating capacity."

At every step of the duplicating process, internal logic in the 9200 would keep track of each piece of paper in the machine. If the machine jammed at some point in duplicating the job, the machine would stop and wait for a human operator to clear the jam. (Thus, the operator did not need to attend the machine all the time but could instead do other jobs, knowing that the machine would stop without creating a catastrophe if something went wrong). Once the human operator had cleared the jam, the 9200 would recycle automatically through the original document, if necessary, to reach

[1] "Xerox Unveils its 'most important product,' " *Business Week*, June 29, 1974.

the point at which it had lost copies during the jam; it would then proceed to replace any copies which had been lost. It would continue from that point to make copies and sort them into the appropriate bins.

Thus, design features of the 9200 included automatic document handling (of up to 50 originals at a time) and limitless sorting (with the two-tiered collator). In addition, the machine could reduce the size of the images or could automatically switch between a normal bin for paper and a reserve bin. It could handle a wide range of paper types without special adjustment. The quality of the copies it produced was considered comparable to that of offset lithography. The system could print and sort up to 120 pages per minute (7200 impressions per hour); it did not require preparation of masters, as did offset presses, but instead worked directly from original documents and made copies on plain paper.

In 1974 the 9200 was available only under a leasing plan, although Xerox was expected to announce a purchase price in 1976. For the leasing arrangement, meters were attached to the 9200 to record the number of originals used and the number of copies per original. The price schedule was based on these meter readings, as shown in Exhibit 1. As suggested by the sample fee calculations in the exhibit, longer run-length jobs had a lower cost per impression, but total operating cost to the customer depended on job mix in a given month.

## The AM 4250

In considering the value of a 9200 to a potential customer, it was important for Xerox managers to consider the performance characteristics of competing systems. These competitors were offset machines which made masters of the pages of the original document and then printed from those masters. The Addressograph-Multigraph Corporation's TCS 4250 was considered one of the chief competitors for the 9200. The 4250 included a mechanism for feeding the originals automatically, another component which made the plates or masters (and which had a reduction capability), an offset duplicator with a rated speed of 10,400 impressions per hour, and an on-line collator. These modules were grouped in a horseshoe arrangement to allow work to flow efficiently from one stage to the next. The platemaker, duplicator, and collator could be operated as a single unit or could be detached and operated separately.

The document handler on the 4250 automatically fed originals to the platemaker which could produce masters at the rate of 17 per minute. (In practice, however, the platemaker usually operated at a much slower speed because it was constrained by the capacity of the offset duplicator to make the required number of copies from each master.) The duplicator could print up to 173 impressions per minute from a single master, but it required an 8-

**EXHIBIT 1**
Price schedule for the 9200

*Installation:* $305
($305 is also charged for removing the machine.)

*Copying* (run lengths of less than 20):
1–5 copies/original: $.0425 (each)
6–19 copies/original: $.0125 (each for copies after the fifth)

*Duplicating* (run lengths of 20 or more):
Each original: $0.16
1–100,000 impressions/month $.005 each
100,000+ impressions/month $.004 each

*Minimum Charges:*
Minimum charges apply to duplicating work only.
First full calendar month after installation: $800
Second full calendar month after installation: $1,000
Each month thereafter: $1,200

*Rebates:*
A 10 percent rebate on duplicating charges is given at the end of each full year of operation, although the rebate cannot reduce the duplicating charge below the monthly minimum.

*Sample Fee Calculations:*
*Job #1:* 10 originals, 19 copies/original

5 × 10 × $.0425 = $2.125
14 × 10 × $.0125 = 1.750
$3.875 total cost of job

$3.875/190 = $.020 cost per impression

*Job #2:* 10 originals, 40 copies/original

10 × $.160 = $1.60
400 × $.004 = 1.60 (assuming more than 100,000 monthly impressions)
$3.20 total cost of job

$3.20/400 = $.008 cost per impression

to 10-second delay between masters for automatic cleaning of the blanket (printing roll). The 4250s automatic collator had 104 sorter bins.

As an example, consider the flow of a job which required 300 copies of a 35-page document. The originals would be put into the document feeder and the appropriate paper would be placed in the paper feeder (which could hold up to 5,000 sheets). The operator might then make a trial run or two to adjust the ink balance and to adjust the machine to handle the particular type of paper chosen. The actual production run would then start. The 4250 would take the first original and would make a master from it. It would then put the master on the offset press and make 104 copies of it, putting one copy into each of the 104 sorter bins. It would then go on to the next page, making a master and printing and sorting 104 copies. Between pages the printing roll would be cleaned (automatically). Once the 104 copies of all 35 pages had been made, the 4250 would have to be stopped (by the operator, not automatically) while the sorter bins were emptied (by the operator). It could next cycle through the document again, making and sorting the additional 104 copies and then 92 copies needed to bring the total to the desired 300. Throughout this process, the skilled operator would have to attend the machine, watching the ink balance and also watching for paper jams. The machine did not stop automatically if a jam occurred, and if the operator didn't stop the machine promptly after a jam, a serious mess would often result.

### Comparing the Xerox 9200 and the AM 4250

In general, the AM 4250 and the Xerox 9200 had somewhat similar design capabilities and, moreover, they were aimed at the same market. Yet, excluding labor costs, the 4250 seemed from the lease schedule (see Exhibit 2) to have a lower cost per copy. (In addition, rental charges for the first three months after installation of a 4250 could count as equity if the customer decided to purchase the system.)

The task of explaining what they thought was a definite superiority of the 9200 was complicated for the Xerox salespeople by the use of productivity matrices, a tool which the Xerox people themselves had introduced earlier for comparing machines. Productivity matrices were tables with run lengths listed along one side and with numbers of originals per job given in the other direction. In the cells of the matrix were the number of impressions per hour and/or costs of a particular machine operating at full efficiency. Even though they showed the 9200 as superior to the 4250 for some job characteristics, these tables had the problem that they did not consider set-up times and costs, level of operator attention required, repair times, and other measures that Xerox felt should be considered in evaluating the 9200.

A brochure used to publicize the 9200 at a trade show of IPMA (the In-Plant Printing Managers Association) showed the different marketing ap-

**EXHIBIT 2**
Rental price schedule for the AM4250

The charges listed below include supplies (not paper) and services.

Each original: $.05

1–110,000 impressions per month: $.01 each

Over 110,000 impressions per month: $.003 each

Minimum fees: $700 for the first full month after installation
$900 for the second full month
$1,100 for the third and following months

*Sample Fee Calculations:*

10 originals, 40 copies/original

| | | | |
|---|---|---|---|
| 10 × $.05 | = | $.50 | (assuming more than 110,000 impressions per month) |
| 400 × $.003 | = | 1.20 | |
| | | $1.70 | total cost of job |

$1.70/400 = $.00425 cost per impression

proach which Xerox managers thought appropriate for the 9200. That brochure listed faster job turnaround, automatic paper-changing, and limitless sorting as some of the important features of the new machine. The brochure then suggested that productivity of the 9200 (or of a competing machine) would be measured in different ways by different CRDs; jobs per month, copies per hour, actual job turnaround time, and output per operator were some of the measures which it suggested might be used. It stated that only a detailed study of an individual CRD could determine the value of a 9200 to that particular shop. The brochure did, however, stress one particular measure of productivity above others: that was *job turnaround* (or the total elapsed time between when a job arrived in a CRD and when it was completely finished and ready for delivery to the customer). The brochure suggested that job turnaround could be measured by the percentage of jobs whose turnaround time was less than various intervals—for example, the percentage of jobs finished in less than four hours and the percentage finished in under eight hours; clearly, as the brochure stated, these measures of productivity depend strongly on the particular job characteristics of an individual shop.

A study of the 9200 by Maxwell Evarts of the Wall Street firm of Dominick and Dominick gave further insights into both the strengths of the 9200 and the difficulty of communicating the machine's true powers.[2] Evarts explained

[2] Maxwell Evarts, *Xerox: The 9200 and the Offset Market,* May 19, 1975.

that he and others had easily understood that the 9200 had considerable advantages for shorter-run lengths, for which the overhead costs in the offset process of making masters and setting up the jobs were particularly significant. In an earlier report he had concluded that 9200's advantage was limited to shorter-run lengths but, he explained, he had changed his mind. The problem, he felt, was that his earlier analysis had been based on an ideal world of machines operating at full efficiency and without disruptions; the real world of duplicating work was much different. In the real world he found that adjustments for ink flow and paper weight were a constant harassment for the offset operator. In addition, accessory equipment (such as the document feeder and the platemaker) was not fully reliable; Evarts claimed to have seen a 4250 document feeder work correctly only once. Finally, the 4250 lacked fail-safe devices and required constant operator attention; the operator had to watch constantly for ink balance and paper jams. Thus, Evarts concluded that the original comparison of costs between the 9200 and the 4250 had ignored the true labor costs with the two machines; the 4250 required constant attention of a skilled operator, while the 9200 required only partial attention of a considerably less skilled operator and left significant chunks of operator time free for other work. Further, he felt that the infinite collating capacity of the 9200 (the two-tiered sorter) made that machine better than the 4250 for even relatively long run lengths.

Evarts was extremely encouraged about the future of the 9200. He identified approximately 45,000 in-house CRDs which had more than one offset machine and which were not occupied mainly with very long run lengths (the printing of special forms) as the hard-core target market for the 9200. The 1974 volume in that market was about 210 billion copies; the estimated growth rate of 10 percent per year would increase volume to 320 billion impressions by 1980. Evarts concluded that the 9200 was so vastly superior for that target market that it would have an 85 percent share by 1980.

The Dominick and Dominick study also highlighted some of the problems of selling the 9200. Evarts himself had clearly and admittedly not understood the potential of the 9200 at first. He suggested that it was crucial to educate potential customers for the 9200 to their true full duplicating costs; because the 9200 would reduce indirect labor and general overhead significantly, those savings had to be considered in addition to the higher machine cost per copy. Evarts suggested that the sales force for the 9200 would require extensive training.

People at Xerox knew that selling the 9200 would also be complicated by the fact that Addressograph-Multigraph and A. B. Dick had been in the offset field for a long time and had established relationships with their customers. Xerox people believed that there was considerable loyalty among potential customers to either AM or A. B. Dick; Xerox would have to overcome such loyalties in order to place their 9200s with these customers. As Carl Lehr, one of the planners working on the 9200, noted, centralized reproduction was a totally new area for Xerox. "We are trying to break into a very traditional market, characterized by great loyalty to the existing suppliers. A. B. Dick and Addressograph-Multigraph are very strong. We believe we have a superior product, but it will be difficult to penetrate this traditionally labor-intensive area."

## Division of responsibilities at Xerox

The Business and Product Development Group at Xerox (or B&PDG for short) was involved in long-range planning and in managing major new products. B&PDG worked with new products from the conception stage through the formal national introduction of the product. The group consisted of several hundred people plus the engineering staff. Engineering, which had several thousand employees, was a subdivision of B&PDG but functioned relatively independently. The engineering offices and the other B&PDG offices were in different locations in the Rochester area.

The Information Systems Group (ISG), on the other hand, was responsible for marketing, sales, manufacturing, and service of established products. ISG had roughly 20,000 employees. The group assumed responsibility for new products at the time of their national introduction (although during the period just before and just after a national introduction ISG and B&PDG had to coordinate work on new products). ISG included the regular salespeople and also the Xerox Consulting Service, an internal consulting group which served the sales staff. The consultants were technically oriented individuals who might be called on by the salespeople to help in selling to large, important accounts.

## The future of the 9200—and the use of a model

Xerox's entry into a new market with the 9200 thus raised problems in understanding and in communicating to potential customers the strengths of the product. In part for that reason, Dave Bliss, who in 1974 was with B&PDG and in charge of the 9200 product planning for that group, had authorized Carl Lehr of B&PDG to work on the development of a computerized model of the 9200 and its work environment. Lehr had been a member of the engineering group at the company before making the highly unusual move "downtown" to B&PDG. If he were to develop a model, he would work closely with the Management Science Department of Xerox, an interval service unit which was in yet another division (the Information Services Division). Accordingly, Lehr began to work with Glenn Alexander, a management science consultant with Xerox, who had been trained in operations research at Stanford and had then gained some experience in that field in the Navy before joining Xerox. Although Xerox managers were already using computer models to aid in marketing their high-speed copiers, Alexander and Lehr felt that a more complete and flexible model of the entire printing operation in a CRD would be necessary for the 9200.

Actually, Bliss and Lehr felt that a model of the 9200 and of any successor products could fulfill three different functions. First, it could serve as a communication device, enabling engineering and marketing to understand and discuss the trade-offs involved in designing and selling a new product. Second, a model could help Xerox personnel understand thoroughly the strengths of their products, thus aiding in pricing and other decisions. Finally, a model could be used to help customers to understand their workloads and to demonstrate to those customers the capabilities of the Xerox products.

Frank Steenburgh, the ISG product manager, commented that the 9200 required a change from Xerox's previous product approach. "The 9200 is a complete system, requiring a quantitative approach to marketing," he said. He explained that in the past it had been appropriate for the sales force to be product-oriented and simply to compare one product with another. For the 9200 the sales force would have to become systems-oriented and to consider the effect of the machine on an entire reproduction department. In addition, they would have to consider the effect of the 9200 on the particular workload and work environment of an individual CRD. Steenburgh and others were concerned about teaching the Xerox sales force to think in terms of systems; however, the sales consultants in the Xerox Consulting Service seemed well-suited for the quantitative approach.

In addition to helping with marketing, a model could help facilitate communication between marketing and engineering at Xerox. Especially because of the physical separation of these two functions within B&PDG, communication became critical. According to Bliss, "Marketing keeps saying, 'I want; I want.' Engineering says, "Okay, but it will cost.' " (And the costs would have to be measured both in money and in time for design and implementation.) Bliss felt that both the engineering staff and the other parts of B&PDG had to have a better understanding of the value of potential design features of the 9200 and of other future Xerox machines.

## APPENDIX

The duplicating department of the Harvard Business School provides an example of an in-plant print shop, or CRD. That facility consists of a front office and a back room. Six people staff the front office; they process orders, maintain files, and perform other administrative duties. Jobs sent to the duplicating department are first processed by the front office. They are then sent either to the back room or to an outside firm for duplicating.[3]

[3] Most CRDs use outside print shops to help manage the workload during periods of very high demand. The Harvard facility is unusual in that it regularly relies on outside printers for the bulk of its work.

**EXHIBIT 3**
Floor plan of the duplicating department

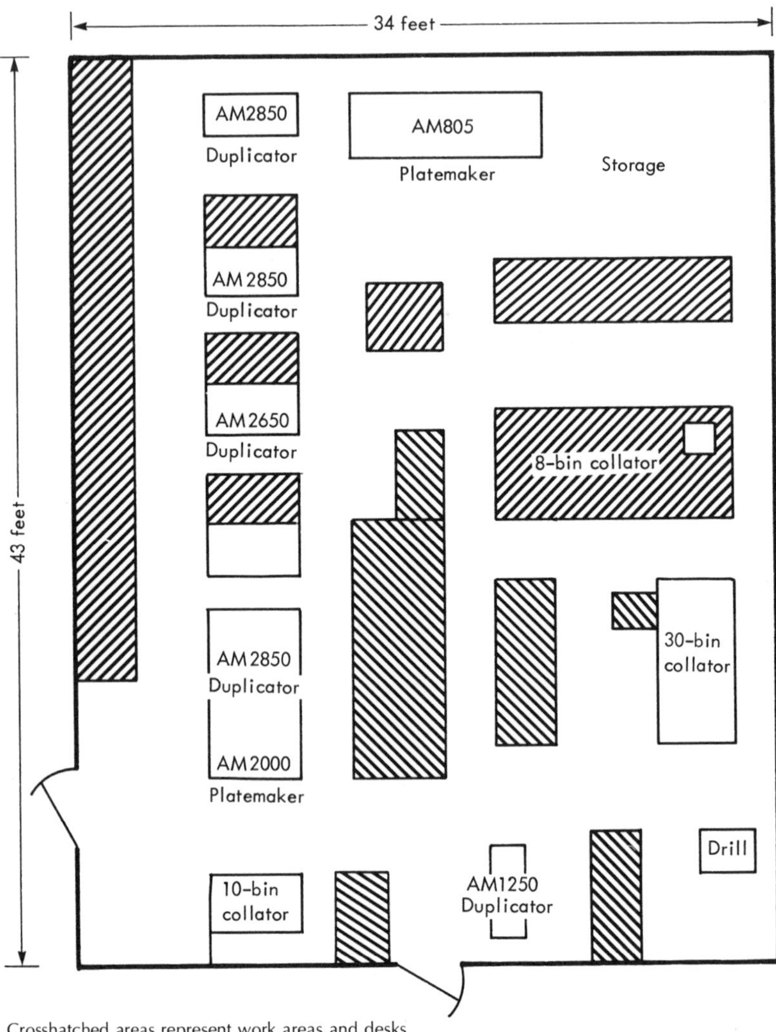


Crosshatched areas represent work areas and desks.

Exhibit 3 shows the layout of the back room of the duplicating department; 13 people work in that area. The flow for a typical job is from the front office to a platemaker to an offset duplicator to a collator to a stapler to a paper punch and then to distribution. More specifically, the order moves first to the electrostatic platemaker (AM805), where a paper plate or master is made for each original (enlarged or reduced if requested). The order then goes to one of four offset duplicators. Before the actual printing begins, the plate must be passed through a chemical solution. Two of the duplicating machines (the AM2850's) have automatic document feeders which pass the plates through the solution and onto the rotating cylinder for printing. Another duplicator (the AM2650) requires that the plates be passed manually through the solution and fed individually to the duplicator. The fourth machine is the slowest, since it requires that the plates be passed through the solution and then placed manually on the rotating cylinder. (However this machine does have greater flexibility than the others in working with different thicknesses of paper.) There is a fifth offset duplicator (an AM2850 with attached platemaker AM2000) which makes its own masters; that machine can also be used just for platemaking if the other electrostatic platemaker breaks down.

For duplex work (for printing on both sides of the paper) the operator must sort the plates into odd- and even-numbered pages. The operator first prints the odd-numbered pages, then turns the copies over and feeds them back into the machine for printing the even-numbered pages.

After duplicating, most documents are collated and stapled. The department has three collators: one with 8 bins, one with 10, and one with 30. The two larger collators have automatic staplers. On these collators, the bins each hold copies of one page of the document; they simultaneously feed one copy of each page to the human operator. The department also uses manual collating; for that process the different pages are placed in order on a table and a human collator picks up the pages for each copy of the document one at a time.

Finally, a large proportion of the copies are punched. A three-hole drill is used to punch approximately 300 sheets of paper at a time. (The duplicating department has experimented with pre-punched paper but found that it caused frequent jams in the multilith process.)

The duplicating department also has a Xerox high-speed copier which is used primarily for short-run, fast turnaround work. As a rule of thumb, run lengths of less than 20 are processed on the Xerox copier, which can produce up to 40 copies per minute.[4]

Exhibit 4 shows the jobs completed on each machine during the week of January 6, 1975. Exhibit 5 shows the distribution of those jobs by number of originals and by run length. The work flow into the duplicating department is highly irregular, with variations by hour, day, week, and month. In addition, productivity of the machines in the department varies because of such factors as paper jams, machine breakdowns, and the characteristics of the individual jobs. (For example, a job with six originals requiring 53 copies per original might take seven minutes to process, while a job with 53 originals requiring six copies per original would take considerably longer.)

---

[4] In addition, there are machines in other locations at the school for handling copying and copy/duplicating. Four Xerox machines perform that work.

**EXHIBIT 4**
Work completed in the duplicating department (week of January 6, 1975)

| | *Monday* | *Tuesday* | *Wednesday* | *Thursday* | *Friday* | *Total* |
|---|---|---|---|---|---|---|
| *Masters produced* | | | | | | |
| AM805 | 511 | 503 | 400 | 493 | 564 | 2,471 |
| AM2000 | 676 | 329 | 628 | 818 | 740 | 3,191 |
| Total | 1,187 | 832 | 1,028 | 1,311 | 1,304 | 5,662 |
| *Impressions printed* | | | | | | |
| AM2850 | 24,031 | 11,761 | 19,320 | 24,263 | 25,009 | 104,384 |
| AM1250 | 19,202 | 27,904 | 14,917 | 14,190 | 6,745 | 82,958 |
| AM2650 | 3,452* | 0* | 20,061 | 14,978 | 9,335 | 82,826 |
| AM2850 | 31,241 | 25,432 | 30,025 | 27,377 | 25,062 | 139,137 |
| AM2850 | 35,440 | 31,263 | 44,087 | 29,986 | 25,681 | 166,457 |
| Total | 113,366 | 96,360 | 128,410 | 110,794 | 91,832 | 540,762 |
| *Impressions collated* | | | | | | |
| 8-bin collator | 30,406 | 22,083 | 14,890 | 18,252 | 17,630 | 103,261 |
| 10-bin collator | 51,380 | 68,520 | 46,724 | 43,683 | 19,133 | 229,440 |
| 30-bin collator | 26,150* | 49,615 | 45,915 | 39,836 | 22,111 | 183,627 |
| Total | 107,936 | 140,218 | 107,529 | 101,771 | 58,874 | 516,328 |

* Machine required service.

**EXHIBIT 5**
Distribution of jobs (week of January 6, 1975)

| *Run length* | *Originals/Job* | | | | | | |
|---|---|---|---|---|---|---|---|
| | *1* | *2–5* | *6–10* | *11–20* | *21–50* | *51–100* | *101–200* |
| 1 | — | — | — | — | — | — | — |
| 2–5 | — | — | — | 1 | 1 | — | — |
| 6–10 | — | 2 | 1 | — | — | — | — |
| 11–20 | 2 | 2 | — | 4 | 7 | 1 | — |
| 21–50 | 36 | 86 | 76 | 102 | 100 | 5 | — |
| 51–100 | 39 | 42 | 30 | 28 | 24 | — | — |
| 101–200 | 34 | 20 | 11 | 22 | 17 | — | — |
| Over 200 | 29 | 20 | 9 | 5 | 5 | — | — |

chapter 5

# BASIC DATA ANALYSIS IN MODEL BUILDING

## O. INTRODUCTION

Some of the basic concepts of data analysis are so useful in model building that we now turn to consider the topic of analyzing data. This discussion is certainly not complete, for entire books and entire courses are devoted to one or another of the topics we consider in this chapter. On the other hand, this discussion does serve to introduce useful concepts and, moreover, suggests the main ways in which the tools of data analysis can be used in computer modeling.

In the first section of the chapter we consider basic summary measures for sets of data. Those measures are analogous to the summary measures for probability distributions that were discussed in Chapter 2 and, in many cases, have the same names we encountered earlier. The first section then proceeds to consider cross tabulation analysis, one of the simplest of the formal tools for data analysis and, perhaps as a result, one of the most useful. The section first introduces the basic process of cross tabulation analysis, along with the major summaries and outputs used with that technique. It then suggests the roles that cross tabulation can play in computer model design.

In the second section of this chapter we proceed to a quick review of regression analysis and econometrics. Again, the aim of the discussion is to show how these techniques fit into computer simulation modeling. The section introduces the basic idea of regression analysis, showing that that technique can usefully be considered as an extension of cross tabulation to be used in the frequent cases in which we have only limited data available for analysis. Similarly, it gives a very brief overview of the types of analysis that constitute econometrics. Finally, the section suggests how these additional techniques can fit into computer modeling.

## I. CROSS-TABULATION ANALYSIS

Many, many problems in business and other fields involve using whatever past data are available (or, at least, relatively easily obtainable) both to aid in *understanding* relationships and also to aid in *forecasting*. For example, we use past demand data to help forecast the demand for a particular product next week. Or, we use past information on the performance of a particular machine under different weather conditions and with different human operators in an attempt to understand why the machine is considerably more reliable on some days than it is on others. Because past data are often extremely informative, the basic tools of data analysis are potentially powerful ones. This section describes cross-tabulation analysis, which is a key tool in data analysis.

As an example, suppose that we are trying to understand the influences on the sales of newspapers at a stand in a busy part of a city; we would also like to forecast future sales. Suppose that we are fortunate and that we have the sales data for the past 50 weeks (or 350 days). In addition, suppose that the news dealer has had ample supplies of papers on those days so that stock-

**TABLE 5–1**
Past sales figures (numbers of papers)

| | | | | | | | | | | | | | |
|---|---|---|---|---|---|---|---|---|---|---|---|---|---|
| 178 | 235 | 236 | 218 | 209 | 177 | 261 | 214 | 228 | 188 | 241 | 233 | 192 | 302 |
| 229 | 214 | 251 | 225 | 188 | 172 | 311 | 193 | 206 | 207 | 221 | 212 | 212 | 287 |
| 197 | 211 | 272 | 200 | 235 | 184 | 255 | 198 | 211 | 226 | 233 | 256 | 155 | 269 |
| 204 | 248 | 259 | 223 | 250 | 187 | 286 | 190 | 193 | 211 | 308 | 208 | 191 | 323 |
| 194 | 201 | 235 | 253 | 184 | 203 | 276 | 171 | 174 | 234 | 234 | 197 | 181 | 315 |
| 203 | 230 | 231 | 212 | 250 | 225 | 286 | 137 | 241 | 225 | 207 | 241 | 237 | 260 |
| 229 | 220 | 225 | 265 | 250 | 197 | 260 | 254 | 205 | 244 | 203 | 282 | 227 | 374 |
| 245 | 252 | 242 | 248 | 259 | 152 | 350 | 196 | 232 | 199 | 249 | 235 | 226 | 274 |
| 218 | 204 | 241 | 201 | 265 | 226 | 321 | 176 | 168 | 176 | 195 | 260 | 208 | 304 |
| 208 | 193 | 217 | 213 | 255 | 233 | 311 | 199 | 261 | 200 | 206 | 276 | 196 | 277 |
| 206 | 209 | 227 | 249 | 292 | 179 | 269 | 254 | 207 | 227 | 194 | 258 | 176 | 273 |
| 162 | 213 | 261 | 229 | 220 | 179 | 310 | 180 | 173 | 263 | 240 | 288 | 232 | 325 |
| 223 | 166 | 219 | 211 | 267 | 213 | 302 | 241 | 255 | 272 | 249 | 202 | 199 | 320 |
| 208 | 234 | 250 | 247 | 236 | 180 | 300 | 209 | 164 | 221 | 232 | 222 | 218 | 319 |
| 152 | 196 | 273 | 210 | 270 | 199 | 291 | 202 | 166 | 259 | 232 | 228 | 208 | 227 |
| 152 | 232 | 213 | 234 | 218 | 242 | 302 | 215 | 174 | 247 | 266 | 227 | 181 | 295 |
| 216 | 124 | 228 | 219 | 276 | 245 | 296 | 220 | 251 | 247 | 200 | 215 | 230 | 260 |
| 234 | 212 | 249 | 243 | 219 | 185 | 322 | 215 | 225 | 249 | 221 | 291 | 179 | 282 |
| 197 | 177 | 235 | 220 | 272 | 184 | 309 | 179 | 229 | 225 | 214 | 282 | 208 | 338 |
| 189 | 224 | 269 | 211 | 249 | 173 | 333 | 192 | 240 | 229 | 228 | 214 | 216 | 354 |
| 157 | 214 | 286 | 229 | 292 | 147 | 292 | 169 | 208 | 260 | 249 | 243 | 181 | 259 |
| 225 | 190 | 217 | 294 | 254 | 197 | 273 | 209 | 281 | 213 | 211 | 286 | 173 | 305 |
| 169 | 150 | 250 | 223 | 200 | 201 | 355 | 194 | 245 | 207 | 174 | 221 | 239 | 313 |
| 187 | 228 | 243 | 226 | 263 | 194 | 316 | 214 | 238 | 193 | 258 | 249 | 210 | 292 |
| 206 | 227 | 209 | 217 | 265 | 160 | 292 | 198 | 191 | 177 | 227 | 194 | 176 | 346 |

outs have not been a problem (and sales can be assumed equal to demand for our purposes). The past sales figures are given in Table 5–1.

In trying to analyze and understand the information in a set of data, a very good first step is to examine the data, carefully. While humans are not precise in their abilities to recognize patterns in data (or just as important, to avoid seeing patterns that are not significant), we nonetheless can recognize some patterns. In addition, careful examination will begin to give us a feeling for the data—the type of values, range of values, etc.

As a next step, we might want to plot the distribution of the values in our sample of data and/or we might want to calculate some summaries of the sample. Figure 5–1 is a cumulative frequency plot for the data from Table

**FIGURE 5–1**

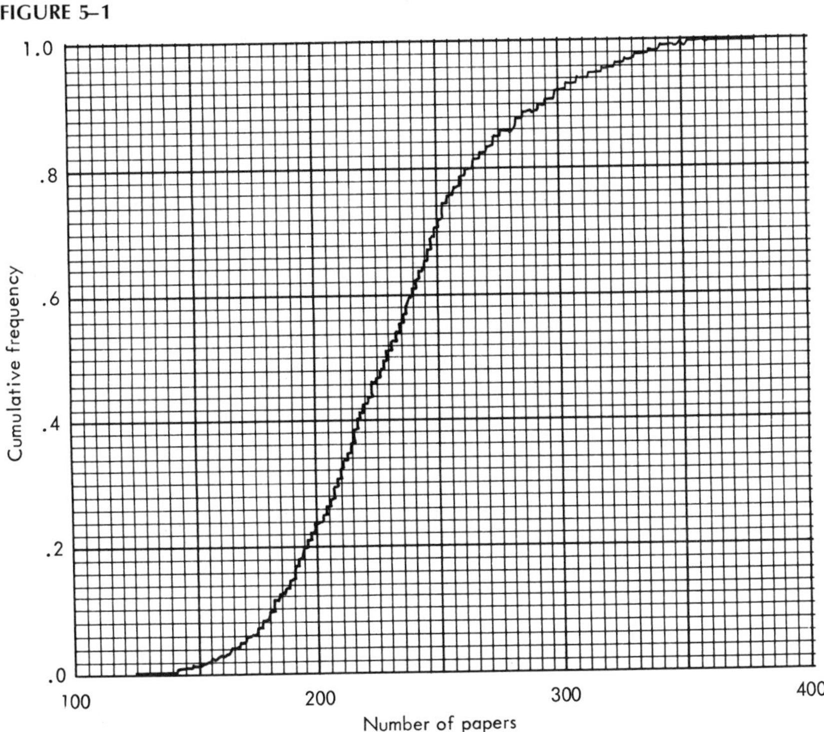


5–1; the curve is a graphic representation of the range of values and the relative frequencies, in the sample of data, of specific subranges within that range. The cumulative frequency curve for a set of data is analogous to a cumulative distribution function for a probability distribution. In the cumulative frequency graph we plot possible data values (numbers of papers) on the horizontal axis. On the vertical axis we show the fractions of data points in the sample that do not exceed specified data values. As was true for cumulative distribution functions, cumulative frequency graphs rise more steeply above more likely ranges of values and less steeply above ranges that are less likely.

Table 5–2 gives some of the most common summary statistics of a set of data. The mean is the average of the values; for the sales data from Table 5–1 the mean is 230.4. The median or .5 fractile can be read from the cumulative

**TABLE 5–2**
Summary statistics

| | |
|---|---|
| Mean | 230.4 |
| Median | 226 |
| Standard deviation | 42.25 |
| Interquartile range | 53 |

curve in Figure 5–1 as 226. There are a number of different measures of the spread of the set of values. One such measure is called the interquartile range; it is defined as the difference between the .75 and the .25 fractiles (or $254 - 201 = 53$ in Figure 5–1). Another very common measure is the standard deviation of the values, which can be calculated as the square root of the average of the squared differences between the individual sample values and their mean. Hence, to calculate the standard deviation of the values in Table 5–1 we first find the mean (or 230.4). For each individual value, we then find the difference between that value and the mean and square the difference. For the first value, this squared difference is $(178 - 230.4)^2 = 2745.76$; for the second it is $(235 - 230.4)^2 = 21.16$, and so forth. Next, we find the average of these 350 squared differences, or 1785. Finally, we take the square root of this average, to find that the standard deviation is 42.25. The reader will recognize the close parallel between the summary measures for sets of data and the corresponding summaries of probability distributions discussed in Chapter 2.

Some of these summary statistics are more useful in analysis of some sets of data, while others are more meaningful on other occasions. The mean and the median are both called measures of central tendency because they provide overall measures of where a set of numbers is located. The median gives what might be considered the middle of a set of data, while the mean gives the average. In summarizing the information in a sample, the mean weights each data point, including what may be unusual data points. For example, the data 1, 1, 1, 2, 2, 2, 3, 3, 3, 2, and the second set 1, 1, 1, 2, 2, 2, 3, 3, 3, 50 have means 2 and 6.8, respectively. The difference in means is entirely attributable to the last number in each set, since the other nine numbers are identical. The second set of numbers includes one particularly large value and hence has a higher mean than does the first set. The median, on the other hand, is not affected by the particular values of extremes of the data; both samples above have median 2. In some data analyses, this property of the median is a considerable advantage. For example, we often start an analysis with a set of numbers which we do not fully understand, and which may contain errors, either because atypical data points were included or because of errors in transcription. In our newspaper sales data, if there had been a very low value and if we found that there had been an unusual strike on the day of the low sales, we might want to exclude the point from our data. Alternatively, if someone had entered the data into the computer and had typed 621 instead of 261, we would not want our analysis thrown off by the aberrant value (in fact, we would want to correct or omit that value). Hence, we might want to use the median as a summary measure of central tendency in order to reduce the influence of extreme (and possibly erroneous) values in initial analyses of data. On the other hand, the mean is a widely used measure, in part because of its general usefulness in further analyses.[1]

Similarly, the interquartile range and the standard deviation have different properties as measures of the spread in a set of data. The interquartile range is easy to calculate and is relatively easy to understand. By definition it includes half of the data points in the sample; and, as was true for the median, the interquartile range will not be thrown off by a few extreme or aberrant values. The standard deviation, on the other hand, involves all the points in a sample of data and so is more affected by extreme values. The standard deviation is not an intuitive measure but it is still the most widely used measure of spread, in large parts because it can be handled analytically in statistical theory.

Once we have calculated various summary measures for our data on newspaper sales and have gained some initial understanding of the sales figures, we might want to proceed to try to forecast sales for another day on the basis of the analysis in Figure 5–1 and in Table 5–2. We can prepare either point or probabilistic forecasts. The single number that we choose for a point forecast should depend on how we feel about (or, how we will be penalized for) the forecasting errors we might make. If we feel that the penalty varies with the square of the error (with penalties for errors of either sign, with relatively small penalties for small errors and rapidly increasing penalties for increasing errors), then it can be proven mathematically that our best bet is to give the mean as our guess, provided of course that we think the sample is representative of what is likely to occur in the future. Thus, the mean minimizes the average squared error. If, on the other hand, we feel that

[1] Another measure that is sometimes used is called the mid-mean. It is the average of all values remaining after what are defined as extreme values have been discarded. The extremes might be defined as the single highest and single lowest values. Alternatively, they might be all values more than some specified number of standard deviations away from the sample mean. Still another possibility is to define as extreme all data points outside the interquartile range. The mid-mean is used in an attempt to include "true" data points that are relatively far from the center of the data and to exclude errors and aberrant values.

it is the absolute magnitude of the error that counts (with both high and low forecasts penalized but only according to the magnitude of the error, not according to its square), it can be shown that the median is the best guess. Often, especially if the economics of a problem are complicated and if we want to consider the possibilities of different errors, we will prefer to look at a probabilistic forecast.

For the discussion that follows it will be useful at this point to introduce another concept using our basic set of sales figures. If we return to the idea of using the sample mean as a point forecast or estimate of other sales figures, we can think of the difference between a particular sales value and the point estimate. This difference is the error we would make if we estimated the particular value by the point estimate: it is called a *residual*. In measuring the effectiveness of a point estimate we often examine the errors we would have made in the past if we had "forecast" each past value with our current point estimate; in this case, we would measure the "past" errors or residuals that would result from estimating the individual past values retrospectively by their mean. Table 5–3 shows examples of the calculation of these past errors

**TABLE 5–3**
Calculation of residuals and residual standard deviation

| *Value* | *Residual (= value − mean)* | | *Residual*$^2$ |
|---|---|---|---|
| 178 .......... | −52.4 | | 2745.76 |
| 235 .......... | 4.6 | | 21.16 |
| 236 .......... | 5.6 | | 31.36 |
| | . | | |
| | . | | |
| | . | | |
| 176 .......... | −54.4 | | 2959.36 |
| 346 .......... | 115.6 | | 13363.36 |
| Average | | = | 1785 |
| Residual standard deviation | | = | 42.25 |

or residuals. It also shows the square root of the average squared error, which is called the residual standard deviation (for it is the standard deviation of the residuals). We discuss residual standard deviation at this point mainly to introduce the concept and so that we can compare residual standard deviations which we obtain with other schemes for explanation and forecasting with the value we obtain at this point.

The data manipulation described above has given us some feeling for the newspaper sales data and has also given us ways to generate point and probabilistic forecasts for future sales values. In some cases, we may stop our analysis with this increased understanding or with the understanding plus forecasts. In other cases, however, we will want to perform further analysis to try to gain further understanding of the process or processes behind the data—and, if we are interested in forecasts, to obtain better forecasts of future values. In particular, we often try to use values of variables to help explain the variable of interest. In the newspaper sales example, we might try to explain the variations in daily sales by trying to identify factors which generate high or low sales. One important factor is the day of the week, and hence we might want to analyze the data further by considering not only the past sales figures but also the days of the week on which they occurred, as shown in Table 5–4.

**TABLE 5–4**

| *Mon.* | *Tues.* | *Wed.* | *Thurs.* | *Fri.* | *Sat.* | *Sun.* | *Mon.* | *Tues.* | *Wed.* | *Thurs.* | *Fri.* | *Sat.* | *Sun.* |
|---|---|---|---|---|---|---|---|---|---|---|---|---|---|
| 178 | 235 | 236 | 218 | 209 | 177 | 261 | 214 | 228 | 188 | 241 | 233 | 192 | 302 |
| 229 | 214 | 251 | 225 | 188 | 172 | 311 | 193 | 206 | 207 | 221 | 212 | 212 | 287 |
| 197 | 211 | 272 | 200 | 235 | 184 | 255 | 198 | 211 | 226 | 233 | 256 | 155 | 269 |
| 204 | 248 | 259 | 223 | 250 | 187 | 286 | 190 | 193 | 211 | 308 | 208 | 191 | 323 |
| 194 | 201 | 235 | 253 | 184 | 203 | 276 | 171 | 174 | 234 | 234 | 197 | 181 | 315 |
| 203 | 230 | 231 | 212 | 250 | 225 | 286 | 137 | 241 | 225 | 207 | 241 | 237 | 260 |
| 229 | 220 | 225 | 265 | 250 | 197 | 260 | 254 | 205 | 244 | 203 | 282 | 227 | 374 |
| 245 | 252 | 242 | 248 | 259 | 152 | 350 | 196 | 232 | 199 | 249 | 235 | 226 | 274 |
| 218 | 204 | 241 | 201 | 265 | 226 | 321 | 176 | 168 | 176 | 195 | 260 | 208 | 304 |
| 208 | 193 | 217 | 213 | 255 | 233 | 311 | 199 | 261 | 200 | 206 | 276 | 196 | 277 |
| 206 | 209 | 227 | 249 | 292 | 179 | 269 | 254 | 207 | 227 | 194 | 258 | 176 | 273 |
| 162 | 213 | 261 | 229 | 220 | 179 | 310 | 180 | 173 | 263 | 240 | 288 | 232 | 325 |
| 223 | 166 | 219 | 211 | 267 | 213 | 302 | 241 | 255 | 272 | 249 | 202 | 199 | 320 |
| 208 | 234 | 250 | 247 | 236 | 180 | 300 | 209 | 164 | 221 | 232 | 222 | 218 | 319 |
| 152 | 196 | 273 | 210 | 270 | 199 | 291 | 202 | 166 | 259 | 232 | 228 | 208 | 227 |
| 152 | 232 | 213 | 234 | 218 | 242 | 302 | 215 | 174 | 247 | 266 | 227 | 181 | 295 |
| 216 | 124 | 228 | 219 | 276 | 245 | 296 | 220 | 251 | 247 | 200 | 215 | 230 | 260 |
| 234 | 212 | 249 | 243 | 219 | 185 | 322 | 215 | 225 | 249 | 221 | 291 | 179 | 282 |
| 197 | 177 | 235 | 220 | 272 | 184 | 309 | 179 | 229 | 225 | 214 | 282 | 208 | 338 |
| 189 | 224 | 269 | 211 | 249 | 173 | 333 | 192 | 240 | 229 | 228 | 214 | 216 | 354 |
| 157 | 214 | 286 | 229 | 292 | 147 | 292 | 169 | 208 | 260 | 249 | 243 | 181 | 259 |
| 225 | 190 | 217 | 294 | 254 | 197 | 273 | 209 | 281 | 213 | 211 | 286 | 173 | 305 |
| 169 | 150 | 250 | 223 | 200 | 201 | 355 | 194 | 245 | 207 | 174 | 221 | 239 | 313 |
| 187 | 228 | 243 | 226 | 263 | 194 | 316 | 214 | 238 | 193 | 258 | 249 | 210 | 292 |
| 206 | 227 | 209 | 217 | 265 | 160 | 292 | 198 | 191 | 177 | 227 | 194 | 176 | 346 |

If we try to analyze the sales data by using the day-of-the-week information, our first step will be to classify the sales figures according to the day of the week on which they occurred. Thus, we will sort the 350 sales figures into seven classes, one for each day of the week. We can then describe the set of data points in any one of the classes using any of the descriptive tools that we used above for the entire set of data. For example, we can calculate the means and standard deviations for the values for each day of the week, as shown in Table 5–5. Alternatively, we could calculate the medians or the

**TABLE 5–5**

| *Day* | *Mean* | *Standard deviation* |
|---|---|---|
| Monday ......... | 200.1 | 25.7 |
| Tuesday ......... | 211.4 | 31.1 |
| Wednesday ...... | 232.7 | 25.1 |
| Thursday ........ | 228.2 | 24.4 |
| Friday ........... | 243.2 | 29.7 |
| Saturday ......... | 197.7 | 24.5 |
| Sunday .......... | 299.4 | 29.7 |

interquartile ranges for the individual classes or we could plot distributions for those classes.

Having sorted the original data into classes according to day and then having calculated descriptors of those classes, we can now ask whether the classification has done us any good in terms of explanation of the data; in other words, we can ask whether we understand the process that generates sales any better when we look at the data classified according to day. In addition, if we are concerned with forecasting sales on future days, we can ask whether the classification scheme will allow us to make forecasts with smaller errors than we would make if we considered only the full set of data without using the explanatory factor of day of the week. To answer the first question, we must define what we mean by saying that the classification scheme explains the data better than the original analysis did.

We usually assume that the classification has helped if it has sorted the data into classes which are more like one another than they are like other classes; that is, we say that the scheme has improved the explanation if it has sorted the larger full set of data into a smaller number of more homogeneous classes. To measure in quantitative terms whether such an improvement has occurred, we generally use the standard deviations of the full set of data and of the individual classes to measure the spreads in those groups. For the newspaper sales data, we find that the standard deviation for the original data is 42.25 while the seven standard deviations for the classes are 25.7, 31.1, 25.1, 24.4, 29.7, 24.5, and 29.7 as shown in Table 5–5. Thus, the classification into seven groups has in fact broken the data into groups which are more homogeneous (have less spread in values than did the original data).

In summarizing the gain in explanatory power that has been provided by a particular classification scheme, we often use a measure that is involved in answering the second question raised above, the question about how much better we can forecast with the classification scheme than without it. For this purpose we generally assume a squared-error criterion. In that case it can be shown that the best forecast for a particular future occasion falling into one of our classes is simply the mean for that class. Thus, we would give a point forecast of 200.1 for a particular future Monday sales figure, a point forecast of 228.2 for a Thursday, etc. Just as we did when we used the overall mean as the base for a forecast when we were considering the entire pool of data, we now proceed to consider the residuals, or the errors that our point forecasts would have made if they had been used retrospectively to forecast in our set of data. Thus, we ask what would be the average error if we used 200.1 as an estimate for all Mondays in the data, 211.4 as an estimate for all Tuesdays, etc. Table 5–6 illustrates how we would find the average squared

**TABLE 5–6**

| *Value* | *Residual (= value − mean for appropriate day)* | *Residual²* |
|---|---|---|
| 178 . . . . . . . . | (178 − 200.1) = −22.1 | 488.41 |
| 235 . . . . . . . . | (235 − 211.4) = 23.6 | 556.96 |
| 236 . . . . . . . . | (236 − 232.7) = 3.3 | 10.89 |
| 218 . . . . . . . . | (218 − 228.2) = −10.2 | 104.04 |
| 209 . . . . . . . . | (209 − 243.2) = −34.2 | 1,169.64 |
| 177 . . . . . . . . | (177 − 197.7) = −20.7 | 428.49 |
| 261 . . . . . . . . | (261 − 299.4) = −38.4 | 1,474.56 |
| 214 . . . . . . . . | (214 − 200.1) = 13.9 | 193.21 |
| | . | |
| | . | |
| | . | |
| 346 . . . . . . . . | (346 − 299.4) = 46.6 | 2,171.56 |
| Average | | 744 |
| Residual standard deviation | | = 27.3 |

error that we would have made in the data base if we had used our seven class means as point estimates.[2] It also shows the square root of the average squared error; as noted above, this value is the residual standard deviation (or standard deviation of the residuals).

[2] In analyzing this classification scheme, we have actually made one choice that was glossed over in the discussion above. In considering the errors about the seven means, we used the entire set of past residuals (that is, 350 past errors, or one for each data point). When we went on to forecast a particular future value we would use the error distribution so constructed. In doing so, we are really assuming that the class means explain all of the significant differences between classes and that the individual errors can then be pooled to form one overall error distribution. In other cases we might want to assume that the error patterns were also different in the different classes. In such cases, when we tried to use the past errors in preparing forecasts, we would use only the error pattern for the particular class we were forecasting. In our current example, this alternative assumption would mean that we would forecast Monday values using the mean for Monday and the past errors for Mondays only, for example. The usual assumption in these analyses is that the error distributions in the different classes are the same so that a pooled measure of error can be used, but this standard assumption is not always the best one and should not be used if the investigator has good reason to suspect different error distributions in the different classes.

If our concern is with forecasting, then we can use the distribution of past errors, together with our point forecasts, to obtain probabilistic forecasts for future values. If our concern is instead with measuring the explanatory power of our classification scheme, we can compare the average errors with the current scheme to the average error we would have made using only the overall mean as a point forecast. To be more precise, we would look at the square root of the average squared error we would have made using the overall mean as the point forecast and compare this figure with the square root of the average squared error we would have made if we had used the individual class means as point forecasts for the data points in their classes. Thus, we compare 42.25 from Table 5–3 with 27.3 from Table 5–6 to see the improvement (or reduction in error) provided by the classification. Often, we look at a fraction representing the reduction in error. We ask what fraction of the original average squared error has been removed by use of the classification. In this example, the average squared error has been reduced from 1,785 to 744. Thus, the reduction of 1785 − 744 = 1,041 is 1,041/1,785 = .58 of the original figure.

One additional very important point should be made before we leave this newspaper forecasting example. In all of the analysis of the newspaper data we have done we have been using the sample of past data. In a way, it is obvious and reasonable enough that we did so; we are concerned with the future sales level in forecasting but we do not yet have data on the future. Hence we do our analysis looking backward into the past. After the analysis has informed us about the behavior of past data, we turn around to the future and use the insights we have gained in order to prepare forecasts. This procedure is often very reasonable, but it does involve a very major assumption that should be made explicitly rather than by default. In using the results about the past to forecast for the future we are assuming that the future can usefully be expected to be like the past. Put more precisely, we are assuming that we have no reason to predict the future differently than we would have predicted the past, before the fact. While such assumptions are often acceptable, they are also often totally unacceptable. Users of data analysis are not always sufficiently careful to think about whether they want to accept such assumptions before they use the results of their analyses for forecasting.[3]

The analysis that was explained above for the newspaper sales data is really a prototype of what is called a cross-tabulation analysis of a set of data. At this point we will return to that example and restate the analysis in the terms of cross tabulations.

In cross tabulations, we start with a set of *data* on some variable (called

[3] There is an added technical problem with the procedure we have described. We calculated residuals and error distributions from the same data we used to find the means for the different days. Such a procedure is really tantamount to fitting and testing a data analytic model on the same data. It will, in general, lead to an understatement of the errors to be expected in the future, even if the future is very like the past.

the *dependent variable*). One way to analyze the data is to consider the entire set and calculate various summary statistics such as the mean and the standard deviation; as we have seen, in doing so we consider the average squared error (or its square root) that we would have made if we had used the overall mean to forecast each of the past data points.

As a next step, we can classify the data in one (or more) ways according to the values of one or more other variables, called *explanatory variables*. In our example, day of the week was the explanatory variable. Each class of data is then a subsample from the original sample. In our example, the sample is the set of all sales figures; the subsamples are the set of all Monday sales, the set of all Tuesday sales, etc. We can then calculate summary statistics for each such subsample. For example, we can calculate the subsample means and standard deviations.

Once we have classified the data, we can calculate the square root of the average squared error that we would have made if we had used the individual class means to forecast the past values from those classes. This figure (27.3 in our example) is called the *residual standard deviation* for the classification. In ways which have not been discussed here, we can also calculate a measure of the standard deviation or *uncertainty* in the estimates of the individual class means; this uncertainty arises because our estimates are based on only a sample of values rather than on an infinitely large supply of data. In addition, we can consider the *number of* past data points or *observations* in each subsample or *cell* of our classification. Finally, we can consider the fractional reduction in the average squared error (as compared with the base of using only the overall mean as an estimate); this value, which was .58 in our example, is called $R^2$.

In performing such cross-tabulation analyses, we sometimes want to explain our dependent variable with more than one explanatory (or classificatory) variable. For example, in the newspaper example we might want to use another factor for weather with only two categories, one for good weather and one for precipitation. We can then think of a two-dimensional classification scheme as shown in Figure 5–2 below. There we show the days

**FIGURE 5–2**

| | *Mon.* | *Tue.* | *Wed.* | *Thur.* | *Fri.* | *Sat.* | *Sun.* |
|---|---|---|---|---|---|---|---|
| *Good weather* | | | | | | | |
| *Precipitation* | | | | | | | |

of the week as one dimension and the weather conditions as another. Each cell in the table now corresponds to a different subsample so that we have 14 such categories. If we sort the 350 data points into these 14 classes we can then proceed to treat the 14 subsets of data just as we treated the smaller number of classes above; we can calculate subsample means and standard deviations and can calculate such measures as the sample residual standard deviation. In principle we could also introduce another explanatory factor and create a three-way classification, and so on. The problem in this procedure is that while additional explanatory factors may in some cases be useful, they have the problem that they increase the number of cells and hence reduce the number of observations in any one cell. Hence, if we use several explanatory variables we may be basing our estimates of means in the individual cells on unreasonably small numbers of data points.

The cross-tabulation procedure can also be used with explanatory variables that are many-valued or continuous rather than few-valued as were the day and weather variables discussed above. To perform such analyses with continuous variables, we approximate such variables by dividing their ranges into a limited number of smaller ranges and then we consider each range of the explanatory variable to define a class. For example, suppose that we are trying to study the weights of a group of adult males. We decide to use height as an explanatory variable. Because height can take on any of an essentially infinite number of values (72.54 inches, for example), we cannot consider each different height value as a separate class. Instead, we group the possible heights into ranges. For example, we might choose divisions (called cutpoints) of 66, 69, 70.5, and 72 inches. Then one class would be all adult males less than 66 inches tall; the next would contain those at least 66 but less than 69 inches tall, and so forth. We could label the height classes 1, 2, 3, 4, and 5 and then we could construct the skeleton classification table shown in Figure 5–3. At this point, we could sort our data on weight into these cells and could proceed just as we did for the few-valued explanatory variables used above to analyze the data in the different cells.

**FIGURE 5–3**

| *Class 1* *(below 66 inches)* | *Class 2* *(66–69 inches)* | *Class 3* *(69–70.5 inches)* | *Class 4* *(70.5–72 inches)* | *Class 5* *(over 72 inches)* |
|---|---|---|---|---|
| | | | | |

In selecting cutpoints for such a classification scheme, we often try to pick values that divide the data points into groups of as nearly as possible equal numbers of observations. We do so in order to avoid basing our estimate of any individual cell mean on an unreasonably small number of data points.[4]

All of the analyses above have simply sorted data into a number of cells and then have studied the characteristics of the data points falling into the

[4] As will be seen below, in other situations we choose cutpoints instead that divide the range of the explanatory variable into segments of equal width.

individual cells. We did not try to study the change in means as we moved from one cell to the next (from Monday sales to Tuesday sales to Wednesday sales, for example). As the height and weight example may suggest, however, cross tabulations can be used as a valuable first step in studying the relation between changes in the dependent variable and changes in the explanatory variables in different cells. For example, we might study the per unit costs for a group of factories making essentially the same product. Suppose the factories differ in size (as measured by total output) and that we think size is an important factor in explaining per unit cost. We might perform a cross-tabulation analysis by classifying the factories into a number of groups by size and then examining the average per unit cost in each class; this analysis corresponds to the cross-tab analyses that we discussed above. In this example, however, we might want to go further and try to use the cross-tabs scheme to try to study some hypotheses about what changes in per unit cost occur with changes in size; thus, we might want to use the cross tabs as a guide or check in deciding the *form of the relationship* between costs and size. One hypothesis would be that costs change linearly with size—for example, that there is the same per unit cost reduction for each change in size. Under this hypothesis, we might construct the table (with equal changes in size from class to class) in Figure 5–4 and then perform a cross tabs to see if the means for the different classes show about the same change for each change of class size.

**FIGURE 5–4**

| *Below 100,000 units* | *100,000–150,000* | *150,000–200,000* | *200,000–250,000* | *250,000–300,000* | *over 300,000* |
|---|---|---|---|---|---|
| | | | | | |

Note that in the example in Figure 5–4 it was useful to have intervals of equal width for the classes rather than to select cutpoints that left equal numbers of observations in different cells. If, for example, the mean for the 100,000 to 150,000 size were $1.18 and that for the next class were $1.10 we would have found a change of −$.08. Under the assumption of linearity we would then expect the next mean (that for the 200,000 to 250,000 class) to be approximately $1.02, reflecting another 8¢ decrease. In many cases, we do not expect such a linear relationship between size and average costs, but instead expect diminishing returns so that changes in costs are not as significant as we continue to increase size. To study such nonlinear relationships we can conduct cross-tabs analyses using what are called *transformations* of the explanatory variables. Diminishing returns corresponds to what are called decelerating relationships, as shown in Figure 5–5.

**FIGURE 5–5**
Decelerating relationships

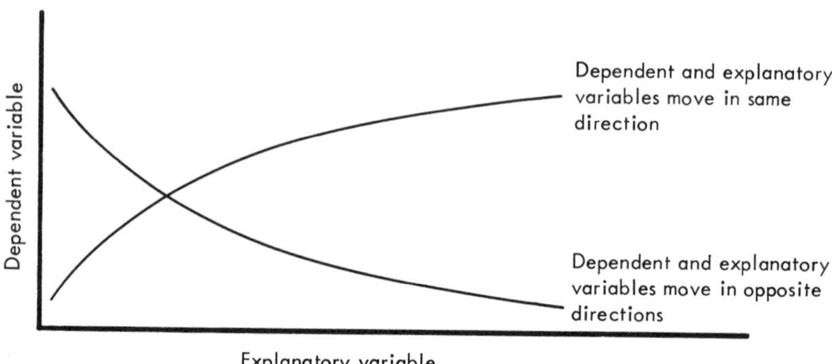


For such decelerating relationships, we might, for example, assume that unit costs were related not to size but to the reciprocal of size. To study such a relationship, we could construct a cross-tabs scheme with 1/size as the explanatory variable, as shown below in Figure 5–6, and study whether the changes in costs as we moved from cell to cell were approximately constant and hence consistent with an assumption of a decelerating relationship. (Note that in Figure 5–6 1/capacity has a range of 1/6 in each interior cell, with capacities in hundreds of thousands.)

**FIGURE 5–6**

| *1/capacity less than 1/3 (capacity over 3)* | *1/capacity between 1/3 and 1/2* | *1/capacity between 1/2 and 1/1.5* | *1/capacity between 1/1.5 and 1/1.2* | *1/capacity over 1/1.2* |
|---|---|---|---|---|
| | | | | |

In still other cases, we may postulate an accelerating relationship between the dependent variable and a particular explanatory variable, as shown in Figure 5–7 below. For such cases we can use some transformation of the explanatory variable such as the square transformation and then construct a table using that transformed variable to define cells.

There are two principal ways in which cross-tabulation techniques can contribute in model building. For one thing, the cross-tabs method can be used in much the way described above for the newspaper data or for the factory cost example: to help us understand relationships among different variables. Such increased understanding should, we hope, lead to better judgments in the model-design process and, as a result, to more useful models. The second way to use cross tabulation in model building is really

**FIGURE 5–7**
Accelerating relationships

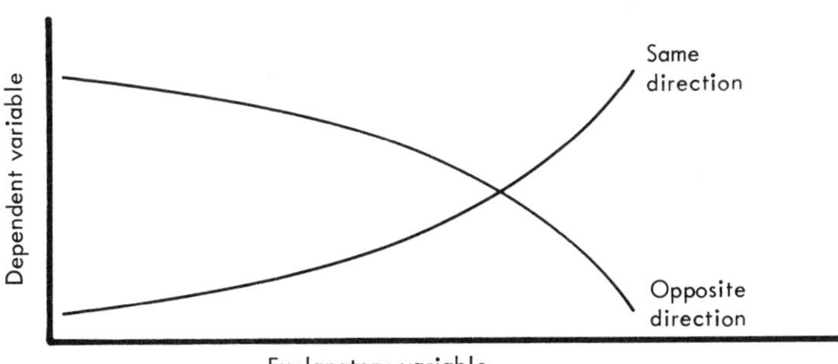


an application of the idea of thinking of data as falling into different cells rather than a full-blown application of the techniques of cross tabs. In some modeling situations it is useful to think of structuring the problem in terms of different cells, even if we do not have the data to perform an actual cross tabulation. For example, suppose that we are trying to predict sales of some product and that the sales forecast will be one input to a probabilistic model. It may be that it is useful to think of the market for the product as consisting of different segments; perhaps light users, medium users, and heavy users of the product category would be a useful conceptual classification. Rather than require model inputs in which the user assessed a distribution for total demand for the product, it might instead be better to require separate input information for each market segment, if we felt that whoever was doing the assessment for input to the model could offer better information on a market-segment basis. In fact, we might want to push the classification idea further. We might believe that the total sizes of the market segments of light, medium, and heavy users were uncertain and, in addition, that we would most probably obtain considerably different market shares in the three segments. If so, then we could build a model that took as inputs distributions for total market sizes in each of the segments and, in addition, required distributions for market share for each segment. In this reformulation we have used the cross-tabs-like idea that the consumers in the marketplace can usefully be sorted into different segments or cells and that the members of one of those cells behave much like other members of the small cell but differently from the members of the other segments, in those aspects of their behavior that are important for our analysis. In choosing some small number of cells that is larger than one, we have avoided assuming that all consumers are alike and will respond similarly to our product, yet we have also avoided the impossible task of trying to consider each individual in the marketplace. A similar procedure of thinking about classifying people or costs or other interesting quantities into a small number of cells is a powerful aid in many modeling situations.

## II. REGRESSION ANALYSIS (AND ECONOMETRICS)

The technique of cross-tabulation analysis requires considerable amounts of data to be useful. For example, in the newspaper example used in the previous section we suggested forecasting sales of newspaper on Mondays on the basis of previous Monday sales. In the terms of cross tabs, we suggested forecasting a future event that would fall into one cell (the Monday cell) of our table by using past data from the same cell of the table. Clearly, this approach is attractive in that it has us forecast a future event from past events that we believe are closely similar to that future occurrence. On the other hand, the procedure does not make much sense unless we have a substantial amount of past data on situations that are satisfactorily like the future one. In the previous section, we had data on 50 past Mondays. We would have been considerably less willing to forecast next Monday on the basis of past Mondays alone if we had had data on only four past Mondays, for example. Thus, we would like some substitute for cross-tabulation analysis to use when we do not have sufficient data to be comfortable with a straight cross-tabs approach. Regression analysis can be thought of as such a tool. Clearly, something must make up for the supposed lack of data; in regression analysis, the basic idea is that we use past data on both similar and somewhat different situations, together with the judgment of the modeler, to substitute for the copious data on similar situations that would have allowed us to use cross tabs.

To introduce the basic ideas of regression analysis we will consider the following example. Suppose that we are trying to forecast sales of apples at a supermarket in order to decide how many pounds of the fruit to order. We feel that it will be most useful to think in terms of pounds of apples purchased per customer; since the volume of customers in any week is relatively stable, we will be able to translate rather easily to total poundage predicted. Suppose that we feel that sales of apples are closely tied to the price charged per pound. We have collected past data on the sales in pounds per customer in the past for several different prices and several different supermarkets. Assume that we are willing to make the very considerable assumption that the past data reflect situations sufficiently close to the one we are planning to forecast that the past data are useful to us. Suppose that the past data on price per pound and pounds sold per customer are as shown in Table 5–7. The table shows data on only ten past occasions; in the terminology of data analysis, it contains ten observations. We would normally want more than ten observations for analysis, but we will use this small set of data for illustrative purposes.

If we did not have the price information or if, alternatively, we had the information but could not determine a good way to use it, the best we could do in forecasting sales for the future would be to use the past sales data alone. Table 5–8 shows how we might retrospectively explain each of the ten

**TABLE 5–7**

| *Sales (lbs/customer)* | *Price (cents/lb.)* |
|---|---|
| .80 | 31 |
| .75 | 31 |
| .50 | 39.5 |
| .40 | 41 |
| .62 | 35.5 |
| .56 | 34.5 |
| .31 | 43 |
| .66 | 37.5 |
| .48 | 37.5 |
| .75 | 34 |

past sales figures by the overall mean of those figures, or .583. The table shows that the average squared error we would make with that scheme applied to the past situations is .0236; the square root of the average squared error is .1537 pounds.

The problem with the explanatory model in Table 5–8 is that it does not use any information on price and, since we have that information and consider it relevant, we would like to incorporate it into the process. We cannot simply use cross tabs. Suppose, for example, that we wish to forecast sales for a price of 40 cents per pound. We have no past data on situations with that price and we therefore cannot forecast the future situation from past ones like it. Even if the future price were to be 37.5 cents per pound (or two pounds for 75 cents) we would not be very happy about trying to use the past data for analogous situations only. True, we do have two observations from the past on which price was exactly 37.5 cents, but two data points do not provide a very firm foundation for forecasting. It would seem far better to try in some systematic way to use all of the data from Table 5–7 in forecasting future

**TABLE 5–8**

| *Actual sales* | *"Predicted" sales* | *Residual* | *Residual²* |
|---|---|---|---|
| .80 | .583 | .217 | .04709 |
| .75 | .583 | .167 | .02789 |
| .50 | .583 | −.083 | .00689 |
| .40 | .583 | −.183 | .03349 |
| .62 | .583 | .037 | .00137 |
| .56 | .583 | −.023 | .00053 |
| .31 | .583 | −.273 | .07453 |
| .66 | .583 | .077 | .00593 |
| .48 | .583 | −.103 | .01061 |
| .75 | .583 | .167 | .02789 |
| Average residual² | | | .02362 |

price. Notice that the problem here arises because of the limitations of our sample. If we had large volumes of data, with many observations for a price of 40 cents and many other observations at 37.5 cents, we would not hesitate to forecast a future situation in which price would be 40 cents from past situations in its cell of a cross tabulation and to forecast a future with a 37.5 cent price from like occasions in the past. Our problem is the limited amount of data that makes cross tabs inappropriate.

The alternative we suggest here is to use the technique of regression analysis. We identify a dependent variable, which in this case is pounds per customer; we also identify one or more explanatory variables, in this case price per pound. We collect whatever useful data we can; we will assume that the data in Table 5–7 are all useful. Then because we cannot focus on a single cell in a table, for lack of data, we instead try to form some judgments about the general form of the relationship between the dependent and explanatory variables. In Figures 5–8 the ten past observations on sales and price have been plotted as points on a graph. Notice that the graph does indeed seem to suggest the expected relationship between price and sales, with higher sales for lower prices and vice versa. If we are now willing to go further and to specify a general functional form describing the relationship between sales and price, we can use regression to determine the particular

**FIGURE 5–8**

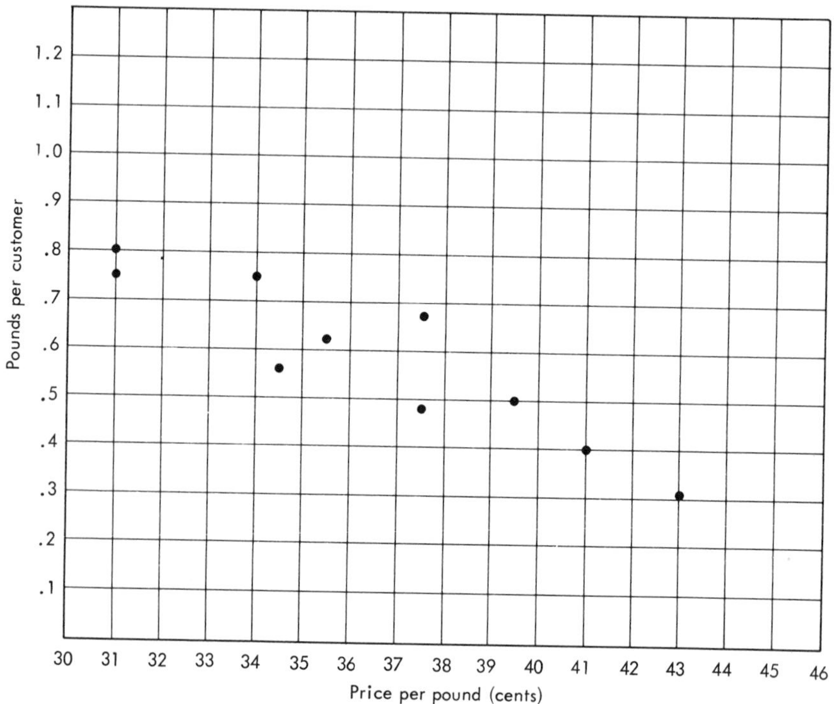

function, from among all of the functions in that family, that best fits the past data.

In the current situation we might make the very common assumption of a linear relationship, or, in other words, a general form of the type:

$$\text{Sales} = \beta_0 + \beta_1 * \text{price}.$$

(Notice, however, that the straight-line form was an assumption, not a conclusion, of the analysis. Other assumptions, including various families of simple curves, would also have been possible.) The standard regression analysis programs that are available on many computers and even on many hand calculators can now determine the particular line that best fits the data. The term *best fit* is interpreted in most regression analyses in a squared-error sense; we ask for the values for $\beta_0$ and $\beta_1$ that would have done the best job of prediction retrospectively in the data base, if errors were counted on a squared basis.[5] For the data in Table 5–7, regression analysis indicates that the best-fitting line is:

$$\text{Sales} = 1.937 - .03714 * \text{price}.$$

This result is interpreted to mean that, as well as can be determined from the past data and from the assumed linear functional form, each time price is increased one cent, pounds purchased per customer decrease by .03714. Table 5–9 shows how the regression equation could be used to "predict" retrospectively in the data base. The scheme gives an average squared error of .00359 and a square root of the average squared error (called the residual standard deviation) of .0599.

In regression, as in cross tabulation, we define $R^2$ as the fractional reduction in the average squared error compared with the forecasting scheme in which we use the mean of the dependent variable as our "predictor." For the regression line of sales on price which we have just fit to the ten observations in Table 5–7, we have an average squared error of .00359, as compared with the .02362 average squared error obtained in Table 5–8, using only the mean sales value as a predictor. Hence the $R^2$ value is

$$\frac{.02362 - .00359}{.02362} = .85$$

[5] To find values $b_0$ and $b_1$ for the coefficients of the line, we notice that for any set of values for the coefficients, the residual on a particular observation is:

$$\text{Sales} - b_0 - b_1 * \text{price}.$$

The sum of the squared errors (with ten observations) is

$$\sum_{i=1}^{10} (\text{Sales}_i - b_0 - b_1 * \text{price}_i)^2.$$

To find the best $b_0$ and $b_1$, we simply use some straightforward calculus to find the coefficients that minimize this sum of squared errors.

**TABLE 5–9**

| *Sales* | *Price* | *"Prediction"* | *Residual* | *Residual²* |
|---|---|---|---|---|
| .80 . . . . . . . . . . . | 31 | .7857 | .0143 | .000204 |
| .75 . . . . . . . . . . . | 31 | .7857 | −.0357 | .001274 |
| .50 . . . . . . . . . . . | 39.5 | .4700 | .0300 | .000900 |
| .40 . . . . . . . . . . . | 41 | .4143 | −.0143 | .000204 |
| .62 . . . . . . . . . . . | 35.5 | .6185 | .0015 | .000002 |
| .56 . . . . . . . . . . . | 34.5 | .6557 | −.0957 | .009158 |
| .31 . . . . . . . . . . . | 43 | .3400 | −.0300 | .000900 |
| .66 . . . . . . . . . . . | 37.5 | .5443 | .1157 | .013386 |
| .48 . . . . . . . . . . . | 37.5 | .5443 | −.0643 | .004134 |
| .75 . . . . . . . . . . . | 34 | .6742 | .0758 | .005746 |
| Average squared error | | | | .00359 |

**FIGURE 5–9**

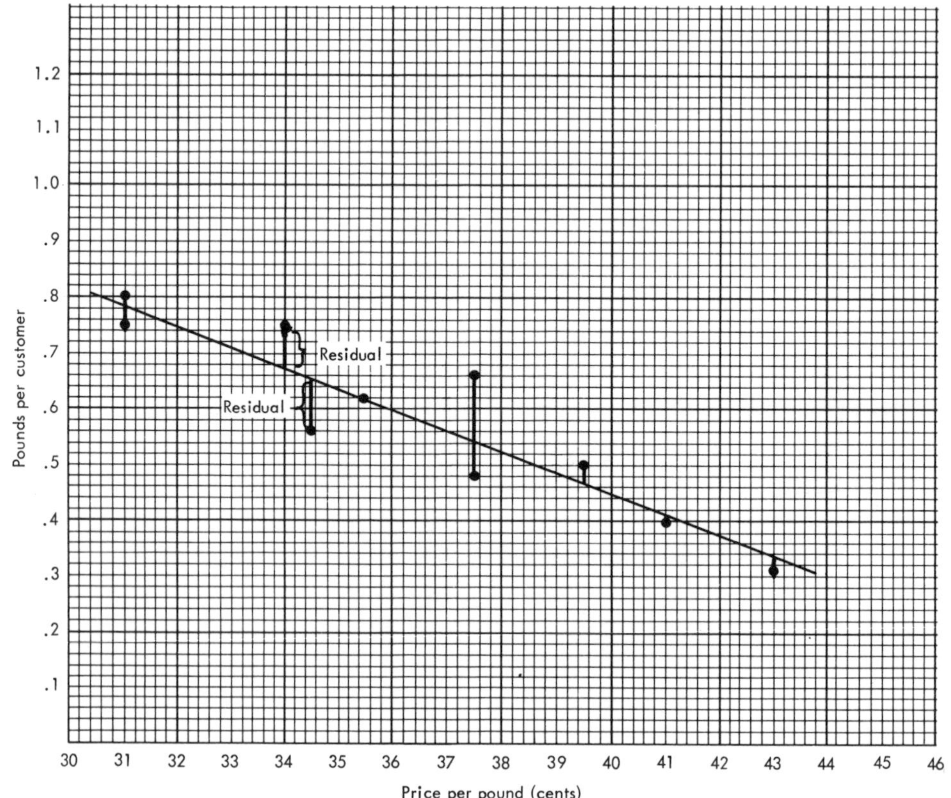

Figure 5–9 shows in graphical terms the regression line and the residuals. The figure includes the ten original data points and the regression line found by computer. It also shows the residuals, which are the vertical differences between the actual data points and the regression line.

We could at this point use the regression line and additional information on how well it fit our data to prepare forecasts for future sales levels, assuming different future prices. Alternatively, we could try to find one or more additional explanatory variables that would allow us to explain the past behavior even better. Suppose that we try the second approach and learn that on three of the occasions represented in our data base there had been special promotions at the supermarkets, with apples being featured together with kits for making candied apples from them. Table 5–10 summarizes the additional data together with the original data on sales and prices.

**TABLE 5–10**

| *Sales* | *Price* | *Special promotion* |
|---|---|---|
| .80 | 31 | yes |
| .75 | 31 | no |
| .50 | 39.5 | no |
| .40 | 41 | no |
| .62 | 35.5 | yes |
| .56 | 34.5 | no |
| .31 | 43 | no |
| .66 | 37.5 | yes |
| .48 | 37.5 | no |
| .75 | 34 | no |

Suppose further that we are willing to make the considerable assumption that all of the past data are useful and, in addition, that the general functional form summarizing the relation of sales to price and to the presence or absence of a special promotion is:

$$\text{Sales} = \beta_0 + \beta_1 * \text{price} + \beta_2 * \text{promotion}.$$

In this equation we assume that the promotion variable takes the value 1 if there is a promotion and the value 0 if there is not. When we introduce a second explanatory variable as we have just done, we can no longer prepare simple graphs of the relationships between the dependent and explanatory variables as we did in Figure 5–8. On the other hand, the computer is still quite able to find the values for the coefficients of the regression equation that give the best fit for the past data. For the data in Table 5–10 the resulting regression equation is:

$$\text{Sales} = 1.822 - .03458 * \text{price} + .06953 * \text{promotion}.$$

Just as we used the first regression equation to prepare retrospective forecasts and to find summaries of fit in Table 5–9, we can use this new equation to find predictions and summary measures as shown in Table 5–11. Most computer regression programs would be able to provide all of this information automatically. The $R^2$ figure in Table 5–11 is computed, using the figure from Table 5–8 for average squared error when the mean sales value is used for explanation; the $R^2$ in Table 5–11 gives the fraction by which that original

**TABLE 5–11**

| *Sales* | *Price* | *Promotion* | *"Prediction"* | *Residual* | *Residual²* |
|---|---|---|---|---|---|
| .80 | 31 | 1 | .8196 | −.0196 | .000384 |
| .75 | 31 | 0 | .7500 | .0000 | .000000 |
| .50 | 39.5 | 0 | .4561 | .0439 | .001927 |
| .40 | 41 | 0 | .4042 | −.0042 | .000018 |
| .62 | 35.5 | 1 | .6639 | −.0439 | .001927 |
| .56 | 34.5 | 0 | .6290 | −.0690 | .004761 |
| .31 | 43 | 0 | .3351 | −.0251 | .000630 |
| .66 | 37.5 | 1 | .5948 | .0652 | .004251 |
| .48 | 37.5 | 0 | .5253 | −.0453 | .002052 |
| .75 | 34 | 0 | .6463 | .1037 | .010754 |
| | | | | | .026704 |
| Average squared error | | | | | .00267 |

Residual standard deviation = .05167

$$R^2 = \frac{.02362 - .00267}{.02362} = .89$$

average squared error has been reduced through use of the new regression equation. Notice that the coefficient for price in the second regression equation is not quite the same as the corresponding coefficient in the first regression equation. Such behavior is generally found in regression analyses with the result that we cannot look at relationships between a single dependent variable and several explanatory variables by considering the explanatory variables one at a time. We must, instead, consider all of the explanatory variables simultaneously.[6]

If, as we assumed at the outset, we are willing to proceed as if the future situations that we are forecasting are much like the past occasions on which we have data, then we can use the regression equation that we have just fit in making predictions for the future. The equation allows us to form point forecasts. For example, for a future price of 40 cents without a special promotion, the equation would give a point forecast of $1.822 - .03458 * 40$, or .439. Some regression programs can provide additional information beyond this point forecast. By considering the various

[6] For more details the reader is referred to other texts covering regression analysis.

factors that lead to uncertainty in the forecast even if the future will be like the past, such programs can provide entire forecast distributions for specific values of the explanatory variables. One such program gave the probabilistic forecast in Figure 5–10 for a future price of 40 cents and no promotion. (In

**FIGURE 5–10**
Probabilistic forecast

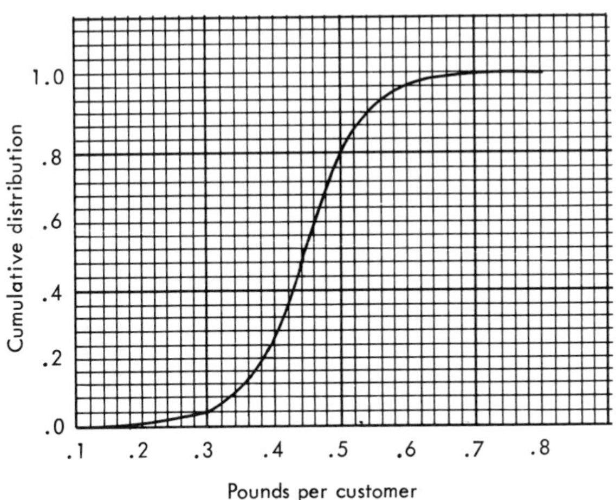


preparing that forecast the computer program combined information on the residuals from the past, on the size of our data sample, and on the extent to which the future price was typical of the past ones; all of these influences help determine the amount of uncertainty in the forecast.)

In summary, then, regression analysis is a technique for fitting functional forms of specific types to sets of data. The general procedure is that the investigator provides a computerized regression program with past data on a dependent variable and on one or more explanatory variables. The investigator also provides an assumption about the general form of the relationship between the dependent variable and the explanatory variables. In the example on apples, we assumed a linear additive relationship.[7] The computer then finds the coefficients for the functional form that give the best fit to the past data in a squared-error sense. The computer provides output information on the coefficients and, in addition, on some summary measures of fit. If the user

[7] Assumptions of additivity and linearity are extremely common in regression analysis. The assumptions are considerable ones, however, and should be made only with care. The reader is referred to books on regression and related statistical techniques for further discussion.

Among the relevant references on regression are: Paul A. Vatter, Stephen P. Bradley, Sherwood C. Frey, Jr., and Barbara B. Jackson, *Quantitative Methods in Management* (Homewood, Ill.: Richard D. Irwin, Inc., 1978), Frederick Mosteller and John W. Tukey, *Data Analysis and Regression* (Reading, Mass.: Addison-Wesley, 1977), and N. R. Draper and H. Smith, *Applied Regression Analysis* (New York: John Wiley & Sons, 1966).

is then willing to assume that the future will be sufficiently like the past, s/he can use the regression results to prepare forecasts for the future; both point and probabilistic forecasts can be found.

As did cross tabulation analysis, regression analysis has two main types of uses in connection with computer simulation modeling. For one thing, regression analysis of past data is often useful in helping us decide what relationships are important in a particular situation; hence, the technique helps in the basic analysis of a problem in which we are making judgments about the problem situation. Regression is more commonly used for a second purpose, that of providing equations that are built directly into a model. For example, if we were building a model for the supermarket described above we might require that one part of a user-specified strategy be the price to be charged for apples. The computer could then use the regression equation to forecast future apple sales. It could prepare a probabilistic forecast of the future sales and, then, on each trial of a probabilistic version of a model, could drawn a particular sales value at random from that forecast distribution. In this example, regression has been used to calibrate the relationship between a decision variable (price) and an important UQ in the problem (sales per customer). In other cases, regression can be used to calibrate relationships among different UQs in a problem. It might be used, for example, to determine that part of one UQ that depended on another uncertainty. Using the type of decomposition idea discussed in Chapter 3, we could then forecast the first UQ as the combination of one part that depended on the second UQ (as shown by the regression equation) plus another part specific to the first UQ. There are many other possibilities for using regression. It should be stressed at this point, however, that while the technique is a powerful one, its use to give equations for incorporation into computer models rests very heavily on the assumption that the past data are relevant and that the relation that fit in the past will continue for the future.

In concluding this discussion of regression and of data analysis, we now turn to a very brief introduction to some of the basic ideas of econometrics. *Econometrics* involves the fitting of statistical models to sets of data, usually economic data. The field can be thought of as the intersection of statistics and economics. It is a rich field, whose practitioners apply existing techniques to economic data and also devise new techniques when they want to analyze sets of economic data for which the existing techniques are inadequate. This discussion is intended to introduce the reader to the types of approaches used in econometrics. It is a very brief summary, intended to provide an introduction to a few of the basic ideas in econometrics. We will not consider econometrics in the same detail that we discussed cross tabulation and regression above.[8]

---

[8] Useful references on econometrics include: J. Johnston, *Econometric Methods* (New York: McGraw-Hill, 1963); and Robert S. Pindyck and Daniel L. Rubinfeld, *Econometric Models and Economic Forecasts,* (New York: McGraw-Hill, 1976).

Much of econometrics involves the fitting of regression models to economic data, and most treatments of the field begin with a consideration of a standard regression approach to finding the coefficients for one equation in which explanatory variables are used to explain the behavior of one dependent variable and then, perhaps, the fitted equation is used for forecasting. The basic regression procedure involves several assumptions about the residuals, or errors left over when the regression equation is used to explain observations (consisting of sets of values for the explanatory and dependent variables). In particular, the user of regression assumes that the mean value of the residuals (over a very large number of relevant observations) is zero. Also, the user must assume that there is no reason, before the fact, to expect that the regression equation will fit observations with one set of characteristics (or values for its variables) better than it will fit observations with other characteristics. This desired property is called homoscedasticity; its opposite is heteroscedasticity. To see this point, consider a simple regression equation for predicting height from weight for adult males. The assumption implies that the equation does not provide a closer fit for lighter men than it does for heavier ones but that knowing an individual's weight would not change our expectation, before the fact, as to the size of the error that we might expect in predicting his height with the regression equation. Finally, use of the standard regression model involves an assumption that the error made by the regression equation in predicting or explaining one observation does not provide useful information about the error it can be expected to make on any other observation. For example, suppose that we are using regression to explain demand for coffee in successive years. This last assumption would be violated if we felt that a year in which the model underpredicted actual demand was more likely than not to be followed by another year of underprediction. In technical terms, we would expect successive residuals to be correlated; the standard regression procedure assumes there is no such serial correlation. As this example should suggest, the assumption that errors on different observations are not systematically related to one another is often a problem in dealing with regression models involving time series data.

In building on the basic single equation regression model, econometrics considers various situations in which the assumptions implicit in the use of that model are violated and the techniques that can be used to get around such problems. In the single equation model itself, econometricians study and use techniques for handling serial correlation between the residual for one observation and that for the next in fitting models to time series data. For example, one very simple technique that sometimes works is to explain or predict differences in the values of a variable rather than the values of the variable itself. We might feel that we could find an equation for changes in coffee prices in which successive residuals would not be correlated. Econometricians also deal with methods for getting around the problem of heteroscedasticity in single equation regression models or with other single equation issues.

Another very large segment of econometrics concerns the issues involved in using regression and regression-related techniques to find the coefficients of more than one equation. It is often the case in economic studies that an economic system can best be described by a set of equations rather than by a single equation. Often the dependent or left-hand side variable in one of the equations will be one of the explanatory variables in another of the equations. For example, consider the following series of equations for relating consumption, investment, gross national product, and government spending, over time.

$$C_t = a_1 + a_2 Y_{t-1}$$
$$I_t = b_1 + b_2 (Y_{t-1} - Y_{t-2})$$
$$Y_t = C_t + I_t + G_t$$

Here $C_t$ is consumption in time period $t$, $I_t$ is investment in period $t$, $G_t$ is government spending in period $t$, and $Y_t$ is gross national product in $t$. The regression coefficients are $a_1$, $a_2$, $b_1$, and $b_2$. The first of these equations says that consumption is a simple linear function of the previous value of gross national product (or national income). The second says that investment is a linear function of the change in national income between the two previous periods. The last equation is an identity defining gross national product as the sum of consumption, investment, and government spending. The fact that these equations involve some of the same variables turns out to mean that the error made in the first of them for a particular period is related to the error made in the second for the same period. As a result, we find that it is not appropriate to try to fit the equations separately to past data. Instead we fit them together, or simultaneously. Much of econometrics involves techniques for fitting such *simultaneous equation models*.

The simple three-equation model above will serve as a means of introducing a few additional terms from econometrics. Notice that in these equations the variable $G_t$ appears only on the right-hand side. This variable is therefore an example of what is called an *exogenous variable*. Exogenous variables take values that are determined outside the system of equations. $C_t$, $Y_t$, and $I_t$ are all determined within the series of equations. Even though they may appear on the right-hand side of some equations, each of them also appears on the left-hand side of one equation. These variables are called *endogenous variables*. Their values are determined by the equations. Finally $Y_{t-1}$ and $Y_{t-2}$ are the previous values of an endogenous variable. They are called lagged endogenous variables. By the time we have reached period $t$, we will know the actual values for these variables. It is also worth noting that while equations may be related, as are those above (because they involve some of the same variables on different sides of the equal sign), sets of equations may also be related and may therefore require some form of joint fitting techniques even if they do not involve the same variables. This type of situation occurs when the analyst believes that the errors the equations will make in explanation and prediction are related to one another.

The processes by which coefficients for a series of equations are fit to data are called *estimation techniques*. A second set of multi-equation techniques involves forecasting with the sets of equations that result from the estimation step. In simple, single-equation regression, forecasting involves having the user give values for each of the explanatory variables and then using the regression equation to predict a value (or perhaps an entire distribution of values) for the dependent variable. The basic idea of the forecasting process in multi-equation models is the same: Values of the exogenous variables are used, in conjunction with the fitted regression equations, to project values for the endogenous variables. The application of this principle becomes considerably more complicated in simultaneous equation models, however. The values for the exogenous variables can be plugged into the equations, but there then usually remain several variables whose values must be found by solving the equations simultaneously. For example, in the following simplistic two-equation model for consumption and income, $C_t$ is consumption, $Y_t$ is income, and $Z_t$ is nonconsumption expenditure.

$$C_t = \alpha + \beta Y_t$$
$$Y_t = C_t + Z_t$$

$Z_t$ is exogenous, while $Y_t$ and $C_t$ are endogenous. In forecasting, the two variables $Y_t$ and $C_t$ must be found jointly. In larger, more complicated, simultaneous equation models, the solution process is complicated. In simultaneous equation models involving lagged variables (such as the three-equation model discussed earlier), the prediction process may involve forecasting an entire series of values for the endogenous variables. In econometrics, the term *simulation* is used for the process of solving such sets of simultaneous equations. (Note that this use of the term is not the general one used throughout this book.) Econometricians use a collection of solution techniques for this purpose.

A final area of econometrics that we will mention is that of *time series models*. In regression and related models we use the values of explanatory variables to explain and predict the values of other dependent (or endogenous) variables. In time series methods, the only explanatory variables are the past values of the dependent or endogenous variable itself. Among the time series techniques are smoothing techniques, in which the next value of a variable is predicted to be some weighted average of the past values of that variable. Other time series techniques involve similar types of operations, perhaps in rather complex combinations. For example, in ARIMA (or Box Jenkins) models, which are currently among the most complicated in use, the time series of the variable of interest may first be differenced. In other words, changes in the variable may be formed. In fact, the series may be differenced more than once, so that changes of changes or some more complicated combination may be used. Then the past series is fit (and the future predicted) by a combination of a weighted average of past values of the variable and a weighted average of past values of the errors. As should be obvious, such techniques become quite complex.

These other econometric techniques are used in computer simulation models in the same types of ways that simple regression equations are used. In some cases, companies use econometric forecasts prepared by outside experts as inputs to company models. In other cases, firms do their own econometric modeling. While the econometric techniques offer another powerful set of tools for use in modeling, their use should be accompanied by the same caveats mentioned above for single-equation regression modeling. The results of such techniques are useful only insofar as the past data are relevant, the form of the relationship assumed is correct, and the future will be like the past, as far as the modeled relationships are concerned.

## EXERCISES

5.1. Design algorithms to find the mean, median, variance, and standard deviation of a set of data.

5.2. Suppose that the newspaper dealer described in section I is trying to decide how many papers to order for next Sunday, and that you are trying to help. Each paper costs the dealer 50 cents; the newstand price is 75 cents. Any leftover papers can be returned for only a 5 cent credit, so that overordering is expensive. Design a simple model that will find a risk profile of the contribution from the Sunday papers for different strategies on stocking levels.

5.3. Design an algorithm that accepts as inputs a regression equation and the set of data from which the equation was found. The algorithm should construct a table like Table 5–11, giving the values of the dependent and explanatory variables on each observation, together with the corresponding residuals and residuals squared. It should find the average squared error, the residual standard deviation, and the $R^2$ figure.

5.4. Suppose that you have fit a regression equation to some data and that you have available a subprogram that will take as inputs a set of future values of the explanatory variables and will provide as output a list of 50 representative values (bracket medians) of the resulting forecast distribution, using the regression equation. Suppose that you are uncertain of the future value of one of the explanatory variables but that you know the future values of all the other explanatory variables. How might you find the implied future distribution of the dependent variable?

case 5.1

# Exercise on Crosstabs: Data File Bonds (Underwriting Data on 2174 Municipal Bonds)

The data used in this study were collected through the use of a questionnaire mailed to 307 different underwriters, 242 of whom replied. It includes data on all municipal bonds issued by these underwriters in the first six months of the years 1964, 1965, and 1966, whose Moody's ratings were Aa, A, or Baa. Issues of less than $600,000 were excluded because they were not rated by the investors' services.

The following explanation of the bond underwriting process is taken from Peter M. Keir and James Kichline, "Interest Cost Effects of Commercial Bank Underwriting of Municipal Revenue Bonds," *Federal Reserve Bulletin,* August 1967. Substantially the same data set is analyzed in this article.

> *The Bond Underwriting Process*. When state and local governments finance through the issuance of bonds, they incur two kinds of borrowing costs. The more important is the interest rate paid to investors (lenders) who acquire the bonds; such payments must be made regularly over the bond's full life. The other type of cost is a one-time fee paid to bond underwriters when the issue is offered. In return for this fee the underwriters take full responsibility for retailing the new bond to investors, and by acquiring the issue outright from the borrower, they assume the market risk that bond prices may fall while the new issue is still being distributed.
>
> Most municipal bonds—whether general obligation or revenue—are offered publicly for competitive bidding. Underwriting groups who compete in such biddings tender a single bid price for the entire issue in the expectation that they can resell it to investors at a higher price. The bid that wins, in conjunction with the coupon rate on the bond, determines the borrower's net interest cost, which covers both the interest yield to the lender and the underwriting fee.[1]

[1] When the new issue is a negotiated rather than a competitive offering, the bid price (and hence the net interest cost) is set by direct bargaining between the borrower and a single underwriting group rather than by sealed bids from one or more groups. Otherwise, pricing considerations on competitive and negotiated issues are the same.

In attempting to set the requisite bid price, the underwriting group first reaches a decision on two other prices. The more important is the reoffering price, which is determined by the yield at which the syndicate thinks it will be able to make an orderly resale of the issue to investors.[2] Obviously, to insure a successful bond offering, the reoffering yield must be sufficiently attractive to elicit participation by enough investors to attain full distribution. Consequently, when setting yield, the underwriting group must accurately assess the prevailing state of the bond market, including the supply of similar securities being offered for sale and the strength of investor demand for such issues.

After determining the necessary reoffering price, the group then decides what fee or underwriting spread is likely to be needed to cover the management and selling costs incurred in distributing the new issue, as well as to compensate the group for assuming the market risk. Allowance for market risk is understandably the most variable element in the spread. Any special factors that seem to increase the chance of a price decline before the issue can be fully distributed will (other things being equal) contribute to a larger spread. Among these are such things as expectations of rising long-term rates, long average maturities, unusually large offerings, and low investment ratings.[3]

Finally, the residual obtained by subtracting the underwriting spread from the initial reoffering price gives the group the price it should bid (with a given coupon assumed). If this bid wins, that price—together with the coupon (or coupons)—determines the net interest cost to the borrower.

Suppose that it is early 1967 and that you are designing a risk analysis model for an investor who wants to analyze portfolios of municipal bonds. You want to be able to input information about the types and amounts of bonds in the portfolio, together with any other needed inputs, and then to simulate portfolio performance over time. As a first step, you have obtained part of data file BONDS. (As a simplifying assumption, you've decided to consider only bonds with ten-year maturities.) File MUNIC contains data on competitively bid issues only. It includes these variables:

---

[2] The reoffering price, taken in conjunction with the bond coupon, determines the yield to final holders. When the new bond has more than one maturity, as most municipals do, the reoffering price is actually an average of a series of reoffering prices set for each maturity. These prices—in conjunction with the coupons for each maturity—provide a series of reoffering yields to investors at different maturity dates.

[3] In evaluating the significance of market risk, it should be noted that the odds that the underwriter will have to sell some part of a new issue at prices below the initial reoffering price are often fairly high, whereas his chances of selling at a price above the reoffering price are virtually nil (unless he is willing to carry poorly received issues in his own portfolio over a period of time and ultimately succeeds in catching a better market.) If bond prices do decline before a new issue has been fully distributed, the underwriting syndicate is terminated. To achieve a full distribution of the issue, members of the syndicate then cut reoffering prices. On occasions when bond prices are changing rapidly, the depth of price cuts needed to float such an issue sometimes carries the reoffering price substantially below the initial bid price, more than eliminating the underwriter's spread on the unsold portion of the bond. On the other hand, if bond prices rise generally while the issue is still in syndicate, investors usually snap up the offering at the initial syndicate reoffering price and underwriters do not benefit.

1. Year of issue (1964, 1965, or 1966).
2. Moody's rating (Aa, A, or Baa).
3. Type of obligation (REV, GOU, or GOL; these stand for Revenue, General Obligation Unlimited, and General Obligation Limited. Payments on a Revenue Bond are guaranteed only to the extent that revenues are generated by the project for whose financing the bond was issued—a bridge, for example. General Obligation Bonds, on the other hand, are guaranteed by general municipal revenues, with or without limitations).
4. Reoffering yield (in present) of the ten-year maturities in the issue.
5. Difference between Moody's 10-year yield index in the week of the offering and the ten-year reoffering yield of the issue.

I. The following tables were obtained when the reoffering yield on ten-year maturities (variable 4) was used as the dependent variable. (The entries within the cells show the average ten-year yield for issues in those cells.)

1. Year as explanatory variable.

| | | |
|---|---|---|
| 1964 | 3.017 | Residual standard deviation = .179 |
| 1965 | 3.004 | $R^2$ = .717 |
| 1966 | 3.622 | 2066 degrees of freedom |

2. Rating as explanatory variable.

| | | |
|---|---|---|
| Aa | 3.080 | Residual standard deviation = .322 |
| A | 3.170 | $R^2$ = .092 |
| Baa | 3.353 | 2066 degrees of freedom |

3. Type of obligation as explanatory variable.

| | | |
|---|---|---|
| Rev | 3.322 | Residual standard deviation = .334 |
| Gou | 3.188 | $R^2$ = .018 |
| Gol | 3.200 | 2066 degrees of freedom |

4. Year and rating as explanatory variables.

| | Aa | A | Baa |
|---|---|---|---|
| 1964 | 2.877 | 2.990 | 3.150 |
| 1965 | 2.871 | 2.977 | 3.130 |
| 1966 | 3.440 | 3.589 | 3.814 |

Residual standard deviation = .141

$R^2$ = .826

2060 degrees of freedom

5. Year and type as explanatory variables.

| | Rev | Gou | Gol |
|---|---|---|---|
| 1964 | 3.088 | 3.005 | 3.032 |
| 1965 | 3.064 | 2.994 | 3.016 |
| 1966 | 3.736 | 3.602 | 3.587 |

Residual standard deviation = .176

$R^2$ = .728

2060 degrees of freedom

6. Rating and type as explanatory variables.

| | Rev | Gou | Gol |
|---|---|---|---|
| Aa | 3.213 | 3.053 | 3.170 |
| A | 3.262 | 3.156 | 3.150 |
| Baa | 3.505 | 3.330 | 3.334 |

Residual standard deviation = .318

$R^2$ = .113

2060 degrees of freedom

7. Year, rating, and type as explanatory variables.

a. Cell means

| | *Rev:* Aa | A | Baa | *Gou:* Aa | A | Baa | *Gol:* Aa | A | Baa |
|---|---|---|---|---|---|---|---|---|---|
| 1964 | 2.934 | 3.065 | 3.223 | 2.869 | 2.981 | 3.135 | 2.886 | 2.960 | 3.200 |
| 1965 | 2.938 | 3.051 | 3.175 | 2.863 | 2.964 | 3.121 | 2.800 | 2.972 | 3.182 |
| 1966 | 3.530 | 3.689 | 3.981 | 3.417 | 3.574 | 3.782 | 3.479 | 3.552 | 3.794 |

b. The corresponding numbers of observations.

| | | | | | | | | |
|---|---|---|---|---|---|---|---|---|
| 16 | 44 | 26 | 115 | 277 | 173 | 5 | 25 | 15 |
| 16 | 50 | 24 | 113 | 278 | 182 | 2 | 32 | 11 |
| 28 | 45 | 32 | 117 | 243 | 159 | 7 | 26 | 8 |

c. Residual standard deviation = .137

$R^2$ = .838
2042 degrees of freedom

II. The following tables analyze the differences between the Moody ten-year yield index and the ten-year reoffering yield.

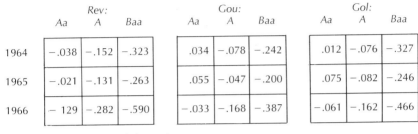

1. Cell means

| | Rev: Aa | Rev: A | Rev: Baa | Gou: Aa | Gou: A | Gou: Baa | Gol: Aa | Gol: A | Gol: Baa |
|---|---|---|---|---|---|---|---|---|---|
| 1964 | −.038 | −.152 | −.323 | .034 | −.078 | −.242 | .012 | −.076 | −.327 |
| 1965 | −.021 | −.131 | −.263 | .055 | −.047 | −.200 | .075 | −.082 | −.246 |
| 1966 | − 129 | −.282 | −.590 | −.033 | −.168 | −.387 | −.061 | −.162 | −.466 |

2. Cell standard deviations.

| Rev: Aa | Rev: A | Rev: Baa | Gou: Aa | Gou: A | Gou: Baa | Gol: Aa | Gol: A | Gol: Baa |
|---|---|---|---|---|---|---|---|---|
| .054 | .080 | .149 | .079 | .070 | .151 | .028 | .075 | .174 |
| .056 | .075 | .089 | .052 | .078 | .130 | .021 | .074 | .147 |
| .095 | .180 | .200 | .097 | .104 | .143 | .074 | .086 | .207 |

3. Residual standard deviation = .108

$R^2$ = .602
2042 degrees of freedom

## Questions

1. Interpret these results.
2. On the basis of this analysis, decide on the inputs, outputs, and basic operation of a risk analysis model for portfolios of municipal bonds.

## case 5.2

# New York Telephone

In 1976 Salvatore Cordo, Supervising Economist for New York Telephone, and his staff were preparing an analysis that would provide part of the basis for a request from New York Telephone to the New York State Public Service Commission to approve an increase in rates for intrastate telephone service in New York. The regulatory apparatus which governed telephone service rates made it important for the phone company analysts to include in their work careful projections of the effects that rate changes would have on telephone company revenues. Therefore, Mr. Cordo had decided to build models of the relation between price and quantity demanded for several types of intrastate telephone service; in other words, he planned to model the elasticity of demand for such services.[1]

New York Telephone was a subsidiary of American Telephone and Telegraph, the parent company of the Bell telephone system. AT&T had operating subsidiaries, such as New England Telephone, in much of the continental United States. The parent company oversaw the maintenance and operation of the interstate long distance telephone lines, while the subsidiaries were responsible for local service. Some of the subsidiary companies were wholly owned by the parent, while others were partially owned by AT&T and partially publicly held. In addition to the Bell companies, the United States had other independent telephone operating companies. These companies provided local service in the regions they served and they also interconnected with the long distance lines of the Bell system to provide interstate service to their customers. Bell system companies accounted for approximately 80 percent of the telephones in the United States, while the remaining 20 percent were operated by independent phone companies.

Two levels of regulation governed the telephone companies in the United States, because under the Constitution, the federal government had authority over interstate commerce, while the states could govern commerce within their borders. Interstate telephone service, provided by AT&T, was regulated

[1] Elasticity is a technical term from economics. The price elasticity for some product or service is the percentage change in the demand for that product or service divided by the percentage price change.

by the Federal Communications Commission. Under the Communications Act of 1934, this seven-commissioner federal agency had been set up to oversee a number of different types of communications activities, including allocation of broadcast licenses and interstate telephone communications. One of the responsibilities of the FCC was to approve or disapprove of proposed changes in the rates charged by AT&T for interstate phone service.

The second level of regulation of telephone services consisted of regulatory commissions in the state, which were responsible for overseeing the operations of the local operating companies. In New York state the regulatory body was the New York State Public Service Commission, which regulated telephone, gas and electric companies, and other utilities.

Because under the law the telephone companies were allowed monopolies in providing many types of services, it was not possible to have market mechanisms set telephone service rates. The philosophy underlying communications regulation was that it was efficient for society to allow such monopolies in areas with sufficiently large economies of scale but that it was then also appropriate for public bodies to oversee the activities of the companies in the public interest. Hence, the telephone companies were required to justify rate increases before the appropriate regulatory bodies.

The basic principle in the regulation of telephone service involved what was called rate of return regulation. In outline, this type of regulation required first that the phone company and the regulatory commission determine the investment base of the phone company. This investment base was called the rate base for the company. The precise way in which the rate base was calculated varied from state to state; it might, for example, be defined as the undepreciated book value of the company's investments in plant and equipment. One of the jobs of the regulatory process was to determine the rate that would be considered a fair return on this rate base. The determination involved consideration of the state of the capital markets and other relevant information. The rate process then required that the company add up its various operating costs and the allowed return on its rate base. This figure provided the aggregate amount which the company could charge its customers for service.

Several factors complicated the rate-making process. For one thing, there was the two-tiered nature of the telephone system, with AT&T and the local companies. When a telephone customer made a long distance call, part of the revenue from that call was assigned to the local operating company in the area in which the call originated, part went to the local company at the receiving end, and the remainder went to AT&T, whose lines provided the middle portion of the communications link. The idea here was to compensate the local companies for the use of their plant and equipment as part of the routing for the long distance call. The question of exactly how to divide the total revenue for a long distance call was a difficult accounting issue that was one of the hard problems in regulation. In addition, this system meant that the local companies would receive part of their revenues under rate schedules which they themselves had not established.

A second set of factors complicating the rate-setting process involved the fact that it was not possible to know, before the fact, precisely what the costs or revenues of an operating company would be. Hence, the target rate of return was in fact only a target. Future rates were set on the basis of past data. Some of the regulatory commissions tried to use this lag in rate-setting constructively in encouraging efficiency by the telephone companies. At the federal level, for example, the FCC had told AT&T that it would be allowed ½ percent of play in the return rate. In other words, if AT&T could make its operations more efficient, cutting costs and thereby increasing its return, the FCC would not intervene to reexamine the rate structure until the rate of return had risen ½ percent above the target. Other commissions handled the problem of delay in rate-setting in other ways. In all cases, it could be assumed that the commissions would review rates if the phone companies returns rose too high. On the other hand, the phone companies could ask for review and rate increases if their rates of return fell too low.

A related complicating factor in rate-setting was that changes in the prices of telephone services would affect the demand for those services. The telephone companies and regulatory commissions would try to set rates that would allow fair rates of return (and only such rates) to the phone companies. To calculate the returns, they needed to estimate revenues and costs. But to estimate revenues they would have to estimate how much of various types of phone service would be demanded by customers at the new rates. It was this problem of estimating the elasticity of demand for telephone services that Mr. Cordo and his staff were analyzing.

At the time, New York Telephone was asking the state regulatory commission to allow it to raise rates. The annual report for the company explained the situation as follows:

> Continuing increases in taxes—particularly property taxes—wages and related costs, depreciation, and other expenses lie ahead. These increases cannot be offset by cost controls alone.
>
> The company needs to earn a minimum of 10.4 percent on intrastate investment. Earnings in that range are necessary to attract the capital for continuing provision of high quality service.

Mr. Cordo would serve as a witness for the rate-setting hearings. He and his staff had prepared exhibits showing the existence of price elasticity in the demand for telephone services. Exhibits 1 and 2 show two of these. Exhibit 1 shows the pattern of the quantity of calls made from coin-operated telephones between 1925 and 1975. In 1951 the cost of such calls had been raised from 5 cents to 10 cents. Mr. Cordo would point out in his testimony that demand had fallen sharply at that time and that the lower demand level had persisted.

**EXHIBIT 1**
Impact of a rate change on local coin public telephone quantity

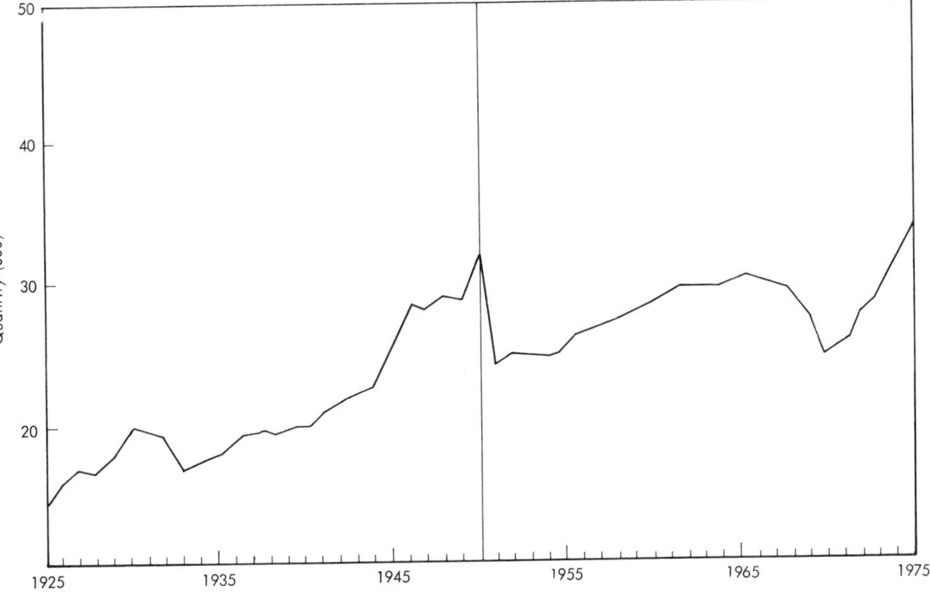

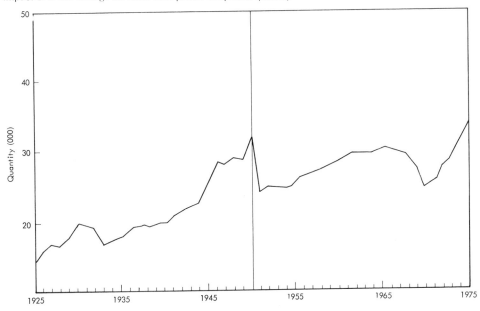

Exhibit 2 shows a similar phenomenon for directory assistance calls before and after New York Telephone instituted charges for such calls in July 1975. In analyzing elasticity for other telephone service, Mr. Cordo felt it would be useful to develop regression equations to explain the demand for various types of phone service and then to use those equations to forecast demand and, hence, revenues under possible new rate schedules. He determined that it would be best to treat separately the demand behavior of different types of intrastate service. He began by considering two customer types: business and residential. In addition, he used three service categories: local service, additional measured unit (AMU) service, and message toll service (MTS). The first service type provided customers with either an unlimited number or else a specified number of calls within a fixed geographical area for a set monthly fee. In the AMU service, customers received a fixed number of message units and then paid for calls beyond that base. The toll service covered non-local (but intrastate) calls such as calls from New York City to Buffalo. The six types of service defined by the different customer types and service types would give six combinations. Mr. Cordo planned to prepare a separate equation for each of these service types. (He would eventually also have to consider demand for other phone company services as well.)

Exhibit 3 shows the data that were collected for possible use in preparing a regression equation for predicting demand for residential local service. The

**EXHIBIT 2**
Directory assistance calls

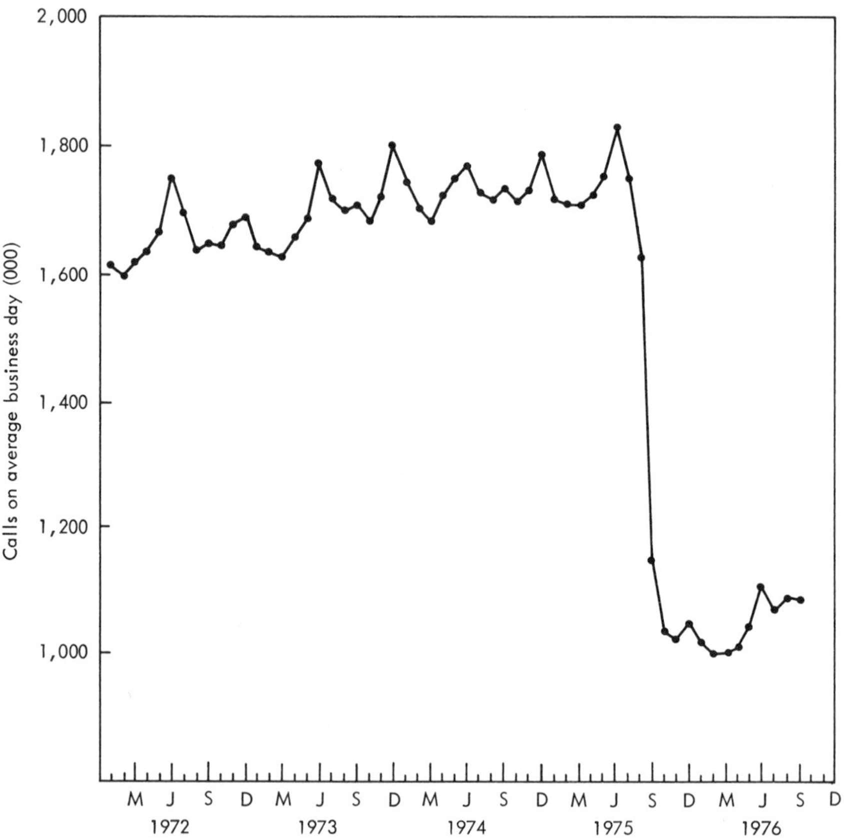


exhibit provides quarterly data. Local service revenues give the receipts from this type of service. The next variable, local service price index, gives the price level for this type of service in relation to the base period of the first part of 1967. The next two variables give general price indices for the New York metropolitan area. They differ with respect to the base they use; the first index gives an average value of 1.00 over 1967; the second index uses only the first quarter of 1967 as a base. The statistics behind these indices were published by the U.S. Bureau of Labor Statistics. The next variable gives personal income in New York, as estimated by the U.S. Department of Commerce. The last variable is a time variable, running from 100 in the first quarter of 1967 to 136 in the first quarter of 1976. Other variables, such as indices measuring the level of business activity in New York, would be available for use in the equations for other services.

**EXHIBIT 3**

Data on residence local services (quarterly averages 1967–1976)

| Date | Local service revenues ($000) | Local service price index (Q1/67 = 1.0) | Consumer price index N.Y. Metropolitan Area (1967 = 100) | Consumer price index N.Y. Metropolitan Area (Q1/67 = 100) | Personal income in New York ($ millions) | Time values (Q1/67 = 100) |
|---|---|---|---|---|---|---|
| 01/67 | 29,516 | 1.000 | 99.1 | 1.000 | 66,823 | 100.0 |
| 02/67 | 29,909 | 1.000 | 99.5 | 1.004 | 67,684 | 101.0 |
| 03/67 | 30,031 | 1.016 | 100.3 | 1.013 | 68,944 | 102.0 |
| 04/67 | 30,759 | 1.039 | 101.2 | 1.022 | 70,170 | 103.0 |
| 01/68 | 31,132 | 1.039 | 102.1 | 1.031 | 72,286 | 104.0 |
| 02/68 | 31,716 | 1.039 | 103.4 | 1.043 | 73,962 | 105.0 |
| 03/68 | 32,107 | 1.039 | 105.1 | 1.061 | 75,458 | 106.0 |
| 04/68 | 32,706 | 1.040 | 106.6 | 1.076 | 77,119 | 107.0 |
| 01/69 | 32,994 | 1.040 | 108.0 | 1.091 | 78,669 | 108.0 |
| 02/69 | 33,802 | 1.040 | 110.1 | 1.111 | 80,165 | 109.0 |
| 03/69 | 33,977 | 1.040 | 111.5 | 1.126 | 81,459 | 110.0 |
| 04/69 | 34,430 | 1.041 | 113.4 | 1.144 | 82,768 | 111.0 |
| 01/70 | 36,786 | 1.072 | 116.0 | 1.171 | 84,054 | 112.0 |
| 02/70 | 38,342 | 1.123 | 118.3 | 1.194 | 86,036 | 113.0 |
| 03/70 | 37,690 | 1.124 | 119.9 | 1.210 | 87,023 | 114.0 |
| 04/70 | 37,746 | 1.126 | 121.7 | 1.228 | 87,198 | 115.0 |
| 01/71 | 37,853 | 1.127 | 123.4 | 1.246 | 89,527 | 116.0 |
| 02/71 | 38,424 | 1.127 | 125.3 | 1.265 | 91,372 | 117.0 |
| 03/71 | 38,965 | 1.148 | 127.0 | 1.282 | 91,718 | 118.0 |
| 04/71 | 38,340 | 1.150 | 127.7 | 1.289 | 91,925 | 119.0 |
| 01/72 | 39,581 | 1.187 | 129.4 | 1.307 | 94,779 | 120.0 |
| 02/72 | 41,030 | 1.212 | 130.7 | 1.319 | 95,228 | 121.0 |
| 03/72 | 41,342 | 1.223 | 132.0 | 1.332 | 96,562 | 122.0 |
| 04/72 | 41,444 | 1.223 | 133.4 | 1.347 | 99,037 | 123.0 |

**EXHIBIT 3 (*continued*)**
Data on residence local services (quarterly averages 1967–1976)

| Date | Local service revenues ($000) | Local service price index (Q1/67 = 1.0) | Consumer price index N.Y. Metropolitan Area (1967 = 100) | Consumer price index N.Y. Metropolitan Area (Q1/67 = 100) | Personal income in New York ($ millions) | Time values (Q1/67 = 100) |
|---|---|---|---|---|---|---|
| 01/73 | 41,535 | 1.223 | 135.1 | 1.364 | 100,493 | 124.0 |
| 02/73 | 42,178 | 1.223 | 138.2 | 1.395 | 102,128 | 125.0 |
| 03/73 | 42,333 | 1.223 | 141.1 | 1.424 | 103,778 | 126.0 |
| 04/73 | 44,617 | 1.282 | 144.5 | 1.458 | 105,919 | 127.0 |
| 01/74 | 48,706 | 1.406 | 149.0 | 1.504 | 107,640 | 128.0 |
| 02/74 | 49,264 | 1.408 | 152.4 | 1.539 | 110,518 | 129.0 |
| 03/74 | 49,552 | 1.409 | 156.8 | 1.582 | 112,995 | 130.0 |
| 04/74 | 49,769 | 1.410 | 161.0 | 1.625 | 114,826 | 131.0 |
| 01/75 | 49,886 | 1.411 | 162.8 | 1.644 | 116,351 | 132.0 |
| 02/75 | 50,651 | 1.411 | 164.4 | 1.659 | 118,747 | 133.0 |
| 03/75 | 51,208 | 1.411 | 167.8 | 1.694 | 121,019 | 134.0 |
| 04/75 | 54,129 | 1.475 | 171.3 | 1.729 | 122,480 | 135.0 |
| 01/76 | 55,310 | 1.511 | 173.4 | 1.750 | 125,417 | 136.0 |

# case 5.3

# National Flood Insurance Program*

In the mid-1960s the U.S. Congress was studying the problem of setting up a program of flood insurance for the country. For decades the federal government had put considerable amounts of money into physical structures meant to help control floods, but those structures could not prevent all floods. The government had not previously been involved in any attempt to provide insurance against floods (although there had been discussions of the desirability of such a program).

The amount of damage each year from floods was considerable; by the mid-1960s it was running over $1 billion. The problem was becoming even worse as more and more areas saw increasing construction on floodplains.[1] Private insurance companies did not offer flood insurance in such areas both because of the large risks involved and because there were not underwriting standards on which to base sound schedules of premiums. In addition, people living in high-risk areas seemed not to understand the high risks of floods in their areas. As a result, it had become standard for floods to occur, causing considerable property damage and causing the affected regions to be declared disaster areas. The federal government would then pour money into those areas in the form of disaster relief to individuals (and businesses). The government might also build new flood control structures for the areas. The new or existing structures would prevent some potential floods but, eventually, waters would rise above the controllable levels and the areas would be flooded again. Again there would be considerable damage; in fact, it was likely that because of increased building on and use of the floodplains since the previous flood, damages would be worse than they had been in the last flood. Again the government would pour disaster relief into the affected areas and the floodplains would be built up again. The cycle would continue.

---

* Much of the background information contained in this case was drawn from the following government sources:

1. 89th Congress, Second Session, Insurance and Other Programs for Financial Assistance to Flood Victims, August 1966.
2. House document 89-465 (1966).
3. Senate Report 93-583 (1973).

[1] See the following section for a discussion of terms related to floods.

There were several objections to the existing system. For one thing, it did not provide incentives to local governments or individuals either to avoid extensive construction on floodplains or to construct buildings in ways meant to reduce their vulnerability to damage from floods to which they wre subjected. An additional, though related, problem was that flood control structures and disaster relief were used by a small fraction of the population but were paid for by everyone. This disparity between users and providers of relief and control measures might have seemed appropriate for single or unexpected disasters but it did not seem appropriate when the recipients used relief to rebuild in the same places, experienced other floods, received additional relief, rebuilt again, . . . . A flood insurance program was interesting in part because it could involve higher insurance premiums for people in higher risk areas and thus better match costs and benefits. In addition, a program might be set up in such a way as to discourage excessive building on floodplains and to encourage local and state governments to plan the use of land more carefully than had been customary.

**Floods and their measurement**

Rivers, lakes, and oceans can all flood adjacent land areas. As an example of the mechanisms through which floods occur, consider the case of a river. Flows in the river are normally confined to the river channel (within the banks of the river) as shown in the first figure (a cross-sectional view of a river and adjacent land).

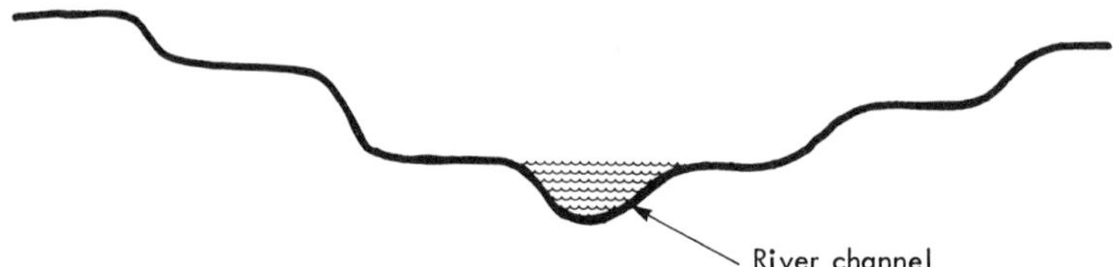


Adjacent to the river channel there normally are flat areas. These areas often have been covered with sediment deposited by the river (in part during past floods). Farther away from the river are land areas elevated farther above the normal level of the river. The land areas near the river and subject to relatively frequent flooding are called the floodplain of the river.

Floods occur when the volume of water in a river is greater than can be contained within the banks. The excess water spills over the banks and is held in the adjacent (or basin) area until it can seep into the ground and/or flow back to the river when the flow volume drops. A moderate flood might at its peak fill the basin to the extent shown in the second figure. On less frequent occasions, the flow in the river might become sufficiently heavy to cause a more serious flood as shown in the third figure.

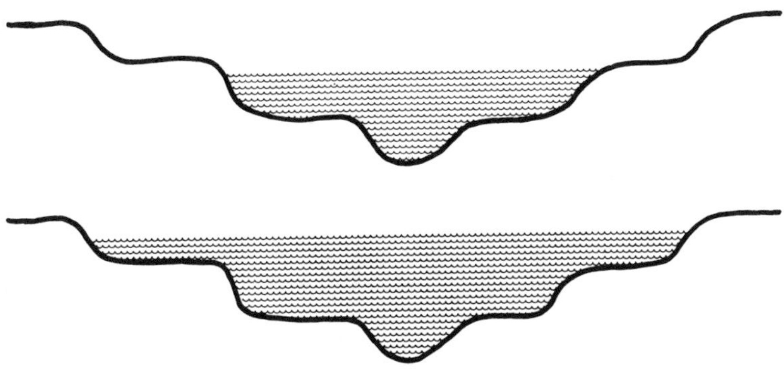

Flows heavy enough to cause flooding can arise when the snow melts late in the mountains whose streams lead into the river. If the snow melts at the same time as the heavy spring rains that are typical of many parts of the country, the resulting volume of flow may be too large to be contained within the river banks. Flooding can also be caused by the extremely heavy rains accompanying hurricanes; in such cases the volume of rain from a tropical storm is itself sufficient to overwhelm the water-carrying capacity of the river channel.

Data on magnitudes and frequencies of floods are available for at least short histories on many rivers. Various government agencies collect such information. The U.S. Geological Survey, for example, regularly measures the flow in many streams throughout the country. When floods occur, streamgagers from the Geological Survey are sent out to measure the depth and extent of flooding as close as possible to the time at which the flood peaks.

Hydrologists often express information about the likelihood of floods of different severities on a particular river in what is called a stage-frequency curve. Such a curve plots the depth (or stage) of water in a flood against the probability that a flood of at least that severity will occur in any given year. These curves have given rise to some potentially confusing terminology; hydrologists speak of a 100-year flood, for example. While the terminology suggests to many people that such a flood is one which will occur every 100 years (and hence, that if a flood of that severity occurred in one year, another flood as bad would not occur again for a century), the term really means only that the *chance* that such a flood will occur in any given year is one in a hundred (i.e., that that depth is the .99 fractile on the cumulative probability distribution function for flood depths).[2]

[2] In fact, if anything, the chances of another bad flood following a 100-year flood are higher than normal because the groundwater level would remain high from the first period of excessive flow and it would be easier than in a dry period for additional flows to exceed the additional water storage capacity of the river basin.

## Damage from floods

In 1966 the Secretary of Housing and Urban Development submitted a report called "Insurance and Other Programs for Financial Assistance to Flood Victims" to the President, at the request of Congress. Four federal agencies had conducted studies of damages from flooding to aid in the preparation of that report. The Army Corps of Engineers, the Geological Survey, the Tennessee Valley Authority, and the Soil Conservation Service had each made special studies for the report. The studies of three of the agencies had focused on questions of how much property was located in flood-prone areas, how valuable such property was, and what relationship there was between the depth of flooding and the amount of property damage which would result. In particular, the studies considered the fact that within a single river basin areas which were lower in elevation and closer to the river had higher risks of flood damage than did higher areas farther from the river. (In the fourth figure, structures on level 1 are exposed to more risk than those on level 2 or on level 3.)

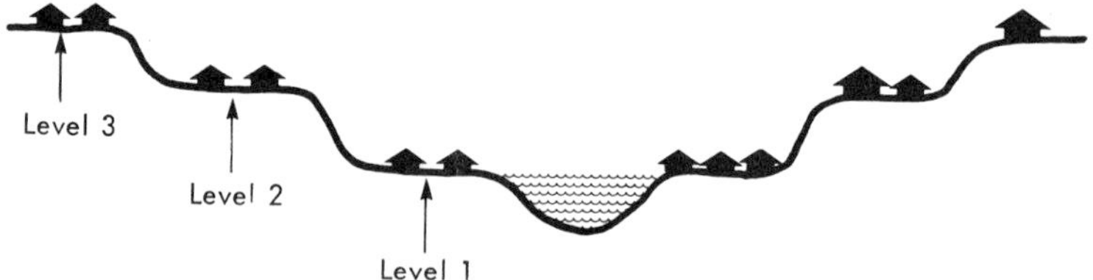


In measuring potential flood damages, the studies had considered what areas (with what values of property on them) would be affected by various depths of flooding. They had considered 48 areas (6 agricultural and 42 primarily urban) which were subject to at least occasional flooding. These areas had different geographical features; they were also marked by different levels of use of the floodplains. As a result, the government had reasonably good information on the relationship between depth of flood and damage in a selection of river basins with different degrees of construction on their floodplains.

## Plans for an insurance program

The planning for a federally assisted flood insurance program involved several parts. The program would have two principal aims, one to encourage more intelligent use of planning for floodplain areas and the other to make voluntary flood insurance available in flood-prone areas at reasonable cost. The program would differentiate between structures which existed at the time of enactment of the program and structures built after that time. For the existing structures the government would be willing to subsidize insurance premium payments to private companies in order to induce the companies to offer the insurance (by making the premiums commensurate with the risks) while at the same time leaving the premiums paid by individual property owners at reasonable levels. In addition, the government might help set up an initial reserve of funds from which payments to flood victims would come and it would "reinsure" the participating insurance companies; that is, the government would pay losses in any given year exceeding some prescribed level.

For new structures in the flood-prone areas the government-assisted program would try to make people realize the full costs of flooding. It would require premiums bearing the full insurance cost (with no subsidy for premiums) for such new structures before granting any federally backed mortgages or other aid. It would also require types of construction meant to provide some protection against flood damages for such buildings.

Under such a program the flood insurance would be issued by private insurance companies and individual property owners would pay their *premiums* directly to those companies. The companies would receive *subsidy premiums* for older structures from the government. Both premiums and subsidies would be put into the *reserve*. When losses occurred the claims would be handled and paid from the reserve by the private companies except that if losses exceeded a prescribed level in any one year, the government would pay losses above that level (payments would go to the insurance companies which would then reimburse the claimants; see the diagram of premiums and payments).

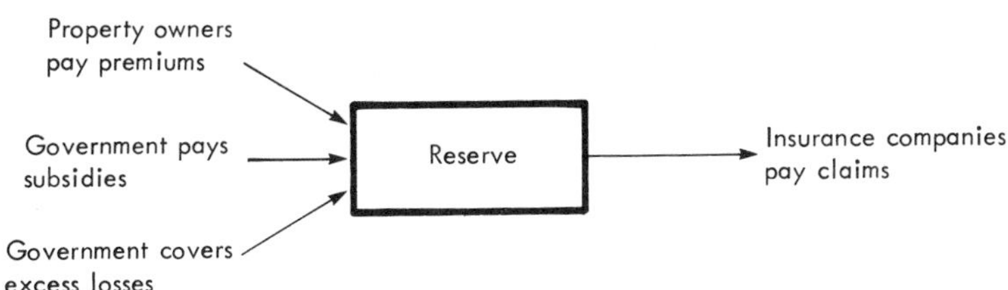


Thus, in setting up the financial side of the program the government and companies had to set schedules of premiums for properties in categories by different levels of risk. (Structures right next to a river were more subject to flooding than structures at slightly higher elevations, for example.) They also had to determine what subsidies would be paid. Finally, they had to set the level of the initial reserve which would be set up for the program (and into which later premiums would be paid and from which damage claims would be paid out) and also the level of yearly losses above which the government would assume losses. Members of Congress and other government officials wanted to understand what various choices for premiums, subsidies, initial reserves, and excessive-loss level would mean in terms of how the reserve fund would behave and, in particular, of how much the government might have to pay into the fund.

## case 5.4

# Korvettes Department Stores*

During the 1974–75 school year, Michael Weingarten, a first-year student at Harvard Business School, had begun to wonder whether regression analysis could be used to help with a problem that had faced him in his former job at Korvettes Department Stores. Specifically, he wondered whether regression could be used to predict sales in new stores, using sales and characteristics of existing Korvettes stores as a guide. By 1976 Mr. Weingarten had done some preliminary analysis showing that the approach looked promising and Korvettes executives wanted to use it to evaluate some proposed sites for new stores.

### Company background

Korvettes was started in 1948 by Eugene Ferkauf and Joe Zwillenberg, two men from Brooklyn, New York, who had served together on a corvette (boat) during World War II. The two took their first initials, changed the "c" in corvette to a "K" to avoid confusion with the Corvette car, and opened the first "E. J. Korvettes" on 48th Street in New York. It was one of the first two discount stores in New York and was a huge success from the start, selling branded merchandise at 20 to 22 percent off. Within the next two years the firm began opening additional stores in the suburbs of New York, where again it met great success. Its customers were largely middle-class people with money to spend and strong price sensitivity. For the time, its stores were large in size; their image was that of full-line discount stores with exceptionally good prices.

In its early years, the operation style at Korvettes was distinctly entrepreneurial in flavor and was marked by an absence of controls and procedures. The offices were marked by enthusiasm and confusion. But, Korvettes had a very salable idea and business was excellent. The firm was turning its goods so fast that it was receiving its customers' money well before it had to pay the distributors from whom it purchased most of its goods.

* This case was made possible by the cooperation of Mr. Michael Weingarten (and that of Korvettes and R. M. Blank Associates).

The period from 1950 to the mid-1960s saw strong years for the company. Its sales expanded to about $600 million. By 1965 it had over 40 stores, mostly in the New York metropolitan area but also in Philadelphia, Baltimore, Washington, Chicago, Detroit, and St. Louis. During the 1950s other discount chains had started, among them Zayre, Topps, Two Guys and others. In addition, during the 1950s and 1960s the major department stores began moving to the suburbs, often to large shopping malls with many stores. An example was Roosevelt Field Shopping Center on Long Island, not far from Korvettes' Westbury suburban store. Roosevelt Field had a million square feet of store space, including a Macy's, a Gimbel's and many smaller stores. Korvettes early suburban stores, on the other hand, were all free-standing along the side of major roads.

As the pressure from department stores and from other discounters grew, Korvettes faced new pressures. It began to promote its merchandise considerably more than it had in the past, emphasizing special price promotions rather than normal day-to-day prices in some cases. The problem of the shopping malls was a difficult one, especially considering the fact that the department stores would not allow discounters into many of the new malls. Many of the discount chains formed during the 1950s had serious problems in the late 1960s and early 1970s. Those stores were generally smaller than Korvettes (perhaps 100,000 square feet versus 150,000 to 200,000 for Korvettes stores). They began and remained supermarket-like in their operation, with front-end checkouts. They were basically self-service stores, with low service, low fashion, low markup, low expense—and low prices. Some of these chains survived the difficult period, but a number, such as Arlans and Interstate, went into bankruptcy in the early 1970s.

During the 1960s and early 1970s Korvettes' image changed somewhat from what it had been in the chain's early history. The firm began to build a few two-story stores that were more like department stores than the early one-story Korvettes had been. Stores included more fashion-goods in clothes and related departments and, in general, moved to a position somewhere between the low-end discounters and the more quality and service-conscious chains like Sears and Penney's. At the same time that some of the early low-end discounters went out of business, in the 1970s, other chains started, often arising from existing retail organizations. For example, K Mart was started from Kresge, while Venture discount stores came from the May Company. This second generation of discounters was considerably more professional than had been the first and they were marked by low expenses and low prices.

Between 1960 and the mid-1970s Korvettes went through several significant ownership and management changes. In the mid 1960s it merged with Spartan Industries, a firm that produced and sold shirts and sportswear. It also operated a chain of 100 discount stores under the name of Spartan-Atlantic. Eventually Charles Bassine, who had come into the firm with the

Spartan merger, emerged as the dominant force in the company and Eugene Ferkauf, the founder, left. In 1971 the firm merged with a real estate development firm called Arlen to form Arlen Realty and Development Company; Korvettes was a division of that firm. Several years later, Korvettes was made a separate corporation, although it was still wholly owned by Arlen.

By the end of 1974, Korvettes was the fifth largest general merchandise discount store chain in the United States. Annual sales were $700 million, coming from 52 stores in 12 different advertising markets. (Since certain metropolitan areas like New York or Washington extend over multistate areas, it is more useful to consider advertising markets than simple political boundaries.) Twenty-two of the stores were in the New York metropolitan area. The company's plans for growth included new store expansion.

In the mid-1970s Korvettes stores continued to sell both hard goods (such as housewares, appliances, stationery, drugs) and soft goods (such as clothing), as it had from the start. The hard goods were still generally name brands; the soft goods sold in discount stores were generally not well-known brands. Discounters in general sold perhaps 40 to 45 percent soft goods at the time, while department stores sold more like 70 or 75 percent soft goods. Margins on soft goods, where fashion was an important factor, were generally better than those on hard goods, and Korvettes' management was anxious to encourage further growth in the proportion of soft goods sold.

Korvettes' customers had changed somewhat from its clientele in its early period. It still had some of the early middle-class, relatively affluent but very price-conscious customers with whom it had had such success at the outset; such customers were particularly interested in Korvettes' hard goods. In addition, however, Korvettes had many lower and lower-middle income customers, including many members of minority groups, who it seemed were particularly apt to shop at the chain. These customers were by and large the ones who bought the stores' soft goods.

Korvettes' executives saw their competition coming from both department stores and other discounters. In the main market area in New York and New Jersey, there were Two Guys discount stores and some small regional discounters, but Korvettes tended to see the department stores as much stronger competition than the relatively few other discounters in the area.

## Store location analysis at Korvettes

Mr. Weingarten had worked as a staff assistant at Korvettes for two years before entering the MBA program at Harvard. In that position, he had had several opportunities to observe the site selection process at Korvettes and had had several prolonged talks with Ray Blank, vice president for new store sites, about some of the problems involved in store site selection. The traditional method by which retailers predicted sales of new stores started with demographic analyses and site visits and studies by the firm's (or others') real estate experts. They would consider the degrees of current and expected future competition, the ease of highway access, costs of the site and other factors. They would also consider the average sales per square foot of space for all existing stores. The real estate experts would judgmentally combine demographic information, site information, and overall average sales rates to come up with an estimate of sales for the new store.

In an effort to make the estimation procedure more accurate, Korvettes also considered the fact that different stores had different trading zones, or zones from which they drew their traffic. For a given size of store, the more people in the trading zone, the greater should be the sales figure, all else being equal. More specifically, Korvettes executives knew that for a typical suburban Korvettes store, 75 percent of all customers came from within a five-mile radius (or a ten-minute drive, when road access was not equal in all directions). Thus, sound forecasting of store sales should, they felt, consider the characteristics of the population of the store's trading zone.

The method of analysis then in use at Korvettes did attempt to consider the trading zone. When a new site was being considered, its trading zone (perhaps a five-mile radius) was drawn on a map. Using computerized census data from a time-sharing service, the firm would obtain income data for the zone and from that information would estimate the zone's expenditures for what was called GAFO (general merchandise, apparel, furniture, and other department-store-type merchandise). In doing so, Korvettes planners used figures for GAFO as a percent of income that were published for various geographical areas; they might in some cases commission studies to check on the validity of those percentages. Then, Korvettes' overall share of GAFO for all of its markets was applied to give the projected Korvettes sales in the market area under study. For example, if Korvettes had an overall 3 percent share of GAFO in the overall market, the sales estimate for the new store would be 3 percent of the GAFO for its trading zone, subject to judgmental adjustment in light of real estate analyses.

Korvettes executives had become more and more aware that even this more sophisticated approach was inadequate, for sales for new stores had been significantly different from what had been projected on the basis of share of GAFO. Looking at the results of the store planning to date, Mr. Weingarten felt that the GAFO scheme ignored the fact that Korvettes attracted lower to lower-middle income people, while higher income groups were more likely to shop in full-line department stores. Thus, it was important to realize that a trading zone with 100,000 households and a median disposable income of $10,000 would represent more business for Korvettes than would a zone with exactly the same GAFO but with 50,000 households and a median disposable income of $20,000. Other characteristics of the trading zone might also influence Korvettes' sales. Korvettes executives believed that members of minority groups (particularly blacks and Spanish-speaking people) were particularly likely to shop at Korvettes. Similarly, since families often bought children's clothing in discount stores (since the clothing would soon be outgrown), family sizes in a trading zone might be important. When he first worked on the problem, Mr. Weingarten did not know how to take the various factors into account and so he did not pursue the matter.

While taking the first-year quantitative methods course in business school, however, he realized that regression analysis provided a method that might be applicable to the problem. He contacted Ray Blank, who had by then left Korvettes to start his own consulting company (R. M. Blank Associates). Mr. Blank was in the process of doing some site location work for Korvettes and was able to make available computerized census data for the trading zones of ten specific Korvettes stores. Mr. Weingarten proceeded to work on that data, despite the small number of observations, with the idea that if the results looked promising Korvettes might find it worthwhile to pay for the collection of data on additional stores. (Such data collection would cost a few thousand dollars.) His preliminary results were encouraging and in 1976 the firm hired Mr. Blank's company to provide data on a larger set of stores. All of these stores were in the general New York area and, in particular, in the suburban parts of that region. Exhibits 1A–1D give some of the census tract data provided by R. M. Blank Associates for those stores. Exhibit 2 gives characteristics of the stores themselves as well as past sales figures. Korvettes divided sales into home furnishings and mercantile sales (everything else). Furnishings had been phased out of some of the stores outside of New York and was not being emphasized by Korvettes. Accordingly, the main interest was in predicting mercantile sales. In an attempt to consider the competitive forces on the various stores, Mr. Robert Warner, senior vice president at Korvettes, had given the competitive information summarized in Exhibit 3.

## New store sites

Korvettes planners hoped to use the past data from the first three exhibits to study the relationship between sales and possible explanatory factors. They then hoped to use their new information in evaluating potential new sites. Two possible sites seemed good candidates for consideration. The first was in Town A, New York. Exhibit 4 gives census tract information for the trading zone for the site and also proposed characteristics of the store. The site was in a densely populated area with good access and little competition. Korvettes believed that GAFO dollars from the trading zone were being spent in significant amounts outside of that zone, which was "understored."[1]

[1] In deciding whether an area was understored, Korvettes planners first found the estimated GAFO for the area, as described earlier. They divided that figure by $60, an estimate of retail volume per square foot. Comparing the result with the estimated actual retail square footage in the area, they determined the relation between supply and demand for department-store-type sales space.

**EXHIBIT 1A***

| Store | Population percent black | Population† percent Spanish | Families with 0–5,000 incomes (percent) | Family incomes 5–7,000 (percent) | Family incomes 7–10,000 (percent) | Family incomes 10–15,000 (percent) | Family incomes 15–25,000 (percent) | Family incomes 25–50,000 (percent) | Family incomes 50+ (percent) | Median family income |
|---|---|---|---|---|---|---|---|---|---|---|
| 1 ....... | 1.4 | 1.2 | 17.1 | 10.6 | 19.5 | 28.2 | 19.6 | 4.2 | 0.6 | $10,480 |
| 2 ....... | 23.9 | 22.4 | 28.0 | 14.0 | 20.0 | 22.4 | 13.1 | 2.3 | 0.2 | 8,204 |
| 3 ....... | 11.1 | 0.9 | 8.7 | 6.6 | 14.5 | 28.8 | 28.8 | 10.2 | 2.3 | 13,495 |
| 4 ....... | 5.3 | 1.3 | 10.7 | 8.2 | 17.0 | 29.6 | 26.3 | 7.0 | 1.0 | 12,362 |
| 5 ....... | 26.0 | 1.3 | 11.8 | 7.9 | 16.1 | 27.9 | 25.9 | 8.7 | 1.8 | 12,563 |
| 6 ....... | 4.4 | 0.4 | 7.8 | 5.0 | 14.9 | 35.2 | 29.6 | 6.7 | 0.6 | 13,151 |
| 7 ....... | 7.7 | 1.0 | 8.1 | 5.4 | 11.3 | 30.4 | 33.6 | 10.2 | 0.9 | 14,142 |
| 8 ....... | 8.4 | 1.1 | 9.9 | 6.7 | 17.3 | 32.6 | 27.4 | 5.5 | 0.6 | 12,474 |
| 9 ....... | 6.3 | 1.3 | 9.6 | 7.1 | 16.4 | 31.1 | 27.1 | 7.8 | 1.0 | 12,730 |
| 10 ....... | 14.4 | 7.8 | 17.3 | 10.6 | 18.9 | 26.6 | 19.7 | 5.7 | 1.2 | 10,610 |
| 11 ....... | 5.1 | 0.7 | 8.5 | 6.2 | 12.8 | 23.7 | 25.6 | 15.5 | 7.8 | 14,771 |
| 12 ....... | 6.7 | 0.4 | 7.9 | 5.3 | 11.8 | 23.7 | 29.2 | 16.4 | 5.7 | 15,413 |
| 13 ....... | 6.4 | 1.6 | 11.1 | 7.6 | 17.4 | 34.2 | 24.8 | 4.4 | 0.5 | 12,036 |
| 14 ....... | 11.2 | 0.3 | 7.4 | 5.5 | 13.8 | 30.1 | 30.2 | 11.2 | 1.8 | 13,873 |
| 15 ....... | 5.9 | 2.9 | 9.0 | 6.3 | 17.6 | 37.9 | 24.0 | 4.5 | 0.7 | 12,251 |
| 16 ....... | 9.8 | 0.4 | 8.3 | 6.2 | 17.1 | 35.2 | 26.3 | 6.0 | 0.9 | 12,617 |
| 17 ....... | 1.4 | 1.0 | 5.8 | 4.2 | 12.2 | 33.8 | 35.1 | 8.1 | 0.8 | 14,117 |
| 18 ....... | 8.3 | 0.6 | 7.9 | 5.6 | 13.5 | 29.8 | 31.3 | 10.2 | 1.6 | 13,851 |
| 19 ....... | 4.1 | 0.3 | 4.5 | 3.6 | 10.4 | 28.9 | 35.4 | 14.4 | 2.7 | 15,710 |
| 20 ....... | 2.8 | 0.6 | 5.8 | 4.4 | 10.9 | 27.6 | 35.1 | 14.0 | 2.1 | 15,347 |
| 21 ....... | 0.6 | 0.7 | 8.0 | 5.5 | 16.3 | 35.8 | 28.9 | 5.1 | 0.5 | 12,821 |
| 22 ....... | 28.9 | 1.1 | 10.5 | 7.7 | 16.1 | 29.9 | 27.2 | 7.4 | 1.1 | 12,618 |
| 23 ....... | 7.1 | 3.4 | 11.7 | 7.7 | 16.8 | 29.8 | 25.9 | 7.1 | 1.1 | 12,318 |
| 24 ....... | 6.6 | 0.4 | 7.0 | 4.9 | 12.0 | 27.8 | 31.8 | 13.2 | 3.2 | 14,690 |
| 25 ....... | 18.4 | 1.9 | 13.3 | 8.8 | 17.0 | 27.4 | 22.9 | 8.6 | 1.9 | 11,972 |

* The census tract data reported here cover a circular area around the store, with a three-mile radius used for stores closer to New York city's center and a five-mile radius used for stores farther from the city. The only exception to this rule is that the data do not include areas within the specified radius but separated from the store by a water barrier.

† In the census tract data, the population is divided into white, black, and other (totaling 100 percent). The classification *Spanish-speaking* can include members of the white or black group. Thus, black and Spanish are NOT mutually exclusive categories.

**EXHIBIT 1B**

| Store | Median rent paid | Median home value | Percent home owners | No cars (percent) | 1 car (percent) | Households with TV (percent) | With washer (percent) |
|---|---|---|---|---|---|---|---|
| 1 ...... | 94 | $27,768 | 10.6 | 47.1 | 46.1 | 91.7 | 40.6 |
| 2 ...... | 70 | 24,063 | 7.0 | 61.2 | 33.6 | 90.2 | 36.8 |
| 3 ...... | 146 | 30,107 | 52.6 | 20.9 | 53.3 | 93.5 | 58.5 |
| 4 ...... | 141 | 29,153 | 19.3 | 39.3 | 51.0 | 92.3 | 36.6 |
| 5 ...... | 127 | 26,801 | 62.9 | 21.8 | 48.2 | 93.6 | 62.7 |
| 6 ...... | 154 | 25,121 | 85.5 | 6.1 | 44.7 | 94.4 | 77.2 |
| 7 ...... | 147 | 35,519 | 67.0 | 8.5 | 40.4 | 92.6 | 69.5 |
| 8 ...... | 123 | 24,767 | 61.4 | 12.4 | 43.7 | 93.1 | 69.4 |
| 9 ...... | 124 | 29,675 | 58.7 | 13.2 | 45.3 | 93.1 | 69.0 |
| 10 ...... | 90 | 31,942 | 13.8 | 44.5 | 43.6 | 91.8 | 40.7 |
| 11 ...... | 136 | 46,883 | 50.7 | 13.2 | 44.1 | 92.8 | 65.4 |
| 12 ...... | 147 | 44,132 | 47.5 | 14.2 | 48.2 | 92.1 | 58.5 |
| 13 ...... | 110 | 26,560 | 52.4 | 19.6 | 55.7 | 92.7 | 69.4 |
| 14 ...... | 131 | 30,382 | 71.5 | 7.4 | 40.2 | 93.5 | 73.7 |
| 15 ...... | 154 | 22,625 | 82.3 | 6.9 | 45.7 | 93.1 | 74.8 |
| 16 ...... | 134 | 25,193 | 64.9 | 8.1 | 43.1 | 93.3 | 68.4 |
| 17 ...... | 154 | 29,644 | 91.4 | 3.1 | 37.1 | 99.1 | 88.4 |
| 18 ...... | 150 | 28,477 | 76.8 | 10.5 | 47.4 | 98.6 | 77.7 |
| 19 ...... | 161 | 31,519 | 90.4 | 4.1 | 34.9 | 98.3 | 85.4 |
| 20 ...... | 138 | 32,805 | 88.8 | 4.5 | 34.1 | 98.0 | 85.1 |
| 21 ...... | 158 | 26,885 | 85.1 | 4.6 | 43.1 | 98.7 | 84.6 |
| 22 ...... | 130 | 25,744 | 69.9 | 20.4 | 50.2 | 98.1 | 68.6 |
| 23 ...... | 111 | 29,973 | 55.9 | 16.7 | 40.4 | 97.3 | 71.2 |
| 24 ...... | 155 | 30,331 | 81.0 | 8.3 | 43.7 | 98.5 | 80.5 |
| 25 ...... | 123 | 27,593 | 38.7 | 26.1 | 44.4 | 96.7 | 61.0 |

The store would have adequate parking space; it could be increased in size from 170,000 to 200,000 square feet gross if sales warranted.

The second potential site was in the Town B Shopping Plaza in New Jersey. The area was densely populated. A new Korvettes store would face competition for some low-end discounters but not from department stores, which were generally considered more of a threat. Exhibit 5 provides information on the trading zone and proposed new store in Town B.

**EXHIBIT 1C**

| Store | With dryer (percent) | With dish-washer (percent) | With air conditioner (percent) | With freezer (percent) | With second home (percent) | Percent adults (over 25) with 0–8 years school | Percent with 9–11 years school |
|---|---|---|---|---|---|---|---|
| 1 ....... | 9.8 | 8.2 | 32.7 | 5.4 | 1.8 | 37.3 | 19.0 |
| 2 ....... | 4.8 | 3.3 | 16.6 | 4.8 | 1.4 | 40.9 | 22.4 |
| 3 ....... | 28.4 | 25.9 | 43.2 | 13.7 | 2.5 | 22.2 | 16.9 |
| 4 ....... | 12.9 | 14.0 | 43.0 | 6.2 | 2.5 | 26.6 | 16.2 |
| 5 ....... | 32.2 | 24.3 | 33.3 | 17.4 | 1.6 | 24.2 | 19.1 |
| 6 ....... | 52.5 | 32.0 | 32.3 | 24.5 | 1.5 | 19.6 | 21.4 |
| 7 ....... | 52.1 | 41.2 | 39.3 | 21.0 | 2.0 | 18.8 | 14.6 |
| 8 ....... | 39.8 | 22.6 | 47.6 | 16.7 | 2.3 | 25.9 | 17.4 |
| 9 ....... | 37.7 | 21.4 | 45.1 | 14.8 | 2.0 | 26.9 | 18.5 |
| 10 ....... | 10.8 | 9.7 | 28.1 | 7.0 | 1.9 | 32.9 | 18.9 |
| 11 ....... | 39.0 | 36.2 | 37.5 | 19.1 | 3.1 | 20.7 | 13.7 |
| 12 ....... | 36.7 | 36.7 | 41.0 | 16.9 | 2.4 | 16.5 | 13.1 |
| 13 ....... | 33.3 | 16.9 | 37.9 | 9.9 | 1.3 | 27.7 | 22.5 |
| 14 ....... | 50.2 | 33.1 | 47.4 | 19.4 | 3.0 | 18.1 | 14.1 |
| 15 ....... | 48.7 | 27.2 | 21.3 | 22.3 | 1.0 | 21.4 | 23.6 |
| 16 ....... | 42.1 | 21.5 | 49.7 | 16.3 | 1.8 | 21.5 | 17.6 |
| 17 ....... | 69.2 | 55.3 | 38.6 | 29.1 | 3.5 | 16.8 | 16.1 |
| 18 ....... | 43.8 | 32.8 | 54.0 | 20.3 | 4.5 | 21.7 | 18.0 |
| 19 ....... | 64.4 | 51.8 | 57.3 | 32.0 | 4.3 | 14.9 | 16.2 |
| 20 ....... | 66.4 | 55.4 | 45.8 | 28.7 | 5.0 | 14.8 | 13.6 |
| 21 ....... | 63.2 | 44.2 | 33.0 | 26.2 | 3.1 | 16.6 | 18.2 |
| 22 ....... | 32.3 | 23.1 | 46.8 | 18.1 | 4.0 | 24.4 | 20.2 |
| 23 ....... | 40.2 | 23.9 | 48.7 | 15.4 | 4.2 | 30.7 | 18.6 |
| 24 ....... | 51.2 | 40.9 | 56.7 | 24.5 | 4.8 | 19.1 | 16.7 |
| 25 ....... | 30.4 | 21.6 | 46.4 | 13.4 | 5.3 | 26.1 | 18.6 |

**EXHIBIT 1D**

| *Store* | *Percent with 12 years school* | *Percent with 13–15 years school* | *Percent with 16+ years school* | *Total population* | *Average family size* |
|---|---|---|---|---|---|
| 1 ........ | 29.2 | 7.4 | 7.2 | 642,990 | 3.2 |
| 2 ........ | 27.2 | 5.0 | 4.5 | 742,557 | 3.5 |
| 3 ........ | 34.4 | 11.4 | 15.0 | 872,388 | 3.4 |
| 4 ........ | 32.3 | 10.9 | 14.1 | 720,417 | 3.1 |
| 5 ........ | 34.5 | 10.7 | 11.5 | 490,775 | 3.6 |
| 6 ........ | 39.4 | 9.9 | 9.7 | 286,402 | 4.0 |
| 7 ........ | 33.9 | 12.9 | 19.8 | 159,397 | 3.9 |
| 8 ........ | 33.0 | 8.8 | 15.0 | 189,767 | 3.7 |
| 9 ........ | 32.7 | 9.7 | 12.3 | 529,803 | 3.4 |
| 10 ........ | 30.5 | 7.6 | 10.1 | 1,113,180 | 3.3 |
| 11 ........ | 29.9 | 12.1 | 23.6 | 132,749 | 3.5 |
| 12 ........ | 31.8 | 13.0 | 25.6 | 336,557 | 3.4 |
| 13 ........ | 34.4 | 7.6 | 7.9 | 308,776 | 3.7 |
| 14 ........ | 33.8 | 12.0 | 22.0 | 229,714 | 3.6 |
| 15 ........ | 38.6 | 8.8 | 7.6 | 243,626 | 4.0 |
| 16 ........ | 36.2 | 9.6 | 15.1 | 280,040 | 3.6 |
| 17 ........ | 38.0 | 12.8 | 16.4 | 216,949 | 4.2 |
| 18 ........ | 36.4 | 10.9 | 13.0 | 517,503 | 3.7 |
| 19 ........ | 38.0 | 12.8 | 18.1 | 201,518 | 3.9 |
| 20 ........ | 35.7 | 14.0 | 22.0 | 179,826 | 3.9 |
| 21 ........ | 37.6 | 12.1 | 15.5 | 165,542 | 4.0 |
| 22 ........ | 34.9 | 10.1 | 10.4 | 647,149 | 3.7 |
| 23 ........ | 29.1 | 8.7 | 12.9 | 210,112 | 3.6 |
| 24 ........ | 36.0 | 11.9 | 16.3 | 421,851 | 3.7 |
| 25 ........ | 30.4 | 9.8 | 15.1 | 607,050 | 3.4 |

**EXHIBIT 2**

| Store | *Selling square feet (000)* | *Annual sales (000)* | *Percent hardgoods* |
|---|---|---|---|
| 1 | 122.5 | $19,221 | 53.3 |
| 2 | 111.7 | 23,637 | 52.9 |
| 3 | 123.4 | 15,607 | 63.9 |
| 4 | 106.0 | 13,326 | 51.5 |
| 5 | 116.9 | 10,161 | 59.5 |
| 6 | 85.0 | 8,640 | 51.2 |
| 7 | 90.3 | 10,811 | 55.9 |
| 8 | 74.9 | 7,371 | 54.6 |
| 9 | 122.8 | 14,877 | 58.6 |
| 10 | 120.9 | 24,194 | 54.0 |
| 11 | 120.3 | 14,797 | 58.6 |
| 12 | 64.4 | 14,843 | 60.5 |
| 13 | 112.6 | 11,673 | 54.7 |
| 14 | 93.8 | 11,203 | 51.1 |
| 15 | 49.1 | 4,684 | 54.3 |
| 16 | 118.1 | 11,009 | 51.2 |
| 17 | 104.5 | 9,674 | 43.7 |
| 18 | 110.1 | 7,985 | 46.9 |
| 19 | 105.0 | 9,011 | 50.0 |
| 20 | 77.2 | 7,271 | 55.1 |
| 21 | 85.7 | 8,757 | 48.7 |
| 22 | 100.0 | 13,238 | 51.1 |
| 23 | 116.1 | 8,441 | 52.6 |
| 24 | 74.1 | 8,109 | 66.0 |
| 25 | 113.2 | 13,416 | 53.6 |

**EXHIBIT 3**

| *Competitive type* | *Stores* | *Description* |
|---|---|---|
| 1 | 1,2,10 | Densely populated areas, particularly good store sites, with relatively little direct competition. |
| 2 | 3,11,12,25 | Good locations in relatively high income areas, with little competition. |
| 3 | 7,9,13,16,19, 20,21,23 | Locations near major shopping centers. |
| 4 | 4,18 | Stores in downtown areas of suburbs. |
| 5 | 5,14,17 | Stores with competition from discounters only (not from department stores). |
| 6 | 6,22 | Stores in shopping centers. |
| 7 | 8,15,24 | Old stores located along the sides of major roads. |

**EXHIBIT 4**
Town A site characteristics

Store size:
170,000 gross square feet
125,000 selling square feet

*Competitive group*
*(see Exhibit 3) 1*

*Population*
40.0 % black
10.8 % Spanish

| Family incomes (000): | |
|---|---|
| $0–5 | 26.6% |
| 5–7 | 14.0 |
| 7–10 | 19.9 |
| 10–15 | 23.9 |
| 15–25 | 13.3 |
| 25–50 | 2.0 |
| 50+ | 0.3 |

| | |
|---|---|
| Median family income | $8,419 |
| Median rent | $80 |
| Median home value | $23,395 |
| Home owners (percent) | 10.1 |

| Cars: | |
|---|---|
| None | 57.0% |
| One car | 36.3% |

| Households with: | |
|---|---|
| TV | 90.0% |
| Washer | 41.8 |
| Dryer | 9.0 |
| Dishwasher | 6.0 |
| Air conditioner | 17.9 |
| Freezer | 6.1 |
| Second home | 1.6 |

| Education (years): | |
|---|---|
| 0–8 | 37.4% |
| 9–11 | 24.1 |
| 12 | 29.0 |
| 13–15 | 5.6 |
| 16+ | 3.9 |

| | |
|---|---|
| Total population | 955,000 |
| Average family size | 3.7 |

**EXHIBIT 5**
Town B site characteristics

Store size:
160,000 gross square feet
120,000 selling square feet

Competitive group
(see Exhibit 3) 5

Population
13.8% black
6.6% Spanish

Family incomes (000):

| | |
|---|---|
| $0–5 | 19.2% |
| 5–7 | 13.0 |
| 7–10 | 22.2 |
| 10–15 | 27.1 |
| 15–25 | 15.7 |
| 25–50 | 2.5 |
| 50+ | 0.3 |

| | |
|---|---|
| Median family income | $9,401 |
| Median rent | $83 |
| Median home value | $18,029 |
| Home owners (percent) | 10.7 |

Cars:

| | |
|---|---|
| None | 44.0% |
| One car | 45.7% |

Households with:

| | |
|---|---|
| TV | 93.6% |
| Washer | 53.6 |
| Dryer | 12.2 |
| Dishwasher | 4.6 |
| Air conditioner | 39.3 |
| Freezer | 5.0 |
| Second home | 4.6 |

Education (years):

| | |
|---|---|
| 0–8 | 40.1% |
| 9–11 | 23.5 |
| 12 | 25.5 |
| 13–15 | 5.2 |
| 16+ | 5.7 |

| | |
|---|---|
| Total population | 431,285 |
| Average family size | 3.5 |

# case 5.5

# Social Systems, Inc.: SIMPLAN

By mid-1976, Social Systems, Inc., of Chapel Hill, North Carolina, had established itself as a supplier of consulting expertise in corporate planning and budgeting. The firm had developed a computer language called SIMPLAN for use in planning and budgeting, and it was licensing the use of that language by clients. The 1975 recession had adversely affected Social Systems, but the firm's business had picked up rapidly as the economy improved, and by mid-1976 its prospects looked strong. Dr. Thomas H. Naylor, founder and president of SSI, and other members of the firm had to decide how to manage SSI's continuing growth and what new directions, if any, the company should take.

## Company background

Social Systems, Inc., was founded in 1971 by Thomas H. Naylor and Horst Schauland. Dr. Naylor was a professor of economics at Duke University. He had been trained as an econometrician and had worked and published extensively in the area of computer simulation. Dr. Naylor was also interested and involved in politics and, in particular, founded the L. Q. C. Lamar Society, an organization intended to promote progressive politics in the South. His initial design in starting a firm was for it to develop and sell a computerized game for use in training candidates. Players of the game would make decisions on how to raise money, what issues to stress, how to use their time, whose endorsements to seek, and other decisions that arise in political campaigns. The feedback provided by the computerized game would help train players in the process of running a campaign.

In line with this plan for the firm, Dr. Naylor had recruited Horst Schauland, a political scientist with additional training in computers, to join him. The two found that the concept of a campaign game was not salable at that time but that, in the pre-election year of 1971, there was a demand for political surveys and for research and background work. The firm found two clients who needed survey work done. Unfortunately, the survey they conducted for the first showed rather clearly that his position was so weak that he should not even announce for the office, while the survey for the second candidate (who had already declared his candidacy) showed that he could expect to lose rather badly. In addition, of course, the end of the 1972 campaign season considerably reduced the market for such surveys.

During 1972, Social Systems, Inc., had undertaken a project of econometric modeling and survey work for the governor of Michigan. That project convinced the members of the firm of how useful it would be to have a more powerful computer language for use in planning studies. Accordingly, in early 1973 SSI began development of a modeling language named SIMPLAN. The programming work was done by two programmers, one of whom (R. Britton Mayo) was still with SSI in 1976 as Director of Systems Development. In July of 1972, Dr. Naylor began running two-day seminars on corporate planning. Participants in those seminars were found through mass mailings (on the order of 10,000 recipients) to the members of professional organizations. They paid several hundred dollars to attend the seminars. Most of the sessions concerned corporate planning in general, rather than the SIMPLAN product, but the new language was discussed briefly. To the surprise of SSI's founders, the seminars made money for the company.

The first installation of SIMPLAN at a customer's site was in April of 1974 at Monsanto. Other installations followed. The company also made SIMPLAN available through commercial time-sharing vendors. Dr. Naylor continued to give two-day planning seminars in attractive parts of the country; SSI continued to publicize the seminars through nationwide mass mailings. The seminars continued to show a positive net contribution and, at the same time, to attract new users of SIMPLAN and of SSI's consulting services.

The recession of 1975 saw a sharp drop in participation in the planning seminars, as companies tried to cut back nonessential expenses. By mid-1976 attendance had recovered, although the format of the seminars had been changed somewhat in the interim. The new format had one-day planning seminars run by Dr. Naylor in various cities throughout the United States. The seminars were publicized through local mailings in the geographical areas in which they were to be held. The sessions stressed the general process of planning and budgeting and ended with a brief discussion of SIMPLAN. Dr. Naylor also ran an annual users' group meeting on planning and SIMPLAN. In the fall of 1976, Betty Feezor, an applications analyst with SSI, was scheduled to begin a series of one-day sessions, in various U.S. cities, specifically on SIMPLAN.

By mid-1976 SSI had 16 employees. SIMPLAN generated approximately 60 percent of the company's revenues, while the seminars provided 20 percent. Another 10 percent of revenues came from straight consulting, with the remaining 10 percent provided by work in conducting surveys. This last activity was not closely linked to the consulting-SIMPLAN-seminars work but was instead an offshoot of the firm's origin as a political consulting and surveying organization. SSI had approximately 20 clients who had paid to use SIMPLAN in-house (on their own computers). The language could be used on several models of IBM computers. SSI granted licenses for in-house use for as little as six months, or, at the other extreme, for permanent in-house use. A six-month license cost $7,500, while a permanent one cost the client $25,000. For the license fee the client received a license for the use of SIMPLAN for the stated period and also installation of the language by SSI personnel on the client's computer (a process that took several days) and a five-day training workshop for up to five participants run for the client by SSI in Chapel Hill. Clients also received system maintenance, occasional telephone consultation, and any new SIMPLAN features added, all for the license period or, for permanent licenses, for one year. Further, license purchasers received a year's membership in the Corporate Modeling Users Group and two slots at any of the seminars. After the first year, license holders could purchase maintenance, SIMPLAN updates, occasional consulting and memberships in a $2,000/year service package.

SSI also sold the use of SIMPLAN on commercial time-sharing services. Originally, the language had been available on different time-sharing systems, but by 1976 SSI was using only Informatics, Inc., for new clients and, moreover, it had switched most of the old clients who had been using other services to the Informatics system. Informatics was a wholly owned subsidiary of the Equitable Life Assurance Society of the United States. It provided software products and computer services, with 1975 revenues at $39 million. The firm's data center was located in Fairfield, New Jersey, where the firm had two large IBM computers and associated peripheral equipment. Through a communications network, the company provided computer processing services to most major metropolitan areas of the United States.

Several different plans were available for use of SIMPLAN through Informatics. Occasional users could use SIMPLAN by paying to SSI a surcharge of 50 percent of certain computer charges paid to Informatics and thus could pay a fee proportional to the amount of use of the language. More serious users purchased licenses for use of the language on Informatics and then paid Informatics variable fees for the computer usage only. License periods ranged from three months (at a fee of $5,000) to 24 months (at $20,000). The license fees included use of the language, a training workshop in Chapel Hill, occasional consulting and, in general, the same package of services as the in-house licenses (except, of course, for installation of the system on the client's computer). There were formulas available for conversion of shorter-term to longer-term licenses (whether in-house or on Informatics) and, in addition, a 24-month Informatics license could be converted into a permanent in-house license upon payment of $5,000, the difference between the two fees. In mid-1976 there were over 20 companies that were users of SIMPLAN through commercial time-sharing services.

## Planning and modeling languages

SIMPLAN was an example of a computer software package for planning and modeling. There were over 50 software packages for those purposes on the market in 1976. A survey by Naylor and Schauland of SSI had shown that nearly 2,000 corporations were using, developing, or experimenting with corporate planning models, primarily deterministic simulation models.[1] These corporations were generally large ones. SSI's customers, for example, were almost all Fortune 500 companies. (It was expected, however, that use of planning languages would spread to smaller firms in the future.)

The various planning and modeling languages had different combinations of features. Almost all of them had the ability to generate financial reports (to produce pro forma financial statements), often with the ability to consolidate information from different parts of a firm into a set of corporate statements. SSI felt that over two thirds of the planning and modeling software packages commercially available were really just report generators.

Other planning packages included other capabilities. One important part of planning and budgeting involves use and maintenance of data, both data internal to the company and, in many cases, external data. Some of the planning packages included capabilities for database management—in other words, the abilities to store data, to update the database, and to make the information in the database available for report generation and other parts of the modeling system. Many planning systems had little such capability, and, in addition, many of the database management systems did not provide modeling and planning options. Some systems, including SIMPLAN, offered database management as well as report generation and other options.

Another set of techniques included in some of the packages involved setting up and solving models. Most packages had the ability to handle what are called recursive models. Such models are sets of equations involving exogenous (or independent) variables and also calculated (or simulated) variables in such a way that once values are known for the exogenous variables, the other (simulated) variables can be assigned values by considering the set of equations in a serial manner. For example, in the following set of equations, PRICE and SALES are exogenous, and the rest of the variables can be found by solving the equations in the order given, once values are available for SALES and PRICE. (In other words, everything needed to solve for the left-hand side variable in one of the equations is either the value of an exogeneous variable or else is the value of a variable found through one of the equations earlier in the sequence.)

[1] Thomas H. Naylor and Horst Schauland, "A Survey of Users of Corporate Simulation Models," *Management Science*, May 1976.

$$\begin{aligned} \text{Revenue} &= \text{Sales} * \text{price} \\ \text{CGS} &= .55 * \text{revenue} \\ \text{EBT} &= \text{Revenue} - \text{CGS} \\ \text{Tax} &= .48 * \text{EBT} \\ \text{EAT} &= \text{EBT} - \text{tax} \end{aligned}$$

Many packages did not, however, have the ability to solve what are called simultaneous models. As an example of a simultaneous part of a model, consider the relationship among debt, interest, taxes, and cash. Assume that we already know net cash before interest and taxes (CBIT), the EBIT, and the starting debt (OLD DEBT). To find the new debt level required we must know how much cash the firm needs. To know that, we must know how much it must spend and, in particular, what the interest charge and taxes will be. But to know the interest charge we must know the debt and to know taxes we must know interest. Hence, we are in a loop—and we cannot just calculate INTEREST, DEBT (the new level), TAXES, and CASH in any serial manner. The following few equations show the problem. They cannot be solved sequentially (or recursively) but must be solved as a group.

$$\begin{aligned} \text{Cash} &= \text{CBIT} - \text{interest} - \text{taxes} \\ \text{Debt} &= \text{Old debt} - \text{cash} \\ \text{Interest} &= .12 * \text{debt} \\ \text{EBT} &= \text{EBIT} - \text{interest} \\ \text{Taxes} &= .48 * \text{EBT} \end{aligned}$$

Very few planning languages had the ability to solve simultaneous models.

Another set of capabilities of some of the planning software involved forecasting. Some languages allowed no automatic forecasting techniques. Others allowed a few simple techniques, such as the use of linear regression with a single explanatory variable. Some systems offered exponential smoothing and related techniques. Some offered regression with several explanatory variables. A very few systems offered various of these forecasting techniques and, in addition, the ability to forecast through econometric models (or entire sets of equations whose coefficients, once they had been estimated through regression and related techniques, would allow forecasting of dependent variables).

Finally, some systems offered the ability to perform risk analyses and a few allowed optimization (through linear programming).

### The SIMPLAN language

In describing SIMPLAN, SSI used the following diagram, on page 409 which shows the modes of operation of the system.

CONTROL mode was the supervisor level of the system and acted as the communication link among the other modes; it corresponded to the monitor

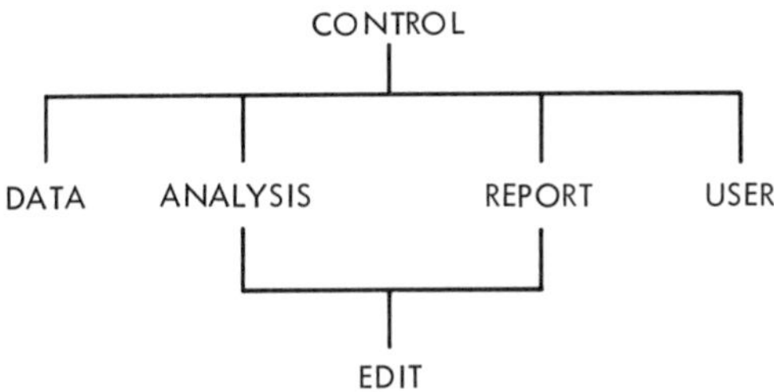


level on a computer system. DATA mode was the part of the package that handled databases. ANALYSIS mode allowed the user to define models and to have the system solve those models. REPORT mode provided for the printing of results in the form of reports. USER mode involved setting security levels and limiting access to parts of the database; it will not be discussed further here. Finally, EDIT mode allowed the user to correct and/or list specifications of models or reports; it could be invoked from either the ANALYSIS or the REPORT mode.

As noted above, the DATA mode provided for the definition and maintenance of databases. SIMPLAN used a system of what were called records and files. A record was really a string of numbers, most often a time series, corresponding to some quantity of interest. For example, a record might be a list of sales figures or it might be a series of annual profit figures. The word *file* within SIMPLAN meant part of a database; a database could consist of one or more files. Each of the types of record in the database could take on different values in the different files. Perhaps the best way to see the relationship among database, records, and files is through an example. An extraordinarily simple database might involve data on SALES, COSTS, and PROFITS. There would be records (or time series) for each of these three variables. The user might want to consider two different sets of figures for SALES, COSTS, and PROFITS—perhaps one set for actual figures and one for forecasts. The user would then have the database contain two files. One file would correspond to actual figures (for each of the three records) and the other would have forecast values. Hence, in this case, the databases can be thought of as having three dimensions—one for time, one for record, and one for file. For each record, there would be one time series of values in the first (actual) file and one series in the second (forecast) file. For SALES, the information would look like this:

| | File 1 | File 2 |
|---|---|---|
| First time period —— | Actual value | Forecast value |
| | | |
| Last time period —— | Actual value | Forecast value |

There would be similar structures for the other records.

The main function of the DATA mode was to allow the user to define records and files in the database. Users specified the numerical data to go into the database and also identification information such as record names (for use in printing reports) and also abbreviations (or shorter names for use in specifying models and reports). The sample protocol at the end of the case shows how the DATA mode was used to set up a particular database.

The main functions of the ANALYSIS mode were to define models (or sets of equations relating variables) and to solve those models. In addition, the ANALYSIS mode provided the capabilities to perform regressions (including solutions of econometric or multi-equation models), as well as time series techniques such as exponential smoothing. The basic idea in this mode was that the user would provide values for the variables which were exogenous to the model to be solved. SIMPLAN distinguished between two types of exogenous variables. "External variables" were variables, such as interest rates, whose values were set outside of the firm being modeled. "Policy variables," such as dividend rates, were variables whose values could be set by the managers of the firm. Users would specify future values for the policy variables. SIMPLAN allowed them either to list values for the external variables or else to determine the values through the forecasting methods it contained. The system would then use the set of equations provided by the user (the model) to determine values for the remaining variables in the model. It might also use the results of regression techniques to find some of the equations to use. SIMPLAN was capable of solving simultaneous as well as recursive models. Once it had solved the model for the time period requested by the user, SIMPLAN would, upon request, save the results for use by the report-writing segment.

Finally, the REPORT mode allowed the user to define and print a wide variety of summary reports of the results of the ANALYSIS section. Hence, SIMPLAN provided for database management, for model definition and solution (of simultaneous as well as recursive models), for various forecasting techniques, and for a wide variety of reports. SSI was just introducing the capabilities for using random numbers in the system. No linear programming or other optimization routines were included.

In a typical run of SIMPLAN to produce pro forma statements, a user might go through the following steps:

1. Set up the required database. Include historical values of variables to be used in regressions or for other purposes.
2. Define a model relating the variables. Perhaps use regression to find some of the coefficients.
3. Use forecasting techniques to project the external variables or else simply list values for those projections.
4. List future values for the policy variables.
5. Solve the model—that is, complete the projections into the future.

6. Define report formats and use them to print out selected results.
7. Change some of the assumptions, returning to one of the earlier steps.

### An example problem

The operation of SIMPLAN is best seen through the protocol from a computer session for analyzing a particular problem. The following example was developed at SSI for use as a case study showing the application of SIMPLAN. The computer protocol which follows shows the use of SIMPLAN for that problem.

Consider a manufacturer of television sets, one color model and one black-and-white model. The company wanted to produce projected annual financial reports for the next five years (1976–80). The Director of Corporate Planning at the firm identified 31 variables whose values could be used to monitor the performance of the company; hence, those variables would be included in the output reports produced by the model. Executives of the firm wanted to consider several outside influences on the firm—in particular, interest rates (both long- and short-term) and national income (which served as a leading indicator of TV sales). They identified nine major policy variables, or variables whose values they could determine and which would have a major impact on the firm. These variables were advertising expenditures, prices of black-and-white and color TVs, the number of shares of stock outstanding, the price to be charged on any stock issues, the dividend rate on stock, a minimum acceptable cash level (below which the firm would resort to additional short-term borrowing), and a decision on whether to raise or retire long-term debt. The following list gives the output variables, external variables and management policy variables chosen for the model:

*Output variables*

| | | | |
|---|---|---|---|
| AP | accounts payable | MA | miscellaneous accruals |
| AR | accounts receivable | NET | net profit |
| BW | black/white TV sales | NPLANT | net plant and equipment |
| CA | current assets | | |
| CASH | cash | NPTSR | net profit to sales ratio |
| CGS | cost of goods sold | OA | other assets |
| CL | current liabilities | OE | operating expenses |
| COLOR | color TV sales | PBT | profit before taxes |
| CR | current ratio | RTAX | reserve for Federal income taxes |
| CS | common stock | | |
| DIV | dividends | RTE | retained earnings |
| EPS | earnings per share | SALES | sales revenue |
| ES | earned surplus | STD | short-term debt |
| INTEREST | interest | TA | total assets |
| INV | inventory | TAX | Federal income taxes |
| LTD | long-term debt | TE | total expenses |
| | | TL | total liabilities |

*External variables*

| | |
|---|---|
| LTR | long-term interest rate |
| STR | short-term interest rate |
| Y | national income |

*Policy variables*

| | | | |
|---|---|---|---|
| ADV | advertising expense | NSHARES | number of shares |
| DPS | dividends per share | PBW | price of black and white TVs |
| MIN | minimum cash balance | PC | price of color TVs |
| NDEBT | new long-term debt | REPAY | repayment of long-term debt |
| NOMINAL | nominal value per share | | |

Each of these variables would correspond to a record within the database. Thus, any one of them, such as ADV, would correspond not to a single value but rather to a time series of values, one for each year. DPS, NOMINAL, EPS, PBW, and PC would be expressed in dollars. Y would be in billions of dollars. BW, COLOR, and NSHARES would be in thousands of units. LTR and STR would be rates; CR and NPTSR would be ratios. The remaining variables would be in units of thousands of dollars.

The modelers decided to project sales of black-and-white and of color TVs through regression analyses involving national income, advertising, price, and sales of the other model (that is, sales of black-and-white models depended in part on sales of color models and vice versa). They also determined a set of assumptions defining the relationships among the variables: for example, they assumed that accounts receivable were 10 percent of sales, that other assets grew by $40,000 per year, and so forth. The following protocol shows how the data were entered into SIMPLAN and the models were defined (including the fitting of regression equations for TV sales). Then, the protocol shows how the model was solved (or projected into the future) and how reports were defined and generated.

SAMPLE PROTOCOL (facing page)

SAMPLE PROTOCOL*

First, the user must set aside space for the database. That part of the dialogue is not shown here.

```
CONTROL.
data
```
} The user requests DATA mode.

```
DATA.
create sales-bw=bw
DATA.
1966=12.3  15.3  15.2  15.4  18.5  20.0  21.3  21.8  23.0  23.7
```
The user asks to create a record with name sales-bw (and abbreviation bw) and then gives the time series for that record, starting in 1966.

```
DATA.
create advertising=adv
```
The user asks to create a record for advertising.

```
DATA.
1666=1600  1760  1792  1840  2000  2160  2240  2272  2368  2400  3000 3000 3000 3000 3000

THE TIME SPECIFICATION MUST BE AN INTEGER BETWEEN 1966 and 1985
DATA.
1966=1600  1760  1792  1840  2000  2160  2240  2272  2368  2400  2000 3000 3000 3000 3000
```
SIMPLAN catches an error in the date

The user has now retyped the line correctly.

The user would then proceed to create records for all variables and to give values for those variables to be used in fitting regressions or for other purposes.

SIMPLAN will list the values in any record if the user gives the DISPLAY command, with a record name.

⋮

```
DATA.
 get color

COLOR IS NOW THE ACTIVE RECORD.
DATA.
1966=17.1
```
} SIMPLAN also allows corrections to the database. Here, the user asks to access the COLOR record and then sets the 1966 figure to 17.1 (the remaining values are unchanged)

⋮

```
DATA.
end
```
After any other needed operations in DATA mode, the user asks to leave that mode. The records have been defined and data have been entered for any records for which values are needed (for example, for policy variables such as advertising).

Here, the user has set up two files for each record (the dialogue for doing so is not shown). One has actual values; the other will contain forecasts.

```
CONTROL.
an
```
Next, the user requests ANALYSIS mode (abbreviating the command)

```
THE DEFAULT TIME RANGE IS 1966 - 1975
ANALYSIS.
est color pc bw adv y

LEAST SQUARES REGRESSION
```
← This is a request to run a regression estimating color sales as a function of price for color, black/white sales, advertising and national income.

* Lower-case text was typed by the user, upper-case by SIMPLAN. Numbers typed by the user have been underlined.

MUCH OF THE DIALOGUE HAS BEEN OMITTED.

```
ESTIMATED EQUATION IS:
   COLOR=0.1334*PC-0.2283*BW+0.0237*ADV+0.0132*Y+11.2709
```

Regression results

| INDEPENDENT VARIABLES | ESTIMATED COEFFICIENT | STANDARD ERROR | T-TEST |
|---|---|---|---|
| PC | -0.1334 | 0.0200 | -6.6704 |
| BW | -0.2283 | 0.1122 | -2.0336 |
| ADV | 0.0237 | 0.0022 | 10.7829 |
| Y | 0.0132 | 0.0017 | 7.7233 |
| CONSTANT | 11.2709 | 3.9949 | 2.0213 |

```
NUMBER OF OBSERVATIONS USED=             10
 R-SQUARED=  0.9999                        F-STATISTIC( 4,  5)=     9302.4648
 ADJUSTED R-SQUARED= 0.9998                DURBIN-WATSON STATISTIC=    1.6503
 STANDARD ERROR=        0.0966             DEGREES OF FREEDOM FOR T-TEST=  5
ANALYSIS.
```

Similarly, the user asks to estimate black/white sales as a function of price, color sales, advertising and national income.

```
est bw pbw color adv y

LEAST SQUARES REGRESSION

ESTIMATED EQUATION IS:

   BW=-0.1210*PBW-0.4989*COLOR+0.0267*ADV+0.0054*Y-7.3610
```

| INDEPENDENT VARIABLES | ESTIMATED COEFFICIENT | STANDARD ERROR | T-TEST |
|---|---|---|---|
| PBW | -0.1210 | 0.0094 | -12.8993 |
| COLOR | -0.4989 | 0.1068 | -4.6693 |
| ADV | 0.0267 | 0.0017 | 15.4040 |
| Y | 0.0054 | 0.0022 | 2.4010 |
| CONSTANT | -7.3610 | 1.4601 | -5.0416 |

```
NUMBER OF OBSERVATIONS USED  =           10
R-SQUARED= .9998                          F-STATISTIC(  4,  5)=   7337.0156
ADJUSTED R-SQUARED=    0.9997             DURBIN-WATSON STATISTIC=   1.8930
STANDARD ERROR            0.0684          DEGREES OF FREEDOM FOR T-TEST=  5
ANALYSIS.
```

NOTE: because COLOR appears in the equation for BW and vice-versa, it would be preferable to estimate the equations jointly, using econometric techniques. SIMPLAN has the ability to do so. SIMPLAN can also VALIDATE such a model by "forecasting" the past with it and comparing the results with actual values (found in another file). An example of validation output follows:

⋮

```
ANALYSIS.
val bw(2) bw
```

The user requests "forecasting" (protocol omitted) and then requests validation

```
MODEL VALIDATION

MEAN ABSOLUTE ERROR =                   0.0206
MEAN PERCENTAGE ERROR =                 0.1216
THEIL'S INEQUALITY COEFFICIENT U =                0.0006
APPROXIMATE STANDARD ERROR OF U =                 0.0006
```

} summaries

| TIME | BW(2) "forecast" | BW actual | DIFFERENCE |
|---|---|---|---|
| 1966 | 12.3377 | 12.3000 | 0.0377 |
| 1967 | 15.3123 | 15.3000 | 0.0123 |
| 1968 | 15.1609 | 15.2000 | -0.0391 |
| 1969 | 15.3931 | 15.4000 | -0.0069 |
| 1970 | 18.4776 | 18.5000 | -0.0224 |
| 1971 | 20.0369 | 20.0000 | 0.0369 |
| 1972 | 21.3036 | 21.3000 | 0.0036 |
| 1973 | 21.7966 | 21.8000 | -0.0034 |
| 1974 | 23.0264 | 23.0000 | 0.0264 |
| 1975 | 23.6823 | 23.7000 | -0.0177 |

Next, the user proceeds to define the model (or set of equations) for the income statement.

```
ANALYSIS.
edit incomemodel
```

← A request to edit a non-existant model is interpreted as a request to create a new model.

```
THIS IS A NEW MODEL.
EDIT.
10 color = 11.270 - .133*pc - .228*bw + .024*adv + .013*y
```

The user lists the model, line by line (Note that this equation for COLOR was found through estimation above)

⋮

Once all the lines were defined, the user would ask to save the model. SIMPLAN will print out the definition on request, as shown below:

```
EDIT.
1
```

← a (shortened) LIST command

```
INCOMEMODEL

 10 BW=-0.1210*PBW-0.4989*COLOR+0.0267*ADV+0.0054*Y-7.3610
 20 COLOR=-0.1334*PC-0.2283*BW+0.0237*ADV+0.0132*Y+11.2709
 30 SALES = PC*COLOR + PBW*BW
 40 CGS = .60*SALES
 60 OE = .04*SALES
 70 INTEREST = STR*STD + LTR*LTD
 80 TE = CGS + ADV + OE + INTEREST
 90 PBT = SALES - TE
100 TAX = .5*PBT
110 NET = PBT - TAX
120 DIV = DPS*NSHARES
130 RTE = NET - DIV
```

These equations give information for the income statement

⋮

The user might then proceed to define a model for the balance sheet items and another combined model for the full set of financial statements. That full model might look like the following:

```
CORPMODEL

 10 BW=-0.1210*PBW-0.4989*COLOR+-.0267*ADV+0.0054*Y-7.3610
 20 COLOR=-0.1334*PC-0.2283*BW+0.0237*ADV+0.0132*Y+11.2709
 30 SALES = PC*COLOR + PBW*BW
 40 CGS = .60*SALES
 60 INTEREST = STR*STD + LTR*LTD
 70 TE = CGS + ADV + OE + INTEREST
 80 PBT = SALES - TE
 90 TAX = .5*PBT
100 NET = PBT - TAX
110 DIV = DPS*NSHARES
120 RTE = NET - DIV
130 CASH = TL - AR - INV - NPLANT - OA
```

```
140 IF CASH < MIN
150 STD = STD + 1.33*(MIN - CASH)
160 ELSE
170 STD = STD(-1)
180 END
190 AR = .10*SALES
200 INV = .20*SALES
210 CA = CASH + AR + INV
220 NPLANT = 95*NPLANT(-1)
230 OA = OA(-1) + 40
240 TA = CA + NPLANT + OA
250 AP = .06*CGS
260 RTAX = TAX
270 MA = 1.25*MA(-1)
280 CL = AP + STD + RTAX + MA + REPAY
290 LTD = LTD(-1) + NDEBT - REPAY
300 CS = NOMINAL*NSHARES
310 ES = ES(-1) +RTE
320 TL = CL + LTD + CS + ES
330 EPS = NET / NSHARES
340 CP = CA / CL
350 NPTSR = NET / SALES
      ⋮
```

These are conditional statements. If cash is less than the minimum, short-term debt is raised by 133% of the shortfall. Otherwise, short-term debt takes its previous value. (-1) means lag one period.

```
ANALYSIS.
de casemodel

ANALYSIS.
ti 1976-1980

DEFAULT TIME RANGE RESET TO 1976 - 1980
ANALYSIS.
mo simul on print on save check

ANALYSIS.
simul bw 23.7 color 34.2

ANALYSIS.
solve corpmodel
```

The user sets the time range 1976-80 and then asks to solve the model.

First, future values must be found for COLOR and BW. The user guesses at the next values to help SIMPLAN in its solution of the equations for the next (and future) periods

The user asks SIMPLAN to solve the full corporate model. SIMPLAN will print lists of all variables in the model. Part of such a list is shown below. After the debugging stage, in which such output is often quite useful, the full print option can be turned off.

CORPMODEL

| TIME | ADV( 1) | AP( 1) | AR( 1) | BW( 1) | CA( 1) | ... |
|---|---|---|---|---|---|---|
| 1976 | 3000.00 | 695.45 | 1931.82 | 32.66 | 11069.19 | |
| 1977 | 3000.00 | 709.38 | 1970.49 | 32.01 | 11988.60 | |
| 1978 | 3000.00 | 720.51 | 2001.43 | 31.38 | 12922.80 | ... |
| 1979 | 3000.00 | 730.11 | 2028.08 | 30.75 | 13876.59 | |
| 1980 | 3000.00 | 740.26 | 2056.28 | 30.11 | 14868.69 | |
| | ⋮ | | ⋮ | | | |

```
DO YOU WISH TO SAVE THE RESULTS?  ENTER YES OR NO.
yes

ANALYSIS.
end

CONTROL.
report
```

The user asks SIMPLAN to save the results

In order to get reports printed, the user must switch to REPORT mode, define the REPORT formats and then ask to have the reports printed.

← Request for REPORT mode

```
REPORT.
edit summaryrpt

THIS IS A NEW REPORT.
EDIT.
10 c 40* 'summary report'
```

The user asks to define a new report called SUMMARYRPT. The following lines define lines of the report.

← the first line has a title in column 40

```
EDIT.
20 *space 2
```

← double spacing

```
EDIT.
30 *tabs 35 by 11
```

← setting tabs in columns 35, 46, 57, etc.

```
EDIT.
40  *width 9
```

← maximum width for numbers

```
EDIT.
50 col 1976-1980
```

← setting the column headings (1976, ...)

```
EDIT.
ch 50 /col/*col/

  50 *COL 1976-1980
```

} the user catches and corrects an error

```
EDIT.
60 header
```

← printing column heads

```
EDIT.
70 *space 1
```

← single space

```
EDIT.
80 underline
```

← underline

```
EDIT.
90 *space 2
```

← double space

```
EDIT.
100 sales
```

← request to print sales figures

```
EDIT.
110 net

EDIT.
120 rte
```

} requests for net profits and retained earnings

```
EDIT.
130 *page
```

← end

```
EDIT.
save
```

← request to save the report definition

```
SAVED.
EDIT.
print
```

← request to print the report

SUMMARY REPORT

| | 1976 | 1977 | 1978 | 1979 | 1980 |
|---|---|---|---|---|---|
| | --------- | --------- | --------- | --------- | --------- |
| SALES | 19318.16 | 19704.87 | 20014.26 | 20280.77 | 20562.82 |
| NET PROFIT | 658.20 | 721.20 | 772.61 | 817.59 | 864.90 |
| RETAINED EARNINGS | 174.45 | 237.45 | 288.86 | 333.84 | 381.15 |

⋮

Similarly, the user could define reports for the income statement, balance sheet and selected ratios. These reports might print as follows:

TV LIMITED

PROJECTED FINANCIAL RATIOS (1976-1980)

| | 1976 | 1977 | 1978 | 1979 | 1980 |
|---|---|---|---|---|---|
| EARNINGS PER SHARE | 2.93 | 3.21 | 3.34 | 3.63 | 3.84 |
| CURRENT RATIO | 1.85 | 1.97 | 2.08 | 2.18 | 2.28 |
| NET PROFIT TO SALES | 0.03 | 0.04 | 0.04 | 0.04 | 0.04 |

TV LIMITED

PROJECTED BALANCE SHEET (1976-1980)
($000)

| | 1976 | 1977 | 1978 | 1979 | 1980 |
|---|---|---|---|---|---|
| ASSETS | | | | | |
| CASH | 5273.7 | 6077.2 | 6918.6 | 7792.4 | 8699.9 |
| ACCOUNTS RECEIVABLE | 1931.8 | 1970.5 | 2001.4 | 2028.1 | 2056.3 |
| INVENTORY | 3863.6 | 3941.0 | 4002.9 | 4056.2 | 4112.6 |
| CURRENT ASSETS | 11069.1 | 11988.6 | 12922.9 | 13876.7 | 14868.8 |
| NET P AND E | 13903.4 | 13208.3 | 12547.8 | 11920.5 | 11324.4 |
| OTHER ASSETS | 504.9 | 544.9 | 584.9 | 624.9 | 664.9 |
| TOTAL ASSETS | 25477.5 | 25741.8 | 26055.6 | 26422.0 | 26858.1 |
| LIABILITIES | | | | | |
| ACCOUNTS PAYABLE | 695.4 | 709.4 | 720.5 | 730.1 | 740.3 |
| SHORT TERM DEBT | 4316.1 | 4316.1 | 4316.1 | 4316.1 | 4316.1 |
| RESERVE FOR TAX | 658.2 | 721.2 | 772.6 | 817.6 | 864.9 |
| MISC ACCRUALS | 199.6 | 249.5 | 311.9 | 389.9 | 487.4 |
| REPAYMENT | 100.0 | 100.0 | 100.0 | 100.0 | 100.0 |
| CURRENT LIABILITIES | 5969.4 | 6096.2 | 6221.1 | 6353.7 | 6508.6 |
| LONG TERM DEBT | 9611.3 | 9511.3 | 9411.3 | 9311.3 | 9211.3 |
| COMMON STOCK | 4500.0 | 4500.0 | 4500.0 | 4500.0 | 4500.0 |
| EARNED SURPLUS | 5396.8 | 5634.3 | 5923.2 | 6257.0 | 6638.2 |
| TOTAL LIABILITIES | 25477.5 | 25741.8 | 26055.6 | 26422.0 | 28658.1 |

TV LIMITED

PROJECTED INCOME STATEMENT (1976-1980)
($000)

| | 1976 | 1977 | 1978 | 1979 | 1980 |
|---|---|---|---|---|---|
| SALES | 19318.1 | 19704.9 | 20014.4 | 20280.9 | 20562.9 |
| EXPENSES | | | | | |
| COST OF GOODS SOLD | 11590.8 | 11823.0 | 12008.6 | 12168.5 | 12337.7 |
| ADVERTISING | 3000.0 | 3000.0 | 3000.0 | 3000.0 | 3000.0 |
| OPERATION EXPENSES | 1931.8 | 1970.5 | 2001.4 | 2028.1 | 2056.3 |
| INTEREST | 1479.1 | 1469.1 | 1459.1 | 1449.1 | 1439.1 |
| TOTAL EXPENSES | 18001.7 | 18262.5 | 18469.1 | 18645.7 | 18833.1 |
| PROFIT BEFORE TAX | 1316.4 | 1442.4 | 1545.3 | 1635.2 | 1729.8 |
| TAX | 658.2 | 721.2 | 772.6 | 817.6 | 864.9 |
| NET PROFIT | 658.2 | 721.2 | 772.6 | 817.6 | 864.9 |
| DIVIDENDS | 483.7 | 483.7 | 483.7 | 483.7 | 483.7 |
| RETAINED EARNINGS | 174.4 | 237.5 | 288.9 | 333.9 | 381.2 |

At this point, the user could change the data, change the models or reports, define new models or reports, ... or end this run of SIMPLAN.

appendix

# DECISION ANALYSIS AND RELATED TOPICS[1]

In general, we make decisions today which we hope will lead to future outcomes which are favorable to us. Conceptually, the procedure we follow is to forecast the future as well as we can and then select the best decisions available, relative to our forecasts. Usually, we can envision many possible future scenarios; surely we want our decision-making procedures to consider all reasonable possibilities. Moreover, we usually feel that some future scenarios are more likely to occur than are others; our decision making should also consider the respective likelihoods of the various scenarios.

What makes decision making in the face of uncertainty about the future particularly difficult is that in most situations the action which would be best if the future turned out one way is not the action which would be best for other future scenarios. Thus, the decision maker's problem is one of selecting actions now when s/he does not know what the future will bring but s/he does know that future events will affect the consequences of possible decisions and, moreover, that for different future outcomes different actions are best. This appendix describes a method for analyzing such problems.

## Example decision problem

In order to have a specific example to use in the following discussion of the decision analysis technique, we will consider the problem of Mr. Joel Williams, the president of the Williams Novelty Company, who is evaluating

[1] For additional material on decision analysis see: Paul A. Vatter, Stephen P. Bradley, Sherwood C. Frey, Jr., and Barbara B. Jackson, *Quantitative Methods in Management* (Homewood, Ill.: Richard D. Irwin, 1978); and Howard Raiffa, *Decision Analysis,* (Reading, Mass.: Addison-Wesley, 1968).

a proposal from his development group for producing a new seasonal novelty for the next season. Mr. Williams has already decided that if the novelty is introduced it will be priced at $1.50 per unit. Further, he has decided that the novelty is not likely to be popular for more than one year, so he has set his planning horizon at one year.

The production department has sent Mr. Williams a report on the machinery which could be used to produce the new novelty; they have identified two options. First, Mr. Williams could use a fairly standard machine which would be leased for the season for $1,000 and which would have a variable cost of $1 per unit. Alternatively, he could use a more automated machine which would lease for $3,500 but would have a variable cost of only $.50 per unit.

The distributor who handles Williams's novelties would automatically buy an initial shipment of 1,000 novelties. After that, he would buy additional novelties in batches of 4,000 each. Mr. Williams is quite sure that the new novelty will not sell more than 9,000 (or the initial batch plus two additional 4,000-unit batches) of the new novelty.

The proposed new novelty is one of many in the company's line, and the revenue from it represents a small fraction of the company's yearly receipts.

## Structuring a decision problem

In analyzing decision problems, we consider two types of components: *act nodes* and *event nodes*. Act nodes represent those parts of the problem where the decision maker can choose; they represent those parts over which the decision maker has *complete* control. Occurrences over which the decision maker does not have such complete control are reprsented by event nodes; examples are the actions of competitors or the severity of next winter. (These parts of the decision problem are also called *uncertainties*.)

Because the decision maker can decide which *action* to take, we do not need to forecast acts, but we do have to enumerate all potentially interesting options for an act node. This problem of generating all of the relevant alternatives for an act node depends for its solution on the judgment and imagination of the decision maker. A more creative manager sees more options for action than does a more pedestrian manager; the process of identifying potential acts is not a mechanical one. One point sometimes ignored is that doing nothing is just as much of a decision as is taking some more innovative action; hence, doing nothing should often be included explicitly in the list of acts for a decision problem.

In Mr. Williams's problem, the possible *acts* are (1) do nothing (do not introduce the novelty); (2) use the standard machine to introduce the novelty; and (3) use the automated machine to introduce the novelty.

The selection of the uncertainties which should be considered explicitly in a decision analysis also involves considerable judgment. In general, we do not want to include (and, in fact, could not include) *everything* that is beyond the complete control of the decision maker—the weather next winter, the competition's decisions, the score of the next world series game. Rather, we should include only those event nodes whose results will help determine the consequences of the actions under consideration. In addition, we should define these event nodes so that their outcomes (or results) can be measured in some unambiguous way; for example, Mr. Williams has defined demand explicitly in terms of units sold rather than as high demand, moderate demand, and low demand. In determining possible outcomes at event nodes two rules should be followed:

1. The outcomes should be mutually exclusive—that is, they should be defined clearly in such a way that only one of the possible outcomes can occur at a time. For example, Mr. Williams defines the outcomes of demand as 1,000, 5,000, or 9,000 items. He does not define them as "1,000 or more," "5,000 or fewer," and "above 5,000," because such outcomes are not mutually exclusive; a demand of 5,000 is both "1,000 or more" and "5,000 or fewer" and so is included in two of these "outcomes."
2. The outcomes should be collectively exhaustive—that is, the outcomes should be defined in such a way that one or another of them must occur. This rule asks that all possible outcomes be considered. (In Mr. Williams's problem, he has assumed that 1,000, 5,000, and 9,000 are a collectively exhaustive set of outcomes.) Thus, in Mr. Williams's problem the uncertain quantity is demand for the novelty next year and the possible outcomes are 1,000, 5,000, and 9,000 items.

Once we have identified the acts and events in a decision problem, we can proceed to consider the interrelations among the various components. A convenient way of doing so is through a decision tree or diagram, which maps out the sequence of act nodes and event nodes in the order in which the decision maker performs the acts and learns about the events. Thus, the tree lays out the parts of a decision problem in the order in which uncertainty about those parts is resolved for the decision maker; the tree involves time sequencing from the point of view of the decision maker.

Decision diagrams are constructed as sequences of act nodes and event nodes. As a matter of convention, an act node is represented as a square with one branch leading from it for each possible action; similarly, an event node is drawn as a circle with a branch for each of the possible events or outcomes. In Mr. Williams's problem, the first thing that will happen is that he will decide which of the three possible acts to take; after that, he carries out that act and learns the actual value of demand. Hence, we draw the tree starting with an act fork. Regardless of which action Mr. Williams takes, the next component is the event fork for demand, so we put an event fork at the end of each of the action branches. Finally, we note that Mr. Williams has decided on a one-year time horizon, so that we end the tree after determination of the first year's demand. (In general, determining the appropriate time horizon is another of the important tasks in any decision problem.) The resulting tree is shown in Figure A–1.

**FIGURE A–1**

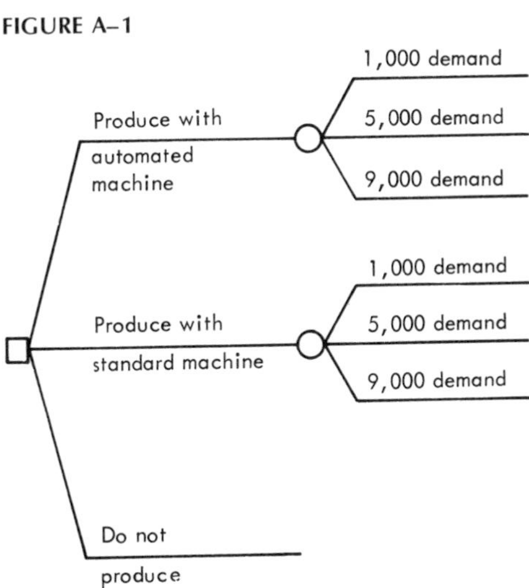


There are frequently different ways of diagramming the same decision problem. For example, in Mr. Williams's problem we could think of a sequence of two decisions: the first a go/no-go decision on whether to introduce the novelty, and, in the case that he does introduce, a second decision about the type of machinery to use. Thinking of the problem in this way gives the tree in Figure A–2.

**FIGURE A–2**

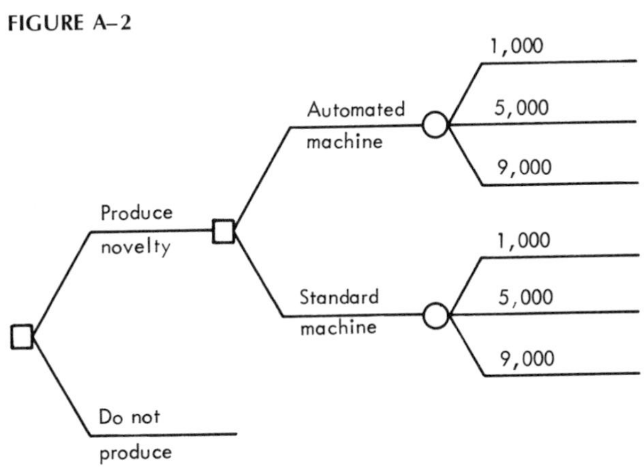

Figure A–1 and Figure A–2 are logically the same and will eventually lead to the same decision. In general, it is often possible (and completely acceptable) to use a series of decision nodes, with no intervening event nodes, in place of a single decision node with many options, and vice versa. Similarly, it is sometimes possible (and again completely acceptable) to use a single event node with many possible outcomes in place of a series of event nodes with no intervening act nodes, and vice versa.

## Evaluating the endpoints

After structuring the problem by drawing a decision diagram, we next evaluate the consequences of various sets of acts and outcomes. As the decision problem unfolds over time, we will follow one or another of the paths through the tree. At any point in the tree, everything "behind" us has already happened and everything in front of us is still in the future. When we reach the end of a path, we can then evaluate the overall outcome. In trying to make a decision, we take trips through the tree in our imagination, trying to determine the values of possible paths. By custom, we put the value of taking a particular path through the tree at the end of that path. These values are called endpoint values.

The first problem in evaluating endpoints is to determine what criterion to use. That decision can become a difficult or controversial one in some decision problems (think of industrial decisions affecting the environment, for example), but in Mr. Williams's problem it is quite straightforward—we will use contribution (revenue minus cost) as the criterion. In general, however, remember that choosing the appropriate criterion is another important area for judgment in structuring and solving a decision problem.

As an example, consider the path through the tree on which Mr. Williams selects the automated machine and then demand turns out to be 5,000 items. We can evaluate the endpoint of that path as follows:

| | |
|---|---|
| Revenue (5,000 * 1.50) | $7,500 |
| Less: Variable cost (5,000 * .50) | 2,500 |
| Machinery cost | 3,500 |
| Contribution | $1,500 |

Thus, we label that endpoint with $1,500. In a similar manner, we can proceed to evaluate each of the endpoints in Figure A–1; the resulting decision tree is given in Figure A–3 (where negative endpoints indicate that Mr. Williams has lost money).

## Probabilities

Our next task is to try to select a strategy for Mr. Williams to give him the best results for his problem. In doing so, we must first determine what we

**FIGURE A–3**

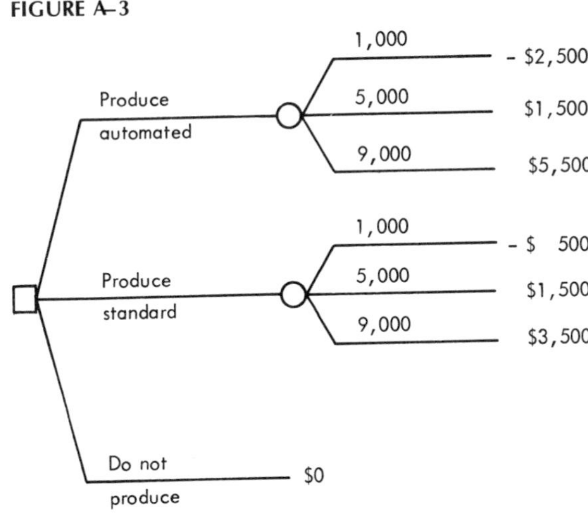


mean by best. In practice, many different rules are used for deciding which of a set of possible actions to take. One rule says to take the action which would be best for the most likely outcome of the events. Suppose, for example, that Mr. Williams thinks that 1,000 units is the most likely figure for demand. In that case, the most-likely-outcome decision rule would say that he should not introduce the novelty on either machine, since the standard machine and the automated machine both give negative values for that demand level. Using such a decision rule, Mr. Williams will select the best act for the actual outcome, whatever it turns out to be, more often than he would with any other rule. Unfortunately, however, using this most-likely-outcome rule can often lead to very bad decisions. First, most likely may not be very likely at all; in a decision problem with many possible outcomes for an uncertainty, any individual outcome may be quite unlikely to occur but still be more likely than any of the other outcomes (all of which are also individually unlikely). In addition, this decision rule does not consider the consequences when the most likely outcome does not in fact occur. We are frequently willing—indeed, anxious—to make a decision which may not be the best under the most likely outcome or even the most optimistic outcome but which gives good results under these or other outcomes while hedging against other possible unfavorable outcomes.

Another rule sometimes used in decision making is called the maximin criterion. Under this rule, we select that strategy which gives the "best worst case"; that is, we ask, for each strategy, if everything goes wrong, how badly off will we be. We then select that strategy which gives the least bad results for this pessimistic view of the future. Since Mr. Williams could lose money if he introduced the novelty, with either type of machinery, the maximin rule tells him to do nothing. Such an outcome is typical with the use of this rule; the rule is so pessimistic that it often dictates no innovation (the do nothing act).

In discussing these two possible rules for selecting a decision, we have really left out from each a major part of the decision problem. In the first, we focused on the *likelihood* of various outcomes but did not consider the consequences or values of achieving various outcomes; in the second, we considered the consequences but not the likelihoods. What we would really like is a rule which considers both the consequences and the likelihoods. We saw in the section on endpoint evaluation that we needed to express consequences in measurable units; our next task is to express likelihoods in measurable units, too, so that we can then try, somehow, to combine the two different measures, considering both consequences and likelihoods.

In order to express a decision maker's beliefs about the relative likelihoods of various outcomes, we use the language of probabilities. Most people have an intuitive feeling that probabilities refer to such things as a toss of a coin or a roll of a die, but in decision trees we are not using probability in that long-run-frequency sense. Rather, we use probabilities to express quantitatively the personal judgment of a decision maker about the outcomes of events. (The probabilities depend on the judgment of the decision maker.) There are a number of techniques aimed at helping the decision maker to express her or his judgments about such events, but these techniques guide and do not replace the judgment.

The decision maker should assign probabilities to reflect likelihoods; an outcome which s/he thinks is twice as likely as another should be assigned a probability twice as high as that of the other. In addition, the probability of something which the decision maker considers impossible should be zero. For convenience, we usually insist that the probabilities for all of the outcomes of a particular event should sum to 1. Assessing probabilities for various events is a skill which a decision maker must learn; the decision maker will already know how to form judgments but s/he will, in general, not know how to express those judgments *quantitatively*. In learning to make quantitative judgments, decision makers will often find it helpful to think about simple choices between gambles or bets. For example, consider Mr. Williams's assessment of the probabilities or likelihoods of various possible levels of demand for the new novelty. We start by offering Mr. Williams a choice of two gambles. In the first, he will receive some very desirable prize if (and only if) demand turns out to be 5,000 units. In the second gamble, we fill a large urn with 100 Ping Pong balls, half of which are red and half of which are green; we then have some individual who is extremely fair select one Ping Pong ball at random and we award the desirable prize to Mr. Williams if, and only if, the selected ball is red. Thus, in the second gamble we select a winning ball with probability .5, the fraction of red balls in the urn. Suppose that Mr. Williams prefers the second gamble. Certainly he will always select the gamble in which, in his best judgment, he has the larger chance of winning. In the second gamble we have seen that his chance of winning is exactly .5; therefore, he must believe that in the first gamble the chance of winning is less than .5. But the chance of winning the first gamble is simply the probability (in Mr. Williams's mind) that demand is 5,000. Hence, Mr. Williams' first choice has shown us that he believes that the probability that demand will be 5,000 is *less* than .5.

We next proceed to another pair of gambles. The first gamble, which depends on demand for the novelty, is the same as the first gamble above. The second gamble also involves an urn filled with 100 Ping Pong balls, but we now use 25 red (and 75 green) balls, with a red ball indicating a win for Mr. Williams. Assume that Mr. Williams now prefers the first gamble. From that choice we can conclude that he believes that the probability of demand of 5,000 units is *greater* than .25, the probability that he would win in the second gamble which we offered.

Continuing in this way we can proceed to find a fraction between 0 and 1 such that, if we put that fraction of red balls into the urn, Mr. Williams is indifferent between the gamble depending on demand and the gamble depending on the red and green balls. This fraction is the probability which Mr. Williams assigns to the outcome: demand = 5,000. Suppose that Mr. Williams selects .3 as this probability. We can then proceed, through analogous series of choices between gambles, to elicit judgmental values for the probabilities of other outcomes. For example, Mr. Williams might, through this process, tell us that he believes that the probability that demand will be 1,000 units is .5 while the probability that it will be 9,000 is .2. (Note that, as usually required, the probabilities for all the possible outcomes sum to 1. If Mr. Williams's initial assessment had given probabilities which did not sum to 1, we would have asked him to refine his values so that they would do so.)

We now have obtained another component of the decision problem, the decision maker's judgment of the probabilities, or likelihoods, of the various possible outcomes of the events in the problem.

### Certainty equivalents and expected value

Having determined the structure of the problem, the consequences and the probabilities, we now proceed to combine consequences and probabilities in a way which allows us to make a decision. In doing so, we must select a criterion to use in deciding whether one option is better than another. If the decision maker selects a particular action, s/he will in general face an uncertain future with various possible outcomes and various probabilities of those outcomes. To allow comparison of different actions and the different uncertain futures accompanying them, we suggest that the decision maker think of these possible futures, one by one. For each, s/he should determine the minimum amount which s/he would accept from (or, for unattractive futures, the maximum s/he would pay to) someone else in exchange for that future. Thus, we would ask Mr. Williams to choose between two deals. In the first, he would make the novelty on the standard equipment; in the second, he would receive some specified amount of money and someone else would have the consequences of producing the novelty in that way. If Mr. Williams is indifferent between the two deals, then he must think that the uncertain future (once he decides to produce on the standard equipment) is worth the same, to him, as the fixed amount. We call that fixed amount Mr. Williams's *certainty equivalent* for the action and its attendant consequences. Note that the certainty equivalent is a personal judgment again; we cannot dictate what a decision maker's certainty equivalent should be.

In a wide range of problems, however, many decision makers feel it is appropriate to use a particular criterion called the *expected value*. The expected value of an action and its various possible outcomes is simply a weighted average of the outcomes, with the probabilities used as the weights. In Mr. Williams's case, the action produce-on-standard has the possible outcomes of −$500, $1,500, and $3,500, with probabilities .5, .3, and .2, respectively. Thus, the expected value of that action is:

$$.5\,(-500) + .3\,(1{,}500) + .2\,(3{,}500) = \$900.$$

The argument in favor of using expected value is that a decision maker should often be willing to play the long-run averages. If s/he faces many decisions which are similar in type and magnitude of consequences, then s/he can play the averages and, in the long run, expect the good breaks and bad breaks to even out. Note, however, that we have assumed that the decision maker will be able to continue "playing"; thus, we implicitly assume that none of the outcomes is so bad that it would, for example, put her or him out of business. We suggest expected value as a criterion only for decisions which are basically routine ones, without any truly dire consequences. Moreover, we stress that any criterion selected should reflect accurately the individual values of the specific decision maker, and, therefore, that expected value should not be used as a criterion if the decision maker feels uncomfortable about playing the long-run averages.

Mr. Williams's problem about producing the new novelty is a routine one for him, and the consequences are not large on the scale of his usual business decisions; therefore, let us assume that he decides to use expected value as a criterion.

### Selecting a decision—averaging out and folding back

Recall that we defined a certainty equivalent as the minimum amount which a decision maker would accept in exchange for some specified uncertain future. Recall also that an act was defined as a part of a decision problem over which the decision maker has complete control (and, thus, the opportunity to select the best choice). These two facts are used to "solve" a decision tree and obtain the optimal decision. We solve Mr. Williams's problem as an example. First, look at the event node for demand which occurs after the decision to produce with automated equipment (that is, on the top path) in Figure A–1. At that node (as at any node in a decision tree) the decision maker looks forward to the future, with the nodes behind her or him representing acts and events which have already occurred. At the specified node, Mr. Williams faces a future with the possible consequences of −\$2,500, \$1,500, and \$5,500, with probabilities .5, .3, and .2. Using the definition of certainty equivalent, together with the fact that Mr. Williams selected expected-value-of-contribution as his criterion, we argue that the entire node can be replaced by its certainty equivalent, as shown in Figure A–4. (The certainty equivalent or weighted average is

$$.5\,(-\$2{,}500) + .3\,(1{,}500) + .2\,(5{,}500) = -1{,}250 + 450 + 1{,}100 = 300.)$$

**FIGURE A–4**

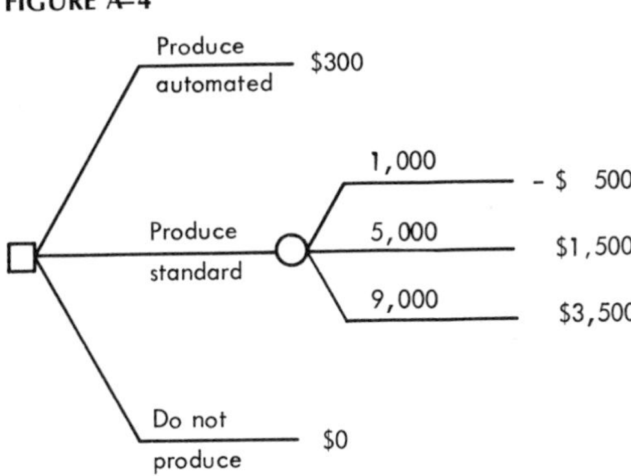


This process of averaging to find the expected value of an event node is called averaging out. The event node after the standard-equipment decision can be replaced by its expected value to give the tree in Figure A–5.

Next, we use the decision maker's control at action nodes to argue that at

**FIGURE A–5**

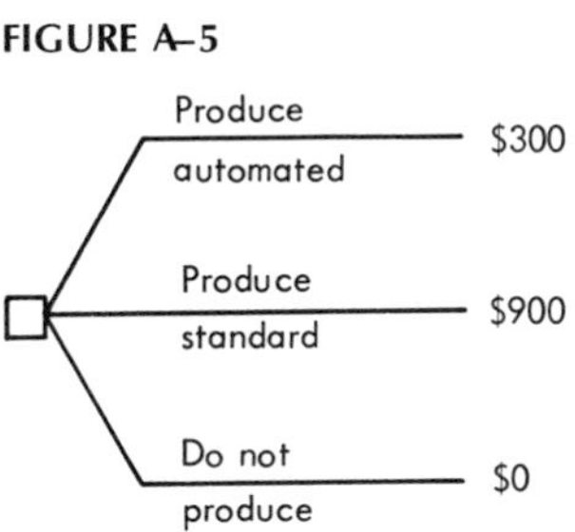

such nodes we should simply select the best-valued alternative. Because Mr. Williams faces expected values of $300, $900, and $0, surely he will select $900. Therefore, we block off the actions resulting in $300 and $0 and label the act node with $900. This process of bringing back the best value at an act node is called folding back. Figure A–6 shows the result.

**FIGURE A–6**

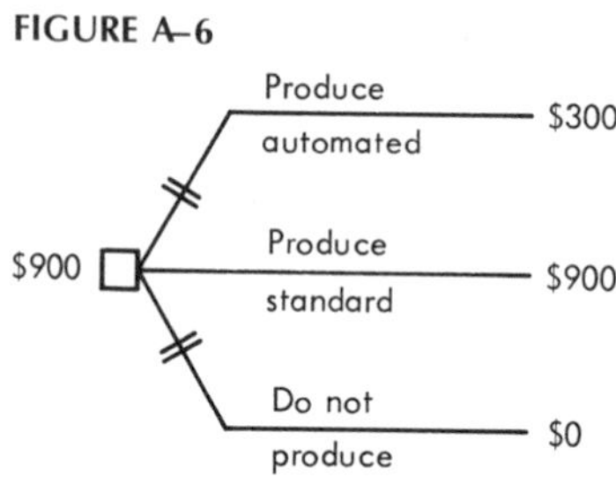


The method illustrated here can be applied in general in decision trees to select the optimal decision. Beginning at the right-hand side of the tree, we proceed toward the left or root of the tree, averaging out at event nodes and folding back at action nodes until we have assigned a value to the entire decision and, in the process, blocked off all undesirable (nonoptimal) actions. The optimal decision is then to take the unblocked path at each act node. In Mr. Williams's case, it is to produce the new novelty on the standard equipment. After we have solved the tree in this way, each node will be labeled with its certainty equivalent, or the criterion value of being at that node; for Mr. Williams, the nodes are labeled with the expected contribution values of being at those positions. The root (or left-most) node of a solved tree will be labeled with the value of the entire deal which the tree describes.

As another example of the analysis of a decision tree, we return to the problem described in Figure 2–5 of Chapter 2.[2] Reading from top to bottom on the page of that figure, the endpoints labeled A through R there are shown in Table A–1 here. If we plug these values and the probabilities into the tree and solve, we find the results in Figure A–7. The optimal strategy is to buy the standard equipment and not to promote even if there is competition.

## Risk profiles

In discussing certainty equivalents and expected value, we saw that it is not always appropriate for a decision maker to play the long-run averages. On some major decisions, and particularly on decisions with potentially dire consequences, most decision makers will want to be conservative or *risk*

[2] See that chapter text for a problem description.

**TABLE A–1**

| Endpoint | Total market | Share | Sales (= total market × share) | Contribution on these sales | Equipment cost | Promotion cost | Net |
|---|---|---|---|---|---|---|---|
| A | 100,000 | .85 | 85,000 | $ 63,750 | $31,000 | $10,000 | $22,750 |
| B | 80,000 | .85 | 68,000 | 51,000 | | 10,000 | 10,000 |
| C | 50,000 | .85 | 42,500 | 31,875 | | 10,000 | −9,125 |
| D | 100,000 | .7 | 70,000 | 52,500 | | 0 | 21,500 |
| E | 80,000 | .7 | 56,000 | 42,000 | | 0 | 11,000 |
| F | 50,000 | .7 | 35,000 | 26,250 | | 0 | −4,750 |
| G | 100,000 | 1.0 | 100,000 | 75,000 | | 0 | 44,000 |
| H | 80,000 | 1.0 | 80,000 | 60,000 | | 0 | 29,000 |
| I | 50,000 | 1.0 | 50,000 | 37,500 | | 0 | 6,500 |
| J | 100,000 | .85 | 85,000 | 85,000 | $50,000 | 10,000 | 25,000 |
| K | 80,000 | .85 | 68,000 | 68,000 | | 10,000 | 8,000 |
| L | 50,000 | .85 | 42,500 | 42,500 | | 10,000 | −17,500 |
| M | 100,000 | .7 | 70,000 | 70,000 | | 0 | 20,000 |
| N | 80,000 | .7 | 56,000 | 56,000 | | 0 | 6,000 |
| O | 50,000 | .7 | 35,000 | 35,000 | | 0 | −15,000 |
| P | 100,000 | 1.0 | 100,000 | 100,000 | | 0 | 50,000 |
| Q | 80,000 | 1.0 | 80,000 | 80,000 | | 0 | 30,000 |
| R | 50,000 | 1.0 | 50,000 | 50,000 | | 0 | 0 |

**FIGURE A–7**

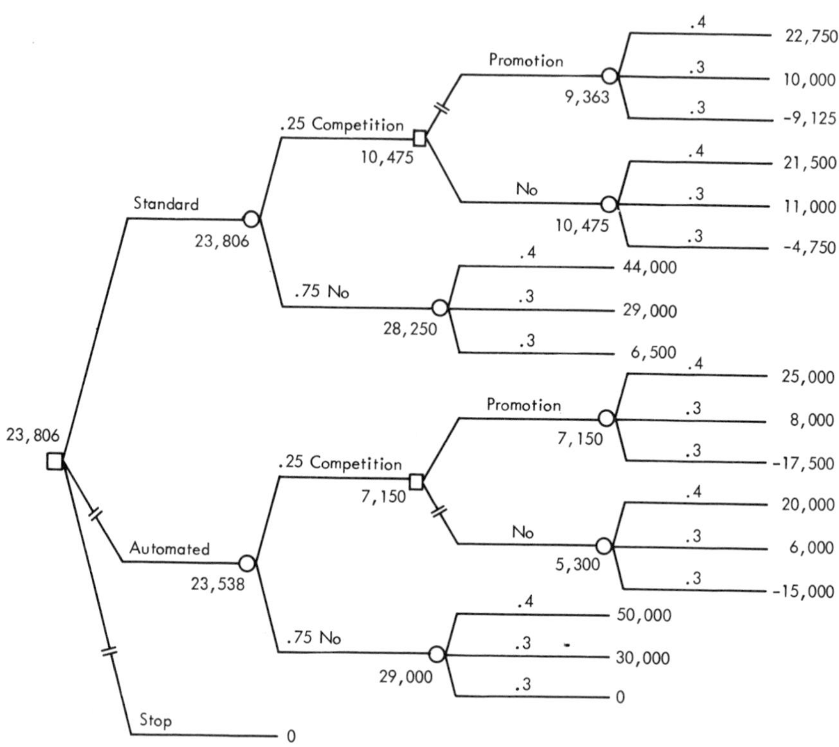


*averse;* they will be willing to sacrifice something in expected value in order to avoid exposing themselves to particularly unattractive outcomes. One step for a decision maker to take in deciding whether expected value is in fact an appropriate criterion for a specific problem is to consider all the possible final consequences and their attendant probabilities. S/he can then consider whether the range of possible outcomes for the selected optimal decision is too wide for comfort—that is, whether it involves sufficiently unattractive consequences with sufficiently high probabilities that s/he is unwilling to risk them. Such a display of possible strategies with their final outcomes and probabilities is called a risk profile. For Mr. Williams, for example, the following table summarizes the risks for each of the three actions.

In this particular problem, Mr. Williams will probably elect to use expected value, for none of the consequences of the optimal act is very bad (the worst involves a loss of $500). Suppose, however, that the decision were a much larger one and that the problem were just like the one discussed above

| *Produce standard* | | *Produce automated* | | *Do not produce* | |
|---|---|---|---|---|---|
| *Result* | *Probability* | *Result* | *Probability* | *Result* | *Probability* |
| −$500 . . . . . . . | 5 | −$2,500 . . . . . | .5 | $0 . . . . . . . . . | 1 |
| 1,500 . . . . . . . | .3 | 1,500 . . . . . | .3 | | |
| 3,500 . . . . . . . | .2 | 5,500 . . . . . | .2 | | |

except that all the consequences were multiplied by 100. In that case, the risk profile for the "optimal" act would be:

| *Result* | *Probability* |
|---|---|
| −$50,000 . . . . . . . . . . . . . . . . | .5 |
| $150,000 . . . . . . . . . . . . . . . . | .3 |
| $350,000 . . . . . . . . . . . . . . . . | .2 |

The "optimal" act now results in a loss of $50,000 with probability .5, so that Mr. Williams might prefer to hedge and do nothing instead. If the consequences became even larger—if they were 10,000 times their original values, for example—then it is quite likely that Mr. Williams would be risk-averse and would be willing to give up the chance at $35 million in order to avoid a substantial chance of losing $5 million.

In more complex decision problems, there will be a series of several act and event nodes in the tree. A strategy for such a problem is a specification of a series of actions (that is, instructions on what to do at each decision node), and risk profiles describe entire strategies, not just the individual actions which make up the strategies. Thus, a decision maker can use a risk profile to summarize the possible final consequences, with their respective probabilities, of the various strategies available. (Examining a risk profile may help to determine that the risks in a specific problem are too great to make expected value an appropriate criterion and, in that case of course, expected value should not be used.) In cases where the decision maker feels that expected value is not an appropriate criterion, risk profiles can be used to aid in the choice of a strategy. The risk profile presents the decision maker with a summary of the final consequences and attendant probabilities for different possible strategies; the decision maker can frequently select one of the strategies on the basis of this information together with her or his attitudes toward the risks it describes.

### Continuous or many-valued UQs

To this point in the Appendix we have considered only few-valued uncertain quantities. However, most of the probability distributions that arise in business problems are continuous or many-valued ones; that is, they assign probability to large (or even infinite) numbers of different values for the uncertain quantity. We now turn to two issues concerning many-valued UQs. First, we consider briefly how a decision maker might arrive at (or assess) a distribution for such a UQ; then we turn to the question of how to use continuous or many-valued distributions in analyzing decision trees.

When there are only a very small number of possible outcomes of an uncertainty, the decision maker can probably just assign probabilities to all possible outcomes. When there are many possible outcomes, however, it would be extremely difficult for the decision maker to assign a probability to each possible value. For example, a decision maker might be concerned with this year's demand for some product, where the demand could conceivably be any number between 1,000 and 10,000. It would be extremely difficult for the decision maker to assign a probability to each individual possible value—such as exactly 4,120 units of demand. Instead, it is more natural for the decision maker to think about probabilities that the UQ falls within specified ranges—for example, that the demand is between 5,000 and 7,000 units, or that the demand is less than 4,000 units. The assessment procedure described here is just a systematic way of finding and using such information about the probabilities that UQs will fall in certain ranges.

The essence of this procedure is to make the decision maker concentrate on a few special ranges of the UQ of interest. The first value which the decision maker selects is the median, also known as the .5 fractile. Thus, the decision maker specifies as the median that number which, in his or her opinion, divides the possible values of the UQ into two equally likely ranges; the UQ, in the opinion of the decision maker, is equally likely to be above or below the median. Note that the median is not necessarily the single most likely value of the UQ. Rather, the emphasis in this discussion is on ranges, and the median divides all possible values of the UQ into two equally likely ranges. One way to select the median is to think about being faced with a choice of gambles. Assume that in the first gamble you will receive $50 if, and only if, the UQ turns out to be less than or equal to some specified value. In the second gamble you will receive $50 if, and only if, the UQ turns out to be greater than that value. If you are entirely indifferent between the first gamble and the second, then the specified value of the UQ is the median of your assessed distribution. If you find the first gamble more attractive, then the specified value is above the median, while if you find the second gamble more attractive, the chance of the UQ being above the specified value is more than one half and so the specified value is less than the median.

Next in this assessment procedure, the decision maker selects other points which divide the range of the UQ into other ranges of interest. In particular, the .25 fractile is that possible value of the UQ which divides the range of possible values into two parts: the chances are 1 in 4 that the actual values of the UQ will be in the left-hand (or smaller) part of the range and 3 in 4 that it will be in the right-hand, or larger, part. Again, it may be useful to think of a choice between gambles. Assume that we know for certain the UQ is below the median. Now think of a gamble in which you will receive $50 if and only if the UQ is less than or equal to a specified value. Alternatively, think of a second gamble in which you win $50 if and only if the UQ has a value between the specified value and the median. If you are entirely indifferent between these two gambles, then the specified value is the .25 fractile of your assessed probability distribution for the UQ. If you prefer the first gamble, then you must think that the chances are greater than 1 in 4 that the UQ will be less than or equal to the specified value, and so your .25 fractile is smaller than the specified value. Similarly, if you prefer the second gamble, then your .25 fractile is larger than the specified value.

The .75 fractile of a probability distribution is the number which divides the range into two parts such that: the chances are 3 in 4 that the UQ value will be less than or equal to the .75 fractile and 1 in 4 that it will exceed that value. A choice between gambles can again be used in selecting the .75 fractile: you should be indifferent between a gamble in which you win if the UQ is between the median and the .75 fractile and another gamble in which you win if, and only if, the UQ is greater than the .75 fractile.

In addition to the .5, .25, and .75, fractiles the decision maker is asked to assess what are called extreme fractiles of the distribution. Most people feel that it is not difficult to make judgments about the extreme values of a distribution, but experience has shown that assessors do have considerable difficulty in making such judgments consistently. For example, you will probably find it very difficult to differentiate between the .99 fractile (which should be exceeded with probability .01) and the .999 fractile (which should be exceeded with probability .001). In fact, most people do not intuitively distinguish between the .99 fractile, the .999 fractile, and the "highest possible outcome." In addition, experiments with large numbers of people have shown that many people give distributions which are too "tight" in the sense that the distribution of possible outcomes for the UQs of interest are not wide enough. You can think about this problem as follows. If you assess the .01 fractile for some UQ, then you are stating that you believe the chances are 1 in 100 that the actual value of the UQ is below this value. Thus, if you assess distributions for many UQs, you would expect each to have a .01 chance of falling below its .01 fractile or, on average, only 1/100 of the UQs should be below their respective .01 fractiles. Most beginning assessors find that when they are told the actual value of the UQ, they are surprised by values below their assessed .01 fractiles considerably more than once in 100 times. Most assessors find that they must concentrate on spreading out their assessed distributions.

This procedure of assessing distribution will probably leave you feeling somewhat uncomfortable. Remember that the procedure is predicated on uncertainty—we are merely trying to give you a systematic way of thinking about your uncertainty about some UQ. Also, remember that any distribution is correct if it adequately and accurately describes *your* feelings about some UQ. Even the warnings about spreading your distribution are intended to help you to express well and consistently your feelings about the value of some UQ—they are not intended to force you to accept anyone else's best judgment about that UQ. In business (and other) situations, it will be true, of course, that some people have better intuition or more knowledge about certain UQs than do others—therefore, a decision maker calls in experts to provide information about parts of a decision problem. The process of training assessors is a separate one, aimed not at giving you intuition but at helping you express the intuition that you have.

## Bracket medians for continuous distributions

The second problem we must consider is the question of how to handle continuous distributions when we are analyzing decision trees. As we have seen, such distributions are most easily described by cumulative distribution functions which assign probabilities to outcomes of the uncertainty in various ranges (in particular, in ranges of the type "all values less than or equal to some specified value"). Figure A–8 gives an example of such a cumulative distribution function.

**FIGURE A–8**

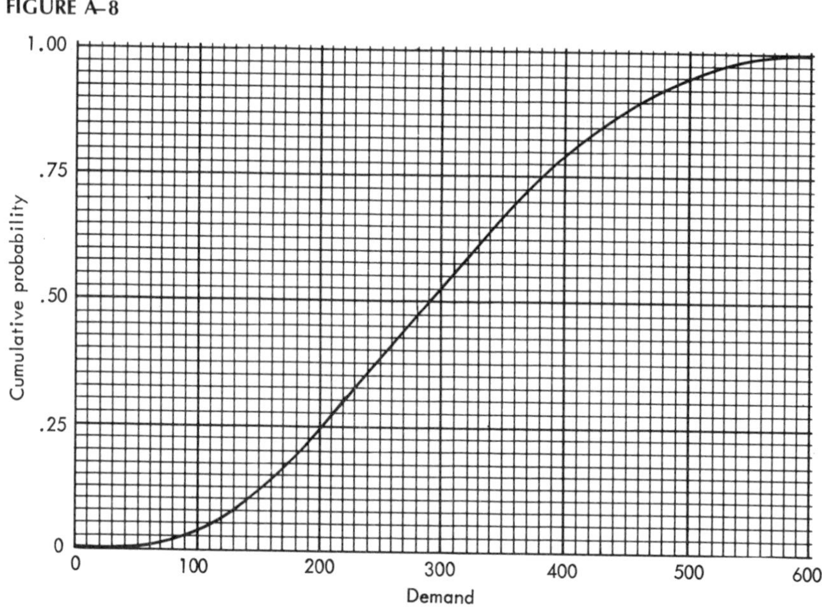

In drawing decision trees we indicate the presence of a continuous uncertainty by drawing a fan, as shown in Figure A–9. While a fan is an adequate tool for indicating the presence of a continuous distribution, it is really not adequate for use in evaluating a decision tree. When we average out and fold back in such a tree, we consider nodes one at a time. For event nodes, we average out the values at the ends of all of the branches leading from those nodes. An event fan indicates an infinite number of possible branches, that is, an infinite number of possible values of the UQ.[3] We cannot calculate and average an essentially infinite number of values, one for each of the possible branches. Hence, to average out at an event fan we must develop a new method for solving trees.

**FIGURE A–9**

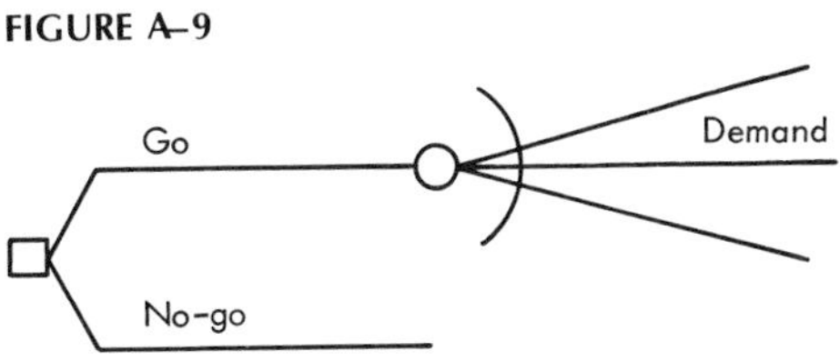


The technique for evaluating trees involving event *fans* is a very simple one. We approximate continuous event fans, with their essentially *infinite* numbers of possible values, by essentially equivalent event *forks* with *limited* numbers of values (and branches). Having replaced the fans by essentially equivalent forks, we simply average out and fold back the way we do in trees without fans. Thus, the problem of handling trees with event fans is reduced to one of finding a limited number of representative values to place on an event fork to replace a specific event fan.

As an example, consider the distribution in Figure A–8. Suppose that we want to select five representative values from that distribution.[4] One way to select the five values is to find what are called *bracket medians* of the distribution. In finding such values, we argue as follows:

If we choose five representative values, we would like each value to stand for (or represent) a set of values of the UQ that are reasonably like one another and like their representative. As a first step we divide the entire range

[3] Actually, a fan indicates either an infinite or else simply a very large number of branches; as we have seen, many-valued UQs are treated for practical purposes as if they were infinite; hence here we consider the case of infinite possible values.

[4] In actual problems we generally have computers available to help with the number work and we can use large numbers of representative values and, hence, obtain very good approximations to the continuous distributions. For illustrative purposes in hand-worked exercises we use five or perhaps ten values. The approximations provided with such limited numbers of values are not very good in many cases—but the number-pushing is kept within reasonable limits. We settle for the small numbers of values because the hand examples are intended primarily for illustrative purposes, anyway.

of possible values into mutually exclusive subranges—such as all values less than or equal to 100 or all values greater than 100 and less than or equal to 200, for example. Next, we must decide how to select the values that divide all possible values of the UQ into the ranges. Again, it should seem reasonable to select the dividers in such a way that the resulting ranges are all equally likely. Thus, if we are choosing five representatives (and hence five ranges) we would want five ranges each of which has probability .2. In the graph in Figure A–8 we can find such ranges by finding the 0, .2, .4, .6, .8, and 1.0 fractiles. Thus, there is a .2 change that the UQ will assume a value between the 0 and the .2 fractile (or between 0 and 185), there is also a .2 chance that the UQ will fall between the .2 and .4 fractiles (or 185 and 255), and so forth.[5]

Having divided the possible values of the UQ into the desired number of ranges, we have only to select one representative value from each range. To do so, we suggest taking the middle of the range in a probability sense. By this we mean that the range from the 0 to the .2 fractile would be represented by the .1 fractile (or 140 in Figure A–8), the range from the .2 to the .4 fractile would be represented by the .3 fractile (or 220), and so on. These representatives are called bracket medians. Table A–2 shows the ranges and the representative values selected when Figure A–8 is approximated by 5 bracket medians.

**TABLE A–2**

| *Cumulative probabilities defining range* | *Corresponding fractiles* | *Cumulative probability of representative value* | *Representative value* |
|---|---|---|---|
| 0.0 and .2 | 0 and 185 | .1 | 140 |
| .2 and .4 | 185 and 255 | .3 | 220 |
| .4 and .6 | 255 and 325 | .5 | 290 |
| .6 and .8 | 325 and 405 | .7 | 360 |
| .8 and 1.0 | 405 and 600 | .9 | 460 |

When we let the representative of a range of values stand for the values in that range, we assign to the representative a probability equal to all of the probability assigned to the range in the original distribution. Thus, the first bracket median of 140 in Table A–2 represents all values from 0 to 185 in the original distribution. Those values had total probability .2. Hence, we will

[5] To be very precise, we would specify which range contains the dividing points (such as the .2 fractile). For example, we might put each dividing point into the left-hand range (of the two ranges it separates).

assign probability .2 to the first bracket median. Similarly, we find that each bracket median should be assigned probability .2 when it represents its entire range of values. Thus, we have arrived at the distribution in Table A–3 for use in approximating the continuous distribution in Figure A–8 above.

**TABLE A–3**

| *Value* | *Probability* |
|---|---|
| 140 | .2 |
| 220 | .2 |
| 290 | .2 |
| 360 | .2 |
| 460 | .2 |

Next we consider how to use these bracket medians in analyzing a decision tree. Suppose that the distribution from Figure A–8 appears at the event fan in the decision tree in Figure A–9. Suppose further that the endpoint value for the No-go branch is 0, while the endpoint value for a branch with a specific demand level is $2 for each unit of demand up to 250, plus $1.50 for each additional unit of demand, minus $400 in fixed cost. To evaluate the decision tree, we first replace the event fan by an event fork with a limited number of branches, each corresponding to a bracket median. With five bracket medians, we would obtain the decision tree in Figure A–10. We then proceed to put the endpoint values on the tree and evaluate it by averaging out and folding back. The results are shown in Figure A–11. For an expected-value analysis, these results indicate that the Go decision is preferable and has an expected value of 152.

Finally, we should note a procedural shortcut. You will note that we used the 0, .2, .4, .6, .8, and 1.0 fractiles to define equally likely ranges. We then selected the middles of those ranges, in a probability sense, or the .1, .3, .5, .7, and .9 fractiles. Once you have understood the reasoning behind this

**FIGURE A–10**

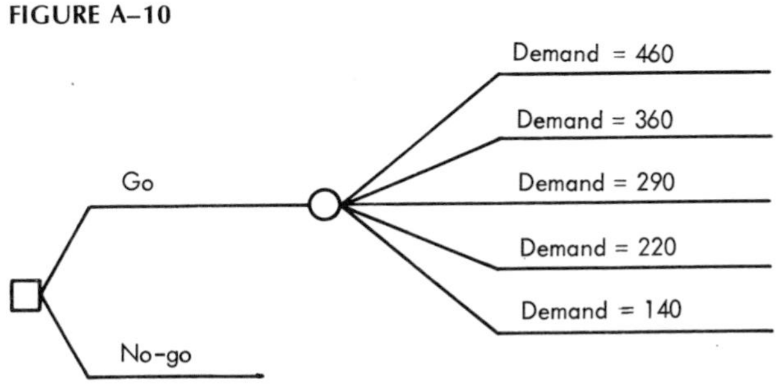

**FIGURE A–11**

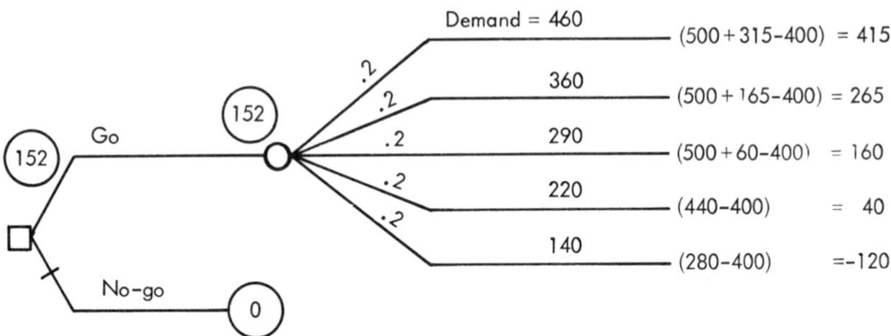


process, you can proceed at once to take the .1, .3, .5, .7, and .9 fractiles and use them as five bracket medians, without first reading off the 0, .2, .4, .6, .8, and 1.0 fractiles.[6]

[6] Similarly, if you wanted ten brackets, the equally likely ranges would be between the 0 and .1 fractiles, the .1 and .2 fractiles, etc., and the bracket medians would turn out to be the .05, .15, .25, . . . , .95 fractiles.

# INDEX

*This book has been set VIP in 10 and 9 point Optima, leaded 2 points. Chapter numbers are 12 and 24 point Optima and chapter titles are 16 point Optima. Case numbers are 14 and 16 point Optima and case titles are 14 point Optima Medium. The size of the type page is 27 by 45½ picas.*